W9-AQL-942

AMERICAN

to the

BACKBONE

AMERICAN

to the

BACKBONE

The Life of James W. C. Pennington, the Fugitive Slave
Who Became One of the First Black Abolishonists

CHRISTOPHER L. WEBBER

PEGASUS BOOKS
NEW YORK

AMERICAN TO THE BACKBONE

Pegasus Books LLC
80 Broad Street, 5th Floor
New York, NY 10004

Copyright © Christopher L. Webber

First Pegasus Books edition July 2011

Interior design by Maria Fernandez

Library of Congress Cataloging-in-Publication Data is available.

ISBN: 978-1-60598-175-8

10 9 8 7 6 5 4 3 2 1

Printed in the United States of America
Distributed by W. W. Norton & Company

for
Harold Louis Wright
1929–1978

CONTENTS

I am an American to the backbone . . .

—James W. C. Pennington

PREFACE

I t should be noted that certain spellings were inconsistent in mid-nineteenth century America, in particular such words as color/colour, labor/labour, etc. When English sources are quoted, the latter spelling is consistently used even if the speaker was an American, but in the United States both spellings were common. "Practise/practice" and "defense/defence" are other words inconsistently spelled in the various texts I have quoted. Whatever spelling was found in the original has been maintained. Among the most difficult matters in that respect is the term "anti-slavery" which appears sometimes as one word, sometimes as two, and sometimes with a hyphen. I have tried to replicate the original and to use the term with a hyphen myself. I dislike using [sic] but at times it seems necessary to show that the error was in the original. It might be noted also that when misspellings occur in quotations from James Pennington or anyone else, the error may well be with the original editor or typesetter.

The following abbreviations have been used in the footnotes:

BAA UDM—Black Abolitionist Archives, University of Detroit Mercy
BAP—Black Abolitionist Papers microfilm. The published version of the
    Black Abolitionist Papers is cited by its full name.
CA—Colored American
FDP—Frederick Douglass' Paper

INTRODUCTION

He had been running for almost eight days and he was tired and hungry. He had been captured twice by slave catchers and escaped. The last food he had eaten was a brief meal provided by the slave catchers three days earlier. Aside from that, he had had only a loaf of bread, a dry ear of corn, and some green apples that had made him sick. He had slept in the woods, in cornfields and under a bridge. And now, north at last of the Mason-Dixon line, he had asked for work and been directed to the house of a Quaker named William Wright.

Standing outside the door that could open a new life to him, James Pembroke (who would later change his name to Pennington) knocked. William Wright opened the door, and behind him Pembroke could see the breakfast table loaded with a nineteenth-century farmer's breakfast. Pembroke asked whether he could find work and Wright responded, "Well, come in then and take thy breakfast and we will talk about it. Thee must be cold without any coat."†

Seldom do two short sentences provide us such an opening into two radically different lives. We can hear them as Pembroke did, both as an invitation and a challenge. He never forgot those words. No white man had ever spoken to him before as one man to another. They opened up for him the possibility of a life in freedom. For the rest of his life, he would remember them also as a standard of caring for others that he should maintain himself. In those words we hear as well the voice of a man who had put his life at risk for principles derived from his faith. William Wright had made his home open to the needs of others; his life was as available to them as the food on his breakfast table. Such stories as theirs should be remembered and told, not least because biographies provide a means of expanding our lives by entering into the lives of others.

---

† This misuse of "thee" (it should be "thou") appears to be Pennington's mistake, as it appears throughout his writing. We will avoid using the notation "[sic]".

AMERICAN

to the

BACKBONE

CHAPTER ONE

Finding Freedom

A s he stood in the slave quarters of Rockland plantation, six miles south of Hagerstown, Maryland, on a sunny afternoon in late October 1827, James Pembroke knew that this was the day that would change his life forever. He and the other members of his family had been beaten once too often. He could remain a slave no longer.

Pembroke reviewed once again the events that had led to his decision. He had seen his father mercilessly beaten for daring to suggest that he would willingly be sold to another owner if his master was dissatisfied with his work. He had been beaten himself when he happened to look up from his work and catch his master's eye. But it was when his master threatened Pembroke's mother with a beating that he decided he could take no more. That happened on a Tuesday. By Saturday he had made up his mind to flee. He rolled up a small bundle of clothes, hid it in a cave a little distance from the house, and decided to leave the next day, Sunday, October 28.

Pembroke, like most slaves in Maryland, was usually given the Sabbath as a day of rest. On the Rockland plantation church-going was not allowed, but slaves could travel a few miles to visit family members on other plantations if they wished. Thus it would not be unusual to see a slave walking along the highway, and Pembroke would be less likely to attract attention than on a work day. With many of his fellow slaves away, all was quiet as Pembroke thought over for one last time the alternatives he had been weighing for weeks.[1]

On the negative side of the balance were the consequences to himself and his family. Should he fail, should he be captured and brought back, there was the certainty of the most severe caning he had ever experienced. He would, in addition, almost certainly be sold south, sold to a harsher master and transported to the cane and cotton fields of the Deep South where the average survival time in the heat and hard labor was a mere seven years. There was, as a result, always a need for more slaves on those plantations, and in Maryland, where the need for slaves was declining, slave owners had turned to breeding and exporting. Pembroke had already seen slaves who displeased his master sold to what was likely to be an early death. He had seen chained gangs, including even children, going by his plantation on the way to Louisiana.[2]

Not least of his concerns were the consequences for his family. They would be accused of having helped him, and how could they prove that they had not? They, too, could be beaten and sold off to a harsher life. But they might suffer whether his escape attempt was successful or not. They would be safe only if he stayed, and even so they would be beaten as usual when their owner was feeling ill-tempered. So those consequences, he had concluded, could not weigh against his plans.[3]

All morning Pembroke had sat in the blacksmith's shop and thought it through yet again. "Hope, fear, dread, terror, love, sorrow, and deep melancholy," he recalled, "were mingled in my mind together." One thing he understood clearly: if his courage failed at this point and he failed to act, no better moment would ever come and he would be a slave for the rest of his life. As the days went by, the obstacles to flight would only become greater. He might soon have children of his own whom then he would be unwilling to leave. Even now he hated the thought of leaving his parents and brothers and sisters behind. Perhaps most difficult of all was the fact that he was so completely ignorant of the larger world. Although he had once lived in Hagerstown for two years as an apprentice stone mason, he had almost no knowledge at all of the world beyond that. He would be striking out for an unknown land in which he would know not a single human being and yet he would be forced to rely on those unknown individuals for his survival.[4]

What little Pembroke knew of the world beyond the plantation had come from conversations overheard when he was an apprentice in Hagerstown, and the stories told by other slaves who passed on information by word of mouth on their Sabbath visits or as they were bought and sold from one plantation to another. Then, too, there were thousands of free African Americans in Maryland, some of whom had traveled to the north and had come back with stories to tell of their experience. Listening to them, Pembroke had learned that there was freedom in Pennsylvania and that Pennsylvania lay somewhere to the north. How far to the north Pennsylvania was, he had no idea. In fact, it was no further north from Hagerstown than Hagerstown was from his home. The border with Pennsylvania, the famous Mason-Dixon line, was only six or seven miles beyond Hagerstown and within easy reach for a young man in a hurry. Yet for all he knew it might have been a thousand miles away. The distance worried him, but he thought he was strong enough to survive or at least to attempt the journey. He was nineteen years old, sturdy and capable, with skills as a blacksmith and stone mason and carpenter. If ever there were a time to leave home, this was that time. He thought he could identify the North Star and he believed he could follow that star and find freedom.[5]

By two o'clock Sunday afternoon, Pembroke was ready to start. Looking around for food he could find nothing but a half loaf of corn bread. He put that in his pocket and went to the cave to collect the bundle of clothes he had hidden there. He looked around one last time. A few children were playing in front of the cabin and his feeling of sadness was intensified by the thought that he would probably never see them again. Nevertheless he began to walk. "The hour was come," he told himself, "and the man must act, or for ever be a slave."[6]

Normally Pembroke might have taken the road into Hagerstown. A slave walking on the road might not normally be questioned on the Sabbath, but the bundle of clothes would have raised red flags for anyone who saw him, so he moved away from the road and made his way through thick woods and across the rough, recently harvested fields. He went slowly, since his original thought had been to stop in Hagerstown to visit his brother and go on after dark. As he walked, however, he rethought his plans and decided not to stop with his brother after all. If he stopped, he would endanger his brother when his escape was made known, and then too his brother might persuade him not to go after all. Pembroke was fond of his older brother and had often turned to him for advice. Merely seeing and talking with his brother might be enough to unsettle him and lead him to abandon his plan.[7]

By the time Pembroke reached Hagerstown, it was dark. By contemporary standards, Hagerstown was a large community, counted in the 1830 census among the hundred largest towns and cities in the United States with a population of over 3,000. Prosperous and progressive city leaders had paved a few streets with crushed stone in the new macadam process, but they had not yet provided street lights, so there were only a few dim lights outside the taverns. The houses were set side by side with little or no space between them, so the densely populated area was not large. Pembroke knew he could walk through town quickly without being seen.[8]

Once through the town, he was well and truly on his way to freedom. He felt "like a mariner who has gotten his ship outside of the harbor and has spread his sails to the breeze. The cargo is on board—the ship is cleared—and the voyage I must make." It was a cloudless night and the North Star was quite visible. And now he knew he must go full speed to be as far from home as possible by the time the sun came up the next morning and he was missed.[9]

Following the road and moving quickly, Pembroke made good progress until about three o'clock in the morning, when a chilly dew came down and he began again to wonder what he had done. "Gloom and melancholy again spread through my whole soul. The prospect of utter destitution which threatened me was more than I could bear, and my heart began to melt." He was still feeling gloomy when the sun began to rise and he found himself in open country with no place to hide except in a corn shock a few hundred yards from the road. Travel by daylight was too great a risk, so he got himself inside the corn shock where there was no room to lie down and no real possibility of sleep. There he squatted all day, fearful and very unhappy. Slowly he ate his bread, trying to make it last as long as possible, but by the time it was dark again not a crumb remained.[10]

Hungry and miserable, he set out again. Now the sky was overcast; he could see no stars at all and had "serious misgivings" about his course. Indeed, the attempt to reconstruct Pembroke's course raises serious questions. If he had gone straight toward the North Star, he would have been well into Pennsylvania within less than twenty-four hours, but when he finally asked where he was, at dawn on the third day, he was told he was eighteen miles from Baltimore. The proverbial crow traveling to Baltimore from Hagerstown would fly somewhat south of due east and be further from Pennsylvania at the end of its flight than at the beginning. Now as then, however, the nearest any road comes to that line runs through the Catoctin Mountains, which rise over a thousand feet above the otherwise gently rolling farmland about fifteen miles east of Hagerstown. Even today the road through those mountains twists and turns as it winds its way around deep ravines and past steep and rocky hillsides. But Pembroke makes no reference to terrain except to say that after his first night, during which he says nothing of any difficulty in finding his way, he was in "open country." It seems hardly possible that he could have traveled through the mountains so easily and, of course, he would have to have been mistaken about the North Star. If, on the other hand, Pembroke did indeed go north into Pennsylvania during his first night's journey, and then, with no star to guide him and doubtful of his course, became confused and began traveling southeast, he might have gotten past the mountains somewhat more easily and still have arrived eighteen miles west of Baltimore on the third day. In that case, he would have crossed and re-crossed the Mason-Dixon line. That famous line is still well marked with three-hundred-pound boulders, but the boulders are set at intervals of a mile and can easily be missed. In the dark it would be a remote chance indeed for a walker to stumble over them.

Wherever Pembroke may have been, and whatever road he was on, he set out again when it was dark, though body and spirit were growing weaker. The night was uneventful, but as dawn broke he found some green apples and a bridge under which to hide. There he spent the day. The green apples, washed down with some water from the stream, disagreed with him and severe cramps made the day miserable. When he set out once again after dark, he was weakened by the stomach upset and lack of sleep. He found himself stopping frequently to rest and sleep for a few minutes, with the result that he made "little progress."[11]

When morning came on Wednesday, he saw a toll booth in the distance and found a twelve-year-old boy who was apparently on duty. He asked where the road led and was told it went to Baltimore, 18 miles away. This astounded him. He knew that it was some 80 miles from Hagerstown to Baltimore and he knew very well that Baltimore was not a good place for a fugitive slave to be. Somehow he had been traveling in the wrong direction, toward danger rather than freedom. Pembroke decided to ask one more question: what is the best way to Philadelphia? "You can take a road which turns off about half-a-mile below this, and goes to Gettysburg," said the boy, "or you can go on to Baltimore and take the packet."[12]

Ten years later, Frederick Douglass would, in fact, manage to escape from slavery by taking the packet boat from Baltimore to Philadelphia, but Douglass had borrowed papers certifying that he was free and he had money for a ticket.[13] Pembroke had neither. For Pembroke, the only sensible choice was to take the turn and head for Gettysburg.

He was relieved to be off on the side road since the road he had been on, he was told, was "The National Turnpike." Here again it would seem that either Pennington's memory is faulty or he was further off course than he had any idea. The National Turnpike was the country's first superhighway, authorized by President Thomas Jefferson, built with government funding, and designed to open the West to trade and settlement. Later in the day, Pennington would discover that he was near Reisterstown, but the National Turnpike ran ten or twelve miles south of Reisterstown. If Pennington had misidentified the North Star at the outset and headed southeast out of Hagerstown, he might have followed the National Turnpike almost from the beginning. If so, he would have found the best route past the Catoctin Mountains and made excellent time, but he would have been moving into ever more dangerous country for a fugitive slave.

Whether Pennington was north or south of Reisterstown when he asked for information, he was obviously not headed north. Turning to the north and following the directions he had now been given, he had gone about a mile when he met a young man with a pair of horses and a load of hay. Drawing his horses to a stop, the young man asked Pennington in a friendly way where he was going. Pennington remembered the dialogue this way:

> "Are you traveling any distance, my friend?"
> "I am on my way to Philadelphia."
> "Are you free?"
> "Yes, sir."

> "I suppose, then, you are provided with free papers?"
> "No, sir. I have no papers."
> "Well, my friend, you should not travel on this road: you will be
> taken up before you have gone three miles. There are men living on
> this road who are constantly on the look-out for your people; and it
> is seldom that one escapes them who attempts to pass by day."[14]

The young man's advice to Pembroke was that he should go a certain distance and then turn off the road toward a house where he would find help.
Clearly the house was a station on the Underground Railroad and the young
man was aware of it and was providing Pembroke with a way to find the help
he needed. But the realization that he had gone so far astray and the warning
about slave catchers had left Pembroke now thoroughly confused. As a result,
he quickly forgot the directions he had been given and decided not to try to
follow them lest he become further lost. He thought he would do better to try
to hide again for the day so he left the road to look for a hiding place. There
was a small patch of woods that seemed to offer a refuge but it was not enough
to provide any real concealment, so Pennington came back to the road. There
were people at work in the fields and he hoped he would not be noticed amid
the activities of a busy day.[15]

That was a bad mistake. After walking another mile along the road, he came
to a milestone marking 24 miles from Baltimore, and near the milestone was
a tavern. It was ten o'clock in the morning and Pembroke was hungry. Under
ordinary circumstances he would have been glad to see a place offering food,
but he was alert now to his danger and set out to pass the tavern as quickly
and quietly as he could. Across the road from the tavern, however, was a field
and in the field was a man digging potatoes. Pembroke was stopped by a shout
of "Halloo!" Although the voice did not sound friendly, Pembroke replied
politely. Again he recorded the dialogue as he remembered it:

> "Who do you belong to?"
> "I am free, sir."
> "Have you got papers?"
> "No, sir."
> "Well, you must stop here."
> "My business is onward, sir, and I do not wish to stop."
> "I will see then if you don't stop, you black rascal."[16]

The potato-digger had already put down his spade and was climbing over
the fence as he spoke. It was obvious that he had no intention of being helpful.
Pembroke "saw that a crisis was at hand." Although he had crafted knives and

guns in his blacksmith's shop, he had brought no weapons of any kind with him, but he was not of a mind to surrender without a struggle. Whether he could outrun his pursuer was uncertain, so he decided he would at least attempt to get some distance away from the tavern where there might be others prepared to interfere with his progress. Then, if necessary, he would find a stone with which to "smite him on the knee." Such a plan was far from ideal, but his work as a blacksmith "had given my eye and hand such mechanical skill, that I felt quite sure that if I could only get a stone in my hand, and have time to wield it, I should not miss his knee-pan."[17]

The pursuer was beginning to be short of breath and was, as Pembroke remembered it, becoming "vexed" at his failure to overtake his prey. Pembroke, on the other hand, was becoming more and more "provoked at the idea of being thus pursued by a man to whom I had not done the least injury." The pursuer made a last desperate lunge that fell short and let out a yell for "Jake Shouster!" There was a small house on the left, and in response to the call, the door flew open. Out came a large man wearing a shoemaker's leather apron and with a knife in one hand. Shouster grabbed Pembroke by the collar and held him while the first pursuer grabbed his arms and held them behind his back. Two men, both larger and stronger than Pennington, now had him firmly in their hands, and one of them had a dangerous weapon. A third man now emerged from the shoemaker's shop and a fourth man came up from the potato field. Surrounded and outnumbered, Pembroke's worst fears seemed to be realized. "My heart melted away," he wrote, and "I sunk resistlessly into the hands of my captors."[18]

The captors dragged him back to the tavern, and word spread quickly through the neighborhood that everyone should "come and see the runaway nigger." Men, women, and children came crowding into the room and one man, taller than all the rest and apparently accustomed to command, suggested a plan of action: "That fellow is a runaway I know; put him in jail a few days, and you will soon hear where he came from." Fixing Pembroke with a hard stare, he added, "If I lived on this road, *you* fellows would not find such clear running as you do; I'd trap more of you." Others in the crowd, however, thought there might be an easier way: let Pembroke save everyone a great deal of unnecessary work, they suggested, by simply telling them where he came from. This he was not willing to do. Unlike many slaves, who used lying as a survival skill, he had been brought up to tell the truth, but he knew that, whatever the law might be, these people had no right to a truth that would be harmful to him. It also seemed to him a very unequal bargain. The captors might be paid a hundred dollars as their reward, but Pembroke would receive a hundred lashes and be sent to the cotton fields of Louisiana. The advantage to them was much less than the cost to him. It was too high a price to pay for truth.[19]

Since Pembroke continued to insist that he was not a runaway, the captors decided they should get legal advice, so they tied his hands and took him to the residence of a magistrate some half mile from the tavern. There was no one home. Disappointed but not discouraged, they decided to consult another magistrate in the neighborhood. Again the distance was not great, but this time the route was across country and involved climbing fences and jumping ditches. Thoughts of a possible reward for their efforts gave the captors energy, but once again they were disappointed. No one was home.[20]

It was now well after noon and the captors' enthusiasm for their work was waning rapidly. Lacking a name for their captive, they had begun to call him "New John" and, still hopeful for some cooperation, they continued to press him to tell them his name and where he was from. It had been hard for Pembroke to cope with the fences and ditches with his hands tied, so they now untied him and urged, "If you have run away from any one, it would be much better for you to tell us!" Pembroke's thoughts, however, were still set on freedom. He was well aware that word of his escape would be spreading and that the information he was refusing to give might come to them anyway at any moment. His escort had dwindled by this time to the original two and, when he saw a patch of woods not far from the road, he decided to try once more to escape. With a quick sweep of his arm he took the legs out from under one man, "left him nearly standing on his head," and got a quick start on the other.[21]

Off they went, over a fence and up a small hill. Since one of the two men had longer legs and was gaining on him, his thoughts turned once again to stones and violence. Just as he was about to look for a stone with which to attack, however, he came over the crest of the hill and found himself at the edge of a newly plowed field with a plowman in position to cut off his escape. Once more he was grabbed by the collar and once more the pursuers caught up. This time he was thrown to the ground. The plowman put his knees on Pembroke's shoulder, the first pursuer came down on his legs, and the other pursuer tied his arms behind him. Kicking, punching, and cursing him, they set off once again for the tavern.[22]

By mid-afternoon they were back at the tavern and appealing again for him to tell them the truth. Pembroke's efforts to escape undermined his protests that he was free but now he had had time to think about another story. "If you will not put me in jail," he said, "I will now tell you where I am from." They made the requested promise and Pembroke told them this story:

> A few weeks ago, I was sold from the eastern shore to a slave-trader, who had a large gang, and set out for Georgia, but when he got to a

> town in Virginia, he was taken sick, and died with the small-pox.
> Several of his gang also died with it, so that the people in the town
> became alarmed, and did not wish the gang to remain among them.
> No one claimed us, or wished to have anything to do with us; I left
> the rest, and thought I would go somewhere and get work.

It was a clever ploy. Some seemed to believe his story while others had no desire to be close to someone who might have smallpox. One or two wandered off muttering, "Better let the small-pox nigger go." The crowd in the tavern became noticeably thinner, but there were still some who wanted evidence and who asked for the slave-trader's name. "John Henderson," said Pembroke, dredging up a name he had heard somewhere. It was a lucky guess. "John Henderson!" said one of the captors, "I knew him; I took up a yaller boy for him about two years ago, and got fifty dollars. He passed out with a gang about that time, and the boy ran away from him at Frederickstown. What kind of a man was he?"

Again Pembroke took a chance and provided a description and again it was satisfactory. "Yes," said his questioner, "that is the man." During this exchange the crowd had continued to dwindle. Jake Shouster's wife had summoned him to dinner and he had wandered off muttering about losing a whole day's work "trotting after a tied nigger." Finally, Pembroke was left with only his original captor, and this man was ready to negotiate.[23]

"John," he said, "I have a brother living in Reisterstown, four miles off, who keeps a tavern; I think you had better go and live with him, till we see what will turn up. He wants an ostler." Ostler has meant various things at various times and places, ranging from someone who takes care of horses to a general hired hand, but, whatever it was he was being offered, Pembroke was quick to agree. "Well," said the captor, "take something to eat, and I will go with you."

The best part of the offer was food; Pembroke had not had a meal since early Sunday, and it was now 4 o'clock on Wednesday. He had no intention, however, of going into a town where there would be newspapers, handbills, and travelers bringing word of escaped slaves, and a jail to hold prisoners. As he ate, he resolved that he would rather die than be taken there.[24]

Pembroke probably never knew it but he had a certain advantage in the fact that the Hagerstown newspaper, the *Torch Light and Public Advertiser*, was published weekly on Thursdays. The next day there would indeed be a notice of a runaway slave and an unusually generous offer of $200 for Pembroke's return. The ad reported that "James Pembrook" had run away on Monday, October 29. Pembroke had, in fact, left on Sunday but Frisby Tilghman, Pembroke's owner, would not have missed him until Monday and therefore would not have imagined that he could yet have reached the Reisterstown area, nor, of course, would he have supposed that he had fled in that direction. The description provided was not altogether flattering:

> about 21 years of age, five feet five inches high, very black, square
> & clumsily made, has a down look, prominent and reddish eyes, and
> mumbles or talks with his teeth closed, can read, and I believe write,
> is an excellent blacksmith, and pretty good rough carpenter.[25]

The ad never used the word "slave"; slave owners had begun avoiding the word under mounting pressure from abolitionists in the North and substituting terms like "servants" or "hands," as if somehow that would calm the rising storm. The ad also reveals a good deal of ignorance on the part of the owner since his slave, in fact, could not read or write.

Most of the other fugitive slave ads that were a regular feature of the newspaper's advertisement pages describe what the fugitive was thought to be wearing. Since slaves owned few clothes there was not much chance that they would dress differently and an observant owner might have guessed, or learned from others, what clothing Pembroke had. The absence of such description, especially since Tilghman would have had many opportunities to observe his blacksmith, seems odd. The "down look" and "mumbles," on the other hand, might have been a natural way for a slave, especially an unhappy one, to respond to his master. Once free, Pembroke had no trouble expressing himself with great clarity.

Over the next three months, Tilghman continued to run the ad. During that time there were notices looking for other fugitives, most with only one name given and with rewards starting at $10, "if taken within the county," and some in the range of $40 to $75. There were two rewards of $100 offered but only one, for "James Pembrook," at $200. Two weeks later Tilghman added that "he received shortly before he absconded, a pretty severe cut from his axe on the inside of his right leg." He also noted that he had placed the same ad in newspapers in Lancaster and Philadelphia.[26] No ads for other fugitives indicated that such action had been taken. Clearly Tilghman wanted his slave back and placed a high value on him. Tilghman kept a bounty on offer, in fact, until the day he died.

None of this news, however, would reach the Reisterstown area until the next day at the earliest. Had they seen the ad and known the size of the reward being offered, Pembroke's captor's friends might have been more motivated to stay with him and help out. As it was, however, they wandered off and left Pembroke with one more opportunity.

When he finished eating, he set out with his captor for the tavern in Reisterstown, resolved in his own mind that they would never get there.

When they had gone about a mile and a half, he noticed that the road ahead entered a thick wood and took a turn. That, Pembroke thought to himself, would be an ideal spot for a confrontation. He would face his captor and "commence action," after which only one of them would be able to go further. Scarcely ten feet from the turn in the road, however, a man on horseback appeared and fell into conversation with the captor. They spoke in German, a common language in Pennsylvania at the time, and so were able to leave Pembroke unaware of the nature of their discussion. When the rider at last spoke to Pembroke, he learned that the man was one of the magistrates they had been looking for fruitlessly earlier in the day. The rider drew himself up on his horse "like a general reviewing his troops, put on a solemn face," and proceeded to examine Pembroke very precisely on the details of his story.[27]

Finally he said, "Well, you had better stay among us a few months, until we see what is to be done with you." The magistrate obviously carried an authority that overrode all previous plans and the making of new plans involved going back once again to the tavern. There the magistrate got down from his horse and went with Pembroke and the farmer into the barroom, where he looked carefully at Pembroke and repeated his examination of Pembroke's story. Apparently well satisfied with the result, he made a new proposal: Pembroke should go and live with him for a short time; he had a few acres of corn and potatoes to get in, and he would pay twenty-five cents a day for help with the work. Any proposal other than jail was perfectly acceptable to Pembroke. It was agreed then that Pembroke would spend the night at the tavern with the farmer, who would take him to the magistrate in the morning.[28]

By this time the sun was setting and the scattered showers of the afternoon had given way to a clearing sky. The farmer had left his hired man in the field digging potatoes alone, but now he felt a need to go and help him load the wagon so they could bring the potatoes into a barn beside the house. Oddly, instead of taking his new servant along to help, the farmer left him in the tavern with a boy about nine years old. The instructions were given in German but it was clear to Pembroke that the boy was to keep a close eye on him.

So now, as Pembroke studied his situation, he found himself in a house by the road with the potato field on the other side of the road. Behind the house and about 300 yards away across an open field was a thick wood. Taking off his coat to make it appear that he was making himself at home, Pembroke then walked around to the back of the house and saw that there was also a garden with a picket fence between himself and the woods. The boy asked why he didn't come in and relax but Pembroke was not feeling able to relax. He countered that he was feeling unwell and asked whether the boy would be kind enough to bring him some water. As the boy went off on the errand, the farmer finished loading the wagon and began working to bring it to the barn. On the way to the barn, the farmer would have to pass in front of the house and leave Pembroke's path from the back of the house to the woods out of his sight. When the boy brought the water, however, the farmer's view was not yet screened by the house. Would the boy be kind enough, Pembroke asked, to get another glass of water? He gave Pembroke a suspicious glance but went off as requested. Meanwhile the farmer was having trouble bringing his horses and wagon across the road made slippery by the rain. Pembroke waited impatiently for the right moment and then, with the farmer finally out of his line of sight, he bolted for the woods. Over the picket fence and off across the fields he went. Behind him, he saw the boy peering curiously over the fence but the farmer was still struggling with the potato wagon and there was no pursuit.[29]

By the time all this had happened, the sun had set and a thick covering of dark clouds had come up. Years later, as he remembered the events of that day, Pennington (as he then was) would think of the passage from the Book of Job that says, "He holdeth back the face of His throne, and spreadeth a cloud before it." He also reviewed the way in which the day's events had led him to tell lies and to imagine doing violence to others and he saw that, too, as evidence of the iniquity of the slave system. Suppose he had been killed in a struggle and had appeared before God's throne of judgment with a lie on his lips and evil in his heart. Any system that would lead a young man who had been brought up to tell the truth and live in peace with others to do and imagine evil was clearly evil itself.

At the moment, however, he had no time to meditate on all this, nor did he have any theological training to send his mind in such directions. He was in a thick wood on a dark night in an utterly unfamiliar place, and the whole area had been alerted to his existence. The woods had a dense undergrowth and it was all thoroughly wet from the afternoon rain. Besides that, there was no star visible and Pembroke began imagining what wild animals might be in the woods and what cliffs he might come upon unseen. He set off to distance himself from the scene of the day's events, zigzagging back and forth in an effort to find a way through the woods. At last he came to a more open area, but now he was wading through marshy ground and leaping ditches. He was thoroughly miserable.[30]

Somewhere near three o'clock in the morning, Pembroke came upon a road just where it forked, and he found that he had to choose one of three ways. The road north from Reisterstown does indeed offer three alternatives, but all of them go to Pennsylvania. Pembroke remembered an old slave superstition that a left turn is unlucky, and yet it seemed to him that the right fork looked just as unlucky in the dark. He chose the middle road and moved on as fast as he could. A breeze had come up to make the chill from his wet clothes even greater and he had not gone far before the crowing of roosters, the barking of dogs, and the distant rattling of wagons on their way to the markets in town made him aware that dawn was not far off.

He looked around and saw that the countryside was now completely open and the only shelter was a small house and barn near the road. To hide in the barn was a great risk, he knew, but there seemed to be no alternative. He climbed up into the loft, which was filled with newly dried corn fodder, and tried to conceal himself. The fodder rustled so loudly with every movement that it seemed to him that those in the house would surely have to hear it.[31]

The farm family, in fact, did not hear him and only a small dog took notice. Pembroke, referring to the dog with an old English word still used by slaves, called the creature a "fice." The word "feisty" has the same origin and conveys the meaning well. It was a small and very aggressive dog ready to yap at any excuse. A fugitive slave in the hayloft provided a very adequate excuse to make as much noise as possible. The dog commenced to bark and Pembroke held his breath, certain the farm family would come to investigate. They, however, were busy getting ready for the day's work and seemed oblivious to the dog.[32]

With the sun now well up and the family going about their chores, it became clear to the fugitive that the farmer was planning to be away for the day. Distracted for a while by activity in the house, the dog stopped its barking until the man had gone. Through the cracks in the side of the barn, Pembroke could see that a mother and two small children were still in the house. The dog now set to work to get their attention by running back and forth between the house and the barn, yapping and raising a fuss. It seemed to Pembroke impossible that the family should fail to get the message, but perhaps they were so used to the dog's noise that they automatically tuned it out. In any event, they paid no attention.

Now Pembroke's thoughts turned to his hunger. The afternoon meal the day before had helped, but that meal, even with the loaf of bread he had brought and the few green apples he had found, was hardly enough to sustain four days of hard travel. Like the Prodigal Son (he reflected later), he might have been happy to fill his stomach with the fodder provided for the cattle—with which, in fact, he was surrounded—but dry corn stalks were more than he could cope with. He thought for a while of presenting himself at the door of the farm house and asking the good woman to have compassion. That, however, could have had fatal consequences, as he well knew, so he settled down to wait out the day. The barn was small and the crevices in its sides were large enough to let a strong breeze sweep through and add to the chill coming from his wet clothes.[33]

More wretched than he had thought possible, he waited through the day until, about mid-afternoon, he heard voices from what seemed to be parties of men passing by on the road. What little he could hear made it very evident that they were talking about him:

"I ought to catch such a fellow, the only liberty he should have for one fortnight, would be ten feet of rope," said one.

Another said, "I reckon he is in that wood now."

Still another said, "Who would have thought that rascal was so 'cute'?"

And all the while, the little dog was running back and forth doing its best to let them know exactly where they could find the man for whom they were looking. Pembroke listened and trembled, but the riders passed on.[34]

Finally, toward the end of the day, the owner of the house returned and began to go about his evening chores. He brought the cow in from the field, fed the pigs, and chopped some firewood while the little dog still tried to get some attention. Several times the man and the dog came into the barn directly underneath Pembroke. Then from the road came sounds as if all the searchers were coming back in one united group. Pembroke recognized the voice of his original captor calling out to the farmer:

"Have you seen a runaway nigger pass here to-day?"

"No," said the local farmer, "I have not been at home since early this morning. Where did he come from?"

"I caught him down below here yesterday morning. I had him all day, and just at night he fooled me and got away. A party of us have been after him all day; we have been up to the line, but can't hear or see anything of him. I heard this morning where he came from. He is a blacksmith, and a stiff reward is out for him, two hundred dollars."[35]

Obviously, the Hagerstown newspaper had been delivered and Tilghman's ad had been seen.

"He's worth looking for," said the farmer.

"I reckon so," said the captor from the day before. "If I get my clutches on him again, I'll hurry him down to [a word Pembroke missed] before I eat or sleep."

But the farmer had seen nothing and had not understood the message the dog was constantly delivering, so the riders moved on down the road. Darkness fell, and once more Pembroke felt free to move on. He came down from the loft and crossed the road into an open field on the other side. The dog had not given up, in spite of the way it had been ignored all day, and Pembroke could not believe, especially after the message from the riders, that no one would pay attention. He moved out into the field some two hundred yards and stopped to listen. A door opened and he stooped to pick up a couple of stones. With a stone in each hand, he made off as fast as he could, but there was no sound of pursuit so he dropped the stones as so much useless ballast.[36]

Now, of course, he was off the road again and dealing with all the problems of thick woods interspersed with marshes. When he came back to the road after several hours, he was so tired that it was all he could do to keep his legs in motion. The mild weather of the first days of the week had been followed by increasing cold, and by early morning there was a heavy frost. Pembroke somehow kept moving, although he was sure he would collapse and fall to the ground at any moment. He came to a corn field that had been cut with the stalks tied together in standing sheaves. Walking into the corn field, he found an ear of dry corn, crept into one of the sheaves, and tried to eat. Even that was beyond his strength, and he fell asleep.[37]

When he woke again the sun was out in full strength. There was no other concealment possible, so he hunkered down as best he could among the corn stalks and set to work again on the dry kernels of the ear he had picked. It was slow going; even his jaws were tired. He spent the best part of the morning gnawing away at the ear of corn, kernel by kernel. All was quiet in the field and on the road until mid-afternoon, when he was again thrown into a panic by a party of hunters who passed by very close to his hiding place with their guns and dogs. When they had shot a bird or two, however, they passed on their way, taking no notice of the terrified fugitive in the corn shock.

When darkness came, he set out again, feeling strengthened by the ear of dry corn but apparently light-headed from lack of food and sleep. He felt that he must at last be nearing free soil and he began to skip and jump and clap his hands and talk to himself. He found himself jeering the slaveholder he had left behind and saying "Ah! ha! old fellow, I told you I'd fix you." The exhilaration passed before long, however, and once again depression gained the upper hand. Now he found himself asking, "But where are you going? What are you going to do? What will you do with freedom without father, mother, sisters, and brothers? What will you say when you are asked where you were born? You know nothing of the world; how will you explain the fact of your ignorance?"[38]

When Saturday morning dawned, Pembroke was aware of a sharper and deeper hunger than ever before, and he resolved to stay with the road whatever the risk might be and to ask the first person he met where he was. The sun was not yet high when he came to a toll booth. Recollection of the events that followed his encounter with a toll booth three days earlier made him hesitate briefly, but he had to know where he was. So he approached the booth and found it staffed by a woman who greeted him in a friendly fashion. Pembroke asked whether he was in Pennsylvania. She replied that he was, so he asked whether she knew where he might find work. Where he could find work, she did not know, but her advice was to continue on for two or three miles and find the home of William Wright, a Quaker. Mr. Wright, she said, would take an interest in him.

Thanking her profusely and paying careful attention to her directions, Pembroke took leave of the woman in the toll booth and walked on. Some half an hour later he found the house to which he had been directed and, screwing up his courage, he knocked on the door.[39]

CHAPTER TWO

Slavery As It Was

When James Pembroke knocked on William Wright's door, he had been running for six days, but he had ceased to be a slave in his own mind long before that. He made that decision on the day his master flogged Pembroke's father. Bazil Pembroke, James's father, had been caring for a small lamb, the smallest of a valuable flock of Merino sheep that was one of his particular responsibilities. The mother had died and Bazil had brought some milk and was stooping over the lamb to feed it by hand when Frisby Tilghman came up. He was in a rage because two of his slaves had come back late from their free Sunday and two others were absent still. To reassert his authority, he was ready to whip anyone who crossed his path.

"Bazil," he said, "have you fed the flock?"

"Yes, sir."

"Were you away yesterday?"

"No, sir."

"Do you know why these boys have not got home this morning yet?"

"No, sir, I have not seen any of them since Saturday night."

"By the Eternal, I'll make them know their hour. The fact is, I have too many of you; my people are getting to be the most careless, lazy, and worthless in the country."

"Master," said Bazil, "I am always at my post; Monday morning never finds me off the plantation."

"Hush, Bazil!" said his owner. "I shall have to sell some of you; and then the rest will have enough to do; I have not work enough to keep you all tightly employed; I have too many of you."

Tilghman had been looking for an opportunity to vent his rage and the last remark was said in an angry, insulting tone of voice that provoked Bazil to challenge him.

"If I am one too many, sir," he said, "give me a chance to get a purchaser, and I am willing to be sold when it may suit you."

That was all the excuse Tilghman needed. He kept a whip under his arm at all times and now he drew it out. "Bazil," he said, "I told you to hush!"

With all his strength, he brought the cowhide lash down on Bazil's back fifteen or twenty times, rising on his toes to bring it down with full force on the last stroke. "By the ——," he spat out with the last stripe, "I will make you know that I am master of your tongue as well as of your time!"[1]

James Pembroke, who was then about twenty years old and about to begin his own day's work as a carpenter, had been getting his breakfast as all this took place and was near enough to hear and see the whole encounter. It changed the relationship between Tilghman and all Pembroke's family. They talked about it among themselves and went about their work with a sadness of spirit that Tilghman could not fail to notice. Determined to break their spirit, he taunted and threatened and made them constantly aware of his power over them. For James Pembroke it was a transforming moment: "In my mind and spirit," he said, "I never was a *slave* after it."[2]

But if Tilghman could break that spirit, he was determined to do so, and to find any excuse to assert his authority. There was, for example, the day when Pembroke was busy in the yard of the blacksmith shop, working to put a new shoe on a horse. Concentrating on his work, he was unaware that Tilghman had come up and was standing, watching, from a small hill nearby, leaning on his cane and with his hat pulled down above his eyes. The horse was heavy and Pembroke, becoming tired, put the horses's foot down so that he could straighten up and take a brief rest. Unaware of Tilghman's presence, he looked up and unintentionally caught his eye. Tilghman exploded in anger.

"What are you rolling your white eyes at me for, you lazy rascal?" he yelled. Taking his cane, he brought it down on Pembroke's shoulders, arms, and legs at least a dozen times before he stalked off, cursing as he went. Pembroke was sore for weeks afterwards. Just as he had seen his father beaten, so his mother, watching from the cottage window, now saw her son beaten. The family was further humiliated.[3]

Although Pembroke was no longer a slave in his own mind after he had seen his father beaten and although his own beating had further alienated him from his owner, it was some weeks later, on Tuesday of the week before he left Rockland, that the decisive confrontation took place. He and his parents had noticed that Tilghman was keeping a close eye on them and that one of their fellow slaves had become the master's spy to report on them even when the master was not present himself. This spy, more Irish than African, had decided to ingratiate himself with Frisby Tilghman in return for special treatment. Indignant at this betrayal, Pembroke's mother spoke to the slave about it and told him that he should be ashamed of himself. This, too, the slave reported to Tilghman, with the result that Pembroke and his parents were summoned into the owner's presence and berated for attempting to intimidate his "confidential servant." When he came to understand that it was Pembroke's mother who had spoken to the other slave, Tilghman threatened her with a flogging should she do any such thing again. Knowing his mother's spirit as well as his master's, Pembroke saw that they were on the eve of a crisis. That was Tuesday, October 23rd. Pembroke thought about it for a few days and by Saturday he had made his decision. He would not continue to be a victim of the system that produced such behavior.[4]

That system was described in detail by Frances Kemble, the English actress who married a plantation owner, and commented perceptively on how the insecurity of the slave owner inevitably led to such outbursts of violence. In her *Journal of a Residence on a Georgian Plantation in 1838–1839*, she wrote,

> I know that the Southern men are apt to deny the fact that they do live under an habitual sense of danger; but a slave population, coerced into obedience, though unarmed and half-fed, *is* a threatening source of constant insecurity.[5]

Ultimately responsible for Tilghman's conduct was the fear all slave owners necessarily had of their slaves. They had good reason to fear. They knew of the slave rebellion that had gained control of Haiti by 1801, of Gabriel's rebellion in Virginia in 1801 that mustered a thousand slaves, and of other conspiracies in Virginia in 1802 and South Carolina in 1816. They would have heard of the uprising in Louisiana in 1811, the biggest slave revolt in American history, in which between two hundred and five hundred slaves, led by a freeman of color, killed two white people and burned down three plantations before they were put down by a militia. They knew that in 1816, fugitive slaves who had been encouraged to flee to Florida by the Spanish had taken over an abandoned fort with its guns and munitions with the result that Andrew Jackson had believed it necessary to send an army unit into Spanish territory with orders to destroy the fort and "restore the stolen negroes and property to their rightful owners." Nearly 300 slaves were killed in the resulting battle but, inexperienced and untrained though they were, they had proved willing and able to engage an organized military force. In 1822, Denmark Vesey, who had purchased his freedom, was betrayed before his planned uprising could be set in motion in South Carolina; but in 1831, 57 men, women, and children were slaughtered in Nat Turner's rebellion before the militia put it down. All this lay behind the slave owners' policy of keeping slaves ignorant and isolated so that word of such events would not spread and encourage further rebellions. Nonetheless, there could be no security in the chattel system because the chattels could never be reconciled to their fate. Fueled in part by their owners' own rhetoric in the recent struggle for American independence, the slave owners' property had dreams of freedom. Thus, as Kemble put it, life in a plantation was a constant struggle, "on the one hand to inflict, and on the other hand to evade, oppression and injustice."[6]

As Pennington himself wrote some years later, "You cannot constitute slavery without the chattel principle—and with the chattel principle you cannot save it from these results. Talk not then about kind and christian masters. They are not masters of the system. The system is master of them; and the slaves are their vassals."[7] Pennington was always careful to indict the system rather than the individual slave owners. He understood that Frisby Tilghman also was trapped by the chattel system as surely as were the slaves. The fact that some human beings were treated as property by other human beings degraded them all. Years later, when Pennington wrote his autobiography, he indicted "the property principle . . . the bill of sale principle" of which "the cart-whip, starvation, and nakedness, are [the] inevitable consequences."[8] Frederick Douglass, in his autobiography, says very much the same thing: "The slaveholder, as well as the slave, was the victim of the slave system."[9]

Even as a young man, uneducated and isolated from any larger world view, Pembroke somehow sensed that it was the system that was at fault. He realized that the system was gradually corrupting his own integrity and that he must escape from that system or be destroyed by it. He had, for example, always tried to be trustworthy and to do work in which he could take pride. His owner had singled him out to learn the blacksmith's trade and he had made an effort to do the best work possible. The skill he had developed had helped, in fact, to reconcile him to the life of a slave. He had a craft and he took an artist's pride in finding new techniques to use. He had often made guns and pistols and blades for penknives, as well as hammers and hatchets and sword-canes, giving each of them a special touch as a work of art.[10] No wonder Tilghman was sorry to lose him. But now Pembroke found that he could take no pride in his work. He could think of nothing but the way his family had been treated and of his determination to get away from the situation he was in.

Pembroke knew very well, however, that his lot could have been much worse. As stories of freedom filtered back from the North, so also stories filtered back from the South of far greater oppression. Tilghman's way of controlling his slaves was mild compared to what happened elsewhere, and Pembroke was still able to say that his general temper was "kind."[11]

One demoralizing aspect of the system, as Pembroke saw it, was the way it undercut whatever effort the slaves might make to improve themselves. If, for example, the family took pride in their daughters and trained them well, the daughters became desirable to the slave owners and overseers and their sons, who were unrestrained by any sense of a common humanity. Then, when the pregnant black woman became embarrassing and visible evidence of the white man's behavior, she was almost certain to be separated from her family and sold into the grueling plantations of the Deep South.

Pembroke remembered that Frisby Tilghman had once owned a beautiful girl who was about twenty-four years old. She had been brought up elsewhere with an owner who was a well-known lawyer of unusual ability. He was, however, also an alcoholic and therefore eventually lost his wealth and had to sell some of his slaves. At that point, Tilghman bought the girl to use as a nurse. Within a year, however, one of Tilghman's sons took an interest in the young woman "for no honourable purposes" and the result was that she had to be sold again, this time to Georgia, to the acute distress of her mother and sisters. Pembroke wrote later that he would "never . . . forget the heart-rending scene, when one day one of the men was ordered to get 'the one-horse cart ready to go into town;' Rachel, with her few articles of clothing, was placed in it, and taken into the very town where her parents lived, and there sold to the traders before their weeping eyes. That same son who had degraded her, and who was the cause of her being sold, acted as salesman, ... While this cruel business was being transacted, my master stood aside, and the girl's father, a pious member and exhorter in the Methodist Church, a venerable grey-headed man, with his hat off, besought that he might be allowed to get some one in the place to purchase his child. But no; my master was invincible. His reply was, 'She has offended in my family, and I can only restore confidence by sending her out of hearing.' After lying in prison a short time, her new owner took her with others to the far South, where her parents heard no more of her."[12]

"Here was a girl," Pennington wrote, "born and reared under the mildest form of slavery. Her original master was reputed to be even indulgent. He lived in a town, and was a high-bred gentleman, and a lawyer. He had but a few slaves, and had no occasion for an overseer, those negro leeches, to watch and drive them; but when he became embarrassed by his own folly, the chattel principle doomed this girl to be sold at the same sale with his books, house, and horses. With my master she found herself under far more stringent discipline than she had been accustomed to, and finally degraded, and sold where her condition could not be worse, and where she had not the least hope of ever bettering it."[13]

It was that same principle that worked against Frederick Douglass when he was allowed to go into the shipyards and earn money. The money he made had to be brought back at the end of the week and given to his owner.[14] Whatever a slave might do to improve his or her lot belonged to the owner. There was no advantage, therefore, to be gained by self-improvement, yet the owner too lost out since he could never hope to see his slaves give him their full potential. Frances Kemble asked a slave one day why he had never learned to read since his father had been able to. "Missis, what for me learn to read?" he answered; "me have no prospect!"[15]

Another aspect of the chattel system was the constant fear in which the owners lived because of the contradictions inherent in that system. They needed to maintain a tight control of the slaves, yet some of the standard punishments other societies might use for that purpose were ruled out. To imprison a slave was to lose the labor for which the slave existed; to execute the slave was to destroy one's own property. Thus the whip or lash became the means of control and must constantly be put to use even in the mildest form of the system. But if stronger force seemed needed, the owners and overseers would use it and, finally, losing patience or lacking alternatives, would damage and even destroy their "property." Pennington speaks of seeing one slave hit with a hay fork,[16] and both Douglass and Pennington recorded instances of slaves being shot. Douglass tells of a slave who ran into a stream to escape a beating and when he refused to come out was shot where he stood and his body left to float in the stream.[17] Overseers and owners were sometimes charged in the death of a slave but, since slaves could not testify in court, they were never convicted.

Pembroke remembered a time when a slave ran away from a threatened beating and the overseer picked up his gun and shot the man in the legs. The slave ran on into the woods but was in so much pain that he came back, hoping the overseer would think he had been punished enough. On the contrary, his owner locked him up for the night and allowed the overseer to tie him up and flog him in the morning. After that, the owner took a sharp instrument, picked out the shot from the slave's legs, and told him it served him right.[18]

There was another slave on the Tilghman plantation, of deep faith and exemplary life, who had a difference of opinion one day with the overseer. When the overseer attempted to flog him, the slave ran into the woods. That happened about noontime. Late in the day, the slave came back quite peaceably. The next morning, Tilghman took a rope and cowhide whip with one of his sons and led the poor old man into the stable where they tied him up. Tilghman then ordered his son to give the slave thirty-nine lashes. He did it in such a way that the sharp end of the cowhide lapped around and struck the old man like a lance in the tenderest part of his side until the blood flowed out. Meanwhile the old man's six-year-old daughter stood by the door of the stable, weeping. In the intervals between blows Pembroke could hear the old man speaking in a low voice, "And lo! he was praying!" At the end of the ordeal, they let the old man down and, leaving him to put his clothes back on, drove the child away from the door.[19] Yet Tilghman is described by Pembroke as being of a "kind disposition."

The circumstances of slaves' lives differed, of course, from place to place and from one era to another, but Pembroke's observations of the life of a slave are similar in many ways to those of others. Frederick Douglass, for example, grew up on a plantation on the Eastern Shore of Maryland, not far from where Pembroke was born, and his circumstances were better in many ways. He had a mistress for a while who helped him learn to read,[20] and he was able to work in the shipyards, away from the plantation.[21] Yet he, also, whipped many times himself, describes the use of the whip, drawing blood from the bare backs of the victims, both male and female.[22] William Wells Brown, another fugitive slave, describes the whip that was used on his plantation in Missouri as having a handle "about three feet long, with the butt-end filled with lead, and the lash six or seven feet in length, made of cowhide, with platted wire on the end of it."[23]

Angelina and Sarah Grimké were sisters who grew up in South Carolina, where their father owned a large estate; but first one, then the other moved north to escape the sight and sound of slavery. They published their recollections in a book called *American Slavery As It Is*, compiled by Angelina's husband, Theodore Weld, a leading abolitionist. The stories they tell bear eloquent witness to Pembroke's analysis of the brutalizing effect of slavery on the slave owners. The Grimké sisters had seen nothing of conditions on the plantation, since their father was an absentee landlord, but wrote rather of what happened within their home in Charleston and what was told them by others. Sarah recalled whipping a slave herself when she was fourteen or fifteen and had felt insulted. Her father had the slave stripped and tied and then ordered his daughter to whip him until he fell on his knees and pleaded for mercy.[24] Angelina tells of a woman who had left the world of fashion and society because of her conversion to Christian faith who, nevertheless, whipped some of her slaves daily in the same room where she would gather her friends to pray. From the window of the room she would look out at slaves in the garden, some distance from the house, and scream at them for an hour or more in a voice that could be heard throughout the neighborhood.[25] They tell also of a serving maid whose ears were slit for some minor offense,[26] of a man who was made to stand holding up one foot and then so tied that if he let the foot down he would be choked,[27] of a female slave locked in a room until she starved to death,[28] of slaves whose wounds became so infected that they could not be brought into the house because of the smell.[29] Sarah Grimké was traveling one day when the coachman pointed to a human head on a pole. A runaway slave had been shot and his head put up as a warning to others.[30] It is by comparison with such stories that James Pennington could speak of his former master as "kind."

> I have no disposition to attempt to convict him of having been one
> of the most cruel masters—that would not be true—his prevailing

temper was kind, but he was a perpetualist. He was opposed to emancipation; thought free negroes a great nuisance, and was, as respects discipline, a thorough slaveholder. He would not tolerate a look or a word from a slave like insubordination. He would suppress it at once, and at any risk. When he thought it necessary to secure unqualified obedience, he would strike a slave with any weapon, flog him on the bare back, and sell. And this was the kind of discipline he also empowered his overseers and sons to use.[31]

Laws and customs also needed to be shaped to keep the slaves under control. Tilghman was one of those who worked to change several local laws in Washington County regarding the control of slaves. One such revision reduced the number of miles slaves were allowed to travel from their plantation on Sundays, when they were traditionally allowed to visit family members on nearby plantations. Tilghman also had the authorities break up a local Sunday school for free blacks which had been established by Methodist and Lutheran churches lest, according to Pennington, "the slaves should get some benefit of it." When Pembroke left the plantation he remembered hearing two sermons but he had never heard of Jesus.[32]

It was not only a Sunday school for free blacks that seemed dangerous to Frisby Tilghman; Christian preaching worried him too. When Jacob Gruber, a Pennsylvania minister, conducted a camp meeting near the Rockland estate in 1818, Tilghman seems to have been one of the Washington County slave owners who accused him of inciting slaves to rebel against their masters and had him arrested. Many years later, Pembroke met with a fugitive who remembered distinctly the words Gruber had spoken and "by which his own mind was awakened to a sense of the value of his soul." Gruber had said to the slaves, "You have precious immortal souls, that are worth far more to you than your bodies are to your masters." Such words might have interested the slaves, but they angered the masters who saw them as an attempt to incite the slaves to rebel.[33]

Ironically, Gruber was successfully defended after his arrest by Roger Taney, who was then a lawyer in Frederick County but some years later served as chief justice of the Supreme Court that issued the Dred Scott decision, requiring a fugitive slave to be returned to his owner. Gruber was acquitted, but some of the slave owners threatened violence if he tried to preach in that area again and he apparently made no effort to do so. Tilghman himself, Pembroke tells us, would ride into Hagerstown to church services if the weather was fine, but he made no effort to speak to the slaves about faith in God, nor was any of the slaves ever given a Bible or tract or religious book. Nor were teachers or clergy ever invited to visit the slaves. Nor were clergy called on when a slave died. The owner might call in a doctor if a slave was sick, but not a minister of religion.[34]

Tilghman had very practical reasons for his policies. Churches, by their very nature, brought people together and enabled them to exchange information. Isolation was essential to control. The less the slaves knew about life beyond the plantation, the less likely it was that they could learn about the freedom that existed elsewhere or learn of the Underground Railroad. Since Hagerstown was an important transportation center with main roads running east and west and north into Pennsylvania, it was, in fact, an important station on the Underground Railroad. There was a black lay minister, Thomas W. Henry, who served at the Hagerstown Methodist Church in 1831 and perhaps earlier. Later he was ordained to the ministry of the African Methodist Episcopal Church and served congregations in Chambersburg, Pennsylvania, as well as a congregation that he established in Hagerstown. Henry was also an active agent on the Underground Railroad. If Pembroke had been allowed to go to church services in Hagerstown, he might well have discovered an easily available way to freedom. No wonder Tilghman, like other slave owners, did everything possible to prevent his slaves from being exposed to the influences and information that came with religion.

There was, of course, no good time to be a slave, but James Pembroke grew up at a time when the conditions under which slaves lived were becoming more oppressive than ever. In the early days of American settlement, slave owners both in the North and South made some effort to educate their slaves and teach them a version of the Christian faith justifying slavery. The American Revolution, however, with its foundational statement that "all men are created equal" and "endowed . . . with certain unalienable rights," set both white and black Americans to thinking about the implications of that statement for the institution of slavery. Then, at the end of the eighteenth century and beginning of the nineteenth, refugees from the Haitian wars of independence began arriving in southern port cities like Baltimore and Norfolk and New Orleans bringing firsthand reports of how African slaves in the West Indies had claimed their freedom. African Americans, encouraged by these reports and the increasingly assertive abolitionist movement, became restive, conspiracies to rebel were formed, and the Underground Railroad began carrying an ever-growing number of slaves to freedom. Whatever the Declaration of Independence might have said, economic interests trumped ideology for slave owners who, as a result, became more repressive in their policies rather than less so. A wave of new legislation swept through the southern states prohibiting not only the education of slaves but their assembling for any religious or social purpose except under the tutelage of approved white leadership. Owners who had used slaves as bookkeepers or in positions requiring some education were now forbidden to do so. Where once it had been thought that education made slaves more useful, now it was agreed that they should be kept in the lowest state of ignorance and degradation, and that the nearer they could be kept to the condition of mere beasts of burden, the better it would be.

Yet the brutalizing influence of this new approach made its impact on the slave owners as well as the slaves. Perhaps the most interesting charge Pembroke later brought against the slave system was the corrupting effect it had on the families of those who owned slaves. In his autobiography, he wrote of the "disastrous influence upon the families of the masters, physically, pecuniarily, and mentally. It seems to destroy families as by a powerful blight, large and opulent slave-holding families, often vanish like a group of shadows at the third or fourth generation."[35]

Pembroke went on to say that he had formed these views while he was still a slave and that the slaves, indeed, commonly discussed among themselves the fact that each generation of a slave-owning family seemed inferior to the one before it. He cited the particular case of a General Ringgold, who was Frisby Tilghman's brother-in-law (Pembroke calls him "General R.," but Tilghman's brother-in-law's name was and is no secret) and one of the wealthiest slave owners in Washington County. He "drove his coach and four" and served several terms in Congress. Although Ringgold had many children, none of them had been trained to play a useful role in the management of the estate. The only one who attained anything like his father's eminence, Pembroke wrote with irony, "was the eldest, who became an officer in the navy, and obtained the doubtful glory of being killed in the Mexican war." As for the general himself, he became addicted to alcohol, used up his wealth, and, at his death, left his widow and daughters destitute and the sons useless for "any employment but in the army and navy." Pembroke recalled walking past the remains of the Ringgold estate one Sunday evening and shivering with horror at its condition:

> To see the once fine smooth gravel walks, overgrown with grass—
> the redundances of the shrubbery neglected—the once finely
> painted picket fences, rusted and fallen down—a fine garden in
> splendid ruins—the lofty ceiling of the mansion thickly curtained
> with cobwebs—the spacious apartments abandoned, while the only
> music heard within as a substitute for the voices of family glee that
> once filled it, was the crying cricket and cockroaches! Ignorant
> slave as I was at that time, I could but pause for a moment, and
> recur in silent horror to the fact that, a strange reverse of fortune,
> had lately driven from that proud mansion, a large and once opulent
> family. What advantage was it now to the members of that family,

that the father and head had for near half a century stood high in the counsels of the state, and had the benefit of the unrequited toil of hundreds of his fellow men, when they were already grappling with the annoyances of that poverty, which he had entailed upon others.[36]

The Tilghman dynasty, it seemed to Pembroke, was following the same path. Frisby Tilghman had once come within a few votes of being elected governor of the state, but he never approached the eminence of his father. He directed his energies not to accomplishments in the wider world but primarily to the oppression of his slaves, especially in creating new laws to limit their freedom. His own children fell even further in ability and accomplishment. A son-in-law died intestate at 36 and one of his sons was sent to West Point to be trained as an officer. After being there a short time, however, he became unsteady, and commenced the study of medicine, but he soon gave that up and preferred to live at home and flog the slaves; and by them was cordially dreaded and disliked, and among themselves he was vulgarly nicknamed on account of his cruel and filthy habits.[37]

All this, it seemed to Pembroke, was evidence of the corrupting effect of the chattel principle. He wrote about that principle years later when he had had opportunity to gain some perspective on the system. It was a system whose principles and consequences have done much to shape American life from the time when the first slaves arrived in Virginia in 1619, even before the Pilgrims arrived in New England, down to the present day. Pembroke, of course, had been born into that system and into a world shaped by slavery, and he himself would also never escape the consequences of that birth and upbringing.

James Pembroke was born on January 15, 1808,[†] on a plantation on the Eastern Shore of Maryland owned by James Tilghman.[38] The Tilghman family had arrived in Maryland 140 years earlier and had become wealthy land owners. James Tilghman's brother, Tench Tilghman, served as aide-de-camp to George Washington throughout the Revolutionary War, and James served as the first attorney general of Maryland in the early years of the Revolution. James Tilghman died in 1809, but a few years earlier he had given land in western Maryland to his son, Frisby, as a wedding gift. He also gave his son some of his slaves, among them James Pembroke's mother Nelly. Since children went with the mother, James Pembroke was taken to the new plantation

---

† This is the date found in the Clergy Register of the Third Presbytery of New York and presumably would have been provided by Pennington himself. His adopted son, Thomas H. S. Pennington, gives the date as 1812, but that seems likely to be much too late since he would not then have been anywhere near 16 when he escaped from slavery in 1829, a date fixed by ads in the Hagerstown paper for his arrest.

when he was about four years old. Bazil, his father, had been a slave on another Eastern Shore plantation but not long after his family was moved to the west, Frisby purchased him and reunited him with his wife and children.

Six miles south of Hagerstown, on a high knoll overlooking the surrounding fields, Frisby Tilghman built a great house for himself. The house, known as Rockland, still stands, beautifully restored, though the slave quarters, which once housed well over two hundred slaves, are gone without a trace. Although Tilghman had been trained as a physician, he chose to become a plantation owner and to specialize in growing wheat. Since the work of the plantation was done by slaves under the supervision of overseers, Frisby Tilghman was free to take an active part in the civil affairs of the newly developing area. He represented Washington County four times in Maryland's House of Delegates and formed and commanded a local militia company. He also served on the board of directors of local banks and was deeply involved in the building of the Chesapeake & Ohio Canal as a means of getting his crops to the eastern cities.

The reuniting of his parents should have helped make James Pembroke's childhood a happy time, at least in comparison with other children born into slavery whose parents were often widely separated and who sometimes never knew their fathers. Both parents, however, worked in the fields and were absent from their home, as a result, from dawn to dusk. New mothers were sent back to the fields within three or four weeks of delivery and infants were often left at the end of a row of crops to be given brief attention by their mothers when they came to the end of the row. Older children were left very much to their own devices. Pembroke's memories of his childhood were, as a result, not happy at all:

> To estimate the sad state of a slave child, you must look at it as a helpless human being thrown upon the world without the benefit of its natural guardians. It is thrown into the world without a social circle to flee to for hope, shelter, comfort, or instruction. The social circle, with all its heaven-ordained blessings, is of the utmost importance to the *tender child*; but of this, the slave child, however tender and delicate, is robbed.[39]

Slave children often played happily with their owner's children until, still at a very young age, the owner's children began to imitate their parents' attitude toward the slaves and assumed an air of authority over their black playmates.

It was also not long before the overseers began to assert their authority over the slave children to accustom them to their authority. It was the business of the overseers to keep the slaves in subjection, and it was therefore a position that not only attracted men with an inclination to anger and violence but also one that developed those tendencies in those who were thus employed. A whip or cane was always in their hands, and they were quick to use those weapons at the least excuse. "They seem to take pleasure in torturing the children of slaves," Pembroke recalled, "long before they are large enough to be put at the hoe, and consequently under the whip."[40]

He remembered a particular overseer named Blackstone who liked to use hickory canes and who kept four or five so that one would be available to his use wherever he might happen to be. Young James Pembroke came upon one of these canes one day and, thinking the overseer had thrown it away, he picked it up and began to play with it as a riding horse. Just at that moment, the overseer came in from the fields and fell upon the child with the cane in his hand, beating him with it severely. After that, he would make a point of chasing Pembroke away whenever he came upon him. The child therefore would often lie for hours in the woods or behind a fence so as to be hidden from the overseer's violence.[41]

A small child was not much use to the slave owner but he could help his parents in various ways. In particular, Pennington used to assist his father at night in making straw hats and willow baskets. Slaves would often work in whatever free time they had to earn a little extra money by making something that could be sold. The income from such small crafts could then be used to provide the family with small items of food and clothing and other "luxuries," which slaves, even in the mildest form of the system, would not otherwise be given.[42]

As for the standard provision made for the slaves by the owners, their food for the week was dealt out by the overseer and an assistant on Monday morning. Pennington tells how each working man would go to the cellar where the provisions were kept and be given three and a half pounds of salt pork (half a pound a day) or, on occasion, twelve herrings (two a day) to last the week. Large loaves of corn bread, known locally as "steel pound bread" and made by one of the women, were also provided, but Pennington notes that in some areas the slaves were given the corn in the ear and would have to grind it for themselves with hand-mills after their day's work was done. Sometimes, for a change, the corn flour was provided in the simpler form of "Johnny Cake," and at other times it was stirred and boiled and given out as mush. No butter, coffee, tea, or sugar were provided and only occasionally milk. An exception to this standard was made only in the two or three weeks of the wheat harvest in the heat of mid-summer when some fresh meat, rice, sugar, and coffee were given to the workers, as well as an allowance of whiskey.[43] Frederick Douglass speaks of a similar allotting of food, though less generous: eight pounds of pickled pork or fish of poor quality for each man or woman every month with a bushel of unprocessed corn and a pint of salt. He remembered being constantly hungry.[44]

For clothing, at the beginning of winter, each slave at Rockland was given one pair of coarse shoes and stockings, one pair of pants, and a jacket. At the beginning of summer, he was given two pairs of coarse linen pants and two shirts.[45] Douglass recites a similar allocation of clothing but notes that children beneath the age of ten were given simply two rough linen shirts for the year with no pants or shoes. If the shirts wore out, as they often did, they went naked.[46]

Once every so many years, one coarse blanket and enough coarse linen for a "bed-tick" would be given to each slave, or each man and his wife. No bedstead or other furniture was provided, so these had to be improvised with whatever materials could be found. No hats or handkerchiefs were provided for men or women. Each working man was given a small "patch" of ground which had to be worked by night. If they wanted vegetables, they had to grow their own.[47]

Slave owners would frequently arrange for some of their more promising young slaves to be sent out to acquire particular skills that could be used on the plantation. The practice also saved them the expense of feeding a child at an age when the child would be less useful. Thus, when James Pembroke was eight or nine years old, he and his older brother, Robert, were sent into Hagerstown to serve as apprentices. James was apprenticed to a stone mason and lived for the next several years with the mason's family.[48] Wealthy Victorian families in England often sent their sons away to school at about the same age so they could gain an education and some social skills. James Pembroke's circumstances were, of course, rather different and the education he acquired was manual, not academic, but, in somewhat the same way as an English child, he gained a new and broader perspective on life. To live in the home of a close-knit white family made him much more acutely aware of the impoverishment of his life as a slave. He also would have had opportunity to see something of the life of a relatively large and thriving community. Among the features of that community was an important slave market where regular auctions took place.

When Pembroke returned to Rockland about two years later, he was set to work with his new skills as a mason to assist in the building of a new blacksmith's shop. The blacksmith was a slave who had acquired his skills in the same way, by being apprenticed out to a blacksmith in the larger community. When the new building was completed, Pembroke continued to work with the blacksmith so as to learn that trade as well. A skilled blacksmith could become an additional source of income to the plantation by doing work for others in the neighborhood. An account book was therefore kept in the shop and Pembroke would study it when no one else was around to see whether he could make anything of the letters and numbers inscribed in it. Thus he taught himself to make a few letters but not to read.[49]

Years later, James Pennington—as he had re-named himself—remembered a constant "indescribable feeling of wretchedness" that he carried with him always, even when he had escaped from slavery. It had made him a very quiet child, but even the owner and his family were aware that there was something more beneath the surface and would say, "That blacksmith Jemmy is a 'cute [meaning "acute" or sharp] fellow; still water runs deep." But not acute enough, he wrote many years later, "to understand the cause of his own wretchedness. The current of the still water may have run deep, but it did not reach down to that awful bed of lava." Or, as he further analyzed it: "There lies buried down in the heart of the most seemingly careless and stupid slave a *bleeding spot*, that bleeds and aches, though he could scarcely tell why; and that this sore spot is the *degradation* of his position."[50]

For some nine years, Pembroke worked as a blacksmith and became highly skilled in his work. He was then sold for $700 to another man who, as it turned out, had not enough work to keep him occupied, and so he was sold back to Tilghman. Tilghman then assigned him to work with a carpenter so that he might learn still another trade. Pembroke had therefore been working as a carpenter for some six months when that day came on which his mother was threatened and he decided he must escape.[51] That sequence of events brought him, after six days of frantic running and hiding, capture and escape, to William Wright's front door.

CHAPTER THREE
Pennsylvania

William Wright opened the door, and behind him Pembroke could see the table loaded with food for a full country breakfast. Tired, hungry, and very nervous, James Pembroke managed to say that he had been sent there to look for work. He would never forget the reply:

> "Well, come in then and take thy breakfast, and get warm, and we will talk about it; thee must be cold without any coat."[1]

Ever afterwards, Pembroke would remember those words when he himself was approached by someone in need.

> From that day to this, whenever I discover the least disposition in my heart to disregard the wretched condition of any poor or distressed persons with whom I meet, I call to mind these words—"*Come in and take thy breakfast, and get warm.*" They invariably remind me of what I was at that time; my condition was as wretched as that of any human being can possibly be, with the exception of the loss of health or reason. I had but four pieces of clothing about my person, having left all the rest in the hands of my captors. I was a starving fugitive, without home or friends—a reward offered for my person in the public papers—pursued by cruel manhunters, and no claim upon him to whose door I went. Had he turned me away, I must have perished. Nay, he took me in, and gave me of his food, and shared with me his own garments. Such treatment I had never before received at the hands of any white man.[2]

Reflecting on it many years afterwards, the former fugitive also wrote:

These words spoken by a stranger, but with such an air of simple sincerity and fatherly kindness, made an overwhelming impression upon my mind. They made me feel, spite of all my fear and timidity, that I had, in the providence of God, found a friend and a home. He at once gained my confidence; and I felt that I might confide to him a fact which I had, as yet, confided to no one.[3]

That fact, which he had not yielded to his captors two days earlier, was, of course, that he was a fugitive slave. It cannot have been a surprise to William Wright. His home, as the toll collector who sent Pembroke to him obviously knew, was an established station on the legendary "Underground Railroad" and he was very accustomed to the sudden appearance at his house of ragged slaves fleeing from their owners. By some estimates, William and Phebe Wright may have helped as many as a thousand fugitive slaves on their way to freedom.

Whether Pembroke had ever heard of the Underground Railroad is unclear. He obviously had no idea that there might have been a station in Hagerstown. If he had heard of the Underground Railroad at all, he certainly had no idea how to locate it and did so finally only "in the providence of God." In finding the home of William Wright, however, Pembroke not only had discovered a link to the invisible conveyor belt transferring slaves from captivity to freedom, but had also come upon a very special community. Wright was a member of the Society of Friends and Quakers who had first settled in what came to be known as "Quaker Valley" in the 1730s. Quakers had once been as willing to own slaves as any Americans, but following the leadership of John Woolman (1720–1772) and others, they had become abolitionists. It may have been for that reason that a neighboring settlement of African Americans grew up on what was known as Yellow Hill. Whether the Friends actively encouraged that settlement or whether, once neighbors, they discovered similar interests, members of the two communities worked together for many years, receiving slaves fleeing the South and sending them on to other Quakers living nearer Philadelphia or to stations to the north and onward to Canada.[4] Canada was the ultimate terminus of the Underground Railroad because, as Pembroke would quickly learn, there was no safety for African Americans in the so-called "free states." Slavery had, indeed, been abolished by states north of the Mason-Dixon line in a gradual process, state by state, after the American Revolution, but when the law abolishing slavery was passed in Pennsylvania in February 1780, it freed no slaves at once and enacted that children born of slaves would remain slaves until their 28th birthday. Thus, when James Pembroke arrived in Pennsylvania in 1827, there were still hundreds of slaves in that state. Even those African Americans who were free had very limited rights: they could not join the militia and, in most cases, could not vote. More important to

Pembroke, however, was the fact that there was a constant danger from slave catchers everywhere. The fugitive slave laws were not uniformly enforced in northern states, but the danger that a fugitive slave might be captured and taken south was nonetheless very real. In theory, slave owners needed a warrant from the county court to take a captured slave back south, and in the years between 1827 and 1834 the Court of Adams County, the county in which William Wright lived, did issue 12 such warrants. But slave catchers did not necessarily bother with the legal niceties; they could act much more simply and directly to gain their ends. It was not unheard of for slave catchers to kidnap not only fugitive slaves but even free blacks and take them south to be sold. In 1845, Kitty Paine, a freed slave from Virginia, was kidnaped in Adams County with her children; bound, gagged, and loaded into a wagon, they were carried back to Virginia and written requests from the Adams County sheriff for their return were ignored.[5]

Pembroke would learn all that very quickly. He would learn as well that William Wright had taken a significant risk in welcoming him. There were fines for assisting fugitive slaves. No one in the immediate community of Quakers and African Americans would betray Wright, but slave holders, searching for their "property," could come into Pennsylvania, enlist the assistance of local law enforcement officials, and conduct a raid on Wright's property. On one occasion, when Wright was sheltering a relatively large party of escaped slaves, such a raiding party appeared and Wright stalled for time, inviting the hunters into his home and engaging them in conversation until the fugitives could be warned and find places to hide. His wife, Phebe, assisting in the effort, asked one of the hunters whether he recognized "the Scripture as the guide of his life." When he replied indignantly that he was an elder in the Baptist Church, Phebe Wright sent for a Bible and lectured him on the sinfulness of slaveholding until his teeth were chattering with fear—and the fugitives on the property had had opportunity to conceal themselves.[6] Even twenty years later, when Pembroke wrote the story of his escape, he referred to Wright only by the initials "W. W." so as to give him some protection against prosecution for his actions.[7]

One immediate consequence of the danger Pembroke was in, even in Pennsylvania, was that he changed his own name to Pennington. The reason for that choice of a new name is not known, but there were prominent Quakers and abolitionists named Pennington, and that may have influenced his selection. He also added, a little later, two initials, "W." and "C." The "W" stood for "William" and honored William Wright, his first benefactor. The "C" stood for "Charles," but that reference is unclear.

James W. C. Pennington, as he would now be known, tells us very little about the next six months; perhaps he was concerned not to reveal too much about William Wright's support for a fugitive slave. Some of what happened, however, seems quite certain. On that first morning, for example, it seems safe to assume that he accepted Wright's invitation to breakfast. He was half starved, and Wright immediately saw that. Pennington says nothing about the meal, however, except that as he sat at the table he and Wright discussed his request for work and the employment Wright might be able to give him. Specifically, Pennington says that Wright set him to sawing and splitting a number of cords of wood piled in the yard.[8]

William Wright had been a school teacher before health problems prevented him from continuing in that vocation and he became a farmer, so help with the physical work to be done on the farm would certainly have been useful. It would have been difficult to make use of the fugitive families or the larger groups that often came, but a strong young man like James Pennington could undoubtedly be of help in many ways. With winter coming on, the splitting of wood and building up of a woodpile to heat the house would have been especially useful. Wright offered what Pennington considered "generous" terms for the work. His experience as an apprentice stone mason in Hagerstown might have given him some basis for judging what was a fair rate of pay, but the experience of earning money on a regular basis would have been completely new to him and the offer of any remuneration would have seemed generous.

At that first meeting, Wright also spelled out for Pennington some of the problems he would face as a fugitive in an area where slave hunters were common. He was now perhaps a dozen miles from the border, but he was not safe. Wright and Pennington therefore agreed on "the way and means of avoiding surprise, in case any one should come to the house as a spy, or with intention to arrest me." Again, no details are provided because, even twenty years later, when Pennington came to write about these events, the Underground Railroad was still delivering its passengers, and bounty hunters who might see a copy of Pennington's story and make use of such information were still active. Wright gave Pennington some sense of security by letting him know that the whole family would be alert to the presence of spies and would take whatever action seemed necessary for Pennington's safety.[9]

Food and warnings were the first priority, but sleep would have been almost as urgent after almost six days with hardly any rest. Wright would have been aware of that need also, and encouraged Pennington to catch up on his sleep. So it was the next morning before the conversation between Wright and Pennington continued.

"Can thee read or write any, James?" asked William Wright.

The short answer, of course, was "No," but Pennington was able to explain that he had tried to learn the letters and numbers by studying the daybook kept in the blacksmith shop to record work done for the neighbors and the amount owed. He was unable to keep the book himself, but he knew that a particular entry had been made when a certain person was in the shop and therefore that the marks on the page must include the name of the individual, the work done, and the amount charged. With no guide to provide a first clue as to the meaning of the those marks, however, he was helpless to make much of them. He told Wright that some five years earlier he had gone so far as to find some paper he could use and to make himself a pen from a quill. When he found that the quill was too soft, he had made another one, of steel. With that equipment, he had taught himself to make some of the letters he found in the book but he did not know the alphabet and he could not write his own name.

"Let me see how thee makes letters," said Wright, handing Pennington a slate and a pencil. "Try such as thou hast been able to make easily."

So Pennington carefully wrote down the letters he had learned: "A. B. C. L. G."

Phebe Wright, who had been watching, exclaimed, "Why, those are better than I can make."

Her husband was also impressed, and said, "Oh, we can soon get thee in the way, James."

So the lessons began. Wright, as a former teacher, was happy to have an eager pupil and set out to teach him reading, writing, arithmetic, and—perhaps to add something more exciting and less familiar—basic lessons also in astronomy. Astronomy and arithmetic quickly became Pennington's favorite subjects. These were tools he could use and Wright would have shown him how to apply them even in his work around the farm. His teacher, Pennington reported, was both "far-sighted" and "practical." His teaching method was conversational. He would illustrate his points with practical examples from the world around them and demonstrate the points he was trying to make with diagrams on his ever-present slate. Pennington throve under this instruction and learned "with ease and rapidity," although the new ideas flooding in upon him brought with them a painful realization:

> I now began to see, for the first time, the extent of the mischief slavery had done to me. Twenty-one years of my life were gone, never again to return, and I was as profoundly ignorant, comparatively, as a child five years old. This was painful, annoying, and humiliating in the extreme.[10]

The more Pennington learned, the more he was aware of the extent of his ignorance, and he was often discouraged. "As my friend poured light into my mind, I saw the darkness; it amazed and grieved me beyond description." It seemed impossible at such moments that he could ever overcome the disadvantage of his upbringing. Wright, however, was not only an excellent teacher but a man who could inspire confidence in his pupil. As a way to encourage Pennington, Wright told him stories of others of African descent who had made names for themselves in spite of their own handicaps. Francis Williams, for example, had been born in Jamaica where, although he and his family were not slaves, education and opportunity were seldom available. Yet Williams had gained admission to Cambridge University and become a recognized scholar, writing poetry in Latin. Phillis Wheatley was another poet whose story Wright told. Born in Africa and brought to Boston as a slave, she had published two volumes of poetry and gained her freedom. Benjamin Banneker, born free but limited in education, had taught himself mechanics and astronomy and written to President Thomas Jefferson urging social justice for Americans of African descent. Jefferson in turn had cited Banneker as an example of what African Americans could accomplish. None of these three had faced the obstacles Pennington needed to overcome, but their stories opened his mind to the achievements of other Africans and helped him believe in his own potential.[11]

The relationship formed over the next few months was both warm and enduring. Pennington and Wright remained in touch with each other afterwards, and when Pennington published his autobiography, some twenty years later, he could report that he had visited Wright twice in the previous four years. He included in the introduction to his book some letters recently exchanged between himself and Wright, and he referred to Wright often as "my friend" instead of by name. Phebe Wright had added a note to one letter saying that their children would argue over which should have the privilege of opening the next letter from Pennington. Wright was still deeply involved in the Underground Railroad and reported that he was currently working with a man from Maryland who was "trying to learn as fast as thee did when here."[12]

Pennington's lessons, however, were brought to an early end by the ever-present danger of slave catchers and one particular incident that brought that danger vividly to life. One evening about 9 o'clock, Pennington had gone to bed in the room above the one in which the Wrights were sitting. He had not fallen asleep, however, when he heard a voice ask, "Where is the boy?" It sounded like the voice of Frisby Tilghman and Pennington was terrified. He sat straight up and listened intently. For a moment there was silence and then he heard sounds that seemed to him to reflect some confusion in the room below. He looked around to see how best to escape and made note of a window at the head of the bed that he could reach without putting his feet on the floor. The window was a single-sash type and opened on hinges. He opened it and waited trembling for some further signal. When the door creaked open at the bottom of the stairs, he put his head out the window. With the sound of a footstep on the stairs he would have been out of the window and on his way to the woods in a flash. What he heard instead was the gentle voice of William Wright saying "James?"

"Here," said Wright, "Joel has come, and he would like to have thee put up his horse."

Joel Wierman was Wright's brother-in-law, also a Quaker, and worked with him to assist fugitives. Like William Wright, Wierman is not named in Pennington's autobiography for fear of making his activities public and exposing him to arrest. As a neighbor and relative with a common concern for the fugitives, Wierman had visited Wright's farm often, sometimes spending the night and frequently arriving without warning, but he lived some ten miles away and so had never before come after dark. Had Wright started up the stairs without speaking, Pennington would have been out the window and gone. Instead, he took a deep breath and went down to deal with the horse. But he could not relax, nor was he able to sleep normally that night. He would doze off briefly and then wake with a start thinking he had heard Frisby Tilghman's voice saying "Where is that boy?" Wright had warned him that there was danger; now he knew it with a vividness that would not leave him.[13]

Over the next several weeks, his sense of insecurity only increased. Each day he felt less safe than the day before, with the result that he could no longer work or study or sleep. Wright tried to persuade him to stay just one more week, but now even he could do nothing to inspire any confidence in his student. Reluctantly, but unable to feel secure with any other decision, Pennington made arrangements to be on his way. It was in many ways a more difficult separation than his departure from his own family. He cared deeply for his family, but they had never been able to provide for him and work with him as William Wright had done. He and Wright had studied together, worked together, and enjoyed each other's company. Pennington said afterwards that he wished he could have spent not six months with him but six years. Yet he could not overcome the fear that he might at any moment actually hear Tilghman's voice, and that constant insecurity was decisive.[14]

Not long after Pennington's departure, the wisdom of his move became clear. Some weeks had gone by and Joel Wierman, the same brother-in-law who had frightened Pennington by his sudden arrival, was staying in an inn some twenty miles further east of Hagerstown than Wright's home when he overheard a conversation. Sitting quietly in a corner of the dining area, Wierman became aware that the conversation between a traveling peddler and some locals had turned to a very particular subject and that they were talking about William Wright. Wierman's report refers to the local resident as "gossiper" and uses the obsolete spelling "pedler." In writing the story down, Pennington again avoids naming people who might be endangered if their work were revealed; he uses Wright's initials and refers to Wierman as "Brother-in-law."

PEDLER: Do you know one William Wright somewhere about here?

GOSSIPER: Yes, he lives — miles off.

PEDLER: I understand he had a black boy with him last winter, I wonder if he is there yet?

GOSSIPER: I don't know, he most always has a runaway nigger with him.

PEDLER: I should like to find out whether that fellow is there yet.

At this point Wierman, who had had his back to the speakers, turned his chair and entered the conversation.

WIERMAN: What does thee know about that boy?

PEDLER: Well, he is a runaway.

WIERMAN: Who did he run away from?

PEDLER: From Colonel Tilghman in Hagerstown.

WIERMAN: How did thee find out that fact?

PEDLER: Well, I have been over there peddling.

WIERMAN: Where art thou from?

PEDLER: I belong in Connecticut.

WIERMAN: Did thee see the boy's master?

PEDLER: Yes.

WIERMAN: What did he offer thee to find the boy?

PEDLER: I agreed to find out where he was, and let him know, and if he got him, I was to receive —.

WIERMAN: How didst thou hear the boy had been with William Wright?

PEDLER: Oh, he is known to be a notorious rascal for enticing away, and concealing slaves; he'll get himself into trouble yet, the slaveholders are on the lookout for him.

WIERMAN: William Wright is my brother-in-law; the boy of whom thou speakest is not with him, and to save thee the trouble of abusing him, I can moreover say, he is no rascal.

PEDLER: He may not be there now, but it is because he has sent him off. His master heard of him, and from the description, he is sure it must have been his boy. He could tell me pretty nigh where he was; he said he was a fine healthy boy, twenty-one, a first-rate blacksmith; he would not have taken a thousand dollars for him.

WIERMAN: I know not where the boy is, but I have no doubt he is worth more to himself than he ever was to his master, high as he fixes the price on him; and I have no doubt thee will do better to pursue thy peddling honestly, than to neglect it for the sake of serving negro-hunters at a venture.

That conversation took place within a month or two of Pennington's departure, but it was two years before he heard of it.[15] Had he known of it sooner, his sense of insecurity might have carried over even into his next residence, in the home of Isaiah Kirk in East Nantmeal, Pennsylvania.[16]

East Nantmeal is still, as it was then, a small community about a hundred and fifty miles east of William Wright's home and about fifty miles northwest of Philadelphia. Wright passed fugitives on toward Philadelphia as well as toward Canada, perhaps because the numerous Quaker population in the Philadelphia area would have provided both security and opportunity. Pennington moved from the one residence to the other in two days and nights of travel, so it is obvious that he was not left to walk or make the trip without assistance. Pennington had worried about finding himself alone and friendless in a new world and with no one to turn to for help. But knocking on William Wright's door had brought him into a wide network of friends. Forty miles east of William Wright's house, another William Wright, also a Quaker, also a station master on the Underground Railroad, might well have provided hospitality the first night. Jeremiah Moore in Christiana, Pennsylvania, thirty miles further east, often received fugitives from William Wright, and it was only thirty miles further to East Nantmeal. Pennington would have made better time on horseback and he might well have learned to ride a horse while staying with William Wright, but it would have been unwise for a black man to travel that way alone, even in a free state. It seems likelier that he was carried in the back of a farm wagon in which he could easily have hidden if strangers appeared on the road.

Three days later, however he traveled, James Pennington came to the home of Isaiah and Elizabeth Kirk.[17] Like the Wrights, the Kirks were Quakers, but they were also leaders in the Quaker community. Elizabeth Kirk was commissioned to serve as a minister, while her husband was involved in administration as an overseer of relief for the poor and of the community's discipline.[18] Pennington arrived at his new home at a time of tension and controversy in the Society of Friends, and Isaiah Kirk was constantly involved that year in attempting to maintain the unity of the local Quaker community, the Uwchlan Meeting.

The divisions in the Quaker community were a direct result of the waves of revival that had shaken American Christianity, first in the 1730s and 1740s and again in the "Great Awakening" that took place between 1800 and 1830. Although the Quaker pattern of worship had not been centered on evangelical preaching, some Quakers began to adopt that style under the influence of the revivalists, and the year 1827, the year in which Pennington became a fugitive and turned to the Quakers for help, was the year in which the Quaker movement finally divided in bitter acrimony and even legal action. The so-called "Orthodox Quakers" adopted the evangelical pattern of preaching, while the followers of Elias Hicks, called "Hicksites," continued the traditional Quaker way of quietly waiting on the Spirit. Month after month, Elizabeth and Isaiah Kirk, as leaders in their local community, were notified of members no longer content with the old way and sent out committees to meet with the disaffected and report back. Month after month, the meeting had no alternative except to vote that the disaffected were no longer members of the Society.[19]

Mrs. Kirk was also active as a preacher. It was said of her that she had a "strong and discriminating mind, and early in life [had] been deeply impressed with the solemn nature of the truths of religion, and the awful responsibility thence arising," which led in turn to a desire to "impress upon others a due sense of the paramount importance of securing a well-grounded assurance of happiness in a future life." Feeling called to the work of ministry, she was commissioned by the Uwchlan Meeting and made trips as far afield as New Jersey and Philadelphia to carry out her work. Between Elizabeth's trips to preach in other meetings and the monthly and quarterly business meetings her husband was involved in, they were both frequently away from home.[20] In the seven months that Pennington spent with the Kirks, there could have been as many as seventy meetings involving one or both of the Kirks, some of them overnight, and one of them, the annual meeting, probably requiring an absence of several days.[21] Perhaps it was because they traveled so much and needed someone to take responsibility in their absence that the Kirks had willingly agreed to provide a home for James Pennington. William Wright would have told them of his confidence in Pennington's ability, and the Kirks quickly learned to trust his judgment and to feel very comfortable leaving him in charge of the farm when they were away on preaching missions or other business. The result was that he was left very much to his own devices and had to pursue his education without much guidance. He relieved the monotony and loneliness by drawing maps of the solar system and diagrams of the pattern of solar eclipses. He also made an effort to teach himself the art of pubic speaking. Much less than a year had passed since he had escaped from slavery and begun to learn the alphabet, yet his image of himself seemed already to include leadership positions in which speaking publicly would be important, so he would go into the barn on Sundays when the family was absent and pretend to be addressing an audience. The experience was frustrating to him since it made him acutely aware of the barrenness of his mind. He had a great desire to speak but very little to say. With few books and no tutor, he lacked the opportunity he now knew he needed to fill the empty spaces left in him by the years of slavery.[22]

Nevertheless Pennington had begun to imagine himself already in the role of leader and even to form judgments as to the adequacy of the Quaker pattern of worship. The only known role models he had were the example of the slave who preached the two sermons he remembered, and whatever limited exposure he had been given to Quaker speakers. Pennington wrote later of how his disappointment with Quaker preaching and the lack of singing at the Quaker meetings had led him to decide not to become a Quaker. That he could make such a judgment would seem to indicate more exposure to religious practice before his escape than he tells of in any of his later writing. Whether he had some further exposure or not, he clearly had only a limited basis for comparison. The two sermons by the exhorter might well have been compared to the Quaker speakers in emotional fervor and found superior, and there must have been singing also or he would not have been aware of its absence in the Quaker meetings.

In spite of the absence of the kind of companionship William Wright had provided, life on the Kirk farm was very comfortable. Since it was farther from any main road than the Wright home, there was less danger that strangers might notice his presence and he was less dominated by the fear of discovery. He did, however, confine himself to the boundaries of the farm and was careful to stay out of sight as much as possible. The frequent absence of his host family meant that he also lacked the tutoring he had been given by William Wright; but with the foundation Wright had provided, Pennington could move along to some degree by himself. The seclusion of the place and the absence of the Kirks left him with time to study. Elizabeth Kirk gave him the first Bible he had ever owned and did take time to meet with him and provide him "much excellent counsel." He spent time, especially in her absence, reading the Bible and committing whole chapters to memory.[23] But Pennington was beginning to imagine larger possibilities for his life than could be realized on an isolated Pennsylvania farm even with all its safety and comfort, and he was ready to move on. He needed now to find a place where he could begin to learn in a much more formal way.

As Wright had done, so too the Kirks made every effort to persuade Pennington to stay with them longer, but he was becoming clearer about what he needed to do and beginning to feel an urgency about moving ahead with his life. The letter of commendation that Isaiah Kirk wrote for him was a concise summary of the ability Pennington had demonstrated and the hope the Wrights and Kirks had for his future:

> East Nantmeal, Chester County, Pennsylvania,
> Tenth Month 5th, 1828
>
> I hereby certify, that the bearer, J. W. C. Pennington, has been in my employ seven months, during most of which time I have been from home, leaving my entire business in his trust, and that he has proved a highly trustworthy and industrious young man. He leaves with the sincere regret of myself and family; but as he feels it to be his duty to go where he can obtain education, so as to fit him to be more useful, I cordially commend him to the warm sympathy of the friends of humanity wherever a wise providence may appoint him a home.
>
> Signed, Isaiah Kirk[24]

Carrying this letter and still with the support of the Underground Railroad, Pennington moved on farther east and north until he arrived in New York City.

James Pennington says in his autobiography that he fled from the plantation in November of 1828 and "past the middle of the month," but the first notice of his fugitive status asking for his return was published on October 27, 1827. He also states that he spent six months with William Wright and seven months with the Kirks, but the testimonial letter Isaiah Kirk gave James Pennington is dated October 5, 1828, less than twelve months after Pennington's escape, so Pennington's dating cannot be completely accurate. Since the autobiography was written and published in England more than twenty years after the events and with no opportunity to consult records, some such minor discrepancies are not surprising. It may also be that Kirk's letter was reconstructed from memory, so that date also may be wrong.

CHAPTER FOUR

Brooklyn, Part I

When James Pennington was captured near Reisterstown, he told his captors that he was on his way to Philadelphia. Six months later, when he left William Wright's home to move on, he says "I wended my way in deep sorrow and melancholy, onward towards Philadelphia." He then spent seven months in East Nantmeal, only forty miles from Philadelphia, living with Isaac and Elizabeth Kirk, who were well acquainted with Philadelphia and had many contacts there. Yet when he left the Kirks, Pennington says only that "Passing through Philadelphia, I went to New York, and in a short time found employ on Long Island."[1] Why did he not spend time in Philadelphia as he had intended?

It is not surprising that Pennington should have wanted to visit Philadelphia. With a population of nearly 80,000, it ranked with Baltimore as the second largest city in the country and had a free black population of 15,000. Besides that, it was the "Quaker Capital," the city founded by William Penn as a refuge for Quakers. Since Pennington had found warm hospitality in two Quaker homes, it was logical that he would be drawn to a city where more Quakers were to be found than anywhere else in the world. Quakers also continued to show a special interest in the conditions under which African Americans lived. A "Statistical Inquiry into the Condition of the People of Color" made by the Quakers twenty years later, in 1849, revealed a community still struggling to overcome the effects of slavery. Almost half the men were "laborers" and almost half the women were "washer-women." But there were also 22 preachers and 11 school masters as well as physicians and dentists, shop keepers and cabinet makers.[2] The first post-Revolutionary War African American leadership had emerged in Philadelphia in the persons of Richard Allen, the founder of the African Methodist Episcopal Church, and Absalom Jones, the first African to be ordained a priest in the Episcopal Church. Jones had died ten years before Pennington left Hagerstown, but Richard Allen was still alive and working to create the first national convention of black leaders when Pennington traveled through the city. Less than two years later, Pennington would come back to Philadelphia to take part in the convention Allen had worked to create. An extended visit to Philadelphia would have enabled Pennington not only to meet more Quakers but also to see for the first time a community of free African Americans, but "passing through" he went on to New York.

To be fair, although Philadelphia might have had much to offer a fugitive slave, there were difficulties as well. Philadelphia was outgrowing its Quaker heritage and becoming a more diverse city in which other attitudes toward African Americans were finding expression. Four years later, when a shipload of freed slaves from North Carolina tried to land in Philadelphia, mobs gathered to prevent them from doing so. White working people saw free blacks as unwelcome competition. Pennington may have discovered that his opportunities in the city would be limited.

New York City was more than twice the size of Philadelphia and the opportunities for indigent newcomers were undoubtedly greater, but the hazards there for a fugitive slave were also great. Slavery had been ended in New York only the year before Pennington arrived, and there were many who were not at all prepared to acknowledge the rights of those who were newly freed. Although slavery had been ended, the state constitution had been revised to eliminate property requirements for white voters but to leave them in place for blacks.

New York, with the largest black population of any of the northern states, had, in fact, a long history of what would later be known as racism. The Dutch had brought the practice of slavery to the colony but had allowed the slaves a good many rights and privileges including marriage, even sometimes with whites, and the opportunity to purchase freedom. When England acquired the colony, most of these privileges were taken away and the result was a violent rebellion in 1712 that lasted for two weeks and was only suppressed by calling in the militia. Thousands of dollars worth of property was destroyed by the rebels through fires deliberately set, and nine whites were killed. When order was finally restored, the English retaliated by arresting 27 Africans and executing 21 of them. The other six, certain of their fate, had already committed suicide. In a published speech made in 1850, Pennington told how less than thirty years after that rebellion, rumors of another rebellion were spread maliciously and for over a year there was a kind of public persecution of African Americans that included insults, abuses, and accusations that led to a series of 160 trials on charges of conspiracy to commit arson and murder. As a result of the trials, 71 were condemned to be banished or sold into slavery, 18 were branded, and 13 were tied to stakes and burned.[3]

As a new arrival in the city, Pennington would have known nothing of that history, but he would quickly have been alerted to the very real danger in his own time. Fugitive-slave catchers were constantly at work in the city, and hardly a day went by when a fugitive was not arrested and sent back to the South. Writing almost twenty years later but at a time when such dangers still existed, Pennington says nothing about how he found his way, but his experience may well have paralleled that of Frederick Douglass ten years later. Douglass wrote of his arrival in the city:

> There I was in the midst of thousands, and yet a perfect stranger; without home and without friends, in the midst of thousands of my own brethren—children of a common Father, and yet I dared not to unfold to any one of them my sad condition. I was afraid to speak to any one for fear of speaking to the wrong one, and thereby falling into the hands of money-loving kidnappers, whose business it was to lie in wait for the panting fugitive, as the ferocious beasts of the forest lie in wait for their prey. The motto which I adopted when I started from slavery was this—"Trust no man!" I saw in every white man an enemy, and in almost every colored man cause for distrust.[4]

Pennington himself wrote simply, "I often felt serious apprehensions of danger, and yet I felt also that I must begin the world somewhere."[5] Douglass was rescued by David Ruggles, an African American grocer who had organized a Vigilance Committee to guard against the activities of slave catchers and to find secure locations for fugitives, often sending them on to safer places as he did with Douglass.[6] Perhaps Pennington also was led to David Ruggles; but whether it was Ruggles or someone else who advised the new arrival, the fact is that he was quickly sent on to Long Island, where he found employment in the home of Adrian Van Sinderen, a wealthy merchant and president of the Brooklyn Savings Bank.[7] Van Sideren's new home on Brooklyn Heights was said to have been a station on the Underground Railroad, but whether that was the case or not—and there were, of course, no records kept of such illegal activity—it is known that Van Sinderen, who had once been a slave owner himself,[†] was deeply involved in several activities on behalf of African Americans. Brooklyn Heights was already becoming what it still remains, a wealthy enclave, home to New Yorkers prosperous enough to be able to live in the quiet seclusion available on the other side of the East River from the frantic activity of the country's greatest commercial center. Numerous ferries

† On April 1, 1817, Adrian Van Sinderen manumitted his slave, Isaac, age 26. Extracts from the records of Newtown, L.I., and other newspaper clippings relating to Newtown, L.I. Brooklyn, N.Y.: Paul Grosser, stationer & printer, 18–. p. 112.

provided quick and convenient transportation to and from the city, still huddled at the south end of Manhattan Island though spreading rapidly to the north. Like most wealthy families, Van Sinderen kept a horse and carriage and needed a coachman to make that transportation readily available. Pennington had shoed many horses and knew something of how to care for them, so his new duties would not have been completely unfamiliar. He probably also was quickly made aware of the fact that his skills as a blacksmith were not necessarily useful even in a city where horses were nearly as common as people. White blacksmiths, like other craftsmen, did not welcome the newly freed slaves into their ranks. Pennington's skills as a carpenter and mason would have been equally unwelcome. Frederick Douglass once claimed that "he could more easily get his son into a lawyer's office to study law than into a blacksmithy. . . ."[8] But Pennington had also split wood and helped care for a farm; work as a coachman would be less physically demanding and also give him sufficient free time to pursue his educational goals.

The greatest attraction of Brooklyn for Pennington was undoubtedly the existence of opportunities for formal education. His autobiography speaks of evening schools, Sabbath school, and private tuition.[9] Pennington was a hungry man confronted with a smorgasbord of opportunities, and he seems to have selected them all. Schooling for African Americans had become available on an organized basis only at the end of the Revolutionary War and was at first provided by white benevolence. In fact, there were few free schools for children of any race, and those that did exist were often considered to be intended for the poor and of such inferior quality that black parents and white alike often refused to make use of them. The New York Manumission Society, however, believed that education for blacks would help dispel prejudice against them and therefore had organized the African Free School in 1787.[10] It was only a grammar school, but the white head master of that school set out to give his black students an education as good as or better than any available to white children, and the school produced such future leaders as Peter Williams, an Episcopal priest, and James McCune Smith, a medical doctor.[11] Higher education, however, was completely closed to blacks; there were no high schools for them in New York State. Williams had had to study privately, and Smith had had to travel to Scotland to acquire professional training. Adrian Van Sinderen was the kind of man who took an interest in this subject and was himself a director of the African Infant School Association. He would have been able to point Pennington toward the schools that would best serve his need.

Night schools and Sabbath schools had been organized with the same goal as that of the African Free School in Manhattan: to raise the educational level of former slaves and thereby decrease the prejudice against them. The Sabbath schools, sponsored usually by churches, had the further agenda of introducing the students to the Christian faith. As in the South, so in New York State, slave owners had been reluctant to allow blacks to be introduced to the Christian faith since it brought with it a desire to gain an education so as to be able to read the Bible. In Pennington's case, Sabbath school education produced life-changing results. Pennington was astonished in the first place to learn that there were three million slaves in the United States and therefore some 700,000 children growing up, as he had done, without an education. He began to wonder whether he could do something not merely for the ten brothers and sisters he had left behind and who remained very much in his thoughts, but for all those thousands of others who continued in slavery.[12]

> I began to contrast . . . the condition of the children sitting around me . . . with that of [the slave children in the south] who had no means of Christian instruction. . . . The question was, what can I do for that vast body of suffering brotherhood I have left behind?[13]

In the second place, but with even larger implications, he began to see himself in terms of the Christian teaching that all human beings are the slaves of sin.

> The theme was more powerful than any my mind had ever encountered before. It entered into the deep chambers of my soul, and stirred the most agitating emotions I had ever felt. . . . The question completely staggered my mind; and finding myself more and more borne down with it, until I was in an agony; I thought I would make it a subject of prayer to God, although prayer had not been my habit, having never attempted it but once.
>
> I not only prayed, but also fasted. It was while engaged thus, that my attention was seriously drawn to the fact that I was a lost sinner, and a slave to Satan; and soon I saw that I must make another escape from another tyrant. I did not by any means forget my fellow-bondmen, of whom I had been sorrowing so deeply, and travailing in spirit so earnestly; but I now saw that while man had been injuring me, I had been offending God; and that unless I ceased to offend him, I could not expect to have his sympathy in my wrongs; and moreover, that I could not be instrumental in eliciting his powerful aid in behalf of those for whom I mourned so deeply.[14]

Pennington was now under the tutelage not of Quakers but Presbyterians, whose Calvinist theology laid out in very clear terms the nature and consequences of sin. His search for freedom from human slavery in this life now began to seem of far less importance than the need to be set free from the bonds of sin and obtain eternal salvation. His concern for his brothers and sisters, and beyond them hundreds of thousands of others, was no longer a matter of their current physical suffering but of their suffering or freedom hereafter. Such a faith did nothing to lessen the need to abolish American slavery but rather intensified it, since those living in slavery were being prevented from hearing the gospel. What role, Pennington asked himself, could he play in setting his millions of fellow sufferers free now so they could be set free eternally? Day after day, these thoughts dominated his mind, but the theology he was imbibing in his Sabbath school and at the church services he attended with the Van Sinderen family helped him find answers. In the first place, he realized, he could do nothing alone; only with the help of an Almighty God could so deeply entrenched an evil be overcome. Secondly, he came to understand that he had no standing at all in the matter since he had not yet been forgiven for his own sins and given grace to come into God's presence in prayer.

> Day after day, for about two weeks, I found myself more deeply convicted of personal guilt before God. My heart, soul and body were in the greatest distress; I thought of neither food, drink or rest, for days and nights together. Burning with a recollection of the wrongs man had done me—mourning for the injuries my brethren were still enduring, and deeply convicted of the guilt of my own sins against God. One evening, in the third week of the struggle, while alone in my chamber, and after solemn reflection for several hours, I concluded that I could never be happy or useful in that state of mind, and resolved that I would try to become reconciled to God.[15]

Pennington had come into contact with Christianity in the midst of the movement known to historians as the "Second Great Awakening." This wave of revival swept the country from 1800 to 1830 and was characterized especially by camp meetings on the American frontier where preachers like Peter Cartwright proclaimed the need for repentance and forgiveness in emotional terms and with dramatic results. Preachers shouted and sinners fell to the ground, wailing for their sins and calling out for forgiveness. Conversion, however, was not always dramatic and sudden; innumerable stories are told of individuals wrestling with their conscience alone as Pennington did until, through prayer and silent meditation, they came to the conviction that their sins were forgiven and they could begin a new life in assurance of their salvation.

Pennington thought he was struggling with these issues alone but, in fact, his employer's family was well aware of his struggle and waiting for the moment to come when he would ask for help or they would see opportunity to offer assistance. In the third week of Pennington's silent struggle, the time came when assistance could be offered. It happened that there would be a guest preacher at the Presbyterian Church the next Sunday, one uniquely qualified to help Pennington resolve his difficulties. The Van Sinderens invited Pennington to join them in listening to Samuel Hanson Cox, and they invited Cox to join them for dinner.[16]

Samuel Hanson Cox was, at that time, pastor of the Laight Street Presbyterian Church in Manhattan and a leading abolitionist. He would later become pastor of a church in Brooklyn and a professor of theology at Union Theological Seminary in Manhattan. Cox was also a leader among the New Light Presbyterians, that element in the Presbyterian Church that strongly supported the call to revival. The First Great Awakening had divided Presbyterians between the so-called New Lights and the Old Lights, who preferred the less emotional and more intellectual pattern that had prevailed in earlier times. Cox took a decisive, and even polarizing, position on these issues. He happened on one occasion to be on a steamboat with John Quincy Adams, then president of the United States, who was traveling from New York to Boston to visit his aging father, John Adams, the former President. The journey required 29 hours and Adams, in those simpler times, was traveling alone. Falling into conversation with Cox, he told him that he thought his approach to religion was "too extravagant, too uncompromising, too severe, too indiscriminate." Cox replied that he was delighted that the conversation had taken such a turn and he would happily continue it in a way that was both "respectful and honest." So, when Adams, who read his Bible daily, said, "I think God is too good to punish men forever," Cox replied, "I think him infinitely too good to lie. Did he reveal the future wrath simply to scare us, not believing it himself?" Adams was not daunted by the arguments of the theologian and told Cox frankly, "Still, I do not believe your version of it." When Cox asked, "What is your version of it?" Adams answered "Anything but yours." "Possibly you may believe it yet," said Cox." "No," said Adams; "impossible."[17] It was the classic confrontation between the two Lights: the Old, represented by Adams, was already moving toward what would later be called "mainline liberal Protestantism," while the New, represented by Cox, would emerge from its frontier background to become a dominant force in American Christianity by the latter part of the twentieth century and be termed "evangelical." New Light Christianity, however, was never simply a religion of frontier revivalism. As expressed by Cox and many others, it could also be highly educated and sophisticated. Cox specifically downplayed the emotional and said:

> I am no advocate for fanaticism, for holy tricks, for mere emotion however strong, for divelling childishness, for devout buffoonery, or any other shameful mode of *practicing* on the stupidity or frailty of the ignorant. The religion of sensation is not-spirituality. . . . The influence of the gospel . . . commands its divinity to the confidence of man, chiefly in three ways—by beneficence, by permanence, by progress in goodness: such an influence . . . is what I mean . . . when I speak of revivals of religion "corporeal excitement," he added, is "incidental and not primary parts or necessary adjuncts of religion. If we *aim* at them, or sanction them in a system of measures . . . they lose their nature, they degenerate into miserable affectation, they disgust man and are an abomination to God."[18]

Cox's version of New Light religion also included a concern for social issues, although for most of the nineteenth and twentieth centuries evangelicals were indifferent to such matters. The fact that Cox and Van Sinderen were both committed to justice for African Americans may well have worked to make Pennington more receptive to their theology. Furthermore, of course, Pennington was a very new student of the Bible and Cox's analysis was simple and direct. Cox had laid out his approach very clearly:

> My general rules of treatment and principles of conduct, in times of religious revival . . . have been and still are: . . . to be very simple and intelligible in the directions given; to feel and exhibit tenderness and sympathetic consideration; to treat their souls as I would my own; to be direct and faithful; to be uncompromising; to explode their excuses, and to show them, if they wish on any ground to decline an immediate and cordial compliance with the gospel, what is the alternative which they shall not decline, the infallible certainty of their damnation, unless they yield their hearts' whole offering to Jesus Christ . . .

Cox liked his hearers to be clear about their situation.

When the Sunday service and dinner were over, Pennington, with no advance notice, was invited into a room with Cox, and the two of them were left alone to see what would happen. Cox was "direct and faithful" but also sympathetic enough not to push Pennington to come to an "immediate and cordial compliance with the gospel." Rather, Pennington reported,

He entered skilfully and kindly into my feelings, and after considerable conversation he invited me to attend his service that
afternoon. I did so, and was deeply interested.

Subsequently, Pennington attended Cox's church in New York once or twice
and met with him several times

as the result of which, I hope, I was brought to a saving acquaintance with Him, of whom Moses in the Law and the Prophets
did write; and soon connected myself with the church under his
pastoral care.[19]

Pennington had now taken a momentous step both for himself and for
African Americans generally. First of all, although he could not have realized it
at the time, he had set himself on the path toward a leadership role in American
society. Ministry was, and would remain for a century and a half, the primary
area within which African Americans could exercise leadership within their
own community, and Pennington was now in position to move toward ordination for ministry. He had also, uniquely, put himself in position to carry out
his ministry in a community in which African Americans were only a small
minority but, paradoxically, perhaps more influential. Other black leaders
like Richard Allen and Peter Williams, serving African American churches,
could have little influence beyond their own limited world. Pennington,
though the particular congregations he served were African American, was,
from the beginning and for the rest of his life, part of a larger church that
was predominantly white, and he would spend a significant part of his time
speaking to white people about his concerns.

So Pennington now had a purpose, not only in terms of his concern for
those still in slavery but in terms of a church community that had some of the
same concerns. For the moment, however, Pennington's focus remained on
his work for Van Sinderen and his effort to obtain an education. That sense
he had from the beginning, of wasted years and the overwhelming darkness
that needed to be rolled back, was more than sufficient to occupy him for a
few more years at least. Samuel Cox, however, had made more than a convert;
he had recruited a leader who would eventually challenge his positions and
surpass him as an orator.

James Pennington, it might be said, had escaped from slavery and begun
his education just in the nick of time. The rapid increase in the number
of free African Americans was creating tensions in the growing cities of
the Northeast and Midwest and forcing black Americans to confront new
issues. Some of the freed slaves came north with special skills. Trained as

blacksmiths, coopers, carpenters, and masons to work on plantations, they found themselves in competition not only with established white workers but with a tide of immigrants from Europe with many of the same skills. White Americans found it difficult to adjust to the newcomers in their midst and responded with harassment and occasional violence.[20] The 1830s were a time of rising tensions in American life, and riots broke out frequently in cities in the North and West in response both to racial tensions and to the growing flood of immigrants from Ireland and Germany and other parts of Europe. The agrarian America of the founders was rapidly becoming an urban society, and a new agricultural community was being established to the west. Andrew Jackson, the first president born in a log cabin, had been elected president in 1828, just as Pennington was settling into Brooklyn. For the first time, America had a president not drawn from the Eastern establishment, representing the rise of a truer, more participatory democracy. The transition would not be easy.

In August of 1827, riots broke out in Cincinnati, and the city authorities decided to solve their problem by enforcing an old ordinance that required Negroes moving into the state to post a bond to guarantee their good behavior and ability to support themselves. The bond was far beyond the resources of laborers of any race and was equivalent to an order for expulsion. Over the next two years, nearly half the black population of Cincinnati, between one and two thousand people, fled the city, many to a hastily organized new settlement in Canada named Wilberforce after the great English opponent of the slave trade.[21] Canada had always provided a northern terminus for the Underground Railroad, but now it became a significant alternative to African colonization schemes. If not Africa, why not Canada? Could the African American community, already divided in its response to the African alternative, come to a common mind about Canada?

At the very moment that this question was demanding an answer, two new voices, one to the north and the other to the south, were adding to the turmoil and setting events in motion that would dominate the remainder of Pennington's life and transform the life of the nation as well.

To the north, in Boston, less than a year after Pennington's arrival in Brooklyn, David Walker, an African American born free in North Carolina, issued a declaration of war on American complacency. He had traveled widely before settling in Boston to make a living selling used clothing. There he had also gained a reputation as a lay preacher. In September 1829, he put his rhetorical abilities to use in a 76-page document entitled *Walker's Appeal, in Four Articles; Together with a Preamble, to the Coloured Citizens of the World, but in Particular, and Very Expressly, to Those of the United States of America*. Here, if they were to read it, white Americans could see in print, for the first time, the depth of anger building up in the black community and be warned of the potential consequences.

> The whites have had us under them for more than three centuries, murdering, and treating us like brutes; and, as Mr. Jefferson wisely said, they have never found us out—they do not know, indeed, that there is an unconquerable disposition in the breasts of the blacks, which, when it is fully awakened and put in motion, will be subdued, only with the destruction of the animal existence. Get the blacks started, and if you do not have a gang of tigers and lions to deal with, I am a deceiver of the blacks and of the whites. . . . [I]f you commence, make sure work—do not trifle, for they will not trifle with you—they want us for their slaves, and think nothing of murdering us in order to subject us to that wretched condition—therefore, if there is an attempt made by us, kill or be killed. Now, I ask you, had you not rather be killed than to be a slave to a tyrant, who takes the life of your mother, wife, and dear little children? Look upon your mother, wife and children, and answer God Almighty; and believe this, that it is no more harm for you to kill a man, who is trying to kill you, than it is for you to take a drink of water when thirsty . . .[22]

Two years later, Nat Turner might have said such things in enlisting supporters for his revolt, but such language had not previously been seen in print, nor was it welcome in either North or South. Throughout the South, a determined effort was made to suppress the *Appeal*. Walker sewed copies of it into seamen's clothing to get it past Southern authorities; but in North Carolina and Georgia, seamen were prevented from even coming ashore. In New Orleans four men were arrested for possessing copies, while in Virginia and Georgia the legislatures considered laws to make the circulation of such material a criminal offense.[23] Even white abolitionists were discomfited to read that "The whites have always been an unjust, jealous, unmerciful, avaricious and blood-thirsty set of beings, always seeking after power and authority" and "I tell you Americans! that unless you speedily alter your course, you and your Country are gone!!!!!" Nevertheless, Walker's vision was not wholly negative: "Treat us then like men," he wrote, "and we will be your friends. And there is not a doubt in my mind, but that the whole of the past will be sunk into oblivion, and we yet, under God, will become a united and happy people. The whites may say it is impossible, but remember that nothing is impossible with God."[24]

No one before had made it so clear that the existing order could not continue indefinitely, but what was to be done? *Walker's Appeal* spoke of more than one possible outcome but offered no guidance to those who might read his words and wish to respond. In April of the following year, however, another African American far to the south, Hezekiah Grice, published a very different document with a specific suggestion: a summons to African Americans to come together in a convention to take counsel for the future.[25]

Like Walker, Grice had been born free, obtained a limited education, and made a living for himself in Baltimore in what would now be called "blue collar" work; he sold ice in the summer and butchered hogs in the winter.[26] For Grice as for Walker, the catalyst for his writing was the work of the American Colonization Society, which had been formed in 1816 to resolve the racial issue by sending black Americans back to Africa. The organizers of that society believed that slavery must be ended eventually but that the freed slaves could never be successfully integrated into American society. Among the founders and early members were such prominent Americans as Senators Henry Clay and Daniel Webster, Francis Scott Key, and the presidents of Princeton, Harvard, Yale, and Columbia. President Madison arranged public support for its work. Fourteen state legislatures including those of Vermont, Massachusetts, and Connecticut endorsed it.[27] Some of those in the colonization movement had naively come to imagine that African Americans would happily embark for a land that most had never known and would see members of the Society as benefactors. Others, Southern slave owners in particular, supported the Society with very different motives. Their hope was that colonization would be a way to remove free blacks from the community and so eliminate the unwelcome witness of an alternative to slavery. A world in which all whites were free and all blacks were slaves would be a simpler world for slave owners to inhabit. Grice and Walker both spoke for the overwhelming majority of African Americans in rejecting such a "solution" to the American dilemma.†

Less than a year after publishing his call to arms and three months short of his 45th birthday, Walker was found dead on the doorstep of his home. A letter to *The Liberator* noted that there were rumors of a reward of $3000 (William

† Theodore Wright, Pastor of New York's Shiloh Presbyterian Church, summed up the feeling of most black people: "The principle of expatriation, like a great sponge, went around in church and state [in 1817], among men of all classes, and sponged up all the benevolent feelings which were then prevalent, and which promised so much for the emancipation of the enslaved and down-trodden millions of our land . . . But, sir, there were hundreds of thousands of men in the land who never could sympathize in this feeling; I mean those who were to be removed . . . They resolved to cling to their oppressed brethren. They felt that every ennobling spirit forbade their leaving them. They resolved to remain here, come what would, persecution or death." Hinks, op. cit., p. 102.

Lloyd Garrison himself had heard numbers from "a credible source" as high as $30,000) offered by southern planters to anyone who would eliminate Walker. Poisoning was suspected but never proved.[†] *Walker's Appeal* had just come out in a third and final edition. It would remain as an important element in the consciousness of whites and blacks in the ongoing debate about the role of slavery in American life, but it would be Grice's proposal that would lead to a specific response and bring the African American community into the debate in an organized and forceful way.

At first, Grice's letter seemed to have made no impact at all. When he mailed out his proposal to leading African Americans in the free states, he told them he would gladly give notice of a time and place for such a convention if their response was positive. But four months went by and not one reply came back. Grice met with William Lloyd Garrison in his Baltimore office to discuss the project, but Garrison picked up a copy of *Walker's Appeal* and said the time had not come for such a book.[28] Then suddenly in August, Grice received an order to come at once to meet with Bishop Richard Allen, the founder of the African Methodist Episcopal Church and by now, at the age of 70, widely recognized as the grand old man of the African American community.[29] Allen himself had responded positively to the first suggestion of a colonization movement, but a mass meeting of 3,000 members of Philadelphia's black community had made it clear that they would oppose it: "Whereas our ancestors (not of choice) were the first successful cultivators of the wilds of America, we their descendants feel ourselves entitled to participate in the blessings of her luxuriant soil."

Allen accepted that judgment and came to believe that Grice's appeal might provide a means to deal with the colonization issue. In addition, he had just learned that New Yorkers were planning a gathering themselves in response to Grice's appeal. A printed circular had arrived, signed by Peter Williams, Thomas Jennings, and Peter Vogelsang, all respected leaders in the city to the north. The circular strongly endorsed Grice's call for a convention, and Allen was worried. If a meeting were to be held, Allen was anxious to have it assemble in Philadelphia. "My dear child," said the bishop, "we must take some action immediately or else these New Yorkers will get ahead of us."[30]

Allen then left the meeting to attend a lecture on chemistry, and the remaining group constituted themselves a committee and issued a call for a convention of the colored men of the United States to be held in Philadelphia

---

[†] The Boston Index of Deaths and the *Boston Daily Courier* listed Walker's death as caused by consumption. Hinks, Peter P., *To Awaken My Afflicted Brethren: David Walker and the Problem of Antebellum Slave Resistance.* University Park, Pa.: Pennsylvania State University Press, 1997, p. 269.

on September 15, 1830, barely a month away. On his way home to Baltimore, Grice encountered a Mr. Zollickoffer of the Society of Friends, who insisted urgently that the proposed convention not be held. The risk was too great of failure, and even if it succeeded, he urged, it would only create new dangers. But Grice would not retreat; the deed was done and the summons had been sent out to every prominent African American known to the Philadelphia committee.[31]

James Pennington was not known by name to the Philadelphians, but a copy of the call was received in Brooklyn and a special meeting was scheduled to consider what response to make. Pennington went to the meeting and, drawing on his experience of speaking to an imaginary audience in an empty Pennsylvania barn, urged the gathering to send someone to Philadelphia. Older members of the gathering were more cautious in their response, but quite willing to send the younger man. Walking home, Pennington thought over the difficulty of going off to Philadelphia for a week when he had obligations to his employer. Van Sinderen was a friend of the African American cause, but he expressed that support in part by his membership in the American Colonization Society, which the proposed Philadelphia meeting would almost certainly condemn. The time available for planning was short since the meeting was now only days away, but Pennington worked out a risky plan. He would fulfill his obligations to his employer by finding a substitute, but he would not tell Van Sinderen of his intentions in advance.

So now, at last, James Pennington would make a visit to Philadelphia, and not as a fugitive slave but as an official representative of the African American citizens of Brooklyn. He arrived at the place of meeting to find an extremely small and select group. When Hezekiah Grice walked up from his boat, having come from Baltimore by ship, he asked the African Americans on the street about the Convention. No one knew anything of it. "Who ever heard of colored people having a convention?" asked one. Grice entered the meeting room to find a gathering of five, the members of the original Philadelphia committee. But Bishop Allen greeted him warmly, and before long Dr. Burton of Philadelphia arrived and asked what was happening. On a hint from Bishop Allen, Dr. Burton was elected an honorary member of the Convention. Half an hour went by and a small group arrived from another Methodist body in Philadelphia, inquiring by what right those present presumed to represent the colored population of the nation. Again Bishop Allen hinted, and a delegate moved that the newcomers be seated as honorary members. But the gentlemen would not be satisfied with less than full membership, so that was duly arranged. Before long, other delegates arrived from Delaware, Boston, Utica, and Rochester—one from each city—and Pennington from Brooklyn. There were no representatives from New York City; Bishop Allen had beaten them out, and they would need a year to get over it. So the Convention was called to order and began its work.[32]

One reason people on the streets were ignorant of the Convention was that publicity brought danger. Some of the delegates had risked not only their jobs but their lives to attend, and mobs could form quickly if word of what was happening came to the wrong ears. For five days the Convention met in secret, but then it was agreed to hold open sessions for the last five days whatever the consequences.[33]

There were two main orders of business: a response to the work of the American Colonization Society encouraging African Americans to emigrate to Africa, and a proposal to encourage emigration to Canada. The Colonization Society was roundly condemned, but the Canadian matter was more difficult. Canada was not simply the northern terminus of the Underground Railroad, but a place where organized efforts had been made already to establish colonies of freed slaves. A committee was appointed to discuss the matter and report back. When they made their report, two days of discussion followed. There were not only great issues of policy to resolve but smaller matters as well. The report had said that "the lands in Canada were synonymous with those of the Northern States," but the word "synonymous" was objected to and the word "similar" proposed in its place. The committee chairman vigorously defended the original wording, but was finally voted down. The Convention then recommended emigration to Canada as an acceptable alternative.

African Colonization schemes needed less debate but were of equal or greater importance at that moment. The American Colonization Society had attracted widespread support; even William Lloyd Garrison was drawn to the movement for a while, and a few African Americans were tempted to see in it a solution to their difficulties. Richard Allen had supported it until persuaded to change his views, and John Russworm, the editor of *Freedom's Journal*, a newspaper founded in 1827 to give African Americans a voice in opposition, startled his colleagues by reversing himself two years later and declaring that he had come to despair of a future for blacks in America and now supported African colonization.[34] The overwhelming majority of African Americans, however, remained opposed to the scheme.[35] A new paper, *The Rights of All*, was created to replace Russworm's journal, and an editorial in the new publication laid out the reasons for their rejection of the Colonization Society's program:

1. "The means are not sufficient to effect the anticipated object."
   In 12 years of existence, the Society had transported only one thousand blacks out of a population of three million, and that

was far less than the increase in black population in the same years.

2. "Since the existence of the Society . . . The coloured population of this country has yearly become more and more neglected." Concern for those in America has been diminished as attention has been directed to the African colony.

3. The removal of freed blacks has reduced concern for emancipation generally.

4. The Society's publicity constantly emphasizes the degraded condition of blacks and so tends to increase prejudice against them.[36]

It was the last issue that African Americans found especially galling, and it reflected a conflict deep in the origins and existence of the Colonization Society. The initial impetus came primarily from the South, where motives for its support were at cross purposes. A significant number of Southerners in those years was opposed to slavery and saw colonization as a way to eliminate it. Other Southerners, slave owners especially, saw the growing number of free blacks as a threat to their "peculiar institution." The existence of free blacks gave the slaves ideas about freedom that undermined the existing order; sending them elsewhere would help maintain social stability. In the North, on the other hand, the predominant motive was to help black people find a land where they could be free to order their own affairs. The American Colonization Society, therefore, needed to send a mixed if not muddled message: black people are a degraded race who can never be part of an advanced civilization, black people can create a free society in Africa and bring the gospel to a pagan continent. But how can people not allowed to acquire an education bring civilization to Africa? Here and there, African Americans were offered an education in return for leaving. Some accepted the education but then refused to go.

Senator Henry Clay of Kentucky, a border-state politician known as "The Great Compromiser" for his efforts to find a middle ground between North and South, put both sides of the contradictory proposal plainly: "Can there be a nobler cause than that which, while it proposes to rid our own country of a useless and pernicious, if not dangerous portion of its population, contemplates the spreading of the arts of civilized life, and the possible redemption from ignorance and barbarism of a benighted quarter of the globe?"[37] How a "useless," "pernicious," and dangerous" population would be able to spread "the arts of civilized life," Senator Clay did not say, but to appeal to its constituency in the North and South alike, the Society needed to promulgate that mixed and contradictory message.

Richard Allen spoke for most African Americans in writing: "This land which we have watered with our tears and our blood, is now our mother country and we are well satisfied to stay where wisdom abounds and the gospel is free."[38] It was in large part in order to solidify black opposition to colonization and speak to white abolitionists like Garrison who initially supported the colonization movement that the Convention had been called. It ended by publishing an "Address to the Free People of Colour of these United States" that appealed to the Declaration of Independence as a charter for all, not white people only:

> . . . being taught by that inestimable and invaluable instrument, namely, the Declaration of Independence, that all men are born free and equal, and consequently are endowed with unalienable rights, among which are life, liberty, and the pursuit of happiness. Viewing these as incontrovertible facts, we have been led to the following conclusions: that our forlorn and deplorable situation earnestly and loudly demand of us to devise and pursue all legal means for the speedy elevation of ourselves and brethren to the scale and standing of men.[39]

That done, the Convention, not satisfied with the response to their invitation, called for another gathering to be held the next June in Philadelphia and then adjourned.

Pennington only spent four days away from his work, so he may not have been there when the final statement was issued. But he returned to Brooklyn to discover that his employer knew more of his activities than he realized. "I was in constant dread," he wrote later, "that I was in the employ of a rich man, who might take umbrage at my daring," and he learned very quickly what sort of employer he had. The meeting that chose Pennington to go to Philadelphia had issued an "Address to the Colored Citizens of the Village of Brooklyn, and its Vicinity" which had been published in the *Long Island Star,* and Adrian Van Sinderen was a reader of that newspaper. In the course of his duties, Pennington went into the library of the Van Sinderen home shortly after his return and found his employer waiting for him. He stood up and pulled his copy of the *Long Island Star* from a shelf. Sitting down again, he said, "James, I want you to explain to me your sentiments." He then proceeded to read the statement issued by the meeting, commenting from time to time on what he was reading.[40] The statement made clear its opposition to the American Colonization Society but the tone was conciliatory. "We do not contradict," it said, "the assertion that their objects . . . are salutary, and benevolent. . . . We truly believe that many gentlemen who are engaged in the American Colonization Society, are our sincere friends, and well wishers." But it pointed out that "Charity begins at home," and asked "what are they doing at home to improve our condition? . . . In our village and its vicinity, how many of us have been educated in colleges and advanced into different branches of business . . . Are we not even prohibited from some of the common labor, and drudgery of the streets, such as cartmen, porters, &c.? It is a strange theory to us, how these gentlemen can promise to honor and respect us in Africa, when they are using every effort to exclude us from all rights and privileges at home." The statement ended with a rhetorical flourish: "[W]e believe that [God] is in the whirlwind, and will soon bring about the time when the sable sons of America will join with their fairer brethren, and re-echo liberty and equal rights in all parts of Columbia's soil."[41] If James Pennington had decided to write a letter to Adrian Van Sinderen, he might well have written just such a statement and, indeed, the authorship may, in fact, have been his.† There was little to offend Van Sinderen but much to make him thoughtful, and it had obviously done so. He asked whether the Philadelphia Convention had endorsed the statement and what position Pennington had taken. "There is to be to-day," he explained, "a meeting of the managers of the Brooklyn Colonization Society, and I have been thinking that if the colored people for whose benefit we intend this society do not approve of it, we had better disband." Writing later of the incident, Pennington used his carpenter's training for a metaphor: "Finding the nail was already driven through the beam, I was not slow to clinch it on the other side." Good as his word, Van Sinderen went to the meeting and discussed the situation with the other officers, who agreed with him that there was no reason to elect officers or continue their involvement in the organization. Unlike some of those involved with the Colonization Society, Van Sinderen was willing to listen to the intended objects of his charitable work and change his mind in view of new information.[42]

However convinced he may have been of Van Sinderen's good will and generosity, Pennington could not have been sure he would still have a job when he came back from his convention. Employers like to be kept informed of their employees' plans, but Pennington did not yet know Van Sinderen well enough to feel free to do that. Fortunately, Van Sinderen was not one to act without listening, and he had obviously learned to respect and value his employee. So Pennington kept his job and could continue his education.

† It is difficult to be sure who wrote what when it comes to the Convention Address. The Address of the Third Convention, which Jennings quotes, was signed by Abraham Shadd, and no reference is made in the minutes to a committee for the address. The Address of the Second Convention is unsigned, although Sipkins served on the committee that produced it.

He would spend a third winter with Van Sinderen and push back further the darkness that still afflicted him. It was clear to Pennington that he needed to remake himself in a new mold as a man who no longer bore the marks of slavery, but that was no short and simple process. "It cost me two years' hard labour, after I fled, to unshackle my mind," he wrote nearly twenty years later; "it was three years before I had purged my language of slavery's idioms; it was four years before I had thrown off the crouching aspect of slavery."[43] Thus he returned to Brooklyn with half the work still to be done and one project for the ensuing year was to finish re-shaping his vocabulary to that of the world of freedom and education.

CHAPTER FIVE

Brooklyn, Part II

For the next three years, James Pennington continued his work for Adrian Van Sinderen and his studies, both in night school and on his own. He was trying to overcome the handicap created by the lack of an education when he was growing up, and that was inevitably a long, slow process. Education, however, was more than reading and writing, it was also exposure to a larger world. The Philadelphia Convention was also an education, opening the vision of a far wider realm of activity and providing him with an introduction to some of the national leaders in the emerging African American community. Conventions of various kinds continued to be an important interest for the rest of his life.

Conventions, in fact, had begun to involve many Americans with a variety of interests in those years. The national political parties began to hold their great nominating conventions in 1831 and 1832. The African American conventions were simply one part of a broader tendency for people to come together around all sorts of issues, local, national, and international. The evangelical impulse that had brought so many people to the United States in the first place ramified in the early nineteenth century into a variety of social and religious causes, including abolition and temperance, education and moral reform. Every cause had its adherents and every devotee felt that he must be heard. Slavery, of course, was a critical issue for many, and it is not surprising that African Americans would have found conventions to be a useful tool with which to attack their own situation. The number of free black people had grown rapidly, from 59,000 in 1790 to well over 300,000 in 1830. A few of these had been able to gain a good education and even a degree of wealth; now they were anxious to call attention to the unequal treatment they were given in spite of their accomplishments, to the lack of opportunity that kept so many others in poverty, and always to the brutal fact of slavery and the millions still in chains.

The 1830 Philadelphia Convention, then, was part of this larger movement. Giving united voice for the first time to the concerns of African Americans, it set an example that was quickly taken up by others in state and local conventions that came together to echo Philadelphia's support for Canadian settlement and opposition to African colonization. In January 1831, New York African Americans gathered to denounce the Colonization movement. "We claim this country, the place of our birth, and not Africa, as our mother country," they resolved, "and all attempts to send us to Africa as gratuitous and uncalled for." They issued an "Address to the Citizens of New York" that said, "This is our home, and this is our country. Beneath its sod lie the bones of our fathers: for it some of them fought, bled, and died. Here we were born, and here we will die."[1] In March, similar meetings were held and resolutions passed in Boston and Baltimore. In May a convention met in Washington, and in early June one was held in Brooklyn. Conventions in Hartford and Middletown, Connecticut, and Wilmington, Delaware, met in July, while in August conventions met in New Haven, Connecticut; Columbia, Pennsylvania; and Nantucket, Rhode Island. African Americans met in Pittsburgh in September and Harrisburg in October. In Rochester, New York; Trenton, New Jersey; and still other cities large and small across the land, African Americans gathered, passed resolutions, sent out general letters, and came away feeling that they had begun to make their voices heard and to change the pattern of American life.

Brooklyn was the last community to hold a convention in the twelve months before the next national convention. When they met in the African Hall on the 3rd of June, James Pennington was one of three who delivered "appropriate addresses" and also one of three delegated to prepare an "Address to the Colored Citizens of Brooklyn, N.Y., and its vicinity." It may have been Pennington's relationship with his employer that influenced the Brooklyn resolutions to speak more gently of the Colonization Society and say that they spoke to the Society "with friendly feelings" and had taken into consideration the objects of that Society before summing up with ironic understatement that the colonization plans were "not essential to the welfare of our race."[2]

"We truly believe," Pennington and his colleagues wrote in their *Address*, "that many gentlemen who are engaged in the Colonization Society, are our sincere friends and well-wishers" and have subscribed because there was no alternative offered, but some, the *Address* suggested, have been so "deluded" as to fail to understand that sending "a parcel of uninstructed, uncivilized and unchristianized people to the western coast of Africa, with bibles in their hands, to teach the natives the truths of the gospel, social happiness, and moral virtue, is mockery and ridicule in the extreme." They called on those to whom their letter will come to ask what impression the first settlers in America "who were wise and learned from Europe" made on the "aborigines of our country." Like the resolutions adopted in Philadelphia the year before and those adopted in the various local conventions, they insisted that under the Constitution "we are already American citizens; our fathers were among the first that peopled this country; their sweat and their tears have been the means, in a measure, of raising our country to its present standing. Many of them fought and bled and died for the gaining of her liberties; and shall we forsake their tombs, and flee to an unknown land?"[3]

The September Convention in Philadelphia in 1829 that provided the impetus for all those local meetings had failed to bring together as broad a representation as Hezekiah Grice and Richard Allen had hoped to assemble. As a result that meeting called for a second assembly to gather in June of the next year, and they agreed to consider it a continuation of the first Convention. Thus the second meeting created a continuing confusion for historians by styling itself "The First Negro National Convention." The Brooklyn meeting was held on a Friday and the national meeting in Philadelphia began on the following Monday. Richard Allen, the grand old man of the first gathering, had died in late March at the age of 71, and perhaps for that reason the sessions were held at the Wesleyan Church rather than Allen's Mother Bethel African Methodist church. The Brooklyn meeting elected Pennington to represent them again, but this time he would go as part of the New York delegation and some of the leaders from the Manhattan community would go with him. In Philadelphia they would hear in person from a new voice in the controversy over slavery.

William Lloyd Garrison, a man only slightly older than James Pennington, had apprenticed as a printer at the age of 13 and at the age of 25 had become the assistant editor of a journal published in Baltimore and called *Genius of Universal Emancipation*. The paper was edited by Benjamin Lundy, a Quaker and a gradualist. Garrison had begun as a gradualist himself and had briefly given his support to the Colonization movement, but he had become increasingly convinced that half measures were useless. Accused of libel because of an article he wrote for Lundy's paper in 1830, he was convicted and, since he could not pay the $50 fine, was sentenced to six months in prison. Arthur Tappan, a wealthy New York merchant and philanthropist, paid his fine for him. Released after seven weeks, Garrison returned to his native New England and began to publish his own paper, *The Liberator*. In the first issue, dated January 1, 1831, Garrison stated his perspective with force and clarity.

> On this subject, I do not wish to think, or to speak, or write, with moderation. No! no! Tell a man whose house is on fire to give a moderate alarm; tell him to moderately rescue his wife from the hands of the ravisher; tell the mother to gradually extricate her babe from the fire into which it has fallen;—but urge me not to use moderation in a cause like the present. I am in earnest—I

will not equivocate—I will not excuse—I will not retreat a single inch—AND I WILL BE HEARD.[4]

William Lloyd Garrison had looked at the compromises made by politicians to avoid facing up to the fundamental dilemma of American life and declared them intolerable.[†]

In spite of hope for a larger and more representative gathering, when the First Annual Convention of the People of Colour re-assembled in Philadelphia for its second session there were only 15 delegates, as compared with 26 in September. New York was better represented, but Connecticut and Rhode Island failed to reappear. On the other hand, William Lloyd Garrison was there with several other white guests who came with their own agenda. Arthur Tappan was one of these guests, and another was Simeon Jocelyn of New Haven, Connecticut. Jocelyn, like Tappan, was a successful businessman. He had studied theology at Yale and then, in 1824, founded the first African American congregation in New Haven. From his years of serving the black community he had come to believe that prayer must find visible and material expression. Eventually, in 1834, he left the congregation in the hands of African American leadership, made a fortune from his dealings in New Haven real estate, and would later help to create in New Haven the first planned, integrated, working-class community in the country.[††] Now he had a vision of a college for black students "on the Manual Labour System"[†††] to be located in New Haven, and he had enlisted Garrison and Tappan to support his ideas.[5] Manual labor schools were a commonly proposed pattern for education in the nineteenth century, and Garrison recalled frequent discussions of such a project when he was living in Baltimore, but no one could imagine raising the necessary funds.[6]

---

† Lewis Tappan said later of Garrison that he had a face that beamed with a look of "conscious rectitude." (Wyatt-Brown, Bertram, *Lewis Tappan and the Evangelical War Against Slavery*, p. 78.) Tappan knew that look because he had a mirror.

†† Much of Jocelyn's real estate dealing involved an area in New Haven then called Spireworth but now called the Hill.

††† The proposal for a "manual labor" school occurs frequently in the various African American conventions but was commended more generally by Joshua Leavitt, Theodore Weld, and other reformers in the belief that a balance of physical labor and education would teach young men the values of discipline and productivity. Weld wrote that exercise "would be a preventive of moral evils *by supplying that demand for vivid sensation so characteristic of youth*, whose clamors for indulgence drive multitudes to licentious indulgence, or to ardent spirits, tobacco, and other unnatural stimulants. It would preserve the equilibrium of the system, moderate the inordinate demands of immoral excitability, and quell the insurrection of appetite." Davis, Hugh, *Joshua Leavitt, Evangelical Abolitionist*, p. 82.

When the visitors presented their plan to the convention, a committee was appointed to meet with them and discuss the project in detail. In due course the committee returned with a favorable report. When the committee asked why New Haven was recommended as the location for the new school, the visitors had given them seven reasons ranging from the fact that the site was "healthy and beautiful" and the inhabitants "friendly, pious, generous, and humane," to the centrality of the location and the possibility that wealthy residents of the West Indies might send their sons there to be educated. Twenty thousand dollars was the estimated cost of establishing the college and Arthur Tappan was ready to contribute one thousand dollars at the outset. He suggested that he could find nine friends to make similar contributions, and colored people might raise the other $10,000.[7] The convention was much impressed with the vision and proceeded to appoint a General Agent with committees in fifteen major cities from Boston to Baltimore and westward to Pittsburgh to assist Tappan in raising the needed funds. There were to be seven Trustees, and the Convention wanted it "distinctly understood" that a majority of them must be "coloured persons." There was a certain nervousness about the fact that the proposal had come from whites and that even here, where black people had set out to define their own agenda at their own convention, the agenda was being preempted by a plan that was not their own.[8]

If Garrison had any lingering doubts about the colonization movement, he had now heard firsthand why African Americans opposed it, and he was fully persuaded. Later in the same month that the Convention was held, he gave a speech in a number of places entitled "Address to the People of Color" in which he elaborated on the themes he had heard in Philadelphia:

> our colored population are not aliens; they were born on our soil; they are bone of our bone, and flesh of our flesh; their fathers fought bravely to achieve our independence during the revolutionary war, without immediate or subsequent compensation; they spilt their blood freely during the last war; they are entitled, in fact, to every inch of our southern, and much of our western territory, having worn themselves out in its cultivation, and received nothing but wounds and bruises in return. Are these the men to stigmatize as foreigners?[9]

The roots of the Colonization Society, he wrote in an article the same month, were persecution, falsehood, cowardice, and infidelity.[10] Garrison was convinced that colonization was not the solution to America's problem, but the battle against colonization would continue down to the Civil War and still draw leading citizens into its ranks: politicians like Stephen Douglas, William

Seward, and General Winfield Scott, clergy like the Episcopal Bishops of Philadelphia, New York, and Connecticut, and always a small minority of African Americans. Indeed, Hezekiah Grice himself would soon despair of American society and emigrate to Haiti.

Yet the clearly stated opposition of African Americans, as expressed in the convention movement, got the attention of men such as William Lloyd Garrison and Adrian Van Sinderen and successfully blunted the Colonization Society's impact. In fact, the Colonization Society had already reached and passed its peak of influence and accomplishment by 1831. The largest number of colonists sent to Africa was 633 in 1827. The following year there were 453 and the year after that 196. After 1832 there were seldom more than 25 or 30 colonists per year. Meanwhile the population of African Americans was growing annually by tens of thousands. Even the number of free blacks was increasing faster than the number of exported colonists. The Society's receipts also had peaked in 1827 when its income was $62,270. Receipts for the following year were less than half that amount, fell to less than $15,000 in 1834, and continued generally at that level thereafter. Ralph Gurley, the Society's Secretary, tried to redirect its appeal to Northerners in 1833 by eliminating Southern representatives from the board and replacing them with Northerners. That move failed, and Gurley's own shift to a clear stand for emancipation and an end to slavery was insufficient to overcome the newly aroused voice of the Negro Conventions and Garrison's abolitionist polemics. The American Colonization Society would continue to serve as a whipping boy for abolitionists, but it was no longer a serious threat.[11]

The condemnation of the colonization movement, however, was not balanced by success in the campaign for a college in New Haven. Philadelphians, including William White, the Bishop of Pennsylvania and Presiding Bishop of the Episcopal Church, wished success to the venture,[12] but it was otherwise in Connecticut. Simeon Jocelyn, believing his fellow citizens in New Haven to be, as he had told the Convention, "friendly, pious, generous, and humane," had failed to consult with them about his vision. He was quickly made aware that the vision was not shared. The fact that Nat Turner's revolt took place that summer sent tremors of fear through Northern communities as well as those in the South. Jocelyn had barely had time to return to New Haven before the outraged citizens came together to make it clear that they were not at all eager to see another college in town. At least part of that concern was a reflection of the importance to the New Haven economy of Southern students at Yale. White abolitionists and African Americans and their property were subject to frequent assault in the days that followed and, when the summer of 1830 was over and college sessions set to resume, the mayor himself, with the support of "the best citizens in New Haven" and a number of professors from Yale, called a public meeting. Some 700 citizens came together with Mayor Dennis Kimberly presiding and passed a resolution claiming that "the establishment of a College in the same place [as Yale and other schools] to educate the colored population, is incompatible with the prosperity, if not the existence, of the present institutions of learning, and will be destructive of the best interests of the city." They further resolved that "the propagation of sentiments favorable to the immediate emancipation of slaves . . . is an unwarrantable and dangerous interference with the internal concerns of other states."[13] Jocelyn and three friends cast the only negative votes. When the public meeting was shortly followed by attacks on the New Haven summer residence of Arthur Tappan's family and a series of attacks on the homes not only of Jocelyn and his friends but African Americans as well, the *Liberator* suggested that "southern medical students" were responsible.[14] Jocelyn had thought that wealthy West Indians might like to support his college, but the mayor and college faculty were quite sure that wealthy Southern planters would be much less likely to send their sons north for an education if there was a college in New Haven catering to blacks. A Christian newspaper in New Haven protested these events labeling them the result of "a prejudice which is the fruit of our own cruelty and crime" that resulted in cutting off "a portion of our fellow beings from knowledge and intelligence and, in effect, saying to the slave owner and dealer, "screw on your fetters and put on the lash in your own way. You shall receive no molestation from this quarter." But that was only one voice, and the voice of the mob was the voice that prevailed. One letter writer pointed out that it was dangerous to make the gospel the rule of life.[15] Jocelyn wrote that "Our beautiful city is clothed with sackcloth. Our proud elms hang their heads."[16]

Concerned by these developments, a committee of New Yorkers wrote to Jocelyn in October for reassurance. What could he tell them, they asked, about "facts or circumstances . . . which in your opinion are calculated to remove prejudice and awaken an interest in the public mind in favor of this enterprise."[17] Jocelyn responded by sending them an outline of the project that he had recently submitted to the *New Haven Advertiser* along with supporting testimonials from "many noble-minded men in different parts of the country." "I am persuaded," he told them, "that the College will be built, though it may be in 'troublous times.'"[18] Not many, however, shared Jocelyn's optimism, and the result was that fundraising was drastically slowed and the next year's Convention had to reconsider the project.

Meanwhile, in Brooklyn, Pennington was deepening his involvement in another convention movement. The Philadelphia Convention had not only condemned the colonization solution to the difficulties of African Americans, but also received a committee report "On the Condition of the Free People of Colour of the United States" that called attention to "the dissolute, intemperate, and ignorant condition of a large portion of the coloured population." The report suggested that African Americans must work to improve themselves by "education, temperance, and economy" and said that "(w)e would therefore respectfully request an early attention to these virtues among our brethren, who have a desire to be useful."[19] Education and temperance would remain concerns of the Convention, as they were for most Americans, whether black or white.

The temperance movement had begun at the end of the 18th century but burst into full bloom with the forming of The American Temperance Society in 1826. Twelve years later, the Society claimed more than 8,000 local groups and over 1,500,000 members. Leading preachers like Henry Ward Beecher were early advocates.[20] Farm workers and immigrants who flocked to the city to find jobs in the growing factories found themselves packed into small apartments with a neighborhood tavern not far away that offered relief from the dull routine of factory work and the tensions of family life in crowded quarters. Drunkenness was a common problem, and the only obvious solution to what was generally seen as a moral failure was abstinence. Though the problem knew no color line, temperance societies, like so much else in American life, were usually segregated. When a "Brooklyn Temperance Association for the people of color" was formed in 1830, Pennington was one of those who helped organize the new society, and when the first anniversary meeting was held on July 20, 1831, five weeks after his return from Philadelphia, Pennington was elected Secretary.[21] Less than four years after escaping from slavery, knowing how to form only five letters but not knowing what they meant, James Pennington was chosen to serve as secretary to his organization. He was learning fast.

Indeed, he was learning to rejoice in his newly acquired power with the pen. In August of the same year, a letter from Brooklyn, dated July 28, 1831, and signed with a modest "P.," appeared in the *Liberator*. Garrison's newspaper was just over six months old, and Pennington wanted Garrison to know that "the more I view the spirit of the 'Liberator,' the more I am convinced of its utility and excellent tendency." "The press," he continued, "is, beyond all doubt, the weapon which will make us triumphant over the petty breastworks of the harpers of inferiority . . . Through the press, we are to show the people of this republic that we are intelligent, and that it is not justifiable in believing that we are not enough so to have our privileges." Pennington's primary purpose in writing, however, was to thank the Editor for correcting the record in relation to the Rev. R. R. Gurley, the Secretary of the American Colonization Society, who claimed to have heard the voice of African Americans in Brooklyn and found a majority favorable to emigration to Liberia.

On the contrary, Pennington told the *Liberator*, Gurley had spoken to an audience of four or five hundred in the Brooklyn Presbyterian Church who slowly drifted away in spite of his pleas that they remain, until not more than fifty remained. When Gurley spoke again in Brooklyn, Pennington was asked to let people know and "solicit their attendance." Pennington was anxious that at least some of the leadership attend so they could quote Gurley in their own statements and went around the community urging African Americans to be present. One man, sitting in a room eight feet wide and ten feet long, told Pennington "he would not walk from his chair to the fireside to hear Gurley again." In spite of his efforts, Pennington counted "but two persons of color present, besides myself," when Gurley spoke, "and they were strangers from Canada." If Gurley and his associates, Pennington concluded in a burst of eloquence, "can so misrepresent the views of any part of a free nation, in order to controvert their rights, then humanity is no more humanity, but transformed into an awful prison-house, whose iron bound gates grate harsh thunders, opening wide for the destruction of innocent people."[22] The rhetoric may seem somewhat overheated, but it came from a man who had just learned to write and who was exploring ways to get attention for his cause and, perhaps, for himself.

Pennington's rhetoric probably drew little notice, but less than a month after his letter was published, Nat Turner's revolt rolled "harsh thunders" and lightning across the Southern landscape, leaving 55 white men, women, and children dead and then nearly 200 African Americans, many of them no part of Turner's small army, who were tortured and murdered by mobs of frightened and angry whites. The longer-lasting consequence was an increase of repressive laws across the south constricting both the liberties of free blacks and the willingness of whites to question the system or offer even such modest alternatives as the colonization movement. Polarization increased and moderate citizens found fewer willing to listen.

Even in Philadelphia with its Quaker heritage, the Turner rebellion produced a violent reaction. In November of 1831 there was a gathering at Upton's Tavern of young white males who were convinced that Turner had not acted alone but only because he and his companions were stirred up by other African Americans in the north who were continuing to create trouble by their incendiary publications. They took note of the actions of other states in the Midwest and South that required free blacks to post a bond to ensure "their good behavior," but felt even that was inadequate. Nor were they satisfied that some had emigrated to Canada, since the British could deploy them against their former owners in the event of another Anglo-American war. They called on their legislature to pass laws preventing blacks from moving to Pennsylvania and expelling those already resident. Some of the Philadelphians who had taken part in the Conventions sent petitions on their behalf to the legislature citing their peaceful reputation and enumerating their contributions to the community. The proposed measures were lost in committee, but similar laws were under consideration throughout the South. The Maryland General Assembly passed a law that "no free negro or mulatto . . . shall come into this State, and therein remain for the space of ten successive days" and making it unlawful for anyone to sell them alcoholic beverages, firearms, or ammunition.[23] The Virginia legislature passed a law to arrest and sell "free negroes . . . convicted of remaining in the state contrary to law," to prohibit any "meetings of free negroes or mulattoes . . . for teaching them reading or writing," and to provide for fines and imprisonment of whites convicted of teaching slaves to read or write.[24] In Boston, on the other hand, Garrison and his colleagues met on January 1, 1832, to form the New England Anti-Slavery Society and adopt a constitution stating that "every person of full age and sane mind, has a right to immediate freedom from personal bondage of whatsoever kind." They added that "we will not operate on the existing conditions of society by other than peaceful and lawful means, and that we will give no countenance to violence or insurrection."[25] But the mere existence of a society dedicated to the abolition of slavery was evidence of the deepening division between North and South.

The full force of the "gathering storm" was still distant, but the evidence was mounting, both in the words of Pennington and his colleagues in the convention movement on the one hand and in the actions of Turner and those who joined with him on the other, that the storm would come. Whether by conventions with their speeches and resolutions or by violent action, African Americans were beginning to make it clear that they intended to take their rightful part in the life of a free country.

But still Pennington's job was as a coachman for Adrian Van Sinderen, and in that capacity he continued to serve through the following year. African Americans in Brooklyn were becoming better organized, and in 1832 they held a public meeting at the end of March, well in advance of the Philadelphia convention, and chose Pennington to represent them again.[26] When June came, he went for the third time to Philadelphia, this time as a member of a New York delegation of five, four from New York and one from Brooklyn. Eight states were now represented, all between Massachusetts and Maryland, and there were 28 delegates as well as a number of visitors. The opening sessions were held in Benezet Hall, a meeting place named for an 18th-century Quaker who had begun teaching night classes for black slaves in 1750 and who later founded the first American anti-slavery society. The Convention continued after the first day at the First African Presbyterian Church, which was made available to them for $1.50 a day. By the time of this third session, Pennington had gained recognition as a valuable member of the gathering. The Convention opened with a roll call and immediately named him to serve with four others as a committee to draft rules to govern the Convention. Several other committees were named as well to carry out Convention business, including another five-member committee to "report to this Convention such subjects as they may deem it essential for them to act on." The resolution calling for such a committee was moved by Thomas L. Jennings of the New York delegation and seconded by James Pennington. In the traditional manner of conventions, when the resolution was adopted, Jennings and Pennington were immediately named to the committee.

The record of the Convention seems to indicate, however, that Pennington may have annoyed his elders with a premature eagerness to make use of his newly gained oratorical skills and hard-won recognition. The Committee to draft rules must have done their work ahead of time, since the same morning session that appointed them also received and accepted their report; but when Pennington's other committee, to report on "such subjects as they may deem it essential to act on," also reported to the morning session, the Convention returned their report to the Committee "for reconsideration" and two new members were added to the Committee to help them do that. The next day, they asked for more time to do their work; but when they came back on the following day they were asked to wait while three visitors to the Convention, two advocates for the Colonization Society, a Philadelphia delegate, and a ship captain who had taken emigrants to Liberia, made speeches. Finally, on the fifth day of the Convention, Pennington was given the floor and presented a list of resolutions for the Convention to consider. These, the minutes report, "produced very tedious debates, and it was finally deemed inexpedient that the same should, at present, engage the deliberations of this meeting." Nothing abashed, Pennington was back two days later with a "summary of resolutions for the consideration of the Convention," but it was decided that there was no longer time enough to deal with them and they would be a "proper subject for the ensuing Convention."

There was, of course, important business to attend to. The Committee appointed the previous year to raise money for the proposed school in New Haven reported that they had done very well until "such an opposition was raised by the white citizens of New Haven" that they had little success afterwards and decided to do nothing further until the next Convention. The Convention heard an eloquent report from Simeon Jocelyn on the need for such a school as he had proposed, and a new Committee was created to raise funds and look for a more suitable location. Pennington then came forward with a resolution, seconded by another member, that the Convention ask the new Committee to obtain as much information as possible about existing schools and report to the next Convention. The minutes report simply that the Convention then adjourned for the morning, and nothing more is heard of Pennington's resolution.

The dramatic highpoint of the Convention came early, in the afternoon of the second day, when the Rev. Ralph R. Gurley of the Colonization Society was given the floor and "addressed the meeting at considerable length, in his usual tone of eloquence" in an effort to remove "some erroneous impressions in the minds of people of color" in relation to the Society. An attempt was made to have him submit his views in writing, but that was ruled out of order by presiding officer Henry Sipkins. Gurley was a Yale graduate, a licensed Presbyterian preacher though not ordained, who served as the energetic agent and secretary of the Colonization Society for fifty years, from 1822 to 1872, believing that he was working to maintain the Union and advance the cause of emancipation. He had traveled to Liberia to help set up the government of the colony and also served four terms as Chaplain to the United States House of Representatives. It was his view that "the consent of the South was indispensable for the safe abolition of slavery; that the work should be done with caution and preparation; that circumstances and consequences should be regarded; that a separation of races so distinct as the coloured and white in complexion, habits and condition is desirable for the happiness of both."[27] In his time, and certainly in his own mind, Gurley was a moderate, working carefully but with a deep commitment in the best interests of all Americans as he understood them.

He was followed immediately by William Lloyd Garrison, who never claimed to be moderate and "who in a most eloquent and convincing speech, proved that the operations of [the American Colonization] Society militate against the interests of the people of color in these United States." The next day another representative of the Colonization Society attempted to persuade the Convention that, while they might have their differences as to the best means of "improving the condition of the people of color," he was ready to assist "in any plan that promised their elevation." Garrison again followed immediately with a rebuttal, quoting the minutes of Society meetings to demonstrate their hostility to the Convention's interests. The Convention found itself listening to representatives of rival white organizations arguing which would best serve the interests of black people. It may have been flattering to be so courted, but the delegates must also have asked themselves whether their movement was being usurped by others. Before the Convention adjourned, Garrison, "their indefatigable friend," spoke once more and was asked to provide a copy of his address for publication. Unlike Pennington, Garrison seemed to have no difficulty in getting the floor and again one wonders whether, however subconsciously, both he and the Convention were reflecting a society in which white males were accustomed to take precedence and black males were accustomed to defer.

In spite of his difficulty in getting the Convention to share his particular concerns, Pennington continued to take an active part, seconding an occasional resolution and, at last, being placed on a three-member committee to write the formal document that would go out to the rest of the country. The odd aspect of that appointment is that a different committee had been named on the first day of the convention and directed to bring back an address to the free people of color expressing the views of the convention. When Friday came, however, no report was made. On the following Tuesday, the next-to-last day of the convention, a new resolution was presented asking again for a committee of three to prepare an address. Apparently the first committee, all distinguished senior members of the convention, had forgotten their duty or had been distracted by more important matters, and a new committee had to be named. Pennington had already given evidence of his eagerness to prepare resolutions, and that made him an obvious choice under the circumstances; but the other two were Henry Sipkins and Frederick A. Hinton, who were the President and 2nd Vice President of the Convention. Were they conferring an honor on Pennington, or making sure that older and wiser heads would prevail? Whatever the strategy was, the committee did its work and presented a statement the next day that was accepted without debate. Five years later, when Henry Sipkins, the first-named member of the committee, died, Thomas Jennings, who had been present with the New York delegation, gave a eulogy that included long extracts from the address of the convention as examples of Sipkins's thought. Perhaps he was the primary author, or perhaps he told Pennington what ought to be said and let Pennington write it. Convention minutes don't always answer all the questions later generations might like to ask. What we do know is that when the convention needed a statement drawn up quickly, they turned to Pennington and two others to get it done, and they did.

That final address to "the Free Colored inhabitants of these United States," expressing the views of the convention, rejoiced in "this glorious, annual event" and "the wisdom of a Divine Providence [that] has protected us during a year, whose autumnal harvest, has been a reign of terror and persecution, and whose winter has almost frozen the streams of humanity, by its frigid legislation." The Address goes on to condemn both slavery and the Colonization Society, whose doctrines they proclaimed to be "an evil for magnitude, unexcelled" and aimed at "the entire extinction of the free colored population and the riviting [sic] of slavery."[28] The Canadian option is treated in passing as relevant only to those in Ohio who were forced from their homes. The United States, they insist, "is *our* own, our native land," and the emphasis must be on gaining an education and improving their ability to take part in its life. The project for a college is commended again in spite of "the disreputable proceedings of New Haven" because "if we ever expect to see the influence of prejudice decrease, and ourselves respected, it must be by the blessings of an enlightened education" and of "that classical knowledge which promotes genius, and causes man to soar up to those high intellectual enjoyments and acquirements" which "is imperishable by time, and drowns in oblivion's cup their moral degradation."[29] It would also have been characteristic of Pennington to stress the value of education.

A final note called on those addressed to "beware of that bewitching evil, that bane of society, that curse of the world, that fell destroyer of the best prospects, and the last hope of civilized man—Intemperance."[30] This, at least, would seem to reflect Pennington's influence, if it is not in fact his writing. His involvement with the Brooklyn temperance society has already been noticed and he would be the author of a lengthy report on temperance at a subsequent convention. The fact that temperance had not been discussed at the convention until it appeared in this final statement would seem to indicate that it was one of the subjects Pennington had tried to bring before the convention. Failing in that effort, he managed to include it in the convention's final report. He had learned that there can be more than one way to gain an objective.

Temperance would become a more central subject of future conventions, but this one broke no new ground. The condemnation of the Colonization Society may have gained new force from the presence of its representatives but had been stated already. Support for the Canadian settlement, the other primary matter at the earlier meetings, was now modified and accepted only for those compelled to leave the country. But Pennington would have been able to return to Brooklyn satisfied that he had begun to have a significant part to play in this national leadership group. He had served on the committee that set the rules for the Convention and the committee that summed up the proceedings and addressed all "the Free Colored inhabitants of these United States."[31] And he had been an illiterate slave less than five years earlier.

CHAPTER SIX

School Teacher in Newtown

lways in James Pennington's thoughts were the millions not yet free and the question of what he could do on their behalf. He wanted to "devise ways and means for their elevation," and the Conventions in Philadelphia had given him one powerful tool toward that end. When the Convention placed him on a committee to write the letter expressing the mind of the Convention, it gave him a pulpit from which to speak to Americans of all colors and conditions, north and south. But the contrast between occupying that pulpit and caring for Adrian Van Sinderen's horse was stark and left him with long hours when his mind was free not only to study and learn but also to imagine and to explore new possibilities. His position on Brooklyn Heights made it possible for him both to learn and to dream, but it was all simply a means to an end that was not yet clear. He thought for a while of going to Africa as a missionary, but how would that help those in chains in America? It was, he thought, "too much like feeding a hungry man with a long spoon."[1]

Through the summer of 1832, Americans, black and white, were temporarily distracted by the arrival of cholera. The disease had been making its way westward across Asia and Europe and had killed 50,000 in England and twice as many in France in the summer of 1831. It reached Montreal on June 6 of the following year and was in northern New York State within the week. Cholera was especially frightening because it was both sudden and deadly. Victims were struck suddenly with various symptoms—fever, muscular cramps, vomiting, diarrhea—and might be dead within hours of the onset of the disease.[2]

As the disease moved southward, those who could flee New York City did so, but it was those who lived in the poorest areas with the worst sanitation who were least able to flee and also most vulnerable. The Dutch Reformed Church called on President Jackson to appoint a public day of fasting, but he saw that as making an establishment of religion, and that was forbidden by the Constitution, so he refused. Bishop Onderdonk of New York nonetheless called for a day of fasting and prayer and issued special prayers for the clergy to use.

One of his clergy did so and was dead three days later, but there were those who saw the scourge as evidence of God's displeasure and noted that while some of "the decorous, the regular, and the pure" had been affected, the heaviest impact was on "the irreligious, the dissolute, and the disorderly members of society."[3] Such terminology, of course, was more of a judgment on those who were different, especially immigrants, the Irish in particular, and blacks, who "lived in the worst housing, under the most crowded circumstances, and were least able to afford good water, medical care, or flight from the epidemic."[4] The New York reformer George Henry Evans, on the other hand, saw the epidemic more accurately "not as God's retribution for sin, but rather as proof of man's inhumanity to man."[5] Early nineteenth-century America was only beginning to understand how society created the circumstances that caused so many of its own problems. Newtown,[†] situated on a stream used to carry off all the garbage and sewage of slums and factories, inevitably saw more than its share of sickness and death. Not until the end of the nineteenth century did civic associations begin to call on the city to clean up "that malodorous locality."[6]

When the dreadful summer was over and life returned to a more usual pattern, James Pennington took another step toward establishing his place in society and moving forward with plans for his future. On October 20, 1832, eight days before the fifth anniversary of his escape from slavery, he married Harriet Walker at St. Ann's Church, Brooklyn. The Rector of St. Ann's conducted the marriage ceremony, but there are no witnesses listed nor is there any information such as the age or address of either the bride or groom,[††] nor are either Pennington or his bride listed in any of the Brooklyn City Directories for the years they lived in Brooklyn. Pennington was, after all, still a fugitive slave living under an assumed name, and Harriet also may have been a fugitive. In those years, even a northern newspaper like *The Long Island Star* still ran an occasional ad for a runaway slave.[†††]

So now Pennington was married and had a steady job, but his colleagues in the Convention were men who were not only married and employed but, for the most part, men who had gained some control of their own lives as small

---

† Newtown is generally the area now known as Elmhurst in Queens County, New York City.

†† Civil registration of marriage was not required in most jurisdictions until the latter part of the 19th century at the earliest, and the Episcopal Book of Common Prayer did not require witnesses until 1979. Nevertheless most marriages at St. Ann's did have witnesses. Cf. Howard, George Elliott, *A History of Matrimonial Institutions*, pp. 452ff.

††† On June 29, 1831, for example, and the following two weeks, the *Star* ran an ad offering a $15 reward for the return of "a negro slave named Tom" who had left his owners in Tea Neck, New Jersey.

businessmen, pastors, and teachers. Pennington, too, had ambitions beyond his employment in the Van Sinderen household and had begun to think of ordination to the ministry "as the desire of my whole heart." He was outgrowing the evening schools and Sabbath schools, having "mastered the preliminary branches of English education," and with thoughts of ordination in his mind he had gone on to study "logic, rhetoric, and the Greek Testament, without a master."[7] He had studied Latin also without a tutor and had surprised Samuel Cox one day by going to him for assistance with a translation of the Greek New Testament.[8] But obviously at some point a teacher would be needed—and hard to find. Pennington could and did employ tutors, but he wanted a formal education and the path in that direction was not clear. Theodore Wright, pastor of the Shiloh Presbyterian Church in Manhattan and the first African American to graduate from an American theological school, had managed to obtain an education at Princeton Seminary, but there were many Southerners at Princeton and the mood was changing. Wright had been physically and verbally attacked in the chapel on his last visit there.[9] Black candidates had been turned away from the General Theological Seminary in New York. Yale had a theological department, but the citizens of New Haven had made it clear that they were not a welcoming community.

As Pennington considered his limited options, he was surprised to find an opening offered in a somewhat different direction. Walking on the street one day as various thoughts revolved in his mind, he met a friend, who said "I have just had an application to supply a teacher for a school, and I have recommended you." "My dear friend," said Pennington, "I am obliged to you for the kindness; but I fear I cannot sustain an examination for that station." But his friend would not be turned away so easily. "'Oh," said he, "try." "I will," said Pennington, and two weeks later he sat down with the trustees to be examined and accepted for the position at a salary of two hundred dollars a year.[†10] "This was," he adds, "five years, three months, and thirteen days after I came from the South."[11] Most remarkable of all, the journey from illiterate slave to school teacher had been made, for the most part, in his spare time.

The school for which a teacher was needed was a brand-new building just erected in Newtown, Long Island, by a wealthy New York merchant, Peter Remsen, a cousin of Adrian Van Sinderen. Van Sinderen had lived in Newtown himself before he built his home on Brooklyn Heights, and he still served as

---

† By way of comparison, William Beecher at the same time took a church in Putnam, Ohio, where he "managed to scrape along on a salary of five hundred dollars a year." Rugoff, Milton, *The Beechers: an American Family in the Nineteenth Century*. New York: Harper & Row, 1981, p. 194.

an elder of the church there. Indeed, Pennington had gone with him to that church, so he had already been in the community at least once or twice before he was hired as a teacher.[12]

Peter Remsen had inherited from his father a spreading estate in Flushing, Long Island, including some of the best farm land in the area with all its farm animals and a large number of slaves. Slaves in the North were not necessarily treated any better than those in the South, and Peter Remsen's father had been as brutal as any Southern slave owner. James Pennington came to know Thomas Johnson, who had been bought in "a lot of four" by the senior Remsen for £100, who then turned a neat profit on the transaction by selling Johnson's mother and sister for the same amount. As a child, Thomas Johnson was often beaten with Remsen's fist or ox goad or whatever was handy. The last time Remsen attacked Johnson was on a Sunday morning when Johnson went to see his wife, who was owned by a neighbor and was very ill. Thus delayed, he returned to find his master getting the horse and carriage ready for the trip to church himself and asking angrily where Johnson had been. "My wife is very ill, sir," was the answer. "Well, let Mrs. Woodhull take care of her nigger wench herself," said Remsen. Feeling himself insulted as a man and a Christian, Johnson answered back, "I think as much of my wife, or Mrs. W's nigger wench, as you call her, as you do of your farm." Remsen lunged at Johnson with his carriage whip, threatening to give him "the butt of this whip over your head," if he were to say such a thing again.[13]

In 1824, three years before slavery was legally ended in New York State, the younger Remsen, who was of a very different disposition and strongly attached to those who had been his slaves, set them free and then hired them back at wages above the average. He employed his former overseer as supervisor at a generous salary that enabled him to begin to buy property for himself and even left the man $500 in his will. Remsen also set aside $2500 to create a new school to serve the African American community. The building for the new school, erected at a cost of $350, was a visible expression of his concern not only for his former slaves but also for the general African American population in the neighborhood.[†] Newtown, like Baltimore, Newport, and other shipping centers where uneducated laborers were needed, had drawn a significant black population. In 1830 there were 477 African Americans in Newtown out of a total population of 2,610. There had been 533 slaves in Newtown

---

† Adrian Van Sinderen had also been a "commissioner of Common Schools for the town of Newtown" when the school districts for the community were created in 1814. It may not be coincidental that a year after Pennington went to Philadelphia and Van Sinderen discussed with him the question "In our village and its vicinity, how many of us have been educated in colleges and advanced into different branches of business," that Van Sinderen's cousin created a school for black children in Newtown.

in 1790 and somewhat over a hundred had been freed over the years before slavery was ended in New York State in 1827,[14] so few of the black residents of Newtown when Pennington arrived would have been long freed from slavery.[†] Pennington would be starting with his students where he himself had started only five years earlier: at the beginning.

So, on the 5th of March in 1833, ignoring a fresh fall of ankle-deep snow, Pennington walked the seven and a half miles from Brooklyn Heights to Newtown, Long Island, and arrived, "teacher-like," at 8:30 to find the door locked and no one there. The trustees arrived shortly afterwards and told him it was important to insist on promptness but it seemed unlikely that he would get any children out for several days in view of the snow. The trustees then presented him with a key, wished him good luck, and left. Pennington opened the door to find a smell of fresh paint. Noticing carpenter's litter still on the floor of the one-room building, he walked the short distance to a nearby store, bought a broom, returned to the school, and swept it out. Since there were still no students, Pennington found "a colored gentleman who had a sleigh" and prevailed on him to take him around the neighborhood to visit the families of the prospective students. The families gave him a cordial welcome but made it clear that he would have to win their support. They had great confidence in Remsen and therefore were quite willing to listen to anyone who came to them with his sponsorship, but it had not occurred to any of them that the new teacher might be black. It took some persuasion on Pennington's part to convince them not only that a black teacher might be adequately qualified but also that an education for their children would be useful. They themselves had lived there for generations without any education so they saw no particular reason to provide one for the next generation.

With Pennington's encouragement, the neighborhood families agreed to send their children to him as soon as the snow melted somewhat and so, two days later, he sat down to begin his new career with nine scholars as unfamiliar with their side of the teacher–student relationship as Pennington was with his. Complicating the work they had to do in this new relationship was a lack of books and writing slates and other basic equipment. Remsen had provided such supplies but he had also founded a school for poor white children and that school, having started first, had appropriated all the equipment. Pennington therefore spent the first day introducing his charges to spelling out

† The Newtown Annual Town Meeting recorded the manumission of a number of slaves in the twenty years before slavery was legally ended in the state. Slavery, in fact, was no longer economical. It was a common saying among Long Island farmers that "in summer time the pigs used to eat up the potatoes, but in winter time the slave did eat all the pigs." *Extracts from the records of Newtown, L.I., and other newspaper clippings relating to Newtown, L.I.* Brooklyn, N.Y.: Paul Grosser, stationer & printer, 18–, pp. 117 and 113.

of the one book he had with him and, like any good teacher, compiling a list of the students' names and getting to know them. That night he went to a store in Brooklyn and spent several dollars of his own money for books and other school supplies—except a rod. He had decided not to acquire that basic teaching aid, "Doctor Hickory" he called it, until it was actually needed and four months went by before he saw no alternative way to "treat the symptoms" of one of his students.[15]

By the third day there were twelve students and Pennington considered himself well launched on his new profession. For a long time, however, he would have to learn his job by experience. He had certainly had opportunity, as a student himself, to observe how others taught, but he had never been instructed in the art of teaching others. Seven years later, he wrote a series of articles for the *Colored American* distilling some of what he had learned for the benefit not only of teachers but also of school boards and parents. Parental support, he had learned, was an essential element in a teacher's success and among African Americans, who had almost no experience of sending children to school, it was of critical importance that they understand the importance of their role. Several of the essays were headed "Errors of Parents," and Pennington had compiled a long list from his years in Newtown. In one essay after another he set those parental errors out, though, he wrote, "I shall try to do it in love."[16]

"One of the grandest of great eras[17] of Colored American parents by which they try the soul of a teacher," wrote Pennington in his seventh essay, is that they will send their children to school as "pets," by which he meant that the parents had not enforced any discipline at home and would not support the rules of behavior laid down by the teacher. The pupil, with an innate ability to play off the authority of the teacher against that of the parent, would take advantage of the situation at every opportunity. Pennington, for example, had required the students to leave their lunch baskets hanging on hooks in one place—"I have found it well," he wrote, "to observe the old maxim, 'a place for everything and everything in its place'"—but one morning a girl placed her basket on her desk to see what he would do about it. Pennington "spoke to her gently:

"P. E., you know it is against the rule.

"E. Well, Mr. Pennington, the children hook [steal] my dinner.

"P. You have the same chance to preserve your dinner as others have; and besides, if you can find one who has taken your dinner and let me know, they will not do it again."

She moved her basket reluctantly and came back the next morning with a large spike in her hand, requesting permission to drive it into the wall above her desk so she could hang the basket there. "Father gave me the spike," she said, "and he says it will not hurt the wall." Pennington thought otherwise and became involved in a long discussion with the girl about the advantages of a warm building without holes in the walls and the harm that could be done to a building by driving spikes into it. But behind the girl testing the rules, Pennington saw her father—"a crookeder stick Adam's woodpile never contained"—who "had sent me his girl as a pet." Clearly she could do as she pleased at home and her father encouraged her to do the same in school. The "truths contained in this case," wrote Pennington, were two: "a deliberate attempt to prostrate the rule of the school" and "a reckless disregard for the preservation of public property."[18]

The same man had come past the school one evening when the students had gone home. It had been his daughter's first day at school, and he and Pennington had not previously met. He tied his horse outside and came in, "exchanged the usual civilities," cleared his throat, and asked whether Pennington would "run me off a line of coarse writing on one slip of paper, and one of fine on another." Pennington looked him in the eye and "read very plainly his design, though he was earnestly assuring me of frankness and friendship." Nevertheless he gave the man the specimens of writing requested. It turned out, as Pennington had suspected from the beginning, that the man was serving as messenger for a group of white people hoping to demonstrate his lack of qualifications. The "clanning together" of "the lower class of whites and lower minded colored people," as Pennington described it, enabled the whites—"stiff-starched with prejudice"—"to stoop and instigate the colored people to such intrigues." A school teacher needed to be alert. Parents would use their children to undermine his authority, and they would allow themselves to be used by others for the same purpose.[19]

It took three months for Pennington to feel comfortable in his new role. He confessed to "strong apprehensions that the business of teaching would not agree with me." The children may have been new to their role as students, but they knew by instinct how to test their teacher. The desks had been arranged, in the traditional way of one-room schoolhouses in those days, facing the walls. Presumably the purpose of that seating plan was to allow the students to do their work without being distracted, but the result was that the children had their backs to the teacher. In the standard one-room schoolhouse (the usual pattern in the first half of the nineteenth century) with one teacher and a range of ages, the whole class would seldom be involved in the same lesson, so there was no need for them all to face forward. Instead, the teacher could go around the room to look over what each child was doing, or the children could be called up one by one to be given work to do or to recite what they had learned. Pennington found it very difficult to keep order with that seating plan. "The little rogues are so expert in taking every possible opportunity to 'cut up,'" he noted, that they would be whispering to their neighbors and unable to see the teacher. Someone coming in, it seemed to him, would have imagined that they were all engaged in playing "Peep O," a children's game like "peek-a-boo" or "hide-and-seek," or whispering to "crickets in the crevices." In short order, Pennington rearranged the desks so they all faced the teacher and no one could look up without knowing the teacher's eye was on her. The teacher's task, he realized quickly, was to keep one step ahead of the ingenuity of the children. "The roguery of the plaugy little chaps put[s] the man to his wits end."

Two things, the newly instituted teacher learned, were essential to the task: a fondness for teaching and a fondness for children. A man not fond of children, Pennington wrote, might become a grouter or a "pate wrapper," but not a successful teacher. It was essential to "gain their affections" and "enter into their sympathies." He remembered an incident toward the end of his first year as a teacher when a boy came to his desk to ask help with "Daboll's rule of three," a system for calculating a fourth term when three terms are known as, for example, the price of five apples when you know the price of two.[20] Pennington, who may have had a bad day, responded in anger to the request: "Sir, you have spent too much time on that sum, you ought to have dispatched it long since. You have been at it an hour and now I must add my five minutes." But by reacting in anger, Pennington became confused himself and spent at least ten minutes writing various things on the boy's slate before he could make it come out correctly. He learned "never again to commence reviewing the plainest sums in a bustle: and by all means to sympathize with a scholar when in a difficulty."[21]

Fondness for children, moreover, could not extend to taking sides. Just as he saw how disastrous it was for parents to treat their children as pets, so it was also a danger for the teacher to have pet students; it destroyed the pupils' faith in the integrity of the teacher, created animosity among the students, and led to the development of parties among the parents for and against the teacher. Here, instead of citing an actual incident, Pennington creates a hypothetical case: A and B get into a quarrel at the noon recess and come to the teacher afterwards to settle the matter. A, the poorer student, is "soundly whipped," but B is let off with "a yell and a stamp." But isn't it strange, Pennington asks, "that those who are the professed trainers of the youthful mind as reasoning beings should overlook the fact that children begin early to reason about the treatment they receive, and they reason correctly."

The animosity between A and B has now been deepened by the teacher's action. B will say to A, "Ah, you got it." but A quite rightly responds, "Well you was just as much to blame as I was . . . You ought to have been whipped as well as I." Out yells Mr. Teacher, "silence there! I did not send you to your seat to riot again. A, I will settle the remainder of your account." B looks at him either with a taunting smile, or a wag of the head. And the feelings will then influence the whole school as other children choose sides and the parents also become involved. "A goes home with his long face on and the furrows of the tears down his cheeks. He looks at his mother as though he wished the question to be asked, 'what is the matter?' . . . He gives his pathetic answer, and out she rails against the favorite scholar, his parents and his teacher." Then A has the consolation that she promises to take him out of school if he is whipped again. A tells B what his mother said and B reports to his mother "and to rights we are in a war of words—So it is reply, reply, reply, and reply again, until the whole district is in a scolding attitude."[22]

Pennington was hesitant to use "Dr. Hickory," but he did "introduce" the doctor "to attend the case of a little fellow whose symptoms had been alarming for several days. He (Dr. Hickory) was always after that employed in the school, though I am happy to say that his bills were always very moderate as the calls were few."[23]

Pennington does not list "ability to learn from mistakes" among the qualities needed in a teacher—and some of the examples may have been witnessed elsewhere and not drawn from his own experience—but it seems clear that he had that ability as well as "fondness for children and fondness for teaching." It was also an excellent background for a future in the ministry.

Teaching was also a way to fulfill a critical part of Pennington's vision for the African American future in America. Issue after issue of the *Colored American* emphasized the critical importance of education. In 1841, an anonymous correspondent wrote: "It is the schools for our children that will abolish slavery. It is the schools which will procure our enfranchisement. It is the schools which will put off and break down prejudice, and ere long, cause a ready admittance of our sons into the workshop, the counting-house, and other places of employment, which are both respectable and profitable. Parents, cannot I excite you to set a proper value upon these excellent establishments? Will you suffer your children to be absent from school one day, or even one hour? My friends, we are a poor people, we are not in possession of houses, or lands, or money, to leave our children; but we can leave them what I think is far better, a good education . . ."[24]

In a similar vein, an unsigned editorial in 1837 estimated that there were 4000 children of school age in New York City, but only some 1000 in regular attendance at school. "This ought not to be the case," said the editor. "There is no people who need education more than we do. . . . We have the best of teachers; men of our own color, who take a national pride in bringing forward their scholars . . . And shall we forego the privilege of sending our youth to such men . . . ?" The editorial concluded with prophecy: ". . . we owe it to posterity. We are not always to be a down trodden people. Our infant sons, should we give them suitable advantages, will be as eligible to the Presidency of the United States, as any other portions of the community: and it is our wisdom, if possible, to give them as ample qualifications."[25]

"Here are excellent houses," said still another editorial, "excellent teachers . . . books, pens, ink and paper . . . and all you have to do is comb your child's head, give him a clean shirt, and send him to school, where he may learn everything necessary to fit him for all the useful purposes of life." "For the neglect of [these privileges] you will certainly have to give an account to God."

But neither warnings nor exhortations could avail much with people whose experience of life was radically different from that of Charles Ray, Samuel Cornish, and Philip Bell, the editors of the *Colored American*. Born in freedom and encouraged by their parents to read and learn, they had encountered numerous obstacles but they had been supported by their parents and had found opportunity. They remained convinced that education was the foundation for a useful life. The vast majority of free African Americans, however, had been born in slavery and found themselves bewildered by freedom and losing out in the struggle for work and the basics of existence with the Irish and other recent immigrants. Pennington had constantly to contend with parents who saw no importance in punctuality and regularity. If their children learned to make a few letters, write their names, and read a few words, they were proud of their achievement but saw no reason to push them further. Pennington provided a hypothetical dialogue to illustrate the problem:

"P. Put your child to school, then, Mr. A., when he is seven years old, and how long will it take him, think you, to master the common school branches?

"A. Two years.

"P. (Only hear the man!) Why most children, sir, at the rate that you parents send to school take a year to learn the alphabet thoroughly.

"A. Well, I should think, with a little attention from the teacher, a smart child could learn a good deal in two years' time.

"P. Before I say any more, let me understand from you, sir, if you please, what you mean by the common branches.

"A. Reading, writing and arithmetic.

"P. You have guessed just less than half way!

"A. Less than half way; why, what other branches are there?

"P. Grammar, geography, and book keeping, and history and astronomy ought to be included. Now, sir, the most reasonable calculation is to allow one year to each branch, on an average. . . .

Extend the branches to the proper list, then, and he wants 'two times two' years more and one to that.

"A. What! Six or seven years to learn the common school branches?

"P. Yes, sir, and I might say more. A child may learn how to learn in six or seven years; but it will take twelve years to become a *finished scholar* in the common school branch."[26]

Pennington compiled a list of "errors of parents"—sending late to school, irregularity in attendance, not encouraging study at home, never visiting the school themselves, and others[27]—but the essential problem was simply a complete unfamiliarity with the very idea of education. Even so, it must have been hard for him to understand why parents would not be eager to provide for their children what he had yearned for and been denied.

Toward the end of May, in preparation for the next Annual Convention, a special meeting was held by "the colored inhabitants of Brooklyn," to act in advance on a request William Lloyd Garrison would make of that meeting. Garrison would be going to England on a fundraising mission for the New England Anti-Slavery Society and the proposed "Manual Labor School for Colored Youth" and wanted to carry with him the broadest possible range of endorsements. So the Brooklyn meeting passed a resolution that rejoiced at the existence of Garrison's Society and its efforts "to oppose the great demon of darkness" and "scatter . . . to the four winds of heaven the broken fragments of slavery and oppression." The resolution goes on to say that the Convention would "earnestly and respectfully solicit the good people of England to contribute to the proposed object" and endorses the efforts of "our indefatigable friend, the able and efficient advocate of our rights, William Lloyd Garrison, Esq."[†]

The resolution is signed by George Hogarth, who was a deacon of the African Methodist Church and a grocer. But the fact that the second "Whereas" speaks in language Pennington often used, of "the blasting influence of slavery, the dark and broad veil of ignorance," and that one of the four "Resolved" sections speaks only of the value of education, and the relatively rhetorical language all make it seem likely that James Pennington was its author.

---

† Garrison had said that money for a manual labor school was "my primary object" in traveling to England and later reported fifteen hundred dollars subscribed and, for the most part, paid, but no one else ever saw the money and no school was ever built. Twenty years later, James McCune Smith was still wondering where the money was. The need, he wrote, was still there but now Garrison was avoiding the issue. "From Our New York Correspondent," *FDP*, February 16, 1855.

When the Third Annual Convention for the Improvement of the Free People of Colour gathered in Philadelphia in June, school would have been in session, but Pennington had found a substitute to hold his job when he went to the first meeting and he must have done the same again. Harriet served as a school teacher a few years later and might have been able to provide the substitute her husband needed. This time James Pennington went to the convention representing not New York or Brooklyn as he had done in previous years, but Newtown. That would seem to indicate that he had moved from Brooklyn Heights to be nearer the school. Brooklyn, however, was represented by two first-time delegates, William Brown and H. C. Thompson. A total of 15 delegates came from New York, but since only five were permitted to represent any community, the delegates were there to represent Poughkeepsie, Newburgh, Troy, Albany, Catskill, and Hudson as well as Brooklyn, New York City, and Newtown. Not to be outdone, Pennsylvania had 18 delegates, judiciously distributed among Philadelphia, Westchester, Carlisle, Harrisburg, and Wilkes-Barre. The competition for leadership between the two areas became heated when questions were raised about the credentials of some of the delegates, and a motion was made that no one be recognized as a delegate unless they had proper credentials from their society or the meeting that elected them. A second resolution was presented requiring that delegates be 21 years of age and an actual resident of the community they sought to represent. In the traditional manner of conventions, the resolutions were referred to a committee which spent a week pondering the matter and then returned with a report which was taken up section by section and adopted.

Once again, the Canadian project was endorsed for some but not for all. The Convention felt it would be better to go west than north: ". . . those who may be obliged to exchange a cultivated region for a howling wilderness, we would recommend, to retire back into the western wilds, and fell the native forests of America, where the plough-share of prejudice has as yet been unable to penetrate the soil—and where they can dwell in peaceful retirement, under their own vine and under their own fig tree." The Convention was nervous of anything that seemed to endorse emigration, even to Canada.

The Colonization Society was excoriated in dramatic language: "The investigations that have been made into that society within the past year, justify us in believing that that great Babel of oppression and persecution must soon cease to exist. It has been reared so high, that the light of heaven, the benevolence of true philanthropy, and the voice of humanity, forbid its further ascent; and, as in ancient times, the confusion of tongues has already begun, which speedily promises its final consummation—and although it has but recently been classed with the benevolent enterprises of this age, it must shortly be numbered with the ruins of the past."

The proposal to create a college had made little progress, in part because committees in Boston, New York, and Philadelphia were working on plans for schools in their area and so had undercut the original proposal. Education nevertheless was recognized as a vital priority, and the need for temperance was emphasized.

William Lloyd Garrison was present again to make his request for endorsement of his English trip in person. He had been busy between conventions. Only a year after creating the New England Anti-Slavery Society (a Massachusetts Society preceded Garrison's arrival in Boston), he had co-founded with Arthur Tappan on January 1, 1833, an American Anti Slavery Society. Since the Convention's endorsement of the Jocelyn-Tappan-Garrison plan had yielded only a storm of New Haven protest, Garrison had persuaded the New England Society to begin planning to create a manual training school for African Americans. Now he asked the approval of the Convention for the fundraising trip he proposed to make to England on behalf of this school. The Convention endorsed his proposal, ignoring the question of how that proposal would be related to the Convention's effort to build such a school.[†]

Although he had inserted a paragraph on the subject of temperance in the Second Annual Convention's formal statement, Pennington had failed to get the attention of previous conventions for a resolution on the subject. This time he was appointed to chair a committee to bring a formal statement that the Convention could issue to the country. A week later the committee returned with a 2000-word statement, a document nearly as long as the Convention's closing letter "To the Free Coloured inhabitants of the United States." The committee reported progress being made in the formation of temperance societies in all the major communities but warned that alcohol was closely linked to poverty and disease. The cholera epidemic of the previous year was cited as a reason to be aware of the "affinity between human disease and strong drink." There were eloquent descriptions of the dangers of intemperance and practical suggestions for forming a national structure to promote the cause. "Those children in tatters, who are cruelly permitted to waste those precious hours, which should be employed in the acquisition of knowledge, who are shivering with cold, or crying for a morsel of bread, are the children of intemperate parents. These impoverished families, these premature graves, are the production of strong drink." The

† Garrison seems to have enjoyed his trip to England but to have raised little money beyond what he needed for his expenses. It seems to be true, also, that Garrison's real purpose in going was not to raise money for a school, but to undercut the Colonization Society's efforts to raise money in England. cf. Fladeland, *Men and Brothers*, p. 209.

committee suggested that the Convention create a parallel society to meet annually at the same time as the Convention to encourage and supervise the national effort and collect statistical information on the progress being made. "If this triumphs," the report proclaimed, "every interest we aim to promote . . . must advance, must prevail. MORAL WORTH IS POWERFUL AND WILL PREVAIL." Thomas Jennings of New York moved that a constitution be drafted to carry out the proposal of a national organization, and he and two others were appointed to do the work needed.

A new weapon in the fight for abolition was mentioned almost in passing: when a resolution was introduced to commend "the indefatigable labours of Miss Lydia White, in her establishment of a free labour store, and that the patronage of all who feel an interest in promoting the cause of universal freedom, is cheerfully recommended to her store. No. 42 North Fourth Street in the city of Philadelphia." The *Colored American* also ran an ad for Pierce's Free Grocery Store in Philadelphia where sugar, coffee, chocolate, molasses, indigo, wines, and "Spanish, Half-Spanish, & Common Segars, & Smoking & Chewing Tobacco" produced by free labor could be obtained. The purpose was to boycott the products of slavery by offering for sale only products of free labor. Such stores had been common in England for some time, but Americans seemed slow to understand the possibility of using economic pressure against the slave states. Northern abolitionists, of course, were still few in number and African Americans had little economic power to use. The economic pressure that England could use against the slave states was far more significant. Garrison and others, including Pennington in another ten years, would travel to England to encourage the use of that lever against the slave states.[28]

When the Convention ended, Pennington returned to Newtown and his school desk, but the goal of ordination had not been forgotten. Events that summer only intensified his interest in a theological education.

Although Samuel Cox had been there at the critical moment to bring Pennington into the church and Pennington had attended his church "a few times," he seems not to have continued in that congregation. Cox was pastor of the Laight Street Presbyterian Church in Manhattan, of which Arthur Tappan and his brother, Lewis, were members, but African Americans were not equally welcome. One day Arthur Tappan was on his way into the church when he noticed the Rev. Samuel Cornish, an African American clergyman and member of the First Presbytery in New York, standing on the church steps. Tappan invited him to come and join him in his pew. "No little excitement," Lewis Tappan wrote in his biography of his brother, "was the result. The devotions of the congregation were much disturbed. The services being over, one or more of the trustees called upon the offending member of the church, remonstrated with him on the gross impropriety he had committed, and requested him in terms very like threatening not to repeat the offence."[29]

No doubt there were pews reserved for African Americans, either in the back or the balcony, and Cornish could have sat there and caused no problem, but he and Tappan had both served as managers of the American Bible Society and it seemed natural to Tappan for them to sit together. Cox attempted to set things right by warning the congregation at his mid-week lecture not to indulge their prejudices. He asked them to consider what complexion Jesus might have had, with the result that he was attacked in a New York newspaper for having said Jesus was a colored man. Cox responded in another paper by noting "How great and . . . anti-Christian" the prejudice must be that would arouse such anger because of a "sentiment guardedly applied to the complexion of Jesus Christ." But Arthur Tappan decided not to repeat his mistake. "Though I advocated the sentiment that as Christians we were bound to treat the colored people without respect to color," he wrote, "yet I felt that great prudence was requisite to bring about the desired change" and therefore he would no longer publicly associate with colored people "till the public mind and conscience were more enlightened on the subject." He would respect "the fastidiousness of the age," though how that would lead to any changes in the age's attitude he did not say.[30]

So Arthur Tappan would continue to attend Cox's church but Pennington would not. He made it a principle always to refuse to accept segregated seating. If he wanted to hear the preacher in a church with segregated seating, he would stand in the aisle or at the back instead. So Pennington would not have been comfortable as a member of the Laight Street Church. The alternative available to him was the First Colored Presbyterian Church, which Samuel Cornish had organized in 1822. Cornish resigned his ministry in that congregation six years later to become senior editor of the newspaper that would become the *Colored American*. He was succeeded at the church by Theodore Wright, who was licensed but not yet ordained. Wright was ordained the following year and installed as pastor in 1830. He would serve there until his death in 1847, and the church would grow from 75 members to well over 400. Except for an AME Zion church with 800 members, Wright's church was the largest black congregation in New York City.

Unlike Samuel Cornish and, indeed, most black clergy of that day, Theodore Wright was seminary-educated. His applications for admission to a number of colleges had been rejected, but Princeton Theological Seminary had accepted him and he had "enjoyed the immediate counsel and support of the beloved Professors, and a delightful intercourse with the students."[31] Princeton Seminary was a graduate school of the College of New Jersey (now Princeton University), which had been founded in 1746 by followers of Jonathan Edwards and supporters of the New Light faction in the Presbyterian Church. Jonathan Edwards himself became president of the college in the last two months of his life. The seminary was founded in 1812, a time when a number of seminaries as well as law schools and medical schools were being created to provide the more extensive education needed with the rapid expansion of scientific knowledge and the growth of an educated citizenry. So Wright, like Cox, would have been of the New Light persuasion and it would be natural for Pennington to find a home in Wright's congregation.

Pennington's arrival, as it turned out, was beneficial to Wright but also a useful step for Pennington toward his goal of ordination. Wright needed help. He had worn himself out building up the congregation. When the rented school room that was used for worship at first grew overcrowded, the Presbytery gave some assistance in the task of acquiring a church building, but most of the fundraising was done by Wright. He visited white congregations throughout the Presbytery in search of the $12,500 needed to purchase a 100-year-old structure on Prince Street that had been abandoned by German Lutherans. By the spring of 1832 he had raised $9,000 and a committee of the Presbytery had underwritten the remainder, but, exhausted by his efforts, he was struck down with an illness so severe that he wondered whether he would survive. From his parents' home in Schenectady, where he had gone to recuperate, he wrote the congregation, exhorting them to remain faithful. Remember how much we have accomplished, he wrote, and think of all those who have not yet been reconciled to God and exert all your energies to bring them into a saving relationship with Christ.[32] Church services meanwhile would have been maintained by clergy like Samuel Cornish who had no regular pastoral responsibility. Almost certainly James Pennington would have begun to take some of that responsibility as well. Cornish had been tutored by a senior pastor in Philadelphia before his ordination, and he in turn had tutored Wright. A promising young man would often have been given opportunity to test his skills as a preacher and pastor so that he could go forward with some assurance of his fitness for the role and with the support of a congregation that had seen something of his potential.

Evidently the combination of Wright's long illness and Cornish's responsibilities as senior editor of a weekly paper left more and more responsibility in Pennington's hands. It was less than six years since he had first heard of Christ, but he had been practicing his skills as a preacher for most of that time and had already seen at least one of his speeches published. By 1832, he had been attending Wright's church for several years and was a familiar part of its life. The transition to more active leadership would have been easy. Among the responsibilities of the pastor was a regular report to the American Home Missionary Society, which had been providing financial assistance to the struggling congregation. In August 1833, it was James Pennington who made that report "to the Secretaries of the A. H. M. S." and, significantly, signed the report "J. W. C. Pennington, Pastor." "The undersigned," he reported, "has regularly discharged his pastoral duties in the Prince Street Presbyterian Church. A pleasant success has attended the preaching. The congregation is somewhat larger than at the last report." He goes on to speak of seven new members and of the death of the Senior Elder, "a deeply pious man, a committed Christian, and watchful and judicious officer. He died in full assurance of hope." In December, he reported, "The congregation is flourishing as usual" and notes the addition of three more members. A special offering had been taken to aid members "wishing to redeem their friends from slavery," and another special offering was planned to assist a congregation in Hoboken.[33] When Wright returned to take up his work again, Pennington was very clear as to his next step. He had already turned his thoughts toward ministry, and the last year had given him direct experience of that calling. Now he needed to find a seminary to provide depth to his education for ministry. He would round out the year as a school teacher, still assisting Wright in the life of the congregation, but then he hoped to enter, for the first time, a program of systematic education toward his goal.

In June the Fourth Annual Convention for the Improvement of the Free People of Colour was held and, for the first time, the meeting was in New York. It was, of course, actually the fifth gathering, and James Pennington was now one of only three delegates who had been present at each. It was the third Convention that had added the phrase, "for the Improvement," to the Convention's title. The change of name was significant. What had been simply a Convention of Free People of Colour with specific political goals had begun to shift its concerns toward self-improvement, and William Hamilton of New York, serving as president of the Conventional Board, emphasized that theme in his opening address: "That society is most miserable that is most immoral—that most happy that is most virtuous. Let me therefore recommend earnestly that you impress upon our people the necessity and advantage of a moral reformation. It may not produce an excess of riches, but it will produce a higher state of happiness, and render our circumstances easier." A Convention which had first met with the clear purpose of contesting the claims of the Colonization Society and supporting those who chose to emigrate to Canada had begun to turn inward. The change may have begun when James Pennington pressed for support for a temperance crusade in the second and third conventions. However worthy the objective, it was not an area in which measurable change could be quickly achieved. It is also, inevitably, more satisfying to attack the faults of others than of oneself. Hamilton said as much in his opening address when he said, "[A]s long at least as the Colonization Society exists, will a Convention of coloured people be highly necessary."

Pennington was appointed to chair a committee to report "such business as may be necessary for them to act upon" and came back a day later with a list of eight goals, in effect an agenda for the Convention. Heading the list of matters to be dealt with was prejudice as reflected in the exclusion of African Americans from equal church privileges and "the disadvantages to which we are subjected in travelling by steam boats and stages." Other objectives were improving the skills and educational opportunities for people of color, support for Garrison's *Liberator*, further analysis of the claims of the Colonization Society, state laws "bearing on the rights and liberties of coloured citizens," a constitution for the Convention, and a convention address. These were still broadly political goals and not radically different from the concerns of previous conventions, but confronting prejudice as it was expressed in daily life and state laws was a new and practical focus. When the subject of moral reform came up, a committee on that subject reported "rapid advancement. Temperance societies are being made the order of the day; gaming and extravagance are being superseded by a judicious husbandry of finances; and idleness and levity are yielding precedence to industry and reflection. Day and Sabbath Schools of an acknowledged reputable character have been multiplied; teachers of colour have been introduced to public patronage; literary societies and libraries have been established . . . and facilities for travelling with comfort are . . . every day increasing." On the other hand, and somewhat inconsistently, they said, "we earnestly deplore the depressed condition of the coloured population of the United States; and they have in vain searched the history of nations to find a parallel." Certainly there was work still to be done.

A Constitution was adopted calling for meetings to be held alternately in New York and Philadelphia, and an address to the free people of color was adopted, proclaiming "our only trust is in the agency of divine truth, and the spirit of American liberty; our cause is glorious and must finally triumph."[34]

CHAPTER SEVEN

Yale

During the mid-1830s, the nation experienced a wave of crime and rioting without parallel in early American history as the violence that had become endemic in American life broke out with increasing frequency and greater force. In the North as well as the South, the possibility of sudden bursts of violence became, like the weather, something that could neither be predicted nor controlled. In 1834, the most violent year, a convent was burned by an anti-Roman Catholic mob in Charlestown, Massachusetts, in August, while pro-slavery rioting swept Philadelphia in October, destroying 45 homes in the black community. In New York, a series of riots in October 1833, and April and July 1834, provided evidence that the constituted authorities were helpless in the face of an angry mob. The mob, however, though it may have been composed of new immigrants and the uneducated and those without a stake in the prevailing order, was often instigated by "respectable" men who, for various reasons, were opposed to the new forces reshaping their world and used the mob for their own purposes. In October 1835, the "gentlemen of property and standing" became a mob themselves when abolitionists assembled in Utica, New York, to create a New York State Antislavery Society. This time it was middle-class professionals, merchants, bankers, politicians, and clerks who attacked the delegates, destroying documents and making it impossible for the meeting to proceed. The delegates retreated to Gerrit Smith's nearby estate in Petersboro and created the Society as planned.[1] In 1837, a New York City mob even rioted over the high price of flour.[2]

In October 1833, a mob, deliberately encouraged by community leaders, had gathered to prevent William Lloyd Garrison from reporting to his followers on his trip to England. The "gentlemen of property and standing" who supported the Colonization Society saw in Garrison and his associates the same Jacksonian virus that seemed to threaten their accustomed preeminence in the national life. They also knew that the mob, composed of recent immigrants and other working people who were in competition with blacks for jobs, could be easily aroused since they, too, felt threatened by the abolitionists. A New York City newspaper editor, therefore, printed and distributed widely through the city a notice calculated to bring out a crowd prone to violence. Although the abolitionists, forewarned, met in another place than the one announced, the mob that gathered was told where they were and stormed that place too, only to find that Garrison and his little gathering had fled. Violence was avoided, but a precedent was created for the future.

April 1834 brought a riot involving clashes between the two political parties and their supporters in a municipal election. Andrew Jackson's election six years earlier had been evidence of a new spirit in American democracy. An extended electorate was determined to have its way and reacted with violence when the traditional leaders of the community attempted to maintain the established order. Since the election was scheduled over a period of three days, the opposing forces had time to organize themselves and work themselves up to a pitch of anger. Polling places were stormed and occupied first by one side and then another. When the mob besieged the Whig party headquarters, throwing rocks through the windows, the mayor arrived with the sheriff and forty watchmen in a vain attempt to restore order, but they, too, were stoned and the mayor and some of the watchmen were badly injured.

The most violent outbreaks, however, occurred in July when a gathering of both blacks and whites assembled in the Chatham Street Chapel one evening to celebrate the ending of slavery in New York State exactly seven years earlier. Once again some of the newspapers deliberately drew attention to the event, inviting others to come and express their views also. An unruly crowd of hostile whites therefore filled the galleries and stamped their feet and shouted to disrupt the meeting. Eventually a fight broke out, lamps and chairs were broken, and some people were seriously injured. The police were notified and this time were effective in driving out the rioters and locking up the church. Some of the rioters moved on to Lewis Tappan's house and threw stones at it.

Five days later, when rumors spread of an integrated anti-slavery meeting in the Chatham Chapel, a larger and far more destructive crowd assembled. When they found no evidence of the advertised meeting, they attacked Lewis Tappan's house again, this time breaking in and hauling furniture out to the street, where they set it on fire. Over the next two days the violence continued; Lewis Tappan's house was burned, and so were the homes of Samuel Cox and another Presbyterian pastor, Henry Ludlow. St. Philip's Church, an African American Episcopal congregation, was destroyed and the churches of Cox and Ludlow heavily damaged. Finally the mayor called in the city militia which, with help from Albany, was able to bring the violence to an end. In the aftermath, the Episcopal Bishop of New York asked Peter Williams, the Rector of St. Philip's, to resign from the Anti Slavery Society on the theory that it was best to avoid provocation. Although he had not been active in the society, Williams did as requested. Tappan moved his family to New Haven and left his house gutted all summer as a mute witness to the lawless behavior that had destroyed it. "It is my wish," he wrote to a colleague, "that my house may remain this summer as it is, a silent anti-slavery preacher to the crowds who will flock to see it."[3]

While all this was going on, James Pennington was making up his mind about what seminary he should attend. He might have been at the Garrison meeting in October but, since he was teaching school and serving the Prince Street Church that fall, he might well have been too busy to attend. For some reason, that church escaped the mob's attention in July. Nonetheless, the riots may have put the Yale Divinity School in New Haven in a better light, since New Haven's response to the manual college proposal had been less destructive than the New York riots, and it was now evident that such violence could occur anywhere.

The riots had one other result that may have been critical to Pennington's decision. Simeon Jocelyn's own house had been attacked by the mob, and he decided that in the inflamed situation in New Haven, he could no longer function effectively as pastor of the black congregation he had founded. Jocelyn therefore moved to New York in 1834 and seems to have allowed Pennington to live in his New Haven home, perhaps in a servant's apartment, and use his library. Ministry in the congregation Jocelyn had founded was provided by David Dobie, a native of Scotland and also a student at Yale, from 1835 to 1837. But Dobie, as a student at Yale himself, would have needed assistance and Pennington would have been able to assist in the church and school, so providing some black leadership and also providing Pennington with a small amount of additional income to meet his expenses. Since indigent students were normally not charged tuition at Yale Divinity School, and since Pennington was not admitted as a regular student but only allowed to audit the courses, it seems unlikely that he would have needed funds for his education, but he would, of course, have had living expenses for himself and his wife. More significant assistance came from Simeon Jocelyn when he enabled Pennington to benefit from his real estate transactions. In September 1832, he sold Pennington two building lots in his Spireworth development for ninety dollars, and in May 1834 he sold him an additional lot for thirty dollars.[†] Pennington sold the first

---

† Surprisingly, this property transaction occurred before Pennington had been hired as a school teacher and while he was still employed by Van Sinderen. There is also a note in the *Liberator* for September 24, 1832, of a letter received from "J. W. C. Pennington, New Haven." All the evidence indicates that he was still living in Brooklyn. It may be that his thinking about seminary had reached such a point that he had been preparing to move, but the school teaching job temporarily delayed his further education.

of these tracts to Richard Thompson of Brooklyn in May 1835 for two hundred dollars, an excellent profit for a two-and-a-half-year investment.[4]

Important also to Pennington in his decision were Yale's status as "the largest and foremost college in America"[5] and the leadership being provided in the Congregational and Presbyterian Churches by Nathaniel Taylor, Yale's professor of theology. If the choice was between Yale and Princeton, Theodore Wright's seminary, the leading theologians in the two schools presented quite different positions, with Charles Hodge, at Princeton, teaching a much narrower Calvinism than that taught by Nathaniel Taylor at Yale. More important still was the fact that Samuel Jocelyn, though he had moved to New York, had been deeply involved in both the black and white communities in New Haven and could provide useful contacts for Pennington. Jocelyn may have felt that New Haven was no longer a community for him, but he knew those who shared his views and who would help Pennington find the support he would need.

Thus when the new school year opened on October 1, 1834, Pennington was living in New Haven and attending classes at the Yale Divinity School. Yale was not yet connected to New York by railroad, nor did it have paved streets or a sewer system, but it was the largest community in Connecticut, third largest in New England, and a center of intellectual activity.[6] Eli Whitney, who lived just north of New Haven, had already invented the cotton gin[†] and was revolutionizing the firearms industry with mass production methodology, Noah Webster was completing his dictionary, and Samuel Morse would shortly invent the telegraph.[7] Nathaniel Taylor, at the Divinity School, outshone them all. It was said that the Divinity School was created for him and an endowment was created for a chair in theology in hope that he would fill it.[8]

Simeon Jocelyn's help was especially useful since Pennington had not been given admission to the Divinity School with such attendant privileges as the use of the library, but allowed only to audit the lectures. He could sit in the classroom but "my voice was not to be heard in the class room asking or answering a question. I could not get a book from the library and my name was never to appear on the catalogue." He referred later to his time at Yale as his "visitorship."[9] The normal expectation for an entering student at the Divinity School was a college degree, which Pennington did not possess. More specifically, first year students at the Divinity School were expected to have learned Greek and Hebrew in college but Pennington, although he was later said to be competent in Latin, Greek, and German, may not have been familiar with

† Ironically, it was the cotton gin that made possible an extension of the "cotton kingdom" into Texas and the southwest and increased the need for slave labor. The widely held belief that slavery would gradually disappear was no longer a reasonable hope.

Hebrew. It seems clear from Pennington's account that he believed color was the reason that he was not accepted as a student, but, if so, it seems strange that Pennington was allowed to audit the classes at all. In fact, the limits imposed on Pennington by Yale, which he speaks of as "oppression,"[10] were probably less onerous than the challenge of gaining a theological education while working part-time and assisting at the church Jocelyn had founded. The ordinary Yale student in those days made very little use of the library in any event. Freshmen and sophomores at the college were not admitted to the library at all, and the library was only open one hour a week. Seminary students could borrow only two books at a time and then only for a fee that was based on the size of the book. Library records of that era show that some students never borrowed any books from the library; those who did normally borrowed *Jonathan Edwards' Works*,[11] since Jonathan Edwards ranked with Calvin himself in Congregational and Presbyterian theology.

Nathaniel Taylor was the most forceful voice in the Divinity School faculty, a select group of four who worked together for well over thirty years and advocated an approach to the Calvinist tradition that became known as "the New England theology." Taylor considered himself a disciple of Edwards, but Taylor did not simply repeat Edwards's teaching; he took a new approach that caused considerable controversy among Presbyterians and Congregationalists. Traditional Calvinism, with its insistence on human depravity and a God who destined human beings to hell or heaven for unknown and unknowable purposes, fit poorly with the entrepreneurial spirit of nineteenth-century America that allowed individuals to shape their own destinies. Taylor lectured instead on "God's moral government" and how God "earned his subject's loyalty by a judicious benevolence." God's power was "reasonable, just, acceptable," and human virtue was understood to consist of "nothing but voluntary obedience to truth; and sin nothing but voluntary obedience to falsehood."[12]

Whether this theology was, indeed, authentic Calvinism was frequently questioned by others, and eventually a new seminary was established in East Windsor by Connecticut clergy who felt Taylor's Calvinism had strayed too far from the tradition inherited from their Puritan ancestors. But Taylor, like Timothy Dwight, the president of Yale College from 1795 to 1817, believed that the only way to win over the students, many of whom had drifted far from the Christian faith, was to engage them in free and open debate and demonstrate a responsiveness to new ideas.

An influx of French ideas at the end of the 18th century had brought with it a general skepticism about religion. Lyman Beecher recalled that "College was in a most ungodly state . . . Most of the students were sceptical . . . Wines and liquors were kept in many rooms; intemperance, profanity, gambling, and licentiousness were common. . . . Boys that dressed flax in the barn as I used to, read Tom Paine and believed him . . . Most of the class before me were infidels."[13] Dwight's willingness to discuss any problem the students might present, combined with the forcefulness of his own personality and his elimination of the fines that had been levied for failure to attend gatherings in the chapel, did much to help win back the disaffected.

Central to the existence of the Yale Divinity School in those years was its leadership position in the New Light school within the Congregational and Presbyterian churches. The division had a long ancestry and had created a Presbyterian schism in 1741. No formal schism took place within Congregationalism since its much looser organizational system left more room for differences. Nevertheless, the Old Light faction had finally created their own seminary rather than send students to study under Taylor. The New Light emphasis on revival and emotional conversion inevitably created a freer atmosphere and a more flexible approach to classical Calvinism. The evolution that led from Calvin to Edwards to Taylor continued through Horace Bushnell (cf. Chapter 9) to such untheological leaders as Norman Vincent Peale and *The Power of Positive Thinking* on the one hand and to diverse forms of evangelical revivalism on the other. It also created room for a growing involvement in social action and political reform.

In 1835, however, the course of studies presented to Pennington and others at Yale was narrowly focused on the Bible and the theology of Calvin and Edwards as interpreted by the faculty of four who remained in place from the opening of the school in 1822 until disability and death opened the way to new voices beginning with Taylor's death in 1858. There were no optional courses at the Yale Divinity School. In the first year, students studied the Bible with Professor Josiah Gibbs and moral philosophy with Professor Taylor. The second-year students continued to study the Bible with Gibbs and began theology with Taylor. The final year's studies then taught the students to apply what they had learned through courses in practical theology with Professors Fitch and Goodrich. There were no courses in church history nor in other religions.

College professors have a certain reputation for idiosyncracies, and seminary professors are at least equally prone to peculiar ways. Since Pennington had not attended the college as an undergraduate, he would not have observed the way Timothy Dwight, on the colder days of winter, would take a seat at the fireplace end of the lecture room and deliver his lecture with his back to the students and his feet to the fire. He would, however, have listened to Eleazar Fitch, whose duty it was to teach the students how to preach. Fitch was a man of such intensity and insecurity that he would never preach without a manuscript—students were sure that without a text he would be unable to speak a word—and would begin in a half-embarrassed, awkward manner, fumbling at the leaves of the Bible and the pulpit cushion, until, like a machine requiring time to warm up, his face would begin to glow and his voice become strong and steady. His lectures on preaching, nevertheless, were considered "unsurpassed in merit."[14] Josiah Gibbs, who taught the Biblical courses, was the sort of scholar constitutionally unable to come to a settled opinion so long as alternative possibilities remained. Taylor once said he would rather have ten settled opinions even if nine were wrong than to leave all ten unsettled "like my brother Gibbs."[15] It was, however, an approach that encouraged students to examine questions with an open mind and fit well with Taylor's own willingness to encourage free discussion and exploration. Taylor himself would sometimes lecture for his full two hours, but more often stop after an hour or so, take out his tobacco box, "refresh himself from its contents," and say to the students before him, "Now, young gentlemen, I'll hear you."[16] At the beginning of his course, he would tell the class:

> In every part of your progress, I invite the utmost freedom on your part. I shall be ready to answer all your questions, remove all doubts, explain what I may have stated not concisely or imperfectly, and if placed in the wrong myself shall most freely acknowledge the same, for we are never too old to learn. At the same time I shall expect to find your object the same as mine, not to support any particular views but the acquisition of truth . . .[17]

George Park Fisher, who knew Taylor as a colleague toward the end of Taylor's career, remembered how Taylor had told him once that he had rebuked one of this students more severely than might have been required and added that "he had been kept awake a great part of the night, by the thought that Christ would not have spoken so. Who will wonder," Fisher added, "that such a man drew to himself the affections of his pupils?"[18]

It was only such warmth of relationships and the quality of the teaching that the divinity school had to recommend it. There were none of the "creature comforts" that modern students expect. Yale campus in 1835 consisted of seven buildings in a row at the northwest corner of the New Haven Green with its two Congregational churches and an Episcopal church. The Divinity School building, actually only a dormitory for divinity students, was begun in 1835 and completed in 1836 to make the eighth structure in the row. There were two dormitories, a chapel, a dining hall, accommodations for the professors, and a building with a room for lectures and recitations. Back of the other buildings was a chemical laboratory and a gallery for paintings collected by Colonel Trumbull. The library was in the attic of the chapel.[19] All of the buildings were designed, in William Wordsworth's phrase, for "plain living and high thinking." There was nothing comfortable or home-like about them. Heating, lighting, and the ventilation of buildings were seldom given consideration in the architecture of the time. Not even sanitation and cleanliness in general were a high priority. Bath tubs were actually "opposed on religious grounds as likely to encourage self-indulgence."[20] Most of the divinity students had to live off campus until the new building was completed, and those who lived on campus were accommodated in "the third loft of the new Chapel" for $25 or $30 a year depending on whether they had corner rooms. When they complained of smoke because of a faulty flue, the rent was refunded—but no mention is made of repairs to the chimney. Students who came from hard New England farms, however, or, for that matter, from slavery in a Maryland plantation, were not generally accustomed to better conditions at home. Also familiar to young men from farming families would have been the challenge of getting up in time to trudge through the winter snow to the chapel in time for the 6 A.M. service in an unheated chapel dimly illuminated by flickering whale-oil lamps.[21] In summer the service was at 5 A.M., and divinity students were as likely as undergraduates to be throwing on their clothes as they raced for the chapel door.[22] Absences were noted, and three were cause for suspension.[23] Students guilty of swearing, playing cards, intoxication, or any immoral conduct could be expelled.

For social life, there were three student organizations called (these were serious-minded students!) the Rhetorical Society, the Society of Inquiry Respecting Mission, and the Society for Christian Research. The first of these was a secret society meeting every three weeks to debate a particular issue. Several times the Rhetorical Society debated the merits of slavery discussing whether the greatest good of the greatest number justifies slavery, whether it is right to assist a slave to run away, whether the Fugitive Slave law is constitutional, and whether slavery in this country has been, on the whole, an evil. Nathaniel Taylor, presiding, affirmed the first question, but the Society did not vote. Inconsistently, the Society voted No on the second question, and Yes on the third. The Society was closely divided on the final question but Taylor voted No. As to whether clergy should attempt directly to influence public opinion, however, the Society was clear that they should not, though Taylor voted No with the qualification: only "as a general rule." Presumably James Pennington would have had strong and different opinions on these issues, but he was not a member of the Society or even the student body. He was an African American participating for the first time, however marginally, in an otherwise all-white society. He would listen and learn during what he called his "visitorship"[24] and have his say at a later date.

The Society of Inquiry Respecting Mission was composed largely of students planning to serve in mission fields, but these were predominantly such frontier areas as Illinois and Iowa. Overseas interest was centered on Asia rather than Africa. The Society for Christian Research concerned itself with learning about the state of religion in various areas at home and abroad. When complaints were made about the length of the resulting reports, it was suggested that in the future, reports be limited to eighteen minutes for foreign mission, ten minutes for home mission, seven minutes for seamen, and five minutes for "people of color."[25] The citizens of New Haven might become riotous about issues of race, but it was not an important issue for the students at Yale Divinity School, at least for those who had been formally admitted.

For students at the Divinity School, the emphasis was almost entirely on the academic enterprise. Except toward the end of the final year, they were not licensed to preach, though they might teach in the Sabbath Schools or provide leadership in a young people's society. Exceptions to the rules also were made for students who needed to earn some money, and clearly Pennington would have been entitled to such an exemption. Students also seem to have been involved in the revivals that took place in the college or larger community almost every year.[26]

The school year during James Pennington's time in New Haven began on the first of October and ran until "commencement" in the third week of August. There were a two-week vacation in January and a four-week vacation in April. This provided two terms of fourteen weeks and one of twelve weeks. Lacking the academic background of other students and needing to work at least part-time to support himself and his wife, Pennington would have had to use vacation time to keep up with his coursework. But for the first and only time in his life, he would have been able to make education his first priority, and it is unlikely that he would have complained. It did mean, however, that he could not keep up with his other interests. When the Fifth Convention met in Philadelphia in June of 1835, Pennington was absent for the first time. But the Convention movement was running out of steam in any event. Reconstituting itself as a moral reform society, it no longer had specific, attainable, immediately relevant goals and therefore did not meet again for eight years. It had, however, accomplished much in demonstrating the ability of African Americans to organize themselves and make their voice heard in the developing debate on the future of American society.

Pennington continued his studies at Yale through two academic years and in June 1836 was presented to the New Haven West Association of the Congregational Church by Simeon Jocelyn "to receive advice from the Association with reference to his undertaking to preach the gospel." The Association had voted two years earlier "that no student at Yale College be examined [for ordination] till he has completed two years of study." In June 1836, Pennington had not even completed two years, but Jocelyn and others may have felt that his practical experience at Theodore Wright's church in New York made the final year's work in pastoral leadership less important for him. The Association voted to consider the matter in the morning, giving themselves the night to think about it. When they met again at 9 A.M., there was further discussion and it was made clear that "Mr. Pennington's desire is to be authorized to perform evangelical labors among the people of color in Newtown, L.I." This, they decided, relieved them of the need to make a decision, since he would not be doing ministry in their jurisdiction. They voted "that he be advised to put himself under the care of the Congregational Association in the city of New York, and to request a license from that body." The clergy of New Haven West did, however, send him on with their blessing, voting "that sofar as we have become acquainted with Mr. Pennington's character and qualifications, we cordially recommend him to the Association in the city of New York."[27]

Coursework for the second year would not have been completed until August, so it is possible that Pennington remained in New Haven until that date, but there would have been no obvious reason for Jocelyn to present him to the Association for examination if he intended to stay for an additional year. Likewise, his "desire . . . to be authorized to perform evangelical labors among the people of color in Newtown, L. I." argues for an intention to return to Newtown in the immediate future, not a year later.

The evidence indicates that Pennington spent a maximum of three years at Yale and possibly only two. In 1971, Kurt Schmoke, a senior history major at Yale (later mayor of Baltimore and now dean of the Howard University School of Law), wrote a published article saying that Pennington spent four years at Yale,[28] but since he was serving Shiloh Church, New York in December 1833, and therefore would not have begun his work at Yale until the fall of 1834 and since he became the agent in Newtown for the *Colored American* in the fall of 1837, it is most likely that he began his time at Yale in the fall of 1834 and returned to Newtown in the summer of 1837. There was also a notice in the *Colored American* in October 1837, that a new church had been dedicated in Newtown with James W. C. Pennington as its pastor. This might argue that he had been there for a year to establish it (in which case he left Yale in the summer of 1836) or that he was called there specifically to take charge of a newly organized congregation (in which case he spent three years at Yale and left in the summer of 1837).

CHAPTER EIGHT

Return to Newtown

The years at Yale had not been easy for Pennington. He had worked long days and given first priority to his studies, but never as a full part of the academic community. Always he was at the back of the room and never was he included in either the organized or informal exchanges that add depth to any program of study. Nonetheless, by the end of three years at Yale, he had gained a better education than most men serving in the ministry at that time. Today it is normal for a theological student to spend three years in seminary studies after completing a four-year college education. In the early nineteenth century, few theological students had a college degree and most clergy had neither a college or seminary degree. Most picked up a bit of "book learning" in one-room school houses when they were available and when they were not needed on the farm. Those who felt called to ministry often studied privately with senior pastors, but others began to preach simply because they felt called to do so and became settled in a parish when a congregation felt the man met their need for pastoral care and worship leadership. The fact that the New Haven West Association had voted not to examine a student who had completed less than two years at Yale indicates that it was not uncommon even for Yale students to try to get by with less than the full program.

By the time James Pennington came back to Newtown, it had been his home for nearly ten years and most of his adult life. He not only knew that small community well, but he had come to know many in the larger community of African Americans and white abolitionists in Manhattan. He had sometimes gone to the national conventions as a representative of that larger community and he had been given opportunity to express himself in their newspaper. But the community of educated African Americans was still tiny and Pennington's reputation in that community was not confined to Newtown or New York.

The Yale school year ended with "commencement" in August. For Pennington, as an unregistered student, there was no graduation ceremony to attend and no certificate of his accomplishments to take home with him except the testimonial to his "character and qualifications" from the New Haven West Association. Even graduation, however, did not provide automatic license to ministry for anyone. Clergy, whatever their education, were licensed by local presbyteries or clergy associations and then ordained, usually in the congregation they would serve. But just as ordination was not linked automatically to seminary education, so ministry was not linked automatically to ordination. Individuals were often licensed to preach long before they were ordained and sometimes simply put to work where there was a need without any formal authorization. This may well have been Pennington's situation in 1833 at Shiloh Church and it may have been his situation as well through the fall of 1837 and spring of 1838.

It seems likely that Pennington went back to Newtown with the hope of resuming his former position. He had been succeeded at the teacher's desk in Newtown by Samuel Ringgold Ward, who would also go on to be an important voice in the black community, but by 1837 Ward had moved to a teaching position in New Jersey and, in 1839, to ordination in the Congregational Church, so the Newtown position was again open.[1] A notice in the *Colored American* in August 1837 reports that the "Rev. James W. C. Pennington will act as agent for this Paper for Newtown, L.I."[2] But Pennington had gone to Yale to study for ordination and returned with a recommendation to the local Congregational association. There was a Presbyterian Church in Newtown but not a church where black people were given equal seating, so Pennington very likely returned with the idea of creating a black congregation. Only a few months were needed to begin that work. In October, the *Colored American* published a letter from Pennington under the heading "Enlargement of Zion": "It will doubtless be interesting to you and to your readers to know that we had the privilege of consecrating a house for divine worship on this place yesterday. Our building is calculated to seat only about 130 persons. We had an able and interesting discourse from . . . [the] Rev. John Goldsmith. We have no Church organized. Members of the several Churches will worship in union. I am engaged to preach to them."[3]

Apparently the need for a church that was welcoming to African Americans took precedence over any particular denominational allegiance. The American Home Missionary Society provided support to the new congregation, and Pennington's first quarterly report to the Society listed twenty-seven members with thirty to forty students in the Sabbath School.[4]

Pennington had returned to New York at a time when African Americans, encouraged certainly by the Conventions held in the first five years of the decade, were making their voices heard more loudly and asserting their rights with new vigor. The issue was no longer simply abolition of slavery, the Colonization Society, and Canada emigration. Now black Americans were beginning to concern themselves with their full rights as citizens, and at last they had a significant voice in the public square. There had been several black newspapers in the city beginning with Samuel Cornish's *Rights of All* in 1829, but none had the life span and impact of the *Colored American,* which first appeared in January 1837. By the spring of that year it had 1200 subscribers, a number that undoubtedly reflected a readership several times that size since the intended audience was made up of the city's poorest inhabitants and each paper would have been passed from hand to hand of those who could read.[5] But now when issues arose, whether it was some petty incident or a major reform that needed action, there was a way to get attention and rally support.

On August 12, 1837, for example, Samuel Cornish was refused a cup of tea in a local restaurant. It was the sort of trivial nuisance that could easily be ignored, especially since, by Cornish's own statement, it was "the first time in my life, that I have been so treated in this city." But it was just for that reason that it needed to be protested. "It remained for a foreigner, in a cellar cook-room, to insult a native citizen of 17 years residence in this city," wrote Cornish, "and to deny a minister of Christ, of gray hairs, and twenty-five years standing in the Presbyterian church, a cup of tea." Cornish knew well that "Contempt will not reach such a man, and pity would be wasted upon him," but the incident could not be allowed to pass unnoticed or it would happen again and yet again and become a way of life.[6]

More important were the laws and customs that kept African Americans from a full participation in the political and social life of the community. David Ruggles, who for years had carried on almost a one-man crusade against the slave catchers who prowled the streets of New York looking for possible fugitives to arrest and return to the south, wrote to the editor to point out that slavery still existed in New York in spite of the law that abolished it. Under the law, no one could bring a slave into New York State to stay for more than nine months. Yet there were slave owners who moved to New York with their slaves and evaded the reach of the law by taking their slaves out of state before the nine months were up and then bringing them back immediately, so enabling them to hold their slaves indefinitely. Ruggles wrote to say that he knew of at least eleven individuals, each of whom was now being held as a slave in that way "as long as he lives."[7]

In November, Ruggles wrote again to raise the issue of the right to trial by jury. Fugitive slaves were often returned to the south by a judge acting alone and without giving the alleged slave an opportunity to summon witnesses and be heard before a jury. The Committee of Vigilance that Ruggles had founded and of which he was often the only member, was raising funds to pursue a case in the Court of Errors, and contributions were needed toward the expenses involved.[8]

More immediately relevant to Pennington were two issues involving the Christian church.

In June 1837, Samuel Cornish reported in his paper on a recent meeting of the General Assembly of the Presbyterian Church, of which he was a clergyman. That church, Cornish wrote, "has become, at length, a slave-holding church. Her Rev. Divines, many of them are slave-owners, if not slave-traffickers; and others are zealous abbettors of this wicked system." Cornish went on to describe the way his local presbytery had voted some years earlier to send their clergy to the General Assembly by rotation so that each would have the opportunity to take part in the larger life of the church and share in "(t)he highest honor the Presbytery could confer upon a member." Time had passed by and newcomers and younger members of the Presbytery had been given their turn, "But alas! the poor editor's turn, has not yet come. Like the Declaration of Independence, the good brethren, did not mean by EVERY BROTHER, A COLORED BROTHER! NOT AT ALL—NOT AT ALL! . . . If our church would escape being cursed of God, she must put away her slavery, and her prejudice against her colored members. She must have the faith of our Lord Jesus Christ, the Lord of Glory, without respect of persons."[9]

Even this, however, might have been of less immediate significance than an article published in August 1837, just after Pennington's return from New Haven, about the Broadway Tabernacle, an enormous church building seating 2,500, which Arthur and Lewis Tappan had erected to bring the evangelist Charles Grandison Finney to New York. "It is with pain and anguish of soul," editorialized the *Colored American*, "that we have seen the southern tiers of pews, in Broadway Tabernacle, crowded with our colored brethren."[10] The Tappan brothers might be ardent abolitionists, but segregated seating in their own church did not get their attention. Tappan had been displeased when other church members objected that he had brought Samuel Cornish in to sit with him, but he would tolerate their prejudices. For Samuel Cornish, on the other hand, it was not acceptable for African Americans to acquiesce in segregated seating in a place of worship. "In doing so," he wrote, "they accept their own degradation. They strengthen the cord of caste, by baptizing it in the house of God." Cornish believed that African Americans had a primary responsibility to support their own church and never to accept segregated seating in others. If they must go to the Broadway Tabernacle or other segregated churches, they should stand in the aisles "and rather worship God with your feet, than become a party to your own degradation."[11] Ironically, Arthur Tappan, having paid to build the church and having accepted segregated seating as he had done at the Laight Street Church, was then excommunicated for attempting to form an anti-slavery group within the congregation. Joel Parker, who had succeeded Finney as pastor of the congregation, believed a strong anti-slavery stand would alienate some of the members and limit the church's ministry. The issue was appealed to the Presbytery, where Parker was upheld, and then to the General Assembly, where Tappan was upheld. But it was typical of Tappan that he would fight a battle over an issue such as abolition while paying no attention to the fact of segregation in his own church. In the same way, he employed African Americans to work for him, but never gave them the training to move beyond the role of unskilled laborer.[†]

Theodore Wright had his own litany of degradation that he recited later that year in Utica, New York, where he had gone to celebrate the anniversary of the founding of the New York State Anti-Slavery Society. His concern went beyond principle to the specific experience of daily life. "Three hundred thousand men," said Wright, counting the free black population, "feel the evils of prejudice . . . The colored man at every progressive step literally runs the gauntlet." He went on to speak of the right to vote, to a trial by jury, to an education for the trades, of the exclusion of black people "from most of the useful occupations in society . . . [and] that throughout this whole state colored children are excluded from common schools."

"Why is all this?" Wright asked his audience. The modern word is racism, but Wright had not heard that word. He had his own term for it: "It is to be traced to the spirit of slavery existing in the breasts of men, even in those who think they have sympathy for the oppressed. Oh! There is enough in this feeling to cause tears of blood to flow from the eyes of those who possess it." Wright went on to cite chapter and verse of his indictment. He told of Mrs. Smith, "a pious woman" who lived in Newburgh and set off to travel with her infant by steam boat to New York. When night came on, she pleaded with the captain for space inside the cabin but was refused. The child died of exposure. Then there was Jeremiah Gloucester, a Presbyterian pastor on a preaching tour of New England, who was also excluded from the steam boat cabin at night. The exposure "threw him into a decline, and he died." He told of others as well: some died, some had their health endangered, some were simply embarrassed or inconvenienced, but it was time for all this to be spoken of and for an indictment to be drawn for action.[12] Rosa Parks, in Birmingham, Alabama, well over a century later, had that same feeling: it's time.

---

† Lewis Tappan's biographer, Bertram Wyatt-Brown, wrote of the Victorian reformers that "The romantic 'interest in unhappy far-off things' that they shared was so keen that it seemed, in contrast to the mythical Antaeus, that they gained strength from their flights above the earth, not from their contact with it." (Wyatt-Brown, op. cit., 258.) He then adds, "Even if Victorian romanticism prevented the English and the Yankee reformers from coming to grips with the evils in their own societies, the evangelicals were at least responsive to evils somewhere." (Ibid., 259.)

James Pennington had a very different experience a year later when he rode the steamer from New York to Newburgh, a town some 65 miles up the Hudson River, to attend a conference of the New York Congregational Association, of which he was a member. In company with several of his ministerial colleagues, he took a berth and stayed on the boat overnight, treated like anyone else. The next day they were met by church members from Mt. Hope, New York, about 35 miles west of the river, who came with wagons to take the clergy to their meeting. Pennington and three other clergy stayed with a farm family where, again, no distinctions were made. The formal meetings were held in the local church. Several candidates for ordination were examined and ordained and each evening one of the clergy, Pennington among them, was called on to deliver a sermon. On Friday they were taken back to Newburgh in time for a 2 o'clock dinner, and again no distinctions were made. But then, with time before the boat would leave, Pennington went to a nearby barbershop where the barber, an African American, had just finished shaving a white client, but he would not serve James Pennington. As the white client watched, the barber "with a slavish and fearful look toward the white man . . . groaned out, 'No, sir, we don't shave colored people.'" Pennington picked up his hat and left but wrote to the *Colored American* to say "what a class we colored people are—so black and degraded that we cannot touch each other! How can we condemn the whites, so long as such a state of feeling exists among ourselves." He had experienced no distinction during the three days of the meeting, at which he was the only African American, nor on the steamer where he had his choice of berths, "no one disputing my right as a man, a citizen, and a traveler." But his question to the readers of his letter was, "What can you and I say to rebuke and persuade a white barber, when our own colored men of the same business have as much prejudice as they?"[13] Like Theodore Wright, unexpectedly denied a cup of tea, and many others before and since, James Pennington was discovering the way racism permeates a society, turning even its victims into collaborators.

These were some of the many issues now being fought out in the pages of the *Colored American* and a few other smaller papers as they reflected the city and larger society around them. As a result of his years at Yale, James Pennington was better prepared now to take part in the struggle and was delighted to find a paper though whose pages he could make his voice heard. For now, he would simply write; eventually he would call for direct action and participate in such action himself.

The immediate task confronting Pennington was to establish himself in Newtown, and that would require a church and pulpit for his new ministry. By the end of October, he had a church in which to preach, and by the following spring he had been formally ordained and installed as pastor. Where a candidate had completed a recognized program of study and had begun to serve a congregation, he would still be examined by a committee of his colleagues, but the outcome of the examination was often taken for granted and scheduled for the same day as the ordination and installation. Pennington was ordained on May 13, 1838,† and his examination may well have taken place that morning.[14]

Over the next two years, Pennington's primary role was as pastor and teacher in the Newtown community, but he was never content to limit himself to one community. While he had been studying in New Haven, the Convention movement he had been so much involved in had died an early death, to his great regret. If he could find a way to revive it, he was determined to do so. The best means available to him to raise the issue was the press, and the *Colored American* was glad to have his contributions. Writing under the name of "Long Island Scribe," essay after essay came from his pen over the next year as he laid out the reasons for a new convention. The first essay, dated February 12, but published on March 22, 1838, noted that another correspondent, "Augustine," who wrote a number of columns suggesting that black people could best establish themselves as farmers, had also proposed a convention. "I have been a member of the 1st, 2d, 3d, and of the 4th convention," Pennington wrote, "and although my wishes were not realized in any of those sessions, I have not been without the belief that the institution was similar to such a one as we must have."[15] Seven more essays followed in which the central argument was that any body of people must be organized in order to make an impact. "The Greeks, the Romans, the Cathagenians, the Egyptians, and as many people of antiquity as can be named, have had their national councils. . . . This, Sir, I maintain, is the most wretched anomaly of our case. Without a seat in any political body in the land, and also without any such body among ourselves, I do not wonder, Sir, that our political condition is so bad; I only wonder that it is not worse!" Conventions, he points out, will nurture and train the political talent needed. "Political talents are always drawn out by being exercised. . . . Let us try it!"[16]

What Pennington proposed in these essays was a very specific plan for what might almost have been a government within a government. "Simply holding meetings and passing resolutions is not sufficient." Instead he suggests associations "in every city, town, village, or place . . . to take the oversight of our moral and political affairs, so far as this may be done, without any collision with the government, whose oppressed subjects we are." These associations would elect delegates to a national governing body with a president, vice president,

† Pennington, Thomas H. S. (op. cit., p. 4), gives the date as May 12, but the Presbytery Register seems more reliable than a later reminiscence.

treasurer, secretary, and executive council empowered to levy a tax as a condition of membership. The national Assembly ("or Convention or Council, or anything else you please"), meeting annually for three or four days, would only have advisory powers but could deal with agriculture and education and "cases of those who are in danger of losing their personal liberty, and all oppressive steps taken by the whites."

There would, Long Island Scribe wrote, be other benefits as well. No need in the community was greater than education, and a convention could create an education society to find out where teachers were needed and make recommendations of qualified men and women. It could enlist the educated men and women already available, like Theodore Wright and Philip Williams, to tutor others in the evening. Pennington suggested that they might find 15 or 20 young men and tutor them for two or three years, thus building "durable monuments."[17] Think also, he writes, of how so many "acquaintances and ties of friendship" were formed when the Conventions were held. Previously isolated individuals, living far apart in Rochester, Philadelphia, New York, and Boston, came to know each other, enabling them to work together on common projects.[18] Conventions, Pennington argues, will build feelings of self-respect and give friends in other countries "extended knowledge of the character of our people."

The series came to an end with a burst of eloquence: "what we do, we must do quickly. Tyrants are reigning—the slaves are bleeding and dying—humanity suffers, and who, O! who can be insensitive? Mr. Editor, intelligent readers, and colored Americans in general, can you be inactive? I know you *will not be—dare not be* inactive!"[19]

Perhaps the most interesting response to these essays came six months later in the *National Reformer*, the monthly journal of the American Moral Reform Society. When the last National Convention met, it had created that Society in its place and then ceased to exist. From one perspective, the focus of African American energy had shifted from specific social and political goals to the less tangible business of moral uplift. From another perspective, the long-standing rivalry between New York and Philadelphia had been won for the moment by the Pennsylvanians. From still a third perspective, William Lloyd Garrison, with his principles of nonviolence, the rights of women, color-blindness, and attacks on the churches for bending too often to the power of the South, had taken leadership away from the more conservative New Yorkers.[20] William Whipper, Robert Purvis, and James Forten, the leading Philadelphians, were successful business men, relatively comfortable with white people. They have been described as *"Philadelphia's Black Elite"* and they were very conscious of that status.[21] Forten had a number of white men working for him in his sail factory. Even Richard Allen, the revered bishop, ran a business on the side.

The leading New Yorkers were primarily clergy like Theodore Wright, Samuel Cornish, Peter Williams, and James W. C. Pennington, or intellectuals like James McCune Smith. Thomas Jennings, another New York leader, was somewhat different as an inventor who ran a drug store. But for the time being, at least, the Philadelphians had taken the leadership, were meeting in convention annually to consider moral uplift, and saw no need to create some other conventions. Noting that "the subject of a 'General Convention' has claimed the attention of many of our most reflective minds" during the past year and that a number of writers in the *Colored American* had "dilated on this subject," the editor of the *National Reformer* wished to inform his readers "that such a Convention will be held in the city of Philadelphia on the second week of August next, where you are most respectfully invited to attend."[22] Their principles, said the editor, "are the promotion of *Education, Temperance, Economy, and Universal Liberty.*" This was fine as far as it went, but then the editor went on to say with more than a hint of a sneer, "If there should be those whose prolific minds leads [sic] them to a more exalted standard of duty and action, we doubt not but their gratification will be enhanced by the association of kindred spirits, that will stand ready to second every righteous effort for our speedy elevation." So the two groupings had gone in different directions and volleys were fired back and forth in the pages of the *Colored American* and elsewhere. There was no olive branch being held out. Pennington's call for a renewed Convention movement had simply exposed the deep divisions within the African American community. For the time being, his challenge went unanswered, and when David Ruggles followed up the suggestion two years later, even further divisions came to light.

But James Pennington had other matters claiming his attention. As soon as he stepped off the Underground Railroad himself, Pennington seems to have stepped back on as a conductor. Adrian Van Sinderen's home on Brooklyn Heights was a station on the Railroad, and Pennington would have been useful to his employer in arranging for assistance to whatever passengers came. Now that he was ordained, Pennington became useful as well in his role as a clergyman. On September 15, 1838, a call came from David Ruggles that a new arrival had come with a bride and they wanted to be married.[23] Pennington crossed over to Manhattan and found Frederick Douglass, newly escaped from Maryland, with his fiancee, Anna Murray, a freeborn woman who had come up to New York ahead of Douglass to wait for his arrival. Douglass had tried twice before to escape and been caught, but this time, disguised as a seaman and with borrowed papers, he had made the journey successfully. He and Murray were friendless in the big city and lacked any of the usual embellishments of a traditional marriage ceremony, but they were delighted to find a clergyman available. Douglass noted later that they had no money for a marriage fee, but that Pennington "seemed well pleased with our thanks."[24] Douglass would go on to become the best known African American orator of the nineteenth century and to publish many of Pennington's essays in the newspapers that he would edit.

In August 1839, Pennington, whose frequently published essays as well as his many contacts through the Convention movement had made him well known, was invited to speak at a major event in New Jersey. On August 1, 1834, Great Britain had ended slavery in the British West Indies, and the impact was felt throughout the United States. It was an ominous warning for slave holders and an event full of hope for African Americans, whether free or slaves. Black communities in the North began to celebrate the date as one of more significance for them than the Fourth of July. These celebrations often drew several thousand people and sometimes included marching bands and a picnic in a grove. Often there were several speakers. African Americans in Newark, New Jersey, planned a strenuous celebration for the fifth anniversary of West Indian emancipation and invited the prominent evangelist Charles G. Finney and the former slave Samuel Ringgold Ward, who would later become a leading abolition speaker and editor, to share the platform with James Pennington.[†]

The celebration began at 6 A.M. with a prayer meeting in the Methodist Church, where those who "once wore the galling yoke of slavery . . . poured out their souls in prayer, for the oppressor, and oppressed, and that slavery might come speedily to an end." At 9 A.M. "a large and respectable audience" met in the Presbyterian Church with singing and a prayer led by James Pennington. Then Samuel Ward was introduced and "spoke for some length" before Charles Finney was introduced and gave an "interesting address for more than an hour." There was then further singing and a benediction by Pennington. Lunch is not mentioned, but food must have been provided at some point to strengthen the gathering for the afternoon's agenda, which began at one o'clock with a procession from the Methodist Church to "the Grove" followed by a band. Perhaps the food was served at the Grove before the afternoon "exercises" began with more singing, and prayer by a local pastor. Samuel Ward was again introduced and "gave a very able and eloquent address" after which A.N. Freeman "delivered the oration." Finally, late in the afternoon, it was James Pennington's turn, and he delivered "a most powerful speech, and was listened to with intense interest." The local pastor then made a few remarks and they processed back to the Presbyterian church to do a bit more singing before a

---

† The event was billed as the "first" anniversary of emancipation in the British West Indies because emancipation was phased in over several years and became complete only in 1838.

final benediction. The reporter provided a vague estimate of the attendance as "thousands of persons, both white and colored," who passed the day "pleasantly without any noise, or confusion, and we hope profitably."[25]

Pennington's keynote speech, subsequently published in pamphlet form, provides the first opportunity to hear him as an orator and see how the instincts that led him to address an empty barn in Pennsylvania had matured. "Why," he asked his audience in the opening sentences, "should we celebrate an event which belongs to the British nation?" Professor Eleazar Fitch at Yale had taught divinity students to organize their sermons with numbered heads and subheads until students complained that they were learning mathematics rather than homiletics.[26] Pennington, in classical fashion, contented himself more simply with three numbered points: that the British rightly saw emancipation as a duty under the law of God, the law of nature, and "the universal consent of mankind," that it was accomplished peacefully, without insurrection or violence, and that the former slaves have proven to be good citizens, "susceptible of liberty." All this is spelled out in more detail, and then, in a lengthy peroration, he spoke of the significance for the world: that "the south is secretly trembling in view of the triumph of human rights in the West Indies" and that when "the eyes of the civilized nations shall be turned with unanimous indignity upon the crying sins of this land," the South will "feel and think differently about her system."

The speech is replete with the clear and rolling phrases of an orator: "[F]ellow citizens, we may truly and confidently rejoice in this event, because it has, in its tendency to destroy oppression, the advantage of the political, commercial, and moral character of the British nation. These give it a hostly power and influence. In proportion as British influence prevails in this land, oppression will continue to feel the shock of this event until it is *dead*! dead!! DEAD!!! America, our country, is afraid of British influence in politics; and for this reason we may expect the continuance of a desperate effort to avoid the political bearing of this event. But the breach is open and the stream will flow. Yes, the breach is open, and it cannot be shut."

But even more notable is the sense of humor, surprisingly somewhat drier and more subtle than in the essays: In describing the transition in the West Indies, Pennington notes that "it is proven to be more impractical to make slave holders into free employers, than it is to make slaves into free men." He speaks of how the United States is bounded to the north and east by British provinces to which slaves have escaped, flying "*from the claws of the devouring Eagle to the jaws of the protecting Lion!* What a contrast. But the time is promised when the lion and the lamb shall lie down together."

This was an address on a political occasion, but the whole address, easily an hour in length, is grounded in Biblical reference and comes at the end to say again that while "this emancipation is a triumph of human liberty . . . it is more. It is evidence that these principles are in the care of God, the Judge of all the earth. Yes, and he, as the faithful executor of his own will, shall ere long dispense the rich blessings of life, liberty, and the pursuit of happiness to every slave in our land."[27] That confidence shapes the speech and makes James Pennington's language different from that of William Lloyd Garrison and that of so many of the abolitionists. There is no need for anger or a call to arms. The event is in God's hands and there can be no doubt of the outcome. Such a confidence could, of course, justify white liberals who preferred to avoid the issue; it could also embolden an African American to move forward, in spite of hardships, in pursuit of justice.

That fall, Pennington was writing essays again as "the Long Island Scribe" but now, perhaps quieted and made philosophical by the rebuke from the Philadelphians, he wrote under the title "The Reflector"[28] and asked his readers to ponder with him why it is that so many human beings, possessed of minds and the power or reasoning, come to different conclusions or remain indifferent to arguments and events that should concern them. Pennington may well have been pondering his own recent experience. He had presented the case for a national convention with logic and conviction, but some had seen the issue differently and some remained indifferent. Why was that? Pennington began with basics, but it seems likely that some of his potential readers would have found their eyes glazing over before the end of the first short paragraph: "All argue that mind pertains to man; that the possession of rational powers is what gives our species the exclusive appelation [sic] man." All human beings, Pennington argues, can reason from facts in the same way. The discovery of a dead body with a fresh wound gushing blood leads people whether in South America or Africa to reason that someone has laid violent hands on him.[29] Then suppose a skillful orator (James Pennington, for example?) announces his subject, brings up his arguments, and "adorns his case with the rich flowers of rhetoric"; unless he is speaking to an English audience and eliciting a response of "Hear, hear," he will still need to wait for the audience to vote on the issue to be sure of his effectiveness.[†] Everyone has a mind and therefore will understand events in the same way, but Pennington suggests that there are different types of hearer, "Reflectus" and "Neglectus," who respond quite differently. The second may see a raging fire and notice the way the firemen do their job and think about the amount of money being lost, while the first thinks to himself, "What devastation! How wondrous are the ways of a wise Providence!"[30] So not everyone will hear and respond in

---

[†] Apparently Pennington had no experience of congregations that responded to a preacher with "Amen" and "That's right" and similar phrases of agreement.

the same way. Nonetheless, he argues, attention is critical. "Inattention is the most ruinous habit of mind imaginable. . . . The first and great thing which is now demanded of us is to fix our attention firmly on the means which have elevated men in all ages and which now give white men the advantage over us." Unless we do that, Pennington tells us, "it is nonsense to go about patching up systems, to talk about getting ahead, or to complain of being kept back."[31]

Pennington knew something about getting a schoolboy's attention. He had taught his scholars a proverb: "If any lad dares/To say I cant [sic]/The rod soon replies/And tells him to try." "The doctrine of the rod," he wrote, "is salutary in helping boys to fix their attentions on their problems. But the mind of a man is not so far different from that of a boy in point of inclination to indolence, as not to need some propelling discipline. Hence, those who have become men but have not put away childish things, are difficult subjects to govern; and, by the way, extremely poor companions in an enterprise where the masculine fixation and dogged determination of men are indispensable."[32] Perhaps he had in mind the childish rivalries between factions both in the colored convention movement and in the anti-slavery ranks.

With that background, Pennington gets down to cases, and it turns out that the readers are being asked once again to think about the value of conventions: a series of conventions was held from 1831 through 1834, the "Reflector" tells us, and much progress was made, but then the convention system was "suddenly abandoned, and the people were off in a flight, catching at a sheet of white paper held out to them from another quarter." The result was that it "turned our people from their noble work of improvement, and set them in chase after shadows fleeting in the wind" with the loss of twenty-five years of progress.[33] Attention had wandered, people lost interest in abolition, and although "two and a half million of our kinsmen . . . are bleeding in bondage" there is little interest in the subject. The *Amistad* case presented the subject of slavery in the most dramatic way possible, but Pennington predicts that people will fail "through sheer inattention" to get the facts straight in their minds.[34] This last of five columns on the subject was written in early December 1839 but not printed until late March 1840. Even the editor seems to have lost interest! But by the time the essay was published, Pennington had decided to move to a different community with a larger audience.

James Pennington's impending move to Hartford would have prevented him from taking part in the annual meeting of the American Anti Slavery Society, even though it was held in New York and he would be affected by the outcome. Only days after his move, the American Anti Slavery Society met in New York at the Shiloh Church and the tensions that had been building in the Society could no longer be contained. A battle of increasing intensity had been going on within the Society for several years between Garrison and his associates, on the one hand, who increasingly rejected the church and clergy as hypocritical for their failure to take a stand on the slavery issue, and Tappan and his colleagues, on the other hand, who supported the Society because of their faith. The Garrisonians also rejected involvement in the political process and advocated a variety of additional causes such as woman's suffrage that the Tappan side rejected. When it came time for the annual meeting in 1840, both sides were ready for a showdown. William Lloyd Garrison chartered a steamboat to bring his partisans down from Boston. He also brought with him a straw to break the camel's back in the person of Abby Kelley, a woman who had become nationally known as a speaker for the abolition cause. When she was nominated to serve on the national business committee, an angry debate broke out with Arthur Tappan, co-founder of the Society with Garrison and its most important contributor, leading the opposition. "To put a woman on the committee with men is contrary to the usages of civilized society," said Tappan. When Kelley was nevertheless elected by a vote of 557–451, the Tappan faction walked out and reconvened the following day in the basement of the church to form a separate organization, the American and Foreign Anti Slavery Society. "The split was not solely on account of the claim that women should vote, speak, be on committees, be officers, etc." wrote Tappan afterwards, "but it was chiefly because Garrison and his party foisted upon the Amer. Anti. Soc. the woman question[†] . . . and the bad spirit shown by the Liberator." It was because Garrison held that there were "subjects paramount to the Ant S cause and he was using the Society as an instrument to establish these notions . . [and] the slave has been lost sight of."[35] African American abolitionists generally supported the new organization but felt that they were being asked to choose between two groups of friends. Some of them attempted to adopt a resolution supporting the delegates of both groups to the World Anti Slavery Convention but others insisted on endorsing only Garrison, Lucretia Mott, and two others with the result was that no resolution was adopted.[36] Gerrit Smith, a wealthy New York landowner and philanthropist, was so disgusted by the "contentious, boisterous and disgraceful" proceedings that he decided "the benefits our anti slavery organization yields are not an adequate recompense for the danger it does our cause, in perpetuating our mutual quarrels; and that it is therefore better that it should be abandoned."[37] Less publicly, a good many others obviously agreed, and neither of the two organizations worked with any great success after that date. State anti-slavery organizations did the most effective work over the next twenty years.

---

† "Women have equal rights with men," Tappan added in a note written up the edge of the paper, "and therefore they have a right to form societies of women only. Men have the same right." Tappan to Welch, op. cit.

There were real disagreements between Lewis Tappan and William Lloyd Garrison on important issues, but their personalities were so similar that they found it very difficult to work together. Both were rigid and narrow-minded and sure that they were right, but Tappan was rigidly set in the evangelical tradition while Garrison was narrowly convinced of the righteousness of new causes. It was never easy to work with either of them for long, except as subordinates and admirers. The confrontation in 1840 seemed to have been instigated deliberately by Garrison, who brought Abby Kelley to the meeting knowing full well that Lewis Tappan would not accept her election.

There was only one issue that united the abolitionists, while there were several that divided them. They agreed that slavery should be abolished, but they could not agree on women's role in society nor on participation in government and political parties, nor on the role of the churches. The Garrisonians accepted women as speakers to mixed audiences and leaders in the society, while refusing to participate in elections or serve on juries, and being fiercely critical of the evangelical churches.[38] A Congregational newspaper analyzed the Garrison party as "haters of evangelical Christianity" who "seem to think that measures directly fitted to destroy the churches of Christ, and set every minister of the Gospel adrift, are to be preferred to measures, which win by light and love the very enemies of truth." The new American and Foreign Anti Slavery Society, on the other hand, seemed to the same paper to be "composed of such men as . . . have a sacred regard for the institutions of Christ."[39] African Americans, for the most part, tried hard to avoid taking sides since both factions supported their cause, but New York blacks were generally supportive of Tappan's group, perhaps as much because he was the local leader and generous in financial assistance as because of ideological agreement. James Pennington was chosen in his absence to serve on the Executive Committee of the new American and Foreign Anti Slavery Society, but blacks were always a small minority on the Board and lacking influence—as they were also within the Garrisonian group. Both the Tappan faction and the Garrison faction had trouble giving real authority to the African Americans whose cause they espoused so vehemently. But blacks as well as whites were troubled by factionalism. Pennington's immediate concern was not the division in the abolitionist ranks but the divisions among African Americans that he would have to face that summer.

CHAPTER NINE

Hartford, Part I

When the invitation came to be pastor of a church in Hartford, Connecticut, James Pennington's first reaction was negative. He had been serving as pastor in Newtown for barely a year and a half and was comfortable there as pastor of a small congregation whose members he knew and cared about. Beside that, he was living at the edge of one of the world's largest and most exciting cities and had been making friends among the leaders of one of the most important and active African American communities in the country. Why should he trade all that for a small and recently organized congregation in an unfamiliar town a hundred miles away? When emissaries from Hartford contacted him about a move to their city, Pennington was willing to explore the possibility. He would travel to Hartford and preach for them and meet with them, but he went with his mind largely made up. On December 10, 1838, he preached at Hartford's Talcott Street Church and on January 7, 1839, he received their call. But he was not ready to move and sent his regrets.[1] The Talcott Street Church had been "making do" with short-term pastorates from the beginning. Clergy, mostly white, who were newly ordained or recently discharged by another congregation or otherwise available had served them for a year or two and moved on. They could continue that pattern for a while, but they remained very interested in James Pennington. There were few well-qualified black clergy anywhere in the country, but Pennington was unusually well qualified and the people in Hartford knew it. He had studied at Yale and been examined for ordination by Connecticut clergy who had talked with their colleagues about this brilliant and deeply committed young man. The Talcott Street congregation knew his reputation, and now they had heard him in person. They waited patiently for thirteen months and interviewed at least one other candidate, but in February 1840 they once more asked Pennington to come and be their pastor.[2]

This time Pennington was interested. Perhaps it was Hartford's persistence in courting him that made the difference, perhaps it was the presence of a somewhat more diverse community with stronger lay leadership, but perhaps it was a series of events that had brought Hartford to the center of the world's attention and made it potentially a much more interesting place to be. When a new invitation came to James Pennington from the Talcott Street Church, Pennington accepted the call. He was unable to come immediately because of specific obligations on his calendar. Pennington had organized a meeting of several Long Island temperance societies in Jamaica, Long Island, at the end of April, and he was scheduled to preside at the gathering and give a major address. If the Talcott Street congregation would wait, however, he would come as soon as possible.

The temperance societies met at the end of April as scheduled and heard the promised speech by James Pennington. In spite of his planned move, he was elected secretary and placed on the "business committee," in a morning session. But the meeting reconvened that afternoon and moved on to new territory by recommending to "the colored citizens of the State of New York" a declaration and a plan for a convention. The declaration asserted:

> We labor under political disfranchisement, and suffer from a discriminating policy of legislation.
>
> We are debarred from the fountains of literature;—these avenues to the arts and sciences which in justice ought to be open to all classes, are closed against us. We are wronged and insulted by the proprietors of public conveyances, in denying us those accommodations which they promise travellers, in considerations of their money.
>
> We are outraged by a system of public caste, which reigns through all orders of the community, the sanctuary of the Most High not omitted.
>
> We will therefore exert our energies in the use of all rightful and reasonable means, to correct the abuses to which we have referred. We owe this to our God, our country, and to ourselves;

Specifically, the declaration called for annual state conventions to meet until these objectives were achieved. James Pennington was convinced of the value of conventions and would continue to work to establish a system not only of state conventions, but of national conventions. Eventually national conventions would be resumed and Pennington would play a leading role in them, but the Jamaica goal of annual state conventions would prove more realistic and effective.

When the Jamaica convention ended, James Pennington left immediately, as he had promised to do in January, to take up his new position in Hartford. Hartford had been of special interest in January 1840, because of a court case as complex as any American lawyers and judges had ever confronted. In the previous summer, a Spanish schooner, the *Amistad*, had been taken over by recently imported Africans off the coast of Cuba. Captured in Africa, they had been brought to Havana, where they were purchased and put aboard another ship to be taken to a Cuban plantation. When one of the a captives asked a bilingual cabin boy where they were being taken, he told them, as a joke, that they were to be cooked and eaten. That was a mistake. With nothing to lose, the Africans managed to free themselves, kill the cook, and capture the captain while two members of the crew escaped. They ordered the remainder of the crew to take them east to Africa, but the crew sailed east during the day and north and west at night until they sailed into American waters east of Long Island. There the ship wandered for several days, lacking resources to head for Africa and unable to find the supplies they needed. More than once they had sent parties ashore seeking food, but they had little to show for it. Coastal ships that showed an interest were frightened off when the Africans waved pistols and cutlasses. Finally, on August 29, 1839, the American Coast Guard brig *Washington* under the command of Lieutenant Commander Thomas R. Gedney came on the scene, took command of the ship, and brought the ship with its passengers into the port of Mystic, Connecticut. The ship might have been taken to New York, but slavery was illegal in New York and not in Connecticut, and Gedney was thinking about admiralty law and salvage rights and the possibility that he might become rich. Judge Andrew T. Judson, who had established a reputation as unfriendly to blacks,† climbed on board the *Amistad*, studied the situation, listened to charges of murder and piracy, and retreated to the *Washington*, where he ordered the Africans held for trial at the Circuit Court in Hartford on September 17. The American legal system, finding itself confronted with an absolutely unique case involving criminal law, property law, admiralty law, and complex questions of jurisdiction, moved slowly while the Africans were lodged in jails, first in New Haven and then in Hartford.

Hartford took on a carnival appearance that fall as crowds vied for a view of the Africans. Hotels were filled with visitors drawn by the novelty of the case. Since this was not to be a criminal proceeding, the prisoners were not

† In the case of Prudence Crandall, a teacher who attempted to enroll black students in her school (across the street from Judson's house), Andrew Judson led the opposition and got the legislature to prohibit any school in Connecticut from enrolling black students from outside the state. He then prosecuted Crandall under that law and had her convicted and imprisoned.

given ordinary treatment; they were free to receive visitors and to be viewed by the curious. The jailer took full advantage of the situation; in the first three days, 3,000 citizens paid twelve and a half cents each against his "expenses" to see these strange people. New York newspapers sent special correspondents to report the proceedings and carried lengthy discussions of the legal issues involved. The three young girls among the Africans were brought into court in tears to hear the lawyers debate the legality of keeping them as prisoners. Roger Baldwin, on their behalf, argued that keeping them as prisoners was "illegal, felonious, and piratical," but nothing was resolved. After several days of motions and pleadings, the September proceedings produced only a date for further hearings in November, and the Africans were taken back to New Haven.[3] Because they were not ordinary prisoners, they were allowed out on good days to get some exercise on the New Haven Green, where they did hand springs and other "wild feats of agility" to the delight of the crowds who came to see them.[4] A New Haven artist, observing the interest of the crowd, capitalized on the excitement by making twenty-nine wax figures of the captives, "perfect likenesses: every muscle, every lineament of countenance is portrayed with all the appearance of life," and exhibiting them along with an enormous diorama in major East Coast cities.[5]

Meanwhile, two federal judges and a grand jury worked through the jurisdictional issues involved in a mutiny on a foreign ship on the high seas.[6] The Spaniards wanted their ship and "property," namely slaves, returned, while Lieutenant Commander Gedney staked his claim to a percentage of the "salvage" rights.[7] Leading abolitionists, often derided for their advocacy of an unpopular cause, seized on the opportunity to turn public feeling in their direction by appealing to a natural sympathy for the victims who had taken action to gain their freedom. Lewis Tappan, Simeon Jocelyn, and Joshua Leavitt, editor of the New York anti-slavery newspaper *The Emancipator*, had quickly formed a committee and issued a public appeal for funds. There would be legal fees, they pointed out, and "other needful expenses. The poor prisoners being destitute of clothing, and several having scarcely a rag to cover them."[8]

Communication with the Africans was a problem that needed to be solved, since one important question was whether they were in fact newly brought from Africa or whether they had been resident in Cuba as slaves for some time. Spain, like the United States, had outlawed the slave trade but not slavery itself. The Spanish "owners" maintained, of course, that they were slaves and being transported simply from one part of Cuba to another. Josiah Gibbs, Yale Divinity School's professor of Biblical languages, spent time with the captives, learned a few words of their language, and then went to New York to scour the waterfront and find someone who could teach him the language of the captives. The committee wrote to Congressman and former president John

Quincy Adams to ask his assistance in the legal proceedings. The excitement about the *Amistad* drew new attention to the fact that the slave trade was far from extinct; indeed, the *Hartford Courant* carried a report that the trade was "as brisk as ever" and "a great number of American vessels" involved.[9]

In November, the District Court met again. The Spaniards had appealed to their government, and their ambassador had suggested to President Van Buren that there was a Spanish-American treaty that must be honored. Van Buren, facing an election year and needing Southern support for his candidacy, was most interested in having the issue go away but would, if necessary, do what he could on behalf of the Spaniards. But the American political system—not easily explained to the Spanish monarch—gives presidents little say in the legal process. The longer the process dragged on, the more Van Buren felt the pressure of his Southern constituents to affirm that the Africans were slaves and therefore property which, under the terms of the treaty, should be returned to the owners. Connecticut lawyers and judges, however, would have to make that decision—eventually. When the Court renewed the hearing in Hartford in November, however, there was a disagreement as to how far off shore the *Amistad* had been when seized, and the only interpreter who had been found was sick and unable to come to Hartford. The matter was postponed until January. Hopeful of a favorable outcome, Van Buren sent a United States schooner, the *Grampus*, to New Haven to be prepared to whisk the Africans away to Havana as soon as the Court had spoken. Meanwhile the abolitionists had also brought a ship into the harbor, determined, if the verdict went against them, to seize the Africans and spirit them somehow to safety beyond the reach of American courts.[10]

Thus, when Hartford emissaries came once more to ask James Pennington to be their pastor, the *Amistad* matter was pending and all eyes were fixed on Hartford and New Haven where lawyers and judges were searching their reference books and pondering their positions. When the Court convened again in New Haven in early January, it spent a week hearing arguments from all sides. Lewis Tappan meanwhile had been in touch with Dr. Richard Robert Madden, a British official resident in Havana, serving on a commission charged with adjudicating slave-trade cases, and familiar therefore with every aspect of the slave trade. Tappan persuaded him that it was important to have his testimony in the case and brought him to New York. To Madden it was obvious that the Africans of the *Amistad* were Mendis, natives of an area of Africa inland from the Liberia coast, and that they could not legally be the property of the Spanish claimants since Spain had outlawed the slave trade. Judson might be no friend of African Americans, but he would follow the law once the facts of the case were made clear to him. He spent the weekend assessing the evidence presented and crafting his opinion. The decision handed down at last on January 13, 1840, was that the ship and cargo must be returned to the owners minus costs, and the salvage payments allowed to Lieutenant Gedney, and without the Africans. They must be "delivered to the President of the United States by the Marshal of the District of Connecticut, to be by him transported to Africa." The Court reasoned that mutiny against an illegal trade, outside American territorial waters, was not a crime that could be prosecuted in American courts. "Cinqueze and Grabeau† shall not sigh for Africa in vain," said the Court. "Bloody as may be their hands, they shall yet embrace their kindred." "What American," asked the Court, "can object to this decree?"[11]

The answer to the Court's question was quick in coming. President Van Buren was no friend of the abolitionists and he had no desire to offend his Southern supporters by setting African mutineers free and conveying them to their homeland. The United States attorney therefore appealed the decision. Roger Baldwin, attorney for the Africans, moved that the appeal should be dismissed on the grounds that the Federal Government had no interest in the matter, but the judge ruled that the government did have an interest in the matter and the appeal ought not to be dismissed.[12] The inevitable long journey to the Supreme Court would require many months, and meanwhile the Africans were moved to Westville, two miles northwest of New Haven.

Through the course of the long legal battle, the Amistad Committee had not neglected the captives. The northern winter had been hard on them and at least a dozen had died, but thirty-six remained and most of them were given the opportunity to learn English and study the Bible. A committee of volunteers worked with them daily to encourage them in their studies. By the following fall, October 1840, the newspapers reported that the Africans were making good progress in learning to speak and read English. The three girls in the group were far behind the others since the jailer had been using them as household help. A Boston newspaper reported ambivalently that "the truths of the Bible . . . exert a greater or less influence on all of them." The same paper suggested "Who knows but God in his wise and holy Providence has thrown them upon our hands, for the very purpose of making them his most honored ambassadors to the dark continent of Africa."[13] The same thought may already have occurred to James Pennington, but it was too soon as yet to act.

Although Pennington's interest in moving to Hartford may have been enhanced by reports flowing down from New Haven about the *Amistad* captives, they were still in jail in New Haven. But Pennington was familiar with

† These names, variously spelled, are those of the two leaders of the Africans. The name "Cinque" has been most often used, but the man's real name seems to have been Singbe (cf. Martin, Christopher, *The Amistad Affair*. New York, Abelard-Schuman, 1970).

New Haven also, and whether the Africans were living in one community or the other, he could hardly avoid an interest in their situation. It must have occurred to him that except for his grandfather's capture by slave traders, he himself might speak the language of these captives and share their customs; indeed, he might have been captured with them. Hartford, closer to New Haven, might have sounded like a more interesting place to be than New York and, unlike New York where there were already strong and well-established leaders in the African American community and Pennington was still a brash young newcomer, it was a place where Pennington might be able to play a larger role with wider support.

Pennington probably did not know that Hartford had once, like the community he was leaving, been called Newtown. He did know—and it would have been an important factor in his decision—that his new home was a center of abolition activity. Almost thirty years earlier, Hartford had hosted a convention of representatives ready to secede from the United States unless the power of the South were curtailed. Delegates had come from all over New England and threatened to leave the union unless the South's extra votes (the Constitution allowed them 3/5th of a vote for every slave, although the slaves themselves couldn't vote) were taken away and unless the Congress were required to muster a two-thirds majority to declare war or embargo trade. The New Englanders were angry about the War of 1812 and its negative impact on their trade with England. In the event, nothing came of it, but the Hartford Convention with its talk of secession was one early indication that the United States were far from united and that Hartford was a well-located center for rallying advocates of the Northern cause.

Nevertheless, after almost twelve years within a short ferry ride of New York City, by far the largest city in the country, the change to a little town like Hartford with a population just under 10,000 and fewer than 500 African Americans must have required some adjustment. Brooklyn alone was four times as large as Hartford. On the other hand, Hartford was the capital of the state with a fast-growing population,† and the new railroad lines that were criss-crossing the country would soon put Hartford on the main lines between New York and Boston and between Albany and Boston. The new rail line from New Haven reached Hartford in 1840 and a "spacious and convenient" depot would open before the year was over. The *Hartford Courant* doubted "whether the Depot of any rail-road company in the Union is so well fitted to accommodate all interested."[14] Soon the line would extend north to Springfield and connect to the line between Albany and Boston. Pennington could still

---

† The *Hartford Courant* of July 16, 1840, reported that the population of the city had increased by nearly 40% in the last ten years, from 6,896 to 9,468.

be in close touch with other leaders in the African American community and in the anti-slavery and temperance societies.

In Hartford, as in Newtown and most significant cities of that era, life flowed from the water. Where an interstate highway now cuts off access to the Connecticut River, there was once an active waterfront lined with wharves. Significantly, the new railroad line also ran along the river and made access to the piers more difficult. But Hartford was still the "head of sloop navigation" on the biggest river in New England and packet boats ran on a regular schedule not only to New York and Boston but even to Albany and Charleston, while other ships carried trade between the city and England, France, and the West Indies.[15] Manufacturing was becoming an increasingly important part of the city's life with a woolen mill on the Little River, a tributary of the Connecticut River, and factories that produced bells and watches and friction matches and Brittania ware, a popular, high-quality type of pewter.[16] The future insurance capital of the country already boasted four insurance companies. Printing establishments turned out thirteen newspapers, two of them daily, and published 800,000 books a year. Hartford was a thriving, growing city, not yet cut off from its rural roots. The same city directory that boasted of 232 stores and 64 "manufactories" also noted in a matter-of-fact way the presence of 1,817 head of cattle and 1,911 sheep.[17]

The "African Church" on Talcott Street was located near the waterfront, the part of town which sailors and transients made most subject to petty crime. Like other American cities in the 1830s, Hartford was subject to riots and mob violence. In 1834 and 1835 the church was plundered by hoodlums who also wrecked several nearby homes of African Americans.[18] The new railroad running a half block away, even with its elegant station, did nothing to make the area more fashionable. The church traced its origins back more than twenty years, but it had never had a settled pastor. Black citizens of Hartford had worshiped at the Center Church as long as there had been any African Americans in the community, but they were required to sit in a separate section of the church, the high-sided box pews keeping them effectively unseen by other worshipers.[19] An anonymous letter to the *Liberator* in 1831 remarked that "There are three classes of people in Hartford—the rich whites, the poor whites, and the blacks. They all have different apartments in the house of God: the poor occupy the back seats, and the colored are seated in the back box, like scabby sheep in a separate pen. So much for Connecticut liberty and Christian equality."[20] In November 1819, black residents had become tired of that treatment and had become numerous enough to imagine a different future for themselves. A small group came together, meeting in the conference room of the First Church, and managed to obtain the services of the Rev. Asa Goldsborough, an African American and Baptist, as their first pastor. In the small black community of Hartford, denominational divisions were a luxury they could not afford. But the tensions between the informal Baptist approach to worship and the more formal Congregational pattern were a continuing problem.

In April of the following year, at the instigation of this new congregation, the managers of the Hartford Sunday School Union voted to establish a Sunday School for "the people of colour," whose children were not welcome in the existing Hartford schools. They were able to obtain a room in a building at the foot of State Street, near the waterfront, where the school began its work in May of 1820. The same room would be used for worship and the space at the First Church, as a result, was no longer needed. No doubt both congregations were more comfortable with the new arrangement.

The meeting room on State Street served the school and congregation for six years but then became unavailable. Fortunately the congregation was ready by that time to take the next step and voted at a meeting held on May 11, 1826, to build a meeting house. Several white friends from the existing congregations were present at the meeting to help the new congregation move through the formal procedures to become a recognized ecclesiastical society. The Congregational Church was no longer, as of 1818, the established church in the state, but there were legal requirements to be met to establish their existence in the eyes of the state and to enable them to sign contracts and deal with other business matters. A simple brick meeting house was then erected on Talcott Street at a cost of $2500. It was located just a few short blocks from the room on State Street and a little further up from the river. The new building served not only as a school house and church but also as a place of assembly for broader community concerns. When African Americans in Hartford wanted to endorse the sentiments of the Philadelphia convention and express their own opposition to the Colonization Society, they gathered at the Talcott Street Church and passed a series of resolutions saying so.[21] Again, on March 14, 1833, a lecture was given in the building by Arnold Buffam, a former president of the New England Anti-Slavery Society, and an offering of $43.49 was received for the work of the Society.[22]

With the erection of the church on Talcott Street, the congregation had a space to call its own but was still without a steady pastor. Black clergy were scarce, and neither black nor white clergy could afford to stay long in a congregation whose income depended on the giving of a small number of members of very limited means. Ten clergy served the congregation over the next twenty-two years. Nevertheless, by 1833, they were able to obtain recognition as a duly organized congregation, and pastors Joel Hawes of the First Church and C. C. Vanarsdalen of the Second (North) Church officiated at a service to celebrate the event. Church members of other area churches took part as well.

Presumably black and white Congregationalists enjoyed equal access to the seating and those who might have been uncomfortable with the arrangement did not attend. Two other Congregational churches had been organized in the intervening years, so the Church on Talcott Street was technically the Fifth Church. The official records of the State Association call it "The 'Colored' (Fifth or Talcott St.) Church" but the City Directories list it as the "African Church," and that was the name the congregation itself used until 1837 when they voted to be called the "Colored Congregational Church."[23] All four names, however, seem to have been in general use.

Though there were now five Congregational churches in Hartford, there were two that played a leading role. The First Church and the North Church together numbered well over a thousand members, and their pastors, Joel Hawes and Horace Bushnell, between them embodied the changing face of American Protestantism. Pennington would find them both generally supportive of the abolition movement but vastly different in other ways.

Joel Hawes, the pastor of the Center Church, had been in Hartford for fifteen years when Pennington came to the community. He had overcome his initial diffidence as a country boy in a big-city congregation to preach a Calvinist judgment on the sins and failings of those before him and become a leading figure in a community which had changed dramatically since he first arrived. When Hawes went to Hartford to serve the Center Church, the city was connected to the rest of the world primarily by the Connecticut River. There were no railroads or telegraph. It could take 14 hours to cover the forty-some miles by stage to New Haven over the available roads, and merchants who had business in New York tried to limit their excursions to two a year and planned to spend ten days to two weeks on the adventure.

Joel Hawes was the senior pastor in Hartford from the time of his arrival in 1819 until he resigned in 1864, three years before his death. The familiar name of his congregation, the Center Church, reflected its place in the community. Hawes was a preacher of the traditional school; his faith made clear and unarguable assertions: the Christian God was Triune and Jesus died to atone for human sin. That, Hawes believed, was what Christianity was all about and there was no reason to change it. Most church-goers in Hartford were quite comfortable with that position. As the population of Hartford grew, so did the membership of the Center Church until, fifteen years after Hawes's arrival in Hartford, leaders in the community came to feel that there was a need for another church. The records show no evidence of dissension; it was simply agreed that the congregation had outgrown the building and therefore a second building should be erected and another pastor called. The new congregation, the North Church, was led briefly by two clergy who made no lasting impression and then, in 1833, called Horace Bushnell to be its pastor.

Horace Bushnell would become one of the best-known voices in American Protestantism and be so deeply involved in municipal affairs that his name is still familiar in Hartford today. Bushnell Park remains what he first proposed in 1853: ". . . an opening in the heart of the city . . ., to which citizens will naturally flow in their walks; . . . a place where children play; . . . a place for holiday scenes and celebrations; . . . where rich and poor will exchange looks and make acquaintance through the eyes; . . . a place of life and motion that will make us more completely conscious of being one people."[24] The Hartford Center for the Performing Arts also carries his name.

When Pennington arrived in Hartford, however, Bushnell was just 38 years old and not yet widely known. Unlike Hawes, he had come to the ministry slowly and almost reluctantly. He had graduated from Yale in 1827, the same year that Pennington escaped from slavery, and briefly tried his hand at teaching school in Norwich, Connecticut, and editing a small commercial newspaper in New York, before returning to Yale as a tutor. He combined his tutoring with the study of law and passed the bar exam in 1831, but then decided to move on to the Divinity School and prepare himself for ordained ministry. It was said of him that he had begun his study for ordination "with no theology and a minimal belief."[25] Nathaniel Taylor's insistence on questioning had fit well with Bushnell's own inclination and by the time he had graduated from the Yale Divinity School in the spring of 1833, he had the beginnings of a theology that would develop, in time, into a complete system that would alarm many of his colleagues. But that would come later. Meanwhile he moved almost immediately from Yale to Hartford to become first continuing pastor of the new congregation. James Pennington had arrived at Yale Divinity School two years after Bushnell's graduation, so they would probably not have met, but they would have studied with the same teachers, thought about the same issues—and come to very different conclusions.

Bushnell had not gone to divinity school simply to learn the accepted answers. Eventually, in 1848, as Pennington was leaving Hartford, Bushnell would give a series of lectures on Christian theology, later published, that drove a wedge between himself and Joel Hawes. Attempting to restate the theology of the Trinity, the Atonement, and the Holy Spirit for a new age, Bushnell set out a formulation Hawes could not accept. Hawes felt that Bushnell's book was "wrong, and on the main points discussed, entirely wrong." Lyman Beecher gave the reaction of the traditionalists more sharply even than Hawes: "It is heresy," he said, "if heresy ever was or could be in the world, or if language could express it."[26] More importantly, Bushnell shifted the entire debate about Calvinist theology by urging a concern for nurture in the faith, a lifelong steady growth rather than a dramatic moment of conversion.[27]

Charges against Bushnell were brought in the Hartford Central Consociation by other churches with the result that the North Church, rather than fight with their neighboring congregations, withdrew from the relationship. It would be some years later, and only after persistent efforts on Bushnell's part, that the relationship would be restored. Hawes had come to the Center Church at a time when New Light and Old Light factions in the Congregational and Presbyterian churches were deeply divided, but he had managed to keep both sides contented. His own sympathies, however, were with the Old Lights, and for several years he engaged in a correspondence with Nathaniel Taylor challenging the "New England Theology" being taught at Yale. If he questioned Taylor, he was even more doubtful of Horace Bushnell. There was no room in his theological system for the new approach Bushnell was proposing. "I do not hate you," Hawes wrote in response to one overture from Bushnell, "in many respects I love you, and wish you all happiness in this life and forever. But we are apart . . ."[28]

For all their theological differences, Hawes and Bushnell seem to have shared a common view of slavery. Neither man had the perspective of the social gospel preaching that rose at the end of the century. Sin for both remained an individual matter and social problems were not their primary concern. They thought slavery was wrong, but they laid their concern on the individual conscience. Connecticut had moved slowly in dealing with slavery and did not finally eliminate it until 1848. It was still legal when Pennington moved to Hartford, and a few slaves were still numbered in the census. A leading member of his church, Joel Mars, considered himself to have been the last slave sold in Connecticut. Slavery was still legal in Connecticut in 1848 when Pennington left Hartford to move to New York. Just before James Pennington moved to Hartford, Joel Hawes became an organizer and founding member of the Connecticut Anti-Slavery Society.[29] He wrote a letter to the *Colored American* to say that "It is now nearly three years since my mind has been decidedly made up in favor of the great principles and aims of the American Anti-Slavery Society." He went on to say that he had not always agreed with all the individual members nor the "spirit and manner" sometimes used to advance its goals, but "I should have lived to little purpose in the world—I should indeed be a most unworthy advocate of the gospel itself, if I had yet to learn how to separate the merits of a cause from the imperfections of its advocates." He went on to express very clearly the twin dilemmas that confronted (and always confront) so many clergy and that had kept him from taking a stand until this point: how to reconcile the "paramount" demands of ministry with the demands of some other worthwhile cause, and how to balance a stand for justice against the possible loss of influence with parishioners who disagree. Nevertheless, Hawes said, in the cause "now every where spoken against" of both the slaves and the freemen, "I wish to have it known which side I am on."[30] He seldom found time for meetings and it seems not to have been part of his preaching, but he always renewed his membership and expressed his interest in the cause. When the *Amistad* Africans came to Hartford, Hawes took up a special collection at the First Church for their support. Bushnell, on the other hand, joined no abolition societies but expressed his support for abolition frequently in sermons that were later published.

Hawes, Bushnell, and Pennington inevitably saw their society from very different perspectives. Hawes's primary commitment was to his theology. He came to the big city from the country and was overawed at first by "the splendor, the noise, and the trials of a city congregation." He feared to offend the "fine folk and fastidious lawyers" who sat before him on Sunday mornings, yet he feared even more not to do so.[31] He would urge them, in his Sunday preaching, to consider the state of their souls, but to do so need not, as he understood it, involve them in considering the world they were making during the other days of the week. "Religion," said Hawes to his congregation, "is a personal thing."[32]

Horace Bushnell also found a comfortable place for his theology in a prospering American economy. New England theology had always seen prosperity as evidence of God's benevolence. Nathaniel Taylor had taught Bushnell that God was reasonable and that human beings chose to be virtuous or not. Bushnell saw no conflict between trade and Christ's teaching. A shrewd merchant, he pointed out in one sermon, could combine his profits with his charity by selling worn, shabby, or leftover goods to the poor at low prices.[33] "Prosperity," he said, "is our duty."[34] But it was always difficult for Bushnell to apply his faith to those in the surrounding community whose lives were less prosperous than his or that of his church's members. He denounced the efforts made by Roman Catholics to establish their own schools; it would nurture "factions, cabals, . . . and contests of force." Common schools, he insisted, were necessary to "bring mutual trust and understanding among all classes." Yet he did nothing to integrate the separate schools for black children and white, and he sent his own children to private schools.[35]

Bushnell did challenge his congregation by taking a public stand on abolition. He had been in his new position only two years when his first published sermon, "The Crisis of the Church," suggested that the principal dangers to the country were "slavery, infidelity, Romanism, and the current of our political tendencies." He prophesied that slavery was a danger that might at "any hour explode the foundations of the Republic."[36] Most clergy at the time were careful to avoid public discussion of so explosive a subject, and few Northerners were sympathetic to the radical abolitionists, but Bushnell was not advocating specific policies; he simply pointed to the problem and urged that respect for the "majesty of the law" and reverence for God were the foundations on which American unity had been built and on which it must continue. Few would argue with that.

The problem for African Americans in the churches of Hartford was not only that they had been directed to the back pews and galleries, it was also the fact that the preaching they heard had little relevance to their daily lives. Hawes, Bushnell, and other contemporary white clergy might deplore slavery and join societies to oppose it, but they saw their ministry as concerned with the souls of the middle and upper class citizens who paid their salaries. "Give me then," said Bushnell, "as a minister of God's truth, a money-loving, prosperous, and diligent trader."

Pre-Civil War Americans, black and white alike, were barely beginning to discover what it meant to live in a multi-racial society, but they had none of the background for understanding what such a world required that Americans would gain over the next two centuries. If Southerners, and many Northerners as well, talked about the inferiority of the Negro race, well-intentioned Northern liberals like Horace Bushnell also had views that would appall Americans of a later era. He was clear about what he called "the obnoxious features in American slavery." There were three such evils that Bushnell was able to distinguish: the denial to the slaves of marriage rites, the lack of protection for life and limb, and the failure to recognize the moral and intellectual nature of black people. Bushnell faulted the slave owner for treating the slave as a tool rather than a human being. Yet these human beings were nonetheless inferior human beings. He expected them to die out before the end of the century as the Native Americans already seemed to have done, unable to compete with the dominant race. The Irish, Bushnell thought, were another example of an ethnic group destined to fail in the struggle to survive and prosper.

The census of 1860 led Bushnell to use a Thanksgiving Day sermon to present his thoughts on the subject with excruciating clarity.

> Emancipation brings no hopeful promise to the colored race. I know of no example in human history, where an inferior and far less cultivated stock has been able, freely intermixed with a superior, to hold its ground. On the other hand, it will always be seen that the superior lives the other down, and finally quite lives it away. And, indeed, since we must all die, why should it grieve us, that a stock thousands of years behind, in the scale of culture, should die with fewer and still fewer children to succeed, till finally the whole succession remains in the more cultivated race? . . . The difficulty is not that single examples of character and manly power, or even of brilliant endowment, do not appear—such examples have appeared

not seldom, in the Indian race—but it is that the race as a whole are too low to get any sufficient spring of advancement. Many are too indolent to work, too improvident to prepare comfort for their families. Many fall into the ways of crime. Others are a prey to the vices of civilization, under which they die prematurely, and get their blood so poisoned as to finally cut away the succession of posterity. In this way, doing what we can for their improvement, they are likely to become finally extinct; passing out of record among us, in precisely the same way as the Aboriginal race themselves.[37]

Perhaps Bushnell was thinking of James Pennington when he allowed that "single examples of character and manly power, or even of brilliant endowment" do appear, but there is little in Bushnell's over-all analysis of African American potential to suggest that he would have understood Pennington's view of the world or offered practical support to the African American community.

Bushnell never joined the Anti Slavery Society. He believed that Christians should work through the church, not secular organizations. But even for Hawes, who had helped found the Society in Hartford, the abolition movement was not a significant part of his life or his understanding of Christianity. When he looked back over the first thirty years of his ministry in Hartford, he was pleased to note that "the state of religion is very much in advance of what it was." There is still among us, he admitted, "a low, vicious class of persons who are as low and vicious as any that have ever found a habitation here." But in "the middling and higher classes" he saw much improvement: "there is far less intemperance than formerly . . . less gambling, less profane swearing and Sabbath breaking."[38] He had nothing to say in his review of thirty years about slavery or the abolition cause or social change in general. He may have had views on such issues, but they were not part of his understanding of his faith and their treatment was not an important part of his moral universe.

Horace Bushnell believed slavery was wrong and thought Christians should work through the church to end it, but he took no concrete actions toward that end. Joel Hawes thought slavery was wrong and helped organize a society to work toward that end, although he seldom went to meetings. They had the preacher's freedom to decry an evil without acting themselves. Confronted with an actual person of African ancestry in their midst, they seem not to have gone out of their way to welcome him or look for ways to work with him toward a common goal.

But James Pennington had plenty to do without worrying about his acceptance by the white clergy of the Hartford area. First of all, he needed a place to live. Then, as now, many congregations provided housing for their clergy, but many others did not. When Horace Bushnell agreed to come to the North Church, he constructed a simple two-story home for himself on property at the western edge of town with a pleasant view of the countryside and distant hills. There was room for a garden where he could make use of his farm upbringing to raise a few vegetables.[39] When Joel Hawes came to Hartford, the pastor was provided with a house on a side street a few doors away from the church on Main Street, and he had only to move in. James Pennington, on the other hand, had to hunt for accommodations and move twice in two years before he could settle into a more permanent home.

The first housing Pennington found for himself and his wife was on the western, growing edge of the city, on the newly opened High Street, in rooms so small there was no space for his books. A year later the Penningtons moved to rooms on Ann Street, slightly closer to the center of town and at the opposite end of the street from Horace Bushnell, in a building used as a "seminary" or college preparatory school for young men. The Penningtons and another family used a rear entrance to rooms not needed by the school. Not until 1843 was it possible for the Penningtons to find a home they could call their own, and even then it required assistance from outside the black community.

The search for housing was complicated by the fact that African Americans were already becoming concentrated in certain less desirable areas. The same pattern is still evident nearly two centuries later. In the 1840s there were two city directories published for Hartford and one of them, which listed no African Americans in its first several issues, then (conveniently for research purposes!) listed "Colored Persons" separately.[†] The first such list included just over 50 names, far fewer than the estimated population, but some African Americans may have been fugitive slaves and so managed to avoid being listed, and others most likely were simply overlooked by editors unfamiliar with certain sections of the community. Many African Americans lived in poorer sections of town that might have been of less interest to the directory's compilers, and many, living in the hotels that employed them as waiters and laborers, might not have been as easily located. Once established, however, the list grew longer each year and by 1847 had grown to 112, still a minority of the estimated African American population of the time. Noteworthy is the fact that the addresses were grouped largely in two areas that are still predominantly African American: Albany Avenue running north and west, and the area south of the capitol building called Frog Hollow. A third cluster

† *Geer's Hartford City Directory* listed no African Americans at all until 1843, and then began to list them separately at the end. Until that year, Geer's, like many residents of Connecticut, preferred not to notice anyone of nonwhite color.

was located in boarding houses and multifamily buildings on streets near the waterfront where there are no residential buildings today. Black people also lived where they worked in some of the large hotels and in servants' quarters in some of the larger homes. The Penningtons were not servants, but the quarters they found for their first two years in Hartford seem to have been of the latter sort.

Quite apart from the obvious tasks of creating a home for himself and his wife and establishing his presence in a congregation that had never had a settled pastor, there was a series of special events that required his attention. Pennington had been in Hartford less than three weeks when a convocation was held at the Talcott Street Church of individuals from New York, New Haven, and Hartford that picked up where the Jamaica meeting the previous month had left off by attempting to recreate the national convention movement. It was a cause dear to James Pennington's heart and he had, of course, written a series of essays over the previous year calling for a new convention, so he may have worked behind the scenes to bring this gathering into being. In Hartford, there was lay leadership as well. Lay church member Charles Johnson presided at the opening session and James Mars at the second. Pennington provided the opening prayer and then was called on with James Mars and Henry Foster to report on the subject of a convention the following evening.[†] That report began by describing American society as the committee saw it: "The American slaveholder is still seated on his throne of blood, reigning at the expense of the rights, happiness and life of the slave. The ramifications of the system are still broad and deep in the so called free states.—We are the party concerned—we are the party that are suffering—we are the party that are bound to ACT in the use of all those legitimate means which God has ordained in the bands of every people."

The report then listed five reasons why a National Convention should be held: "that it had been done successfully already," that it was method "sanctioned by the usage of all ages," that without it "we are totally defenceless and at the mercy of our enemies," that "indiscriminate connection" with abolitionists fails to serve the purpose, and, most significantly, "We cannot delegate the protection of our rights to others." James Pennington, Amos Beman, and Isaac Cross were appointed a committee of correspondence to negotiate with those in other cities who might be interested and to agree on a time and place for the proposed meeting. It was, however, stipulated that the place be a "central" one and that the date be in August. The proceedings were to be published in the *Colored American*, the *Liberator*, and the *Emancipator*.[40] The first National Convention in Philadelphia had been organized with only one

† Henry Foster is listed in the city directories as a tailor; Mars and Johnson are not listed.

month's notice, so three months may have seemed adequate for a new one. As it turned out, it was not.

One month later, a call went out for a "National Reform Convention of the Colored Inhabitants of the United States of America" to be held in New Haven on the first Monday of September. "Where man's inhumanity to man Makes countless thousands mourn," the summons to the convention proclaimed, "there is great necessity of individual, collective, unanimous and energetic action in Freedom's cause." There were nearly a hundred signatures from some twenty cities in New York, New Jersey, Pennsylvania, Connecticut, and Ohio.[41] Unfortunately there were no signatories from New Haven, the proposed site of the projected meeting. That was bad planning. Three weeks went by and "A Voice from New Haven" reported to the Colored American that "one of the largest and most respectable meetings of the colored people of New Haven" had assembled on July 26 and declared that they considered the proposed meeting in their city to be "inexpedient, and uncalled for." They believed that more time was needed to prepare for such a meeting but they also noted that "it would have been an act of common courtesy to have consulted the colored citizens of this place as to the propriety of holding the Convention here." They would be glad to host a meeting next year, they said.[42]

What went wrong? Amos Beman had been present at the Hartford meeting in May that called for the New Haven meeting, and Amos Beman also signed the New Haven statement in July expressing disapproval of a New Haven convention. But Beman did not sign the New York summons to a convention that went out in June with a specific date and place. Further, the New Haven protest claimed to be responding to a notice of the meeting in the July *Colored American* which would indicate that they not only had not been consulted before a date was set but also did not receive the first notice that went out. All that was bad enough, but David Ruggles made it worse by sending a renewed notice of the proposed September meeting in New Haven that took no notice of the "Voice from New Haven." The New Haven citizens were now even more upset and let the planners know it.

James Pennington got the message and led his cohorts in a hasty and not altogether dignified retreat. The *Colored American* published a notice "To the Public" over Pennington's signature withdrawing his name and those of others from Hartford from the convention call. Their names had been added, he said, before they were ready and before "the correspondence we were engaged in was matured." But some of the manifestoes now being published, he said, reminded him "of the heavy-handed Dutchman, who seeing a fly biting his neighbor's horse on the back of the neck, smote it with the eye of the broad-axe; thus in killing the fly, levelled the horse to the ground to rise no more!"[43]

The whole affair was made more complicated still by a summons from a different group of New Yorkers to a state convention in Troy, New York, in the middle of August. The Jamaica convention had suggested the first Monday in September; but why, then, did the Hartford plan call for a national convention on that date? Clearly there had not been sufficient consultation. The New York Convention planners, unlike the Hartford planners, had carefully laid the ground for their meeting in a series of local conventions throughout the state. They also had a very specific agenda: the franchise for African Americans. Theodore Wright, Henry Highland Garnet, pastor of a church in Troy, New York, and a number of others had been working toward this event and believed that public sentiment was ready to support them. A petition was drawn up and presented to the New York legislature by Garnet, who felt the reception was favorable. The next April, however, the legislature voted forty-six to twenty-nine against enfranchising New York's black citizens. Undiscouraged, the New York leadership called another convention for the following August. The New York initiative would set an example for Connecticut, and James Pennington began to confer often with Garnet. They were two pastors of congregations in the center of their states, in or near the state capital, with similar concerns and of similar age, though Garnet was eight years younger. Both had been born in slavery and traced their ancestry to a grandfather who had been a tribal chief. Both had also been greatly influenced by Theodore Wright, and both would later serve as pastor of the Shiloh Church.

In late August, those in New Haven issued one further statement, noting that James Pennington had withdrawn his name and the names of the Hartford signers from the call to a New Haven Convention, while David Ruggles and a majority of the New York signers had renewed the call for a New Haven convention in a statement that seemed to them to deny "the existence of acumen or originality enough" among the citizens of New Haven to have "raised the voice." They charged the citizens of New York with using intrigue and said they considered the whole situation both "insulting to the citizens of New Haven" and "a foul and mischievous charge on the hitherto unsullied character of New York."[44] James Pennington seems to have been the primary force behind this attempt to revive the convention movement, but he was apparently not in a position, in the midst of a move from one city to another, to coordinate the various personalities and agendas. In the process of trying, however, feelings were hurt and egos bruised, and it would take time for people to settle down and try again.

Meanwhile, in July, there was a formal installation ceremony. In keeping with the congregational style of church government, the event began in the morning with a formal examination of the candidate by a committee. Five pastors and six deacons or delegates represented Hartford area Congregational churches, while Theodore Wright came from Shiloh Church in New York with W. P. Johnson, a lay delegate. Deacon James Mars represented the Talcott Street Church. Papers were presented showing that Pennington had been called and giving his response. Certificates provided evidence that he had been ordained and was a member in good standing of the New York Congregational Association. Nonetheless, the local association needed to satisfy itself that the candidate met their standards also. Like the committee that had examined him in New Haven when he finished his course of studies and the committee on Long Island that recommended him for ordination, the committee inquired into his theological views, his experience of religion, and his reasons for seeking ordination. Joel Hawes of the Center Church conducted the examination, and the candidate was then excused while the committee discussed their evaluation of him. A report sent to the *Colored American* by a member of the Talcott Street Church, who was present and had been present at many similar occasions, said that he had never heard a candidate to equal Pennington. His answers "seemed to be implanted by the Holy Spirit—they were easy, simple, deep, and profound." When the committee finished its work, they "expressed their high satisfaction as well as astonishment at the very able manner that he acquitted himself" and voted unanimously to approve of his qualifications.[45]

As in Newtown, a negative outcome was not expected in these events and the installation, which must have required some planning and the issuance of invitations, took place the same afternoon. Therefore the participants reconvened at 3 P.M. to hear a sermon by Theodore Wright and a charge to the new pastor by Joel Hawes. Horace Bushnell provided the introductory prayer and read the Scriptures. Pastors McLean and Sprague of the Third and Fourth Churches took part as well, but other denominations were not represented.

Choral and instrumental music also marked the occasion. The *Colored American*'s correspondent reported that it was all done "in a solemn manner . . . as if they felt they were transacting business for eternity." The report also noted that there was a large congregation of both "white and colored yet none seemed to find any inconvenience."[46] That was different from the usual pattern of church life in Hartford at the time, since white Christians commonly did feel it was inconvenient to assemble with people of color unless separate provision were made for them in a gallery or other separate area.

The Hartford clergy did come together to take part in Pennington's installation, but they did not rush to welcome him beyond that or to include him in the their social or ecclesiastical life. Hawes and Bushnell and the other Congregational clergy in the Hartford area belonged to a loosely structured

"Hartford North Consociation" which met annually, usually in June, to conduct its limited business. Clergy and lay delegates from the churches came together to receive reports from the various congregations and to make grants to needy churches and worthy causes. Pennington was in Hartford in June 1840, since he took part in a meeting at his new church there on May 18, but he was not present at the Consociation gathering a month later. Nor was he present at the Consociation meetings in 1841 or 1842. There may have been a logistical reason. Included in the Consociation were some two dozen congregations in an area of at least forty square miles. Meetings lasted the better part of two days and were seldom in Hartford. In view of the distances involved, ten to twenty miles for many of those attending, overnight hospitality was usually arranged for the clergy with local church members. But who would provide hospitality in their home for an African American? Pennington knew how his friend Theodore Wright had been treated in the New York Presbytery where hospitality was provided for the other clergy at meetings but Wright was left to shift for himself. Samuel Cornish, who had organized Wright's congregation between 1821 and 1826 and continued to be part of the Presbytery, told how he and Wright had been treated:

> I have seen a minister of Jesus Christ sitting in Presbytery, with his white brethren in the ministry, who, though it had been announced that full provision was made among the church members for every brother . . . yet [was] left by himself in the church for three successive days, without dinner or tea, because no christian family could be found in the church, who would admit him to their table, on account of his color.[47]

White clergy and lay people alike, however well-intentioned and opposed to slavery, could not see African Americans as people like themselves. So, in Hartford, other newcomers were welcomed to the ranks, but not Pennington. That would change in 1843 when the Consociation was divided, but for the first three years there is no evidence that Pennington was included in the life of the church beyond his own congregation.

Three years later, Pennington told an international gathering, "If I meet my white brother minister in the street, he blushes to own me; meet him in our deliberative bodies, he gives me the go-by; meet him at the communion table and he looks at me sideways."[48] Only a series of remarkable events would change that pattern.

There was one more non-parochial event that engaged Pennington's attention in his first months in Hartford. The national convention plans had fallen apart, but somehow a state temperance convention came together for a three-day meeting beginning on the same date that the National Convention planners had hoped to use. Pennington had delayed his coming to Hartford to take part in a Long Island Temperance Convention in April. On the first Monday in September, a Connecticut State Temperance Convention took place at the Talcott Street Church and Pennington was elected president for the coming year. The state of racial relationships was evident in the fact that the State Temperance Convention was made up entirely of African Americans, while a Hartford County Temperance Society met in June and August with a white membership. The disagreement between Hartford and New Haven over a National Convention clearly had not seriously disrupted personal relationships, since Pennington served as president of the gathering and Amos Beman of New Haven was one of five vice presidents. Pennington presided at five sessions, at one of which Beman offered the prayer, while Beman presided at one session and Pennington offered the prayer. Also present as an honorary member of the convention was Theodore Wright of New York, who offered a prayer, moved a resolution, and addressed one session of the Convention "in a spirited and eloquent manner."[49]

Although the convention was centered on temperance, the delegates felt free to discuss other issues, some of which would certainly have been addressed at the proposed national convention. The resolution offered by Theodore Wright stated that "the holy principles of human rights, as maintained by the abolitionists of this country, are at once the hope of the slave and of the nominally free of our land" and that "the patient endurance" of the abolitionists "excite our gratitude to God—and claim our hearty cooperation."[50] "After considerable discussion," a resolution was also adopted calling on "the colored people of this state to petition the legislature at their session in 1841 to grant us the elective franchise." A committee was created to oversee efforts toward this end and subcommittees were created in all the communities represented to obtain signatures for a petition to be presented to the state legislature.

While James Pennington was involved in the planning and carrying out of these various events that summer, other meetings were being held nearby that would have been of great interest to him but to which he was not invited. Joel Hawes, as previously noted, had been among the founders of the Connecticut Anti Slavery Society. Subsequently, a Hartford County Anti Slavery Society was founded that held a meeting at the end of June with representatives from eleven towns and three other counties. Apparently there were no black citizens present. A strange resolution was passed saying that "the prejudice which so extensively prevails in this country against the colored man, is not prejudice against his peculiarities, whether of color, or feature, but prejudice against a proscribed and degraded class, color being the circumstance which identifies him with that class." In a more positive mood, they "hail[ed] with joy the recent act of the General Association of this State recognizing the sinfulness of slavery, and immediate emancipation as its proper remedy."[51] The Society met again at the end of the year and re-elected Joel Hawes one of three presidents. If on the one hand they were not ready to include black citizens in their membership, they faced the fact on the other hand that many of their fellow white citizens were also not comfortable with them. Many churches refused to allow them to use their buildings for meetings. At Newington, "those present (not excepting the ladies) were obliged to seek shelter from the rain, under those roofs which were erected for the protection of horses." Other churches, they report, were opened for the first time "to the defamed, persecuted and despised, who have come out, in the face of obloquy and reproach, and pleaded the cause of those who cannot speak."[52] "The friends of the down trodden slave," the report continued, "still meet with opposition from every quarter." Nonetheless, they called for resolutions to be circulated throughout the state calling on the legislature to amend the constitution to "repeal all laws making distinction on account of color."[53] But that was unlikely to happen when those supporting such action were divided four ways, with two white factions disputing the proper way to work against slavery and two black factions disputing what sort of conventions to hold.

Although the plans for a national convention and the reality of a state convention must have occupied a significant amount of his time, Pennington was not only getting to know a new congregation and provide a ministry to them, but beginning to provide leadership for the "African School," held in basement rooms of the Talcott Street Church. In theory, the Hartford common (public) schools were open to black and white alike. In practice, the treatment given black children was such that their parents had petitioned in 1830 for the creation of separate schools, and eventually two such schools were created in Hartford.[†] In theory, the African schools were provided for by public funds. In fact, not even buildings were provided, and the schools made do with whatever space could be found in the basements of the Talcott Street Church (called the "North African School") and the African Methodist Church (called the "South African School"). The Talcott Street school had been fortunate for several years to have Amos Beman as school master. Beman's grandfather had won his freedom by serving in the Revolutionary War, and his father was pastor of a Congregational Church in Middletown, Connecticut, where Wesleyan University is located. Beman might have thought

---

† The records show two schools operating by 1840, but it is not clear when they actually began to function. cf. White, David, "Hartford's African Schools, 1830–1868." *Connecticut Historical Society Bulletin*, Vol. XXXIX, (1974).

about studying at Wesleyan himself; but just before he would have been old enough, the college had attempted to enroll a black student and met such opposition by the other students that the black student, Charles Ray, was asked to leave. Another white student, L. P. Doyle, who was upset by the incident, then set out to tutor Amos Beman himself, with the result that both he and Beman endured repeated threats and bullying until, after six months, the threats became so ominous that they gave up the effort. It was at that point that Beman moved to Hartford, where he was employed as schoolmaster at the Talcott Street Church from 1831 to 1835. Still seeking a better education for himself, Beman then moved to the Oneida Institute in upstate New York, one of the few academic institutions that welcomed black students at that time, and spent three years studying with other future black leaders like Henry Garnet and Alexander Crummell. Returning briefly to Hartford, he traveled on to New Haven with letters of commendation from Horace Bushnell and Thomas Gallaudet, founder of the Hartford Asylum for the Deaf, hoping to study for ordination at Yale, and arriving just a year after Pennington had left.[†] The Temple Street Church apparently employed Beman on a temporary basis for two years while he audited courses at Yale, as Pennington had done. The Talcott Street Church considered him as a candidate for its pastor but chose Pennington instead. Beman was then installed as pastor of the Temple Street Church in New Haven, where he served for nineteen years.

Pennington arrived at the African School with a far better background and more experience than anyone before him. But Amos Beman had been gone by then for five years, and the school had suffered from teachers with little more knowledge than their students. Pennington would have to rebuild the program and would have to contend as well with a supervisory board for many of whom the African Schools were a minor responsibility and who had no particular aspirations for the students. One strong supporter on that board was Seth Terry, a Hartford lawyer, who was involved in a number of local charities and who was able eventually to help Pennington acquire an adequate house. But others were often obstacles to the creation of a smoothly functioning program.

The challenge of beginning again as a school teacher and dealing again with parents and school committees led Pennington to recall his first days as a teacher seven years earlier and to begin a series of articles for the *Colored American* titled "Common School Review." The first of these essays appeared in the June 17, 1840 issue, and must have been written very soon after Pennington's arrival in Hartford. The series would eventually extend to fourteen

---

† The "letter of recommendation" from Bushnell commended Beman but added that if Yale felt unable to accept Beman, he would "quite understand."

essays over the next year and a half and range from simple reminiscence and a frank acknowledgment of his own beginner's errors in Newtown to a catalog of "errors of parents" and the duties and failures of school committees. Pennington might not have stopped to think before writing that the Hartford congregation included individuals who not only read the *Colored American*, but parents who discussed them with their children. A little boy came to him one day asking who the "Silas Simons" was that he had mentioned in a recent column. He wanted to know "how near that case came 'to home.' 'Don't be alarmed, Billy,'" said Pennington, "'I have not begun to throw bombs toward your part of the town directly yet.'"[54]

But bombs were being thrown quite intentionally not only toward parents, but also toward the school committee responsible for the Talcott Street school. The first committee failure discussed may have been a very immediate problem: "that of inviting teachers without the prospect of supporting them. You cannot take a more decisive measure to blast forever the prospects of young men who bid fair to be useful. It is unjust, and cruel as death, to send 30, 60, or 100 miles, and invite a young man to come and take charge of your school, parade him before a committee for examination, set him to work with the promise of pay, and then, after three or six month's arduous labor, turn about and tell him you cannot pay. This is robbing a man of his time . . ."[55] Such strong language might seem to reflect personal experience, but the trustees of the Newtown school had Peter Remsen's money available and the Talcott Street school committee theoretically had tax money to spend. Pennington, however, had developed a broad range of acquaintances with his visits to the Philadelphia Conventions and his years at Yale. He is not speaking of his own experience when he goes on to say, "I knew a teacher once who was sued at law for the amount of three weeks board by a man who had six children in the school he taught. This same man was a member of the school committee, was in good circumstances, and the teacher's salary was less than $200." A teacher should be paid "a competent salary," he wrote, yet "Many seem to have the strange notion that a teacher ought to labor for less than another man." Pennington had also known teachers who were required to go around the district and collect school fees themselves. "You know that you cannot make your teacher collector, without bringing him into quarrels with many in your district. Then why try it?"[56]

Pennington devoted two whole columns to the subject of the teacher's compensation. The writing is heartfelt and blunt; more significant, it is written to committees and trustees who would often have been white. "If you employ a shoemaker to make a pair of shoes, you *must pay* him. If you employ a tailor to make a coat, you *must pay* him. If you employ a builder to build a house, you *must pay* him. If you fee a lawyer to plead a case, you *must pay* him or else your attention will be called to the law relating to legal obligation in contracts . . ." You cannot fail to pay the teacher, Pennington points out, and still "make your district respectable. A wise man, in the emergency, will conform to the sacred maxim, 'if you find your hand in a lion's mouth, you must take it out softly.' But I presume you would not find a man speaking very softly after he has been so fortunate as to get his hand out of so unpleasant a place. Will the complaints of an ill-treated teacher be creditable to you?"[57]

Committees also need to be responsible for the furnishing of the school room. Pennington started his career in a new building with new desks. Not every teacher is so fortunate. By the time he came to Hartford, the African Schools had been operating for at least ten years and equipment was no longer in pristine condition. "Rickety desks," Pennington wrote, "are a great evil. It occasions bad writing, blotting of books, and many quarrels among scholars. Here comes Tim Allyn with his book; he has filled a page with a motion to write without a second, and hence it is not fit for a blind Jew to look at through a pair of leather spectacles. Well, out cries the teacher, 'Why Tim! why Tim! what does this mean?' 'Jeb kept all the while joggling the seat,' says Tim. 'I did not,' says Jeb. 'Silence,' responds the teacher, and all is still, but there is the copy, mean and provoking as ever."

Pennington's critique moves on to slapstick: "Boys are fond of playing tricks upon smaller ones. A chap will get his foot fixed against a seat, and give it a hoist, and away it goes, with a whole batch of 'young ones' over on the floor, whamety-bang a-lang. Then for rubbing shins, scratching heads, and pronouncing the vowels, 'A! E! I! O! Ah! Tom Johnson pushed our bench over.'"[58]

Books and slates and good stoves, too, are essential equipment. "Why is it that a school-room should be rigged off with a stove that would not answer even in a grog shop! All the patched-up, broken-winded, three-legged, half-doored, no-piped, broken-hearted, old plated, outlandish, and out of fashion things in the shape of stoves are to be found in our school-houses? I ask again, why should this be?" Good equipment is essential, Pennington argues, if a teacher is to be expected to succeed in his work. "And you may as well send a lame dog to catch a fox as to require a man to teach without them."[59]

In these columns, Pennington is a preacher using all the tricks of the trade—proverbs, humor, repetition, exhortation—and all of it with the passion of someone who sees others being abused and believes he can make a difference. Wisely, he uses humor to defuse the instinctive defensiveness with which parents and committee members might otherwise react. But Pennington, like any good preacher, believes he knows something others need to hear. As he came toward the end of the series, he received a first issue of a new magazine for African American parents, teachers, and committees titled *The Journal of Education and Weekly Messenger* and interrupted his planned series to give the editors the benefit of his advice. They should first of all simplify the title by omitting the second half: "It is like a little boy with a big head as it is now." And then the editor should be named and should sign his articles, and the journal needs more solid matter: "scientific essays, thoughts on the best modes of training and governing schools, specimens of correspondence, or letter writing, and practical composition, etc." All this, Pennington goes on, should be published not weekly but monthly or quarterly. Otherwise readers are being asked to subscribe to two weekly journals and would be better served by a column on education (such as Pennington happens to be writing?) in the *Colored American.*[60]

With this series of fifteen articles, appearing intermittently over a period of a year and a half, James Pennington made it clear that he had not intended to step off the large stage by moving from the New York City area to Hartford. He had opinions and he meant to make himself heard.

Meanwhile, James Pennington and his wife would make do with the situation as they found it. The two school rooms were in the basement of the church and "Mrs. Pennington" is listed as an assistant. In a two-room school house with students at various levels of progress, an assistant could be very helpful. The African School Committee, which included Joel Hawes as a member, visited the schools on a regular basis and one of the members, Thomas Robbins, a clergyman, left the reports of his visits to the Connecticut Historical Society, of which he was a member. His first visit, in 1844, came after James Pennington had resigned the position to find more time to respond to the growing number of invitations to speak elsewhere, so Augustus Washington, a member of the congregation, was serving as the teacher,[†] but his report would probably have been similar had Pennington been present. In his first visit, Robbins notes that there were 33 students present out of 56 registered and that attendance was "irregular"; a year later he found 55 present of 78 registered. The room, he reported, "needs ventilation," and there was "a deficiency of books," though the teacher had supplied a number. Ten children were "learning their letters," and some of the older children were "good scholars." The students, in Robbins's opinion, were being "judiciously instructed" and there were "proper religious exercises," but he was disappointed that there was no singing. At the South

---

† Augustus Washington was perhaps the best-educated member of the congregation, apart from Pennington himself. He had studied at the Oneida Institute and at Dartmouth but had to leave Dartmouth and move to Hartford in 1844 to earn an income. He taught for only two years and then resigned to establish himself as a photographer using the new daguerreotype method. His portrait of John Brown is one of the best-known images of the famous insurrectionist. Washington made a great success of his business but resigned in 1854 and moved to Liberia, where he served in the government and died in 1875.

African School, the children sang "like black birds." On other visits, Robbins found students doing well in grammar and American geography and making progress in their spelling. Washington, he believed was "a competent good teacher" who "deserves to be encouraged."[61]

Pennington, however, was far from satisfied. He knew what education could accomplish and saw it as vital if African Americans were to make any progress. In 1846 he made a formal application to the Hartford School Committee for a proper building, properly supplied. The committee eventually did provide better equipment and, in 1852, a new building; but in 1868 a state law required children to attend school in their own district regardless of race, and the separate African school was finally abandoned.[62]

The division in the ranks of the Anti Slavery Society that spring over whether or not to take part in the political process was directly relevant to the fact that 1840 was a presidential election year and there were some who felt the abolitionists should run their own candidate. Given a choice between the incumbent Martin Van Buren who, though a New Yorker, was dependent on Southern slave owners for his election, and William Henry Harrison, who had pressed for slavery to be legalized in the Indiana Territory, one faction preferred the tactic of choosing the lesser of two evils while others thought it would be better to nominate someone they could support in good conscience, however unlikely he might be of election. The Garrisonians would take no part in the political process, calling instead for a new constitution and, if necessary, a division between the North and the South. Other abolitionists thought it better to try to make their voices heard. Thus the Liberty Party was formed with the support of Arthur Tappan and his colleagues, and nominated James G. Birney, a former slave owner from Kentucky. Birney won just 7,000 votes out of nearly two and a half million cast, or three tenths of one percent. For James Pennington, however the issue was not which candidate to vote for but the right of African Americans to vote at all. The campaign for the franchise would now be added to his list of causes, and he would work actively toward that goal in both New York and Connecticut.

CHAPTER TEN

Hartford, Part II

The year 1841 got off to a bad start. The Connecticut River was still Hartford's primary lifeline to the world and the source of its prosperity, but the river refused to be taken for granted. It would on occasion rise up and assert itself, sweeping away whatever had been placed too carelessly within its reach.

Late December 1840 and early January 1841 had seen much snow and very cold weather; the river was frozen solid. On Tuesday, the fourth of January, a farmer at Springfield, Massachusetts, just 25 miles above Hartford, drove a team of horses across the river on the ice. But then the weather turned warmer, the snow began to melt, and on Thursday there was heavy rain. As the river rose, the ice was forced up and broke in huge masses that went swirling down the flood. The banks of the river north of Hartford are low and the river was soon flooding out into farmland and then down into the city. The water rose so rapidly that many, it was reported, "had barely time to leave their beds and retreat to the upper rooms, where they remained without fire or food until they were relieved."[1]

James Pennington lived on the west side of town, away from the river, though his books and papers, for lack of space in the small rooms he and his wife had rented, were stored on the third floor of a building on Front Street, nearest the river. When the school day ended on Thursday, he walked home through the rain, unaware of the impending disaster. Friday morning he went to the church, but at noon, when he walked over to Front Street as usual to spend some time with his books, he was shocked to find he would need a boat to get to the house where he kept them. The books and papers were on the upper floor of a frame house on a brick foundation with a wing at the back. The Johnson family lived in the wing and the Cross and Patterson families in the main part of the building. All three families were members of the Talcott Street Church. By noon on Friday, the Johnsons had already abandoned their quarters, while the other two families had moved up to the second floor. The water was still rising rapidly and Pennington became fearful for his materials. But where there is a river, there will be boats. There were church members who used rowboats to supplement their diet with fish from the river, so they were prepared for such an emergency. Two church members took pity on their pastor and, making their way to the house in a rowboat and scrambling in an upper window, their "intrepid exertions" saved his library. By midnight the water was still rising and the Johnson's wing of the building already swept away with everything in it. The Crosses and Pattersons, hearing ominous sounds from the foundation, abandoned their part of the house as well.

For two blocks west of the river, houses were surrounded by ice and water with only the upper stories visible. Outbuildings and barns were capsized or swirling in the flood; some were simply swept away. Cats and dogs climbed onto slabs of ice and pieces of wood while small boats made their way through the water to save what they could from the water and to take people out of second and third story windows.[2] The same weather system produced "freshets" throughout the northeastern United States. From Massachusetts, New York, New Jersey, and other parts of Connecticut, reports came in of bridges swept away and houses, sawmills, and stables carried off by rivers that had burst out of their banks. From the Delaware River in Pennsylvania came reports of a town that had lost sixteen out of twenty houses and "the inmates gone with them. Those who heard them, say that their shrieks for help was most appalling."[3] The last such flood had been forty years earlier. Pennington made note of the Biblical time span and, in a report he wrote for the *Colored American*, he quoted Psalm 95: "Forty years long was I grieved with this generation."[4]

On Saturday, the water, which had reached 26 feet above the low-water mark, began to go down and the "scene of confusion and distress" could begin to be sorted out. A committee was formed by the Common Council of the city to "examine into individual cases of distress" and solicit assistance. They believed at least a hundred families had lost everything and would need "charitable assistance for some time to come."[5]

Hardly had the waters receded when the *Amistad* case was back in the news. Moving at the stately and untroubled pace of the Connecticut River in summer, the Supreme Court had yet to deal with the matter, but rumors circulated wildly. On January 16, Arthur Tappan's newspaper, the *New York Journal of Commerce*, worried that "It is rumored from Washington that these poor fellows are, after all, to be given up to the Spanish authorities. We cannot believe it, and will not, till it come to pass.[6] But Tappan, it turned out, was borrowing trouble.

Pennington's more immediate concern was for the papers snatched from the flood. His first book was on the verge of publication and he had no desire to see the precious manuscript go swirling off down the river. A notice in the *Colored American* in early January said that the book, based on lectures the author had given in several cities, was "now in press and will soon be out." Those interested were told they could place orders for it "at fifty cents a single copy."[7] But the printer's office, at the corner of College and State Street, was a short block and a half from the river and almost certainly had been submerged. Except for the last-minute rescue provided by the parishioner's boat, the manuscript might have been lost completely. But the papers were saved from the flood, the printing office was dried out, and a month later *A Text Book of the Origin and History, &c. &c. of the Colored People* was in print as promised.[8]

The book was an important first attempt to tell Americans, black or white, something that needed to be said: that African Americans also had a history and one in which to take pride.[†] Others, especially in the last half of the twentieth century, would produce far more extensive studies, but this little book of just under a hundred pages and fewer than 20,000 words created by itself a new field for historical study. "Black History," which now occupies a month in the calendar, begins here.

A Text Book of the Origin and History, &c. &c. of the Colored People is not really a "textbook" as modern students would think of it, a dispassionate presentation of material on a given subject. Pennington says it is a "text book" because he has "aimed to state facts, points, and arguments, simply, rather than go extensively into them." It is a book that provides texts as a preacher might do as the basis of an argument, not the argument itself. There is no intention to develop the arguments and substantiate them in detail. The Colonization Society might be said to have provided James Pennington's text and defined his subject matter. From the beginning, that Society had brought together individuals with a wide variety of motives, but there was general agreement among them that African Americans faced "unconquerable"[9] and "insurmountable"[10] prejudice in America that would keep them in a subordinate position forever. Some also gave free expression to that prejudice in speaking of "inferior blood" and a need to "remove threats of insurrection

---

[†] An African American named Jacob Oson, who taught a school for black children in New Haven for a number of years, delivered a lecture in 1817, first in New Haven and then in New York City, entitled "A Search for Truth; or an Inquiry for the Origin of the African Nation." This essay, published in New York, queries whether "my people and nation" are "such a vile ignorant race of beings, as we, their descendants, are considered to be" and speaks of the arts and sciences that once flourished in Africa. Much briefer and very different in shape and language from Pennington's work, it remains possible that he knew of it and that its inadequacies led him to produce his own much more substantial work. (Burkett, Randall K., "The Reverend Harry Croswell and Black Episcopalians in New Haven, 1820–1860," *The North Star: A Journal of African American Religious History*, v. 7, n. 1 [Fall 2003].)

and prevent intermarriage."[11] Such widespread opinions could not go without a response. This "text book" was intended first of all to provide its readers with the facts they need to overcome false statements often made about black people and, second, to look at prejudice itself and set it in context of "the total subject of human rights."[12] "Prejudices are to be uprooted, false views are to be corrected, and truth must be unveiled and permitted to walk forth with her olive branch."[13]

James Pennington's first agenda, then, is to set out a basic history of "the colored people," "who and whence" they are. This history, inevitably, is limited by the historical knowledge available at the time and by an approach to the Bible that would no longer commend itself to many. Because it was commonly argued by slave holders that Africans were descended from Cain or from Ham or the Canaanites and that each of these was under a curse and committed to slavery by the Bible, Pennington sets out to demonstrate through Biblical genealogy and geography that no descendants of Cain could have survived the flood, that a curse on Ham was not intended for his descendants, and that Africans are not Canaanites. Here, the book is indeed a "text book," laying out the argument in numbered headings and subheadings that would have delighted Professor Fitch but are less likely to intrigue a modern reader. In terms generally accepted until at least the latter part of the century, the reader is shown that Africans are descendants of the Biblical Cushites or Ethiopians who were amalgamated with the Egyptians. The argument is documented with frequent references to such familiar, contemporary authorities as *Biblical Geography, Rollins' Ancient History*,[†] and *Rollins' History of Carthage*, as well as the ancient authorities Herodotus and Josephus.

Why have Africans fallen behind Europeans? Pennington's analysis is that they were undone by polytheism. "When a man has adopted the idea of more gods than one, he has unhinged his mind from every thing like truth." Other more recent scholars have suggested that the rise of modern science was made possible in Europe because an underlying faith in one God led people to look for unity in observable phenomena and so to discover the "laws" that made modern physics possible. Pennington looks at the other side of the coin and argues that it was polytheism which led to "blindness of mind . . . looseness of morals . . . divisions . . . [and] animosities." "There is no reason," he writes,

---

† On p. 22, the text cites "*Robbins' Ancient History*" but this must be a typographical error. *Rollins' Ancient History* was a well-known, standard text and is cited elsewhere. No other references to *Robbins* have been located. "*Biblical Geography*" is probably E. F. C. Rosenmuller's *The Biblical geography of Central Asia: with a general introduction to the study of sacred geography, including the antediluvian period*, translated from the German by N. Morren, with notes by the translator. Edinburgh: Thomas Clark, 1836–1837.

"why we should dodge the truth on this subject. If our ancestors have made a mistake, we can have no reason for closing our eyes against the fact, but rather let us profit by it."[14]

Even so, Pennington does not accept the notion "that the Africans have been enslaved because they are fit only for slaves." On the contrary, he notes that the Spaniards introduced slavery to the New World when they made slaves first of the "aborigines" or Native Americans. It was only when the Spaniards needed a further supply of slaves that they looked to Africa as a source. "Indians," he notes, "were stolen from the coast of New England and sold at Malaga" before the first English settlement of New England and before the first slaves were imported to Virginia.[15]

All this, however, leaves the principal issue unexamined: "Are colored Americans, in point of intellect, inferior to white people?" Pennington sets out to demonstrate that "the notion of inferiority, is not only false but absurd, and therefore ought to be abandoned." He recognizes that "we are inferior in attainment" and that circumstances may produce a loss of the "habits of, and taste for enlightened education," but he will not accept the notion that "there is *an inferior order of intellect*"; indeed, he goes on to argue that civilization arose in Africa, in Egypt, and moved from there to Greece and Rome and elsewhere. Even after the rise of the slave trade, explorers have "visited that country [Africa] since it has begun to be drenched with blood by the man stealers, and have seen the arts in a highly cultivated state." He cites 13 authors who have given accounts of African kingdoms and their resources but, without taking time to give further details, simply cites five examples of Africans of blood unmixed with Europeans who in the 17th, 18th, and 19th centuries had distinguished themselves in art and literature. Oddly, he does not cite two of the Africans William Wright had told him of to inspire him when he was beginning his studies, although he does mention one of them, Francis Williams, at a later point. Thomas Jefferson, he notices, had a different opinion of black intellect, but Jefferson's arguments are dismissed as "a budget of confusion."[16] Whatever Jefferson's reputation may have been, Pennington was not reluctant to cross intellectual swords with "the sage of Monticello."

Yet Pennington relies finally on an argument from a different aspect of the Bible: that humanity was created in one act and it is "inconceivable that different orders of intelligence should have been produced by that action." And here we begin to hear echoes of Nathaniel Taylor's lectures at Yale. Pennington writes about the "moral government" of the world and how there is one moral law all are required to learn and obey and therefore all human beings must be capable of learning and following that law. And now Pennington, the preacher, is in his element: "Then it is one Lord, one law and one race of moral beings over whom this one Lord administers this one law. Who then, is the idolater? Who is the blasphemer? Who is the Sabbath breaker? Who is the murderer? Does it matter in the sight of God and in His dispensation of rewards and punishments, whether he is of Africa, Asia, Europe or America? Does God slacken his hand upon the idolatrous colored man? Does the sword of justice fall more lightly upon him for his sin of idolatry than upon the European, or upon the American? Nay 'his law is truth,' Psalm cxix.142, and 'the Judge of all the earth does right.' Gen. xviii.25."[17] Yes, God's law is equal for all, but Pennington would have his readers notice that in America it is enforced even more strictly against blacks than whites, so whites thereby acknowledge that blacks are as capable as themselves of responding to God's will. On this subject Pennington gives St. Paul (almost!) the last word: "one Lord, one faith, one baptism, one God and Father of all, who is above all, and in you all. But to every one is given grace according to the measure of the gift of Christ. Ephes. iv. 7. What! To the colored saint too, Paul? How you do talk against Americans!"[18] Pennington may be writing a "text book," but he has always a preacher's ear for the language of his audience.

If, then, black and white are alike in ability and responsibility, one subject remains to be dealt with, and that is prejudice. Except for a very brief, and seemingly incomplete, chapter on the origins of differing skin colors, the balance of the book is an examination of "American prejudice against color . . . its nature, its tendency, and its cure."[19] A review in the *Colored American* a few weeks after the book was published expressed the opinion that the author of the book had spent too much time on his discussion of prejudice and might usefully have spent more time in his treatment of black history, "the historical part being but little understood, while all are more or less familiar with the nature and character of prejudice."[20] A modern reader is likely to feel that the opposite is true. The historical part of the book may be badly out of date, but prejudice is still deeply ingrained in our society. James Pennington's analysis of prejudice still speaks to any who will listen.

Pennington writes that there is no need to repeat what others have said about prejudice: "that it is hating the image of God" and "founded in a will to tread down the weak and poor." He sees it also as "selfish" and "ill willed." But, most importantly, he tells us, "If any who are filled with this prejudice should deny this, it only proves that they do not know what is in their hearts."[21] And what is in the heart has consequences in "insubordination, bloodshed, and murder." For those who dispute him, Pennington asks, "What kind of a spirit was that which beseiged [sic] our houses with brickbats, stones, and deadly weapons, broke up the Canterbury school, put a rope around Garrison's neck, burnt Pennsylvania Hall, and shot Lovejoy? Was there no insubordination, no bloodshed nor murder in all this?"[†] There are other consequences as well: "blindness of mind," injustice, dishonesty, hypocrisy, brutish and uncivil manners, "sacraligion," blasphemy, and "hatred for the truth." All this, he sums up, "is carrying the total nation down to a state of refined heathenism," for "who is a heathen but him who acts as if the God of heaven did not hear, see, and govern him?"[22]

Pennington has stories to tell to illustrate and justify these claims. He recalls, for example, the time when he was begged to come to a white family in the evening and give their children lessons, "But, O! it would not do to let this be known, nor for those children to go to his school." And he remembers also the times when he went into a church hoping to hear a sermon or join in prayer but found himself sneered at or ushered to "the negro pew." "The more I do think of it," he writes, "the more my soul sickens."[23]

Such is the diagnosis: there is a disease affecting the "vitals of the nation." But, Pennington says, "that a cure is possible we sincerely believe." For a cure to take place, "the truths of the Bible must be brought to bear more directly upon it. Hatred and injustice are condemned by the Bible." "He that hateth his brother is a murderer." "Let the truth of the Bible, then, deeply probe, and pierce their consciences, that they may be set right and saved from condemnation."[24]

That last appeal shapes the final section of the book. White people also must be made aware of their sins and repent, but "Colored people must bear and forbear." Proposing an approach to the evil of slavery and prejudice that would emerge again as the central emphasis of Martin Luther King, Jr., Pennington says, "The writer can only say for his own heart, I have come in contact with prejudice at almost every step, and God is my record, that I regard the haters of my people only with pity . . . I owe them nothing but good will. If I could deliver them from their blindness and folly and turn their hatred into love, I would do so, but not a hair would I rend from their head, though justice to my cause should slumber till the great day of Almighty God." He tells a story that was told him by "a pious slave" from Maryland: that "while the legislature was discussing in an evening session, an oppressive law which was afterwards passed against colored people in that state, he and others held a prayer meeting in a grove . . . to supplicate the blessing of God upon these men in power. How excellent. It is a pattern. It is an excellent one. What was Christ doing for men when they were murdering him?"[25]

---

† There is a general reference to the riots in New York, Philadelphia, Cincinnati, and elsewhere, and specific reference to the community disruption of a girls' school in Canterbury, Connecticut, in 1834, the mobbing of Garrison in Boston in 1835, the burning of Pennsylvania Hall, Philadelphia, when abolitionists met there in 1838, and the shooting of Elijah Lovejoy, an abolitionist printer in Illinois, in 1837.

The book might well have ended on that note. Oddly, it goes on to a brief section titled "Is there any difficulty in accounting for our complexion?" Pennington says, quite rightly, that "Much has been said on this subject that may be called nonsense. The reasoning, or rather guessing, has been a tissue of foolery." Pennington cites some two dozen authors who have explored the subject and refers to Nathaniel Taylor's emphasis on common sense. "I would rather be a black man with common sense," Pennington writes, "than a white man with a head full of nonsense." In an age that knew nothing of genetics and chromosomes, however, not much except nonsense was available. A Vermont writer, "S. Williams," a few years earlier, had inferred that black complexion would change to white from intermarriage in five generations or 126 years, "but by climate, without intermarriage, four thousand years." Pennington adds that he is sorry that "while Mr. Williams was in the way of calculation he did not give us a guess concerning the prospect of the whites to change our complexion to theirs on the supposition that they had met us in Africa." And there, with two brief notes about Portuguese and Jewish descendants becoming black by long residence in Africa, the book comes to an end.[26]

There is no summary or conclusion of any kind. One wonders whether the last few pages did, in fact, get carried away in the water. But it remains a remarkable performance by any standard. The argument is clear and logical, the authorities cited are numerous, and the author not only provides ample material for those who need to answer the racists surrounding them but does it with good will, charity, and humor. "The book is an interesting little volume," says the reviewer in the *Colored American*, "and every colored person ought to have it. It will . . . furnish them with arguments in proof of the origin and character of our race, and the identity of men who are prominent subjects of profane history. . . ."[†] One twenty-first-century scholar goes further and calls it "one of the best indictments of racism in antebellum America."[27]

If it is hard for a modern reader to understand why such a book was needed, that reader needs to examine some of the other contemporary literature available. A far thicker book than Pennington's was written two years later by Josiah Priest, a prolific and widely read author at the time. Staggering under the title, *Slavery as it relates to the Negro, or African Race, examined in the light of circumstances, history and the Holy Scriptures; with an account of the Origin of the Black Man's Color, causes of his state of servitude and traces of his character as well in ancient as in modern times: with Strictures on Abolitionism*, Priest's book assures us that Africans are, indeed, descendants of Canaanites who were descended

---

† In recognition of his debt to the *Colored American* for providing him with a place to express his views and make himself known, Pennington contributed fifty copies of "*A Textbook of the Origin and History &c. &c.*" as a donation to the paper's support. The *Colored American*, March 20, 1841.

from Ham, who, unlike Noah's other two sons, was born "a negro with all the physical, moral, and constitutional traits which mark and distinguish that race" and cursed with all his descendants. The first apostles, he tells us, went north from Jerusalem, to the Greeks and Romans: "Is this not a proof of the superiority of the white blood above that of the African?"[28] Priest put in print what many Americans believed. Pennington's book was a first, modest, but far better buttressed by scholarship and authority, attempt to deal with a vast cloud of ignorance and prejudice.

How had James Pennington found time to research his subject, lecture on it in various cities around the state, and produce even this small book while getting acquainted with his new parish, organizing a statewide temperance conference, working to resolve tensions in relation to a national conference, writing columns for the *Colored American*, and still been able to find time to eat and sleep? Whatever the secret was, there was no opportunity to relax once the book was published. The Supreme Court's long-awaited *Amistad* decision was finally handed down in March, and with it came new responsibilities.

The Amistad Committee had prevailed on John Quincy Adams to assist Roger Baldwin in presenting their case to the Supreme Court. Adams had retired as president a dozen years earlier and was now 73 years old, but he had "retired" to a seat in the House of Representatives and had served as a constant irritant to Southern members by presenting resolutions against slavery although the House had adopted a "gag rule" that such petitions would not be discussed. It was Baldwin who made the legal argument to the Court; but Adams, aware of the political dimensions of the case, felt some further argument was necessary. He had spent weeks researching various legal aspects of the case but had come at last to feel that he no longer had the ability to bring it all into a clear and compelling focus. "I have neither time nor head for it," he said one day to Francis Scott Key—"nothing but heart." But that was also what was still needed when Baldwin had made the legal case.[29]

Adams would not repeat the legal issues, but rather he would center his argument on the simple theme of justice. For over eight hours in the course of two days, Adams made an impassioned appeal to the consciences of the justices. He reminded them that one of the principal complaints made against George III in the Declaration of Independence was "that he had made laws for sending men beyond seas for trial." Yet was not President Van Buren now seeking to do exactly that, and where would that lead? "I submit to Your Honors," said Adams in an argument that will awaken thoughts more than a century and a half later of prisoners transported to Guantanamo Bay by presidential authority and the sort of justice that might be meted out there (also, of course, in Cuba), "that if the President had the power to do it in the case of Africans and send them beyond seas for trial, he could do it by the same authority in the case of American citizens."[30] He ended by recalling how he had first spoken to the Court nearly forty years earlier. Even Chief Justice Story, who had served on the Court for thirty years, was not on the Court when Adams had last addressed it. "At that time," said Adams, "these seats were filled by honored men indeed, but not the same. They are all changed. . . . Where are they? . . . Gone—gone; all gone. Gone from the services which they rendered to their country to appear before a tribunal where they must answer for all the deeds done in the body . . . I fondly hope that they have gone to receive the rewards of eternal blessedness . . . In taking, as I suppose, my final leave of this Bar and of this Honorable Court, I can only ejaculate a fervent petition to Heaven that every member of it may go to his final account with as little to answer for as these illustrious dead, and that you may every one receive the sentence—Well done, good and faithful servants, enter into the joys of your Lord."[31] It was all quite irrelevant, but even justices of the Supreme Court, as Adams well knew, can be moved by passion as well as reason.

There were three Southern justices on the Court at the time (and one vacancy), but the only dissent in a 7–1 decision handed down on March 9, 1841, came from the Pennsylvania member of the Court, Henry Baldwin (no relation of Roger). Chief Justice Story, also a Massachusetts man, wrote and read the Court's decision: that the Africans on board the *Amistad* were free individuals. Kidnaped and transported illegally, they had never been slaves and must be released. Although Justice Story had written earlier that ". . . it was the ultimate right of all human beings in extreme cases to resist oppression, and to apply force against ruinous injustice," the opinion in this case more narrowly asserted the Africans' right to resist "unlawful" slavery. The Court ordered the immediate release of the *Amistad* Africans, but overruled the lower Court's opinion that the president was obligated to return them to Africa. So they were free at last, but they were still in Connecticut, and the Amistad Committee that had vowed to defend them found itself with a new problem: how to return 36 Africans to Africa. John Adams thought the government should provide a ship for the purpose. The government had been ready enough to provide a ship to take the Mendis to Cuba. But President Van Buren had failed to win reelection, William Henry Harrison, sworn in as president five days before the Supreme Court decision, had died after only a month in office, and now the president was John Tyler, a Virginian. None of these was likely to have sent a ship to return the Mendis to Africa, but with Tyler in office it was certain that help for abolitionists could not be expected from Washington.

For the moment, the Committee moved the Mendis,[†] as they were generally referred to in the press, to the village of Farmington, just west of Hartford. It was no closer to Africa, but it was an area where more support could be found. Citizens of Farmington had become so involved in the Underground Railroad that one historian has called it the "Grand Central Terminal" of the system.[32] Now they provided housing in a "barracks" adjacent to the cemetery. The three girls in the group were housed in private homes, though it took some time, and even a new appeal to the courts, to free them from the jailer who had become accustomed to using them as domestic help. Rooms over a local store were transformed into a schoolroom so that lessons in English and Christianity might be continued.[33] Farmington was also a mere ten miles from Hartford, so there would have been some opportunity for James Pennington to travel out to Farmington and meet the Mendis, these exotic strangers who might be his cousins.

The Amistad committee hired a teacher and set the Mendis to work learning English, studying the Bible, and earning some funds themselves by working in local farms. Lewis Tappan and his Amistad Committee were in no hurry to arrange for the Africans' departure. They hoped to send them home only when they were thoroughly Christianized and meanwhile to use them in a fundraising campaign for the cause of African mission. Now the Amistad Committee would be challenged to move Africans not simply to Canada or to safe havens in the United States, but back to Africa. They had had to raise funds already for the Mendis' support and legal defense, but now even more funds would be needed. Tappan was in touch with the principal American missionary society, the American Board of Commissioners for Foreign Missions (ABCFM), an organization chartered in 1812 and supported by Congregational, Presbyterian, Dutch Reformed, and other Protestant churches, but he insisted that support could not come from churches that accepted money from slave owners. The Mendis themselves, of course, could be coopted to help. Tappan took them to New York and exhibited them at his Broadway Tabernacle at 50 cents a look.[34]

James Pennington, who had not been a central actor in the drama to this point, now came on stage with a more creative idea: not simply to send the Africans back, but to send missionaries with them to help create a new Christian society in Africa. The grand scheme of the previous year having fallen flat, however, this scheme was put forward much more tentatively, even indirectly, looking for signs of broad support before going forward. Three weeks after the Supreme Court decision was handed down, Pennington sent a letter to

† The Africans seemed to come from the Mendi area of Africa, part of present-day Liberia and Sierra Leone.

the *Colored American* headed "A Thought By The Way." Noting the "signal act of Divine Providence which has, to our great joy, brought about the liberation of the citizens of Mendi," Pennington wrote that he was "humbly of the opinion" that it created "solemn obligations to commence Missionary operations in Africa." "I have, for the last ten years," he wrote, "been looking daily for an opening which would enable us to do something in this way without countenancing Colonization. I think here is such an opening . . ."[35] Not only, Pennington suggests, are the Mendis now being prepared to go back to Africa as Christians, but perhaps others could be trained also in a school that might be continued in Farmington. But it's only a suggestion, he tells Charles Ray, the editor: "What do you think of it? Speak a word."

The response was all he could have asked for. The next week's issue of the *Colored American* carried an editorial with a solid endorsement of the proposal. "Brother Pennington thinks that here is an opening for the colored people of this country to do something towards Christianizing Africa, and without countenancing colonization." It would be "disconnected with speculative enterprises, to lead to deceive, to defraud the natives . . . disconnected, too, with powder and ball and rum, and with colonization and slavery. . . . Here, also, is an opportunity for those Christian abolitionists of this country, who love the cause of missions, who long to do something towards Christianizing Africa, but who cannot conscientiously contribute their money into the treasury with the contributions of slaveholders—who cannot support missions, in part sustained by robbery and the price of blood."[36]

But Pennington hardly waited for a response. On the 5th of May members of the Talcott Street Church and a few other churches gathered in the church basement to take the first steps. A Methodist pastor opened the meeting with prayer and James Pennington then spoke briefly and informally of his sense of urgency in response to the opportunity that had been presented to them. He was quite accustomed by this time to speaking to gatherings of every size, but he had much less experience of presiding at a meeting or serving as the one in charge of an organization. It was unlikely under the circumstances that anyone else would be chosen as leader, but Pennington was unassuming and deferential. "Something," he said, "must be done; and unless I can see our whole people, and this church particularly, more interested in this work, I don't know but that I shall have to go myself." He went on to speak of the way great enterprises have often had very small beginnings and the basic philosophical truth that everything must have a beginning in order to exist. Still proceeding informally, he suggested that in order to be businesslike they should select a chairman. Not surprisingly, the meeting quickly chose James W. C. Pennington for that role. He said a few words about the Christian duty to be engaged in a mission and then recognized several others to speak before offering some suggestions that he had "hastily noted down" as to what ought to be done. The immediate goal, however, was simply to agree to call a larger meeting and to pass appropriate resolutions. The resolutions were brief and the opening clause summed up the purpose: "Whereas, It is a matter of vital importance to the spiritual interests of Africa, and the honor and success of the Gospel in that country, that a mission should be established in the interior, disconnected with the stations on the coast; and, whereas, Divine Providence has now, in the case of the citizens of Mendi, (late Amistad captives,) most evidently opened a wide door for access to the heart of that country, therefore . . ." Three short resolved clauses created a committee of three to issue invitations and make other arrangements.[37]

The call to the conference, published in the *Colored American*, found Pennington at his most passionate:

> We pray that no consideration of mere temporal interest may deter any from coming to this Convention. Whatever political privilege we are contending for; whatever social enjoyment we seek; whatever occupation we may be engaged in—let all be laid aside for a few days, while we come to the rescue of the perishing souls of our fellow-men. Let the artist forsake his studio, and the merchant his counting-room; let the student forego the fascinations of literature, let the mechanic quit his workshop, and the husbandman his rural domicil [sic] and healthful occupation. Let one and all come, for necessary all our several employments are, and desirable as the objects we seek must be, what are these when put in counterpoise to the salvation of the immortal soul of man? Lighter than the buoyant air! Less than nothing, and vanity! To deny or to doubt that we can effect anything, is to deny and to doubt whether we are capable of fulfilling the end and aim of our existence, and to question the sincerity of our devotedness to the religion we profess . . .[38]

The most passionate response to this passionate appeal came from "Augustus" in Brooklyn, who wrote to Pennington and Augustus Hansen, the planning committee, to express his enthusiasm and to frame it in the largest context of African history and culture. "The crisis, I believe, has fully arrived," he wrote, "and the time is at hand in which the providences of God imperatively call upon us to do something to press forward the moral engine which is to evangelize, to civilize, and bless benighted Africa. Although the darkness of midnight has settled for centuries over her wide domains—the sun of her glory has been obscured for ages—her sons and daughters preyed upon

by the ruthless hands of European and American avarice and oppression—
the light of her science and her arts extinguished and obscured by the flames
which rose from the 400,000 volumes of the Alexandrian Library; and her
inhabitants left to grovel through the dark labyrinths of ignorance, superstition,
and idolatry—the death slumber of ages is broken, and she is to stand again,
redeemed, disenthralled, regenerated and enfranchised by the irresistible and
omnipotent spirit of the gospel of our Saviour."

"What are we doing?" he asked. "We who sustain a relation so peculiar,
so dear, and so responsible? She stretches out her bleeding arms to us, and
trembling, stands in speechless agony, begging for the bread of life. She looks
imploringly to us for help, her looks expressing all her heart's desire, with eyes
suffused with tears, 'more eloquent than learned tongue or lyre of sweetest
notes.'" "Augustus" himself thought he would be unable to attend but was
urgent that the project go forward: "Go on, then, dear brethren, in advocating
the laudable cause in which you are engaged. Every thing around you seems to
bid you, Onward! onward! Do something—do it—do it now! Press forward
into the vast field of moral action and missionary benevolence, and fight
manfully in the cause of our Lord."[39] If the delegates themselves would come
with such enthusiasm, it would bode well for the outcome of the convention.

Even before the call to convention was issued, the challenge was also taken
up by an anonymous writer calling himself "Onesimus," the name of the slave
who was befriended by St. Paul. Anglo-Americans, he wrote, can boast of a
"bright array of names in the list of devoted men who have taken their lives
in their hands, and gone to distant barbarous lands to promote the happiness
of men of every language and of every clime. But what have we done? What
have Africans, and the descendants of Africans in America done toward evan-
gelizing the world?"[40] Over the following weeks, a succession of letters and
editorials supported the proposal. Onesimus, who may well have been James
Pennington since the letters were posted from Hartford and had something
of the same style,† wrote lengthy epistles almost every week and supportive
letters arrived also from pseudonymous correspondents in Philadelphia and
Pittsburgh. Henry Garnet in Troy wrote in support, although he was unhappy
that once again a meeting in Hartford had been scheduled too close to the
date of a meeting already scheduled in Albany.

---

† It is also probably significant that the sequentially numbered columns are sometimes
signed "Onesimus" and sometimes not. On August 21, in an unnumbered column,
Onesimus says that he has completed the task he set himself, but in November one more
numbered column appears without a name to take up a subject the writer says he had
promised in a previous number to deal with. There is also a short letter from Onesimus
in June correcting several typographical errors in his last column. Pennington, in his own
name, exasperated the editor on another occasion with a similar fussiness.

Forty-three delegates, both black and white, from six states and a variety of churches duly arrived in Hartford on August 18th and were joined by Cinque and four others of the Mendis.

They unanimously endorsed the plan for African mission and created a board with James W. C. Pennington as president and eight vice presidents representing several churches and including Morris Brown, the second bishop of the African Methodist Church. Theodore Wright was the treasurer, Amos Beman was corresponding secretary, and Lewis Tappan, who had not been present, was named as one of two auditors. The other auditor, George Hogarth, came from the African Methodist Church in Brooklyn. The Union Missionary Society is sometimes hailed as the first such organization formed by African Americans; but perhaps it was more significant as the first organization formed by African Americans that was designed to reach out beyond the concerns of the American black community.

But James Pennington was not putting all his energy into either the mission society or his parochial work. Among the papers rescued from the flood was the work of another author, a young member of his congregation, who was a teacher in the other African school, usually called the South African School, but also known as the Elm Street School. Ann Plato was an aspiring writer, twenty-one years old, whose father, Alfred Plato, was a leading member of the Talcott Street Church.[41] Seeing that her pastor had become an author, she asked him for help in publishing a collection of her own writing, and he was happy to provide support and encouragement. Distinctions of race were not usually Pennington's style, but in this case he is proud to point out that Ann Plato is black. "I am not in the habit," he writes in his foreword, "of introducing myself or others to notice by the adjective 'colored,' &c., but it seems proper that I should just say here, that my authoress is a colored lady." He was amused by her name and asks, "As Greece had a Plato why may we not have a Platoess?" More seriously he writes, "She has done well by what nature has done for her, in trying what art will add. The fact is, this is the only way to show the fallacy of that stupid theory, that nature has done nothing but fit us for slaves, and that art cannot unfit us for slavery! My authoress has followed the example of Philis Wheatly, and of Terence, and Capitain, and Francis Williams, her compatriots. These all served in adversity, and afterwards found that nature had no objection, at least, to their serving the world in high repute as poets . . . She has a large heart full of chaste and pious affection for those of her own age and sex; and this affection is largly [sic] interspersed over the pages of her book. If you will reciprocate this affection you will, I doubt not, read this book with pleasure and profit."[42]

Plato was the second African American woman to have her poetry published; Phyllis Wheatley (1753–1784) had preceded her. Like Wheatley's poetry, Plato's verse is remembered more for the author's race than the quality of the writing. Pennington says she is "of modest worth," but there can be no question that Ann Plato had some ability as a writer and this small collection of poems, essays, and biographical sketches gives evidence of an unusual thoughtfulness and skill with language. She writes too much of death and the grave for modern taste, but any woman of twenty-one who can write biographical sketches of three friends who have died is likely to speak more of the shedding of tears and the shortness of life than a similar modern writer. Even so, Plato is less sentimental than a good many of her contemporaries. What she does not write about, and modern writers criticize her for it, is race. But perhaps it is evidence of her secure sense of herself that she is able to write instead about matters that transcend racial difference: her work as a teacher, a visit to a country farm, and the changing seasons. She writes "A good education is another name for happiness," and how many young people know that? There are reports by the Hartford School Committee of visits to her classroom and commendations for her work, but nothing else is known concerning Ann Plato. With James Pennington's assistance, she helped open the way for many others to follow.

A continuing concern for Pennington was the flow of fugitive slaves to his door and the efforts of slave holders and slave dealers to reverse the flow. In June, he wrote to the *Colored American* with stories of children ten and eleven years of age who had been tempted aboard a boat in the Hudson River near Poughkeepsie by a promise of oranges or a request for a package, only to find themselves locked in the hold and carried off to Kentucky. Years later, they had escaped and come back to tell their stories, only to be taken again near Albany by the same man, John Cutter, and to escape a second time. Pennington wrote to ask, "Do we not need more vigilance and watchfulness to keep our children and friends from falling into the vile hands of the slaveholder? . . . What were the free citizens of Albany about, when two free citizens were kidnapped in their streets? John H. Cutter comes on to New York about once in two years; would it not be well to keep a look out for him?"[43] There was, of course, a Vigilance Committee in New York City, but it could not be aware of every danger and its work had not extended up the river to Poughkeepsie and Albany. Pennington had a particular reason for these concerns: there was always the danger that he himself might still be located by his former master. But no African American was safe in any Northern community; the existence of slavery in the Southern states changed the quality of life for those who were technically free but still not free of danger.

A related problem was the difficulty clergy always face, of separating the genuinely needy from the imposter. In 1845, Pennington and Moses Breck posted correspondence in the *Christian Freeman* concerning a man who had come to both of them claiming to be a fugitive slave and seeking assistance. Pennington had judged the man to be "an imposer upon the friends of humanity," seeking "to swindle them of their money." The man, Richard Thompson, claimed to be from Lynchburg, Virginia, and to need several hundred dollars to buy his wife's freedom, but Pennington heard nothing of a southern accent and noted that the papers the man presented were in the same handwriting and full of the same errors though they were attributed to different men at different addresses. But two or three days later, a man with the same name had come to Breck with a recommendation from a pastor in Springfield. He told Breck he had escaped to Canada with his wife and then been captured, taken south, escaped again, and now needed money to get back to his wife in Canada. Breck had provided assistance and had heard that the man had reached Montreal, that his wife was not there but a short distance away and was going happily on his way. Breck knew Pennington well enough to be sure he would not "willingly injure a poor oppressed fugitive," but thought he had been "rather hasty" in this case. Pennington responded that he most certainly would not knowingly injure a fugitive because "I am a fugitive myself," but he noted that the stories the man told didn't jibe and either it was not the same man or he had changed his story. "I am not yet convinced," he wrote, "that I have been too hasty."[44] But he had revealed himself publicly to be a fugitive for the first time and thereby risked his freedom. The danger would grow as the Southern states put increasing pressure on the Northern states to enforce fugitive slave laws and to add new and stricter laws to those already in existence.

The naming of Lewis Tappan as an "auditor" had been an interim solution to his absence from the meeting and unwillingness at first to cooperate with the plan for a new mission society. He had thought the plan was premature and Tappan still hoped for support from the primary existing agency, the American Board of Commissioners for Foreign Mission (ABCFM), though he insisted that the Board would have to reject support from slave owners. A November meeting in Boston, however, made it very clear that the Board was not willing to forego Southern support. Tappan was outraged. They have taken a stand, he noted, on "the Sabbath, the Indians, the Caused of Temperance, Revivals of Religion &c as if [these] were greater obstructions to the conversion of the world than American slavery! When will the churches of this land open their eyes . . . upon the series of outrages perpetrated upon the principles of an anti-slavery gospel?"[45] What was obvious to Tappan was not obvious to many others, who saw it as a distraction in their work of proclaiming the gospel. One missionary, stationed in "Tabreez, Persia," wrote to say that he saw no reason for "missionaries far and long away from their native land . . . to become parties to such exciting subjects as that of domestic slavery." He felt it would only make enemies for themselves and for the cause that required "the judicious application of all their powers."[46] But other missionaries wrote in support of the new society and Tappan, now that the ABCFM had made their views clear, was now willing to serve in his usual capacity of managing the money for the new society.

The enormous task of creating and funding a new society was not, however, the only task on Pennington's agenda. Even as the Convention was meeting, announcements were appearing in the *Colored American* and elsewhere that the sixth anniversary of the Connecticut State Temperance Society of Colored Americans was to be held at Bridgeport on September 6, less than three weeks after the Union Missionary Society's founding meeting had closed. The fifth anniversary meeting had chosen Pennington as president, so he set out to rally his troops. With a typical flourish, the announcement of the meeting exhorted its readers: "Sons of old Connecticut, awake! arise! and let us work. We have much to do, and that too which is highly important. Come up to the mark, and acquit yourselves like men in your own cause." But he could also be realistic, so it is not surprising that the meeting was postponed to the end of the month. He had set a demanding agenda for the delegates from the various temperance societies around the state. They were requested to furnish their reports—"as full and as accurate as possible"—on the state and progress "1. Of the temperance cause. 2. Of education. 3. Of the mechanic arts. 4. What has been done towards obtaining the elective franchise. 5. The number of colored freeholders in each town. 6. The proportion of adults that can read and write." A "little exertion between this and the time of the meeting," he told them, would make their reports more useful.[47]

William Johnson, who had been traveling the state to drum up subscribers for the *Colored American*, reported that he had been at the meeting and that, "Notwithstanding the storm, the presence of seventy ladies from abroad, as well as the city of Bridgeport, added much to the life of the Convention. One lady hired a horse and carriage to bring her intemperate husband up to the shrine of teetotalism; and, joy to tell, he was broke down, and like a man, he threw off the shackles of rum, and stepped forward, in tears of true repentance, as we believe, and signed the pledge! And a happier couple I don't know as I ever saw. I saw him the next day, still rejoicing."[48] As to James Pennington's agenda, Johnson filed no report.

But Pennington had added to his other responsibilities the task not only of raising funds to pay for the Africans' return voyage but also of finding missionaries to accompany them. One suggestion, from the Executive Committee of the new society, was that Pennington himself go as a missionary. That idea had, of course, occurred to Pennington ten years earlier, but this was a much more direct challenge in the form of a letter from the Committee. Pennington responded that he had taken the matter under consideration "earnestly and prayerfully . . . asking counsel of God, and reflecting on the subject in all its bearing, both upon Africa and America." "I love the Mendians," he wrote, "I love their country. At first my heart was bent to go, indeed it is now while I am writing, but I have had to yield." His conclusion was that "my calling is with my suffering brethren in this land." He noted that he had only recently begun his ministry in Hartford and that the newly formed missionary society also "will need much labor to make it go."[49]

Pennington was not unopposed in his efforts. At the same time that he was attempting to find missionaries to accompany the Mendis and had one member of his church expressing interest, the Colonizationists were also active and had recently persuaded two members of his congregation, including one of the deacons, to go to their colony in Liberia. Even the columns of the *Colored American* brought evidence of opposition. "Americanus" wrote to ask what kind of religion the Society would carry to Africa. Would it be "the religion that not only sanctions, but sustains and protects American slavery?" What evidence was there, the writer asked, that Christianity had been a blessing to African Americans in the United States? If it were to be the form of Christianity known to Americans, "I humbly protest," wrote Americanus, "against such a wicked and abominable crusade against 'the rights of man.'"[50] It was exactly the viewpoint of William Lloyd Garrison and his supporters, and it left James Pennington and his colleagues squeezed between the conservative, white-dominated churches and mission societies on the one hand that were reluctant to offend slave holders, and the Garrisonians on the other hand who saw no good in the churches at all.

Pennington, continuing the series of columns on African missions in the *Colored American*, put forward one more reason for supporting the mission to Africa: that African Americans were judged by the condition of their kin in Africa. "If the vast peninsula of Africa ," he suggested, were "one consolidated empire; and if its ninety millions of population possessed regularly organized and well disciplined navies; enjoyed the light of education; were conversant with the circle of the sciences; familiar with the fine arts; and, above all, illuminated—though but partially, even as this land—by the benign ray of Christianity; what mental vision is there so obtuse that may not see" how different the feelings of others would be toward Africans in America? Pennington singled out especially the right to travel without indignities and the sacrilege of the "Negro pew." The conversion of Africa, he believed, would transform America as well.[51] A pastor in Newton, Massachusetts, was so moved by a missionary sermon he heard James Pennington preach that he sent a poem to the *Union Missionary Herald*. The first and last verses contain the basic message:

> They tell us that we do not feel
>> For Pagans o'er the wave;
> As if our hearts are turned to steel
>> While bleeding for the slave.
>
> But no! 'tis universal man
>> We love and toil to save:
> For 'tis a part of God's great plan
>> To disenthrall the slave.[52]

For the present, Pennington, Tappan, and their colleagues at least had the human-interest story on their side, and they did their best to make use of it in the short time available. The Mendis, knowing the Court had set them free to return to Africa, were becoming increasingly restive at the continued delay and fearful of spending another winter in New England. By the end of October, a missionary had been found, and in November the Africans were sent off on one final fundraising campaign around New England. Sixteen public meetings were held in less than two weeks in Boston, Salem, Lowell, Worcester, Northampton, Springfield, Hartford, and a number of other cities as well. Nine of the African men and boys and one of the girls, traveling with Lewis Tappan, their teacher William Raymond, and a member of the Farmington committee, edified their audiences by demonstrating their English-language abilities in reading from the Bible, repeating prayers, and showing samples of their handwriting.[53] A reporter for the Lynn *Record* went to the Marlboro Chapel in Boston to see the captives and wrote that it was "the best entertainment we ever witnessed in that place. It was worth going fifty miles to see."[54]

By the end of November, two additional missionary couples had been found. Henry Wilson, a tailor, and his wife were members of Pennington's Hartford congregation and would go out as teachers. The Federal government had been asked to provide transportation for the Mendis since President Van Buren had been quite ready to repatriate them to Cuba, but President Tyler, a Virginian, could find no constitutional authority to help them go home. The Mendi Committee therefore chartered the *Gentleman*, a three-masted ship typical of the Atlantic trade in that era, at a cost of $1840. While the ship lay anchored off Staten Island taking on provisions to supply the mission for a year, one final rally was held in the First Church of Farmington at which Joel Hawes preached a sermon on "caste" and another $1300 was raised.[55] Then the Mendis climbed aboard a boat to go down the river to New Haven and on to New York for several more days of meetings and fundraising.

On the next Sunday afternoon, November 21, they attended an afternoon service at the Shiloh Presbyterian Church and listened to a missionary sermon by James W. C. Pennington. The offering was dedicated to their support and a farewell was spoken on behalf of the church by Theodore Wright, the pastor. That same evening they were taken to the Broadway Tabernacle where Lewis Tappan had gathered an overflow crowd, "not a spot large enough for one's feet, the pulpit and pulpit stairs not excepted, but what was occupied."[56] James Pennington led the prayers, and the Mendis read a psalm and a passage from the Sermon on the Mount. There was even a spelling bee to demonstrate what had been learned. Then a member of the committee gave the history of the *Amistad* and one of the Mendis told of his capture in Africa, the horrors of the Atlantic voyage, the fight to take over the *Amistad* off the coast of Cuba, and the end of the voyage off Long Island. The Mendis sang a familiar hymn, "When I can read my title clear," and one of their own songs as well. Simeon Jocelyn, of the Amistad Committee, instructed the missionaries to keep the faith, teach the natives, and avoid involvement in commercial matters. Cinque spoke at some length, expressing his thanks and promising to help the missionaries, speaking in his own language while Kinna, one of the other Mendis, translated. A New York newspaper report spoke of "His rapid enunciation, the expression of his countenance, the flashing his eye, and the significancy of his gestures and movements in certain passages of his address," and "his ability to touch with a master's hand the finer chords of the human heart;—for when in the conclusion of his remarks, he expressed a sense of his obligations to the Americans for their kindness to him and his people, and bade them farewell for ever, his manner was subdued and touching, and affected those who are well acquainted with him, to tears."[57] The pastor of the Broadway Tabernacle then preached a missionary sermon, and the assembly closed with the singing of a favorite hymn that summed up the self-confident triumphalism of nineteenth-century Christianity:

> From Greenland's icy mountains, from India's coral strand;
> Where Afric's sunny fountains roll down their golden sand:
> From many an ancient river, from many a palmy plain,
> They call us to deliver their land from error's chain.
>
> What though the spicy breezes blow soft o'er Ceylon's isle;
> Though every prospect pleases, and only man is vile?
> In vain with lavish kindness the gifts of God are strown;
> The heathen in his blindness bows down to wood and stone.

Shall we, whose souls are lighted with wisdom from on high,
Shall we to those benighted the lamp of life deny?
Salvation! O salvation! The joyful sound proclaim,
Till earth's remotest nation has learned Messiah's Name.

An offering of sixty dollars was received to support the missionaries.[58]

The next night a similar meeting was held in the African Methodist church, but this time the congregation gathered around the Africans at the end to shake their hands and wish them well in the voyage to their mutual homeland. And yet two more evenings were spent in that fashion in other parts of the city before the Mendis were finally allowed to climb aboard the *Gentleman* and sail down the harbor, though Lewis Tappan and members of the committee still accompanied them, exhorting them and praying with them until they came to the lower harbor where, with one last embrace, the Mendis were allowed to go, as they had attempted to do two and a half years earlier, to the east and Africa at last.[59] †

So the Mendis were returned to Africa, but now Pennington and the new missionary society were faced with the greater problem of supporting a Mendi mission. The publication of a new magazine to publicize the work and solicit assistance was a high priority, and the first issue of the *Union Missionary Herald*, edited by Josiah Brewer, a former missionary and editor,†† appeared in January 1842. The first issue of the little magazine, published in Hartford and selling for three cents within a hundred miles and five cents in more distant places, contained a complete record of the origins of the society, including the minutes of the founding meeting and the constitution. The cover laid out its purpose: "containing the proceedings of Evangelical American Missions, Not connected with Slavery; and a general view of Other Like Benevolent Operations." There were letters of support from future African Methodist bishop Daniel Payne, Joshua Leavitt, and others. There was also a map of western Africa showing the location of the Mendi land and a report on Mendi customs. The last page listed donations from some twenty-five

† The mission to the Mendi homeland was not an unqualified success. Many of the Mendis were scarcely ashore before they put off their western clothing and disappeared into the bush. Cinque himself went back to his tribe and became a tribal leader in the traditional way. Only at the end of his life did he come back to the mission to die. One girl later returned to America to study at Oberlin and returned to Africa as a teacher. The missionaries persisted with some success, but Pennington's hope to see "in every valley, and on every hill top, fair temples of the living God, and hear the ransomed tribes of every tongue with rapture shout their glad hosannas" would remain a vision.

†† Josiah Brewer was born in Berkshire County, Massachusetts, in 1790 and died in Stockbridge, Massachusetts, in 1872. He was graduated from Yale in 1821 and was one of the first to volunteer as a missionary to Turkey for the American Board. He was the first to introduce schools and the printing press.

supporters, including ten dollars for a "life membership" in the society for James Pennington from the members of the Talcott Street Church, totaling $47.34. Easier for the Talcott Street congregation to manage was to send boxes of used clothing and similar materials for the missionary's family and converts, a standard technique in the support of nineteenth-century missions. Pennington wrote a letter to accompany one such box suggesting that each of the "Chiefs" be given "a piece of spotted cloth, a large table spread, and a few yards of handsome plaid."[60] More substantial assistance came from Josiah Brewer, a former missionary in Turkey and a member of the Amistad Committee, who pledged $500 and committed the resources of the Amistad Committee to the new society with a promise of repayment within a year.

Clearly, however, fundraising would be a problem. Pennington suggested that each black congregation contribute $100, but if the Talcott Street Church needed an annual subsidy of $100 from the other Connecticut Congregational churches, it was unlikely that even they could contribute regularly at that level. Two significant initiatives were taken to address the financial problem. In the first place, James and Harriet Pennington donated a building lot in New Haven to the Society. This was one of the three building lots Simeon Jocelyn had sold Pennington to help with his finances during his studies at Yale. Purchased for thirty dollars, the land was probably worth several times that amount and seems to have been leased to provide the society with a stream of income.[†] The other initiative was a fundraising tour by Augustus Hansen. Hansen was the son of a British merchant and government official and the daughter of a tribal chief in Ghana. Educated in England, he had come to America to take a commercial position that failed to materialize. Appalled at the treatment black people received in the New World, he remained nevertheless in New York City and became active in various reform movements. He had moved to Hartford in 1840 to be tutored in theology by James Pennington and had assisted in the formation of the Union Missionary Society. Seeing the need for a broadened base of support, he set out on a speaking tour through the surrounding states to promote the society's program.[††]

The financial difficulties the Society faced were compounded by the rather different operating styles of the two central figures, James W. C.

---

† A note signed by the Penningtons, dated January 12, 1842, promises the donation but the deed, selling the land for one dollar to Amos Beman for the Union Missionary Society, was executed on November 16, 1842. The land was sold to Pennington by Simeon Jocelyn in May 1834. The deeds are on file in the Connecticut State Library.

†† Hansen was ordained to the priesthood of the Episcopal Church in 1842, translated two of the gospels into a West African language, and returned to England at the end of the year. He later served as a missionary and in government posts in West Africa (Ripley, op. cit, v. III, pp. 286–287).

Pennington and Lewis Tappan. Tappan was a businessman concerned for the bottom line, while Pennington was a preacher who commended and practiced living by faith that God would provide. Correspondence went back and forth between them. From Pennington to "Brother Tappan" went hopeful letters listing small contributions that would probably be coming: a pledge of ten dollars from Pennington himself; a hundred dollars from the Connecticut Anti-Slavery Society, which was attempting to resolve its debts but seemed likely to fulfill its pledge eventually; the possibility of raising another sixty or seventy dollars (including Pennington's pledge of ten) if "Brother Raymond"[†] could come to Hartford to speak.[61] "I merely refer in good faith to these facts," Pennington wrote. From that point of view, it looked like almost two hundred dollars; for Tappan's purposes in paying the bills, it looked like much less. From Tappan to Pennington went letters worrying about even smaller amounts. There was a "Dear Brother" letter asking about "a few pounds" that had been collected in England by Joseph Sturge and sent on to Tappan through an intermediary toward Pennington's expenses. Now Sturge had written to Tappan to ask about it, since he had not received any acknowledgment and wondered whether the money had been delivered. "I have no recollection of receiving the money," Tappan wrote to Pennington; "Have you any?"[62] Since the money had been directed to Tappan for Pennington, it is hard to see how Tappan could blame Pennington for its disappearance. If it had reached Pennington second or third hand, he would presumably have spent the money for his expenses as needed without realizing that Sturge wanted to know it had arrived. Abolitionists traveling in England to raise money for the cause frequently had to spend most of what they had raised simply to pay their expenses, and few records were kept. Unfortunately, Tappan, for all his generosity to a variety of causes, was a tight-fisted businessman who wanted to be able to account for every penny, and he had the notion that African Americans were careless with financial records. It didn't help that Pennington, needing money for the Society's expenses, wrote him a few weeks later to ask for "a short term loan." "I have not a dollar on hand except borrowed money," Tappan responded. "I cannot comply with your request."[63] Petty matters like this served to confirm his opinion of the financial abilities of African Americans, but it had far more to do with the different priorities of a businessman and a preacher than it did

† Presumably William Raymond, who had taught the Mendis in Hartford and gone out as one of the Mendi missionaries with his wife. They returned almost immediately because their only child had died soon after their arrival in Africa, but back they went to the Mendi mission at the end of November 1843. Raymond played a leading role in giving the young mission a secure start, but he died in Africa after just four years at the age of 31.

with race.† Eventually this difference in style would produce unhappy consequences.

So ended James Pennington's tumultuous first full year in Hartford. He had published one book, edited another, written numerous articles for publication, and organized a national, ecumenical mission society. He had not been troubled, however, with the need to fit in meetings of the Hartford Clergy. One of those meetings had been in the home of Joel Hawes, a few blocks from where Pennington lived; sixteen clergy were present, but not James Pennington. The fact that Joel Hawes and Horace Bushnell were opposed to slavery was apparently unrelated to the question of actually meeting with someone of color. At their 1839 meeting in the home of Horace Bushnell, the minutes report that "The Association had a pleasant conference on several questions relating to the subject of slavery."[64] James Pennington might have helped the clergy understand the issue on the basis of first-hand information, but the conversation might not have been as "pleasant." In 1840, again, "Friendly conversation was had on the subject of slavery" and the clergy suggested that a state convention of the clergy ought to be called to discuss the subject. There were eighteen clergy present, including Hawes and Bushnell, but again Pennington was not there. Although four of them had taken part in Pennington's installation, it seems not to have occurred to them that a relationship might have been created.

† The fact that a donation to the *Liberator* in 1837 came from "H. Pennington" seems to indicate that even at home it was Mrs. Pennington who did the bookkeeping. Cf. *Liberator*, March 11, 1837.

CHAPTER ELEVEN

The Mendi Mission

I n May 1741, Jonathan Edwards preached a sermon to a small gathering at a private home in Northampton, Massachusetts. Toward the end of the sermon, one or two those present became, as he wrote to a friend, "so greatly affected with a sense of the greatness and glory of divine things, and the infinite importance of the things of eternity, that they were not able to conceal it; the affection of their minds overcoming their strength, and having a very visible effect on their bodies. . . . the affection was quickly propagated through the room; many of the young people and children that were professors appeared to be overcome with a sense of the greatness and glory of divine things, and with admiration, love, joy and praise, and compassion to others that looked upon themselves as in a state of nature. And many others at the same time were overcome with distress about their sinful and miserable state and condition; so that the whole room was full of nothing but outcries, faintings, and suchlike."[1]

It had been well over two centuries since the first Pilgrims and Puritans had landed in Massachusetts, and the rather austere pattern of life they had created had not always worn well. As the years went by, there was a growing concern for younger generations who could not bring themselves to make the commitment required for membership in the covenant community. The self-reliance required to survive in the scattered New England farms, and the self-confidence following on the work of Isaac Newton and others who seemed to demonstrate that human beings could come to understand the mysterious universe, had led to a growing negligence of religion that deeply concerned Edwards and others. The revival that began under Edwards's preaching in Northampton and under the itinerant preaching of the English evangelical preacher George Whitefield, who spread what is known as "the Great Awakening" up and down the eastern seaboard, offered a clear and simple message of salvation endorsed by emotional experience. The "New Lights," as they came to be called, produced a wave of revival that changed the nature of American Christianity.

Another century passed by before James Pennington was introduced to Samuel Cox but, once again, revival was in the wind. This time it was the self-confidence produced by the American Revolution and the specifically irreligious attitude engendered by the French Revolution that were of concern to Christian leaders and led them once again to appeal to the emotions as well as the mind. This time the "Awakening" began at a place called Cain Ridge in Kentucky and radiated out in a tumult of revival with outward manifestations beyond those that had surprised Jonathan Edwards.

Samuel Cox and the professors at the Yale Divinity School were not much given to the outward displays that were common on the unsophisticated frontier. Cox wrote that "corporeal excitement is incidental and not primary parts or necessary adjuncts of religion. If we *aim* at them, or sanction them in a system . . . they lose their nature, they degenerate into miserable affectation, they disgust man and are an abomination to God."[2] But whatever the outward manifestations might be, Cox and Nathaniel Taylor and the New Light Presbyterians and Congregationalists were still followers of Jonathan Edwards, and seasons of revival were expected to occur at regular or irregular intervals. Between the beginning of the Great Awakening in 1741 and 1838, when James Pennington had just left Yale and Professor Fitch sat down to enumerate, it was possible to count "twenty distinct effusions of the Holy Spirit at Yale, most of them in the nineteenth century."[3] Seminarians, after all, spend three years of intense concentration on theological matters and the state of their spiritual life. A revival every two or three years, then, may have had as much to do with the cycles of seminary experience as with the otherwise unpredictable outbreak of spiritual fervor.

Nevertheless, the newly ordained clergy carried out with them an expectation of renewal, a "powerful work of grace," a "spiritual awakening."[4] There were many terms all seeking to describe a life-changing event in which the individual came to a new and deeper conviction of God's presence and power, and that power was demonstrated in a range of ways. There were individuals dedicating themselves to mission on the frontier or in remote continents, small groups gathered regularly in prayer, and larger groups intent on a variety of social reforms such as the Negro National Conventions, the Temperance Movement, the Anti Slavery Societies—and even the Colonization Society. The Connecticut General Association's *Annual Report*, however, wishes to make it clear that these revivals were carried out with appropriate New England restraint: "These scenes of religious awakening are without exception spoken of as having been marked by an entire absence of noise and extravagance, by deep and solemn thought and that profound engrossment of the understanding and the heart which furnishes reasonable assurance that the rational soul is wrestling with the awful power of the world to come."[5]

Whatever happened in Connecticut churches would not upset Samuel Cox or frighten the horses!

But times of renewal did take place. Joel Hawes, at the Center Church in Hartford, counted ten "awakenings" during the forty-six years of his ministry there[†] with a net gain of over five hundred members in the first fourteen years.[6] The reports of the local and statewide Congregational church associations often took note of evidences of special revival, though they also noted that these evidences were not universal but limited to some churches and certain places. Eighty towns in Connecticut experienced such revivals between 1820 and 1822.[7] A typical account of the General Association stated that "The churches . . . are reported generally as enjoying the outward elements of prosperity in a very satisfactory measure" but "[i]n one or two churches, seasons of special religious interest have been enjoyed . . . [W]e have to lament that no general or powerful outpouring of the Holy Spirit has been vouchsafed us."[8] Lacking a general outpouring, other methods were tried. In 1831 a systematic approach was developed in Hartford that required a four-day program with prayer meetings in the morning and preaching in the afternoon and evening. Smaller meetings were also held in the parish and "distressed souls" were visited by parish elders.[9] James Pennington sometimes walked past a church in the midst of such a revival and stopped in to listen. The Center Church, was not far off the direct route from his home to the Talcott Street Church, so if revival was going on, he would have noticed. He never sat down, because he would have been directed to "the Negro pew," but Pennington was always eager to learn, and from his post at the back, he could hear a variety of well-known preachers and learn something of their different ways of interpreting their faith and exhorting others to repentance and renewal.

There were several congregations in the Hartford area that experienced such seasons in the early period of James Pennington's time at the Talcott Street Church, and the annual reports indicate that "seasons of refreshing" had visited that congregation also and resulted in striking growth. The report for 1840 filed the following year showed 52 members, an increase of five over the previous year, but the report for 1841, Pennington's first full year in Hartford, shows 130 members, twice as many men and almost three times as many women as the year before.

In spite of the time required for school teaching and for all his non-parochial activities, his congregation had grown remarkably. The annual report for 1840

---

† In the first of these revivals, Hawes sent for help from Lyman Beecher, a senior colleague and enthusiastic revivalist. The messenger roused Beecher in the middle of the night and his wife awoke to find him half-dressed and saying, "Wife! Wife! revival, in Hartford and I am sent for!" (Mitchell, op. cit., p. 42).

had listed a total membership for the Talcott Street Church of forty-seven. In April of 1843 Pennington wrote to Joshua Leavitt that "My church has about trebled its number. We have had a very precious revival this past winter, which added about thirty to the church, we trust of such as shall be saved."[10]

Talcott Street, of course, was a congregation that had never had a duly installed, seminary-trained pastor. E. A. Tyler, who had served the parish in the previous year, had had notable success in other churches, but he was dividing his time between the church and his duties as editor of the Congregational Church's newspaper. James Pennington may also have been spending a good deal of his time on his writing and organizing, but evidently the congregation, which was, after all, much involved itself in his temperance and missionary work, was thriving in the new relationship. "Seasons of refreshing" may have made a difference, but surely a new, well-trained, and energetic pastor made a difference as well.

The standard Pennington set himself was reflected in a sermon he preached not long after his arrival in Hartford. Amos Beman, who had taught school in the Talcott Street building, was being installed as pastor of the Temple Street Congregational Church in New Haven in the fall of 1841, and Theodore Wright preached the sermon. William Johnson, the Church School Superintendent of Wright's congregation, was present and reported to the *Colored American* that it was "one of his happiest efforts." Wright's text was, "I am not ashamed of the gospel," and Johnson reported that "When he came to that part where the bleeding slave is to be the preacher's client, no quill is competent to give a description of his burning eloquence. It appeared to me that all might have raised on their feet. In breathless silence, every eye was upon him, as if to see how far in divine sublimity he was going before he stopped." Pennington, because of his connections to both the new pastor and congregation, was called on to give the charge to the congregation, and Johnson told his readers that Pennington "put in his scythe, and never stopped, crooked or turned, until he got through and came down from the pulpit. He walked into the domestic circle of the church just as if he was at home and told them, like a father, that they should never criticize their pastor for activities outside the church although they might make his pastoral calls less frequent"; these also were a part of his ministry. "He also told them how beautiful and delightful it was to dwell together in unity. He was very solemn and affectionate, as he most always is, but sharp as a two-edged sword."[11]

Pennington had learned about pastoral ministry from Theodore Wright and the faculty at Yale, and from his own experience at Shiloh and in Newtown. His own new congregation provided greater resources to work with in his ministry than he had had on Long Island. Unlike the Newtown congregation, composed largely of recently freed slaves, the Hartford congregation included men and even women with some education and leadership ability. When the first Convention of Colored People condemned the American Colonization Society, a gathering a month later at the Talcott Street Church echoed that condemnation in a resolution that expressed a readiness to "resist all the attempts of the Colonization Society to banish us from this our native land" and "transport us to the pestilential shores of Liberia."[12] The congregation was not yet officially organized and relied on visiting and short-term clergy for services, but there were lay leaders quite prepared to express themselves in a national forum. Henry Foster, a tailor, served as chairman of the meeting. Among the other members of the congregation were Augustus Washington, who had studied at Dartmouth and created a reputation for himself in the art of daguerreotype photography, Ann Plato, a writer and poet, and William Saunders, also a tailor, who had served on the executive committee of the Connecticut Anti Slavery Society and was one of the first African Americans in Connecticut to support Garrison's *Liberator*.[13] James Mars, a deacon of the church, had also published a book about his life and how he laid claim to being "the last slave sold in Connecticut."

The Hartford City Directory shows that by far the largest number of African Americans in the city were "laborers" (21 of 88 names listed), with tailors (5), "cordwainers" (shoe makers, 5), and waiters (3) the only other significant occupations. But many of these were chafing against the limitations imposed on them by the larger society and were as "upwardly mobile" as it was possible to be in their circumstances. Holdridge Primus, for example, was a laborer, but he and his wife Mehitable had a daughter, Rebecca, who became a teacher. She went south after the Civil War and founded the Primus Institute in Royal Oak, Maryland, with the support of Hartford's Freedmen's Aid Society, to help create one of the new educational structures needed where there had been little provided. Noteworthy also is the fact that thirty-two men from the congregation served with the 29th and 31st colored volunteer Infantry Regiments and were present at Appomattox Court House when Robert E. Lee surrendered to Ulysses S. Grant to bring the Civil War to an end.[14]

Talcott Street Church may have had able leaders, but it had none of the wealth that supported the Center Church and North Church. Pennington had not been told when he went there that the congregation had been subsidized annually by the American Home Missionary Society and that an annual report was expected. When they asked for the usual report in April of 1841, Pennington had to tell them that he was unaware of the relationship but would provide whatever information they needed. He told them that the last year had seen sixty "hopeful conversions," thirty added by profession of faith or letter of transfer, 105 in the Sabbath School, and one hundred who had taken the temperance pledge. The congregation had also contributed six dollars to the Amistad Committee and six dollars to support a congregation in Toronto, Canada. There were also 500 volumes in the Sunday School Library.[15] The report of the Home Missionary Society shows that it contributed to the support of a number of "feeble" churches in the state, including one hundred dollars annually to the "Congregation of Colored People" in Hartford. "Feeble" seems an unfortunate choice of words for a congregation whose members had so recently emerged from slavery and were still so limited in opportunity but who had, nonetheless, organized themselves into a congregation, built a church, and established a common school. Nor was the congregation simply receiving, however. The Home Missionary Society received an annual contribution from the congregation of twenty-five dollars in some years and fifty in others,[16] and contributions went off frequently in response to special appeals.

As the congregation was growing with Pennington's leadership, so also was the school. Indeed, the school was bursting at the seams. In March of 1862, Pennington published a report to the Committee and members of the "Colored Second School District, Hartford," listing an enrolment of 95 "children and youth" with an average daily attendance of 65. These students were being taught in a space less than three times the size of the average 21st-century American living room.[†] In that space, somehow, the children were divided into four principal groups according to their level of progress, and the youngest two classes were subdivided further between boys and girls. The youngest groups spent their time primarily in learning their letters and doing "easy sums" on slates. At the other end of the scale was the first class, composed of eighteen to twenty of the "best scholars of both sexes" who were learning the rules of grammar, practicing composition, and studying geography, especially that of the United States. In arithmetic, they worked out on the blackboard and their slates "the most difficult parts of Daboll's Arithmetic from Reduction onward."[17]

Pennington concerned himself not only with academic performance but also with "the morals of the school" and raising the level of self-respect. Toward this end, he created a jury trial system and brought offenders over seven years old before a jury of their peers for judgment. The result, in Pennington's opinion, was "happy." "Boys dread as well as men to come before a jury with law and testimony crying for vengeance. A year ago, fighting and swearing were fearfully prevalent in the school; and now there are only three or four boys who occasionally *forget themselves*."[18] "How faithfully I have discharged my duties," Pennington told his readers, "I have to rely upon you to say. I can

---

† The average American living room is said to be 16' × 16' or just over 250 square feet. The Talcott Street school had a room 36' × 22' or 792 square feet, including a 6' × 10' entrance space.

only add that I have taxed the last nerve of my body and the last faculty of my mind to give satisfaction."

Of equal importance in Pennington's report is the inadequacy of the facility and equipment. The rooms themselves are "anything but calculated for a school." Clearly the space was too small; not only that, but the only desks were nailed to the wall three feet high and two feet wide and quite beyond the reach of the smaller children. The seats, of various sizes and shapes, were obviously chairs that had been discarded by others. Pennington had already written in the *Colored American* about his unhappiness with the standard seating plan in which the students sat facing the wall instead of the teacher. With the desks nailed to the wall, there was little alternative. More difficult still was the lack of adequate lighting and ventilation. The space was a basement room divided into two sections. Kerosene lamps would have burned out the oxygen in the room and the windows were small and high up. By four o'clock of a winter afternoon "there is not enough light to read ordinary print." Pennington "hoped that an object so important to the health and advancement of your children will have your serious attention at an early day."[19] But the parents had little influence where decisions were made. They had asked for separate schools because their children were seldom admitted to the ordinary schools. Now the children had schools of their own but without adequate financial support, and the school committee, even if concerned, could not easily gain the resources needed to improve conditions.

Pennington did find allies, however, in the white community. Most notable in this respect was Seth Terry, a Hartford lawyer, a deacon for many years at the North Church and then for twenty years at the South Church, and someone who was always ready to come to the support of a good cause. Terry was one of the founders of the Hartford Sunday School Union, and was actively involved with the America Board of Foreign Missions,[20] the Hartford Charitable Society appeal, the Temperance Convention, the Union Prayer Meeting, the Hartford Orphan Asylum, the Beneficent Society, the American Asylum for the Deaf and Dumb, and the American Colonization Society.† So universally respected was he that he was cited as "one of the oldest and most respectable lawyers in Hartford" in a standard ad for a cure for rheumatism in the *Hartford Courant*.[21] Terry was a member of the Hartford Committee with oversight of the African schools and supported Pennington in the effort to persuade the city government to provide additional funding, but it took several more years to get that help.

Seth Terry was able to provide more immediate help in another area: James and Harriet Pennington's quest for adequate housing. After making do with

† He was treasurer of the Colonization Society in 1841, but was probably unaware of the stand taken against its work by James Pennington.

the equivalent of servant's quarters for the first two years, Terry found a way to obtain a good house for Pennington closer to the church. As a lawyer, he was handling the estate of someone who had recently died, and the estate included a house that had been rented to others. Terry was also handling financial matters for Noble Jones, a waiter at a Hartford hotel and a member of the Talcott Street Church. Jones, who was single and earning a good income between his wages and tips, had gone to Terry with the request that he invest Jones' money for him. Thus when Terry became aware of the Penningtons' need for housing, he was able to suggest that Jones might help his pastor buy the house. With those funds available and a house that could be purchased from a friendly lawyer instead of a prejudiced real estate dealer or owner, James and Harriet Pennington were able to move to 35 Village Street, a double frame house painted yellow and located a short few blocks from the church.[22] The other half of the double house could be rented out to help pay the mortgage.[†]

When spring came, Pennington traveled to New York City for the second-anniversary meeting of the American and Foreign Anti-Slavery Society. The leadership involved the usual names. Arthur Tappan presided, and Simeon Jocelyn, the corresponding secretary, read the annual report after an opening prayer by Theodore Wright. Lewis Tappan presented a series of resolutions that was passed without dissent, and reports were read from the *Amistad* Africans who had reached Sierra Leone. Efforts were being made to settle on a permanent location, and the missionaries had had no serious illness. There were reports that some of the Mendians "had rushed into their former licentious habits," but the missionaries were "full of hope" and pressing ahead. Other reports were read from missionaries in the West Indies and Sandwich Islands (Hawaii). James Pennington gave the major address on the occasion.[23]

Behind the scenes, however, the Union Missionary Society was moving or being moved away from the founding vision. That vision had been of a predominantly African American society devoted to African mission, but whites would be welcome—indeed, without their financial help it was hard to see how the new venture could survive. Lewis Tappan was not present at the initial meeting and at first demurred when asked to serve as a treasurer. He, also, knew the financial challenge involved and was far from convinced that the project could succeed. He was, nevertheless, named as one of two "Auditors" and, since the Amistad Committee, now the "Mendi Committee," already had a structure with Lewis Tappan as treasurer, it was agreed to merge

---

† On April 1, 1844, the ownership was adjusted by the transfer to Noble Jones of an additional quarter of the ownership. (Hartford Town Records, v. 69.) Elizabeth Bolles, who had been living in the building, continued to do so for another year and then was succeeded by William Mitchell, a waiter at the City Hotel.

the two committees and let Tappan serve as treasurer of both. The result was that critical decisions would be made in New York and that, while James W. C. Pennington was president of the organization, it was, increasingly, Lewis Tappan who controlled it. Appealing for support primarily to African American congregations, the finances of the new society were always precarious at best, and in September 1846 the Union Missionary Society Executive Committee acted to merge the organization with several other societies to form the American Missionary Association.† Pennington continued to be listed for a few years as a member of the Executive Committee, but Lewis Tappan was the treasurer and the guiding hand. Reports continued to be published regularly from the Mendi mission. New missionaries went out and many missionaries died, but the work continued. Now, however, there were reports also from the Sandwich Islands and Siam where missionaries opposed to slavery turned to the new society for support and from Jamaica and the American West.[24] The new society still refused to accept contributions from slaveholders and could boast of an integrated membership and board of directors at a time when that was rare. After the Civil War it was instrumental in founding eleven colleges for the freed slaves including Fisk University, Howard University, and Hampton Institute. It may not have been exactly what James Pennington had envisioned and it may not have found a continuing place for his talents, but its creation must be listed among his most important achievements.††

The Underground Railroad had probably brought fugitives to Pennington's door in Newtown. In Hartford his home was a major station. The summer of 1842, however, brought a somewhat different case to public attention in Hartford. A slave named Nancy had been brought to Hartford by a Georgian named Bullock to care for his small children. James Mars's wife did laundry for the Bullock family and Mars himself worked in a store owned by members of the Terry family. When two years had gone by, friends of Nancy's learned that the Bullocks were about to move back to Georgia and take Nancy with them. One of those friends came to James Mars and asked him to sign a petition for a writ of habeas corpus so that Bullock would have to come before a judge

---

† The other societies combined in the AMA were the Amistad Committee, the Western Evangelical Missionary Society, created in 1843 to work among Native Americans in the Northwest Territory, and the Committee for the West India Missions, which began work in Jamaica in 1837. All of these had it as a founding principle to refuse to receive "the known fruits of unrequited labor." *Liberty Standard*, November 5, 1846 (*BAP* 8264).

†† The AMA became increasingly associated with the Congregational Church, which, in 1957, merged with several churches to become the United Church of Christ. The AMA maintained its distinct identity until 1999, when a restructuring of the United Church of Christ folded it into its Justice and Witness Ministries division.

and explain why Nancy should be kept in slavery in a state where slavery had been abolished. Mars signed the petition and immediately, as he put it in his autobiography, "had a fair opportunity to see how strong a hold slavery had on the feelings of the people in Hartford. I was frowned upon; I was blamed; I was told that I had done wrong; the house where I lived would be pulled down; I should be mobbed; and all kinds of scarecrows were talked about, and this by men of wealth and standing." Mars, however, "kept on about my work, not much alarmed." When the five-member court assembled ten days later, there were two votes to send Nancy to Georgia and two to set her free. The chief judge, however, ruled that slavery was no longer tolerated in Connecticut and Nancy was free. The judge's ruling, Mars wrote, "made a change in the feelings of the people. I could pass along the streets in quiet."[25]

James Pennington went to Nantucket that summer, perhaps to preach in a local church, and on Sunday evening he went to the Friends Meeting House to hear a speech by Lucretia Mott, a Quaker well known at that point for her advocacy of the abolition movement, and was much impressed. The next day he wrote to the *Nantucket Inquirer* under the heading "God is no Respecter of Persons," to urge others to take the opportunity to hear her on Tuesday when she would speak again. Her language, he wrote, was "eloquent yet simple, glowing yet chaste—and uttered too in the sincerity of real affection; every word of it must have sunk deep into the spirit of everyone present—and I doubt not that the meeting was to all, whites as well as blacks, a season of copious refreshing from God. I know that I went away from it, for the time at least, a better man."[26] By contrast, a few weeks later the American Anti-Slavery Society held its meeting in Nantucket and a very different spirit prevailed. William Lloyd Garrison and Frederick Douglass were principal speakers, but so was Stephen Symonds Foster, one of the most extreme and vitriolic of the abolitionist orators. It was apparently his oratory that triggered a series of violent events that the authorities failed to control. So many stones and rotten eggs were thrown in the windows while the mob shouted and jeered that meetings had to be adjourned and moved. One woman was hit in the face with a brickbat. Earlier that year there had been riots in Cincinnati over the issue of fraudulent bank notes. It was a violent era and mobs were quick to form for a variety of reasons.

Some of the most remarkable events in that violent summer occurred in Philadelphia in the aftermath of an attack by an Irish mob on African Americans celebrating the anniversary of the end of slavery in the West Indies. Before the violence ended, there were two attempts to set fire to a temperance headquarters, Moyamensing Hall, built to serve the black community. When the riots were over, the city convened a Grand Inquest that decided the Hall was dangerous to the surrounding property and ordered that it should be pulled down. James Pennington was outraged by the spectacle: "in the open light of heaven, encircled by the commissioners of Moyamensing District, with their ensigns of office, men with ladders, fire-hooks, crowbars, &c demolish a Temperance Hall, built by self-denying reformers and devoted to the special objects of temperance reform." Why was such a hall declared "dangerous to the community"? Pennington wanted his readers to know that "It is notorious that there were between four and five hundred groceries, non-descript taverns, etc., kept by Irish dealers in ardent spirits who have been practicing a most fiendlike system of complicated rum selling and extortion upon the colored people . . . The rumsellers found that if this Temperance Hall and its self-denying lecturers and agents floated, they must sink." If further evidence were needed of the danger of the building, the Inquest noted that there had been two attempts already to set it on fire. In "the present excited state of feelings," the Philadelphia officials decided it was better to remove the African American Temperance building than the Irish "grog shops."[27]

Later that year a more famous case drew attention in Boston. On October 4, 1842, a slave named George Latimer escaped from Norfolk, Virginia, with his wife and made his way by ship to Boston. His owner, James B. Gray, posted ads and Latimer was recognized. Gray then went to Boston and caused Latimer to be arrested without any legal process and placed in the Leverett Street jail, while he began legal procedures to return Latimer to Virginia. In Boston, however, unlike Hartford, there were mass demonstrations on Latimer's behalf and there were "gentlemen of property and standing" who took up the case and worked for Latimer's release. Finally, when a judge ruled that Latimer must be returned to his owner, arrangements were made instead to purchase him. So Latimer was set free, but the interest aroused by his case created a movement aimed at changing the laws that tolerated slavery. Sixty-five thousand petitioners called on the Massachusetts legislature to outlaw any official assistance to slave owners and to initiate a movement to amend the United States Constitution to remove the state of Massachusetts from any connection with slavery.[28]

James Pennington responded to these incidents with a simpler but more radical proposal: to recognize that the clauses of the Constitution allowing slavery are invalid. On November 17, while Latimer was still in jail, Pennington preached a Thanksgiving Day sermon that had little to do with the traditional Thanksgiving Day themes and everything to do with the legal basis of slavery. On moral and Biblical grounds, Pennington proclaimed the Constitutional clauses dealing with slavery to be a "covenant with hell" and told his audience (and readers, since the sermon was immediately published) that "covenants involving moral wrong are not obligatory on man." The "sermon" was in fact not a sermon in the usual sense at all, but rather a dry and didactic analysis of the argument, often made in the North and made by the judge in Latimer's case, that fugitive slave laws were based on the Constitution and must therefore be obeyed even in states where slavery was no longer legal. Pennington had learned at Yale to see God as the "moral governor of the universe," and he would now bring that theology to bear directly on the case at hand.

"Covenant agreements," said Pennington at the outset of his sermon, "do not necessarily make a thing right." Nathaniel Taylor's concern for "God's moral government" is central to Pennington's argument. If a thing is right, he reasons, it is so because of "our duty as subjects of God's moral government" and would be right and our duty whether there were a covenant or not and whether we were even willing to do it or not. On the other hand, if a covenant is morally wrong, no solemn covenant can make it right. "God neither wills or commands any thing that is wrong" and "No law, Covenant, or agreement, can legalize wrong." All this is laid out in the opening sentences in a clear and logical sequence with no rhetorical flourishes. Quoting the specific language of the Constitution,[†] Pennington sets out, like any good preacher, to demonstrate three points: 1) what is involved, 2) that it is a moral wrong, and 3) that it has no obligation in the sight of God.

Against the authority of the Constitution, Pennington sets the authority of the Declaration of Independence and the Bible. The Declaration of Independence had asserted that "all men are endowed by their Creator with . . . life, liberty, and the pursuit of happiness." That, in turn, is rooted in a universal truth: It "has its foundation in the nature of God, of man, and also of things." Here it is worth noticing that Pennington uses as an illustration the example of "a man from the state of Maryland" whom we would assume to be free since we see that he is a man and we have agreed that all men are born free. But now comes another man from Maryland to claim the first man as property. None of Pennington's listeners knew that the first man was their preacher and that the second man was still looking for him. Preachers often use stories from their own lives as illustrations, and the fact that it's a first-hand account adds interest. Pennington was not yet free, however; not free under the law and, therefore, free to give his story the added interest of stating it as his personal experience.

So the issue is the right of one man to claim another as property and this, said Pennington, "cannot be done! A thief may successfully carry off another man's property, but that does not ESTABLISH his right." But that is what the Northern states have covenanted to do "and it is *wrong*, morally wrong."

---

† No person held to service or labor in one state, under the laws thereof, escaping into another, shall, in consequence of any law or regulation therein, be discharged from such service or labor, but shall be delivered up on claim of the party to whom such service or labor may be due. *United States Constitution*, Article IV, Section 2.

It is wrong and therefore it is not binding. This clause of the Constitution is a dead letter. The framers of the Constitution had no right to require an immoral action. Pennington points out that the Declaration of Independence is, in effect, a statement that actions of the British king and legislature could not compel American obedience to and appealed, as he is doing, to a universal moral law and "the Supreme Judge of the world."

The first of the three points was not divided. The second had four subsections. The third section, with nine subsections, would have rejoiced Professor Fitch's heart. But finally the preacher comes to the fore. He has used language from the prophet Isaiah to call this section of the Constitution "a covenant with death and an arrangement with hell." Now he cites "the bleeding hearts and the manacled limbs; the nakedness, the starvation, the darkness of mind, the premature death, and all the LOSS OF THE IMMORTAL SOUL."

The sermon ends with a reference to George Latimer "shut up in Boston jail . . . without the benefit of the ministry! Yes, mark it,—while we are giving thanks, this man is denied the common humanity extended even to criminals!"

But Pennington's sense of humor breaks through even here: "But where is this scene? In Virginia? No! But in Massachusetts!—Oh! speak that lowly; don't let Charles Dickens hear that, lest he write another volume of 'Notes on America.'"

With that, he ends: The Constitution "authorizes these things to be done in sight of Bunker Hill Monument. Shades of Warren and Putnam, revive, and shed us another breath of your immortal fire, to purge the shrine of freedom!

"God of Liberty, save us from this clause, and thanks shall be thine forever! Amen."[29]

It wasn't really a sermon and it wasn't at all about Thanksgiving. It was a careful, reasoned statement of a basis for passive resistance to the evil of slavery. Something that is legal, Pennington argued, may nevertheless not be moral, and moral is what matters. There had been denunciations of slavery before, but nothing quite like what this speech provides. It was printed (with footnotes and an update on the Latimer case) and widely distributed. William Lloyd Garrison almost immediately added Pennington's basic text to his masthead: "A covenant with death and an agreement with hell." But unlike Garrison's diatribes, Pennington's speech was a reasoned appeal to reasonable people. He did not denounce the Constitution as such; on the contrary, he called himself a constitutionalist who was only concerned to point out a defect in it. There is no suggestion of a path forward, but if a law has no power to bind, there must be consequences. It would be still a dozen years before Pennington himself would act on the basis of his reasoning, but when the crisis came, he had already left himself no alternative except to resist an immoral law.

CHAPTER TWELVE

England

Hartford might have been considered a distant and "provincial" city by a New Yorker, but when James W. C. Pennington moved to that city, it gave him a prominence in national and even international affairs he had not had before. His call for the creation of a missionary society and his selection to lead it was probably the primary factor that led the Connecticut Anti-Slavery Society to choose him as a delegate to the Second World Anti-Slavery Convention to be held in London in June 1843. Large meetings in Troy and Hartford endorsed the choice, and so did the Union Missionary Society. The American Peace Society took advantage of the opportunity to add Pennington to its twenty-six-member delegation to a General Peace Convention to be held in London just after the Anti-Slavery Convention.† "Four commissions!" Pennington wrote to a friend. "Who is sufficient for these things? Pray for me. Ask my dear people to remember me daily with earnestness at the throne of grace."[1]

None of these endorsements carried any weight with the railroad that relegated him to the baggage car on his way to New York. He described it as "a little dirty dark carriage."[2] The ship from New York treated him better, allowing him to experience equal treatment in transportation for perhaps the first time in his life. Pennington had written to Joshua Leavitt, editor of *The Emancipator* and co-founder of the New York City Anti-Slavery Society, expressing the hope that they could travel to England together, and Leavitt had published Pennington's note and his cordial response in his paper. Leavitt, who had been chosen as a delegate by the Massachusetts Anti-Slavery Society, told his readers that he would be "extremely happy in the company of so worthy and able a minister of the gospel," but nevertheless he embarked from Boston for Liverpool on the steamship *Hibernia*,[3] and so was not on the same ship as Pennington, who left from New York on May 10 on the packet ship *Montreal*

† There were 292 delegates from Great Britain and six from the continent of Europe.

with three other colleagues: William Johnson of the New York Vigilance Committee and two clergy, H. H. Kellogg of Illinois and Jonathan Blanchard of Ohio. On two Sundays he was even able to conduct services for the other passengers.[4] Following the Gulf Stream to combat a "brisk headwind," they reached London on schedule three weeks later.[†] Pennington reported that the trip was uneventful and the company good.[5] [††]

Arriving in London on the third of June, Pennington found "comfortable lodging" in a boarding house and went to visit the Rev. John Morison of Trevor Chapel, Chelsea, with a letter of introduction from Samuel Cox. Morison, a Scotsman in his early fifties "known for his bold and fervid utterances on the platform . . . and support for the abolition of slavery in the USA,"[6] wanted to know what position the American clergy took in relation to slavery. What excuse do they have, he asked, "for not bearing a decided testimony against these sins?" Some say, Pennington responded, that it is "a political question. Because it is supported by the laws of the land, we may not touch it." Yes, said Morison, "but any question may become a political one. The powers that be might make a law that we should not preach the gospel, and so the question of preaching would be a political offense. But would we obey that law rather than God?" It was a neat point, and Pennington would use it himself as soon as he returned to America.

"Are you engaged for tomorrow evening at 6 o'clock?" Morison asked.

"I am not."

"Will you preach for my people?"

"I will, Providence permitting."[7]

But Pennington had no engagement for the morning either, and so he went to Surrey Chapel, an independent Methodist and Congregational church established fifty years earlier in Blackfriars Road, Southwark, London, when the site was still surrounded by open fields. By 1843, the building had been surrounded by a vast industrial sprawl, but it remained an influential center for various activities. The non-denominational governing board of the enormous, round building[†††] with a seating capacity of some three thousand made it available for musical events, and a number of charities, associations, and societies

---

† In 1838, a steamship called the *Sirius* made the journey across the Atlantic in 19 days, about the same time a sailing ship would have taken. Most travelers in 1843 still relied on wind and sail.

†† Fladeland, Betty, *Men and brothers; Anglo-American Antislavery Cooperation.* Urbana: University of Illinois Press, 1972, p. 285, says that Pennington was forced to travel in steerage, but Pennington makes no mention of it and Fladeland cites no source.

††† The first pastor said the building was round so there would be no corners for the devil to hide in. It was also a more practical design for preaching since it allowed more seating close to the pulpit.

also used it, some on a regular basis. William Wilberforce, the leading voice in Parliament for abolishing slavery and the slave trade, and his friends had made Surrey Hall their central London base, and a number of anti-slavery meetings had been held there. The pastor in 1843 was James Sherman, and Pennington had read a book of his and wanted to hear him preach. June 4 that year was the day of Pentecost (known in England at that time as Whitsunday), so the chapel was holding a communion service and, though there had been no previous contact, Pennington found himself called on to assist the pastor in distributing communion to the church members. This was a new experience. Never before had James Pennington been asked to assist or preach in a predominantly white congregation.

That evening, he had his second such experience when he preached as requested at the Trevor Chapel. The next day, he returned to Surrey Chapel to speak to a congregational meeting and lay out for them the reality of church life in America. "In America," he told them, "if I were disposed to do so, I could go either to the Roman Catholic or Socinian [Unitarian] places of worship, and be kindly received; but I could not go either to the Episcopalian [sic], Presbyterian, Methodist, Congregational, or Baptist churches, without being reminded that I was a colored man, and therefore not permitted to enjoy the privilege of worshiping God with them as I have done with you."[8]

Pennington was invited to come again to Surrey Chapel the following Sunday, the day before the Convention was scheduled to open, and preach the sermon, which he did, choosing as his text the words "Behold, I stand at the door, and knock."[†]

The First World Anti-Slavery Convention had been held in London in 1840. The British abolitionists had fought and won their own long struggle for abolition by bringing slavery to an end throughout the empire on August 1, 1838. That being done, they looked around for new fields to conquer and discovered that slavery still existed in Brazil and Cuba and other places as well, but most especially in the United States of America. Although these countries were beyond the boundaries of the worldwide empire the British were creating, the thought of correcting others is even more appealing than correcting one's own faults, so it was agreed that the whole world should now be guided by the British example and that an international conference should be called to begin this larger crusade. New societies were formed to promote the campaign, but the English were as divided as the Americans on the proper approach to take, and shortly they also divided in the same way. The more conservative organization was the British and Foreign Anti-Slavery Society, formed in 1839 and based in London. Lewis Tappan and his associates had

† Revelation 3:20

chosen the parallel title the American and Foreign Anti-Slavery Society to indicate their alignment with the British society. Other, more radical groups, were better represented in Scotland and Ireland.[9] This division was only one example of the many ways in which the British and American abolition efforts reflected and influenced each other.

The "British connection," formally dissolved though it may have been by the events of 1776 and the following years, remained a critical component of American life and thought. In terms of social reform, it was often British groups that led the way and even supported American groups financially. Wendell Phillips, perhaps the most persuasive of the abolitionist orators, said, "British Christians are the sheet anchor of our cause."[10] "We rely much, very much, under God upon the rebuke of Great Britain for the destruction of slavery among us," wrote Henry Stanton to the British Society.[11] And the British were delighted to rebuke the rebellious Americans and to listen to visitors tell them about the failures of American society. Most of the Americans involved in the fight against slavery made at least one journey across the Atlantic in the two decades before the Civil War,[12] and many of their British opposite numbers traveled to America to study the situation for themselves and confer with American abolitionists about ways and means. Often, as Garrison and several black abolitionists had done, they went specifically to raise money. American abolitionists also copied techniques that the English anti-slavery campaign had invented, like consumer boycotts, investigative reporting, and mass mailings. These had not been used before to accomplish a social purpose, but they were quickly copied by Americans and are still used to promote a variety of causes.[13]

England and the United States had acted in concert to abolish the slave trade,[†] though the British were far more diligent about enforcing it. The British, of course, had the world's most powerful navy, and they were quite willing to employ it to see that the trade was stamped out. A naval watch was created off the west coast of Africa to search for slavers, apprehend them, and free their prisoners. Treaties were also established with Holland, Denmark, and Spain that allowed for the search of suspect vessels, whatever flag they were flying. The American navy was much smaller and much less diligent as well. American shipyards, it was well known, were still building ships for the trade. Some of these were sold to nationals of other countries, but some were still operated by Americans with papers and even token crews from other countries for display in the event that they were stopped. The result of British efforts to suppress the trade was, of course, to make slaves more valuable and the slave

† Great Britain abolished the trade as of May 1, 1807, and the United States as of January 1, 1808.

trade more profitable. So the trade continued. It was worth the risk of losing an occasional ship for the money that could be made from those that came through. When slavery also was finally outlawed in British possessions, that, too, had international consequences. If cotton and sugar could be produced more cheaply by slaves, those who relied on free labor were at a disadvantage. Clearly the effort to eliminate slavery required the international coordination of plans and programs.

When the First World Anti-Slavery Convention assembled in London's Exeter Hall, a significant delegation of Americans was on hand, but a difficulty arose when it was noticed that many of them were women. Women had been active in the British anti-slavery crusade, as in America, but had usually formed their own societies. They had not taken leadership positions in the men's organizations. The London organizers had heard about the difficulties caused by the presence of William Lloyd Garrison's feminine supporters at the American Anti-Slavery Convention only a few weeks earlier and therefore had made it clear that the delegates to their Convention "do consist exclusively of Men."[14] But the Garrisonians had won the fight for women's right to participate fully in the American Anti-Slavery Society and saw no reason to despair of winning the same battle in London. Lucretia Mott, Abby Kelley, Elizabeth Cady Stanton, and others were therefore certified as delegates by the American Anti-Slavery Society and presented their credentials, with the result that the Convention was thrown into a turmoil and spent its whole first day debating whether, in fact, it would be appropriate to seat the ladies. When the majority agreed that it was not appropriate, the ladies removed themselves to the balcony, where they remained as a very visible presence and were joined from time to time by such English sympathizers as Lady Byron and the novelist Amelia Opie. When William Lloyd Garrison arrived late and was told what had happened, he and several other male delegates declined to take places on the main floor and joined the ladies in dramatic protest in the balcony.[†]

When a second convention was called for 1843, Garrison's name was not on the invitation list, nor were the names of any women. The British and Foreign Anti-Slavery Society extended its invitation to its namesake, the Tappan-dominated American and Foreign Anti-Slavery Society, created in 1841, and the various state chapters affiliated with it. Lewis Tappan himself decided to go to England to represent the New York Society. The Connecticut Anti-Slavery Society had been created in 1838, significantly later than the societies in Massachusetts, New York, and Ohio, and as a result of the events

† Although Garrison joined the ladies in the balcony, when his traveling companion on the ship to England, Charles Lenox Remond, was forced to go steerage, Garrison did not join him. (Fladeland, op. cit., p. 263.)

surrounding the *Amistad* affair. Prominent among the Connecticut founders were citizens of Farmington who were providing housing for the Mendis and had a long history of involvement in the Underground Railroad. Having become acquainted with James Pennington in the course of the *Amistad* affair, it seemed to them that he was the obvious choice to represent them in England. African Americans were not well represented in the delegations that appeared in England for either of the World Conventions. Robert Douglass of Philadelphia and Charles Remond of New York attended in 1840, and James W. C. Pennington, the single Connecticut representative, was one of a very few such delegates in 1843.

The Second World Anti-Slavery Convention, like the First, was held in Exeter Hall. Like Surrey Chapel in size, though much newer having been finished in 1831, it was a building able to accommodate some three thousand people, and it also was frequently used for religious and philanthropic meetings. It had become the usual meeting place for the Anti-Slavery Society; indeed, the name "Exeter Hall" had became a synonym for the anti-slavery movement.[15]

Although it was billed as a "world" convention, the 1843 gathering was so primarily because of its concern for the abolition of slavery throughout the world. In his opening address, read for him by Joseph Sturge since he had recognized at the last moment and "with tears" that his health was too frail to enable him to be physically present, Thomas Clarkson, the revered founder of Britain's abolition movement, reviewed the progress of the cause in the Empire and far beyond. Russia, Brazil, Denmark, and Tunisia, among others, were recognized as having made progress in eliminating slavery. But for all this world-wide focus, the delegates were almost entirely from England, with a handful of Americans, a few representatives from Scotland and Ireland, and one from Haiti. And their attention was centered largely on slavery in the United States. Questionnaires had been sent out to provide background information, and individual delegates had been assigned topics on which to report. Answers to questions about the nature of slavery and the internal slave trade in the United States were submitted by the executive committee of the American and Foreign Anti-Slavery Society and published in a 480-page book to be circulated in Great Britain and other countries as well. Copies were also presented to colleges, schools, libraries, and other public institutions. William Jay was asked to report on legal issues, Theodore Weld and Gerrit Smith to report on religion, John Greenleaf Whittier on literature, and Joshua Leavitt on the relationship between free trade and abolition.[16]

The planning committee had asked James Pennington to report on the "Free People of Colour" in the United States, and that statement was submitted and accepted early in the Convention's proceedings. Although the full report was not published, it evidently spoke plainly about such matters as the "negro pew" that had long irritated Pennington, and he did take the floor on the third day to give an oral summary of his written report. He was very blunt in reporting white attitudes toward black Americans and seems to have set out deliberately to shock his audience by quoting what he called "a Jim Crow definition:

> "'—Do what you will,
> The nigger will be a nigger still.'"
> He added that "it was also said, 'Take a nigger, cut off his head, oil him, broil him, throw him into an oven, he will be a nigger still.'"
> These, he said, were "Americanisms."

He proceeded to provide statistical summaries of the situation in various American cities and to discuss the various relationships between African American congregations and the different churches, Episcopal, Congregational, Baptist, and Presbyterian. Here several clergy delegates interrupted to try to clarify the situation. If the connection is maintained, do white churches admit colored members to communion? Are they admitted to communion at the same time? Are the exceptions to this rule increasing? Pennington answered each question in a few words and then went on to tell the story of a distinguished African Methodist clergyman who had been assaulted while sitting in a railroad car and thrown out with no reason ever given. Here Joshua Leavitt interrupted to verify the story and the esteem in which the victim was held.

In making his report, Pennington was interrupted frequently by cries of "Hear!" and "Hear, hear."[†] It was not a completely negative picture that he presented. He cited recent court decisions, decisions of the higher courts especially, that had been moving in the direction of impartial justice for all without regard to color, and he noted that discriminatory laws were being repealed in the Northern states. He made a very direct and practical appeal to British citizens to be vocal and active in questioning Americans about these conditions whenever they traveled to the United States or when they welcomed American visitors. "Tell them," he said, "how they stand toward the world, and ask them what they are doing to abolish slavery." Recalling the Biblical story of the man who fell among thieves and was rescued by the Good Samaritan, he suggested that British travelers should go to America as Good Samaritans and use their influence with white Americans to make a difference for black citizens.

---

† African Americans in Baptist and Methodist churches were accustomed to punctuating a sermon with "Amen!" and "That's right" and similar phrases, but Congregationalists, black or white, were quieter. This may have been Pennington's first opportunity to speak to so responsive and affirming an audience.

Slavery in America, Pennington said, has been called a "domestic question" but it is, in fact, a question for all mankind: "As America has dared to make laws inconsistent with the rights of humanity, to abuse and degrade humanity, I feel warranted in appealing, and I do appeal, to the world for justice against such laws and wrongs to humanity. (Loud and long-continued cheers.)" Pennington concluded by saying that "the literature of the colored race had been spoken of" and he was therefore presenting to the Convention his *Text Book of the Origins and History of the Colored People* and his sermon on "covenants involving moral wrong." The Convention then appointed Pennington and a few others to make a report to the Convention on the best way to use the statement that had been submitted.[17]

The committee reported back that it accepted Pennington's summary of the achievements of the "free people of colour" in spite of the handicaps they faced and recommended that an address should be sent to the American churches "earnestly and affectionately entreating them to lay aside those unlovely and unchristian prejudices which have been so long entertained" and to "concede to their coloured brethren their equal, social, and religious rights, and to dwell together with them in harmony and love."[18] That report in turn was adopted by the Convention.

Joshua Leavitt's was one of the leading American voices at the Convention, and his focus was on American policy in Florida toward the Seminole tribe and on the possible annexation of Texas. Abolitionists saw that as an extension of the slave holders' power and believed that the British could help avert it by offering support to the Texas government in exchange for the abolition of slavery. "The annexation of Texas," he told the delegates, "is deemed by us to be the *articulum stantis vel cadentis*; it is that by which slavery is to stand or fall in our country." But the Convention was, as Pennington was, more interested in people than policy and offered only mild support for the abolitionists on the Texas issue.[19]

On Friday of the first week, Lewis Tappan spoke and told the Convention (what they had already heard from Pennington) "that if he were to take brother Pennington . . . into any of the churches of America, it would throw the congregation into a holy horror. (Hear, hear, laughter, and cries of shame.)" Tappan did not tell the Convention that his brother had, in fact, done almost exactly that on one occasion in the church they both attended, but that he had not repeated his mistake.

The Anti-Slavery Convention was followed immediately by the fourth annual meeting of the British and Foreign Anti-Slavery Society, also in Exeter Hall. A long address by George Howard Viscount Morpeth, who chaired the meeting, was the principal order of business, but Amos Phelps, Joshua Leavitt, and Lewis Tappan were among the Americans present who spoke to the assembly.† Tappan spoke at some length about the efforts being made to annex Texas, an independent republic at that point, and to extend slavery to that area. He had already taken advantage of his wealth and contacts to meet with the British foreign secretary, Lord Aberdeen, and to urge on him the importance of preventing the further spread of slavery into Texas.[20] At the Conference, he implored Great Britain to "step forward and use her moral influence in putting down slavery in Texas and throughout the world." The border states of Virginia, Maryland, and Kentucky, he told the delegates, would abolish slavery except for the hope of being able to raise slaves to sell to the Southern states and Texas. They are raised there, he told the delegates, "and then sent to the southern market, just as cattle is here sent to Smithfield. (Sensation)."

James Pennington then "rose, amid applause," to move a resolution on efforts being made to encourage the emigration of Africans to the West Indies and Indians to Mauritius. These programs he denounced as a "new form of slavery." Africa, he said, needed its people to develop its resources. But Pennington had been given permission to speak more broadly, and so he went on to speak of an approaching "world crisis" and, concerning himself again with people rather than policy, went on to develop an analogy between the human race and a human body, suggesting that the world was in crisis because not all members of the body had been given opportunity to develop equally. The African member of the body, for example, had been dismembered, causing "mutual disease, mutual agony, mutual trouble throughout the body."[21] "What is the remedy?" he asked. "It is direct, it is close, it is reasonable. Restore the dismembered limb. (Cheers.)" As for the "great crisis," he suggested that "the hand of Providence" had been placed on the car of human progress so that it could proceed no further until all passengers were in. Or it is like a ship, he went on to say, with a hundred passengers who are registered and have paid their fare. If only fifty are onboard, "shall the ship sail without the rest?"

Remarkable in this speech is the ease with which James Pennington, who fifteen years earlier was stumbling through the dark woods and swamps of Maryland with a price on his head, had made himself completely comfortable in addressing an English audience presided over by such a member of the nobility as George William Frederick Howard, 7th Earl of Carlisle KG PC and member of the Privy Councils of the United Kingdom and Ireland. This was different from speaking to a hypothetical audience in a Pennsylvania barn, but James Pennington continues as if it were the most natural thing in the world to say "I am persuaded that if the noble lord were commander of the ship, he would not weigh anchor till all were aboard. (Cheers.)"

† The published report lists only Lewis Tappan as an American among those at the meeting and then adds that "several gentlemen of colour were present."

This speech is also remarkable for the way in which Pennington grounds his political statements in his faith and, in so doing, avoids putting the noble lord on the spot. The noble lord and his colleagues in government are not the ultimate authorities. "I rejoice," he continued, "to know that God is the Commander of the ship, and that he says the anchor shall not be weighed, a sail shall not be hoisted, until all the passengers are embarked. (Cheers.) My race constitute the rejected passengers, and if the noble lord were among the fifty, he would protest against the sailing of the vessel until the remainder were aboard. (Cheers.) And on board they must go, or the ship cannot sail."

The speech ended in the sort of reconciling hope that would also mark the speeches of Martin Luther King Jr. more than a century later although Pennington's appeal, made to a largely evangelical audience, was more directly theological. "Though I have a country that has never done me justice, yet I must return to it and I shall not therefore recriminate. It has pleased God to make me black and you white, but let us remember that whatever be our complexion, we are all by nature labouring under the degradation of sin, and without the grace of God are black at heart. (Hear, hear.) I know of no difference between the depraved heart of a Briton, an American, or an African. There is no difference between its colour, its disposition, and its self-will. There is only one mode of emancipation from the slavery of sin, from the blackness of heart, and that is by the blood of the Son of God. (Hear, hear.) Whatever be our complexion, whatever our kindred and people, we need to be emancipated from sin, and to be cleansed from our pollution by the all-prevailing grace of God. I bless his name, that in Christ there is neither Jew nor Greek, Barbarian or Scythian, bond nor free, but all are one. (Long continued applause.)"[22] He had first seen that relationship between sin and slavery when he first heard the gospel in Brooklyn. The proper relationship between the need for freedom from sin and freedom for slaves would remain an issue among Christian abolitionists. Evangelicals like Tappan and Leavitt were prone to begin with the notion that if only slave holders were converted, slavery would disappear, then, after some years of effort and little direct result, they would move on to a more pragmatic and political approach. Others, however, remained convinced that only by converting the sinner could the sin of slavery be eliminated. Garrison rejected all political action and Tappan moved only reluctantly toward involvement in politics. It had seemed to him for years that to take political action was potentially to compromise one's ideals. If we were to form a third party, he wrote to Joshua Leavitt in 1845, "It would be thought, and in many instances justly, that we were not disinterested in advancing the cause of the slave and the free people of color, but were aiming after the distinctions and the emoluments of office." He thought it was obligatory to vote but saw no reason to believe that "separate political action is necessary, expedient or obligatory."† But Leavitt had become a supporter of direct political action and was a founder of the Abolition Party in 1840 (later the Liberty Party), which would nominate candidates for president and vice president of the United States.

James Pennington, on the other hand, without the right to vote, would agitate for the franchise but continue to center his work in the church.

As a minister of a non-episcopal church, Pennington also felt free to respond to a bishop who mused publicly about his feeling that somehow slavery would continue to exist to the end of the world. "If that be so," said Pennington, and "in the judgment of so great a theologian as your lordship it is to be so, it is high time we gave the white man a taste of it; and as the black man has had it in the former part of the world, perhaps it would be right to let the white man have it in the latter part."[23]

London in June of 1843 was host to a succession of conventions. After the World Conference on Slavery and the annual convention of the British and Foreign Anti-Slavery Society, the next order of business was the First General Peace Conference which took the last three days of the week. Here, as with the World Anti-Slavery Convention, Pennington was an official delegate and, for the third time that week, took the opportunity to make a major speech. His focus for a number of years had been on his ministry and his role in the abolition and temperance movements, but his early exposure to Quaker pacifism had left its mark and continued to shape his thinking as it had in his speech on immoral covenants. The speech was typically eloquent and colloquial by turns. "War never settled a principle," he told the delegates; "war never settled any question of right . . . conquests gained by the sword, never stayed settled." He told them that he had heard how a conference of Indian chiefs had urged that "there was no use in contending with Gen. Jackson, for there was no man like him. One chief said, 'I have *licked* him thirteen times, but he won't stay *licked.*' (Laughter.) So it was with war. War, as war, might conquer a people, but they would not stay conquered"; it was a failure as policy because it could not attain its objective. It was up to Christians, he said, to work to eliminate the "repulsive . . . unjust and pernicious spirit" that led to war. He went on to show the connection between war and slavery and concluded with "an eloquent appeal in support of the principles of peace."[24]

The beginning of the next week found Pennington with Lewis Tappan, Joshua Leavitt, and Amos Phelps at the White Conduit house in Finsbury, a famous cricket ground and garden just north of London, where there was a gathering to honor parliamentary supporters of universal suffrage and to raise

† Letter from Lewis Tappan to Joshua Leavitt in the *Pennsylvania Freeman*, December 18, 1845.

money for the universal suffrage campaign. Blacks in Britain had the same opportunity to vote as whites, but that was an extremely limited privilege. In 1843, less than 15% of the adult male population of Britain were able to vote, and that was a consequence of a reform act eleven years earlier when less than 10% of adult males had the franchise. Women were beginning to organize to demand equal rights, although it could be argued that "equal" was still far from complete. Thus the Finsbury meeting did not ask for equality but for "universal suffrage." Tea was served late in the afternoon to a select gathering of two hundred and fifty larger donors, then the tables were cleared and nearly five hundred more were admitted for sixpence each. Pennington, "received with tremendous cheering," told his audience that he came from America "whose liberty was trumpeted all over the world," but that since whites had a monopoly of the suffrage, he could sympathize with others who had no right to vote. It was the law of the Romans, Pennington said, "that every citizen should be heard in their assemblies," and "surely the people of England were not now more ignorant than the Romans." A monopoly of the suffrage, he went on, "was offensive to God and oppressive to man" and should be "swept from the face of the earth (loud cheers)."[25]

Two intense weeks of almost daily meetings, morning, afternoon, and evening, at four major events dealing with abolition, peace, and suffrage were followed by a few days without formal events, but on the first Monday of July, Pennington was back at the Surrey Chapel for a tea in his honor attended by some six hundred members of the congregation. After tea had been served, there was hymn singing and prayer before James Sherman, pastor of the Chapel, and Pennington both spoke, Pennington saying that he was embarrassed by their great kindness to him. Sherman then presented Pennington with a set of Bible commentaries "elegantly bound" on behalf of himself, the elders, and the members of the congregation. Sherman then read a letter to James William Charles Pennington signed by all the members of the Chapel congregation and begging him to accept the books "as a testimony of our sincere regard for your person and ministry." The lengthy letter deplored the circumstances of colored people in America and expressed "an utter inability to account for the anomalous circumstances that the minister who begat you in the Gospel . . . those who ordained you . . . and some also who occupy the most exalted and useful stations in America, who gave you letters of commendation to us . . . should nevertheless refuse to allow you to minister to their people." They went on to resolve unanimously that it had been "their peculiar privilege to receive from their brother, Mr. Pennington, at the sacramental feast, the emblems of the Redeemer's dying love and listen to his instructions as an ambassador of Jesus Christ." They "affectionately urge[d]" American pastors and churches to receive him, "remembering that believers of all nations and of all colors" are "fellow citizens with the saints and the household of God."

The gathering was, in effect, a sendoff for Pennington as he embarked on a circuit of cities and towns to the north and east which would take him into the beginning of the following month. Over the previous forty years, the anti-slavery forces in Great Britain had established a regular pattern for such journeys, sending various speakers out to raise money and gain support for their effort to persuade Parliament to abolish the slave trade and slavery. A few African Americans had already followed that well-trodden path, and Pennington had only to walk in their footsteps. With some eighty antislavery societies scattered across the British Isles, it would not be difficult to fill a month with speaking dates.

Pennington began his tour by moving northeast from London, toward East Anglia and what had traditionally been the heartland of English evangelicalism, the area from which many of the first New England settlers had come. Distances were not great even for those days, but there were glitches nonetheless. In mid-July Pennington was scheduled to speak in Ipswich, 80 miles from London, but for some reason arrived a day late. He did, however, manage to have a visit with Thomas Clarkson, the "grand old man" of English abolitionism, who lived near Ipswich.

Clarkson it was who had dismounted from his horse on his way to London to sit down by the side of the road and think through the matter of slavery and his obligations as one who had begun to understand its evil. He had graduated from St. John's College, Cambridge, in 1783 and remained in residence, planning to continue his studies and to be ordained in the Church of England. Learning of an essay contest on the slave trade, he entered it, wrote a carefully researched paper in Latin, and won the prize. He had been "wholly ignorant" of the subject when he began, but became so obsessed with it that he kept a candle burning at night so that he could get up and jot down thoughts as they came to him. Having won the prize, he could not move on to the next subject but found his thoughts coming back again and again to the horror of which he had learned. But then, while riding toward London, he asked a question that not all academics make after doing their research and writing a paper: "what should I do about it?" "A thought came into my mind," he wrote of the experience later, "that if the contents of the Essay were true, it was time some person should see these calamities to their end."[26] He tried to rid his mind of the subject, but the question still came back: "Are these things true?" The answer was immediate: "They are." The consequence was inescapable: "Then surely some person should interfere."[27] Clarkson was twenty-five years old at the time and he would spend the rest of his eighty-six years "interfering." Working closely with William Wilberforce as the Parliamentary leader, he led the effort that resulted in the end of the slave trade in 1807 and of slavery, after almost forty years, in 1833.[†] Eighty-three years old and worn down by his long years of toil in the abolition cause, Clarkson had been too feeble to attend the conference in June. Even in 1840, although he was the principal speaker at the First Anti-Slavery Convention, delegates were asked not to cheer or applaud him for fear of tiring him and they had stood in silent tribute when he entered and when he left. He was not, however, too tired to receive Pennington at Playford Hall, his country estate near Ipswich, and Pennington always counted it as the high point of his trip.

From Norwich, Pennington's itinerary went west through the Midlands for almost 200 miles to Worcester, where he was a guest of the anti-slavery society, and then northward to Leeds, an important transportation center nearly 200 miles north of London. The Leeds Anti-Slavery Society had gathered at the end of July at the Queen-street Chapel to hear a report from their delegates to the London Convention. One delegate to London told of the hope that Texas might be admitted as a free state with beneficial results to slavery in the rest of the country, and another reported on a correspondence that had been going on between Methodists in England and Methodists in Virginia. The English Methodists had let it be known that they were unwilling to be in communion with any church that tolerated slavery, and the Virginians had responded first, that that was an unwarranted interference in their affairs, and second, that slavery was misrepresented and that slaves in Virginia were "fat, lively, happy, and cheerful." This the English Methodists had rejected as an obvious misrepresentation, since they had read of a number of runaway slaves. Intercommunion was not making good progress between the two Methodist bodies.

The Leeds *Mercury* reported that "The Rev. James William Charles Pennington then came forward and was received with loud applause." His speech on that occasion was probably typical of many he made during his visit. He explained the division between "free states" and "slave states" and described the limitations on the freedom black people had even in the "free" states. He spoke of the pursuit of fugitive slaves, of the lack of a vote in many of the Northern states, the constant discrimination encountered in travel, the lack of access to education, and of the existence of the "negro pew" in so many churches. All the great denominations, he said, had their hands "stained with human blood." There were many kind-hearted people, he explained, in the Northern states, but they also were enslaved by the slavery system. As he had done at the Convention, he also spoke optimistically of progress being made

---

† Slavery was technically abolished in 1833, but the emancipated slaves remained indentured until 1838.

and concluded with expressions of gratitude for the warm welcome he had received in Britain. He said he would tell his comrades at home that all the world was not like America. "Homo sum," he told the audience in a saying more familiar to English collegians than to fugitive slaves; "nil humanum alienum puto; I am a man; and I regard nothing as foreign to me relating to the family of man." A local reporter wrote of Pennington that everything about him was impressive.[28]

Six days later, Pennington had come halfway back to London to celebrate the first of August with the Birmingham Anti-Slavery society. The end of slavery throughout the British Empire was celebrated in Birmingham somewhat less elaborately than in Newark, New Jersey, but the Birmingham Society had played a leading part in the British abolition campaign and did want to celebrate their accomplishment. Joseph Sturge, a Quaker, described as "a great lumbering bear" of a man with a "hearty laugh and vigorous handshake," was there for the occasion. He was a leading figure in the Birmingham Society as well as in the national campaign. He had traveled several times to the West Indies and Jamaica and once to America to see slavery for himself. Sturge had been a founder of the British and Foreign Anti-Slavery Society which, in turn, had organized the first World Anti-Slavery Convention. Joshua Leavitt, who had been traveling separately since the meeting in Finsbury, was also present in Birmingham, and both he and Pennington addressed the crowd in the Ebenezer Chapel on Steelehouse Lane. Pennington told of his experience in attempting to gain an education, how he had to find teachers and pay them himself, and how he had been given permission to study at Yale as a favor but was not allowed to be counted as a regular student. He commented also on the exchange of letters between English and Virginia Methodists that he had heard of the night before in Leeds, and was indignant that the Virginians would attempt to persuade anyone that slaves could be happy in their condition. He told them also that he had heard only the night before of 500 ministers seceding from the Methodist Church for its unwillingness to take a clear stand on slavery, and that he considered this to be "glorious news" and evidence that more and more Christians were committing themselves to oppose slavery. "God has thrown the leaven of truth into the American conscience," he said, "and conscience will overthrow the whole system itself." Finally, he wanted them to know how important their influence was on events in the United States. Emancipation in the West Indies had made it clear to the southern slaveholder that he now stood alone, and slaves also knew what had happened and were encouraged by it. He told them of the numerous fugitives he had assisted and of his surprise at how well informed they were about such matters.

The next day, the Birmingham Peace Society held its first Annual Meeting in the Cannon Street Chapel with many of the same speakers as the previous night. Joseph Sturge was called to chair the meeting, and officers were elected for the coming year. James Pennington was called on and said many of the same things he had said in London, including his story about General Jackson and the Indian chiefs, but this time he went on to speak of how members of the same tribe in Africa had found themselves fighting each other simply because they happened to be in the territory of European nations at war with each other. He made a particular point of the relationship between war and slavery. Joshua Leavitt was there as well and spoke more practically of the will of the people which was, he maintained, for peace.

Pennington and Leavitt departed Birmingham by train the next morning to take ship from Liverpool on August 4th. This time they would travel by steamship, though separately again; Leavitt on the *Hibernia* and Pennington on the *Great Western*, a six-year-old steamship with side-wheel paddles and four masts for auxiliary sails. Pennington had barely stepped off English soil and onto the ship when he was reintroduced to American customs. He had paid the full first-class fare, but there was no stateroom for him and he would have to take his meals in the steward's pantry. In place of a proper berth, he was given "not even any tolerable protection from the weather . . . nothing but a sort of recess where merchandise had been tumbled in—affording not even a decent place for a beast."[29] Other travelers must have protested to the captain, because Pennington was reassigned to share a cabin with a slaveholder from Kentucky who, in turn, took himself off to sleep on a sofa. Pennington, in spite of the indignation of Southern passengers was also given a seat at the ship's dinner table.[30]

CHAPTER THIRTEEN

New Beginning in Hartford

T he *Great Western* arrived in Boston at 5 P.M. on August 22. James Pennington posted a note immediately to Lewis Tappan and then traveled on to New York, where he reported on his journey to a large congregation at the Broadway Tabernacle and visited Lewis Tappan in his office before returning home to Hartford. Back in Hartford, he received a letter from an irritated Lewis Tappan, who had embarrassed himself by telling friends that James W. C. Pennington had been awarded an honorary doctorate by an English university. Apparently the books presented to Pennington at Surrey Chapel had become, as they crossed the ocean, an honorary doctoral degree conferred by a non-existent "Surry University." As these rumors circulated, Tappan, assuming they were accurate, repeated them to friends and then, when the Hartford *Courant* carried a report of the honor, he made the same statement publicly. Whatever Pennington told him in his office was inadequate, and he wrote to demand a further explanation: "Will you gratify my interest, by informing me what actually took place on the subject in England? What college proposed conferring the degree, or what persons informed you so? What you wrote out respecting it? What authority the Hartford paper had for making the announcement? In what form you declined the proffer of the degree, and to whom?" Why was there such a concern over a simple misunderstanding? Tappan's letter makes evident his fear that "enemies" will be able to use the situation as evidence that black people are getting beyond themselves. If there was a degree, they will hold it up as evidence that Pennington is getting conceited, and if there was no degree but only a rumor, they will claim that Pennington, in his pride, had instigated the rumors. Tappan feared an "assault" by "enemies of the people of color—of abolition—and myself." The last of these was probably his first concern, and a valid one since he himself had circulated the erroneous report. As a white American of the nineteenth century, his own feelings may not have been that different from those of his "enemies."

Pennington wrote to the papers immediately to set the record straight. "[T]here is no College or University in England named 'surry' . . . I am not aware that the degree of D.D. has been conferred on me by any institution." It had, however, been spoken of by friends with "highly respectable literary connections," but "at my request it was dropped." Contributing to the error, he told the *Hartford Courant*, was the fact that he had found himself listed in English handbills and newspapers as "doctor"; on one occasion he had even been introduced to a public meeting by that title, but he had corrected the error whenever possible. Missing the point entirely, the *Courant* duly reported that "Mr. Pennington states that he declined the proffer of the degree of doctor of divinity conferred upon him by the Surry University."[†] There were, nonetheless, as Tappan had feared, those who chose to believe that Pennington had appropriated the title himself and that it was evidence of a certain lack of humility on his part. The fact that he wrote immediately to the newspapers to correct the error would indicate that the criticism was more indicative of the racial attitudes of others than of any justifiable concern about arrogance on his part.[1] Of course, corrections never catch up with errors; in March 1844, more than half a year later, an Ohio abolitionist newspaper said of Pennington that "while at a convention [in England], he had the degree of D.D. conferred on him."[2]

As James Pennington was nearing Boston on the last few days of his return voyage and looking forward to being home again, events were taking place in Buffalo that he would almost certainly have been involved in had his absence been a few weeks shorter. He had worked to rekindle the Convention movement, and in his absence a fire had blazed up. Henry Garnet's work in New York State, encouraging local gatherings as a basis for a larger convention, had borne fruit, but the result was probably not at all what James Pennington had in mind. Pennington and Garnet had become friends and talked together about what needed to be done but had gone about it in somewhat different ways. Pennington relied more on the written word to attract support and prepare the way, but Garnet depended more on the spoken word. Pennington organized a mission society to convert Africa, while Garnet organized local gatherings to change New York State law. It may be that their very different experiences of coming out of slavery to freedom had shaped their different styles, or perhaps

† The *Hartford Courant* had reprinted a report on August 25 from the *New Haven Morning Courant* stating that "Rev. Mr. Pennington . . . the colored clergyman of Hartford . . . received the degree of Doctor of Divinity from the Surry University." The paper also reported that he had been "admitted as a cabin passenger [on the Great Western], having received the same accommodations and treatment that the other gentlemen received from the worthy captain." My grandmother used to ask, "Is it true, or did you read it in the paper?"

it can be ascribed to the mystery of differing human behaviors that we speak of as "personality."

Pennington had come out of slavery to be accepted by Quaker families and introduced to a quietist approach, deeply committed to justice but equally committed to peaceful methods. Garnet, on the other hand, who was a few years younger than Pennington, had been brought out of slavery as a child when his family managed to escape and brought him to New York City. They were helped along the way by Quakers, but Henry was only nine and the Quaker teachings made little impact. In New York he entered the African Free School, where he studied with such future leaders as James McCune Smith and Alexander Crummell. Smith would go on to study medicine in Edinburgh and become a doctor, while Crummell overcame hierarchical resistance to become an Episcopal priest. Garnet, on the other hand, had been forced by financial pressures to go to sea as a cabin boy. While he was gone, a relative of his master tracked the family down and attempted to seize them. Garnet's father and mother escaped by jumping from an upper window, but his sister had been captured and barely escaped being taken back into slavery. When Garnet returned, he found their home abandoned, the furniture stolen or destroyed, his father in hiding, and his mother recuperating under the care of a neighbor. In a rage, Garnet spent some of his earnings on an enormous knife and charged wildly up and down Broadway, hoping the slave owners would try to capture him so that he could have his revenge. Friends calmed him and took him to a Quaker home on Long Island, where he was indentured for a time but so badly injured in an accident that he had to use a crutch for many years and finally to have one leg amputated. But Garnet had an inquiring mind and managed to be tutored for a while on Long Island and then to study again in New York, though in a school where black and white students were taught separately. For a while he studied in a Phoenix School created by Theodore Wright, Peter Williams, Jr., and Samuel Cornish, and then he went to New Hampshire where a new interracial academy had been created by abolitionists. After a good beginning, Garnet and some of the other students from New York made speeches at a July 4 meeting of the New Hampshire Anti-Slavery Society that so enraged the local farmers that they brought their oxen and hauled the academy building into a swamp and burned it. Expecting further trouble, Garnet got a shotgun and when a band of horsemen rode by one night and fired at the house where he was staying, Garnet, still angry, returned fire. Peace was restored, but Garnet and the other students were ordered to leave the state within two weeks. These harrowing attempts to gain an education led him at last to the peaceful setting of the Oneida Institute, newly established on an interracial basis in upstate New York. There Garnet, Crummell, Beman, and others were given a rigorous classical education and, although less successfully in Garnet's case, imbued at the same time with that mixture of nonviolence and resistance to evil that characterized William Lloyd Garrison's abolitionism. Under the influence of Theodore Wright, Garnet was ordained at last in the Presbyterian Church and called to a ministry in Troy, New York, centrally located near Albany, the state capital. There, as the basis for a renewal of the national convention movement, he set to work to build a network of local abolition societies and "committees of correspondence" throughout the state modeled after those that had moved the colonies toward the Revolutionary War.[3] So Garnet was working toward the same goals as Pennington, but with a more grassroots approach to developing the movement. By 1840, enough progress had been made to hold a state convention focusing attention on the right to vote. Unlike Connecticut, where African Americans had no right to vote—where, in fact, slavery was still legal—New York allowed them to vote if they owned a certain amount of property. Garnet and his colleagues therefore were seeking only to amend the law, and they won substantial support for their proposal in the New York State Assembly. Legislators they had spoken with had led them to expect success in their quest, so they were unpleasantly surprised when it turned out that they had misread the legislators and the measure had been defeated by a vote of forty-six to thirty-nine.[4]

Had his expectations been less high, Garnet might have taken defeat more easily. Instead, he used his next opportunity to express his anger. His efforts to recreate the Convention movement had moved on after the state convention to produce a National Convention of Colored Citizens that met in Buffalo in August of 1843. Garnet welcomed the delegates with a keynote speech that was long remembered. Where other speakers at this conference and the preceding ones had addressed themselves primarily to free African Americans and urged them to work on self-improvement, Garnet directed his address to the slaves and called on them to seek freedom by force of arms if necessary. He was ready, he told the delegates, for "war to the knife and knife to the hilt." "If you would be free in this generation," he said, "here is your only hope. However much you and all of us may desire it, there is not much hope of Redemption without the shedding of blood. If you must bleed, let it all come at once—rather die freemen, than live to be slaves. . . . Brethren, arise, arise. Strike for your lives and your liberties. Now is the day and the hour. . . . *Rather die freemen than live to be slaves.* Remember you are FOUR MILLIONS." The closing lines were equally alarming to the many cautious delegates: "Let your motto be RESISTANCE! RESISTANCE! RESISTANCE! No oppressed people have ever secured their freedom without resistance. What kind of resistance you had better make, you must decide by the circumstances that surround you and according to the suggestion of expedience. Brethren, adieu. Trust in the living God. And remember that you are four million."[5]

Garnet had said similar things before, but this was a national convention and delegates from border states worried that they could not return home in safety if such words were spread abroad as their sentiments. A motion was carried to refer the address to a committee for revision and Amos Beman, who had come from New Haven, worked with Frederick Douglass in an effort to tone down the published text. After much debate, a motion to endorse even the revised speech was defeated. But endorsed or not, the speech had been made and was widely reported. Garnet told the delegates he would publish it himself with the names of any who would sign it—and, several years later, he did.[6] The Convention adjourned on the nineteenth of August, three days before Pennington's ship reached Boston. He would quickly learn that in the division between the moral reformers and the political activists, the activists had now gained the larger share of attention. But his immediate task was to report on events in England and pick up the parish and school work that he had left to others for three months.

The Talcott Street congregation heard a full report within a week of their pastor's arrival in Boston and responded immediately by sending a lengthy letter to the Surrey congregation, expressing their appreciation for all that congregation had done for their pastor and for the letter of greeting and good will that he had brought with him from them. Their letter of response became an opportunity to affirm for the English congregation "the correctness of what you allege to have learned of the disabilities under which all people of African descent labor, whatever may be their character or education." They listed the lack of the elective franchise, "the laws and customs of business corporations, colleges, and above all, of churches. . . . when we come into the house of God, and find there the 'negro pew,' we are injured and wounded beyond measure." The frequency with which Pennington had been invited to preach in English pulpits was contrasted with the fact that in Connecticut he had been invited to preach only by the pastor of the congregation in Derby and the chaplain of the state penitentiary. Signing the letter with Pennington and many others were the deacons of the church, James Mars, Henry Foster, Henry Plato, James Isaac, and Harriet C. Pennington.[7] The last name is of special interest since women did not normally serve in that position at that time.

A full report was also made to a state Anti-Slavery Convention in Middletown, Connecticut, in mid-October with 170 delegates on hand, one third of them clergy and most of them white. The influence of his English experience was clearly evident as Pennington challenged the pattern of segregation that was taken for granted everywhere in America but not to be found in England. "I observed closely," he told the delegates, "and kept an 'eye out' always, and I discovered not the least sign of prejudice against color." He told them how he had preached in over a dozen churches, and preached from the pulpit that

Whitefield had used,[†] how he had "accepted many invitations to select parties among the middle classes," attended their Bible society meetings, traveled their railroads, and freely entered their coffee houses. In America, by contrast, "On every hand I meet a frown. I am hedged about by a cloud as black as Egyptian darkness, and by a breath as cold as death itself. . . . We bring no railing accusation, but we have a right to ask the reason why." He spoke of the way African American Christians had been helped to build small schoolhouses and churches—"or rather to shoulder the debt" for them—and how it seemed to him that often it was done "to get us out of the way." "I may as well speak out my convictions," he told them, and then he proceeded to say the things he had not said publicly before. It seemed to him, he told them, that he was "an excommunicated man . . . I have tried to make myself useful and agreeable as a Christian—have tried to avoid anything wrong. . . . For years, I have not been able to go into the pulpit—to the communion table, or to the mercy seat, but as a complainant." Now, at last, the pent-up anger began to pour out. "Talk of peace! There can be no peace till we are righted." And it was not a matter for someone else to deal with, he told them. It was their responsibility to act. He remembered his meeting with John Morison of Trevor Chapel and told the delegates how he was often asked in England, "What was the thing now wanting in the United States to accomplish the abolition of slavery? I answered, for ministers and churches to act. What excuse do they give [he was asked] for inaction? Some say it's a political question. And what do you say to that?" He gave them Morison's response: "Anything may be made a political question." English Christians had not let fear of political involvement deter them. An Englishman had told him that they felt "as much bound to labor for the slaves, as if they were at their own door." The question he left with his audience was why they had not acted to deal with injustice that was indeed at their door.[8] Garnet might be challenging the slaves to resist, but James Pennington had a more immediate way of life to challenge, and that was the pattern in the life of the church that made distinctions based on color. In England he had seen firsthand that such distinctions were not inevitable; now he would challenge them in America. The journey to Britain had shown James Pennington another way of life, a church and society in which black and white were treated equally, at least in such matters as transportation and access to the pulpit. He was more aware, as a result, of the daily discrimination he encountered in America and more ready to confront it and work for change.

---

† George Whitefield (December 16, 1714–September 30, 1770) was an itinerant minister who helped spread the Great Awakening in Great Britain and, especially, in England's North American colonies.

With Pennington's words ringing in their ears, the convention adjourned until morning and then became embroiled immediately in a debate over whether to substitute the term "emancipation" for "anti-slavery efforts" in the minutes of the previous day's proceedings. Mr. Crocker thought the latter term a "bug-bear" for many people. Mr. Burleigh, however, thought the English language was studded with "bug-bears" and eliminating them all would leave the language colorless. Mr. Colton sought to resolve the issue by adding the word "judicious" before the term "anti-slavery." After much parliamentary maneuvering, the minutes were adopted unamended with only two negative votes. That being resolved, the convention became involved in a seemingly endless and dispiriting debate over whether it was or was not appropriate to refuse fellowship to slave owners. If Pennington had hoped for a clear call to Connecticut Christians to take a united stand for justice, he would have been disappointed. Individual clergy, however, had heard his challenge and taken it to heart, with the result that Pennington began to be invited to preach from their pulpits and to exchange pulpits with him. Dr. Porter of Farmingdale exchanged pulpits with Pennington the following spring, and he was able to speak of at least a dozen such invitations and exchanges within the next year.[†]

Change took place also in the Hartford clergy association. Through the first two years that Pennington served in Hartford, there seems to have been no formal relationship between him and the other clergy or between his congregation and theirs. In 1843, however, the pattern of church life was reorganized. The Consociation was divided in two and a new Hartford Central Association was formed. The new grouping involved less distance to travel and made more frequent meeting possible. That new alignment and the memory of the Middletown meeting seem to have led the other clergy to bestir themselves at last to invite James Pennington to their meetings. In December of that year, at the first meeting of the new clergy group, two and a half years after his installation, Pennington was present and was officially received as a member by transfer from "an Association in New York."[9]

Once the relationship was established, Pennington was apparently treated like any other member. It had been the custom in the former two-day meetings for one of the clergy to preach a sermon. Clergy seldom have the opportunity to listen to someone else's preaching and to consider different styles and understandings, so they often take advantage of their

† Lewis Tappan wrote to Thomas Clarkson shortly afterwards and cited the exchange of pulpits involving James Pennington as one of a long list of "symptoms of advance" of the anti-slavery cause. (Tappan, L. To Thomas Clarkson, February 28–29, 1844. *BAP*, 3/482.)

meetings to learn from each other. The shorter meetings, however, made full-length sermons too time-consuming, so sermon outlines or "skeletons" were offered instead. "Skeletons to be presented," we read in the minutes, by "Brs. Pennington, Sprague, and Spring," at the next meeting.[10] For the uninitiated it might conjure up a surprising vision! At his first meeting, Pennington was assigned to present a "skeleton" for the benefit of his colleagues at their next gathering.

At their meetings, the clergy also discussed a variety of matters of interest to them if not, perhaps, to many others. In September 1844, for example, two of the members read dissertations on the subject, "Are election and foreordination in any sense grounded on foreknowledge?" That meeting was held in Farmington, only about ten miles west of Hartford, but a distance that might have been difficult for someone lacking a horse and carriage—or an offer of a ride from a neighboring cleric. Pennington was not present. At the next meeting, four of the clergy, including Pennington, were asked to write on the subject, "Is the happiness of the agent the motive to action in right conduct?" In August of 1846, the minutes record several typical assignments: "Brother Pennington was appointed to write on the topic, Ought a minister knowingly to unite in matrimony a believer with an unbeliever?" and "Br. Seward to write on the question, What is the import of the phrase 'the blood of Christ,' as used in the New Testament, the moderator to write on the subject, For what precisely is the atonement a substitute as respects those who finally perish?"[†] In September of the following year, on the other hand, the minutes report that "Br. Clark read a dissertation on the question, 'Is slaveholding in all circumstances incompatible with chh [church] membership? The question & dissertation were made the subject of free remarks by the brethren in their turns.'"[11] James Pennington was present and undoubtedly gave his colleagues the benefit of an informed opinion on the subject when his turn came. Unfortunately, the papers Pennington and others presented on these various subjects have not been preserved, but it is evident that the Hartford clergy were impartial in providing him with opportunities to display his theological abilities and not shy about discussing slavery in his presence.

Much is made in various studies of Pennington's life of the fact that the Central Hartford Clergy Association "twice elected James Pennington as moderator," as if this were evidence of the Association's openness and a recognition of Pennington's leadership. A fuller analysis leads to a rather different conclusion. On the first of these occasions, in January of 1845, there were only five clergy present, not including the moderator. Pennington was therefore chosen to serve as moderator pro tem; and after he had opened the

† Punctuation, etc., as in the original.

meeting with prayer, it was decided, for lack of a larger number, to adjourn. Moderator pro tem of an adjourned meeting is a modest honor at best. In fact, serving as moderator for such a gathering was not a significant honor, in any event, or evidence of the willingness of the white clergy to recognize Pennington as their leader. Then as now, the task of chairing such a gathering was and is commonly delegated to the more junior members, but Pennington was not so "honored" until 1847 when he had been serving in Hartford for seven years.[12] The coveted assignments, then as now, were to serve as representative of a local association at the higher levels of church structures, the annual and less frequent state and national conventions that provide for travel to larger cities and opportunity to meet with other distinguished leaders. Those assignments came to James Pennington only in connection with the abolition societies and not from his ecclesiastical colleagues.

But after his visit to England, Pennington's relationship with the larger church was changed, and the changed relationship went two ways. If Pennington was more willing to challenge his exclusion from other pulpits, he was also more willing to challenge those clergy who acquiesced in the institution of slavery by excluding them from his pulpit. Before the year was over, the Talcott Street congregation had resolved that no slaveholder would be allowed to receive communion in that church nor be admitted to the pulpit. Slavery, they said, was "contrary to the Bible, the purity of the Christian religion, and the clear rights of the enslaved" and the system in the United States was "as foul as ever existed in any country in any age," but "many professed ministers of the Gospel and disciples of the meek and lowly Jesus" are "continually visiting, mingling, preaching and communing among us at the North." Therefore, they resolved "that no Slaveholder shall be admitted to our pulpit or communion and fellowship." "We cannot fellowship with slaveholders as Christians in good and regular standing without being partakers in their guilt."[13] Obviously such an action would not affect many slaveholders—though it was not unknown for such individuals to visit African American congregations in the North—but it would send a message to other Congregational and Presbyterian churches particularly and have some impact on decisions made at higher levels. The Presbyterian church had been and would continue to be torn over the issue of fellowship with slave owners, with some contending that they should have no relationship with those guilty of such sin and others arguing that they could only influence them if they remained in communion. The Talcott Street Church had now cast its vote on the subject.

The Amistad affair had also introduced James Pennington to one man who was willing to work with him to challenge the customs of the Connecticut church. John Hooker was sixth in a direct line from Thomas Hooker, who had led the first settlement of the state, and, as the husband of Isabella

Beecher, he was also related to the various Beechers including Henry Ward Beecher and Harriet Beecher Stowe. The first American Hooker had been dissatisfied with the Massachusetts settlement and led his followers out to establish a colony at Hartford with a freer, more democratic way of life. John Hooker, only twenty-four years old when James Pennington came to Hartford, was equally ready to challenge the establishment and to listen to James Pennington's report on the contrast between American and English ways. A few years earlier, a black man had come into the church on a Sunday and Hooker invited him into his pew. He was told afterwards that he had "done more to break up the church than anything that had happened since it was established." Nevertheless, when Pennington began openly expressing his unhappiness with the segregated ways of Connecticut churches, it had been the pastor of Hooker's church who was among the first to invite Pennington to his congregation to preach, and Hooker reported that "we were all astonished at seeing the pulpit thus occupied."[14] Hooker was astonished but not unhappy. He would become a valuable ally to Pennington. And now a number of congregations were as astonished as the one in Farmington to see a black man in their pulpit.

Preaching was, of course, one way of making an impact. Pennington's simple presence in the pulpit sent a message to white Americans. But it was not a place, as Pennington understood it, for political statements, and the audience was limited. He had discovered early in his career that he could amplify his opinions by sending letters and articles to newspapers, the *Colored American* chief among them. The *Colored American*, however, had succumbed at the end of 1841 after a notable run of six years, and there was nothing to take its place. *The Union Missionary Herald*, although dedicated to foreign missions, had filled the void in some sense in 1842, but it also had run out of funds. White abolitionists had the *Liberator* and the *Emancipator* and the *Anti-Slavery Standard*, but there was no paper belonging to African Americans. Returning from England with new energy and new ideas, James Pennington decided that he would try to fill the void himself. Having met with Thomas Clarkson and come away overawed, as all who met him were, by the great man, he decided to call his paper *The Clarksonian* and wrote to Clarkson to ask for a letter to signify his support. Clarkson responded that he had little energy left, but he approved the project and expressed his support.

The first issue of *The Clarksonian*, in December 1843, however, featured a long letter to Thomas Clarkson from Pennington giving him a report on recent events in the United States. The Middletown Convention was first on the list. Pennington wrote that the purpose of the gathering was "to bring Christians on a common abolition platform, where they can work in peace like valiant men without being annoyed by various frivolous disputations such as woman questions &c, &c, &c." The Middletown gathering had been distracted by questions far more frivolous than that, but it was difficult for black abolitionists to take a broad view of their struggle and see it in a larger context that might include woman suffrage as well. Slaves were sold in the market, whipped, and beaten. Men like Garnet and Pennington had been there and experienced it, and it had made them single-minded. Pennington had obviously approved the ground-breaking selection of his wife to serve as a deacon, but that was not an equal priority for him. The abolition struggle was his central concern, and Pennington wanted Clarkson to know why Christians seemed to provide so little leadership. The root of the difficulty in finding common ground, he wrote, was that the "non-professors" had taken an early lead while the clergy and churches were divided as to committing themselves to the abolition cause, and now some of them had "scruples" about being rebuked by the "non-professors" for coming lately to the struggle. Garrison might be right, but his strident anti-church position made many of the clergy reluctant to be seen taking his side in the abolition struggle and thereby admitting that he had been right all along and they had been slow to see it.

A second issue to be resolved—the "Alpine point," according to Pennington—was the question of fellowship with slave owners. A resolution was adopted at Middletown saying that they would have no fellowship with slaveholders, but it was in the future tense. There were still many clergy who felt that there were "worthy exceptions" among slave owners, and Porter of Farmington had quoted the absent Joel Hawes of Hartford as saying "those who are good enough for Christ are good enough for me." Pennington found this strange language indeed from an evangelical pastor. "Theologically speaking," he asked, "who of us is good enough for Christ?" How, Pennington wanted to know, could a slaveholder show his faith except by his works and, in particular, by setting free his slaves?

He wrote also of the state of negotiations with Texas, which he thought the current president (John Tyler of Virginia, who became president on the death of William Henry Harrison but had no widespread support) might move forward since he had so little to lose.

Most interesting, however, is what Pennington says of himself and his changed approach since returning from England. "I have cast off my modesty as a moth-eaten garment," he told Clarkson, "and repented of it as a sin which I have been indulging in too much, far too much. I must speak and write freely for myself."[15]

The Clarksonian, unfortunately, failed to provide a platform for that writing. Published on a monthly basis, it drew contributions not only from Thomas Clarkson but also from Amos Beman and Henry Garnet, but it exhausted the resources available by the end of 1844 and Pennington was forced to merge his fledgling paper with another small anti-slavery sheet that also failed to survive for long.† Through the next year, Pennington wrote at least three times to Clarkson, addressing him as "venerable father," "My great and good friend," and "Most excellent Father of my cause." The letters reflected a close friendship between the two men; Pennington sending "kindest regards to Mrs Clarkson, your daughter and grandson," and Clarkson sending "best wishes for the health and prosperity of yourself and family."[16] Clarkson sent at least two more letters to Pennington as well as a general letter to American abolitionists. In February 1844, he lamented his failing health—"the powers of my mind becoming every day weaker and weaker"—and told Pennington that this was "the last letter, I fear, I shall ever be able to undertake."

But in this "last letter," Clarkson was determined to denounce slavery as "the greatest evil with which any country was ever cursed" and to point out how slavery demoralizes a society and destroys its moral sense so that its people "become unprincipled . . . driven to infidelity and. . . . make themselves despised by all the civilized world." He was concerned also for the impact of slavery on the free people of color and wanted them to know that the people of England "sympathize with them in their misfortunes" and consider prejudice against color as "most infamous, most unjust, most wicked." He said that because arguments of both religion and expediency had failed, he had resolved to try to shame Americans into acting. Pennington is welcome to print the letter in the *Clarksonian*, but Clarkson warns him that he may make enemies for himself and his paper by doing so.[17] Clarkson would, in fact, live on for two more years. In October 1845, he wrote to an American woman to say he could not write a letter for a fair she was planning because he was writing the story of the abolition of slavery in England after the abolition of the slave trade in 1807. Typically, having said his health was too fragile to take on a letter to the fair, he promises that he "will endeavor to steal a few moments at intervals" to work on it.[18] Before he died in September 1846, at the age of 86, he would write at least two more letters to Pennington, though only Pennington's responses have survived.

In September 1844, Pennington wrote optimistically to Clarkson agreeing with a recent statement of John Greenleaf Whittier, the Quaker poet, "that our cause never went on so rapidly." He cited the fact that few fugitive slaves are recaptured although "they run away in increasing numbers every day" and that the churches are "becoming deeply ashamed of their conduct and that "abolitionists are very rapidly increasing in influence." The plan to annex

† An editorial in another abolition newspaper (*BAP*, 7300/8046) speaks of a "7th number" of the Clarksonian, but no surviving copies have been located.

Texas, he wrote, had "completely failed" but would be decided in the next election, though British diplomatic influence would also be important. He noted also that charitable contributions were being directed more and more toward those organizations that took a clear stand against slavery such as the new Union Missionary Society. He was optimistic also about the growing circulation of the *Clarksonian* and the lectures he had been able to give in a number of places "to shame the whites and encourage my colored brethren." He reports also that he has been taking part in African American conventions every month, at which the purpose is "to find ways and means to improve." There had been five thousand at a temperance convention in Catskill, New York, in August, and a similar gathering will take place at Norwich, Connecticut, in September.

Constant traveling was also reflected in Pennington's last letter to Clarkson, written at the end of the year. He reported that he had just returned to Hartford after three weeks away, "as my custom is, every winter season," visiting "my colored brethren" in Albany, Troy, and Schenectady in New York, and Pittsfield, Lenox, and Springfield in Massachusetts. He had spent a week or more in Troy as a guest of Henry Garnet and his "amiable family,"† and attended a convention in Albany with Lewis Tappan, Joshua Leavitt, Gerrit Smith, and "other distinguished friends of the slave." He told Clarkson that the Massachusetts legislature had sent agents to Charleston, South Carolina, and New Orleans to test the constitutionality of laws under which colored seamen from Massachusetts had been arrested by appealing to the federal courts. "Popular violence," however, had forced the agent in Charleston to "quit his post." "Alas, alas, dear friend," Pennington wrote to Clarkson, "for my wicked and unreasonable countrymen!"[19]

Still more traveling was reflected in a letter written earlier to Joseph Sturge. In May of 1844, Pennington had gone to Philadelphia and found himself witnessing further unrest in the City of Brotherly Love. "We have had more serious and disgraceful riots at Philadelphia," he wrote; "I assure you it was one of the most melancholy scenes I ever witnessed in my life . . . To see men, women, and little children flying for fear of violence to their persons was painful." The violence was part of a series of riots in May and July of that year between a group calling itself the "Native American Party" or "nativists" and recent Irish immigrants. The Roman Catholic bishop had protested in November of the previous year against the daily reading of the King James Version of the Bible in the public schools and asked that Roman Catholic

---

† A discussion of this visit and the value of conversation and "mental communion" with other clergy was printed in the *Clarksonian* of December 14, 1844, and preserved in *Amos Beman's Scrapbook* (cf. Bibliography). Nothing is said about whether Harriet went with him on these journeys.

children be allowed to use the Douai version and to be excused from religious teaching. Anti-Roman Catholic groups spread word that the bishop was trying to remove the Bible from the schools, and when the Native American Party held a meeting in a mostly Irish section of the Kensington area of the city, a group of Irish attacked the platform the speakers were on and the nativists called on Americans to defend themselves from "the bloody hand of the Pope." Two churches, a rectory, a convent, and a school as well as several homes were burned down before soldiers arrived to put an end to the violence.

Once again, municipal authorities seemed puzzled as to how to deal with the trouble. The *Pennsylvania Freeman*'s editor wrung his hands in despair: "Philadelphia," he wrote, "is ruled by the mob; and it is *farcical* to pretend that civil law protects, in the *least* degree, the property or persons of our citizens. The police are powerless and the military about as inefficient. The mob *kill* whom they choose, *burn* what they choose, and *do* just as they choose, for there is no power to restrain or check them."[†]

More constructively, the Philadelphia *Public Ledger* editorialized that "In all our civil commotions, the authorities and peaceful citizens look on till the disorder threatens to demolish the whole social fabric. Nobody becomes alarmed until every body is in danger . . . In too many of the cases the rioters have been allowed to *fight it out*. All this is wrong. Prevention is better than cure . . . The first object of government should be to prevent a mob from assembling; the second, to intimidate it and disperse it immediately."[20] But the lesson was not quickly learned, and riots continued to be a regular feature of American city life. On July 11, Philadelphia's city council passed an ordinance to give the city a regiment of infantry and at least one full troop of horses to preserve the peace, but the remedy lay not so much in available manpower and weapons as in a willingness to use force early and in a government not somewhat disdainful of the "lower orders" or even supportive of one side or the other.

Pennington had left the city by train for Harrisburg on the evening of May 8th and could see the Roman Catholic Church burning and hear the bell fall from the tower. Although the violence this time was aimed at the Irish, less than two years earlier it had been aimed at African Americans, and Pennington found it interesting to compare the two episodes. A few days before he left, Pennington had been looking out the window and had seen a black man using his horse and wagon to rescue some of those who were threatened. Asking who this was, he was told that it was Peter Lewis, who, two years earlier, had been assailed by the mob himself and so beaten with clubs and brickbats that he was "taken up for dead." He had survived, however, and now had come to the

† *Pennsylvania Freeman*, May 9, 1844.

aid of white people in danger. Pennington noted to Sturge that the Irish had joined in the assault on the blacks but that the blacks had not been involved in the anti-Irish riots.

Because he owed so much to the Quakers himself, Pennington reported that he was "deeply pained for the reputation of Philadelphia as it will affect that of the Friends." "Why is it," he wondered, "that Philadelphia acts so? Is it the acting and her character? Who has formed that character?" He told Sturge that he had decided it was a "criminal deterioration" of the principles of Penn, Foxx, and Benezet.[21]

A very different aspect of James Pennington's activities that year is reflected in letters that reopened the earliest chapters of his life. When he stood in the plantation in Hagerstown resolving to make his escape, he wrote years later that there had been "two great difficulties that stood in the way." He had "a father and mother whom I dearly loved,—I had also six sisters and four brothers on the plantation." Pennington had not forgotten his family in his freedom; but when he attempted to communicate with them, his letter was intercepted and the family members sold away. But one day, as he was doing research on Southern slave laws in the Hartford office of the secretary of state, he came across a Maryland law in which his parents were specifically mentioned. Frisby Tilghman had sold them to Mississippi but later repurchased them and, since Maryland law forbade the importation of slaves, a special statute was needed to make an exception in their case. So his parents were back at Rockland. The news, Pennington wrote, "awakened my mind to great excitement."[22]

It was about this point, in 1844, that James Pennington went to John Hooker and told him what he had never told anyone, even his wife, for fear of exposing himself to danger and disturbing her with "disquieting fears." "Under the most solemn injunction of secrecy," he told Hooker that he was a fugitive slave and that he was never free of the fear that he might be captured and taken back into slavery, indeed the burden of "harassing apprehensions" had been growing with the South's constant attempts to strengthen and enforce the fugitive slave laws. "I felt this much relief," he wrote later, "Thank God there is one brother-man in hard old Connecticut that knows my troubles."[23] And Hooker was a man who might be able to help. The discovery that his parents were again on the Tilghman plantation raised the question whether it might be possible to purchase not only their freedom but his also. Hooker agreed to see what could be negotiated and wrote to Tilghman, giving no indication of Pennington's assumed name or location, and offering to purchase Nellie, Bazil, and James. Tilghman's response indicated that he had some knowledge of Pennington's whereabouts and that James was "an ungrateful servant," but the price of servants was high at the time and James was a first-rate blacksmith, worth at least a thousand dollars so, under the circumstances, he could not take less than five hundred dollars.[24] He made no mention of the parents. The sum was beyond what Pennington considered possible and, when further negotiations brought no progress, he decided to abandon the effort. He did, however, write two letters, one to his family and one to his former owner.

In his letter to Frisby Tilghman, Pennington chronicled the events that had led to his escape, reviewing his own conduct and taking opportunity to brag a bit about his skill as a blacksmith:

> It is important for me to say to you, that I have no consciousness of having done you any wrong. I called you master when I was with you from the mere force of circumstances; but I never regarded you as my master. The nature which God gave me did not allow me to believe that you had any more right to me than I had to you, and that was just none at all. And from an early age, I had intentions to free myself from your claim. I never consulted any one about it; I had no advisers or instigators; I kept my own counsel entirely concealed in my own bosom. I never meditated any evil to your person or property, but I regarded you as my oppressor, and I deemed it my duty to get out of your hands by peaceable means.
>
> I was always obedient to your commands. I laboured for you diligently at all times. I acted with fidelity in any matter [with] which you entrusted me. . . . During the time I served you in the capacity of blacksmith, your materials were used economically, your work was done expeditiously, and in the very best style, a style second to no smith in your neighbourhood. In short, sir, you well know that my habits from early life were advantageous to you. Drinking, gambling, fighting, &c., were not my habits. On Sabbaths, holidays, &c., I was frequently at your service, when not even your body-servant was at home.

But in return for this, Pennington wrote, he had suffered only abuse:

> You struck me with your walking-cane, called me insulting names, threatened me, swore at me, and became more and more wrathy in your conduct, and at the time I quitted your place, I had good reason to believe that you were meditating serious evil against me.

But Pennington's purpose in writing was not to seek revenge or simply to denounce Tilghman's conduct. Instead, his purpose was to point out to

Tilghman that even though the country was divided as to the existence of a Biblical warrant for slavery, there were many who believed that it was condemned. That being the case, Pennington suggested to Tilghman that it would not be wise to take the chance of approaching God with the blood of others on his hands. Pennington was writing, he said, "to convince you of my perfect good will towards you" by reminding Tilghman "in the most kind and respectful terms" of his "coming destiny."[25] Using the terms that he had learned from Nathaniel Taylor at Yale, Pennington told his former master that all human beings "are in a state of probation; our great business is to serve God under His righteous moral government. Master and slave are the subjects of that government, bound by its immutable requirements, and liable to its sanctions in the next world, though enjoying its forbearance in this."[26] That being the case, he should remember that he is "soon to meet those whom you have held, and do hold in slavery, at the awful bar of the impartial Judge of all who doeth right. Then what will become of your own doubtful claims? What will be done with those doubts that agitated your mind years ago; will you answer for threatening, swearing, and using the cowhide among your slaves?"

Pennington listed by name those whom Tilghman would meet hereafter: "Uncle James True, Charles Cooper, Aunt Jenny, and the native Africans; Jeremiah, London, and Donmore, have already gone a-head, and only wait your arrival."[27] And Pennington will be there also. "Sir, I shall meet you there. . . . I assure you that the thought of meeting you in eternity, and before the dread tribunal of God, with a complaint in my mouth against you, is to me of most weighty and solemn character." Pennington signs the letter "with kind regards . . . yours respectfully, J. W. C. Pennington."[28] Nowhere, oddly, does he identify himself by his slave name or explain his new name to Frisby Tilghman. In fact, although he signs his full name, he addresses the letter to "Colonel F——T——, of H——, Washington County, Md." as if it were Tilghman, not Pennington, who needed concealment. Of course, anyone interested could easily find out who "Colonel F——T——, of H——" really was. But this letter was first published as an appendix to *The Fugitive Blacksmith* and no one is identified in that publication except Pennington, not even William Wright, the Quaker who first opened his door to a runaway slave. What makes some sense of all this is the fact that *The Fugitive Blacksmith* was published in England when James Pennington had gone there specifically to escape his vulnerability to the Fugitive Slave Act until he could buy his legal freedom. Since that involved specific negotiations with Tilghman, it no longer mattered whether Pennington's new name was revealed, but to use Tilghman's name might have annoyed him and slowed the process.

There was a second letter written by James Pennington in 1844 because of the unnamed event that "awakened my mind to great excitement," and this one was to his family, whose loss he referred to as that of "the sun and moon and eleven stars from my social sky."† He wrote to his family for the same reason that he had written to Frisby Tilghman: a concern for their eternal destiny. He told his parents that they "cannot have much longer to live in this troublesome and oppressive world," nor can they "bear the yoke much longer." He wanted them to know of the Gospel, which offers "the prospect of a different destiny from what you have been called to endure in this world." He cited the words of the Book of Job: "There the wicked cease from troubling, and the weary are at rest . . . and the servant is free from his master."†† Whenever he baptized a child, Pennington told his family members, he had wished that they were among the number, and whenever he preached the Gospel, he had wished that they could have been in the congregation. He told them not to believe those who twist the Gospel to make it seem supportive of slavery; rightly understood, it is not. He also thanked his parents for "those mild and gentle traits of character which you took such care to enforce upon me in my youthful days . . . [A]t the age of thirty-seven, I find them as valuable as any lessons I have learned."[29] He said nothing to them of the possibility that they might still gain their freedom, but these were public letters and no place to write of escape plans; if he was able to be in contact with his family at all, he would have been able to offer them some possibility of escape. He had escaped himself and hundreds of others did so every year; surely it was not impossible for his family members as well. But if this letter is evidence of some sort of plan being made to rescue his family, it was a long time before it was carried out.

† Of course, Pennington had ten brothers and sisters, not eleven, but he is making a reference to Joseph in the Book of Genesis, who dreamed of his parents and brothers as the sun, moon, and eleven stars. (Genesis 37:9)

†† Job 3:17, 19.

CHAPTER FOURTEEN
Hartford, Part III

n the election year of 1844, abolitionists were faced with several unappealing options. The two main parties were the Whigs and the Democrats, and both of them, striving to be truly national parties, capable of carrying both Southern and Northern states, were unwilling to take a stand on the issue of slavery. In 1840, Whig efforts to alienate no one had led them to nominate an elderly and inoffensive general from Indiana named William Henry Harrison and to appeal to the south by naming John Tyler as his running mate. Tyler was a Virginian and a man who had spent most of his career in the Democratic Party. When Harrison died after a month in office, the country found that John Tyler, almost unknown outside his own state, was their president, the first to come to the office because of the death of his predecessor. Tyler quickly alienated Northern liberals by vetoing much of the legislation proposed by the Whigs and finally by announcing support for the annexation of Texas early in 1844. As a result, the Whigs did not nominate Tyler in 1844, but instead, still looking for Southern votes, chose James K. Polk of Tennessee, a slave owner, though not one who was outspoken on the issue, as their presidential candidate. The Democrats, who had lost behind Martin Van Buren in 1840, nominated Henry Clay of Kentucky, who had also been a slave owner but who had worked to forge compromises on the issue as a leading member of the Senate. Clay lost support in the South by opposing the annexation of Texas, while Polk sought to appeal to North and South by calling for the annexation of not only Texas but Oregon as well.

Given those choices, abolitionists were divided over the question of whether to participate in the political process at all. William Lloyd Garrison had long been opposed to involvement in the political process and advocated a separation between North and South, while Lewis Tappan and others preferred to become involved in the political process by means of a new, third party that was specifically opposed to slavery. This new entry in the field, the Liberty Party, chose James G. Birney of Kentucky, a reformed slave owner, as their leader in the 1840 election but garnered only seven thousand votes, fewer than one percent of the votes cast. Many abolitionists failed to see this as a useful path to follow. Why throw your vote away on a candidate who can't win, they asked, when you can have some influence on the outcome by voting for the lesser of two evils?

James Pennington, like most African Americans in New York, had not followed Garrison when the American Anti Slavery Society divided, even though his pacifist inclination might have led him in that direction. Torn between the two polarizing figures of Lewis Tappan and William Lloyd Garrison, it was easier to follow the local leader, Lewis Tappan, especially since he had so generously employed his money on their behalf. Even so, Pennington, as a pastor and pacifist, might have preferred to stay on the sidelines, especially as African Americans had no vote in Connecticut anyway. Eighteen forty-four, however, was different in several ways. In the first place, Roger Baldwin, who had served with John Adams in the legal battle over the *Amistad* captives, was the Whig candidate for governor of Connecticut and there was hope that he, if elected, would work to extend the franchise to African Americans. In the second place, Lewis Tappan had been persuaded to become more deeply involved in political action by his conversations with English abolitionists at the first World Anti Slavery Conference and was now prepared to give strong support to the Liberty Party, which had again nominated James G. Birney.[1]

In the midst of these issues, James Pennington found himself with a new platform and a new partner. The *Clarksonian* had failed, but Pennington was not alone in believing that African Americans needed a newspaper of their own, and an arrangement was therefore made to produce a paper with James McCune Smith of New York as co-editor and to publish issues alternately in Hartford and New York. Bringing together James W. C. Pennington and James McCune Smith was a creative idea. Pennington had proven skills as a writer as well as international relationships with leading abolitionists, while Smith was perhaps the best-educated African American of his day, having followed a thorough elementary and secondary education in New York schools with several years of study at the University of Glasgow. He returned to New York having earned a bachelor's degree in 1835, a master's degree in 1836, and a medical degree in 1837, and then capped his studies in Scotland with a medical internship in Paris. Smith, too, while developing a medical practice in New York City for both white and black patients, would find time to write voluminously on issues of race in America. His 1841 lecture to the New York Philomathean Society on "The Destiny of the People of Color" set high goals in claiming that "We are destined to write the history of this republic, which is still, in letters, a mere province of Great Britain. We have already, even from the depths of slavery, furnished the only music which this country has yet produced. We are also destined to write the poetry of the nation, for . . . our faculties, enlarged in the intellectual struggle for liberty, will necessarily become fired with glimpses at the glorious and the true, and will weave their inspiration into song." Prophetically, he then went on to foresee Martin Luther King Jr.: "We are destined to produce the oratory of this Republic; for, since true oratory can only spring from honest efforts in behalf of the RIGHT, such will of necessity arise amid our struggles—no holiday speeches in which shall be uttered eloquent falsehoods, garnished untruths, and hollow boastings . . . on the contrary we shall utter the earnest pleadings of down trodden humanity, seeking security from wrongs, too long inflicted, no longer to be endured."[2]

Nevertheless, the paper Smith and Pennington produced, named the *Star*, disappeared almost without a trace. It exists only in the writings of a contemporary, Martin Delaney, who remembered the co-editing arrangement but not even the name of the paper, and in a single excerpt reprinted in Garrison's *Liberator*. That excerpt, however, is a full and careful statement of James W. C. Pennington's views on the Liberty Party and the 1844 election. Pennington had two main points to make, and Garrison would have liked them both: that the Liberty Party's immediate goals were unrealistic, and that the leaders had, in any event, forsaken their stated goal of abolition. The Liberty Party was founded to work for abolition, but Pennington points out that the federal government is generally agreed to have no power to abolish slavery in the states, so even if the Liberty Party happened to win an election, it could do nothing about slavery at the national level. Recognizing this, the Party had set two preliminary goals: to abolish interstate trade in slaves, and to abolish slavery in the District of Columbia. But Pennington argues that this is useless, since slaves could still be traded within the states and because unscrupulous men would continue to find ways to trade in slaves, even between the states, as long as there was a demand for them. As for the idea that abolishing slavery in the District of Columbia would make an impact, Pennington points out that many slave states border free states but were not influenced by that fact, so adding the District of Columbia to the free states would make very little difference. These immediate goals are clearly unrealistic, but Pennington's critique goes much further. He argues that the Liberty Party has, in any event, abandoned its principles and is more concerned to win elections than to accomplish change. "We believe," he wrote, "that the [L]iberty men hate whiggery, more than they hate slavery, and that they love office more than they love anti-slavery."[3] Lewis Tappan either ignored Pennington's views or was not aware of them even months later. Writing to Pennington in answer to a request for a small loan, he went out of his way to report enthusiastically about some speeches he had recently made on behalf of the Liberty Party and boasted that "the anti slavery cause rolls on." But Tappan's political commitment cut no ice with James Pennington. As an outsider to the system, he could see clearly what insiders like Tappan failed to see: that to place any hope in a third-party gambit was to face certain disappointment. The article ends with a typical display of learning and rhetoric. In a day when most educated people knew Latin, Pennington would be understood and appreciated when he offered an interesting variation on a familiar quotation from Virgil's *Aeneid*. Virgil had written "Timeo Danaos et dona ferentes" (I fear the Greeks even bearing gifts). But Pennington writes: "Timeo Danaos et dona sequentes" (I fear the Greeks even seeking gifts) and translates it freely, "We fear these office-seeking liberty men." To make himself very clear, he adds a rhetorical flourish: "We doubt the sincerity of men who can make the bleeding hearts of suffering slaves, and the sympathies which those slaves excite, a means by which they shall gratify their vaulting ambition."[4] Even the members of this small party, unlikely to win an election any time soon, seemed to James Pennington to be more interested in gaining office than in making a difference in the lives of the suffering and he, outside the whole process, was free to say so. The cost of differing with Lewis Tappan was another matter.

The Liberty Party could, however, make a difference in the outcome of the election by drawing votes away from Whig candidates, and it did exactly that. When Pennington wrote to Thomas Clarkson in September 1844, he noted that "The abolitionists have no hope of electing Mr. Birney, but they will certainly come near enough to it to affect both of the other parties and . . . decide the fate of one of them."[5] That was prophetic. The Whigs had lost an election in Connecticut earlier in the year because of the abolitionist vote, and they lost the general election in 1844 because of the number of Liberty Party votes in New York State. Had New York State gone to the Whigs, they would have won the election, but they lost New York by five thousand votes and the Liberty Party drew fifteen thousand votes that could have gone to the Whigs and made Henry Clay president instead of James K. Polk. When Pennington wrote again to Clarkson in December, he made no mention of the election, but he had rightly foreseen the death of the Whig Party.[6] The Whigs would manage to win one more election, in 1848, by copying their tactics of 1840 and nominating a popular retired general, Zachary Taylor, who, like Harrison, would fail to live out his term. The third-party movement would continue to grow in strength until, under the banner of the Republican Party, it became the second-largest party in 1856 and placed Abraham Lincoln in the White House in the election of 1860. Meanwhile, the Liberty Party, seduced by the vision of power because of its greatly increased numbers in 1844, turned away from its initial vision toward more pragmatic politics, disenchanting its idealistic founders, and gradually fading away as a significant political force.

In the State of Connecticut, the election of Roger Baldwin in 1844, running as a Whig, might have given James Pennington a more realistic reason to hope for progress. Here was a state governor and a member of a major party who was a committed abolitionist and known to believe in the right of African Americans to the franchise. In keeping with his principles, Baldwin asked the legislature to give black citizens the right to vote, but the legislature gave short shrift to the request and the governor made no further effort to change either the laws or the legislators' minds.

The other New England states were well ahead of Connecticut on issues of race. James Pennington did the research to show how far behind it lingered and published a summary of his findings two years later. Massachusetts and Maine had had no slaves since 1790. Only Rhode Island and Connecticut still had a few slaves in 1840. But Connecticut alone, of all the New England states, limited the right to vote to white males. Even convinced abolitionists, however, seemed to feel that there was no more to be done about that for the time being. When the Connecticut Anti Slavery Society met in May 1845, shortly after the legislature had declined to take action on the franchise, there were no resolutions presented on the subject of reforming the election laws. The predominantly white association held its first session at the Talcott Street Church and opened with a prayer by J. W. C. Pennington, but when they considered a resolution on the political process, it made no reference to the recent action of the legislature. Instead, the gathering resolved simply that it was the duty of every voter to employ the ballot box for the overthrow of slavery but not, apparently, to use that power to enable black citizens in Connecticut to vote.[7]

The other resolutions of the Society were also strangely indirect in their language. "We know of no Constitutional reason," they proclaimed, "why we should not use all the means in our power for the overthrow of slavery"; but they offer no suggestions as to what might therefore be done. "If lawful efforts to promote liberty, justice, and morality be right," they told the world, "then are we as abolitionists right." But why did they phrase it so tentatively? They agreed that "at no period of human history, have men seen such unanimity of exertion by the nations of the earth for its [slavery's] extermination from this world as the present," but they adjourned without committing themselves to any such exertions.[8]

William Lloyd Garrison had written that "I do not wish to think, or to speak, or write, with moderation," but the Connecticut Anti Slavery Society seemed unwilling to give offense if it could be avoided. They made it clear that they were not Garrisonians when they resolved that "we desire neither the dissolution of the Union, nor the downfall of the churches." The Society demonstrated its commitment to providing equal opportunity for its black members by selecting James Pennington for three dubious honors. He was chosen to serve on its nominating committee with John Hooker and three others, elected secretary and treasurer for the coming year, and appointed to serve on a three-member committee for liquidating the Society's debt.[9] In spite of the moderate fuss being made by the Connecticut Society and other anti-slavery organizations, the country as a whole and the churches in particular were still a long way from even understanding the evil of slavery, let alone acting effectively against it. A lengthy article in an English publication spoke of the American churches as "the bulwark of slavery" and noted that "It has come upon many of the religious and benevolent societies of America, as a novel idea, that it is wrong to buy, sell, or work slaves to support theological seminaries or Christian missions." The article cited news from America of a gang of slaves being sold by an Episcopal Church and of the American Board of Missions expressing gratitude for a legacy of slaves to be worked by the Society, or sold for its benefit. It also described a proposal to build a mission school by using four extra hours of labor from slaves each day, two before daybreak and two after dark, so that there would be no additional cost for the project.[10] When such things happened in the Southern states, it is hardly surprising that such evidences of equality as the right to vote were long withheld in the North and that the Connecticut Anti Slavery Society and Connecticut legislature were satisfied to pass moderate resolutions.

Free blacks in the North cared about the status of the slaves not only because they were of the same race but because they knew that none of them would be seen as equal while some were still enslaved. In 1846, the Connecticut legislators chose to free themselves of further responsibility on the subject of the franchise by calling for a popular referendum. New York State had taken that course the year before and the voters had resoundingly defeated the proposal to let African American voters be freed of property requirements. Encouraged by that example, the Connecticut legislators removed reference to color from the state's constitution to clear the way for a change in the laws and then, since any further action on their part was certain to annoy a significant number of voters, turned the matter over to the electorate to decide for themselves whether it should be legal for anyone not white to vote. Pennington, Amos Beman, and Joseph Brown, a lay member of Beman's New Haven congregation, published an appeal to the voters of the state that called America a "cutaneous democracy," where human rights are based on the color of the skin. "We do not believe, they wrote, "that the color of the skin is an indication either of virtue, wisdom, or justice . . . but . . . as a physical manifestation for which an all wise Creator is alone responsible." They pointed to the fact that they were taxpayers and that since "taxation and representation should go together, the surest way to degrade us is to disenfrachise us, that the most direct way to make us bad citizens is to treat us as aliens." "We appeal to you in behalf of the tarnished honor of this State," they write, "to wipe this stain from her escutcheon."[11] In spite of the logic of their appeal, voters in Connecticut were in no mood to move forward, and the proposed change was defeated by a vote of almost five to one. "Good old Connecticut," as Pennington liked to call it, was not ready to change its good old ways.

Amos Beman looked at the result and was outraged not only by the result but by the fact that nine-tenths of the Irish residents in Connecticut voted against the colored man. African Americans looked at Irish Americans and thought they were seeing a natural ally. As the Irish struggled for freedom from the British, so the African Americans also were engaged in a fight for liberty. As the Irish immigrant struggled to find employment in America, so did the black refugee from the South. To the Irish, the situation seemed very different: they were white and therefore entitled to oppress the blacks and so feel themselves to be one rung up the ladder. Beman did understand the psychology of it: opposition of Irishmen in America to colored men is "not so much an Hibernianism as an Americanism. Abuse of the colored people is popular, and the pecuniary interest of many of the Irish is promoted by imitating the bad example of their pro-slavery American teachers. Let them be severely rebuked, but in all justice strike the most guilty party the hardest blow."[12]

In a letter to Joseph Sturge a year later,[†] Pennington commented, "We have just closed an important struggle in this state for the right of suffrage, and I am ashamed to tell you that we have lost it by strong majority. I have been a faithful and orderly citizen of Conn. for eight years, but the good people of the state are not willing to trust those of my brethren whom I have labored to elevate and myself to cast our votes. There are 65,000 white voters in the state of Connecticut. The whole number of colored voters would be about 1,000 and yet our 65,000 white superiors are afraid of us 1,000 inferiors; afraid to give us a chance to show ourselves patriots! What a beautiful example of consistency in the whole situation! But this is the effect of slavery as we feel it even at the north. Better days will not come until the south is free."[13]

While white Americans worried about the election, James Pennington was, to all outward appearance, going about his business as usual, speaking at various gatherings, firing off letters and articles to the press on issues large and small, and involving himself in every aspect of the abolition movement, not forgetting the missionaries in Africa. In June of 1845 he sent a letter to Thomas Lafon promising boxes of cloth to be used to "conciliate the feelings"

† Showing the influence of his time in England, Pennington whimsically gives his return address as "Pembroke Place, 35 Village Street, Hartford."

of local chiefs.[14] On July 5, 1844, he offered a prayer at a temperance meeting of over three thousand African Americans in Catskill, New York, and on August 1 he was a featured speaker at a celebration of the end of West Indian slavery in New York City.

Pennington was going about his business, but there was growing evidence that he needed a change. In September 1845, he was present at the annual meeting of the Connecticut State Temperance Convention at the Talcott Street Church and was scheduled to speak, but before the end of the first day he asked to be excused on account of ill health and because he had been engaged in activity which required "the full extent of his mental powers all day." It is the first evidence that his energy was not inexhaustible. Before the end of the second and final day of the Convention, he came back to move an amendment to the group's constitution and join in a discussion of several resolutions, but plans were already well along to spend time away from the parish and constant pressure of abolitionist activities. Meanwhile, in October 1845, he was present at a Convention of the Friends of Liberty in Boston. At the end of the month, the American Board of Commissioners for Foreign Missions met in Quincy, Massachusetts, and attempted to set at rest forever the question Lewis Tappan had pressed on them two years earlier: is support for missions inconsistent with support for slavery? Leonard Woods of the Andover Seminary prepared a report that declared it to be the duty of the Board to prosecute the work of saving souls without attempting to "go any faster than the consciences of the people become enlightened," or to interfere with the civil condition of society. Calvin Stowe, Harriet Beecher Stowe's husband and a member of the faculty at Lane Seminary in Ohio, said he would "sooner die than say a missionary ought to enter his open protest against all the evils he may come in contact with. Jacob lived with four women at once. Had there been an organized church there, would Abraham and Jacob have been excluded? These examples are for our instruction, and they give us just the light we need in this matter."

It was not the light James W. C. Pennington needed; he was not impressed with these authorities and wrote to the *Christian Freeman* to point out at some length the fundamental contradiction in the position taken by the Board and several leading churches that distinguished between slavery and slaveholding. It was sinful in their opinion to buy or sell a slave but not intrinsically evil to be a slave owner. The churches, Pennington wrote, were trying to have it both ways: to denounce the slave system as evil while not condemning the individuals who were both church members and slave owners. If "men made in the image of God [are] heathenized, and starved; families in a state of concubinage, &c, it is useless," he wrote, to "talk metaphysics" and say that the relationship of owner to slave is not sinful. "It would answer the object of practical religion quite as well, to stand by the sick bed of a peasant and talk Greek to him." "I belong to the school which desires the reformation and salvation of the slaveholder, not his destruction," Pennington concluded, "But in the course above, there is not the least tendency to reform him. . . . All I ask, is that our theologians may possess that most precious jewel, called consistency."[15]

On a far more trivial point, Pennington found time to write another letter to the same paper pointing out that a number of leading British abolitionists had been awarded honorary degrees by several American universities while American abolitionists had not been similarly honored. The University of New York, Jefferson College, and the College of Delaware are mentioned as having honored several English abolitionists while such deserving Americans as Joshua Leavitt, Jonathan Blanchard, and Amos A. Phelps had been neglected, apparently because, as American abolitionists, they were considered controversial. Pennington points out that the English are beginning to disparage these American degrees with nicknames such as "The Water Doctor" for a man who had been given a degree by Watertown College.[16]

While he was expressing his views on these and other matters in public, Pennington was involved in negotiations with his congregation for a radical change in his life. Even before he gave evidence of exhaustion at the Temperance Convention in September, the planning had begun for a break from the congregation. Sabbaticals for clergy would not become standard for another century and a half, but James Pennington needed one and was wise enough to know it. At the August meeting of the Hartford Central Clergy Association, he notified the members that he was asking his congregation for a two-year leave of absence to further his education, and they provided him with an official certificate and testimonial commending him as "a brother beloved and member in good standing . . . to the sympathy and fellowship of the people of God, wherever Providence shall cast his lot."[17] On November 2, he preached an hour-long sermon to his congregation that was later published as "A Two Years Leave of Absence or A Farewell Sermon." The sermon is, for the most part, a standard analysis of a text[†] with its importance to Christian living constantly emphasized. The moral governance of God, as always, remains a central point. Under that moral governance, the congregation is told, "You must learn to apply the word of God to overt acts," and "the last and the greatest of the curses

---

[†] "And now, brethren, I commend you to God, and to the word of his grace, which is able to build you up, and to give you an inheritance among all them which are sanctified." Acts 20:32. The words are from St. Paul's farewell to the leaders of the church in Ephesus.

that must be dealt with" is slavery.[18] Here, once again, Pennington is at his most eloquent: "Is the word of God silent on this subject? I, for one, desire to know. My repentance, my faith, my hope, my love, and my perseverance all, all, I conceal it not, I repeat it, all turn upon this point. If I am deceived here, if the word of God does sanction slavery, I want another book, another repentance, another faith, and another hope! I speak very reverently, and from a deep and mournful reflection." "I am not bound to show," he continues, "that the New Testament authorizes me in such a chapter and verse to reject a slaveholder. It is sufficient for me to show, what is fully acknowledged by my opponents, that it is murdering the poor, corrupting society, alienating brethren, and sowing the seed of discord in the bosom of the whole church . . ." He quotes an exposition of slavery by the Synod of Kentucky that reported, "This system licenses and produces great cruelty. Mangling, imprisonment, starvation, every species of torture . . . There are now in our whole land two millions of human beings, exposed, defenseless, to every insult . . . They suffer all that can be afflicted by wanton caprice, by brutal lust, by malignant spite, and by insane anger." Once again, Pennington is eloquent in his appeal to a larger audience than the one before him: "Two hundred and thirty long, dreary and bloody years have passed away, during which eight generations of us have sunk, starved, beaten, mangled, brokenhearted, and bathed in blood to the grave. At this day of reform, revivals, missionary operations, political renovations, and literary excellence, when we rise up and cry to these men on Christian principle, enough, enough, O do let the past days of your bloody doings suffice; slacken your hands, let us go that we may make friendship, and do a little for the glory of God before the day of account comes with us both."[19] But this is a farewell to his congregation, and at the end he speaks very personally to them: ". . . live unitedly in the fear and love of God; . . . keep your church pure; be examples of public and private piety; train your children right; pray much; pass the fugitive along, support the temperance cause, stand by the Union Missionary Society, pray for the Mendi mission and brother Raymond." He urges them to pray every night for the Raymonds and ends with four verses of the familiar evangelical hymn:

> Blest be the tie that binds
> Our hearts in Christian love
> When we asunder part
> It gives us inward pain;
> But we shall still be one in heart,
> And hope to meet again.[20]

As a preface to the printed sermon, Pennington attached a one-sentence letter that he had sent to the congregation in August requesting to be dismissed so as to be able to spend two years in classical studies, resigning his salary for that period of time but leaving open the possibility of returning to his ministry. He attempts also to deal with the inevitable questions: Why are you doing this? Where are you going? For these, the answers are unclear. He tells them that he hopes to deal with the fact that he is still a fugitive from slavery and hopes to spend the first few months in attending to certain business with a view to relieve himself from that increasingly unhappy situation. He tells them that if a slave owner set out to capture him, he is confident that he could raise the money to purchase his freedom and "if I wanted daggers to defend myself, I could raise ten thousand of the truest hearted and hardest handed men in Connecticut . . . But I am not at all the proper sort of subject for the kind of excitement consequent upon either of these modes." He intends to act on "my own plan," but will say nothing more about it.[21] As to his intention to pursue classical studies, Pennington tells his congregation that "I entered the ministry and public labors at a time when all the avenues of learning were closed. The means of thorough learning are now within our reach. I am still a young man. Our part of this nation is yet in its elements, to be moulded. And the last half of the present century will be our great moral battle. I go to prepare for that."[22]

The next morning, Pennington was busy with all the last-minute details that have to be taken care of before a journey. He wrote to the *Christian Freeman* to report the availability of a major gift. An "aged and pious member" of a Congregational church in the state was creating a Board of Trustees that included James Pennington to administer a legacy of several thousand dollars "to advance the cause of learning among the colored people and Indians." Pennington had been authorized to act in any preliminary measures that might be taken so long as the donor's name was not revealed. He wrote, therefore, to announce the legacy and to request further donations and a gift of land. Black clergy, he wrote, had proved themselves, but there remained a need for education. "What is the next step," he asked, "in the onward course of the colored man? I answer, sound scholarship. What next? Sound scholarship. And what next? Sound scholarship."[23]

If Pennington was to be away for two years pursuing sound scholarship for himself, he would have little opportunity to act on the proposal and there is no further record of it. Nor did anything visible come from his sermon of the night before, although it was published and widely distributed. He had outlined two specific goals for his sabbatical, but the strangest part of this strange episode is that in the following months Pennington's status as a fugitive slave was not resolved and nothing was done to further his classical education.

The matter of his status as a fugitive remains a mystery. A few years later it would be resolved by others on his behalf, but no record survives of what Pennington meant to do or whether he made an attempt at that time that was unsuccessful. As for the goal of a classical education, that was probably derailed by Pennington's discovery of a letter that had been sent to Governor Slade of Vermont by Nathan Lord, the president of Dartmouth College. Pennington had been urged to go to Dartmouth, by a friend named Baird and perhaps by Augustus Washington in his congregation, who had studied at Dartmouth a few years earlier. He had been strongly inclined to go, but when he saw the letter from Nathan Lord, he changed his mind. Governor Slade had sent a letter to Lord about two black students he hoped could study at Dartmouth and Lord had replied that they would be accepted; he had written to their pastor in Philadelphia consenting to receive them. He went on to say that the college usages in respect to the admission of students are entirely impartial. "We make no distinction in regard to nation or color. The African and Indian are as freely received as the Saxon, if possessed of the requisite literary and moral qualifications."

Had Lord written nothing more, all would have been well; but Lord did not stop there. He went on at some length to say that "experience has not been very satisfactory in regard to negroes." One had graduated a few years earlier with honors, but two others had failed "from fickleness, inconstancy and unsound morality." On the rather slim basis of experience with three individuals, he told Governor Slade, "We doubt the fitness of Africans, in their present state of civilization, for the grave and considerate pursuit of students. We doubt the expediency of attempting to educate many of them beyond the level of their race." He thought "they will need cultivation as a people, for centuries, before many of them will be able to hold their way with long civilized and Christian Saxons, if indeed that is ever to be expected, which I doubt." And still he rambled on about the need "to help a struggling people" and their preference not "to have a flood of blacks at this college" although they were willing to "risk inconvenience" because "it is right that negroes should be educated in proper circumstances. We dare not refuse them. We would not for Christ's sake." Toward the end of his unfortunate letter, he suggested that "we are apt to exaggerate before hand the difficulties of doing well. Lions," he told Governor Slade, "are wild only in the desert. On the king's highway, if found at all, they are chained." And with that mysterious thought, he ended his epistle.[24]

Governor Slade, an adamant opponent of slavery, apparently was not amused by Lord's musings on racial matters and passed copies of the letter to others, with the result that one came to James Pennington and changed his plans drastically.† He left Hartford as scheduled but did not go to Hanover. Instead he sent back to a friend a copy of the letter from Nathan Lord with the request that he forward it to William Henry Burleigh, editor of the *Christian Freeman*, along with Pennington's comments. Needless to say, James Pennington had been outraged. He told his friend that he had heard about the letter and decided at first not to read it when it came to him rather than be prejudiced against the college. When he did read it, he tried still to think of it as one man's opinion rather than an expression of college policy, but was prevented by Lord's constant use of plural pronouns as if he wrote for the faculty or trustees. If he were younger, Pennington wrote, he would "not shrink for a moment from taking my place in a class at Dartmouth . . . nor should I consider it robbing Saxons of their blood-rights or titles, to excel, or try to excel them." But with limited time and means, he was not prepared to make the effort required to disarm President Lord of his prejudice. "I have no wish," Pennington wrote his friend, "to excite prejudice against [Lord] as a gentleman and a scholar, but I feel bound to demand justice for my people and myself." He thinks he has a right to know what knowledge Lord and his colleagues have of black people in their remote section of the country as a basis for his judgment, and how many black students had ever entered Dartmouth. "If two failures decide the character of millions," Pennington asked, "what would he have me do with the thousands of literary failures which have taken place among the Saxons? . . . Were all the patriots of the American army disgraced because an Arnold once commanded among them? Is the Vice President's chair unclean because Aaron Burr once sat in it?"[25]

By the time he wrote his response to Lord's letter, Pennington had changed any plans he might have made to visit Dartmouth and was well on his way in the opposite direction. His next letter, dated February 10, 1846, came from Kingston, Jamaica, where he arrived in mid-December, a bare six weeks after his farewell to the Talcott Street congregation. Whatever efforts he had

---

† Also not amused by Nathan Lord's letter was Augustus Washington, who thought that the reference to two students who had failed "from fickleness, inconstancy and unsound morality" included him. He wrote a long letter, published in the *Charter Oak*, to Theodore Wright in which he told the story of his efforts to acquire an education without support from his family and turned aside often by prejudice. He explained how he had been forced to move frequently by lack of funds or support and recited, ironically, Lord's charge of "fickleness and inconstancy" as he did so. He explained that he had been forced to leave Dartmouth for lack of funds and had dutifully paid all his remaining bills, although "it is said that several thousand dollars are due at Hanover from other students. But no one, as yet, has charged me with a want of mediocrity in my studies or dishonesty in other respects. . . . If any further reply is necessary to the cause of the failure of two negroes myself, as one of the two meant, I am ready for a fair investigation; but no ex parte one."

planned to make in regard to his fugitive status must have fallen through quickly and the letter from Nathan Lord must have discouraged him from looking further for a welcoming institution and facing ignorant racism again. Instead, he arranged with the Union Missionary Society to go to Jamaica as a traveling missionary and observer. Seven years earlier, James Pennington had made his first major speech at a celebration of the abolition of slavery in the West Indies; now he would see for himself the society he had hailed and in which recently freed slaves were playing an important part. These plans, too, must have been made suddenly since neither his wife or his congregation was told about them at the time. Ships traveled frequently between Hartford and Jamaica, so Pennington could have made plans easily.

Jamaica is the third largest Caribbean island after Cuba and Hispaniola, but much smaller than either. It is the third largest nation in the Western Hemisphere in which English is the dominant language, but Jamaica is a small country, not even as large as Connecticut. Like the Southern states, its economy had been heavily dependent on one labor-intensive crop and on slave labor to produce that crop, though the crop in Jamaica was sugar rather than cotton. England had taken Jamaica away from Spain in the 17th century but had never seen it as a place like Virginia where an English settlement might be planted. They saw it, rather, as a possession to be exploited. The wealthy land owners often stayed in England and sent out overseers to run their plantations for them. There were American plantations run in that way also, but far fewer. Frisby Tilghman at least lived at Rockland himself with his family and had a personal relationship, however unpleasant, with his slaves. The English who were plantation owners in Jamaica preferred on the whole to keep their distance and, as a result, even in the seventeenth century, blacks outnumbered whites in Jamaica; by the nineteenth century they outnumbered whites by almost twenty to one. Americans had watched the abolition of slavery in Jamaica with hope or fear, depending on their attitude toward slavery, with abolitionists trumpeting any favorable news and the pro-slavery side pointing to every negative sign as evidence that slavery could not safely be abolished in the United States. Most impressive from the abolitionist point of view was the fact that the transition had been accomplished without violence. The former slaves had moved peaceably into their new status and made no attempt to avenge themselves on their former masters. On the other hand, abolition had inevitably had serious economic consequences. Many of the plantation owners, having to pay free laborers, could no longer make the profits they had made with slaves and therefore allowed their plantations to decay. Many of the freed slaves took up subsistence farming which added very little to the national economy, although it left them much better off as individuals. The transition from an economy based almost entirely on the sugar industry to a more diversified agriculture therefore looked to the Southern slave owners like a disaster, but may, in fact, have been simply a difficult transition to a better balanced and healthier society.

What struck James Pennington on his arrival was the sight of a society in which black people played a wide variety of roles that, even in the Northern states, were almost completely out of reach. There were shop keepers and small businessmen and even policemen. Black citizens, by the time of Pennington's visit, already comprised a third of the legislature. Black and white lawyers presented cases to juries on which black and white Jamaicans sat together to decide cases.[26] There had, however, been many reports to the States from those who looked at emancipation in the West Indies as a failure, who attributed the declining economy to the indolence of the black population. Pennington thought the accounts being circulated in the United States were too bright on the one hand and too dark on the other. The great questions Pennington had come with were those being asked in the United States: "Are the colored people peaceable . . are they willing to work for fair wages . . . are they . . . good citizens . . . Is there anything in the condition and the conduct of the colored people that can be seized upon by the American slaveholder, as an argument to justify him in continuing his oppression?"

In response to all of these questions, Pennington's observation was "Things are working well. I speak without hesitation! They are working well." He had seen men, women, and children in the cane fields and going to market and could report that "they are by no means a lazy people. They do more work," he wrote, "than any class of men in America. I do not except the Irish laborers on the public works." People he had visited in their homes and schools and chapels were "very happy and cheerful, and withal very peaceable." Pennington's primary interest, of course, was the work of missionaries. Before emancipation, there had been fewer than fifty clergy, most of them representing the Church of England, in a population, slave and free, of half a million. With the abolition of slavery, missionaries came in increasing numbers and by the time of Pennington's visit there were some two hundred, the majority now of various evangelical churches, but still far too few to serve so large a population. American Congregationalists had established five mission stations immediately after the end of slavery in Jamaica with a supporting committee in Massachusetts. Pennington visited all of them and reported to Payson Williston in Massachusetts that he found the missionaries there entirely responsible for the temperance effort in the island and leading efforts also to improve the educational system. To Lewis Tappan he wrote, "O my brother, how great the work is. It is a wonderful field."

In Kingston, Pennington had English contacts as well. A large Baptist congregation was served by Samuel Oughton, a Baptist, who had been sent out as a missionary by the Surrey Chapel. Oughton had arrived in Jamaica in 1836, during the emancipation process and had been imprisoned for his criticisms of the conduct of some of the magistrates. When the planters tried to drive wages down, he told his congregation that rather than work for less than a day, they should let canes rot in the fields and the ships go back empty. When Oughton's activism was attacked in England, Joseph Sturge had come to Oughton's defense.[27]

Pennington would have found his way quickly in Jamaica with the help of Samuel Oughton and the international abolitionist network. Whatever his purpose in coming had been, he quickly found employment, not only in the churches, where he was asked to preach in Baptist and Wesleyan chapels seating between fifteen hundred and two thousand five hundred people and seldom saw an empty seat,[†] but also on behalf of the government. The governor of Jamaica, James Brice, Earl of Elgin and Kincardine, asked Pennington to go on a tour of the principal cities and towns to lecture on the subject of education. Lecturing on behalf of the government, Pennington was also observing on behalf of the Union Missionary Society and finding opportunity in the changing circumstances of Jamaican life. "I cannot tell you," he wrote to Amos Phelps, a Boston area abolitionist pastor, "the extent of the field which opens up before me here."[28] The London missionary societies that had been willing in the past to build churches and chapels and pay the salaries of missionaries were increasingly leaving such matters to the local population. As a result, Pennington found that Jamaicans were looking more and more to America for assistance. The recent arrival of the five Congregational missionaries seemed to be evidence of American ability to take up the slack left by the London societies.

Pennington had visited Brother Thompson at Eliott Station and found him erecting a building that would provide him shelter at one end and allow room for worship at the other. There was a terrible lack of books for arithmetic, spelling, reading, and writing. He wondered whether it might not be simplest to print books for them in Hartford. With freedom, the black population was also anxious to see black preachers in their pulpits. "We have more liberty," they told Pennington, "but you have more education . . . [so] send us some of your men. We will take care of them well, and . . . make returns to you some other way." "Colored brethren or abolitionists would be able to do much," Pennington realized, "but it would have to be done while the new society was still being formed; now is the time to thrust in the new plough."

---

† "Chapel" in English usage refers to buildings used by congregations not of the established church (Church of England) and has nothing to do with the size of the building.

As he surveyed this developing situation, however, it seemed to Pennington that there was a lack not only of preachers or missionaries, but of a leadership that understood how to "embody their religion . . . so as to make religion available for the purposes of reform." He had certainly seen a good deal of Christianity in the United States that made no difference for society as a whole, and he saw it also in Jamaica, but Pennington's faith had been shaped in a different tradition from the time of his first meeting with William Wright through his conversion by Samuel Cox and into his years with Theodore Wright. Even Nathaniel Taylor, with his talk about "the moral governance of God," understood faith as having consequences beyond individual conversion. In Jamaica, however, the few clergy on the island were mostly representatives of the established church (Frederick Douglass described them as "state paid hirelings") who had little interest in changing their comfortable world. Abolition in Jamaica had come as a result of the efforts of Christians of both the established and dissenting traditions in England, but not those of Jamaica. The result of this history was that Pennington found a vast amount of sincere personal religion but nothing with a larger understanding of the social dimensions of Christian faith. "Ministers were expected to preach well, leaders were expected to teach well, and a private Christian is expected to attend chapel, and contribute well. Personal piety," he knew, "would not be enough to transform society as well as individual lives."[29]

From Kingston on the south coast to Annotto Bay on the north coast and then eastward to Montego Bay in the northwest, Pennington traveled freely around the island, speaking about education, preaching in the churches, and writing long letters to individuals in the States that quickly appeared in various journals. There were plans to be made for future relationships between American blacks and those in Jamaica, but there was the new experience of complete freedom in a society where black people were the vast majority and no laws restricted their movements or their aspirations.

When Pennington wrote to Amos Phelps at the end of February, he had not yet been to Montego Bay, and he had plans to visit other places as well. He expected these journeys to take him about three weeks and that he would then "take the first chance home." On that schedule, he might have been home sometime in April. In fact, he was still in Jamaica some two months later when word came that his wife had died on June 5. He did take "the first chance home" after that, but the funeral had been held on the day after Harriet's death and he came home to an empty house. Harriet had been 36 years old. There were no children. Harriet had kept track of the family finances, helped teach the children at the Talcott Church school, and served on the Board of Deacons, but otherwise has left no record of her accomplishments. For at least ten years, James Pennington never told her that he was a fugitive slave because he was concerned that she would worry about him, and he apparently had not told her in advance that he was going to Jamaica. Fifteen months later, he mentioned her death in a letter to Joseph Sturge, saying, "I met with a serious loss about 15 months ago in the death of my loved companion." He undoubtedly said similar things privately to others. To Lewis Tappan he wrote that she had "a pleasant death," meaning, presumably, that she died without much suffering and in assurance of faith. For a prolific writer, Pennington is remarkably silent about his personal life.

Lewis Tappan wrote to sympathize but was unable, as usual, to refrain from saying exactly what he was thinking, regardless of consequences. "I sympathize with you in the death of your wife," he wrote, "and rejoiced to learn that her death was so happy. She should be glad to see you back with your people." So far so good, although there was a bit of a barb in that last sentence. But Tappan was unable to resist passing on a conversation he had had recently with "a mutual friend," who told him that "two things had struck him very unfavorably" [about Pennington]. The first was "information you sent over from England, that Pennington had received a doctorate" (which, of course, he had denied), and the second was "leaving your people and your wife without their knowing where you had gone to, when you went to Jamaica." They had known very soon, however, as the letters came back, and there might not have been opportunity earlier. But Tappan assumes the criticism to be valid and assumes it his job to pass the criticism on. Was he angry that Pennington had been critical of his involvement in the Liberty Party, or does it simply reflect his critical attitude toward blacks in general? Others might have felt that a condolence letter was not the ideal vehicle to pass on a third party's personal criticism of another, valid or not, but Tappan said he would like Pennington to see it as evidence of friendship: "You see how faithful I am in informing you of these things."[30] Friendship would become increasingly difficult as Tappan continued to find new opportunities to display his faithfulness.

The proposed two-year leave of absence to pursue classical studies might have taken a sudden detour to Jamaica and another shock with his wife's death, but Pennington had not abandoned the plan and told a correspondent in England in September 1847 that he had been "closely engaged in some classical studies, and in maturing my mind for future conflict." Apparently he had gone back home to Hartford and made arrangements to study privately or to engage tutors as he had done years earlier. He could not, however, avoid the constant demands on his time that went with the Talcott Street Church's reputation as a primary station on the Underground Railroad. Village Street was not far from Talcott Street and two or three fugitives came to his door almost daily. One Thursday his doorbell rang at 6 A.M. and four young men were there, part of a group of twenty-five who had arrived in New York only a day or two earlier. Two days later, again at six in the morning, a family of seven was on his doorstep: "a father and mother and five interesting children ranging up to a daughter of seventeen."[31] The fugitives always arrived destitute and needed time and care to be prepared for the next stage on the Railroad. Some did stay in Hartford, but others were sent on to Massachusetts or Canada. Classical studies were constantly having to be put aside for the immediate needs of these refugees from the South. Pennington believed that they were actually providing the South with a safety valve by expediting the flight of the most discontented rather than letting their despair spread to others.

Pennington also continued to attend meetings of the Hartford Central Clergy Association; in fact, he missed no meetings after his return, though he had missed some earlier. It would have been a distraction from his classical studies and was certainly not essential to his ministry, but the occasional contact with a collegial group undoubtedly helped fill the hole left by Harriet's death. If the Hartford clergy were supportive of their bereaved comrade, the strictly formal minutes of their meetings show nothing of it. The July meeting was held only a month after Harriet Pennington's death, but the minutes make no mention either of her death or of Pennington's return from an extended absence. At the August meeting, the minutes record "Brother Pennington appointed to write on the question Ought a minister knowingly to unite in matrimony a believer with an unbeliever?" The next meeting was in October in West Hartford, and Pennington, with Joel Hawes and Horace Bushnell both present, read the paper assigned, having taken time away from his other studies, presumably, to do it. In June of 1846, his colleagues chose him as moderator for the coming year. It was a position without much honor, as has been pointed out, but in a society that generally ignored the presence of black people, it was not completely insignificant.

Less consistent with the idea of sabbatical was an effort on Pennington's part to do something about the government's neglect of the African schools. Augustus Washington had become the teacher in the North African School during Pennington's absence and continued in that role after his return, earning a commendation from the school visitor. But the hopes entertained in the creation of separate black schools had not been realized and although the school visitors had noted the lack of books, the stuffiness of the school rooms, and general inadequacy of the facilities, they had made no specific recommendation to deal with the problem. In 1846, therefore, James Pennington took time out from his classical studies to petition the School Society of Hartford to meet its obligations, telling them that conditions were "exceedingly irregular, deficient, and onerous." For years, he told them, the School Society had done nothing except turn over to the African schools a small share of the public fund and leave them to their own devices with the consequence that the schools had been unable to provide adequate quarters and competent teachers. The Society responded immediately by increasing the tax rate so as to be able to provide two better-equipped schools. The result was some improvement in materials supplied and six years later separate school buildings. Not until several years after the Civil War did the state pass a law requiring students to attend the school in their own district regardless of race and thus bring to an end the segregated school system.

Pennington's absence from the country briefly, and from his various ministries for the better part of two years, had only increased the difficulties of the fledgling Union Missionary Society. It was quickly evident that there simply was not an adequate base in the black community to support the sending and maintaining of missionaries either abroad or in the home mission field. Lewis Tappan, with a treasurer's eye for the bottom line but a committed evangelical's zeal for spreading the gospel, searched for a solution. Clearly there was missionary work to be done that the American Board of Commissioners for Foreign Mission was not doing and that missionaries whose consciences bothered them in regard to support from slaveholders were reluctant to undertake. Pennington's experience in Jamaica only confirmed the need for American workers in new fields. Tappan and like-minded white evangelicals, of course, still had no vehicle for foreign and domestic missionary work. They could not support the ABCFM since it would not excommunicate slaveholders, and they could not be quite comfortable in the African American UMS in spite of its specific invitation to white Christians to join with them in mission. Tappan's solution was to leave the UMS aside for the moment and to persuade Pennington and others that the time was right to call a broadly representative convention to think creatively about the best way to pursue the work of mission. If a merger could be arranged of several smaller mission societies with the UMS, perhaps an integrated society could be formed that would attract broader support and be able to undertake a broader field of work.

A convention was summoned therefore to meet in Albany in early September. Representatives came from not only the UMS but also the Western Evangelical Missionary Society, dedicated to mission in the American West, and the West India Missionary Committee. The work of these societies was presented and discussed and principles were agreed on for governing the work of Christian missions. Perhaps the most significant principle agreed on was one that is still divisive in American Christianity: the relative weight, or even existence, of "social sins." Those who attended the convention in Albany wanted it clearly understood that societies as well as individuals can go astray. "Christianity," they proclaimed, "wages an uncompromising warfare against all forms of sin, public as well as private; social, political and organic, as well as individual, sins sustained, authorized, legalized, and even required and enjoined by civil rulers, as well as sins forbidden and punished by them; and ministers of the gospel, Christians and Christian churches, should themselves abstain from and reprove in others, the one class of sins as fully as the other . . ." Obviously this stand had implications for the institution of slavery, but the statement of principles could be applied as well in the mission field. The converted slave master must be "prepared to break the bonds of the slave," but also "the proud Brahmin must embrace fraternally the man of low caste," the polygamist must "obey the seventh commandment," and "the oppressive ruler" must "dispense justice to the subject." It would be "a perversion of Christian institutions" to receive such "flagrant, habitual, and determined transgressors into the churches, under the idea that they are converted, while refusing to abandon their cherished and darling sins" in the vain hope that "the great moral transformation" will be worked out afterwards. The statement went on to say that there was no justification for expecting missionaries to sacrifice more in the cause of evangelism than Christians at home or for mission boards at home to dictate the details of a missionary's life "on the other side of the globe" when they would not do that for clergy at home. Such distinctions, the convention agreed, were a "false, unscriptural, and mischievous error."

The new organization set out broad principles but gave particular attention nevertheless to American society. "We have been accustomed," they said, "to regard Christianity as established in this country. But what fearful crimes, public as well as private do we witness, and what multitudes professing the purest faith . . . are practising these crimes." In particular, they drew attention to the three million "of our colored brethren in slavery the most malignant and cruel in existence" in whom "the image of God is effaced" while "the religion of a large portion of the country defends the atrocity." "To bear such crimes in silence," the statement continued, "or fellowship them" is enough "to paralyze the faith and hope of the church." "Our mission is first with ourselves," the convention agreed; it would be wrong to discipline the intemperate while having fellowship with the slaveholder.

To propagate these principles, a new organization, the American Missionary Association, was created. The list of missionaries supported included ten in Jamaica, six in India, two in the Mendi mission, two in Canada, one in the Sandwich Islands (Hawaii), and several unnamed serving "feeble churches in the west." Charles B. Ray in New York City was the only individual listed under "Home Missions." From the outset, it was an integrated society with Theodore Wright, Samuel Ringgold Ward, Samuel Cornish, and James W. C. Pennington, serving as members

James W. C. Pennington. *Image courtesy of the author.*

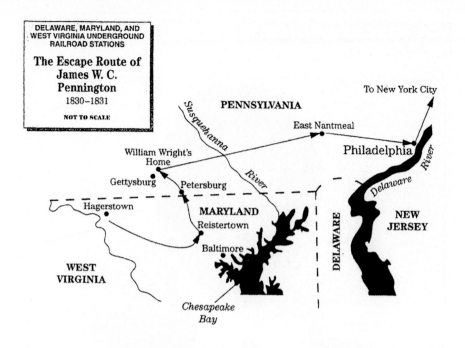

ABOVE: Escape route of James W. C. Pennington. *Image courtesy of the author.*

BELOW: The ad for the return of James Pembroke, published in *The Hagerstown Torch Light and Advertiser*, used the same stock picture to illustrate all such ads and there were several in every issue. *Image courtesy of the author.*

200 Dollars Reward.

RAN AWAY from the subscriber living near Hagers-town, Washington county, Md. on Monday the twenty-ninth of October, a ne- gro man named JAMES PEM-BROOK, about 21 years of age, five feet five inches high, very black, square & clumsily ma le, has a down look, prominent and reddish eyes, and mumbles or talks with his teeth closed, can read, and I believe write, is an excellent blacksmith, and pretty good rough carpenter ; he received shortly before he absconded, a pretty severe cut from his axe on the inside of his right leg. Any per- son who will take up and secure him in the jail of Hagers-town shall receive the above reward.

November 1. FRISBY TILGHMAN.
1—tf.

ABOVE: William (1788-1865) and Phebe (1790-1873) Wright, who welcomed James Pennington to freedom. *Images courtesy of the Adams County Historical Society.*

BELOW: Samuel Hanson Cox (1793-1880) received James Pennington into the Christian Church. *Image courtesy of the author.*

ABOVE LEFT: Amos C. Beman (1812-1874), a colleague of James Pennington, who served churches in New Haven and Portland. *Image courtesy of the author.*

ABOVE RIGHT: Henry Highland Garnet (1815-1882), a colleague of James Pennington, who succeeded him as pastor of the Shiloh Church, New York. *Image courtesy of the author.*

BELOW: The Abyssinian Church in Portland, Maine. *Image courtesy of the author.*

29. 6th Avenue
New York Oct 18th 1854
Rev. J. M. Kebbs D.D.

Sir, I have, since I met you at that interesting ordination, called at your residence several times, but have always failed to find you at home. I called a few days since on a special errand. It was in relation to the enterprise of your laborious Co presbyter Mr Wilson, He anxious to have his Presbytery, buy, or lease the Church edifice in Thompson St for his people. This, I hope, will be done

1. The objection may be raised, that Mr Wilson is not a popular preacher: but my testimony is that he is an excellent Pastor, a cautious, judicious, and good adviser, and leader of a flock just such an one as is needed among the better class of our people

2. Thompson St will be a good position for him There is a large colored population in that region of the city.

3. The Jews are ready to buy it at $13.000.

4. You can get it, at $12.500 good title; or lease it for 3 or 5 years at $600 per annum.

5. There is a house in the rear and other apartments which will rent, for 4, or 5 hundred dollars.

6. The Church edifice can be leased seperate from those at a rate proportionally less, but it can be bought seperate,

Dr. I would call on you and urge these matters, but I am obliged to go to Connecticut to day and shall not return till the last of the week. But I must call your attention to one other consideration, it is this; we do need one more efficient coll Presbyterian Church in this city. This is in your power to give.

I have in person presented these general views to both Drs. Alexander and Potts.

I am dear Sir

Yours Respectfully

J. W. C. Pennington

Letters from James W. C. Pennington to J. M. Kebbs. *Images courtesy of the author.*

Joel Hawes (1789–1867), pastor of
the Center Church, Hartford,
Connecticut, 1818–1867.
*Image courtesy of the Connecticut
Historical Society.*

John Hooker (1816–1901), the lawyer
who purchased James Pennington.
*Image courtesy of the Connecticut
Historical Society.*

Horace Bushnell (1802–1876),
pastor of the North Church,
Hartford, Connecticut, 1833–1859.
*Image courtesy of the Connecticut
Historical Society.*

James McCune Smith
(1813–1865), New York
doctor and abolitionist.
*Image courtesy of the New
York Historical Society.*

James McCune Smith

Lewis Tappan (1788–1863)
was an influential antebellum
abolitionist. He was an active
participant in the *Amistad* case
and he and his brother founded
Oberlin College, open to
blacks and whites alike.
Image courtesy of the Author.

ABOVE: *Amistad* captives on New Haven Green. *Images courtesy of the author.*

BELOW: New York City draft riots, July 1863. *Images courtesy of the author.*

of the board. Lewis Tappan was installed as secretary and, of course, as treasurer.[†] "It is intended to give the intelligent & excellent men of color their full share in our cause," wrote Tappan, but gradually the black members of the board were relegated to minor and honorary positions. "Tappan and his friends could not resist taking charge," wrote Tappan's biographer; "that was their nature."[32]

As always, while still pursuing classical studies, Pennington also found time to write letters and to concern himself with missionary work in Africa. In August 1847, he wrote about the need to educate "talented and pious colored men to serve in Africa." That led him to note that there was a lack as well of black clergy of any kind. The 23,000 African Americans in New England had only three churches and only one, presumably Pennington himself, trained within New England. At a time when the American churches were putting enormous energy into foreign mission and missionary work on the American frontier, it does seem surprising that so little effort was made to minister to a population living next door—or even in servants' quarters behind the same door. A few years later, Pennington summed up the situation with the categorical statement that "Not one of the American denominations has ever undertaken any systematic measures for the Christian instruction of the free people of color. There are no provisions for educating ministers and teachers to them."

People of color were apparently invisible to people who were white. If a publisher could produce a city directory for Hartford that included no names of colored persons even as a separate category until 1844, it was obviously not hard to overlook them also as a significant mission field. Here again, the fact that the vast majority of black people in the United States were held in slavery made it difficult for those in the north to be recognized as human beings of equal value.

By September of 1847, Pennington's sabbatical was effectively over and he journeyed down to New York to help complete the transition of the Union Missionary Society into the American Missionary Association. The Union Missionary Society held its final meeting and approved of the merger on the morning of the 19th and that afternoon at 4 o'clock the American Missionary Association held its first Annual Meeting. James W. C. Pennington was chosen as one of five vice presidents while Simeon Jocelyn, Arthur Tappan, Henry Garnet, and a number of others formed

---

† The AMA continued to thrive "thanks to the skill of Lewis Tappan." In 1852 it had five missions in the foreign field with sixteen ministers, sixteen physicians, and thirty-three assistants. It had established a mission in Kentucky and even had an agent distributing Bibles to black and white alike in the slave states. (Wyatt-Brown, p. 294.)

an executive committee but Lewis Tappan was the treasurer and would be at the center of the decision making.

In October, the next National Convention of Colored People and Their Friends was being held, and Pennington traveled west to Troy, New York, to take part. The early rivalry between Philadelphia and New York for leadership had been settled in favor of New York. There was only one Pennsylvanian on hand, while 46 were present from the host state and fourteen from Massachusetts. James W. C. Pennington and Amos Beman represented Connecticut, and single delegates represented five other states. Perhaps Henry Garnet had done his work too well in organizing New Yorkers, since over two thirds of the delegates were from New York. Though he was not yet 32 years old, he had clearly moved into a central position of leadership. The fact that the Convention was meeting in his city and his church was further evidence of his importance to the movement.

Garnet called the meeting to order and then stepped back to let others preside and be chosen as officers. He was being respectful of his seniors, but the ringing words of his 1843 "Address to the Slaves," although it had not yet been published, still echoed in the delegates' minds.[†] This would not be a convention that created similar waves, but would move more cautiously to take small steps forward and respond to more immediate and practical matters. After Nathan Johnson of Bedford, Massachusetts, was chosen to serve as president and James W. C. Pennington as one of three vice presidents with James McCune Smith of New York and Peyton Harris of Buffalo, the meeting quickly became involved in an extended debate about the establishment of a national newspaper in which, oddly, James Pennington took no part. The *Colored American* had expired and the *Clarksonian* had never gained a significant audience, but Frederick Douglass, who opposed the resolution, was about to begin publishing the *North Star*,[††] which would be renamed *Frederick Douglass' Paper* and survive until 1860. The debate continued all afternoon and evening and was not resolved until well into the morning session of the second day, when the resolution was adopted by a vote of 27 to 9. "We lead the forlorn hope of Human Equality," they resolved; "let us tell of its onslaught on the battlements of hate and caste; let us record its triumph in a Press of our own." James Pennington and James McCune Smith, who had been trying to do that very thing, were then appointed to serve on a committee of seven to carry out the

† The address was published in 1848, and there were rumors that John Brown helped finance it.

†† In view of his own difficulties in finding the *North Star* when he left Hagerstown, it is interesting that Pennington wrote Douglass to commend the choice of a name for his paper and express the hope that it would "be . . . what the *North Star* is in the heavens— brilliant, dignified, standing in bold relief . . . So it is also to the flying bondman . . ." Letter to the *North Star*, January 7, 1848.

intention of the Convention, but no funds were provided and nothing seems to have happened as a result. The first issue of Douglass's new paper managed to provide a long report on the Convention while saying nothing of this long debate. Much of the money to create his paper had come from supporters in England, and now those who wanted a black press would have one from the first printing establishment in America ever owned by colored persons.

After that inauspicious start, a report on education, still pursuing the dream of an African American college, was adopted by a closer vote of 26 to 17. Garnet supported the idea of colored academies but questioned the need for colored colleges since enough other colleges were now open to them. Pennington said nothing and recorded no vote. The evening was spent listening to the first four of an impressive seven-man roster of featured speakers: Henry Garnet, Frederick Douglass, Amos Beman, and Alexander Crummell. James Pennington became more active on the third day, presenting a resolution on commerce and then being called on to preside at the day's sessions. Resolutions on Commerce and Temperance were passed without significant debate, but the resolution on Commerce, presented by Pennington, offered a new and imaginative possibility for black progress in response to a proposal he had brought back from Jamaica for a Jamaica Hamitic Association. Until this point, international matters had been largely questions of the colonization or emigration of African Americans to other places. The letter Pennington had brought from Jamaica offered no specifics and, again, nothing concrete seems to have resulted, but this seems to be the first suggestion of the benefits to be gained by international black cooperation.

Having dealt quickly with Commerce and Temperance, the delegates then bogged down in extended debate over the choice of a city for the next meeting. A series of votes was required as first Rochester, then Pittsburgh and Cleveland, were voted down before Newark, the site first proposed by the committee, was approved, 25 to 15.

The report on Agriculture produced more debate since Gerrit Smith, a wealthy and generous New York land owner, had offered 140,000 acres of land in the New York State Adirondack region to provide 40- to 60-acre plots for 3,000 African Americans. The committee recommended "to our people that they forsake the cities and their employments of dependency therein and become cultivators of the soil, as the surest road to respectability and influence." In a country whose population was still ninety percent rural, it made sense to advocate land ownership as the best route to independence, and Smith's donation was a remarkable act.† The land, however, was rocky and mountainous, not ideal for agriculture, and although 3,000 settlers were

† Smith did lay down some restrictions: those taking up his offer must be between the ages of 21 and 60, not already land owners, and not "drunkards."

less than one percent of the free black population, it proved impossible to find that many who had both the interest and the skills to make good use of it. James Mars of Hartford was one of those who thought seriously about the possibility of such a move. He had farming skills and could sell his house and land in Hartford to buy a piece of Adirondack land, but after some exploratory correspondence with Smith, he decided against it. He was concerned for the education of his children and had hoped to find "a place not entirely unsettled." But that was the dilemma. Until Smith could attract a population to settle his land, it was unattractive to people like Mars who would have to forfeit advantages to move. The best-known settler on Smith's land was John Brown, who was not black but was allowed to move there in order to provide leadership and agricultural guidance. Brown, however, quickly moved on to Kansas and then Harpers Ferry.

Having cleared away these matters, the Convention moved on Friday afternoon to the central question always before it: how to abolish slavery. The mood of the Convention, indeed the nature and direction of the entire black abolition movement, was the issue in the debate that developed on the best means of ending slavery in America. With time on Saturday needed for the usual housekeeping resolutions, the debate extended into the Friday evening session, and James Pennington and the other two orators scheduled to bring the Convention to an inspirational end found themselves preempted by the need to define fundamental priorities. The resolution presented, decrying violence and bloodshed and insisting on the primacy of moral suasion, brought Henry Garnet to the floor with several objections to the language of the report, in particular the phrases "shedding of blood" and "moral suasion." Garnet had made the debate necessary by the unresolved conflict over his "Address to the Slaves" four years earlier at Buffalo, and the phrasing of the resolution seemed designed to repudiate his acceptance, even encouragement, of violence. As at Buffalo, there were strong feelings on both sides. Garnet was not lacking support, and after hours of debate through an afternoon and evening session, the resolution was sent back to committee. Pennington had not spoken; Frederick Douglass had taken the lead in support of the resolution, and his position was summed up in the first issue of his new paper: "PATIENCE and PERSEVERANCE shall be our motto." On the final day, the committee report was brought back transformed into a position paper to be considered further by a committee of one, Frederick Douglass, who was charged to report at the next Convention. Meanwhile the Convention agreed with a statement that was much more like Douglass than Garnet. "The human voice," the report stated, "must supersede the roar of cannon. Truth alone is the legitimate antidote of falsehood. Liberty is always sufficient to grapple with tyranny. Free speech, free discussion, peaceful agitation, the foolishness of preaching these, under

God, will subvert this giant crime." The Convention believed that slavery would die when people sufficiently understood its nature. "Our only hope for peaceful emancipation in this land is based on a firm, devoted, and unceasing assertion of our rights, and a free, full and determined exposure of our multiplied wrongs." The statement closed with words that seemed designed to replace Garnet's call for "RESISTANCE! RESISTANCE! RESISTANCE." This time the key word was "agitate, agitate!! AGITATE!!!" Nevertheless, the Convention did include a resolution "That the Convention recommend to our people the propriety of instructing their sons in the art of war."[33]

CHAPTER FIFTEEN

New York, 1848–1849

On March 25, 1847, Theodore Sedgwick Wright died in New York City at the age of fifty. He had been the most widely respected leader among African Americans in New York, served as a mentor to James Pennington and Henry Garnet, and provided a voice of wisdom and moderation in the counsels of the Anti Slavery Societies and Colored People's Conventions. While he "poured out his whole heart in supplication for the oppressed," he prayed constantly for slaveholders as well. The church he had served for seventeen years was the largest African American congregation in the Presbyterian Church.

Lewis Tappan wrote an obituary for Theodore Wright in which he remembered having taken a distinguished Southern lawyer who was an elder in the Presbyterian Church to a service at the Shiloh Church. After hearing the prayer and the sermon and "observing the respectable appearance of the congregation and the neatness of their place of worship," he had exclaimed, "What a sight; what an excellent prayer and discourse; how respectable everything appears here. I was never in such a place before . . . I am determined that I will not live as I have done, &c." Ministers and elders, black and white, thronged the church for the funeral service. Few clergy, Tappan wrote, were "more holy and beloved."[1]

The leadership of the Shiloh Church spent very little time deciding that James W. C. Pennington was their first choice as Wright's successor. They had known him since his earliest days as a Christian, had heard him preach often over the years, knew of his writing and international travels, and were so confident that he could provide the leadership they needed that they waited only a few weeks before extending a formal call. It was not so easy for James Pennington. He had asked for a two-year leave of absence with the expectation on both sides that he would return to the Talcott Street Church afterward. By April 1847, he had not yet completed that two-year leave and felt obligated first to use the full time he had asked for and then, indeed, to return to Talcott Street as promised. The

Shiloh congregation did have at least one other obvious option, and that was to call Henry Highland Garnet, another younger pastor who had been mentored by Theodore Wright. Garnet was also familiar to them and had also given evidence of his oratorical skills and leadership abilities. It was Garnet who preached the sermon at Theodore Wright's funeral. But Garnet was more volatile and controversial, and the congregation needed unity. If Pennington was not available, they, like the Talcott congregation in 1839, would wait until he was.

Not until he had completed his plan of study, taken his part in the 1847 Convention in Troy, and returned to full-time ministry could James Pennington even begin to think about what might come next. His thoughts about his future ministry were also complicated by his decision to marry again. Almira Way, like Harriet, had been a teacher in the Talcott Street school, and it seemed best to Pennington, in view of their marital plans, to move away from the congregation and community where he had lived with Harriet in order to begin a new life in a new place. The next time the Shiloh congregation approached him, he told them he would come in March 1848, one year after Theodore Wright's death.

On March 7, therefore, Pennington presented his credentials to the Third Presbytery[†] of New York, answered "the constitutional questions," and was received as a member.[2] The installation followed three days later. At the Presbytery's next meeting, James W. C. Pennington was appointed to serve as a member of the Committee on Experimental Religion, in other words one of the committee to examine the credentials of candidates for ordination—a remarkable testimony to the respect Pennington's new colleagues (all white) had for his faith and learning.

Faith and theological accomplishment would not be much direct use, however, in the first challenge facing the new pastor. The same April meeting of the Presbytery received a committee report recommending that the church property should be sold at auction because of planned changes in the street and repairs needed in the building.

Before he could give full attention to that, James Pennington had personal business to attend to. He returned to Hartford to marry Almira Way on May 7 in the spacious home of Henry Goodwin, the former owner and editor of the *Hartford Courant*. Joel Hawes conducted the service.[††] The bride, tall and slender, wore a brown silk dress, and the traditional wedding cake was pronounced "very grand" by one who attended.[3] James Pennington returned

---

† In the Presbyterian system, congregations in a local area are united in a presbytery in which each congregation is represented by an elder and a minister.

†† The location may indicate that Almira Way had been a servant in the Goodwin household or that Joel Hawes made the arrangement with Goodwin. Weddings were not held in Congregational churches at that time.

to New York not only with a new wife but also a newly adopted four-year-old son. Thomas H. Sands Pennington was the child of Sarah Blackstone Sands, who had died on March 28 at the age of 31 and on her deathbed asked that Pennington adopt her son.[†]

Augustus Washington spoke for the Talcott Street congregation when he wrote, "I may be selfish, yet I cannot but regret exceedingly that he should feel it his duty to leave this people, whose pastor he has been for the past eight years. He has ever secured the confidence and respect of the whole community, and has had one of the most orderly, respectable, and intelligent audiences that I ever knew. He is a sound theologian, a good self-made scholar, and a gentleman: aside from pastoral duties, actively engaged, heart and hand, in temperance, education, anti-slavery, and all the reforms that tend to improve, refine and elevate society. He is one of the ablest men in the country and perhaps has never been properly appreciated by us till now. . . . He cannot but do good wherever he goes."[4]

Certainly there was ample opportunity to "do good" in New York. The city had nearly doubled in size, from almost 300,000 to almost 500,000, in the twenty years since James Pennington had first known it and was thirty times the size of Hartford. The African American population of some 15,000 was more than fifteen times that of Hartford, but the occupations engaged in by that population were very similar: servants, waiters, washerwomen, and laborers were the largest categories by far. The 1860 census showed only seventeen African American school teachers and even fewer clergy. The Shiloh Presbyterian Church counted some five hundred members, but they were far from wealthy, and one of the primary challenges facing their new pastor was the one that had worn down Theodore Wright at so young an age: raising money to pay the church's debt. The challenge was magnified by the action taken by the Presbytery to sell the church. The city was planning to widen the street, and the building, bought by the congregation when another church

---

† There is a frustrating lack of information about Harriet Pennington, Almira Way, Sarah Sands, and Thomas Sands. Harriet is the only one of them listed in any of the Hartford City Directories. There is no record of cause of death for either Harriet or Sarah Sands (records were kept in those days only of death by murder, suicide, or accident), nor is there any record of the adoption of Thomas Sands. A waiter named Raphael Sand, working in a Hartford hotel, is listed in the Directories as living at 2 Ann Street rear, where Pennington had lived earlier, but there is no certainty that he was the husband of Sarah or father of Thomas. Since he continued to be listed for several years after her death, it seems odd that he would not have taken responsibility for a son unless, of course, he and Sarah were separated—or not in a relationship in the first place. Thomas H. Sands Pennington, who became a druggist in Saratoga Springs, N.Y., and died in 1900, is listed in the United States census record of 1850 as born "about 1844" and in the 1860 census as being sixteen years old. Thomas is the source of a brief but important memorandum about his stepfather.

community abandoned it, was in serious need of repairs. But "the principal reason" given by the Presbytery's committee was that "a very large portion of the Congregation reside in the upper part of the city, at a great distance from the present location of the church." The critical fact was that the black population was moving north as the city grew and the church, at the corner of Frankfort and William Street, where the ramp to the Brooklyn Bridge would be located twenty-two years later, was being left behind. The old building, described by one observer as having "nothing about it very inviting," but capable of seating 1500 people,[5] was sold for $14,175 and the proceeds were used to pay off the mortgage and other debts, leaving $10,000 "with which to secure another church edifice."[6]

Pennington found housing for himself and his family on West Broadway, a few blocks from the Shiloh church, but the center of black population was already north of 14th Street, two miles away, and the horse-drawn trolley cars that were becoming popular did not welcome black customers. The time-honored solution to this problem as New York City grew was for the church to follow its members. One church after another moved out of lower Manhattan and often moved further north a second or third time to keep up with the rapidly shifting center of population. Within three weeks of Pennington's arrival in Manhattan, the Shiloh congregation had arranged to move to a new building on Prince Street, approximately half way to 14th Street. It was a better location but still far from ideal. The Third Presbytery, of which Shiloh was a member, noted cheerfully that the site was ideally suited to attract "a large portion of the destitute of the city." Certainly the destitute needed the church's ministry, but they would not provide much help in dealing with the debt of $14,500 that the congregation had assumed in order to buy the new church. Attendance did increase and the church school doubled in size, but raising money would now become a continuing concern for the new pastor.[7]

Financial matters would also dominate the relationship between Pennington and Lewis Tappan, since contributions for the American Mission Association often came to Pennington and had to be forwarded to Tappan as treasurer. In June, for example, Pennington sent a note enclosing contributions to the American Missionary Association of ten dollars from the Abyssinian Congregational Church in Portland, Maine, and three dollars from the same church's Sabbath school. The Shiloh congregation could not afford a secretary to handle such small matters, but Lewis Tappan would watch them closely.[8] Tappan was also a near neighbor now. He had moved to Brooklyn after his Manhattan home was destroyed, but his office was still in the commercial district.

For the time being, Pennington and Tappan could continue to work together where their views coincided—as they usually did on the abolitionist agenda. Eighteen forty-eight was again an election year, and abolitionists had reason to be deeply concerned about the direction the national government was taking. The question of what to do about Texas, debated at the World Anti Slavery Convention in London in 1843, had erupted in a full-scale war between the United States and Mexico. Texas, infiltrated by American settlers, had declared its independence from Mexico in 1836 and had been admitted to the Union as a slave state in 1845. In the following year, President Polk deliberately sent American forces into territory still claimed by Mexico. When they were fired on, he asked Congress for a Declaration of War on the grounds that "Mexico has passed the boundary of the United States, has invaded our territory and shed American blood upon American soil." Abraham Lincoln, a new member of Congress from Illinois, like many others of the Whig party, wanted to know exactly where the attack had occurred and where American blood had been shed. "Show me the spot," he demanded. Even Robert Toombs, a Whig Congressman from Georgia who would later become an ardent secessionist, declared: "This war is nondescript. . . . We charge the President with usurping the war-making power . . . with seizing a country . . . which had been for centuries, and was then in the possession of the Mexicans. . . . Let us put a check upon this lust of dominion. We had territory enough. . ." James Pennington called it "the Slavery War."[9] He and other abolitionists were united with most Northerners and many in the South in seeing the war as an attempt to extend the territory in which slaves could be held and to increase the number of members of Congress who could be relied on to vote in the interest of slave owners. Henry Thoreau went to jail rather than pay taxes to support the war and wrote his famous essay "On Civil Disobedience" to explain his stand.

By the time James Pennington moved to New York, the war had been ended by the Treaty of Guadalupe Hidalgo, signed on February 2, 1848, and ceding to the United States not only the land Texas claimed north of the Rio Grande, but also the present-day states of California, Nevada, and Utah, as well as parts of Colorado, Arizona, New Mexico, and Wyoming. In return, Mexico received $18,250,000. To all outward appearance, the slave states had won an enormous victory in opening so vast a territory to their "peculiar institution." Indeed, even the Whig Party seemingly endorsed the war by nominating as its next candidate for president Zachary Taylor, one of the leading generals of that war.

Lewis Tappan, however, had not been won over. Engaged in politics now in a way he had not been earlier in his career, Lewis Tappan drew James Pennington and others into an attempt to make the Liberty Party a more significant force in American life. He created a Washington newspaper, the *National Era*, to be the printed voice of the party, and raised money both in the United States and England to pay the editor's salary and expenses. Taking a moderate position, the newspaper gained a wide circulation but alienated those with more forceful views. Attempting to control the Liberty Party as he controlled so much else in his life, Tappan persuaded the party to set aside James Birney, the candidate of 1840 and 1844 who had never won an elective office, and nominate Senator John P. Hale of New Hampshire, a recent convert to the anti-slavery cause. In early July, the new paper printed a lengthy appeal "To the Friends of Liberty" signed by Arthur and Lewis Tappan, James W. C. Pennington, Simeon Jocelyn, Charles B. Ray, and six others. In somewhat turgid language, the signers said they "beg leave to offer some considerations to the friends of impartial liberty." Rejecting the Garrisonian notion that there was nothing to be gained by participation in electoral politics, the statement advocates "the power of the ballot box" and argues that "the prayers of good men can be acceptable at the court of heaven only when they vote as they pray." Printed also as an eleven-page pamphlet, the Appeal expressed confidence that "the great body of the people of the free States are beginning to see that their rights and liberties are in jeopardy . . . and vowing eternal hostility to the extension of slavery." They proclaimed their candidate to be "honest, capable, and independent" and asked, in less than ringing prose, "Why not, then, unite with the friends of Liberty, in giving him the entire Anti-Slavery vote of the country? He might be elected . . ."[10] To anyone who looked at the national mood realistically, it did not seem likely.

Meanwhile Martin Van Buren, voted out of the presidency eight years earlier but unable to resist the possibility of returning to the White House, had moved toward an anti-slavery position and set out to gain the nomination of a new combination of factions calling itself the Free Soil Party and campaigning with the slogan "Free Soil, Free Speech, Free Labor, and Free Men."[11] Hoping that this new party would serve its purposes, the supporters of the Liberty Party joined in a convention in Buffalo in August that opposed the extension of slavery in the territories and denounced "the reckless hostility of the Slave Power." Delegates then chose Van Buren rather than Hale, with the result that the disillusioned remnants of the Liberty Party nominated Gerrit Smith. Frederick Douglass saw no hope in any of these alignments, but Samuel Ringgold Ward used the columns of Douglass's paper for "An Appeal to the Colored Voters of New York" on behalf of Gerrit Smith. "It is difficult to see," he wrote, "how a man who . . . exerted his utmost power to consign our brethren of the *Amistad* to a Cuban gibbet in 1840, can, without the least . . . intimation that he would not do the same again . . . be a fit candidate." Gerrit Smith, on the other hand, was a known quantity: an "outspoken, uncompromising, impartial and truly practical philanthropist." "Yes, turn your eyes from the little huckstering, wirepulling, aristocratic, pro-slavery politician . . . to one who loves you, and gives . . . HIMSELF to us and our cause."[12] There was indeed nothing of the typical politician about Smith. He apparently told a friend that if he were president he would end the war, withdraw the troops, disband the army and navy, replace the tariff by direct taxation, give the public lands to the needy, abolish naturalization laws, and deny public office to anyone who supported the sale of liquor or owned slaves.[13]

None of these maneuvers and appeals made much difference to the electorate, who gave Van Buren only ten percent of the vote and Gerrit Smith a tenth of one percent. Zachary Taylor, the war hero, defeated Lewis Cass, but died after 16 months as president, leaving Millard Fillmore, almost as unknown then as today, to serve out his term.[†] As a resident of New York State, Pennington could have voted if he had owned property valued at $250, but whatever property he owned was in Connecticut.[††] His support for Tappan's political efforts seems to have been confined to his signature on the July appeal. The article he wrote in 1844 denouncing Liberty Party candidates and saying that "they love office more than they love anti-slavery" would certainly have applied as well or better to Martin Van Buren and other Free Soil candidates in 1848. James Pennington was an active and vocal advocate of causes but not of personalities or parties.

Uninvolved though he may have been in the political campaign, he found himself needing to do damage control when it was over. Gerrit Smith emerged from the 1848 campaign so disappointed with the support he had been given by abolitionists that he decided to withdraw entirely from the associations he had supported, including the American Missionary Association. James Pennington took it upon himself to appeal to Smith to reconsider. The "many humble colored Christians interested in the support of that society," he told Smith, "have never voted pro slavery tickets." The AMA was created "to stand on the side of the oppressed, and to furnish them a gospel pure from any blood but that of the Son of God . . . If in any way it should as a body give sanction to oppression, I will leave it. . . Is it true my dear friend, that you cannot overcome your scruples?"[14] But Smith was in a sulk that would lead him to support John Brown rather than the timid politicians around him.

For Lewis Tappan and business people like him, New York City was primarily a commercial center, but for James Pennington it was a central point in the escape route taken by fugitive slaves. The Shiloh Church and the Pennington home nearby (Pennington had moved from West Broadway to 29 6th Avenue to be closer to the church building) were an important station in the

---

† Taylor was a slaveholder but opposed extending slavery to the territories. Fillmore proclaimed his hatred of slavery but thought it had to be protected under the Constitution.
†† The property qualification did not apply to white voters. James McCune Smith had appealed to black citizens to purchase the necessary property to enable them to qualify, but the amount was the rough equivalent of $7000 in today's dollars and few servants and laborers had that amount available. "Convention of Colored Citizens," *Christian Freeman*, May 22, 1845.

Underground Railroad. Nor was it simply a matter of sheltering escaped slaves and sending them on, but of outwitting slave dealers and finding sympathetic magistrates. In December 1848, John Lee of Frederick County, Maryland, came to New York as representative of an association of Maryland slave-holders to test the New York laws. Two men in his employment then seized a young man named Joseph Belt who was walking on Duane Street at 8:30 in the morning. Without bothering about any legal process, they took him to a hotel on Broadway where he met John Lee, and then to Long Island, where they brought him before a judge two days later and accused hm of stealing a coat. Unfortunately for their purposes, they had found the wrong court. Judge Edmonds dismissed the case on the grounds, first, of illegal arrest and, second, on the grounds that he had no reason to take it for granted that slavery was legal in Maryland. Lee had an attorney with him and a copy of the Maryland laws, but Edmonds said he had no evidence that the copy they presented was, in fact, published by the Maryland state authorities. Lee's error was to present Maryland law rather than base his case on the Constitution of the United States and federal law. Pennington wrote to Frederick Douglass,† to note that if the judge had been less sympathetic, Belt might have been taken back into slavery on "purely constitutional grounds. Mighty God—what a government," he commented. The fact that Douglass, Belt, and Pennington all came from Maryland led him to add, "These Maryland scamps must be met and conquered. What do you say to forming a *Maryland* society at the North?"[15] New Yorkers met and adopted resolutions condemning Belt's arrest as an "alarming outrage" which, they said, "affects the security of every colored man, woman and child in this city." No colored persons, they resolved, should allow themselves to be arrested as a slave or on any charge without due process of law.[16] But Belt was outnumbered, and New York City had only begun to learn what kind of policing was needed to maintain order in a city of that size and complexity. That black New Yorkers were aware of their rights and able to meet in protest was useful, but far from an adequate response to the threat they identified.

Appeals came also to Pennington from people who saw him as the pastor of a large New York congregation concerned for fugitive slave problems and therefore a potential source of help for them with their own various needs. In December 1848, a letter came to him from a George Williams in Chilli-cothe, Ohio, who seemed to have some acquaintance with Pennington and had written to him and to Gerrit Smith to ask for financial help in rescuing

---

† The letter is signed "Yours, in haste" and was written in such haste that Pennington forgot that the year had changed and wrote "January 5, 1848" and omitted one of his middle initials.

his relatives from slavery. He had rescued his sister but needed $300 for his sister's daughter and another $1000 for his brother. He expressed the hope that Pennington would "bring the subject before the public mind" and write to Smith asking for a subscription paper. "Remember me to Mrs. Pennington," he writes, "and let me know what you can do." Ironically, Pennington, who had been unable to purchase his own freedom, was now expected, because of his position, to be able to provide such assistance for others.[17]

New York was also the central stage in the ongoing conflict with the Colonization Society. Never able to raise adequate funds or to send any significant number of settlers to Liberia, they were still able to command attention and attract an occasional black leader who despaired of change in America. When President Roberts of Liberia came to New York in 1848, he was given the freedom of the city, something that black Americans themselves did not have. Henry Garnet was one of those who was having second thoughts on the subject of colonization. In February of 1849, Garnet wrote to Samuel Ward to say that his mind had changed in some respects on the subject of colonization. He was now prepared to say that Liberia's existence could be "highly beneficial to Africa," that "the new republic will succeed," and that every treaty President Roberts of Liberia negotiated with a European power "goes far to create respect for our race throughout the civilized world."[18] When Garnet also wrote to Frederick Douglass asking what objection he had "to the civilization and Christianization of Africa," Douglass responded indignantly, "The African Civilization Society says to us, go to Africa, raise cotton, civilize the natives, become planters, merchants, compete with the slave States in the Liverpool cotton market and thus break down American slavery. To which we simply and briefly reply, we prefer to remain in America . . . You go there, we stay here, is just the difference between us and the African Colonization Society, and the true issue upon which co-operation with it or opposition to it must turn."[19] †

Actions and statements such as these required a response, and in April James Pennington presided at the Shiloh Church over a meeting called specifically to express the mind of the "Colored Citizens of the City of New York" on the subject of colonization. He opened the meeting by charging that the Colonization Society had made a treaty with Liberia, giving them control of public

† The contrasting personalities of Douglass and Garnet led to increasingly acrimonious exchanges. In September 1849, Garnet wrote to Douglass: "I know, sir, that in your hot pursuit after a worthless, and a transient, fame, you would sometimes stoop to mean things, but I never dreamed that you would ever sink so low, that you would have to reach up, on tip-toe, to find that level of meanness where common knaves are inclined to pause. Ah, sir, the green-eyed monster has made you mad." "'Calling him out,' and He Comes," *North Star*, September 7, 1849.

lands in that country, and that the Society continued to complain of the lack of support given them by African Americans. Other leaders, speaking at great length, added further charges, and not until the second night was it possible to pass resolutions repeating the stand taken years earlier in Philadelphia at the first convention Pennington had attended: those who have a desire to go to Africa are free to do so, but most of those born in America consider themselves to be Americans and are unwilling to be coerced into leaving.[20]

Several speakers at the meeting referred specifically to the activities of a Colonization Society agent in England and the need to counter his representations. That may have been decisive for Pennington, who had been exploring the idea of another English trip for some months and now decided that the time had come. There was a World Peace Conference scheduled to be held in Paris in June. Pennington could represent the American Peace Society, as he had done before, and take advantage of the opportunity to travel the speakers' circuit again in England to raise money to assist the resettlement of fugitives and to help pay down the Shiloh Church's debt. The constantly growing pressure to catch and return fugitive slaves was another critical factor in Pennington's decision. It was well known by this time that Pennington himself was a fugitive, and in New York City he was more exposed than he had been since his first months in Pennsylvania. He had talked the matter over with John Hooker in Hartford, who had urged him to go abroad until arrangements could be made for his freedom.† The decision was made before the Anti-Colonization Society mass meeting, since the resolutions adopted at that meeting included a statement that "we fraternally commend the Rev. J.W.C. Pennington to the confidence and sympathies of British Christians, as a firm friend of his people in America."

The central resolutions, however, condemned colonization in no uncertain terms: "the testimony of our generation of the people of colour is entirely, uniformly, and absolutely against the scheme of African colonization . . . we will not remove to Africa except by the exercise of force." Toward the end of

---

† John Hooker (*Some Reminiscences of a Long Life*, p. 39) tells a somewhat different story of the events leading to Pennington's trip to England. In Hooker's account, when Pennington confided his status to him, it was agreed that Pennington should go to Canada while Hooker opened negotiations with Frisby Tilghman, to purchase Pennington's freedom. Tilghman's response was that "Jim" was a first-rate blacksmith, easily worth $1000, and he would settle for no less than $500. This, Hooker says, was "so much beyond Pennington's ability to pay, that it was thought best for him to go on to England without returning to Hartford." Hooker, however, is writing fifty years after the events he describes and seems to have conflated two separate attempts to negotiate Pennington's freedom. Hooker did attempt to negotiate a purchase while Pennington was still in Hartford, but the record is clear that he went on to New York from Hartford, spent a year at the Shiloh Church, and then went to England.

the session, the delegates adopted a resolution offered by James McCune Smith calling on the Congress to appropriate a sum of money to send not themselves but the agents of the Colonization Society "to the land of their forefathers . . . [as] disturbers of the public peace."[21]

The decision to travel again to England must have been under consideration for a number of months, perhaps even before the move to New York. Lewis Tappan had written a "Dear Brother" letter to Pennington in March of 1848 to complain that he had gone to the West Indies without advance notice and now seemed to be thinking about a trip to England but had not consulted Tappan. "Your movements are mysterious," he wrote. "When you went to the West Indies I, in common with many of your friends, wondered at your voyage. . . . Still you are a freeman, and have an undoubted right to go to England or anywhere else without disclosing the objects of your voyage. . . . Have you not some plan in view to raise money in England? If so, dear brother, is it not best to open the subject to your friends & co-laborers here that, in their correspondence with English friends, they may speak of you & your plans unambiguously?" What Tappan could never understand was that his benevolence might be seen in any sense as a burden by its recipients, but the assumption of a right to know and advise is not very different from a right to control. A fugitive slave would be sensitive to such matters, but there was no way Tappan could have understood that. His concern, he assured Pennington, was entirely in Pennington's interest: "I write to you as a brother beloved, wishing you to do at all times that which is honorable to yourself, to our brothers the people of color, and to those you are intimately associated with on committees etc. Frankness with those thus situated is a duty. Is it not? By what road do you expect to go!"[22]

Surely one factor, however subliminal, in the decision to travel to England again was the need to escape that sort of hectoring for a while. A more obvious factor was Pennington's status as a fugitive slave. He had revealed that status to the world during his first English trip—it was an asset there as it never could be in America—but it deprived him of whatever security his changed name, education, and ordination provided. In Hartford, distance from the centers of business and communication also provided some security, but now he was in New York where slave catchers lurked constantly. It was a daily anxiety, an added source of stress that he could try to ease by his ceaseless activity, but he remained a black man in a white world, a man who could be stopped at any moment and taken back into slavery, for whom the law provided little protection, and there was nothing he could do that would change that fact. He remembered all too well that frightening evening in Pennsylvania when he had heard sounds downstairs that might have signaled the arrival of slave catchers and had stood poised on the window ledge ready to leap down and run for his life. That was more than twenty years ago, but nothing he had accomplished had made him more secure than he had been then. The burden of that anxiety was only increased by the knowledge that he had been free of it for a while in England. There was one place, he knew, where he could go about the business of living without any need to consider whether this place or that would be barred to him or whether he would be suddenly arrested and dragged back into slavery. Whatever obvious reasons there were to go to England, there were those silent factors that made the stated objects more persuasive.

Apart from these personal reasons, there were, of course, specific purposes to be served: he could raise money to help pay the church's debt; the "free produce" movement was gaining momentum and he could be an advocate; he could also speak out against the efforts of the Colonization Society's agents, who were always at work to enhance their image and gain support. More specifically still, there was a Peace Conference scheduled for Paris in August. By the spring of 1849, Pennington had been pastor of the Shiloh Church for a full year and begun to make his mark on the congregation and the city. He had also lived with his new family for a year and enjoyed again the comfort and security of married life. But now the reasons to travel seemed to outweigh those to stay at home. With or without permission and understanding from Lewis Tappan, James Pennington would go to Europe again.

CHAPTER SIXTEEN

Great Britain, 1849–1851

James Pennington's second trip to Great Britain was very different from the first in one respect at least: he had a family with him. He and Almira had been married less than three months, so this might have been considered a honeymoon trip—though longer than most such trips, even in a day when a "Grand Tour" of the continent was not unusual for newlywed couples with adequate means. There is no record of their trans-Atlantic journey, but by mid-June they were in London and Pennington was already writing back to the New York papers about his experience. On his previous trip, he had been impressed most of all with the freedom he had to travel and to be accepted everywhere without regard to color. This time he was impressed first of all with an incident that reminded him of the long reach of the slave system.

Pennington had stopped one day in the office of the British and Foreign Anti Slavery Society in the center of London and had been introduced to a recently arrived American fugitive slave. The man had attempted to escape from slavery in Louisiana some two years earlier but was caught, given one hundred and sixty lashes, and put in an iron collar for six months. Determined still to be free, he had managed to hide himself on an English ship, where he was discovered only after the ship had been at sea for three weeks. The captain "appeared to be enraged" and ordered him flogged, but when all was ready he said, "Well, I don't see any place left to flog" and treated him well instead. On arrival in Liverpool, the captain kept him concealed until dark and then gave him clothes and money and put him on a train to London, where he came to the Anti Slavery Office and it was arranged for him to go to one of the British Islands where he could begin a new life in freedom.

"What struck me with great force—I may say, alarming force," wrote Pennington, was the fact that the captain had felt it necessary to hide the fugitive even in Liverpool. "Here," he continued, "you see American slavery reaching forth its bloodstained hand all over the world, feeling after its victim, and seizing by the throat all who dare aid him." There was no point, he understood more clearly than ever, in seeking to escape from slavery to some other part of the world. "We must meet it on the continent and conquer it there, or we are dead men, go where we may!"[1]

The fears raised by that story were amply justified by another incident that summer that demonstrated the reach of the slave states beyond any question, although Pennington only heard of it the following year. He had just finished giving a lecture in London in early April 1850, when a young man who worked in the Custom House told him a story from his own experience. Just as in the story told to Pennington at the Anti Slavery Society's office, a ship had sailed for London from a Southern port and far out at sea had discovered a slave hidden in the hold. The slave was quickly imprisoned on the ship and remained there while the ship came into the St. Katherine's docks, London, unloaded its cargo, took on a new cargo, and sailed for America.

Pennington asked what reason was given for keeping the man imprisoned for the four or five weeks it took to unload and reload the ship and then taking him back to slavery. The answer was that the slave owner had discovered his loss and sent a message by a steamer that reached London first. The letter threatened the ship's master with dire consequences if he failed to bring the slave back, and the master, a young man, commanding his first ship, did not dare risk the loss of his job. The customs officer himself had been unwilling to "get into any hobble" with the captain for fear of creating difficulties for him.

"This story," Pennington wrote to William Harned, a New York publisher of anti-slavery materials, "melted my whole soul away to water. Think of the gallant fellow, perilling his life . . . And when the bark strikes the rock-bound coast of Albion's Isle and anchored within sight of the palace of the British Queen and within five minute's walk of the very spot where Lord Mansfield pronounced, 1772, his celebrated decision, that as soon as a slave touched British soil he is free—there is no freedom for him!"[2] Safely on shore himself, Pennington was safer in England than America, and he would not return to New York until the haunting fear of capture could be brought to an end.

The Peace Conference in Paris was still almost two months away, so Pennington settled in with his family to preach and speak as invitations came, but also to begin a new project. Now, at last, he would write the story of his escape from slavery. Since his status as a fugitive slave was now a matter of open record, he could tell his story and use it to good purpose. One reason for his journey was the need to raise money to pay the church's debt, and a public that would flock to hear anti-slavery speakers might well be willing to buy a book as well. In fact, there was already some precedent for such a venture. Two other fugitive slaves, Frederick Douglass and William Wells Brown, had already published their stories, Douglass in 1845 and Brown in 1847. It seemed to Pennington that an account of his escape from slavery would be of particular interest to young people. He would shape the story for them and publish it inexpensively to gain the widest circulation. Pennington's account would also be different in placing his story within a specifically Christian frame of reference: slavery is not simply an evil, but a sin, "a sin not only against man, but also against God."[3] The "providence of God"[4] is a constant theme, and the book ends with the plain statement of that purpose: "My object in writing this tract is now completed. It has been to shew the reader the hand of God with a slave . . ."[5]

Between late June and early November, the only certain dates for Pennington's activities are those of the Second General Peace Congress which met in Paris from the 22nd to the 24th of August. Pennington traveled that summer in Germany and Belgium as well as France, and it seems likeliest that those places were visited after the Conference and that the time beforehand was spent in England working on his biography. The Conference in Paris drew, inevitably, a primarily French-speaking audience; Pennington had not studied that language, but he did have a knowledge of German that would have been of use when he traveled further east. News accounts of the Congress report the presence of twenty American delegates and "800 Anglo Saxons." England, France, and America had been at war with each other thirty-six years earlier, and hostilities between England and France were a tradition extending through the centuries, so this gathering, even though governments were not officially represented, was an historic occasion and celebrated by the French hosts with all the ceremonies of an imperial court; the palaces and gardens of the emperors were made available to the Congress. Indeed, Louis-Napoléon Bonaparte, who had recently been elected president of France, would shortly become the last French emperor.

This "Second Peace Congress" was not the successor of the one Pennington had attended in 1843, but rather was the second of a series of conferences organized principally by Elihu Burritt, an American reformer. Burritt, like Pennington, came from Connecticut, had been trained as a blacksmith, and was largely self-educated.[†] He had organized the first Peace Congress in Brussels the year before and firmly believed that the world was ready to begin an era of universal peace. William W. Brown and Alexander Crummell were among the American delegates to the Paris Conference. Burritt had invited the Archbishop of Paris to preside at the Congress, but the archbishop had declined for reasons of health. Also realistic about the state of the world, the archbishop had written to commend the delegates for their efforts but to suggest that "alas! The time has not yet come when it will be completely possible

---

† 19th-century references to "the Learned Blacksmith" are references to Burritt, not Pennington.

for the nations to enter upon the path of peace. Perhaps war will continue for many years longer to be a cruel necessity. But it is allowable, it is praiseworthy, it is noble" to seek an end to "these fratricidal contests."[6]

Lacking the presence of the archbishop, Victor Hugo presided and opened the meeting with an eloquent speech that led one Englishman to say to another, "I can't understand a word of what he says but isn't it good?"[7] When translated into English, it offered a glimpse of a future:

> . . . when war will seem as absurd and impossible between Paris and London, between Petersburg and Berlin, between Vienna and Turin, as it would be impossible and would seem absurd today between Rouen and Amiens, between Boston and Philadelphia. A day will come when you France, you Russia, you Italy, you England, you Germany, you all, nations of the continent, without losing your distinct qualities and your glorious individuality, will be merged closely within a superior unit and you will form the European brotherhood, just as Normandy, Brittany, Burgundy, Lorraine, Alsace, all our provinces are merged together in France. A day will come when the only fields of battle will be markets opening up to trade and minds opening up to ideas. A day will come when the bullets and the bombs will be replaced by votes, by the universal suffrage of the peoples, by the venerable arbitration of a great sovereign senate which will be to Europe what this parliament is to England, what this diet is to Germany, what this legislative assembly is to France. A day will come when we will display cannon in museums just as we display instruments of torture today, and are amazed that such things could ever have been possible.[8]

Hugo would have been delighted by the post-World War II development of a European Union but baffled, undoubtedly, to find the use of torture still being debated in the United States in the twenty-first century.

It was late on the second day of the Congress that William Wells Brown came to the platform. Brown had slipped off a steamboat in Cincinnati in 1834 and had become an active agent for the Underground Railroad in Buffalo, New York. A strong believer in nonviolence and moral suasion, he had become a popular temperance and anti-slavery lecturer and had come to Paris on his first overseas venture. Although he had not been listed among the speakers, he was recognized and said he would not have thought of taking up the time of the delegates except for the importance of saying something about the "war element" that condemned three millions of men in the United States to slavery. Noting that slavery had been outlawed in almost every country of Europe, he stated his belief that condemnation of war would lead to the emancipation of the American slaves.

James Pennington came next to the platform and also apologized for "trespassing on the meeting at that late hour," but he had been asked to speak in support of a resolution calling on "ministers of religion to endeavour to eradicate from the minds of all . . . those political prejudices and hereditary hatreds which have too often been the cause of disastrous wars." He began by pointing out that such actions are not that simple because, in the present state of the world, it would take great moral courage to speak against war. The love of war, he said, was seen by many as a mark of patriotism. He pointed out, as he had done six years earlier at the First General Peace Convention in London, that "war settles nothing," but he also analyzed the way in which patriotism can become an obstacle to peace. "He is an unfortunate man," Pennington told the delegates, "who has no country; and . . . who having a country does not love it." The long struggle with the Colonization Society, however, had helped African Americans clarify their own thinking about love of country. "But this love of country," Pennington went on, "is capable of great abuse. . . . Mere politicians act upon the principle . . . that as patriots we must stand ready to meet them in defence of our country. Here lies their grand fallacy. Why should we take this for granted? Is it not equal to taking it for granted that the gospel is not adapted to change men, that they will not agress upon each other? . . . They seem to forget that it takes more moral courage to keep the peace than it does to break the peace and to fight battles. And the former is the kind of courage ministers of religion need to teach the principles of peace in the face of the war-spirit of the age." Pennington noted the sheer numbers of slaves in the Western Hemisphere and told the delegates that twelve million slaves could certainly "disturb the peace" of the forty million among whom they live. Nevertheless, he told his audience, "We, all things considered, prefer to keep the peace, and choose God as our arbiter. The sword settles nothing. Physical force, however powerful, substantiates nothing. But the arm of God does. . . . The Bible, the high code of civilization, decides the principle, it does not license the use of the sword up to 1849, or 1850, or to any other point of time. It decides the principle that it is wrong and wicked; and dooms it to be beaten into a ploughshare. Who shall assume the responsibility to preserve it for five, ten, or twenty years longer? We shall not be found fighting against God, even though all the swords in the world were at our service."[9]

The French, according to the reporter, were surprised by the English and American custom of giving "three obstreperous hurrahs" on certain occasions. Pennington was familiar with that and had also been exposed on his earlier visit to England to the local custom of interrupting speeches with various signs of approval. Some reports of his speech duly indicate cries, presumably from the "Anglo-Saxon" delegates, of "Hear! Hear!" and "Bravo!" as well as "painful sensation" and "new sensation" in response to his discussion of the horrors of slavery. The speech ended, he was also "shaken heartily by the hand" by the Abbe Duguerry, the pastor of the French Protestant church, M. Coqurel, and others on the dais.

Saturday evening was given over to a soiree at the chateau of Alexis de Tocqueville, the author of *Democracy in America,* which had been published in 1835, who was currently serving as Foreign Minister of France. No one took note of any conversation between de Tocqueville and Pennington, but they would have agreed on a number of issues. De Tocqueville, only a few years older than Pennington, had traveled the United States at the age of 30 and seen very clearly what another foreign student of American life a century later would call "the American dilemma."[†] De Tocqueville had written:

> An old and sincere friend of America, I am uneasy at seeing
> Slavery retard her progress, tarnish her glory, furnish arms to her
> detractors, compromise the future career of the Union which is the
> guaranty of her safety and greatness, and point out beforehand to
> her, to all her enemies, the spot where they are to strike. As a man,
> too, I am moved at the spectacle of man's degradation by man, and
> I hope to see the day when the law will grant equal civil liberty to
> all the inhabitants of the same empire, as God accords the freedom
> of the will, without distinction, to the dwellers upon earth.

De Tocqueville had also seen clearly the inability of the Colonization Society to colonize African Americans elsewhere as fast as their numbers in America were increasing. Among the hundreds of guests that evening, there would, unfortunately, have been little opportunity for Pennington to bring de Tocqueville up to date on the state of the American democracy or challenge his host's view that African Americans could never attain equality in the North.

The plainly dressed Quakers and simply dressed Americans wandering past the tapestried walls and through the illuminated gardens were able to meditate on the continuing inability of the French to decide whether their future lay in democracy or with the surviving institutions of the *ancien regime.* Interested though they were by the opulence on display, the American delegates, who thought of Sunday as a day for sober worship and restraint, made their adieus to M. and Madame de Tocqueville before midnight on Saturday, "thus setting

† Myrdal, Gunnar, *An American Dilemma; the Negro Problem and Modern Democracy.* New York, London, Harper & Brothers, 1944.

an example to the Parisians," the *Courant*'s reporter noted, "of a respect for the day, which was soon to follow."[10]

On Sunday, James W. C. Pennington was given the opportunity to preach in the American Protestant church in Paris, and William Wells Brown was gratified by the impression he made on a congregation that had not previously heard an African American in the pulpit. "His sermon on that occasion," Brown remembered, "was an elegant production, made a marked impression on his hearers, and created on the minds of all a more elevated idea of the abilities of the negro."[11]

The following day the delegates were taken to Versailles, where the fountains, normally deployed only on Sundays, had been restrained until Monday lest the Americans be offended. A report published in the *Hartford Courant* was so overwhelmed by the fountains of Versailles and the extensive gardens that little attention was given to the speeches of the delegates. "The parks and gardens of Versailles must not be judged by New York parks or Boston Commons," the *Courant* instructed its readers, "nor by Mont Auburn or Green-wood. We can only compare them to our western forests." Equally dazzling to the American eye were "the splendor of its interior, its rich tapestries, its enormous mirrors, and its gorgeous couches." In stark contrast to the splendid surroundings and "starred and trinketed ambassadors" were the soberly dressed Quakers and, indeed, the sober principles of the "Anglo Saxons" who insisted on observing their sabbath. Thus ended the formal aspects of the event. Some of the delegates continued on to visit other parts of Europe, while others returned to England or America.[12]

There were also two post-Congress receptions held, one by Foreign Minister de Tocqueville and a second hosted by the British delegates to honor the American delegates. The latter became, in effect, a "rump" session of the Congress, with a number of speakers expressing views they had not been able to express earlier or had only thought of afterwards. William Allen, a Massachusetts clergyman, took the opportunity to tell the British delegates that it should be understood that it was the state governments, not the federal government, that were solely responsible for the existence of slavery. William Wells Brown took the opportunity to correct Allen in a letter to a London paper in early September, thus broadcasting to the British public a statement that would otherwise have had only a limited audience.

American visitors and reporters were appropriately impressed by the elegance of the surroundings and distinguished Europeans, and trusted the speeches made and friendships formed would have some lasting value, but William Lloyd Garrison had only very faint praise: "[I]t will probably do some good, but I fear it will prove a somewhat sentimental affair, and proceed rather mincingly in its work . . . Still, any agitation of the Peace question must do good, and serve to open the eyes of the people to the horrors and iniquities of war. But into what a baptism of blood is Europe about to be plunged!"[13] Garrison was better, however, as an agitator than as a prophet; Europe's "baptism of blood" was still 75 years away, while America's was far closer.

Conventions, of course, have value as much for the personal relationships formed as for the resolutions passed. During the Congress, James Pennington had met Professor Friedrich Wilhelm Carove, a vice-president of the Congress and a member of the theological faculty at the University of Heidelberg. Carove, a protege of G. W. F. Hegel, had been imprisoned for seven years earlier in his life for speaking out against xenophobia and anti-Jewish speeches made at the Wartburg festival. Heidelberg had been the first European university to offer a professorship to a Jew when they invited Baruch Spinoza to take such a position in 1673.[14] It was also the first university to create a chair of natural and human rights. The idea of recognizing James W. C. Pennington with an honorary degree was, therefore, not unnatural and was discussed, though it is uncertain whether Carove or Pennington initiated the conversation. Where the story of a degree from the "University of Surry" had come from was remains unclear, but it had irritated Lewis Tappan, and Pennington had never succeeded in putting down the various rumors that circulated about it. All the confusion, however, had planted the idea firmly in Pennington's mind, and now there was an opportunity to bring the long-dormant idea to fruition. From Pennington's perspective, the point would be to recognize the intellectual abilities of African Americans. Whenever a black man stood up to speak, it seemed still to be a surprise to a white audience that indeed such a man could not only speak, but speak both grammatically and even powerfully. Even the correspondent of the English *Anti Slavery Standard*, in reporting William Wells Brown's speech, expressed that sort of surprise in writing, "The thing that most interested us, as it will your readers, was the success of our friend William W. Brown in addressing the audience."[15] A doctorate from a major European university would then be one more piece of evidence for Pennington to point to as evidence that color and intellect were not inversely related. Carove's motivation was very different: it would be a means by which Europe could begin to atone for its "terribly heavy guilt" in robbing Africans of their "sacred human rights."[16] As Carove and Pennington talked, it became clear to both that they had a common interest in this project, and Carove thought he could accomplish it.

Carove returned to Heidelberg to set in motion the process of awarding a degree, while Pennington traveled briefly in France and Belgium before returning to London. *The Fugitive Blacksmith; or Events in the History of James W. C. Pennington, Pastor of a Presbyterian Church, New York, Formerly a Slave in the State of Maryland, United States*, was ready for publication, and Pennington would be able to use the book to create new opportunities to speak and equally use his speeches to promote the book. The dramatic tale of Pennington's escape from slavery was an immediate success and by mid-October a second edition was called for.[17] Setting aside, to some extent, the idea of writing for children, Pennington added to the second edition a preface stating again his theological purpose and spelling out in some detail the nature of slavery in general, not only what he had experienced himself.

> The question may be asked, Why I have published anything so long after my escape from slavery? I answer I have been induced to do so on account of the increasing disposition to overlook the fact, that THE SIN of slavery lies in the chattel principle, or relation. Especially have I felt anxious to save professing Christians, and my brethren in the ministry, from falling into a great mistake. My feelings are always outraged when I hear them speak of "kind masters,"—"Christian masters,"—"the mildest form of slavery,"—"well fed and clothed slaves," as extenuations of slavery; I am satisfied they either mean to pervert the truth, or they do not know what they say. The being of slavery, its soul and body, lives and moves in the chattel principle, the property principle, the bill of sale principle; the cart-whip, starvation, and nakedness, are its inevitable consequences.[18]

Pennington was especially concerned to answer all those who worried about being unfair to the "kind" and "Christian masters." Slavery was all of a piece and evil through and through: no kindness or Christian faith on the master's part could eliminate that essential character. By July of 1850, nearly 6,000 copies had been sold and a third edition was published.[19]

Returning to London after the Peace Conference, Pennington divided his time between the publication of his book and speaking engagements, often making appearances with William Wells Brown. Brown was not as effective a speaker as Pennington, but he had a series of "panoramas" of slavery created for him by American artists and reproduced in England which he used to illustrate his talks. There were pictures of a slave gang being driven past the Capitol in Washington, of a free man caught by slave traders and being auctioned off, of slaves picking cotton with a woman being whipped at a whipping post in the background, that were far more dramatic and memorable than his words would have been.[20] Acting on behalf of the Free Produce Association in addition to his efforts to raise money for the Shiloh Church's debt, Pennington spoke in Halefield, Newcastle, Alnwick, Berwick, Morpeth, Hull, Derby, Birmingham, Stourbridge, Manchester, Leicester, and Leeds, exhorting his audiences to purchase free in preference to slave-labor produce.[21] In November he was traveling through the English Midlands and finding it difficult to keep in touch with his publisher, who complained that he had sent him two notes without an answer. When he caught up with his mail, Pennington wrote the publisher that he had sold five hundred copies of the book and would show himself at the office as soon as possible. Meanwhile, friends in the Midlands were trying to keep him for themselves and provide enough work for him so that he would forget about London. In the first two weeks of November, he had been in Boston, Lincoln, Mansfield, and Newark, typically preaching three or four times in each place and giving lectures on peace, anti-slavery, and temperance. In Newark, his audience for a lecture on peace was some 1200 individuals.[22]

London, however, would not serve well as a permanent base. The largest city in the world, with a population approaching two and a half million (five times the size of New York), could not long pay attention to anyone. The Anti-Slavery Society was definitely interested in the cause of the Americans, but it was also concerned with the serfs in Russia and efforts to make the Spaniards keep the anti–slave-trade treaties they had signed. In addition, there were always new visitors from America with stories to tell, and the new star of the lecture circuit was William Brown, who drew two or three thousand to a talk in Worcester in October. Before long, Henry Garnet would also arrive. Scotland was less sated with celebrities and better able to provide a home away from home for Pennington and his family. By the end of the year, Pennington was in Edinburgh; that city and Glasgow, less than fifty miles away, would remain the center of his activities for the next year. It would seem that he settled on Glasgow as a home away from home, since he gave the office of the Scottish Temperance League in Glasgow as the address at which to write him.

While Pennington had been involved in the English Midlands, Professor Carove was petitioning the faculty in Heidelberg. Europe, he argued, "has to atone for a terribly heavy guilt for the wretched sons of Africa who since [sic] centuries have been robbed of their most sacred human rights. We must therefore take every opportunity that offers itself to help the robbed ones to their rights, to give to the freed ones as far as possible a repatriation for guiltlessly suffered insults and indignation."† He attached to his petition copies of Pennington's published work: the address celebrating emancipation in the West Indies, the history of the colored people, the sermon on immoral covenants, and *The Fugitive Blacksmith*. Attached also to the petition was an article from an English paper noting (with that typical mixture of praise and condescension that has been noted before) that Pennington's language "is

---

† Presumably the German original is somewhat less awkward than the translation.

such good English, is so correct and so impressive and deep that they would do honor to a born Englishman of clerical experience and regular education."[23]

Carove told the faculty that Pennington's interest in the degree was based on a desire to "encourage the entire colored population of the United States," not "on account of any personal merits nor for personal distinction."[24] "Would not Germany," he asked, "like to be the first one to give a strong push to our endeavors by recognizing the struggle of my people using all its powers to educate my brothers and to evangelize them and to lift them up?"[25] Voting "salvo meliori," the faculty concurred as of November 5, 1849, and the degree was awarded on December 19. "You are the first African who has received this dignity from a European University," the faculty told Pennington in conferring the degree, taking occasion to congratulate themselves as well by adding, "and it is the University of Heidelberg that thus pronounces the universal brotherhood of humanity."[26]

Back in England, Pennington wrote to the papers, acknowledging that "it is not usual for a gentleman, on receiving an honorary title, to take any notice of it through the newspaper press," but that "I believe the circumstances will satisfy me in departing from the usual course." The whole purpose of the exercise, of course, depended on publicity. Unless the award were widely noticed, it would fail to serve the purpose of encouraging others. "I am only to be regarded as receiving it," Pennington wrote, "in trust for my People, and as an encouragement to the Sons of Ham to rise with others in the acquisition of learning; in this view I accept of it in behalf of the Negro race, throughout the world, and especially in America." He went on to pay tribute to the German settlers in America, not one of whom, to Pennington's knowledge, in Pennsylvania or Missouri, had become a slaveholder.[27] †

By the time the notice was printed, Pennington had returned to Scotland and was in the midst of a series of lectures. Midway between Christmas and New Year's Day, the citizens of Edinburgh in those years felt able to attend lectures, and on December 27th they filled the capacious Queen Street Hall with a "highly respectable audience." This was the second in a series of lectures, and Pennington's theme was the sinfulness of slavery. The fifth, sixth, and seventh of the Ten Commandments, prohibiting murder, adultery, and theft, were all violated, he argued, by those who kept slaves. He told his audience "that his own grandfather and father were stolen as slaves, and that he himself was born a slave in the State of Maryland. He contended that every slaveholder held to his slaves the relation of a thief." That slaveholding also involved murder

---

† Somewhat confused by the proliferation of "New" places around the world , the *British Banner* printed Pennington's letter and listed him as "Pastor of Shiloh Presbyterian Church, New Zealand."

was evidenced by the fact that the average life span of a slave was ten to fifteen years less than that of other Americans. "Was it not murder," he asked them, "to take a man's life and send him to his grave before his time?" As for adultery, "The foulest transactions," he told them, "took place in a state of slavery. He could lay his hands on American documents which he would be ashamed to read in his private study, and much less could he read them to such an audience as that now before him." That said, he went on to discuss the claim often made by supporters of slavery, that the Epistle of Paul to Philemon condones slavery. Pennington disagreed with those who believed that Onesimus, the subject of the epistle, was a slave, but those who justify slavery, he continued, should be careful since the argument could cut both ways. If slavery is not a sin, then slaveholders themselves were "as liable to be slaves as the negroes. (Applause.) No man was safe—the minority was at the mercy of the majority." He ended his address by making the matter a question for every individual in the audience: "would any one whom he was addressing like to be a slave? If not, then let every one aid in extirpating the evil. (Applause.)" The audience adopted a resolution to have Pennington's lectures printed and showed their agreement with the theory that slaveholding was sin by voting to hold no fellowship with churches that took slaveholders into their communion.[28]

The Christmas season apparently made little impact on the lives of the citizens of Edinburgh. The next day, the Ladies' Emancipation Society of Edinburgh met to transact various business items with Charles Cowan, Esq., M.P., presiding. They heard year-end reports—"at considerable length," according to the newspaper—on the tracts they had issued, the meetings they had held, and a memorial (not described) that had been sent by "the ladies of Britain" to the Queen, and then stayed to hear a talk by James Pennington on the evils of slavery. Those who might have heard him the day before undoubtedly heard some repetition: he spoke of his experience of slavery and urged support for a commercial boycott of slaveholders, but there was new material as well. Pennington seemed constantly to find new ways of looking at the evils of slavery and providing his hearers with some dramatic picture of the horrors of the system. For this occasion, Pennington had an image around which to build his talk instead of the Ten Commandments. Slavery, he told them, was a monster with four legs, "a commercial leg, an ecclesiastical leg, a political leg, and a literary leg." Each of these was important, but the commercial leg was a particular concern for Pennington and one of the stated reasons for his presence in Britain. The campaign for "free produce" and a boycott of the products of slavery was a central theme throughout his visit. Charles Cowan, Esq., M.P., presided at the meeting, and other reports and speeches were made to the ladies by "the Rev. J. R. Campbell, . . . the Rev. Mr. Arthur, Baptist . . . [and] the Rev. H. Grey." If any of the female members of the Ladies' Emancipation

Society spoke, it was not noticed by the newspaper reporter. The last speaker ended the meeting after Pennington had spoken by reading "an elaborate paper on the subject of slavery" and then telling the audience that "the title of Doctor of Divinity had just been conferred, by the University of Heidelberg, on their worthy friend, Mr. [!] Pennington." The announcement was greeted with applause and "The meeting shortly after separated."[29]

The proceeds from sales of the *Fugitive Blacksmith* and honoraria from lectures and sermons were proving the usefulness of Pennington's journey. In four months, enough money had been raised to cut the Shiloh Church's debt in half. But conditions in the United States were rapidly becoming more dangerous, and there could be no thought of returning until his freedom could be purchased. While Pennington was lecturing in Edinburgh, Senator Henry Clay of Kentucky, known as "The Great Compromiser," was making one last effort to establish common ground between the Northern and Southern states. Dealing with such diverse matters as the admission of new states and the rights of slaveholders, it excited such passions in the Senate that one member drew a pistol and was only prevented from firing it by the swift intervention of other senators.[30]

For James Pennington, the critical part of the legislation was a tightening of the fugitive slave laws that put every African American in the North in danger. An individual could be seized on the testimony of an agent of the owner without any supporting documentation and brought before a commission entitled to deal with the case "in a summary manner." The alleged fugitive could not testify in his behalf or bring witnesses. Even bystanders were compelled to assist when asked and were subject to heavy penalties if they refused. Concealing a fugitive, providing food or shelter, or hindering the proceedings were equally punishable. Bonuses were also provided for law enforcement officials who captured slaves. This law applied to all fugitives, no matter how long ago they had escaped. For the better part of the year, the various parts of Clay's compromise were debated, and not until September was the Fugitive Slave Law adopted. But the Southern legislators and the Northern compromisers who were seeking to eliminate the causes of intersectional irritation by terminating the constant flow of fugitives to the North had succeeded only, in the words of one observer, in scattering "50,000 sparks . . . among their powder barrels."[31] Increased efforts on the part of slave owners to capture fugitives set off riots in Boston and elsewhere. Over the next ten years, Harriet Tubman and others only worked the harder to free slaves and bring them north.

As for James Pennington, who had gone to Britain in part to escape the earlier fugitive slave laws, these draconian provisions, in the words of his friend John Hooker, "filled him with new apprehensions as to his own fate on his return to New York."[32] He had planned to return to New York that year and had written his friend George Whipple† saying, "I long much to see you again."[33] But it would take many months now and much effort by friends in both Scotland and America to make that possible.

In February, James Pennington spoke to the Young Men's Christian Association of Glasgow and used the occasion to give perhaps his most systematic exposition of the history and evil of slavery. The speech was embellished with such rhetorical flourishes as "the darkest outlines of the midnight shades that mark the horizon of man's fallen state" and (speaking of the Pharaoh of Egypt) the nice alliteration of "his malicious movement in murdering the male children." The story Pennington told was set in the context of a history that began with the Jewish captivity in Egypt—"only the Jews in Egypt, and the Negro in America" have not "sunk and perished under slavery"—and dwelt at some length on the savage suppression of the so-called "negro plot" during the early years of the British occupation of New York.††

It has been often suggested that the British liked to listen to American abolitionists because, having outlawed slavery in Britain long before, it enabled them to look down on their American cousins. Pennington, however, gave them no such opportunity for self-congratulation. In discussing the state of African Americans in New York under British rule, he pointed out that "The first 130 years of his heavy bondage was borne under the British crown." The "barbarous" suppression of the "negro plot," he carefully reminded his audience, was an attempt "made by men administering justice under the auspices of the British crown, to exterminate this people."

Pennington followed his horrifying account—of men burned at the stake for a conspiracy never either proved or carried out—with a careful statistical summary of the increase in black population from the time of the first importation of slaves to Jamestown in 1620 to the census of 1850. Half a million slaves at the time of the American Revolution had now become nearly four million. The parallel with the increase of the Hebrews in Egypt was evident. But Pennington wanted his audience to see also the differential increase, larger in some states than others, because of the importation of slaves from the more northern slave states to the cotton states of the deep South. And then he asks them to notice that the natural increase in population does not occur in the cotton South, indicating that a very high percentage of the slave population

† George Whipple (1805–1876) had been a professor at Oberlin College (1836–1846) and then was corresponding secretary of the American Missionary Association for thirty years. After the Civil War, he helped found Hampton Institute and served as president of the board from 1868 to 1876.

†† See discussion in Chapter Four.

has died prematurely. Pennington's figures would indicate that "168,916 men, women and children, were actually killed and worn out prematurely on the cotton and sugar plantations of the far South."[†]

Pennington wanted his audience to see not only the evils of slavery but also the indomitable character of this so-called "inferior race." Once the northern states had emancipated their slaves, there set in a "tide of exits" with an average of over two thousand slaves each year reaching the North and, in most cases, Canada. The slave states had "called to their aid all the elements, implements, and agents of power, malice, vengeance, and destruction that earth and hell could invent . . . They have chased their victims to the Red Sea with blood-hounds and fire-arms; they have shot them from trees, while swimming rivers; they have followed in gangs into the cities of the North." But opposed to this, "In this great work of self-emancipation, the slave evinces all the great elements of mind out-scheming mind, iron will, penetrating judgment, power of endurance, quick invention, profound insight of human nature, physical and moral courage, and practical knowledge of heavenly bodies."

Pennington turned next to their progress in "popular education, agriculture, commerce, mechanic arts, and Christianity." His own experience in the realm of "popular education" provided opportunity for Pennington to tell stories that would enable his audience to hear typical American voices and understand what ordinary African Americans had to contend with in attempting to improve their situation. Briefly he outlined the way the American school system was organized, with funding provided in each state and no federal control. Then he asked his audience to "picture a scene in a town" where a school is located.

"Here is a fond mother," he suggested, "who has a darling child whom she is anxious [to] train for useful purposes." Telling her husband that their child is now five years old and has learned his letters, she suggests that "he must go to school." The next morning, therefore, mother and child set out for the school, only to be greeted "by sneers on the part of the white boys, and she is told that 'the school committee have voted not to admit coloured children.' How can this mother turn away from that school-house door, with her trembling boy while civilized white boys and girls are making wry faces at them. And heaping upon them all the reproaches they can by their superior talents invent. 'What's that nigger wench want here?' 'That little darky coming to school! Guess if that little nig comes here, I'll leave the school pretty quick.' 'My father's one of the committee, and he said nigger children warn't coming to school.'

[†] Pennington's numbers come from a briefly published New York newspaper called the *Buffalo Republic*. Pennington's speech was published with several statistical tables that make his argument here much easier to understand.

"Nor does it stop here. Each of these little civilized Anglo-Saxons [note that Pennington speaks of "Anglo-Saxons," not "Americans"] goes home with mouth opened for news, and eyes stretched like one who had seen sights unseeable.

"The girl to her mamma. 'Why ma, what do you think?'

"'Well, what is it now?'

"'There was a little nigger brought to school to-day.'

"'Well, the teacher didn't take him in I hope?'

"'No indeed, his mother had to take him away again. Oh what fun we had about it; I had to snicker right out a laughing; indeed the whole school didn't do much else all day.'

"'Well, I do hope for the land's sake we shan't be troubled with any niggers in our school, if there is any black children goes to school there, you certainly shall not go.'"

Pennington then pictured a similar scene in the home of the committee member's family.

"'Oh! Father, there was a black boy brought to school this morning; it was Bill Simpson's son, his mother brought him.'

"'Well, what did teacher do?'

"'Why he sent him off . . . I didn't hear exactly what he said to her at the door, but anyhow they soon cleared out.'

"'Bill Simpson's boy you say? . . . I'll speak to him about it; don't see what he wants to crowd his children into the school for; he knows blacks never have been admitted; there's the effects of these abolitionists urging these blacks forward.'

"Mother. 'Well I think niggers better be made to know and keep their places. I shall never consent to have our children go to school with niggers.'

"So the matter goes from family to family until . . . this becomes a question of general interest. With Simpson it is a question of right, not one of propriety, and he does not wait for Mr. Committee-man to see him; but he calls on the school committee himself, and makes a respectful representation of his grievance. He wishes simply to know why his child has been excluded from the public school. Why, he is told that no coloured children can be received into the school.

"'But why not, sir?'

"'Oh, why, because many white people will not send their children.'

"'Must I then rear my child in ignorance, because some whose skins are not coloured like my own objects to its entering school with their children? Is it not as much my duty to educate my child as it is that of white parents to educate theirs? And, above all, I ask, have I not a right to send my child to the public free schools?'

"'Well, you know it has not been usual to admit coloured children to school, and it will only create an excitement and *make it worse for you.*'"

This last remark was, Pennington told his audience, "a genteel hint to be aware how he insists upon his right to send his child to the school, lest he awaken the mob spirit, and thus be severely chastised for his conduct."

How will a man "placed in such circumstances" act, Pennington asked. Briefly he outlined the alternatives: a privately employed teacher, a move to another town where black children are admitted to the public school, suing the school committee, or the calling of a public meeting to organize a separate school for black children. This last can be objected to as "yielding to the wicked conduct of the whites" but provides a long-term solution in enabling black children to become qualified to compete on equal terms in the larger society. Here, again, Pennington is drawing from his own experience as he describes the way the black schools "challenge examinations" and "invite these same school committees, teachers, and scholars who have rejected us . . . [to] come . . . see . . . hear . . . and confess we are up with them." This, he concludes, is what we are doing "in the work of civilization."

The remaining areas of social life—agriculture, mechanical arts, and commerce were dealt with much more briefly. Pennington speaks of the skill of black farmers on Long Island, the "blacksmiths, carpenters, cabinet-makers, tailors, and bootmakers" who can be found "in almost any number in New York and Connecticut, and the skilled sailors who are "manning the ships of our princely merchants, and bringing the wealth of the Indies to their warehouses." He boasted that "We furnish the best seamen in the world," but prejudice prevents them from moving up the ladder to first mate and captain. Likewise in the places of business, and here Pennington may well have had Lewis and Arthur Tappan in mind, the merchant "will never give him the same chance to work his way up to the clerk's desk, and to a partner's place."[†]

Lastly, Pennington spoke of Christianity, pleasing his audience, no doubt, by calling it "the highest and the most perfect form of civilization" and then setting them on edge by adding that "tried by this standard, we are compelled to confess that we have not on earth one strictly civilized nation; for so long as the sword is a part of a nation's household furniture, it cannot be called strictly civilized; and yet there is not a nation, great or small, black or white, that has laid aside the sword." It is not the issue of warfare, however, that is Pennington's primary criticism of the so-called Christian and civilized nations,

---

† In 1853, for example, one of thee secretaries in the office of the American and Foreign Anti Slavery Society resigned and another white man was installed in his place. Ethiop commented, "What a pity it is that the black cannot occasionally get a sup or two of the anti-slavery pap that is ladled out in this city! Why is this?—Is it incompetency on the one part—prejudice on the other, or what? Or is the hungry white crowd so large that the black specks pass unobserved by the chefs in command?" "From Our Brooklyn Correspondent," *FDP*, April 15, 1853.

but that of prejudice. Viewing the black experience in America, one would expect the result would be "turn coloured people in masses to infidelity." Yet the fact is that, on the whole, this has not happened, but that they have created their own churches and that there are many African American churches of almost all the major denominations. Some have remained within the particular denomination while others, Methodist and Baptist especially, have separated themselves from the parent denomination and yet are regulated in the same way as the churches from which they seceded. "Our pulpit," he continued, is systematic, doctrinal, expository, and "aims to be practical. It reaches life and applies the truths of the gospel to it in all its springs. We teach our hearers that the church is the only true reformatory organization in the world . . . [and] we insist upon the duty of aiding in all the great reforms of the day, and the objects of benevolence."

The final portion of this address was used for the most part in a defence of the Bible and Constitution as anti-slavery documents. "Now, we say, the idea that God has handed down a book from heaven to licence each man of our common species who can make a raise to be a slavetrader, is monstrous—it is ungodly. But . . . we receive it with joy for the light it contains; we read it, we study it, and we do not believe there is a particle of slavery in it. We stand in the midst of those who hold the contrary, and solemnly protest against the views they promulgate." Indeed, Pennington claimed, by disputing the idea that the Bible sanctions slavery, "We believe we are doing a service to the whole human family," for "if the New Testament sanctions slavery, it authorizes the enslavement of the whites as well as us."

As for the Constitution, "We, the free people, alone are sustaining the fundamental maxim of the American Republic, 'That all men are born free and equal.' If we, being born in America, cannot live upon the soil upon terms of equality with the descendants of Scotchmen, Englishmen, Irishmen, Frenchmen, Germans, Hungarians, Greeks, and Poles, then the fundamental theory of the American Republic fails and falls to the ground; and the door once opened to kick out the people of colour, let others be prepared for their turn."

"We do not expect," he concluded, "to remain in slavery . . . We expect to overcome the spirit of caste and enjoy full American liberty . . . I have shown you a people who are practising, more faithfully than any other, the true Christian law of moral power—I mean the law of forgiveness and endurance of wrong. There is no solitary case on record of a minority, with justice on its side, being crushed, while adhering to the law of forgiveness and endurance. It is not in the nature of God's moral government to permit such a thing. On this grand basis the coloured people of America are safe for their future destiny. The American oppressor may destroy himself; but destroy the coloured man he never can." And then, as he had often done before, James Pennington called on his hearers to pray for the oppressor. "Perhaps we have too much neglected this powerful means. These men are not only profoundly wicked, but they are labouring under a most perilous delusion. They are to be pitied; and prayer is to be one means of saving them, if saved at all." The slave power's position is like that of the Pharaoh at the Red Sea, but "your prayers may save them from a fate similar to his."[34]

Although concentrating his efforts in southern Scotland, Pennington traveled occasionally to London and the Midlands and also kept up a correspondence not only with his various friends in Britain but with those in the States as well, reporting on American events to those in Britain and to those in America on what he had seen in Great Britain. He wrote to George Whipple in New York about a church he had visited in Edinburgh where he was asked to attend a meeting of the Juvenile Missionary Society connected with the congregation. The society was composed of children aged fifteen and under, chose its own officers, and raised money for missionary work. Pennington was impressed that "The indomitable little Scots have raised over $500 the past year by pennies" and "sustain several teachers in foreign fields." "[W]ould it not increase a missionary spirit in our churches?" he asked Whipple, to have a similar program. "Children love to have something to do, and parents love to see their children exciting an interest."[35]

Since Whipple was also on the board of the American Missionary Association and was interested as he was in African mission, Pennington told him of reports that had come back to Scotland of their mission to the Calabar region of Africa. It was an area, Pennington reported, of "high promise" but some "difficulty in getting laborers." Members of the Scottish mission board had asked whether they might find missionaries from America for Jamaica as well as Africa. "I did not like to discourage them," Pennington wrote, but he had had to tell them how few qualified Americans there were. He wrote also, with some amusement, of letters he had seen describing a "very interesting state of things" involving the young king in Calabar. "This royal youth," the letters said, "has resolved to adopt Christianity and especially in regard to marriage that he will have but one wife instead of the number his father had which is a rule of Calabar royalty. This is likely to make a little trouble. The old king says that Mr. Waddell may teach all his children white man fashion but the oldest son who is to succeed him must keep to Calaban fashion or the people will not have him as their king. To obviate this the young men has determined not to marry at all. Let us pray the Lord will settle this little snarl without either compelling the youth to go back to polygamy, or adopt a course so dubious as celibacy."[36] It was one thing, Pennington noticed, to urge the need for making Christians of Africans, but another to confront particular aspects of cultural differences!

In April, Pennington wrote Whipple again, passing on stories of devoted missionaries who had served in Africa and Tahiti and who had remained at their posts in spite of conflict not only with the French but with their own mission boards. The problems the Scots faced were different from those in America, but political issues and misunderstandings between devoted Christians created hazards in both areas.[37] It was easier to escape from slavery than to escape the conflicts between well-intentioned Christians and abolitionists sure of their own righteousness but unable to abide the differing perspectives of others within the same cause. James Pennington had tried, with some success, to avoid the battles between Garrisonians and Tappanites in America, but he had found himself on the Tappanite side often enough to incur the wrath of Garrisonians. It sought him out even in Scotland. Since he was living in Glasgow, he worked with local abolitionists to organize the Glasgow New Association for the Abolition of Slavery and, having launched that society, he went on to recruit a women's auxiliary. After all, if there was a Ladies' Emancipation Society in Edinburgh, why should there not be a similar society in Glasgow, Pennington asked himself. The new society then hired Pennington as a lecturer, which gave him a more stable income and somewhat more control over his schedule.

The creation of a "new" association implies the existence of an "old" association, and indeed there was a Glasgow Emancipation Society in existence, though largely inactive; it had held only one public meeting in the past three years.[38] The GES, however, was Garrisonian, and the creation of the new society brought to the surface the continuing divisions within the abolition movement. Pennington was connected with the more conservative British and Foreign Anti Slavery Society based in London and allied with the American and Foreign Anti Slavery Society in New York. The Garrisonians had usually found more support in Scotland and it was outrageous to them that Pennington should be poaching on their territory. Wendell Phillips, perhaps the most famous orator for the Garrisonian position, wrote to an English friend that "Pennington is with you just what he was here, self-seeking, trimming & utterly unreliable."[39]

Phillips and others seemed to be unable to accept successful efforts by individuals unconnected to their particular organization. Parker Pillsbury was another minister and social reformer who had represented the American Anti Slavery Society (Garrisonian) and condemned those who failed to affirm the Garrisonian creed. Samuel Ringgold Ward took the issue on in uncompromising language in a letter to Frederick Douglass, asking:

What was the animus of Parker Pillsbury's strictures upon Dr. Pennington, Rev. H. H. Garnet and myself? Why, it seemed that we three Maryland lads had been to England, had said that Garrison and coadjutors were infidels, and had actually been well received where he had not!! Now honest anti-abolitionists would have called all this in plain, unmistakable, uncanting language, "negro insolence." Who does not see that is just what Mr. Pillsbury meant. Mr. P goes on to complain that we have collected money for colored Churches and for fugitive slaves, where he cannot collect for the American Anti-Slavery Society and then tells the Glasgow Examiner that we ought not to have money for any [such] purposes, but it ought to be given to his Society. "Who is equal to us?" is the English of that. But more, Dr. Pennington belongs to the Presbyterian Church, Mr. Garnet has settled in a parish in Jamaica, and Mr. Pillsbury "is informed" that I am going to settle as a planter in Jamaica. He says that were we abolitionists, we should neither settle over parishes nor upon plantations. Of course, then, we are not abolitionists, i.e., we are not subject to the dictation of Mr. Pillsbury and his coadjutors. I ask, once more, is not this the animus of the overseer? Is it at all akin to the idea that a negro is so equal to an Anglo-Saxon, that he may go where he pleases, move his own field and method of labor, and succeed as well as he can? No! The chief complaint against us is, that we do succeed, and, possibly, may do yet more. What did we run away from Maryland for? To succeed or to fail? You and Dr. P and Garnet are answering that question daily.[40]

Garrisonians nevertheless began to search for a chink in Pennington's moral armor and attempted to show that money given to him was not being properly directed. Had money raised for the Shiloh Church, they wondered, been properly remitted? Andrew Paton, a member of the old society, wrote an American friend suggesting he try to find out. "If not, get some of them stirred up to insist on having what money he has collected remitted to them without delay. Ascertain what he writes them as to his money and generally inform me."[41]

The GES wrote to William Wells Brown and organized a meeting in Glasgow in January 1851, at which they launched a vigorous attack on Pennington and the New Society. Pennington agreed to meet with them to try to resolve differences, but although he failed to satisfy his opponents, they lacked sufficient evidence to agree on a specific plan for pursuing the matter.[42] The informality and multi-sidedness of Pennington's work would have made any very precise accounting for funds difficult if not impossible. Offerings were often taken at his meetings, but when he had spoken about the abolition movement, the free produce movement, the price of his own freedom, the peace movement, and the New York Vigilance Committee, what would the offering be for, especially when he had his own living expenses, including now a wife and son, to deal with and the necessary expenses of the local abolition, free produce, and peace societies? It seems unlikely that either side in the squabble could have satisfied a careful audit. William Lloyd Garrison never satisfied questions about the money he raised even on his first trip to England, organized for the specific purpose of raising funds for a "manual labor school." No school was ever created and it seems likely that Garrison failed to raise any significant funds beyond those necessary for his own travel and other expenses.

But James Pennington had a full schedule in Scotland and England and no time to indulge in partisan squabbles. When a request came in May from J. R. Baillie in Ipswich that he attend a meeting of the Young Men's Peace League, he thanked Baillie for "this mark of respect," recalled with pleasure his visit to Ipswich in 1843, but regretted to say that he would be engaged in Scotland the whole month of June and in England for July and part of August. He hoped he would be able to visit Ipswich, he said, because he would like to give a talk on slavery as a breeder of war.

When the newly organized Glasgow New Association for the Abolition of Slavery gathered in June, Pennington made a major address analyzing the ways in which slavery in the United States might be abolished. It was commonly suggested that the owners should be compensated for their loss of property, but Pennington dismissed that idea as impractical. The Northern states would dismiss that idea, since they had abolished slavery without compensating the owners and would hardly support compensating Southern owners. Furthermore the cost would make such a plan impossible. Britain had compensated slave owners in the West Indies, but estimates of the cost for such a program in the United States ranged between one and two billion dollars, and "who was to meet that bill?" Pennington inquired. "If they should mortgage every inch of personal and real estate in America they could not do it." The second alternative was a slave rebellion or foreign invasion. Pennington wanted to be clear that that was "not his choice." The third alternative was what he called "a grand exodus" following the example of the slaves in Egypt. Pennington noted that he had followed that example himself and the "tide of negro emigration from the South to the North would still roll on. No power would be able to arrest it. It was propelled by the philosophy of human nature, of common sense, civilisation, and of Christianity." People everywhere, he was confident, would surely "give the negro a crust of bread on his flight, and a blanket to cover his nakedness, or a place to shelter him."

This was not, of course, a realistic answer to the question Pennington had asked his audience to consider. He reported himself that there were more slaves in America than the entire population of Scotland. If it was unrealistic for the Colonization Society to think of transporting three million Americans to Africa, it was not much more realistic to imagine that number of people successfully escaping to the Northern states and to Canada in any reasonable period of time. Pennington still held on to "the darling thought," he told his audience, that "some of the beautiful West Indian islands" might be a place of refuge for freed slaves. But how would they get there, and where would there be room enough for the numbers involved? He offered no answers to these obvious questions. But his purpose was not to provide ultimate answers to the problem of American slavery. His purpose was to help launch the new society and encourage them to support the free produce movement and do whatever other good they could. It was, in many ways, a "dream" speech and, like Martin Luther King Jr.'s great speech on the Washington mall over a century later, he envisioned a day when they could raise a shout of triumph, "Jehovah hath triumphed, his people are free!" He resumed his seat, the local paper reported, "amid rapturous applause."[43]

Traveling to England at the end of June, Pennington was able to work with his editor on the third edition of the *Fugitive Blacksmith*. Six thousand copies had been sold, and everywhere he went people showed him copies they had bought, so it was selling well. The fact that it was being summarized in lengthy reports in various newspapers may have hurt sales as much as they helped.[†] By September, he was back in Scotland, writing to the Glasgow *Christian News* about various white abolitionists who had been imprisoned or murdered for their beliefs and actions. He mentioned W. L. Chaplin, who had been imprisoned in Washington, D.C., for helping two slaves to escape, Charles Torrey, who was sentenced to hard labor in Maryland for his abolitionist activities and died in prison three years later at the age of 33, Daniel Drayton, who attempted to help a group of seventy-seven slaves escape from Washington on the *Pearl*, and Elijah Lovejoy, who was shot and killed by an anti-abolitionist mob in Illinois when he attempted to produce an anti-slavery newspaper. "The monstrous destroyer," he wrote, "is not content with the thousands it destroys in the persons of the slaves—men, women, and children; but it is found of late years that it has a peculiar relish for white men who have the heart and the talent to use the pen and the tongue against it. Amongst its white victims have been men of the highest legal, ministerial, and popular talents and acquirements, and still its bloody hand is reaching about after its prey. Where is the dismal game of death and destruction to end?" The newspaper spoke of Pennington's career and noted that he liked to introduce himself as the man who "ran

† Chambers's *Edinburgh Journal*, for example, devoted five newspaper columns to a summary of the book with long sections quoted verbatim but without quotation marks.

away with himself."[44] Pennington could make good use of humor, but he also understood that it was important to show white victims of slavery as well as black in building a sense of outrage and winning support for his cause.

James Pennington's colleague, Henry Highland Garnet, had arrived in Britain that summer, traveling at the request of the Free Produce Association, to serve as their agent and promote the boycott of the products of slave labor. Joseph Sturge, seeking to revive the free produce movement, had tried to make such an arrangement with Henry Bibb, another fugitive slave and itinerant lecturer, in 1848 but had been unable to complete a plan. Since Pennington's arrival, he had done what he could to promote the Association's goals but could not give it his whole attention. Now Garnet could take primary responsibility and Pennington would help when he could.

In August, Garnet and James Pennington traveled together to Germany to take part in the third Peace Congress, meeting this time in Frankfurt. Lacking the palaces and gardens of Versailles to impress the delegates, the German hosts opened what public gardens and museums they had, including a museum containing portraits of all the German emperors. One day was set aside for a trip to Heidelberg—Pennington's second trip to that city—and another for a visit to the fortress at Mayence[French for Mainz]-on-the-Rhine where they also saw Gutenberg's birthplace.

On the evening after the trip to Heidelberg, a special meeting was arranged in a public hall in Frankfurt to allow an American delegate, never named in the article, to state his views on the slave trade and slavery itself. With Joseph Sturge presiding, the speaker told his audience that he saw the British efforts to eliminate the slave trade was not only an "utter failure" but an "aggravation of the evil." It was his view that laying a heavy tax on the price of slave labor would so reduce its value that the whole system would collapse, but he saw no prospect of the British government taking such action. His solution therefore was to "Christianize and civilize the African nations" so that "having their minds regulated by the gospel, and their attention drawn to agriculture and the useful arts," they would no longer be interested in fighting each other and selling their captives into slavery. This also, however, he saw as a "distant prospect," and the only alternative was for Europeans to abandon the use of sugar, tobacco, rice, and cotton produced by slave labor and for the government to tax it so that the system of slavery would "greatly and speedily" collapse. At this point another Frankfurt citizen arose to suggest that a shop or shops should be set up to sell free produce at the same price as slave produce, since he was sure the former would be much preferred. If there were losses involved, he was sure that he and others could make them up at the end of the year.

The meeting was reported to have been pleased with all this and ready to go on their way with a sense of a job well done, when still another speaker came forward, this time an American who said that he also was opposed to slavery and the slave trade, but he felt that the British public and Europeans generally were shown only the dark side of slavery, but it had a *bright side*† also. He told a story about an English visitor who had expressed a wish to see the social condition of the slave population and was advised to visit some of their churches. When he did this, he saw "a well dressed, deeply interested, and apparently a happy people." Expressing his pleasure, he asked again to see the slaves and was told that those *were* the slaves. "Then," said the visitor, "I shall be an anti-slavery man no longer." When the speaker sat down, a Quaker rose up and moved that Dr. Pennington be asked for his comments. This was agreed to, and Joseph Sturge ruled that the meeting would continue.

He had seen such churches himself, said James Pennington, but they were congregations of free people, not slaves, since slaves could hold no property in churches or anything else under American law. Then Pennington cut to the heart of the slavery question with a clarity and eloquence often missing when the debate was sidetracked to issues of the quality of slavery rather than the fundamental injustice of the institution. "But the question was not as to the degree of comfort here and there possessed by slaves," Pennington pointed out; "it was not, how well are they clothed here, and fed there—but are they their own or their master's property—are they men and women, or things, goods, and chattels, in American law? A family might be well under a master, he might die, he might fail in business, and to-morrow that family might be sold at the auction block, and husband and wife, parents and children be torn from each other's embrace, never more to meet in this world. But were all just as his American friend had represented, it exhibited after all no bright side, for assuredly slavery had none—it was dark throughout. There were congregations of Christians, admitted to be Christian churches, the followers of Christ, and yet other professed Christians claimed the right to own them, and dispose of them as goods and chattels! The people of God claiming the right to enslave their brethren in Christ, whom he had made free! It was a crime that outraged humanity, and insulted high Heaven the more, because they were the freemen of Christ!" Pennington advised the gentleman to "go home and study the question of *property* before he ventured again to show *the bright side* of American slavery!"[45]

Henry Garnet followed with some specific material from an official report, but when the original speaker tried to reply, Joseph Sturge told him it was "too much" for him to attempt to contradict two speakers with first-hand experience, besides which his speech had little to do with the purpose of the meeting—which then closed with a vote of thanks to the chairman.[46]

† Emphasis in the original.

When the Peace Congress ended, Garnet and Pennington were asked to stay on and take part in two public meetings on the subject of slavery. A German banker and abolitionist saw the opportunity to provide some education for his countrymen on the nature of American slavery as two fugitives from that system had known it. An Evangelical church was made available but proved to be too small for the crowd that assembled; hundreds were left outside. Speaking through an interpreter (presumably Pennington's knowledge of German was not adequate for public speaking), Pennington made the familiar point that slavery is always oppressive, no matter how "kind" the master, and outlined the legal position as a result of the fugitive slave law about to be enacted. Garnet described the influence of slavery in "degrading the minds of all who participated in its evils, whether as masters or as slaves, and illustrated his views by many affecting details." Both Garnet and Pennington tactfully spoke of the lack of participation in the slave system by German immigrants. "There appears," they told their German audience, "to be a natural kindness and true humanity in the German mind, which spurns from it the odious idea of trading in human flesh and blood, and getting wealth by those means." They spoke of the "respect and veneration" with which Americans turned to Germany, translating their literature, and "anxious to show deference to the intelligence which is continually flowing out from the ancient Fatherland."[47]

Back in England, Garnet sent the editor of the *Non-Slaveholder* a diary of his work in September and October organizing free produce societies in one place after another. "The demand for free labor articles," he wrote, "is increasing daily."[48] Pennington and Garnet sometimes spoke together, but one gathering, in September in Sunderland, was so large that the two wound up speaking separately in adjacent churches.[49] And even though Henry Garnet was now present specifically to support the free produce movement, Pennington continued to deal with that subject as he had before. At an anti-slavery meeting in Newcastle in September, he told the audience that he was delighted to hear that manufacturers in Lancashire were responding to the boycott by "anxiously looking to new fields for the supply of cotton."[50]

Both Garnet and Pennington, however, had to address the newly enacted Fugitive Slave laws as well as their other issues and educate the British public about the implications of that legislation. Henry Garnet wrote to Gerrit Smith to tell him that news of the Fugitive Slave Law had been greeted in England "with a storm of indignation and contempt."[51] With prophetic insight, he told Smith that "This extreme measure will hasten the downfall of slavery." At the Friends' Meeting House in Gloucester in October, a "crowded meeting" listened to Pennington give a brief lesson in American history and the odd circumstances that the same men who "proclaimed to the world the grand principle that all men are born free and equal" had "utterly overlooked" the application of that principle to the very people they themselves held in bondage. Indeed, in that same document, they essentially declared that negro slaves were personal property and any attempt by the slave to escape could be punished by the state or by the owner. In the early history of the Union, owners freely tracked runaways and took them back but, over time, Pennington explained, Northern citizens "began to resent as an outrage the scenes which the recapture of escaped slaves brought before their eyes." The result was the passage of laws providing *habeas corpus* rights to the runaways so that they could no longer be carried off without being brought before a proper tribunal and having it proved to a jury that the individual was, in fact, a fugitive. Juries, however, were often unwilling to make a finding that would send back the fugitives who had "thrown themselves upon the hospitality and compassion of humane and Christian men," with the result that thousands of slaves had been able to build decent lives for themselves in Northern communities while the slaveowners "chafed under a law which brought their cruel and unchristian system so much under the eye of the public." The new law, Pennington explained, eliminated any such safeguards and enabled the slave owners to drag fugitives and even those accused of being fugitives back to the South. Pennington offered himself as an example, telling how he had won his freedom, educated himself, and developed a productive ministry, but now, "whilst preaching in his pulpit he may be seized and borne off, and his flock left to relapse into the ignorance from which his pious labours have done so much to rescue them." The *Gloucester Journal*, in reporting this speech, told its readers in self-satisfied tones that "Dr. Pennington's address was characterized by moderation and good sense, and, but for his features and colour, no person would have supposed him to be anything other than a very well educated and sensible Englishman."[52]

Remarkable in these reports is the interest of the British public in American affairs. Just after Christmas of 1850, James W. C. Pennington was the featured speaker at a program in Kelso, a small market town on the Scottish Borders. The meeting had been called to consider sending a petition to the Parliament requesting the government to enforce its treaties against the slave trade with Cuba and Brazil. The presiding officer of the meeting told the audience that such "enthusiasm was manifested" in Perth and Glasgow and "other important places . . . that it might fairly be presumed that no question in modern times had created more interest." Any report on the speaking schedules of the American emissaries in Britain should include some reference to the setting of the speech since Pennington, Garnet, Brown, and others were seldom the only speakers on a program and the nineteenth-century Scots and English, lacking television and other modern amusements, had an amazing ability to sit through a long evening of speeches. The first speaker in Kelso explained at some length what the treaty was and why it might not be enforced. Maintaining a British squadron off the coast of Africa to capture slave ships and send their cargoes back to Africa was expensive, and the House of Commons had recently voted to discontinue the practice. The House of Lords had disagreed and the issue was therefore still pending. James Jarvis, a local pastor, spoke to the subject for about an hour. The resolution was then adopted, but not before it had been seconded and explained by a speaker who went on at some length about the specific requirements of the treaties in question. Then another resolution was moved and seconded with further lengthy speeches. When James Pennington was finally introduced, the audience must have been sitting for at least two hours, but he was received "with loud and hearty applause" and was "repeatedly cheered" in the course of his address. In view of the evening's purpose, Pennington spoke to the subject of the treaty obligations of Britain and America, noting that treaties between England and the United States entitled the citizens of each country to all the freedoms of the other. He saw himself as the beneficiary of those treaties since he had been able to live freely and travel freely in Britain. English citizens, on the other hand, did not enjoy such freedom in America. He spoke of how British sailors, if they were black, would be forbidden to land in Southern ports and would be imprisoned if they did. He also showed his audience a notice recently posted in North Carolina concerning Harry, a runaway slave. The owner was offering $125 for his capture and $150 for his head. He had a copy of the warrant for Harry's arrest in his hands as he spoke, dated June 1850, a year after Pennington's arrival in Britain. His American friends kept him well supplied with material for his speeches. The warrant for Harry's arrest, he told his audience, was not only enforceable in North Carolina but in Pennsylvania and New York as well. Implied but not stated was the fact that such a warrant could be executed also for James Pembroke, also known as James W. C. Pennington. Earlier in the month he had written to the newspapers with a story of an elderly preacher, a former slave, who had "sunk under the fear" of being carried back into slavery and had died.[53] Pennington told his readers it was the equivalent of murder, and no doubt he saw himself as threatened by the same fate as Harry and the elderly preacher.

News from New York would, of course, take several weeks to reach Great Britain, so Pennington would not have heard of an early test case for the Fugitive Slave Act in New York City. Harry Long, a waiter in the Pacific Hotel in New York, was arrested at the request of an agent of a Richmond, Virginia, doctor and brought before Commissioner Hall, a commissioner appointed under the new law. After some legal wrangling, William Jay and another lawyer procured a writ of *habeas corpus* requiring Long to be brought before the Supreme Court of the State of New York. Coming before that court, the lawyers argued that Hall was not such a commissioner as the law required, since he was empowered under a general rule appointing all clerks and deputy clerks commissioners. Jay argued that there needed to be a specific appointment. Instead of arguing that point, the commissioner took his case to the Circuit Court, where the judge adjourned the court and tried the case as a commissioner under the new law which could not be appealed. Acting in that capacity, the judge handed the prisoner over to the slave catcher, who carried him off to Virginia the next day. Whether he was or was not a fugitive, he found himself no longer a waiter in a New York hotel but a slave in Virginia. Under the new law, the best legal counsel and the highest courts in the State of New York had failed to save Long from slavery.[54]

Pennington wanted his audiences to understand his fear and to know also that their influence made a difference in America. He "knew Jonathan[†] too well," he told his hearers, to think that their opinion made no difference. Such resolutions as they were passing that night would "speed their way across the Atlantic" and let Americans know how their actions were seen. He wanted to make them aware of the horror of a system that could offer a reward for a man's head, and he wanted to persuade them that their influence made a difference in America.[55]

But James Pennington had no desire to spend his life persuading British audiences of their potential influence. His goal was always to use his own influence in his own country. The Fugitive Slave Act may have prevented him from returning as soon as he had planned, but its passage was evidence that he must find a way to purchase his freedom. It was also true that he had taken responsibility for a congregation nearly three years earlier but had given them only one year of ministry. Not surprisingly, they were anxious to have him back or to make other arrangements. John Hooker had tried once before to be helpful in this respect but had been daunted by the amount of money asked. In the fall of 1850, Pennington asked him to try once again, and he discovered that Frisby Tilghman had just died and that the matter was in the hands of William Clarke, the administrator of the estate. Clarke was quite willing to settle the matter at a reasonable price but felt unable simply to emancipate Pennington. It would be necessary, he informed Hooker, for him to sell James Pennington to someone else. He added that he would like to close up the estate and would settle for $150 and wondered to whom the bill of sale should be made out.

Meanwhile, congregations throughout Berwickshire had set out to raise the money needed and in less than three months had collected almost £100. £55 was sent to Hooker and the remainder set aside to defray the cost of Pennington's journey home. When Hooker was notified of this success, he sent a junior partner in his law firm to Maryland with ample funds to complete the transaction. Before long, the younger lawyer had come back with a document giving ownership of James Pembroke to John Hooker. Bemused by the new status he had acquired, Hooker wrote a long letter to the Hartford *Daily Courant*

---

† "Jonathan" was common British usage for American before "Uncle Sam."

reviewing the history of Pennington's development, from slave to fugitive to pastor and doctor of divinity, and the negotiations which had made Hooker the owner of a slave. And now, wrote Hooker, "it remains for me, by deed under my hand and seal, to 'create him a Peer of the Realm.'" But first, Hooker would indulge himself in a bit of whimsy: "I shall, however, defer the execution of the instrument for half an hour, till I have walked up and down the whole length of Main Street, to see how it seems to be a slave-holder, especially to own a Doctor of Divinity. Possibly during the walk I may change my mind and send him back to a sugar plantation." Hooker signed the letter, "very respectfully yours," and then added a "P.S." "I have returned from my walk. The deed is executed. Jim Pembroke is merged in Rev. Dr. Pennington. The slave is free—the chattel is a man." But Hooker could not resist a further playful bit of legalese: "I spoke of half an hour's walk. I must confess that my return was a little hastened by the thought, which suddenly struck me on the way, that perhaps the 'legal relation' I had rashly assumed was a '*malum in se.*' I thought for a moment of going for consolation to one of the 'lower law' divines,† but feared it might end in my sending the Reverend Doctor to the auction-block."[56] The deed of manumission was duly executed and recorded in the Farmington town records and stands there, Hooker wrote, "for the wonder of future generations."

Hooker found one further occasion to enjoy the strange transaction in which he had been involved. It was after he had returned to New York that Pennington was invited to speak at an August 1 celebration of West Indies emancipation, and Hooker was there, at a grove in the suburbs of Hartford, with a few other white people and about two hundred African Americans. After Pennington had spoken, Hooker was spotted in the crowd and a "clamorous call was made for 'Mr. Hooker.'" "I went upon the platform," Hooker wrote in his memoirs, "and prefaced my short speech with a few words, as follows: 'Before I make a speech, my friends, I want to set you right about an error you have just fallen into. You all know that Mr. Pennington was once my slave. Now it is one of the elemental principles of slavery that the slave can own nothing. Everything that he acquires, or thinks he acquires, passes through him to his master. Even the mule that he got with his own earnings belongs to his master. Now from when I set Mr. Pennington free I merely took my hands off from him—merely let him go. I did not give him anything. Thus the doctorate of divinity, which, as his master, I owned, remained with me, and did not go by his manumission to

---

† *Malum in se* is the legal term for a matter that is "evil in itself," and the "lower law" is that which obtains in a region, as opposed to the "higher law" which is everywhere recognized. In theology, the higher law is God's law and the lower law is the human legal code. Hooker is suggesting that by acquiring a slave he had become a participant in the evil of slavery and therefore hurried to rid himself of a possible corruption.

him, and I hold it still. So, when you next call us out on an occasion like this, I want to have you call for 'Rev. Mr. Pennington' and 'Rev. Dr. Hooker.'"[57]

It was January of 1851 when the legal arrangements were completed, but some time afterwards that the actual documents arrived in Great Britain. Not until June did the committee in Scotland finally come together for a festive celebration of Pennington's freedom, but "a joyful time they had of it." The meeting was held in Dunse (Duns), the county town of Berwickshire, in the East United Presbytery Church, which was "crowded to excess" for the event. William Ritchie, the pastor of the church, described the "terror and dismay" that the Fugitive Slave Act had spread among the colored population of America and the feeling of insecurity it had engendered. "This is the state of things," he said, "from the peril of which we desired to rescue our beloved Dr. Pennington. . . . You have seen him. I ask, could you endure that that meek and manly countenance should be again marred with the tears of a slave? (Hear, hear.) You have heard him; I ask, could you endure that that eloquent and persuasive voice should be again heard uttering the groans of a slave ? You know his character and gifts; I ask, could you endure that that tender heart should be wrung with anguish, that those fine talents should be lost to the church . . . You have shown by your liberal efforts for his ransom that this was an ill you could not bear." Henry Ward Beecher, the speaker said, had made the mistake of asking a New York audience that sort of question in the previous month—"Would anyone send Dr. Pennington back again to slavery?"—and heard voices in his congregation respond "I would" and "I too." That had not been the response in Scotland, the speaker told the gathering, and he was now able to present the deed of manumission to James Pennington.

Pennington, in response, spoke of the way in which the American churches had failed to respond to the challenge of the African Americans in their midst. Not one of the American denominations had ever undertaken any systematic program for the education of the free people of color or providing ministers and teachers for them. He spoke of the difficulties he had encountered in his time at Yale and how he had been engaged ever since as an "Anti-Slavery pastor and preacher" while serving in various anti-slavery and vigilance committees. He told them how in Great Britain "I have wrought in your pulpits, I have wrought in your school rooms, yea, and that my right hand might not forget her cunning, I have wrought a little in some of your blacksmiths' shops." He suggested that he might have introduced the subject of slavery into more pulpits than any previous American visitor and served as an advocate for the cause of the slave in three other countries of Europe. Expressing gratitude to his hosts and his American supporters, he moved on to Glasgow, where supporters representing abolitionist, peace, and temperance groups gathered for another farewell celebration. With that, he brought his long exile to an end.[58]

CHAPTER SEVENTEEN
New York, 1851–1852

Word that James Pennington's new freedom had been officially celebrated in Scotland traveled first, of course, to John Hooker in Hartford, and then to New York, where Lewis Tappan was somewhat embarrassed to find that his *American Missionary* magazine was not first to publish it. This was, in fact, inexcusable, since Hooker's colleague had stopped in New York on his way back from Maryland to exhibit the bill of sale he had acquired for a Doctor of Divinity and Tappan had been the first to see the document, aside from the bearer of it. The *American Missionary* spoke of that visit in July as occurring "the other day" as if it had been a recent event, but the messenger had returned to Hartford after seeing Tappan, Hooker had completed the legal work, and the manumission papers had been sent on to Scotland, where their receipt had been celebrated in June. It must have been months earlier that Tappan had been made acquainted with the proceedings. Frederick Douglass's *North Star* had told its readers in April that Pennington had requested Hooker's help in returning to America. Douglass had picked the news up from the *Pennsylvania Freeman,* which had it from the Congregational Church's *Religious Herald,* published in Hartford.[1] Hooker's own account had been sent to the Hartford *Daily Courant* on June 3rd and then picked up by the *New York Independent,* another religious journal, and published there. By the time Tappan published the story in the *American Missionary,* it was decidedly old news.

Tappan called the bill of sale he had seen a "truly American curiosity," but equally curious was the way Tappan treated the news.[†] "If any apology is needed for our publication of the following article," he wrote, "it may be found in the fact that Dr. Pennington is a member of our Executive Committee"—as

---

† The article in the *American Missionary* is unsigned and Tappan was not technically the editor, but he often pinch-hit as editor, wrote frequently for the paper, and would surely have approved of whatever was written in it, whether he wrote it himself or not.

if the story might not otherwise have been newsworthy. The three paragraphs of the article itself were oddly focused away from Hooker's achievement and Pennington's freedom and toward Tappan's agenda: denouncing the "atrocious Fugitive Slave law," suggesting that it was now time for Pennington to come back to New York, and chiding the Third Presbytery and New York Christians in general for their apathy in regard to slavery and the suffering it caused. "We hope Dr. Pennington will now lose no time in returning to his own native land," Tappan urged, "and to the church of which the Holy Ghost has made him the overseer. . . ." Having been unable to control Pennington's departure, he still hoped to control his return.[2]

Pennington's Heidelberg doctorate irritated not only Lewis Tappan but the Garrisonians as well. Rumors circulated that it had been promoted by the British and Foreign Anti Slavery Society, whose members had made James Pennington their "special protege." But at the root of the Garrisonians' problem was the rapid decline in their support in Scotland. Contributions that had once gone to the Garrisonian strongholds in Boston and Philadelphia were now going to Frederick Douglass in Rochester and to the New York Vigilance Committee and other organizations aiding fugitive slaves rather than Garrison's supporters.[3] Jealousies and rivalries of various sorts continued to trouble the abolition movement. In New York, Lewis Tappan, unable to abide Garrison and his supporters, also continued to concern himself with the financial affairs of African American leaders.

No sooner was James Pennington back in New York than he found himself involved in two meetings a week apart with Lewis Tappan and others, having to do with money he had collected in Jamaica. Pennington had been back from Jamaica for four years; and he had spent two years of that time in England. Samuel Oughton was there from Jamaica, and so was Bartholomew T. Welch, a leading Baptist pastor from Brooklyn.[†] The first meeting was on September 1; when they met again on September 9, John Hooker was also there from Hartford, and Tappan noted in his journal that he "devoted most of the day to this business."[4] Tappan does not say what the issue was or whether anything was resolved; presumably it was not, since the whole matter came up again four years later.

The New York to which James Pennington returned in mid-August was growing faster than ever, with immigrants flooding in from the mid-century wars and revolutions in Europe. It was, as it has always been, a city with extremes of wealth and poverty. Lewis Tappan and his friends could live in mansions on Brooklyn Heights, but William J. Wilson, a school teacher and

† Bartholomew T. Welch was also President of the American and Foreign Bible Society. cf. Haynes, D. C., *The Baptist Denomination*, p. 327.

civic leader, who wrote a stylish and often caustic "Brooklyn Correspondent" column for *Frederick Douglass' Paper* under the pseudonym "Ethiop," also looked down from Brooklyn Heights and saw the city's poverty:

> Miserable loafers rub their eyes and shake their tattered garments to the breeze; and as it freshens, wretched women pull their more wretched apologies for coverings closely about them, shiveringly pass on; squalid children, once white, but now difficult to tell of what color, and painful to behold, crouch before each successive blast as it winds its way to their half-naked bodies. Alas, it is a sad reflection, that amid so much *brick and mortar*—amid so much splendor, there is so much of misery and degradation; society is organically diseased here. I venture to say that there is more wretchedness, more misery, more degradation, here in this metropolis amidst the superfluity of philanthropy and religion, than can be found in any whole nation outside of Christendom. Vice and folly stalk abroad at noon day, and *christianity* hides her head behind the veil of the temple until each returning Sabbath. Society here needs renovating, *soul* and *body* . . .[5]

The New York lawyer and diarist George Templeton Strong, on the other hand, saw only progress:

> How this city marches northward! The progress of 1835 and 1836 was nothing to the luxuriant, rank growth of this year. Streets are springing up, whole strata of limestone have transferred themselves from their ancient resting-places to look down on bustling thoroughfares for long years to come. Wealth is rushing in upon us like a freshet.[6]

What Strong and many others failed to notice was that the freshet of wealth rushed in to lift some higher but left many others drowning. The Irish immigrants,[†] escaping the potato famine in Ireland and willing to do any work available for a pittance, were making it increasingly difficult for African Americans to find and hold jobs in the city, and slave catchers made their lives more perilous still. The Fugitive Slave law and other "compromise" legislation of 1850 had only increased tensions between the North and South; protest

---

† In 1826 the United States received 10,837 immigrants, of whom 5,408 were Irish. In 1842 the potato famine sent over 50,000 Irish immigrants. (Smith, op. cit., p. 737.) Between 1845 and 1855 over two million European immigrants arrived in America, half of them Irish and most of the rest German. (Williams, Robert C., *Horace Greeley*, p. 125.)

meetings were held in many communities and newspapers raged against it. The *Ohio Standard*, noticing the way in which every citizen was required to assist in the arrest of fugitives, editorialized, "We are all Slave Catchers . . . The law does not permit you to stand neutral in this controversy between Slavery and Freedom."[7] The *Hartford Courant* wrote "It is kidnapping made easy. . . . Under this law, no colored man is safe . . . Does any man believe this law will not be used to drag free blacks into slavery?"[8]

Incidents describing exactly that aspect of the new law were widely reported, and every attempt to enforce it only increased the anger. From Pennsylvania came a report of the systematic abduction of "poor neglected colored children" to be sold in Washington so that "from outward appearances . . . (t)hey take into slavery more ever year than all the Anti-Slavery Societies take from it."[9] In Ohio, a farmer was fined $1200 for giving nine fugitives a ride in his wagon. In Florida, a man who tried to help seven slaves escape by boat to the Bahamas was chained in prison for fifteen days, pelted with eggs in a pillory, and branded on his hand with the letters "SS" for "slave stealer."[10] In Boston, a waiter named Fred Wilkins, or Shadrach, was seized at his place of work and rushed to the courthouse, near a black residential area. Word spread quickly, and even as lawyers were obtaining a court delay, a group of fifty-some African Americans invaded the courtroom, lifted Shadrach on their shoulders, and carried him out to a waiting carriage that bore him off to Canada and safety. President Fillmore, outraged, immediately ordered that those who had enabled the escape be brought to trial. Charges of treason were instituted but reduced to a misdemeanor and ultimately dismissed.[11] Two months later, however, another Boston man was dragged from his bed by slave hunters and abducted before any alarm could be given. Nonetheless, when news of the incident spread, the city was "thrown into the greatest excitement" and "Seven of the most popular abolitionists were arrested and locked in prison."[12] "The cradle of liberty," said one abolitionist paper, has become "a slave hunting ground for kidnappers."[13]

But the Fugitive Slave Law was strongly supported even in the North. In New York City one hundred leading merchants formed the Union Safety Committee, issued statements, and organized lectures to call for support of the compromise and the return of fugitives to the South.[14] Their goal was to defend the Union—and their commercial interests.

But how should African Americans respond to the Fugitive Slave Act? It was all very well to provide support for individuals, but what long-term policy should they now adopt? For some, the answer was to think again about colonization. Augustus Washington, Pennington's Hartford admirer, was not the only one to decide that there truly was no future for African Americans in America. They had worked hard to improve their situation and to call patiently for change, but the response had been ever more forceful measures to establish the power of the slaveocracy and to increase the insecurity of the free black population. Washington's daguerreotype business was thriving as members of Hartford's elite came to him for their pictures to be taken and, often, framed in silver. William Lloyd Garrison was among those who stopped in for a portrait to be made. But Washington looked around with a growing despair as it seemed to him that every "avenue to wealth and respectability" was closed to the black population. They could not participate in government or, except rarely, attend college, and now the iron hand of the federal government was even supporting kidnappers who threatened the peace and order of free black communities. In 1841, he had said, "I abhor with intense hatred the motives, the scheme, and spirit of colonization," but a few years later he was pondering the value of settlements in Canada, Mexico, the West Indies, and elsewhere in the hemisphere. By July of 1851, he had concluded that if black Americans were "ever [to] find a home on earth for the development of their manhood and intellect it [would] first be in Liberia or some other part of Africa."[15] In 1853, he moved to Liberia, where he again found success as a daguerreotypist and served as well in the Liberian Congress.

Evidence of this changing outlook was the creation by a New York group of an organization called the "United African Republic Emigration Society" (subsequently known as the "Liberian Agricultural and Emigration Association"), acting at first independently of the African Colonization Society, but later turning to that ancient enemy for support. Governor Washington Hunt of New York also saw a new opportunity for the ACS and went to the New York legislature for funds to assist its program. The inferiority of free blacks, Hunt insisted, was a result of their history and would lead to the extinction of the race if they were not separated from whites. "The instinct of nature, too powerful to be countenanced by the refinements of abstract reasoning, proclaims," he concluded, "that the two races must sooner or later be separated."[16] The New York *Tribune* and other papers expressed their agreement.[17]

To cope with the emergency, black New Yorkers held a series of meetings and organized a "Committee of Thirteen" to provide leadership. Resolutions were passed denouncing both the governor's plans and the ACS while calling on African Americans to stand fast and continue the fight against slavery and discrimination. After much weighing of pros and cons, another resolution was passed calling on African Americans to leave the city with "its seductions, its oppression, and baleful atmosphere" and "seek to expand our elbows, our lungs, and our energies in the free air of the rural districts." Another resolution created a committee to present a proposal for a mutual savings bank. Still anther resolution called for a day of fasting and prayer. Perhaps the most striking evidence of the growing hopelessness was a resolution stating that "all history teaches us that every people should be prepared to defend themselves by a knowledge of the use of defensive weapons" and urging the young men of New York and Brooklyn "to organize military companies." The last of these resolutions was adopted at a meeting in the Shiloh Presbyterian Church in Pennington's absence. As usual, there were denunciations of colonization plans and especially the notion that African Americans generally "trace our ancestry to Africa alone. We trace it," they pointed out, "to Englishmen, Irishmen, Scotchmen, to Frenchmen, to the German; to the Asiatic as well as to Africa. The best blood of Virginia courses through our veins."[†] They insisted again, as they had done often before, "That this is our native land: that here we live and have lived; that here we hope and have hoped; and that no amount of persecution had driven or will drive us to any inhospitable region."[18] But the way to a realistic future was far from clear. One of the meetings was honest enough to say "We are so mixed up in the heat and the smoke of the battle, that we can see too little of our absolute or relative position."[19]

In the midst of such confusion, James Pennington was not surprised when a friend asked him whether the fact that several European governments had recently recognized Liberian independence might have changed his views on colonization. Pennington told his friend that his views were unchanged and then took the opportunity to write a letter to *Frederick Douglass' Paper* explaining why they were not. He put no trust in European governments. France was now again an Empire, and the Prussian Kaiser had recently deprived Germans of their liberal constitution. There was no reason to expect that they would promote democracy in Africa. But he gave much more attention to the way England had been moving into South Africa. "It is now found," Pennington wrote, "that the Briton going to Africa loses all his kindly and generous feelings for the Negro." What, then, became of the colonizationist theory that Africa was available to the American black? "You push us in this country, and we must get out of the way . . . You say we must separate from the Saxon by going to Africa. But the Saxon is there! The real land-stealing, unscrupulous Saxon is even in Africa and is pushing his way into the interior! They are Saxonizing Africa!" What, then, became of the colonizationist theory

† Later in the year, James McCune Smith corrected Horace Greeley, who had suggested that free blacks should dedicate themselves to civilizing the "land of their forefathers." Referring to "the hundred thousand whites who will pass this night in the embrace of black women," Smith asked, "Did you mean foremothers?" (James McCune Smith to Horace Greeley, September 1, 1851. *BAP.*) The modern ability to decode DNA provides statistical evidence of this mingling of races. Among African Americans the Y-chromosomes are about one third European; but the mitochondrial DNA, which comes from the female line, is only about six per cent European. In other words, genetic studies confirm that white slave owners exploited their female slaves. ("Who Killed the Men of England: the written record of history meets genomics, evolution, demography, and molecular archaeology," Jonathan Shaw, *Harvard Magazine*, July–August 2009, p. 33.)

that the races must develop separately? Pennington ironically cited, as he often did, the proverbial saying, "Consistency, thou art a jewel!"[20]

In this time of confusion, America looked for leadership to an accidental president, the third to hold that office in less than two years. Millard Fillmore, a rather obscure New York State politician who had been defeated in a campaign for governor and was serving as comptroller, had been nominated for vice president to secure the New York State vote for the Whig Party and then had inherited the presidency when Zachary Taylor died after a mere sixteen months in office. The fact that the newest occupant of the White House was a Northerner and a New Yorker brought no benefit to African Americans. Like so many other Northern politicians in those years, he was not one to challenge the existing order. "God knows that I detest slavery," he said, "but it is an existing evil . . . and we must endure it and give it such protection as is guaranteed by the Constitution."[21] Thus the Fugitive Slave Act seemed to him an appropriate way to placate the South and preserve the Union. Lewis Tappan called it "the Fillmore Act" because Fillmore, as vice president, had presided over the Senate debate on the so-called "Compromise of 1850" and then signed it into law after he became president.

Tensions within the churches were continuing to rise as well. Methodists in 1844 and Baptists in 1845 had divided over slavery. Presbyterians, already divided between the New Light and Old Light factions, became further divided by the slavery issue. Garrisonians, as has been said, scorned the divided churches, while even those churches that had taken a strong stand against slavery were often unable to satisfy the strongest abolitionists. "Come-outer" groups were formed in many places by dissatisfied members of a number of churches. Some of these kept a denominational identity, as did the Free Methodists and Free Mission Baptists, while others were united more by their opposition to slavery than by any theological position. Only a few weeks before James Pennington's return to New York, a major convention of anti-slavery Christians drew 250 delegates from eleven states to Chicago. The famous evangelist Charles Finney was there, and so was Lewis Tappan. Delegates took turns denouncing the major denominations and mission boards for their failure to condemn slavery and expel slaveholders, and for their willingness to accept money contributed by slave owners. Individual Christians were condemned as well for their participation in churches that had failed to take a clear stand on the issue. The churches' failure, it was charged, gave "respectability to slaveholding" and the individuals who remained in such churches, they maintained, tended to lose their anti-slavery fervor. The charge that those who failed to come out were "more attached to a sect, than they are opposed to slavery" would shortly be made against James Pennington, and angry letters would be exchanged in *Frederick Douglass' Paper*.

Conventions similar to the one in Chicago were held, often annually, in various states through the 1850s. Slavery and fellowship with slave owners were condemned, and disobedience to the Fugitive Slave Law was counseled. Some agreed with Garrison that the Constitution was a pro-slavery document and that disunion was the course to follow, but Garrison continued to condemn the churches as well for their moral failure and to insist that, except for the come-outers, Christian churches had failed to live up to their profession.[22]

If evidence was needed that the time for compromise was past, it was provided by an incident on September 11, 1851, in Christiana, a small town in Pennsylvania just north of the Mason-Dixon Line and in countryside that Pennington had probably traveled through on his journey from the home of William Wright to that of Isaiah Kirk. It was an area of steep wooded hills and scrubby ravines, difficult to traverse but perfect cover for runaway slaves. William Parker, a fugitive slave from Maryland, had settled in the area in 1839 and assisted a number of other fugitives in succeeding years. In 1849 he willingly took in four fugitives from the estate of Edward Gorsuch, a Maryland church deacon and a slaveholder reputed to be kind in his treatment of slaves. Nevertheless, they were slaves; therefore, they wanted freedom and Gorsuch wanted his property. When Gorsuch learned their location in the summer of 1851, he went to Philadelphia for the proper papers and recruited a United States marshal and two assistants to join with him, two family members, and two neighbors in an attempt to retrieve his property.

Gorsuch apparently saw the affair as a matter of honor involving his good name and reputation. What he did not know was that William Parker was a valued member of a community prepared to defend itself. For blacks who lived so near the Mason-Dixon line, the danger from slave catchers was very real. Earlier in the same year, kidnappers had brazenly invaded the home of a black couple, knocked down the woman, and carried the man off without bothering with any papers or legal procedures. Understandably, the three thousand black people who lived in the area had formed a mutual protection society under Parker's leadership and arranged for signals to be given in time of danger. Parker, who was described by a local white abolitionist as being "bold as a lion, the kindest of men, and the most steadfast of friends," was regarded by local African Americans as "their leader, their protector, their Moses, and their lawgiver all at once."[23]

The preparations Gorsuch had made for his expedition had drawn attention, so William Parker was warned that trouble was coming. When the marshal appeared on his doorstep and identified himself, Parker's response was, "If you take another step, I'll break your neck." Eliza Parker, William Parker's wife, fetched a horn and began to blow it to summon help, and shots were then exchanged, though it is unclear who fired first. Local residents began to come across the fields, some with pistols, shotguns, and rifles, some with rocks or scythes. Among those who came to the scene were the local miller, Castner Hanway, and Elijah Lewis, the postmaster and a Quaker, both of whom were white and unarmed. They had simply heard that Parker's house was surrounded by "kidnappers" and had come to see what was happening in the neighborhood. As tensions mounted, Hanway was heard to shout, "Don't shoot! Don't shoot!" But the marshal, who had asked for assistance from the white men and been told they had no desire to become involved, let them know that they were committing a federal crime by failing to assist him. Hanway responded that he had better leave before blood was shed, and the marshal seemed prepared to do so, but Gorsuch was intent on pressing the issue and moved forward. More shots were then fired, Gorsuch was killed, and his son and at least two of Parker's allies were badly injured.

Knowing they would now be facing a far stronger force, Parker, the fugitives, and some others promptly fled to Canada. They crossed Lake Ontario in a steamer from Rochester, New York, with help from Frederick Douglass, who was given Parker's pistol as "a memento of the battle for liberty at Christiana" and a token of appreciation. Meanwhile, in Pennsylvania, reinforcements arrived for the marshal. As many as half a dozen blacks were captured and sent off to slavery while thirty others, three whites and twenty-seven blacks, were arrested and charged with treason.[†] James Pennington, newly returned from the quiet hills of Scotland, was immediately caught up in the Christiana Affair and, in a remarkable transformation of outlook, went to work with Charles B. Ray to help raise money for the defense of men accused of violence, both black and white. Significant to him was the fact that black citizens had organized and fought for their freedom. Like many other pacifists, when war finally came he could not fail to support the cause of freedom even if it violated his pacifist principles.

Arrayed against the defendants was the full force of the federal government. President Fillmore himself instructed Daniel Webster, the secretary of state, to see that the best lawyers were provided to the prosecution. The government was anxious as always to impress the South and, having convinced a grand jury to indict thirty-eight men for treason, brought charges first against Castner Hanway.[††] Hanway, however, could not easily be shown to have committed treason. He had no weapon and had taken no violent action,

† The federal government charged "treason" to impress the South with their support for the Fugitive Slave Law. The government defined high treason as "any combination or conspiracy by force and intimidation, to prevent the execution of an Act of Congress, so as to render it inoperative and ineffective." *NAS*, December 4, 1851.

†† Ironically, the trial was held in Independence Hall in Philadelphia, a place where treason had once been committed by the Founding Fathers. Among the counsel for the defense was Thaddeus Stevens, later to become a leading Republican voice in Congress.

nor had he encouraged others, though it was argued that his mere presence as a white man had encouraged the blacks. There was some justification for that belief, but the jury, having spent nearly a month listening to the evidence and arguments,[†] took only fifteen minutes to find Hanway not guilty, and charges against the others were finally dropped since the principals were safe in Canada and there was little local support for the prosecution. Pennington and the Trustees of the Prince Street Church gave a public reception for the defendants to celebrate their victory, and Pennington wrote triumphantly to his friends in Scotland, saying "We have just closed another grand drama in the strange history of American slavery . . . the government stands before the country and before the whole world clothed in shame." It was a victory not without cost. Pennington pointed out that the nearly four months Hanway had spent in jail had destroyed his health and that the cost of his defense had "exhausted his property."[24] The black prisoners also had substantial debts and had been deprived of their normal earnings; at least one was near death as a result of his ordeal. While Pennington worked with vigilance committees in Philadelphia, New York, and Rochester to provide assistance for the black defendants, a nearby Quaker meeting paid the costs of the white defendants, two of whom were Quakers.[25] Months later, Pennington was still trying to raise funds for the former defendants from John Jay, Horace Greeley, and others. By that time the defendants were in Canada, but still destitute and in great need of help.[26]

William Parker wrote his own account of the incident in 1866 and boasted that ". . . my rights as a freeman were . . . secured by my own right arm." The incident is spoken of today as the "Christiana Riot," but to many at the time it seemed more like the opening skirmish in a war that loomed ever closer on the horizon. "No single event before John Brown's raid," one historian has judged, "contributed more to the decline of confidence in the nation's ability to resolve the controversy over slavery without wholesale resort to arms."[27]

Nothing, of course, was resolved by the Christiana incident, except that partisans on both sides were outraged by what had happened and tensions heightened. Through that same summer and fall, stories continued to be published about both fugitives and free men being carried off by slave hunters. In August, in Buffalo, a cook named Daniel who worked on a Great Lakes ship was bludgeoned and carried off to Kentucky after a brief legal proceeding.[28] In Poughkeepsie, New York, in September, a young tailor was arrested and, after a brief legal procedure, taken to South Carolina.[29] In Busti, New York, in October, a man named Harrison was carried off.[30] In December, a young woman, recently married, was arrested and taken to Kentucky,[31] and two

† The trial opened on November 24, 1851, and concluded on December 17, 1851.

fugitives from Maryland were taken in Pennsylvania on a Sunday, though in that case one escaped from his captors.[32] Each incident further enraged Northern feelings. Even those who saw no great harm in slavery seemed to feel that this taking up of fugitives from their community was a violation of their own security.

Partly to look for a better understanding of these violent events but perhaps also to enable him to catch up on American events after so long away, James Pennington convened a meeting of ministers and members of black Presbyterian and Congregational churches at the Shiloh Church on November 18 to "consider the condition of those churches in this country" and "to collect facts and statistics in relation to the interests and usefulness" of these churches. Pennington, Amos Beman of New Haven, and E. P. Rogers of Newark were constituted a committee of three to correspond with other churches and ask them to respond to a series of questions. Statistics of membership were requested and the existence of mission, temperance, and education societies. The critical questions, however, were:

1. To what extent has your church and congregation been affected by the Fugitive Slave Law?
2. Has the present colonization agitation affected your people so as to incline them to leave in any numbers for Africa, the West Indies, Canada, or the Gerrit Smith lands?
3. Do you think the spirit of the American Colonization Society has increased among the whites in your place?[33]

Meanwhile, just a few days before that meeting,† James Pennington was involved in a curious incident after an ordination service that he had taken part in with other members of the New York Presbytery. It was a routine ecclesiastical event but took an unusual turn at the end when Pennington was introduced for the first time to one of the other clergy participants. As they exchanged the usual pleasantries about places they had lived, people they had known, and churches they had served, they suddenly realized that they had known each other when they were children over forty years before in Hagerstown, Maryland. Some of Pennington's fellow slaves had been hired to work in the home of the other man's family and the two boys had had what the newspaper report delicately called "some degree of that familiarity which subsists between the white children and the domestic servants of the households in slave states." From that beginning, the two boys had grown up

† The ordination of the Rev. James Sinclair took place in the Spring Street Church on November 13, 1851.

and followed very different courses to become pastors of large Presbyterian churches in the same city and to share in the ordination of a young man entering that same ministry. The service being over, the two men stood there in the emptying church deeply engrossed "with great mutual respect and cordiality" in their conversation. Behind the headlines and the resolutions were human beings whose lives had come together in a strange way. The story, widely reprinted, served to draw attention to the fact that black and white, freed slave and privileged white, could work together in a common cause and respect each other as human beings in spite of the structures and passions that produced so much fear and violence in the world around them.[34] It was a small but human incident in a society that was losing sight of that humanity in its anger and fear.[†]

Perhaps it was that same internal tension that made Americans turn with relief to the visit of the Hungarian patriot Lajos Kossuth, who arrived in New York on the frigate *Mississippi* on November 11. The story of a rebel and patriot fighting against the powerful forces of the Austro-Hungarian Empire was bound to appeal to Americans—as it had appealed to many in England, where enormous crowds welcomed and cheered him, though not Queen Victoria, who was nervous about popular uprisings and those who promoted them. Torn between a politician's desire to be seen with a popular hero and the need to remain on good terms with the queen, the prime minister chose to support Kossuth and resign his office. France, under the Emperor Napoleon III, on the other hand, had refused him passage. Somehow it was arranged that Kossuth would be brought to America by a ship of the United States Navy, but Kossuth caused controversy wherever he went. Daniel Webster, who was secretary of state, spoke admiringly of Kossuth, while Millard Fillmore as president apologized to the Austrian chargé d'affaires for what he explained was simply Webster's individual opinion.[35] Fillmore had a diplomat's need to be cautious, but most Americans could unite in scorn for the distant Austrian Empire and support for the heroic Hungarians; it cost them very little and made them feel much better about themselves than they felt when they looked at their own divisions.

Abolitionists consulted with each other about the possibility of using Kossuth's visit to their advantage. Daniel O'Connell, the Irish patriot and liberator, had specifically linked the cause of Irish freedom with that of the

---

† There is, however, a letter from Pennington to the Rev. Jeff Kebbs, referring to "that interesting ordination" at which they had met and seeking help for another black congregation that hoped to lease a church for their use. Pennington was writing because he had called several times and never found Kebbs at home. It was one thing to be cordial in a church building and another, apparently, to be of real assistance. (Pennington, J. W. C. to J. M. Kebbs, *BAP*, 9:0150.)

American slaves;† perhaps Kossuth would do the same. Gerrit Smith thought the effort should be made to contact the Hungarian and persuade him that he could serve the cause of liberty in the United States. Henry Bibb, editor of a black newspaper published in Canada, thought that if Kossuth saw,

> as he must, that some of the most philanthropic and devoted men . . . are being tried for their lives in Boston, Buffalo, and Philadelphia for aiding Refugees to escape from chattel slavery and refused to sympathize with them . . . and connive at it by accepting the presents and congratulations of their oppressors, he will prove himself to be unworthy of our sympathy. We cannot believe in the patriotism of the man who condescends to receive favors and congratulations from slave[-]holding despots, who are decidedly more tyrannical than the arbitrary power from which he has fled. . . . A true patriot . . . cannot be expected to leave this country without expressing his detestation of the groveling hypocrites who constitute the slave-holding portion of the Union; for if Kossuth is really what he professes to be, he cannot hold sentiments, in common with avowed liberty destroyers.[36]

Pennington, more of a realist, thought it unlikely that any abolitionist would be able to get near enough to Kossuth to explain the parallels between Hungarian and African American oppression. Already a variety of other Americans with an agenda had been in touch with prominent Hungarians in America and taken control of his program. "I fear," Pennington wrote to Smith, "we cannot raise force enough to break through the troop that will be around him."[37]

Certainly no abolitionists were included in the official party that welcomed Kossuth to New York, or in the reception hosted by the mayor, or in the parade up Fifth Avenue. The *New York Times* described the welcome as one of "the most magnificent and enthusiastic ever extended to any man in any part of the world." Linking all that with the abolition cause would indeed have been a triumph, but the abolitionists were not the only group with such an idea. Over the next week groups of every sort—"religious, civil, social, political, and academical"—besieged him. There was even a delegation of Floridians who complimented him on how well he understood their

---

† Some of O'Connell's words might well have been spoken by James Pennington: "My days—the blossom of my youth and the flower of my manhood—have been darkened by the dreariness of servitude. In this my native land—in the land of my sires—I am degraded without fault as an alien and an outcast." (O'Connell, J. (ed.) *The Life and Speeches of Daniel O'Connell.* Dublin, 1846, v. I, p.185.)

concern to preserve their own institutions from "the enemies of constitutional freedom." "Could he fail to understand this?" asked the *National Anti Slavery Standard*. "Could he help feeling that these slaveholders meant that they accepted his silence as the price of their homage?"[38]

Whether he understood the Floridians or not, he seemed to understand very well the dynamics of American society and where the power lay. He had not come, he said at the outset, "to meddle with whatever party question of your own domestic affairs." In other words, he made it clear, as the *National Anti Slavery Standard* translated that phrase, that he would take no stand in relation to the American way of condemning every sixth child "to grow up, live and die, in a state of personal degradation and mental darkness, compared with which the restraints placed on Hungarian freedom of action and thought, were perfect freedom and the fullness of light . . . While he is appealing to the people of the United States for their intervention between his countrymen and their tyrants, he is careful to let them know that he has no intention of intervening between them and the victims of their tyranny."[39]

Nevertheless, Kossuth did receive a deputation from the black community and, in spite of Pennington's pessimism about breaking through to the Hungarian hero, he found himself in his presence with Lewis Tappan and three others in a delegation from the American and Foreign Anti Slavery Society. A strategy had been devised that the delegation had hoped would give them some claim to Kossuth's sympathy. They would read a polite and deferential "Address of the Coloured People to Kossuth," saluting his efforts on behalf of Hungarian freedom and suggesting that that cause was also "the common cause of crushed, outraged humanity."[40] Having read this very vague statement, a letter was handed to Kossuth that made a more explicit link between the cause of Hungarian freedom and African Americans by claiming that no part of the American people held him in "greater veneration" than those who "acknowledge the divine obligation of doing justice and showing mercy to all men, irrespective of race and complexion." Nevertheless the letter said that they had no "desire to connect you with any party of this country . . . and no reply is desired." But Kossuth outsmarted them. He glanced at the letter and, seeing its purpose, suggested that since this was a public occasion it would be good to read the letter aloud. Tappan "exhibited signs of surprise and vexation" but did as requested. Kossuth then responded by thanking them profusely for not trying to "entangle me in any party question" and for understanding his basic principle that every nation has the right "to dispose of its own domestic affairs," after which he shook hands all around and ended the audience.[41]

Kossuth had come, of course, with one objective only: to gain specific American support, arms and money, for his cause. Americans instinctively sympathized with him and his cause, and his appeal to that instinct was direct

and open. When he was told that he would review the New York militia, he
responded, "Oh God, how my heart throbs at the idea to see this gallant army
enlisted on the side of freedom against despotism; the world would be free,
and you the savours of humanity. And why not?" There were of course, many
reasons "why not," from the parting warning of George Washington against
"entangling alliances" to the impending need for that militia to preserve
the Union. But Kossuth had only one concern and would play to American
heartstrings for sympathy and support. "If you consider these claims not sufficient to your active and operative sympathy," Kossuth concluded in his major
New York speech, "then let me know at once that the hopes have failed with
which Europe's oppressed nations have looked to your mighty and glorious
Republic . . . that I may hasten back and tell Europe's oppressed nations, 'Let
us fight forsaken and single handed . . .'" [42] But that was the message Kossuth
was given. William Jay spoke for many in a letter to the American Peace
Society: "I regard Kossuth as a great man, and trust he is a conscientious
one. . . . But while I do justice to his talents, earnestness and patriotism, I
am compelled to believe that he is asking what it would be a sin and a folly
to us to grant." [43] The United States was not yet prepared to intervene in the
affairs of other nations, and Kossuth went on his way without the support
he had come to obtain.† So, too, did the American and Foreign Anti-Slavery
Society; indeed, the whole exchange left abolitionists sniping at each other
as to the success or failure of the strategy. William Lloyd Garrison expressed
disapproval of the way Tappan had handled the matter, and Tappan and
Garrison exchanged angry and public letters in the *Liberator*.[44] A New York
abolition paper condemned the approach and congratulated William Jay for
not signing the statement although he was a member of the AFASS Board.
That drew a sharp response from Jay, who said he had entirely approved of
the statements presented to Kossuth and had not signed them only because
he was "unable to be present." Abolitionists as far away as Ireland weighed
in with a resolution expressing "grave disapprobation" for the way in which
the American delegation had allowed Kossuth to avoid committing himself
to the cause of freedom in America. The Irish society believed that the
Americans had set a "dangerous precedent" and done "serious injury" to
their cause by "absolving him from any expression of sympathy" with "the
downtrodden millions of republican America." [45]

Lacking any such expression of sympathy from Kossuth and having gone
to great effort for nothing, Tappan, Pennington, and others returned to the

† The diarist George Templeton Strong was another who resisted what he called "Magyar-
mania." It seemed to him that "other 'causes' have a prior claim on a New Yorker," such
as "Dr. Muhlenberg's hospital" and "distressed individuals around us . . . in this city and
county whose appeal is stronger." (*The Diary of George Templeton Strong*, pp. 76–77.)

central issue that remained what it had been twenty years earlier in Philadelphia: the status of free black people in the North and the continuing downgrading of that status by the insistence of colonizationists that blacks would be better off in Africa, and America would be better off without them. A trickle of settlers continued to flow to Liberia, and from time to time a leading African American despaired of progress in America and joined them. James Pennington also was willing to consider alternatives to the United States but continued to look south rather than east and to see the island of Jamaica as a better choice than Africa. In December, he met with Samuel Cornish[†] and W. W. Anderson, an English lawyer practicing in Jamaica, to discuss emigration from the United States.[46] The subject of emigration continued to come up but never seemed a really practical solution to the problem. After all, Jamaica was already well settled and the cost of transporting any significant number there would have been as prohibitive for Pennington and his colleagues as emigration to Africa was for the Colonization Society. A meeting that same month in Brooklyn to discuss a common stand on colonization only revealed further divisions. One speaker who assailed all institutions, whether of the Church or State, that favored pro-slavery doctrines in any degree included in his condemnation James Pennington and Samuel Cornish for their membership in the Presbyterian Church and held that only emigration to Africa provided a solution.[47] But no one knew how to move three million people even if they were willing to go. Finally, solutions would have to be found, as Pennington had always insisted, in the United States.

In January 1852, the Committee of Thirteen called for another meeting, this time at the Abyssinian Baptist Church in Manhattan. "There are traitors among us," they announced, "colored men united with our oppressors—men who, to satisfy their selfish ends, to put money in their purses, are uniting their influence with those who would drive us from our country."

James Pennington, who was not one of the Committee, opened the meeting with prayer, denounced "the foul system of colonization," and expressed his trust that "they would yet have their privileges acknowledged in this country, and that they would no longer hear the doctrine that it was necessary for them to go four thousand miles to be made men." Resolutions were offered denouncing "a few renegade colored men" who would recommend "an ignominious flight to the pestilential shores of Africa." Pennington returned to the platform to support the resolutions and to read from his statements of twenty

† Cornish founded the first black newspaper in the United States with John Russwurm in 1827, calling it *Freedom's Journal*. In 1829 he moved on to edit *The Rights of All*, and later the *Colored American* from 1837 to 1839. In 1822 he founded the first black Presbyterian congregation in Manhattan, and he was also a founding member of the American Anti Slavery Society.

years earlier and reaffirm them. He spoke also of the fact that the Colonization Society had transferred a million acres of land to the Republic of Liberia
but reserved the right to hold half the area in trust. How, he asked, could the
Republic claim to be an independent state if the Colonization Society controlled so much of the land? "This is your home," he told the gathering. "Here
you are bound to raise your children. This is the cornerstone of your future
prosperity." He "concluded amid much applause," and the meeting continued
with one speaker after another denouncing colonization, until midnight came
and the chair announced that "in decency, it was time to adjourn and to go
home with the ladies."[48] Nothing new had been said, as Pennington had made
very clear by simply repeating his own speeches from twenty years earlier; but
as long as the Colonization Society continued to promote its viewpoint, the
opposite side would need to be heard, if only to build up their own morale.

The New York City meeting was followed before the end of the month
with a meeting in Albany of the State Convention of Colored Citizens. This
time James Pennington was chosen to preside and the subject, once again, was
colonization and Governor Hunt's endorsement of it. The Convention agreed
that the Governor was wrong not only in his recommendation of colonization
but in his basic statements of fact. Contrary to his statement that the black
population was declining and headed "like the Indian race . . . [for] permanent
extinction," the census figures showed an increase in every decade except one,
the decade from 1810 to 1820, when slave owners had moved some five thousand slaves south to avoid having them set free when the state ended slavery
within its borders. If declining numbers indicate a population unable to survive
in New York State, they called the governor's attention to the decline of the
population of Montgomery County, New York, in the last census and wondered
to what part of the world those citizens should be removed.

Contrary to the governor's statement that they were "Debarred from all
participation in public employment . . . rejected from most of the institutions
of learning and religion, . . . shut out from social intercourse and condemned
to a life of servility and drudgery," the statement pointed out that African
Americans did "in proportion to our attainments" hold public employment
and even win elections in some places. As to the institutions of religion and
learning, the letter made the interesting point that where black citizens had
been rejected, it had been uniformly on the plea that Southern students would
not come if black students were there, but the institutions needed the Southern
money. This, the letter points out, "is palpable proof of the chains which the
South has forced upon men of science and sanctity in our State." It was not
that black people were not qualified or would not be accepted, but rather that
even Northern institutions and white citizens were enslaved by the South's
"peculiar institution."

The address goes on for three double-columned pages, providing statistics and specific details on the various aspects of the governor's misconceptions. How, they ask, could the governor think they were "governed by laws they have no share in framing" when they had had the right to vote since the state's laws were first adopted? The property qualification limited that right to some degree, but 80% of black citizens were able to vote if so inclined. They would have thought that the votes they cast for him, hoping for a liberal interpretation of the Fugitive Slave Law, would have earned his gratitude and "made some impression on his patriotic memory." It was, however, when it came to the governor's statement that they were "shut out from social intercourse" that the statement was most amusing. It was quite possible, they assured him, "that social intercourse can exist apart from the class of our fellow-citizens who monopolize the higher offices in the gift of the people." In other words, people do talk to each other even if they don't live in Albany. They not only talk to each other, they fall in love with each other and in New York City and Brooklyn "intermarriages between the 'two great races,' have become so frequent as to interfere with the usual classification in census-taking." If the governor was right in discerning an "instinctive antipathy" between the races, they wondered also how he would explain the fact that so many African Americans were no longer of pure African ancestry—fewer, they suggested, than could still claim pure French, German or Irish descent.[49]

In addition to the convention statement, Pennington, as president of the Convention, sent an abridged version to the papers that appeared in the *Liberator* in March and perhaps other papers as well. Summing up the response to Governor Hunt, Pennington argued that a state appropriation for the Colonization Society would be 1) unconstitutional, because there was a provision of the state constitution forbidding grants to "individual associations," 2) unnecessary, since African Americans had the means to take themselves elsewhere if they wished to go, and 3) unwise, because the Colonization Society was a "fraud" that "keeps alive an army of agents who live by plundering us of our good name." Co-signed by the Convention secretaries, it kept the issue before the public and provided a convenient summary for those who had not taken the time to read the much longer Convention statement.

Whether Governor Hunt paid much attention to the Convention address in any form is impossible to tell, but as each new evidence of blindness to the actual racial situation in the United States drew another eloquent response from the African American leadership, it was at least more difficult for the white leadership to continue to reveal its ignorance so openly. Ultimately, of course, the response to the governor and others like him would be made by the black citizens themselves as they went about their business and proved their ability to play their part in the long-term project of creating a truly color-blind society. One of Frederick Douglass's pseudonymous contributors, "Observer," believed that what mattered was simply money. "To exert an equal influence, and secure equal respect with the people of this country, can only be done by our becoming their competitors in energy and enterprise. . . . The time has come when we must not only demand the rights of men, but act the part of men . . . We are Americans, and here let us work out that glorious destiny, even now to be seen in the distance, which awaits us . . . I feel proud of our destiny which the black man may accelerate, but which neither Governor nor Legislature can avert."[50]

The continuing battle over the place of African Americans in the national life made enormous demands on James Pennington's time and energy. To preside over a state convention, take part in local meetings, issue statements, write letters, keep in touch with other leaders, and plan strategy could easily have become a full-time job, but Pennington had decided many years earlier that his vocation was to ministry, and that remained the center of his life. Frederick Douglass, William Lloyd Garrison, and others centered their lives on the struggle for the abolition of slavery as writers, editors, and speakers. Pennington did all those things also but could never give it his full attention. There was always a congregation that came first. The role of pastor tends to recede into the background in the telling of Pennington's story because the role as abolition leader was far more public. The records of meetings, the speeches, the letters remain as evidence of that public role, while the records of parish ministry were seldom visible outside the community in the first place and have far less often been preserved. But it is possible to see something of that ministry, and it is important to fill in that part of the story as fully as possible.

The Shiloh Presbyterian Church was a large congregation. Pennington reported something over four hundred members, but membership involved more than simply attending services. To become a member involved meeting with the church's "Session" and making an acceptable statement of faith. Typical quarterly reports speaks of one or more "hopeful conversions," as well as one or two added by profession of faith and by a letter of transfer. Pennington reported attendance at church services to be over seven hundred, and that would not have included the several hundred children in the Sabbath School[†] or the individuals who were unable to come every Sunday because of their work or their health or their lack of a deep commitment. It would be reasonable to estimate the Shiloh community as well over a thousand individuals, perhaps

---

† The Sabbath School should be understood as something more than a modern Sunday School. Sabbath Schools were often called on to provide basic education for those unable to attend a public school and therefore would need teachers and a library. In his first quarterly report, Pennington speaks of the need for more teachers and says that the school's library is good, although he does not know the number of volumes.

twice that number, who might turn to the church in an emergency and consider James Pennington to be their pastor.

Because the Shiloh Church was the poorest in the Presbytery, it received some financial assistance from the Presbytery from time to time and from the American Home Missionary Society on a regular basis. In return for that support, Pennington reported quarterly to the AMHS. The surviving reports are never as full as the first report Pennington made to the Congregational Consocation in Hartford, but they do help to fill in some of the details of his ministry. In one report, for example, he speaks of "preaching on an average twice on the Sabbath," giving one lecture a week, and making "pastoral visits daily among the sick and destitute colored people in various parts of this city." Since Shiloh was the only Presbyterian Church in the metropolitan area that welcomed and included black people, members came from Hoboken in New Jersey and Williamsburg and New Town on Long Island, and Pennington's pastoral visits took him to those areas as well in a day when there were no subways or rapid transit lines. The temperance cause remained an important part of his ministry as it had been from the early days in Newtown. "All our members," Pennington reported, "take the pledge on uniting with the church."

Some aspects of pastoral care in Presbyterian churches are shared with the elected representatives of the congregation called elders, who serve with the pastor as the Session. In the nineteenth century and well into the twentieth century, the Session dealt with the individual lives of church members in matters that would seldom be considered appropriate today. The Session records for Pennington's years at Shiloh Church have disappeared, but the immediately following years' records are available and reveal the sort of matters that would have concerned James Pennington and his Session also.

In the last two meetings of 1857, for example, the Session admitted one new member when she made a profession of faith and another when she "renewed her covenant" after an absence of several years. Sometimes the Session simply spent time in a "profitable conversation" about the religious condition of the church. In the first meeting of 1858, the Session received more new members and resolved not to let the church be used for "concerts of secular music, or for any exhibition of a theatrical or dramatical character." All that is not much different from what would be on the agenda of a modern Session.

Early in 1858, however, the Session found itself also dealing with charges of a "dramatical character" concerning events in real life and not in the theater: Julia Roberson, a member of the congregation, was charged with having violated the Seventh Commandment ("Thou shalt not commit adultery"). The Elders, therefore, appointed one of their number to visit the accused and report back three days later. Pastor Garnet agreed to call on her as well. Three days later the Pastor and appointed Elder came back to tell the Session that it was "their painful duty" to report that the charge was true. Accordingly, the Session called Julia Roberson to come and answer the charge in person.

Three more days went by and the Session met again and Julia Roberson was there to tell them exactly what had happened, sparing no details. She and Phoebe Butler had gone to a room with Gilbert Eston and "had criminal licentious intercourse with each other." Indeed, she told the Session that Elston had succeeded in "accomplishing her ruin": she was pregnant. The Session therefore voted unanimously to expel Julia Roberson from membership and investigate the subject further by summoning Phoebe Butler. Perhaps Elston was not a member, since he was never cited for his role in the event. Phoebe Butler, however, "denied the whole statement in every particular" and was ready "to take a solemn oath" to that effect, though she was unwilling to meet with the Session to discuss it. The Session therefore met again four days later and voted to suspend Phoebe Butler's membership for violating the Seventh Commandment. But that did not end the matter. A week later, the Session met to deal with charges brought against Phoebe's father, Jacob Butler, who was also an Elder, for accusing the Session of acting unjustly in connection with his daughter. Not content with having one rather difficult matter to deal with, the Session also summoned another Elder, J. H. Tate, to explain why he had been absent so long from their meetings.

Those matters were settled over the next few weeks as Elder Butler "settled his differences" with the Session and Elder Tate explained that he had been absent due to sickness and "wounded feelings" and was also forgiven. In March and again in May, new members were admitted, but in September Session meetings became more interesting again as Elder Butler's son, Jacob Butler Jr., was judged "guilty of being intoxicated" and L. B. Matthews, the superintendent of the Sabbath School, was ordered to resign because he was declared "guilty of ante nuptial fornication." The Session also asked the Choir to take note that no one could serve with them who was "guilty of profane language." Elder Tate was asked to resign since he had not apparently gotten over his wounded feeling and was still missing meetings. Meanwhile Mrs. Cordelia Hughes presented a letter charging Mrs. Ferguson with slander and profanity.

And so it went. Before the year was over, the church school superintendent came to express "sincere regret and heartfelt sorrow" and be admonished and warned "to watch and pray." The Session would not reinstate him in his post but agreed to consider the matter settled and promised to "make this action known to the church." The Mesdames Ferguson and Hughes made "mutual concessions" and a "desire for reconciliation," so that matter was settled. But Edward Hays was charged with "unChristian conduct," Mrs. Sarah Gibbs had apparently used the church for a concert of secular music in spite of the Session prohibition, and former Elder Tate was now accused of intemperance.

Hays, Gibbs, and Tate were cited to appear and answer charges. The picture presented by the carefully preserved minutes of the Shiloh Church Session is one of a community striving earnestly to keep the Ten Commandments in the midst of a thriving city where wealth was on ostentatious display but not available to them. For the members of Shiloh Church, the world, the flesh, and the bottle were available to provide inexpensive release from the austerity and hardships of daily life, and they were not always able to live up to the ideals they had accepted. Not all the seven deadly sins are clearly represented in the petty situations the Session found itself dealing with, but pride, lust, envy, and sloth were certainly evident. The Session was remorseless in asking members to face up to their failures but generous in offering forgiveness when members confessed their sins and expressed repentance.

While we can only assume that the personal, pastoral issues of 1857 were not significantly different from those a few years earlier when James Pennington was pastor, we do know very exactly what the financial issues were that confronted the pastor of the Shiloh Church in those years, because Pennington needed to report those to the Presbytery. His quarterly reports show us a congregation of very limited means attempting nonetheless to reach out to the needs of others. Each of the reports speaks of offerings collected for purposes beyond the parish budget. Although the congregation was struggling to pay its bills and reduce its debts, it never allowed its vision to be narrowly centered on its own needs. The American Missionary Association remained important to Pennington. When missionaries returned from the Mendi mission in Africa, a special service was held to hear from them and an offering of $10.88 was received for their work. In remitting the amount to Lewis Tappan, Pennington apologized that it was not more but said that there had been "frequent and several large collections for different objects within a short time."[51] These included a special offering of $120 for the church's debt and an "assessment on account of the Prince Street sewer" of $130, but more typically the special offerings were $70 for the Sabbath School, $46 for "the colored orphan asylum on Fifth Avenue in this city," and a pledge of $25 "for the aid of the Hoboken Church" that had been partly raised in the quarter reported and would be completed in the next quarter.[52] Twenty-five dollars was a more significant amount then than now, but to raise it in six months would only have required three or four cents a week from each member of the congregation. A skilled carpenter at that time might have earned a dollar a day or slightly more, but most members of the Shiloh congregation were not skilled laborers. The wage for common laborers was approximately seventy-five cents.[53] The fact that raising a few dollars for a sister congregation was a difficult task provides some measure of the poverty of the congregation's members. At the end of the year, Pennington wrote to the *New York Evangelist* to speak of his expectation that the church would soon be self-supporting and to list, in addition to those he had reported to Tappan, contributions of $46.00 to the Colored Orphan Asylum, $33.20 to aid the Lemmon slaves, $12.00 to aid the Hoboken Church, and $9.35 to aid "a young man from the South in purchasing the freedom of his brother-in-law." It would "greatly improve our position among the churches," Pennington wrote, when the debt was paid off, "but we should do much more."[54]

Challenging though these circumstances might have been, Pennington spoke of the Sabbath School as "flourishing" and its "prospects . . . [as] quite flattering," while the congregation was described as "gradually increasing in numbers."[55] By the end of the year, he was pleased enough with the progress being made to write to the *New York Evangelist* of his expectation that the congregation would soon be "self-sustaining" and able "to take a respectable stand among her wealthy neighbors as a producer, or helper in the various schemes of Christian benevolence." "We should do much more," he wrote, but they were moving in the right direction. With the support of the Session and Trustees, the congregation was being asked to contribute to "some general object" at least once a quarter, and nearly two hundred and fifty dollars had been received as a result. In addition to those already mentioned, there had been an offering to assist a group of fugitive slaves and another to help a recent fugitive purchase his brother's freedom. The "ladies of the congregation" were doing their bit by holding a fair in the church basement to help in the "extinction" of the debt.[56] Meanwhile, however, Pennington admitted that the assistance of the AHMS was still needed and "payment quarterly will oblige me."[57]

Centered though he was on this ministry and its demands, Pennington did continue to find time for other engagements. One of the most interesting of these was the installation of Amos Freeman as pastor of the Siloam Church in Brooklyn toward the end of July. Among the participants were Samuel Cox, Pennington's one-time mentor, and Pennington himself. Ethiop reported on the event for *Frederick Douglass' Paper*, but some background must be filled in at this point.

When Samuel H. Cox and James W. C. Pennington first met, in the home of Adrian Van Sinderen, Cox had the reputation of an ardent and early abolitionist. In the riots of 1834 in New York City, Cox's home had been burned by the mob and he himself barely escaped being beaten. But in May of 1846, he was chosen as moderator of the General Assembly of the Presbyterian Church, and that summer he sailed to England to represent that body at a meeting of the Evangelical Alliance in London. In the course of that meeting, a resolution was introduced providing that no person holding slaves or defending slavery should be admitted to its membership. At once, Samuel Cox was on his feet and to everyone's surprise denounced the resolution. The mover inquired if this could possibly be the same man once known for his abolitionist views, and Cox responded that he was the same man but "by the blessing of God, had been delivered from the blindness of fanaticism, and . . . was proud to stand forth to denounce a resolution which would shut out from their fellowship such a noble body of Christians as the people of the Southern states of America." The resolution was voted down, but Samuel Cox became a target of scorn thereafter among his former associates.

That same month, Cox attended a meeting of the World's Temperance Convention in Covent Garden, London, and crossed swords with Frederick Douglass in his new role as defender of slave owners. Douglass was not a delegate to that gathering but, being in the audience, was called on to speak and used the occasion to point out that three million Americans, because of slavery and prejudice, were "placed beyond the pale of American temperance societies." Moreover, free black citizens in Philadelphia, when they attempted a parade to bear witness to their temperance convictions and draw others into their ranks, were "brutally assailed by a ruthless mob . . . their ranks broken up, their persons beaten, and pelted with stones and brickbats . . . one of their churches burned to the ground and their temperance hall utterly demolished." There were cries of "Shame, shame, shame" from the audience and of "Sit down" from American delegates on the platform. Cox, "greatly exasperated"[58] by the alternate view of American reality that Douglass presented, wrote to the *New York Evangelist*:

> What a perversion, an abuse, an iniquity against the law of reciprocal righteousness, to call thousands together to get them, some certain ones, to seem conspicuous and devoted for one sole and grand object, and then, all at once, open an avalanche on them for some imputed evil or monstrosity, for which, whatever the wound or injury inflicted, they were both too fatigued and too hurried with surprise . . . to be properly prepared. I say it is a trick of meanness! It is abominable!

Douglass, in due course, responded with equal heat:

> Sir, you claim to be a Christian, a philanthropist, and an Abolitionist. Were you truly entitled to any one of these names, you would have been delighted at seeing one of Africa's despised children cordially received and warmly welcomed to a world's temperance platform, and in every way, treated as a man and a brother. But the truth probably is that you felt both yourself and your country severely rebuked by my presence there; and besides

this it was undoubtedly painful to you to be placed on the same platform with a negro, a fugitive slave . . . If it be true, I sincerely pity your littleness of soul.[59]

Back home in Brooklyn, Cox wrote more calmly to the *National Anti Slavery Standard* to lay out his revised position with greater care: "I think no better of the [slavery] system than I used to do, praying God of his mercy, and in his own way, to remove it from our country, and the world; yes, I pray for its utter annihilation. . . . Some ultras I view as extravagant, malignant, and infidel; as well as traitors to the country and its best interests. . . . Measures of which the tendency is to make a bad worse; or to exasperate the feelings rather than convince the mind; or to alienate the South, and dissolve the Union . . . I cannot and will not favour or abet in any way. I like no passionate or furious demonstration." Of slavery, he wrote, "It is a huge ulcer on the national body politic. It will never cure itself. It will kill us, or we must kill it. It is the grand incubus of the nation." But Cox had no solution to offer beyond a prayer: "God grant in mercy, not judgment, his own guidance in the means, and his own deliverance in the end."[60] That would hardly satisfy the Lewis Tappans who were sure they had God's guidance, or the William Lloyd Garrisons who were unwilling to wait for it.

Abolitionist papers took delight on reprinting statements Cox had made in earlier years. The *National Anti-Slavery Standard* took to enlivening its columns with retrospectives on "Dr. Cox Twenty-Five Years Ago" when he had written "a man who would trade in man would buy and sell Almighty God himself for thirty pieces of silver, and virtually does so whenever he vends or purchases 'his image' of humanity"[61] and "Dr. Cox Sixteen Years Ago" when he had extolled William Lloyd Garrison as "the friend of man and the foe of oppression."[62] If he had defended the pious Southern slave-owner in London in 1846, ten years earlier he had written: "I hesitate not a moment to say that other things being equal a slaver of any description ought to be excluded from the communion of the church."[63]

Not satisfied to make him look foolish by quoting him, the *National Anti-Slavery Standard* lampooned him directly, saying "The spirit of absurdity and vanity never before so took possession of any man. Such perfect abandonment to utter foolishness, such magnificent self-inflation, such reckless disregard of common sense, such windy abuse of mother-tongue, and such complete reliance upon overwhelming nonsense, approaches almost to the sublime." An editorial in the *Cleveland True Democrat* reprinted in *Frederick Douglass' Paper* went further in saying: "Of all the coxcomical, pedantic, windy, weather-cocking divines to be found in either of the three worlds, the Rev. Samuel H. Cox, D.D., of

'Rusurban, Brooklyn,' must be in our opinion, decidedly and most unmistakably the paragon."[64]

What Samuel Cox had come to believe was undoubtedly what most American Christians have always believed: that the common customs and practices of the country cannot be contrary to their faith since they live in a "Christian country," and its customs and practices must, therefore, be Christian. The idea that Christian faith might require significant changes in one's behavior was, and is, uncomfortable and divisive. If Southern Christians went faithfully to church, then slaveholding could not be a sin. When resolutions condemning slavery came to the General Assembly of the Presbyterian Church, Cox gaveled them down as out of order.[65] When a resolution was finally passed that called for the Southern presbyteries to report on such matters as the number of slaveholders in their membership, how many slaves they owned, what respect is shown for the marriage bond, whether baptism is administered to the children of slaves professing Christianity, and similar matters, Cox produced a statement that deplored every effort to make slaveholding an issue. "The gospel," he proclaimed in a statement that would certainly have surprised St. Paul and many others, "is less anti-error than pro-truth; that the way to get darkness out is to put light in, and not to waste the strength of the Church in a vain war on darkness."[66] In 1853, the anti-slavery forces finally succeeded in bringing the issue to a vote and carried their point by a two-to-one margin—yet somehow the church did not split until the Civil War divided the country itself.[67]

Nevertheless, Cox was a skilled orator, and his church in Brooklyn remained popular with those who sought to compromise the great national issue. On Thanksgiving Day, Ethiop went to hear him and reported that Cox had given thanks for the Union as "the best under heaven!!! Best for the black man; best for the red man; best for the white man; best for the good man; the bad man," and had added "that the amount of good produced to the blacks, in their transition from Africa to this country, making them thereby what they now are, was incalculable; and that they ought to be thankful for it." "After this," wrote Ethiop, "I took my hat and left."[68]

But Ethiop was there in July the next year for the installation of the new pastor of Siloam Church. Whether Cox and Pennington had met at all in the twenty-some years since Pennington had become a Christian with Cox's guidance is unknown. Cox had lectured twice in Hartford when Pennington was there, but there is no evidence that his former student was present.[69] Now they were together on the same platform, but their lives and convictions had drifted far apart. Ethiop reported the event with gusto. Nothing pertaining to church matters, he reported, could take place in Brooklyn without Cox being assigned a part "which he always performs so ably," and on this occasion he had been called on to give the charge to the pastor. Given that there were "some past offences to heal among the colored people, it was natural to expect the Dr. would do well—his very best; and we were not disappointed," wrote Ethiop.

Ethiop was not, of course, a wholly disinterested observer, but he had given Cox full credit and his assessment of James Pennington's preaching at the peak of his career is worth quoting in full.

> The next speaker was to be Dr. Pennington, who, as you know, was a black man . . . Dr. Pennington arose, and after a few well-timed remarks, laid down his positions and thence proceeded to pronounce one of the most splendid discourses that has ever been my fortune to listen to. Dr. Cox, who is a very thin-skinned man, turned alternately red, purple and white, after the similitude of a camelion; and well he might. For the first time he had been distanced in the popular race—he had not fully counted upon his man. Again; our present and destined position in this country, as defined by Dr. Pennington, so unlike anything he had ever heard before; while so clear, yet to him so startling and so new, yet so convincing that the old Dr. was fairly routed horse and foot . . . Little I know did Dr. Cox think, that the quiet, meek looking boy, walking often some three miles on the Sabbath, and taking one of the humblest seats in one of his pompous synagogues to listen to his preaching, would have become at this day the able and learned Dr. Pennington, capable of facing him and flooring him too. But such is the course of things. While the Dr. P. theme rose in grandeur and magnificence as he proceeded, his voice deepened and mellowed into indescribable sublimity, till at last theme and speaker alone retained place in our thoughts; and like the setting summer's sun, they ended, shedding a golden hue over all. Dr. Cox made a second attempt, but it was no go. . . . And now let me ask, do we appreciate such men as Dr. Pennington? Are we like the whites in this respect?[70]

There were obviously many who did "appreciate such men as Dr. Pennington," and his schedule reflected it. In mid-August, shortly after the Brooklyn installation, he made a trip to Detroit, journeyed from there to Hartford, returned to New York for the first Sunday in September, and was in Cleveland three days later for a convention of "Colored Citizens of the State" of Ohio. Railroad travel was a good deal easier in the nineteenth century than it is in the twenty-first, but Pennington's schedule was such that he arrived in Cleveland on the morning of the Convention and had to leave that same afternoon.

James Pennington apparently saw himself to be more an educator than an exhorter. Frederick Douglass and William Lloyd Garrison might go forth to rally the troops, but Pennington went to Cleveland as the keynote speaker at the State Convention to teach history and provide an "instructive address . . . on the part which colored people have taken in the struggles of this nation for independence and its various wars since." He produced what the convention minutes called "sundry antique papers, collected by him with great pains from the archives of the State of New York, showing that some thousands of colored people in that State, thirty years before the Declaration of Independence was promulgated, were charged by the King of Great Britain with conspiring against his authority," with the result that "some were banished, and others were hanged." Pennington went on to show his audience a petition by the citizens of Connecticut after the Revolution asking the state government to "comply with the promise . . . made to them of freedom" in return for their assistance in the battle. Then he read from a paper in which George Washington certified the services of black soldiers at the end of the war. In short, he "claimed for his race the honor of being the first of Americans whose bosoms were fired by the Spirit of American Independence."[71] A knowledge of what is now called "black history" was a frequent theme for James Pennington. He had done the research, and he used his opportunities to teach others what he had learned and what they needed to know about themselves and the significance of their past.

The Cleveland Convention opened another channel for Pennington by creating a newspaper to serve that city and the other African American communities in the Midwest, and persuading him to serve as a Corresponding Editor. At the time there were only two other black newspapers in the entire country. Samuel Ringgold Ward in Canada, Amos Beman in New Haven, and Martin Delaney were among the familiar names of those persuaded to serve as correspondents and contributors. *The Aliened American* published its first issue in April 1853 and survived as a weekly newspaper for two years. The first issue promised "to aid the educational development of Colored Americans; to assist in the enforcing of an appreciation of the benefit of trades [industrial education] and to aim at our Social Elevation. We have a work to accomplish, which, however Law may facilitate, it can never, itself, wholly finish."[72]

Toward the end of the year there was a major event to celebrate in the election of a deeply committed abolitionist, Gerrit Smith, to Congress. Pennington had been traveling that summer and sent a brief note to Smith in August, hoping to arrange to visit him on his way from Detroit to Hartford. When that failed to work because "I was unsure at what station to get out," he wrote another longer letter instead, inviting Smith to come to the Shiloh Church to give a lecture "On the duties of the people of color as related to the Agriculture of this country." "I wish," he told Smith, "to direct the attention of the colored people to their great secular mission in this country—namely removal from the large cities." Smith's proposed agricultural community had elicited only a small response, but Pennington believed the movement toward the land would slowly build as reports of success filtered back to the cities. Pennington promised an audience of 1000 to 1200 on any date Smith might name between the middle of October and the middle of November. It would serve also, he thought, as an indirect way to reopen the battle against the colonization of system.

That proposal, however, was swept aside when Smith was elected against all odds to serve in Congress. He had been nominated for president by a faction of the Liberty Party in 1848 and 1852, but in 1852 he was also nominated against his wishes for Congress and defeated both the two major party candidates by over two thousand votes, becoming the only abolitionist ever to hold that position. "I had reached old age," he told the voters in a letter acknowledging his election. (He was 55 years old.) "I had never held office. Nothing was more foreign to my expectations, and nothing was more foreign to my wishes, than the holding of office." Since they had elected him, however, he felt he must serve, and so he outlined for his supporters what he called "my peculiar political creed": that there is no possible legal basis for slavery, that men and women, black and white should have equal right to vote, that trade restrictions were unnatural and sinful, that the United States should, by her own Heaven-trusting and beautiful example, hasten the day when the nations of the earth shall 'beat their swords into ploughshares and their spears into pruning hooks,'" that "the building of railroads and canals and the care of schools and churches fall entirely outside" the sphere of government and should be voluntary, and that every officer of the government from president to postmaster "should be elected directly by the people."[73]

Whatever other citizens may have felt about such a platform, abolitionists were thrilled. "We can find no language to express our appreciation of the election of this God-like man, to Congress," said one abolitionist paper. "Oh, that Wm. Lloyd Garrison, Lewis Tappan, Wendell Phillips and Samuel Lewis might be placed side by side with him in Congress."[74] James Pennington used similar language in a sermon he wrote for the next Sunday, and which he sent to Smith in advance, in which he would tell his congregation that "I regard this as the hand of God! Yes, beyond peradventure. It is the hand of God. He has been stirring our political elements and His Mighty Hand which holds the hearts of all men has brought this thing right side up with care. In this train of matter God has not wrought a mightier thing for us in 50 years." So overjoyed was Pennington by this unexpected event that he went on to express "yet another wish, and that is to have a colored man in the legislature of New York." That, he thought, could be accomplished if he could persuade enough African Americans to move to the rural areas where they might form a majority of the electorate. The fact that they were already a majority in some areas of the South, though without the vote, may have made the idea seem a reasonable wish for the foreseeable future. Therefore Pennington told Smith, "I shall not venture to pray for my colored Assemblyman until I have a first prayed ten thousands out of the cities. At present my joy is full and God be glorified."[75]

As Pennington was writing that letter on November 7, dramatic events were unfolding elsewhere in the city that would involve him in a historic legal case. Jonathan Lemmon, a Virginian, had decided to move to Texas and came to New York with his wife and eight slaves belonging to her to take a ship for Texas. The slaves were placed in a boarding house where the African American community became aware of their presence and brought a writ of *habeas corpus* for their release. This was not a matter of fugitive slaves that would have come under the new law dealing with such cases, but rather an issue of the right of any individual to hold slaves in New York State. Louis Napoleon, an illiterate New York African American, brought the legal action on behalf of the New York Vigilance Committee and with the assistance of Chester Alan Arthur, the future president, and John Jay, grandson of the great chief justice of the Supreme Court. Judge Elijah Paine took a week to consider the case and then, in a long and carefully researched opinion, ordered that the slaves be released. "All men by nature are free," Paine ruled, and the State of New York had repealed in 1841 whatever protection might have been granted to slave owners and slaves in transit. Therefore slaves brought into the state must be set free.

James Pennington wrote to a Scottish newspaper about the trial and verdict, calling it "one of the most important slave cases ever brought before our courts" and describing the reaction to the judge's ruling. "Within there was a shout; without there were three cheers. The officers said hush, but it was of no use; ten thousand hearts, relieved after eight days intense uncertainty as to the fate of eight souls, could no more be restrained (being under black skins) than the mighty waters of the Clyde or the Firth when they break over their bounds. And oh, Mr. Editor, if you could have heard some of the expressions and prayers and preachings that I heard in the Park just as these eight liberated slaves came out to go into the free world . . . Let me tell you only three out of many. One old coloured lady said—'Well, if that judge don't get into heaven, no man will ever enter into that holy place.' Another said—'God will surely bless the soul of that judge.' Another said—'Well, that judge shall never pay another cent for cleaning his office as long as I live.'" There was a public reception for the eight at the Shiloh Church and a collection made of $45 for the benefit of the freed slaves.[76]

Southern politicians were, of course, outraged. The governor of Georgia saw it as a cause for war, and the governor of Virginia thought it tended to dissolve the Union. The Virginia Legislature authorized its attorney general to appeal the case, and this was done; but not until April of 1860 was a final decision rendered by the New York State Court of Appeals. Long before that time, the Lemmon slaves had arrived in Canada, and James Pennington had been deeply involved in getting them there. By the time the writ of *habeas corpus* was granted, plans had been laid and a basic fund collected. Almira Way Pennington, although her husband had told Gerrit Smith in his letter the previous week that she was "only in tolerable health," was assigned the task of accompanying the group as far as Hartford, where they were placed "in the legal care of Hooker and Hawley and in the social care of Messers Brown, Gardner and Crass, colored men." Among those Pennington turned to for help in defraying the cost of the legal work and travel was Horace Greeley, the controversial editor of the *New York Tribune*. Again it was Almira Pennington who played a part by carrying the letter to Greeley, telling him that only $15 had been available to send with the freed slaves and that the "poor laboring men" whose families had received them ought not to be "unduly burdened." One hundred dollars, Pennington told Greeley, "must be remitted" as soon as possible. He added a P.S. saying that he felt "some solicitude" in the matter, since he had personally pledged Hooker that he would be reimbursed.[77]

Adding to the rising tension between North and South had been the publication of Harriet Beecher Stowe's depiction of slavery in *Uncle Tom's Cabin*, a "sentimental" portrayal in the best sense of the word: an appeal to the emotions in the easily digestible form of a story. The writing appeared first in serial form in June of 1851, and the whole book was published in March of 1852. In the first year of publication, 300,000 copies of *Uncle Tom's Cabin* were sold and the Philadelphia diarist Sidney George Fisher called it "the great book of the year" and reported that "it is read by all classes, in cottages and palaces . . . & has been translated into every language of Europe, including Russian."[78] There were also critics, of course, especially in the South, who questioned its accuracy. In response, Stowe assembled supporting materials and published *A Key to Uncle Tom's Cabin* in 1853. In her search for corroboration, Stowe wrote to James W. C. Pennington and received in response a long letter[†] in which Pennington spoke more directly about his feelings than he had ever done before. "O, Mrs. Stowe," he wrote, "slavery is an awful system. It takes man as God made him; it demolishes him, and then mis-creates him, or perhaps I should say mal-creates him." "I see that you have been a close observer of negro nature," he went on, noting her analysis that she

† Pennington's letter is dated November 30, 1852.

had never seen a slave "how ever careless and merry-hearted, who had not this sore place, and that did not shrink or get angry if a finger was laid on it." He spoke of his own "feeling of wretchedness . . . some feverish sore" growing out of the constant assertion of black inferiority. When he went to Jamaica and saw black men serving in the legislature and on juries, there was "a sensible relief" until someone said, "This is nothing but a nigger island" and "my old trouble came back again." He told her how he had gone to England and traveled in Europe seeking "to banish that troublesome old ghost entirely out of my mind." He was determined that "I'll be a man, and I'll kill off this enemy which has haunted me these twenty years and more." As he traveled in Europe and was treated simply as a human being without regard for color, he, in turn, had "put myself into the harness, and wrought manfully in the first pulpits, and the platforms in peace congresses, conventions, anniversaries, commencements, & c; and in these exercises that rusty old iron came out of my soul and went 'clean away.'" Now, he wrote, "I have now no more trouble on the score of equal manhood with whites."[79] Yet as the record of James Pennington's writing and speechmaking and constant travel is assembled, it is legitimate to ask whether the "old ghost" was in fact gone or whether a compulsion to prove his worth to himself and others was not the driving force.

CHAPTER EIGHTEEN

New York, 1853-1854

The most momentous three years of James W. C. Pennington's life began like those of a reclusive scholar, not a leader of societal change. From his home in Manhattan, he sent off a letter to a number of newspapers as well as "several American, English, Scotch, German, and French travelers and scholars" asking for opinions as to the accuracy of statements he proposed to make in a "revised and enlarged edition of the work of the celebrated GREGOIRE, (formerly Bishop of Blois, Member of the Conservative Senate of the National Institute, of the Royal Society of Gorttinguen [sic], etc., etc.,) entitled 'An Inquiry Concerning the Intellectual and Moral Faculties &c, of the Colored Race.'"† Gregoire had asserted that the Greeks had included under the name of Ethiopian "all men of a black color," and he asserted that in writing, manners, customs, and worship the Egyptians used the same forms as "the Negro" although "their color was somewhat whitened by the influence of climate."[1] Clearly he was still working on the ideas he had first put forward in *A Text Book of the Origin and History, &c. &c. of the Colored People* twelve years earlier and finding corroboration in the work of a contemporary French scholar. If, however, Pennington ever completed this project, there is no record of it. It seems likely that events overtook him and he no longer had time to devote himself to scholarly research.

† Henri Gregoire (1750–1831), a friend of Thomas Jefferson (Dershowitz, p. 134), was a remarkable leader through the French Revolution and in the years following. He proposed bringing the King to trial and urged his condemnation, though not his execution, and continued to dress as a bishop and say mass even during the Reign of Terror. He believed that Roman Catholicism was not irreconcilable with political liberty. He also published numerous pamphlets and books on the subject of racial equality, and was an influential member of the Society of the Friends of the Blacks. On Gregoire's motion in May 1791, the Constituent Assembly passed its first law admitting some wealthy free men of colour in the French colonies to the same rights as whites [Wikipedia]. Gregoire's essay, "An enquiry concerning the intellectual and moral faculties, and literature of Negroes," was translated and published in Brooklyn in 1810.

The new year brought with it another distinction and duty when New York's Third Presbytery elected James Pennington to serve as moderator for the six-month term of office. The moderator is simply the presiding officer at a meeting of the presbytery and has no role outside the meeting; but in New York at that time, to put an African American in that position was still noteworthy even though the venerated Theodore Wright had also served in that position some years earlier.[2] Lewis Tappan, who must have forgotten that Wright had held the same post, was thrilled.[†] "Our colored countryman," he wrote, "has recently been elected Moderator of the Third Presbytery in this City, a body composed of a large number of the most influential Presbyterian ministers among us. This is a sign of the times."[3] If it was a sign, it was a sign of small progress on a long road.

The congregation continued to grow, but it had not yet reached a point at which it could dispense with the assistance of the American Home Missionary Society. Pennington reported that the congregation could pay the pastor's salary of $500 a year[††] and its obligations to the presbytery[4]; it could raise money as well for missions and church extension and occasionally "for the aid of persons wishing to redeem their friends from slavery"; but it was "severely tried in the pecuniary point of view" because some of its "most industrious members" had been absent for much of the time and unable to contribute. Pennington anticipated their return and felt certain that the congregation would soon be "self-sustaining." "A pleasant success," he told the Society, "has attended the preaching." In April, fifteen new members were added, ten by profession of faith, in June seven more, and in August another seven new members were reported. In November, Pennington reported that two young men had begun studying for the ministry under his direction.[5] Milton Badger, the secretary of the AHMS, wrote back commending Pennington on his labors and promising the requested support.[6]

All the outward evidence spoke of a thriving congregation that took appropriate pride in its pastor's accomplishments. In February, the ladies of the congregation organized a special tea "gotten up in the good old Scotch style" and presented their pastor with a handsome pulpit gown and black suit that they had ordered from Edinburgh. Ethiop was on hand for the event and expressed the opinion that the gown was "an elegant affair, surpassed perhaps by none in the city." Mentioned also was the fact that "quite a number of white persons—both ladies and gentlemen—were present and mingled

---

[†] Tappan had noted Wright's election to the position in an obituary he wrote for the American Missionary less than six years earlier, in 1847. (Tappan, Lewis, "Obituary," *American Missionary*, May 1847.)

[††] William Beecher, brother of the famous Henry Ward Beecher and pastor of a rural congregation in the Midwest, was said to have "scraped along" on the same amount.

freely in the festivities." Samuel Cornish and Charles Ray, former editors of the *Colored American,* were called on to speak, as were Amos Freeman of the Siloam Presbyterian Church in Brooklyn and the pastor of a German Presbyterian Church. Between the speeches, the church choir sang, and when the speeches were finished, a series of resolutions was offered and unanimously adopted, expressing joy in the occasion and expressing trust that "we will go forward in well-doing, believing his [God's] purposes will be consummated in the universal salvation of our sons and daughters . . . And that they shall yet be dignified with all the honors and immunities of Church and State in the American Republic."[7]

That dignity was not easily gained in mid-century America, but James Pennington and his colleagues continued to press for it whenever they saw an opportunity. Having so recently returned from Britain, where there was no established pattern of segregation in public transport, Pennington was especially sensitive to the constant inconvenience and irritation of the situation in New York City. Horse-drawn omnibuses[†] carried passengers up and down the avenues, but African American passengers were not provided with equal access. Some cars had banners on the sides saying: "Colored People Allowed in this Car,"[8] but such cars were few and far between. Sometimes black passengers could board a standard car and be accepted; sometimes they were made to stand on the platform at the end of the car, exposed to the weather; sometimes they could ride for a while and then be forced off because a white passenger complained or because an aggressive trainman suddenly noticed who was on board.[9] Pennington's strongest weapon was always his pen. He had deployed his pen first on this subject in September of 1852 in a letter to the *New York Evangelist* reporting on a recent experience that had broken through his usual patience. "You are aware," he wrote, "that I am pastor of the Presbyterian Church on the corner of Prince and Marion streets in this city. My congregation extends from No. 1 Pearl street to 65th street,[††] and from Hoboken to Brooklyn and Williamsburg; so that in the discharge of my pastoral duties, I am constantly called to different points, and from one extremity to the other of this immense field. And yet, sir, according to usage in this community, I cannot avail myself of any of the lines of omnibuses, or any of the multiplying lines of railways in this city." As a result, he had found

---

† Horse-drawn "omnibuses" began operations in the 1820s on Broadway and spread from there to the other major avenues. By the 1850s there were some 700 such vehicles, carrying about twelve passengers each. In bad weather passengers were packed in "without regard to comfort or even decency," but many were still left waiting, sometimes for hours. Streetcars running on rails, but still horse-drawn, began to be used in the 1850s. (Weil, François, *A History of New York,* p. 99.)

†† This was the northern limit of the city's expansion at the time.

himself unable to complete his rounds on schedule on Thanksgiving Day. He
had been responsible for a morning service in Newtown, Long Island, and a
second service at three o'clock that afternoon in the Shiloh Church on Prince
Street. Having completed the service in Newtown, he came back across the
East River on a ferry and found a bus that would have gotten him to Prince
Street with five minutes to spare but "was rudely refused" and had to walk the
mile and a quarter. As a result, he arrived long past the announced time and
"in a very uncomfortable state, both physically and mentally, for my work."
A few weeks earlier, he had been asked to take part in a funeral service for
a teacher in the Orphan Asylum who had died recently. He was notified of
the service only at noon when he was making a parish call in the lower part
of Manhattan. Going home at once to change for the funeral, he could have
reached the Orphan Asylum in time by bus but, again, was unable to use
one. He stopped at a carriage stand near his house to attempt to negotiate for
a hack, but $1.50 was the lowest cost he could get and that was beyond his
means. He therefore walked the entire distance "in painful excitement . . .
under the burning sun of one of our hottest days, getting there after the hour
and not fit for service."

These were only two of many stories he could have told. Other angry travelers told frequently of their own experiences in the various black newspapers.
Frederick Douglass, for example, always made it a point to seat himself in one
of the cars for the general public and, as a result, "I was often dragged out of
my seat, beaten and severely bruised, by conductors and brakemen." He made
it a point also to resist, holding on to the seat when trainmen used force. On
one occasion he described himself as so "interwoven with the seats" that he
imagined it must have cost the company twenty-five or thirty dollars to repair
the damage, and finally the superintendent of the rail line ordered the trains to
run through the town where Douglass lived without stopping.[10] But Douglass
apparently never sued the company for his treatment.

"Why is it," Pennington asked, "that a man in the service of one of the
largest congregations in the city, has to submit to such a system of oppression?
It is not because I smoke segars[†] in the 'busses, as I see some white men do.
It is not because I carry a pet dog with me and say to every one, 'If you love
me you love my dog'—not excepting finely dressed ladies in the 'busses. But
it is simply and only because I am a black man, obediently carrying about in
my person the same skin, with the same color, which the Almighty has seen
fit to give me.

"But seriously, Mr. Editor, it is a hard case that a man should be compelled,
in the public service, to walk ounce after ounce out of him every day, and not

† "Segar" was a common nineteenth century spelling for "cigar."

be allowed to avail himself of the public conveyances designed to save time, health and life." His predecessor, Theodore Wright, Pennington added, "had his life shortened several years by this oppressive usage,[†] and I feel that I am walking in his footsteps" and digging for myself "an untimely grave . . . Will the members of a Christian public object to me, a minister of Christ, using the facilities of a public conveyance, while about my Master's business? . . . I ask for simple justice at the hands of my countrymen."[11]

That story, under the heading "A Hard Case," was reprinted in a number of newspapers including the *New York Daily Times*. Harriet Beecher Stowe referred to it in *Key to Uncle Tom's Cabin*, published the following year, when she wrote of the troubles of "that very laborious and useful minister, Dr. Pennington," who has "been often obliged seriously to endanger his health by walking to his pastoral labors, over his very extended parish, under a burning sun, because he could not be allowed the common privilege of the omnibus, which conveys every class of white man, from the most refined to the lowest and most disgusting." "Let us consider," Stowe went on, the number of Christians who theoretically "consider Dr. Pennington . . . a member with them of the body of Christ [and] these Christians are influential, rich and powerful; they can control public sentiment on any subject that they think of any serious importance . . . It is a serious question, whether such a marked indignity offered to Christ and his ministry, in the person of a colored brother, without any remonstrance on their part, will not lead to a general feeling that all that the Bible says about the union of Christians is a mere hollow sound, and means nothing."[12]

The *Maryland Colonization Journal* also reprinted the story but was not sympathetic: "He says he rides with the white people side by side in European cities, but is only denied the privilege in New York. Why then settle in New York? He is not a native of the city, no ties of birth or early association retain him there . . . The fact is, the home for such men as Dr. Pennington, is not New York city, nor any city on the broad American Continent. Broad fertile Africa is the true home of the black man. He says his predecessor in that ministerial charge was brought to an early grave by these very hardships which he has voluntarily offered to undergo. Then why accept the charge and why complain after accepting?"[13] But the Maryland editor, himself presumably also an immigrant or descendant of an immigrant from another continent, failed to understand that black people as well as white could love the land of

---

† Henry Garnet charged that Theodore Wright's wife had been "indirectly murdered" by her exclusion from a cabin while traveling to Rhode Island on a steamboat on Long Island Sound and thus exposed to the weather on a stormy night. She was, Garnet said, "a lady of delicate and feeble health [who] on her return home . . . took to her bed and died." ("Outrage Upon the Stonington Railroad." *North Star*, April 14, 1848.)

their birth and be determined to fulfill its promise. Peter Vogelsang, a leader in the New York African American community, summed up their views of Africa once by saying, "None of us would go, even if they promised to make us kings in Guinea; we are Americans and will remain such."[14]

It was, however, one thing to know oneself to be an American and another to be treated like an American. How to move toward the American dream of "certain unalienable rights" was the problem. Clearly the promise of "liberty and justice for all" was not fulfilled when streetcars and other facilities were segregated, but complaints and resistance, to this point, had been futile. In 1845, "a colored man named McFarland" had brought charges of assault and battery against a Sixth-avenue Railway conductor. He had boarded the "Colored People's Car" but then deliberately moved into the car directly behind that was reserved for white people, to test whether "persons of his shade could ride on the white folk's car or not." When the conductor threw him forcibly from the car, he brought legal action charging the conductor with assault and battery. The case was duly heard and promptly dismissed by the Justice, who ruled that the complainant had deliberately provoked the assault and that the conductor had used no more force and violence than was necessary to "eject the obnoxious passenger."[15] There was little point in seeking a legal remedy if the case was simply dismissed and the established pattern affirmed.

Ethiop thought the solution to the problem of segregated transport was to form a black aristocracy. "I cannot ride in the stage, says one. I am kicked from the steamboat table, says another. I am dragged from the cars, says a third. Now, bad as this kicking or dragging process is, who that has had a moment's reflection upon the subject, but knows that a black aristocracy, and nothing short of it, would soon remedy it. Steamboat and railroad stocks would, in the regular course of things, be as much in their hands as others. Their interests and the *white's* would be in common; and of necessity, would bring a change and similarity of feelings between the parties. In fine, the present party lines would be broken up, and others drawn—not black and white, but thrifty and thriftless; for this, despite of all that may be said to the contrary, is but the true bent of our social polity, which nothing can change."[16]

In fact, Ethiop may well have been right. Certainly the growing economic power of the black community in the twentieth century had as much to do with the civil rights revolution as the sit-ins and other protests. But it was not a solution of any immediate value to the impoverished community of pre-Civil War African Americans like James Pennington who often found no place to ride even at the back of the car.

Having appealed to the public on the basis of his experience, Pennington— still relying on the power of printed words—tried a somewhat different, lighter approach. Since the *Times* had reprinted his complaint, he would offer them a humorous story in the dialog form he used so often and so effectively. A Baptist preacher, he wrote, also African American, had been called to travel up to 60th Street "in the course of his pastoral duties" and, "being weary" and anxious to be home as soon afterwards as possible, he boarded a Broadway omnibus and found only one passenger, a white man.

The passenger said, "I suppose, now, you thought I would object to your coming in here."

Pastor W. responded: "Well, sir, I do not know that I had any right to suppose that you would be so unkind."

Passenger: "O, I would just as soon ride with a coloured man as with a white man. It makes no kind of difference to me."

So the car proceeded on down Broadway with passengers, all of them white, getting on and off, and the car filling and emptying until they were far down town and the pastor, as the other passengers had done, pulled the string to alert the driver and handed up his coin as they had done, but held it up, in his case, with black fingers. The driver was startled:

Driver: "Why, I did not know that you were there!"

Pastor: "Well, you know it now, don't you? Don't keep me waiting; here's your money—take it and let me go; I am in a hurry."

"Here there was a pause of a minute or two, which was broken by a hearty laugh from ladies, gentlemen, and all in the 'Bus. The scene ended by the 'Bus-man fingering the [coin] from the black fingers."

And that, Pennington concluded, proved his point: that public conveyances exist to accommodate citizens traveling to their homes and businesses, and color is irrelevant to that purpose.[17]

Less dramatic or critical to daily life, but illustrative of the multifaceted aspect of prejudice, was a concert in New York's Metropolitan Hall by Elizabeth Greenfield. Greenfield had been born a slave in Mississippi, but when her owner moved to Philadelphia and became a Quaker, she set Greenfield free in compliance with Quaker principles yet ignored the Quaker objection to music to pay for voice lessons for her former slave. Like Marian Anderson in the same city a century later, Greenfield began to sing at small gatherings and attracted such attention that a concert tour was arranged. In Buffalo, New York, she drew a capacity audience, and although one local paper suggested it had to do with the "novelty of an African-American opera singer and . . . the area's support for abolition as much as to her singing abilities," another paper described "a voice of great purity and flexibility, and of extraordinary compass; singing the notes in alto, with brilliancy and sweetness, and descending to the bass notes with a power and volume perfectly astonishing." Jenny Lind, "the Swedish Nightingale," was touring America at the time, and it was not surprising that Greenwood was quickly dubbed "the African Nightingale" and "the Black Swan." The New York concert, however, was arranged for a white audience, and Pennington thought he spoke for all black New Yorkers in writing Greenwood to say that "the undersigned [five African American pastors] profoundly regret that themselves and their numerous coloured friends are denied the privilege of attending your concert." Pennington, presumably with Lewis Tappan's cooperation, offered the Broadway Tabernacle as a site and asked whether Greenwood would be willing to repeat her concert there on the following day with no one excluded. If she were willing to "decline further benefit" for herself, he suggested that the proceeds, after expenses, be divided between the Home for Aged Colored Persons and the Colored Orphan Asylum.[18] Greenwood responded immediately, expressing regret that "the colored people of the city" had been barred from her concert and agreeing to sing the next day and let the proceeds be used "for any charity that will elevate the condition of my colored brethren."[19]

The *National Anti Slavery Standard* obtained a report on the first concert from a white friend who was able to attend. Greenfield, he reported, had appeared timid at first but "the first sound of her voice was agreeable, not disappointing—surprising! . . . She showed great power and compass—the audience were pleased, amazed, gratified, overcome!" Ethiop reported that he had been unable to attend that concert since "birds of the same plumage" as the Black Swan "were not permitted to flock thither."[20] The *New York Tribune* was unable to resist noting that swans, in fact, do not sing, but went on to say, "She has a fine voice, but does not know how to use it. Her merit is purity and fulness, but not loudness of tone. Her notes are badly formed in the throat, but her intonation is excellent." The *Tribune* thought, "It is a voice that ought to be cultivated in Europe, and ought to stay there."[21] But that was because the reporter could not imagine a day when a black artist would be fully accepted in American concert halls. New York authorities were so nervous about their city's ability to cope with the event that a large force of police was on hand to cope with any possible trouble.[22] Beyond some raucous laughter as Greenfield entered the hall, there was, however, no disturbance. If the proposed second concert was held, no New York paper, even the *Anti Slavery Standard*, reported the event; but two years later she was back in New York and did sing twice at the Broadway Tabernacle, each time to a mixed audience, "ebony and topaz in equal proportions," according to Philip Bell, writing as "Cosmopolite" for *Frederick Douglass' Paper*. Bell, who had helped Samuel Cornish found the *Colored American*, was impressed with the singer's range, "a flexibility of voice in the musical world, compassing, it is said, thirty-one clear notes."[23]

Whether James Pennington was on hand for one of the concerts that vindicated his earlier protest is not known. The crosscurrents of Manhattan life that brought a fledgling singer to his attention one day brought a much stranger case to his doorstep soon afterwards. Jane Trainer, a ten-year-old child, was brought to New York by a Mrs. Rose Cooper, alias Porter, a woman admitted by her counsel to be a prostitute. The girl's father, apparently a free man though his wife was a slave, followed the pair to New York to claim custody and obtained a writ of *habeas corpus*. But Cooper had connections with the shady side of New York's power structure, and Captain Isaiah Rynders, a colorful figure who could organize gangs on behalf of Tammany Hall, managed briefly to block the serving of the writ.[†] Cooper had apparently won the girl's confidence, and Rynders so intimidated the Manhattan judge who was asked to sort things out that he said it was beyond his competence and needed to go to the Supreme Court. Nonetheless, he suggested that the child be placed in neutral custody and, over the objections of Mrs. Cooper, she was placed in the custody of James Pennington, who tried to enlist Lewis Tappan's influence on behalf of the girl's father.

Judge Seward Barculo of the New York Supreme Court, sitting in Brooklyn, had no patience with all this. Told that the writ could not be served because the officer who held them would not give them up and his emissary feared for his life, he ordered that new papers be drawn "and if it be necessary, take every able-bodied man in Kings County to assist you in carrying it out." Told that the child preferred Rose Cooper to her own parents, Barculo exclaimed, "What, will you tell me that when my child goes into a neighbor's house, and is there detained by bribes of sweetmeats and toys, that I cannot claim her and take her home?" Not only did Charles Trainer take his daughter home, but by the following January he had managed to extricate his wife from slavery and bring her to New York. A celebration was then held at the Shiloh Church with James Pennington offering prayers and scripture, and Lewis Tappan providing both a history of the case and a lengthy denunciation of the local justice system. "Eminent counsel," Tappan said, had "twisted and distorted the laws for gold . . . judges feared to do their duty . . . men wealthy and influential escorted the bold woman from her home of shame to the courthouse . . . while bullies and rowdies constituted themselves her body guard." The little girl was then brought forward for all to see, and Pennington ended the evening by speaking for the family and asking for contributions for their benefit.[24] [††]

While all that was going on that spring, Pennington had been busy in the planning of a convention in Rochester and working also on the sermon

† Rynders's "sluggers" intimidated voters and were said to have been responsible for swinging New York State's electoral votes to gain the election of presidents Polk, Pierce, and Buchanan. Buchanan appointed him U.S. Marshal of the Southern District of New York, and Rynders Street in New York's vice district was named (appropriately!) in his honor.

†† In March a jury awarded Charles Trainer $750 damages from Rose Cooper, who by then had moved on to California. "The Trainor [sic] Case," *New York Times*, March 3, 1854.

that he would preach to New York's Third Presbytery to mark the end of his term of office as moderator. The Presbytery met on Sunday, July 3. People in those days stayed home to celebrate 4th of July weekends, and the Presbytery sermon provided Moderator James W. C. Pennington with an opportunity to define his relationship to the Presbyterian Church and his understanding of the church's role in society. That sermon is also perhaps the nearest we have to a Sunday sermon from Pennington. It lets us see how he went about the task of interpreting Scripture and applying it to the concerns of a congregation, although this was, admittedly, a special occasion and unique congregation. The sermon, published afterwards, shows us a craftsman constructing his address very carefully along classical lines and challenging his audience without asking them to move further than he recognized was possible.

Pennington's text comes from the story of Jesus' "cleansing of the Temple" in Jerusalem, an occasion on which he took violent action to drive the money changers out and his disciples remembered a verse in the Psalms that says, "The zeal of thine house hath eaten me up."† Pennington begins by retelling the story in his own words and then focusing on the word "zeal." What follows is on one level a rather dry exposition of the meaning of the word but, if the audience was listening carefully, they would have heard an analysis of the difference between James Pennington's approach to social change and that of the Garrisonian abolitionists. Zeal, Pennington told his audience, "is an impassioned ardor in the cause of God. It is opposed to apathy, sloth, and indifference. It is opposed to mere fanaticism . . . It is not the noise of a professor filling the ears of his auditors. It is not the fanaticism of one in haste to give notoriety to a bad cause." Zeal, as Pennington defined it, was not necessarily evident from outward appearance, because it is an element added to the natural temperament. One person may be impetuous by nature, but that is not necessarily Christian zeal. The power of Christian zeal lies in its practical usefulness and therefore, while it has "the bravery of the warrior, the courage of the martyr, the boldness of the patriot," it is also marked by discretion. Here Pennington, demonstrating the range of his theological reading, quotes the great 16th-century Anglican theologian Richard Hooker, who had defined discretion as involving "prudence and knowledge to govern one's self, [and] also management." The preacher then spends a significant part of the sermon illustrating his definition of zeal in the life of Christ and the apostles, carefully laying a foundation for his principal point. Coming down almost to the present time, his final illustration is the story of "that great Presbyterian divine, Dr. Chalmers," who had seen the need to reach out to the poorest parts of the city of Edinburgh and created a

† John 2:17, Psalm 69:9

model program drawing rich and poor together that Pennington himself had visited four years earlier.

This vivid and almost contemporary example of Christian zeal led Pennington to present three areas that should concern his fellow clergy. First, he spoke about the needs of New York City where new churches were being built for the expanding and affluent uptown areas while old churches were being abandoned and demolished in the downtown areas where the new immigrants and other poor people were able to find housing. Churches are more needed than ever, he told his congregation, in the downtown communities; not the sort of elaborate temples being constructed further north, nor "pauper churches," but "neat, and substantial, and attracting" churches with clergy who have "zeal to the work of the office." Never before, he continued, have clergy with such zeal been so needed because, second, "There is a crisis coming for which we have none too much time to prepare." Surprisingly, this reference in 1853 to a coming crisis turns out to have nothing to do with the rapidly approaching Civil War but rather with concerns that might have weighed more heavily with many of his colleagues: "the tide of intemperance is rising" and "Sabbath desecration cries to Heaven for the wrath of God upon this land." Even more narrowly, Pennington inveighs against "the prevalence of military funerals on the Sabbath."

Pennington's priorities in this sermon might well be questioned, but he was attempting to carry his hearers with him and, having spoken of concerns that might be uncontroversial, he moved on at the end of his sermon to an area where his concerns might not have been as widely shared. Finally, he spoke about slavery. His position, he points out, is well known, but at a recent General Assembly a coalition of seventy-six had called for a survey to determine the number of slaves held in Presbyterian churches. This had been an extremely controversial matter and strongly resisted by representatives of the Southern congregations, but Pennington sees it as a "question of *facts* which the Presbyterian *world* has a right to know . . . Common-fame says that Presbyterians in this country own 80,000 slaves . . . and that these Presbyterian slaves are liable to all the evils of the system—no church, no Christian ministry, no Bible, no marriage, no parental control over children." Clergy like himself who have traveled abroad "have been made to smart with the odium of this common-fame report. Now," he said, "we wish to know whether this thing is true. Our Southern Presbyterians can give light on the subject; this we ask them to do at present. It is *just, kind,* and *reasonable.* If they have clean hands, let us see them."

Pennington asks his fellow Presbyterians first of all to establish the facts, and then "there is one thing we need to learn, namely how to discuss slavery without getting angry, and . . . look at the subject theologically." He wants them to understand that the wider Presbyterian world is of one mind, agreeing that slavery is wrong and finds no support in the Bible. This surely should give pause to those who think otherwise. He expresses a confidence in the system that the Garrisonians would have derided, but Pennington might have challenged them to show what concrete results they had to show for their approach. Pennington's way is different: to challenge moderately, to seek consensus, to point to accomplishments, and to call his colleagues to move forward together. "I rejoice," he tells them in the closing paragraph, "to know that our church is the friend of progressive opinion, and the time will come when she will be as united on this subject as she is on those of missions, temperance, Sabbath, consecrations, etc." Moderate though this stand was, it had not been easy. "No member of this Presbytery has felt more keenly the uncomfortableness of his position than I have . . . but the conviction I have just expressed has hitherto induced me to trust in the workings of our system to bring us unanimously to the ground now occupied by our United Presbyterian brethren in Scotland, and other bodies of Christians in that country and this." The Presbytery in the six months he served as moderator had, he told them, been more "harmonious and prosperous" than in many years. He cited specific accomplishments— churches organized, young men ordained, pastors installed. Of course, it is never enough. "Had we more of this consuming zeal of Christ . . . what a different world this would be!"[25] But the world was not becoming different enough soon enough to satisfy those whose zeal found expression in far more extreme positions and who would center their attacks increasingly on Pennington in the next few years.

James W. C. Pennington had begun his career as an activist for the cause of African American rights at the first national convention in Philadelphia in 1830. The high point of that career came three days after his sermon to the Presbytery, when he was chosen to preside over the Colored National Convention held in Rochester, New York. The division in the convention movement between the Philadelphian concern for moral improvement and the New York emphasis on social action had at last been largely overcome, and Philadelphia was represented by four able and experienced delegates. New Yorkers nonetheless dominated the Rochester Convention, with eighteen delegates from five cities. Massachusetts also was represented by only four delegates, none of whom, of course, were allies of William Lloyd Garrison. Nine states, all of them Northern, sent delegates.[†] Frederick Douglass was there, and so were

† The first convention had included delegates from Maryland and Virginia. The "Call for a Colored National Convention" was signed by 42 individuals from nine states. The official minutes do not list the delegates. William J. Wilson (Ethiop) was a delegate and states that there were 140 delegates from eight states. The names listed here are those of signers of the "Call."

James McCune Smith, David Ruggles, Amos Beman, Charles Ray, Robert Purvis, and William J. Wilson, better known as Ethiop. Henry Garnet was absent; after spending two and a half years lecturing in England, he had moved on to Jamaica as a missionary. Of the 140 delegates present in Rochester, only James Pennington and Junius C. Morrell† had been present in Philadelphia 23 years earlier.

In 1830, the Convention had been chiefly concerned to take a strong stand against the work of the Colonization Society and secondarily concerned to approve emigration to Canada. Condemned by black leadership though it was, the Colonization Society continued its work, and the battle against it continued through the 1850s. R. R. Gurley, the executive secretary of the American Colonization Society, even came to Rochester to advocate his society's position, but only a handful of the delegates attended an evening meeting when he was given opportunity to present his views. The focus in 1853 had shifted necessarily to the Fugitive Slave Law—"the most cruel, unconstitutional, and scandalous outrage of modern times," the Convention called it[26]—and, even more importantly, the ongoing struggle to gain recognition as citizens of the United States with the same rights as those of other colors. A growing number of African Americans had given up that struggle and had come to believe that emigration was indeed the answer to their problems, though even those usually preferred emigration to Canada or Jamaica or Haiti or even Kansas to Africa. These destinations had never been recommended by the American Colonization Society because Southern slave owners had no desire to see free black communities prospering so close to the slave states and becoming both magnets for fugitives and also beacons of black freedom, stimulating unrest among the slaves. Thus the primary division in the black community in the last decade before the Civil War, and for a long time after it as well, was between those who saw their future in America and those who did not. Rival conventions were sometimes held, and Henry Garnet, returning to the United States after three years in Jamaica, would become a leader in the emigration movement.

Those on both sides of this division had, inevitably, much in common, whether they recognized it or not. Both were, in effect, advocates of black nationalism. The emigration faction, of course, was concerned to build black nations in the Caribbean or Africa, while those who remained convinced that their future was in America were also becoming increasingly centered on creating a free black society, though, in their case, within the white society that oppressed them. Their ultimate goal was still to become fully part of that society, but if that goal was still distant, perhaps the creation of a parallel

---

† Morrell had been among the Philadelphia representatives in 1830 and had served as secretary to the Convention. He had moved to Brooklyn by 1853.

black society as an interim step would be useful. The Rochester Convention therefore created on paper a parallel black society with its own government: a National Council made up of elected representatives, four from each state, and with its own President, Vice-President, Secretaries, and Treasurer. There were to be Committees on a Manual Labor School, Protective Unions, Business Relations, and Publications that would meet monthly. The National Council was to meet at least every six months, receive reports from the Committees, and make plans "for the general good." All this was to be supported, ironically, by a poll tax of ten cents on voters as well as donations and fees. Members of the Council and its sub-councils and committees in each of the states were to be charged one cent a week. Elections to the Council would be held every two years beginning on November 15.[27] To flesh out this structure, the Committee on Business Relations was to establish an office and create a registry of "colored mechanics, artisans, and business men" and of all persons willing to employ colored men, and "to teach colored boys mechanical trades, liberal and scientific professions, and farming." The Committee on Publications was to collect "facts, statistics, and statements," as well as histories, biographies, and books by colored authors and provide a "Library, with a Reading Room and Museum." Once again, as in 1831, there was to be a Committee on a Manual Labor School that would "incorporate itself as an Academy," create a Board of Trustees, procure funds, select a location to include a farm, and hire instructors.[28] There was even to be a quasi-judicial arbitration system to enable African Americans to resolve their problems without appeal to the Federal court system.[29] Ethiop was amused by the way the delegates had taken the draft plan back to their hotel rooms and returned the next day to urge minor amendments: "a member who fancied . . . he saw a hole in the plan would get up to apply a patch; then another would rise to piece out an invisible corner; here a member would attempt to clip off an excrescence; there one would supply a deficiency; this one would come forward to enlarge—that one to curtail." But James McCune Smith "brought it safely through" and was rewarded with the Presidency of the new Council.[30]

Whatever its deficiencies, it was at least a specific plan. "Our warfare," they said, "is not one where force can be applied." It required instead organization and a clear plan of action to make white Americans aware of their claims and responsive to them. "Our white fellow-countrymen do not know us," they pointed out in a summary that remained largely true long afterward and is still true for many. "They are strangers to our character, ignorant of our capacity, oblivious of our history and progress." They set out to remedy this problem by pointing "with pride and hope, to men of education and refinement, who have become such, despite of the most unfavorable influences; we can point to mechanics, farmers, merchants, teachers, ministers, doctors, lawyers, editors, and authors, against whose progress the concentrated energies of American prejudice have proved quite unavailing."[31]

The need was not only for white Americans to recognize this achievement, but for African Americans themselves to amplify this accomplishment by providing structure and guidance for those emerging from slavery and unprepared, after generations of deliberate deprivation, to make use of the opportunities of freedom. They knew they would find more of opposition than support in the larger community. "We must open our own avenues," they recognized, "and . . . educate our own minds." "We must emerge from menial positions to the pursuit of commercial and other elevating branches of trade."[32] This was, in brief, a convention with a purpose and a plan to move toward that purpose. Even the *New York Times* admitted, "the Convention is earning the reputation of being practical and business-like."[33]

The plan for a National Council was ambitious but produced little in the way of concrete results. Realistically, however, how much foundation was there for so comprehensive a plan? The American democracy had been created on a broad base of self-sufficient farmers and small businessmen in a society that valued education and made at least a minimum education widely available. European democracies were built slowly and painfully, with many mistakes and backslidings, through the gradual creation of an educated middle class. The vast majority of African Americans in 1853 (over three million) were still held as slaves and prevented from acquiring an education or enjoying a stable family life, while the 170,000 who were free (imagine Chattanooga, Tennessee, with perhaps half a dozen college-educated citizens and only one trained doctor) were still almost entirely laborers. It was a small and fragile base on which to create a functioning democracy. In 1903, W. E. B. Du Bois would popularize the term "the talented tenth" in projecting the creation of a leadership group that could help realize the goals held up by the Rochester Convention half a century earlier, but there was as yet no "talented tenth" to bring the Rochester goals to reality.

Most conventions, however, are called to inspire as well as to plan. If the ambitious plans were never quite fulfilled, the inspirational aspects of the 1853 convention were probably sufficient in themselves to justify coming together. Each convention also provided a sort of benchmark of progress, its reports and resolutions indicating the changing concerns of the larger community. The first conventions had been content to assert the promise of America's foundational documents and to call for "elevation" of African Americans and a greater fulfillment of the promise. By 1853, the Convention was making far more specific demands: access to schools and colleges and churches and work places, trial by jury, unrestricted suffrage, the right to serve in the militia and navy, equal opportunity to claim land in the West, and, very specifically and fundamentally, the abolition of slavery and repeal of the Fugitive Slave Act. The Convention's "Address to the People of the United States" (not only to Colored Americans as in earlier conventions) summed it up by pledging that the delegates would "use all and every means consistent with the just rights of our fellow men, and with the precepts of Christianity" to gain their objectives. "We are," they insisted, "and of right ought to be American citizens. We claim this right, and we claim all the rights and privileges and duties which, properly, attach to it."[34] To leave Rochester with such goals openly stated and shared with a large group of others would give new strength to the delegates as they went back to work in their various scattered communities.

It is probably not surprising that there is no reference to James Pennington in the minutes of the meeting except the statement at the beginning of most sessions: "President in the chair."[†] The president of a convention does not normally make speeches or become involved in making motions. The same logic may explain why the report of the one committee Pennington chaired "did not come to hand in time to be printed in the order in which it was reported to the Convention." That report, the longest report to the Convention, did "come to hand" in time to be included in the printed Convention report, and dealt with the always contentious issue of colonization. Typically, Pennington attacked his subject indirectly and took the opportunity to review the history of colonization, beginning with the Dutch colonization of South Africa "with gun and sword in hand" in the seventeenth century. White people, he reminded his readers, were the original colonizers, and not with benevolent purposes. After the Dutch in South Africa came "two new schemes of colonization carried out in the eighteenth century in Africa": one by the British, who "commenced *colonizing whites*," and one by the Americans, who "began to turn their attention to Africa, for the purpose of *colonizing free colored persons*." The British colonization of Africa is dealt with at great length with quotations from both British and African sources portraying the way in which a peaceful people were forcibly dispossessed and, often, enslaved. The report then moves on to a much briefer description of the current policy of the American Colonization Society which pretends to oppose slavery, yet never utters "one word of rebuke to slaveholders" while speaking of the removal of free blacks as a "high and exalted obligation, enforced by the duty of self preservation to both races." Of special concern is the argument made by the Society that the Liberian government was now well established and recognized by the governments of Britain, France, and Prussia. The Report points out that, in fact, the Liberian government is largely under the control of the Colonization Society and that, in spite of the talk of "Africa for the Africans," Britain and France are rapidly

† Some sessions were chaired by the vice president, Amos Beman.

acquiring the best land in Africa for white Europeans and the Liberian government, in the same way, is pushing out the natives of that country and subjecting
them to colonial rule. "The truth is," the Report states in summary, that "the
Liberians are in league with the worst enemies of Africa's dearest interests."
After this rather indirect treatment of the subject of colonization, and perhaps
as evidence that little had changed on either side of the argument, readers
are then referred to William Lloyd Garrison's publication of 1831, *Thoughts
on African colonization*, and, especially, the section of that work titled "Voices
from the Colored People."[35]

Frederick Douglass' Paper called the Convention "unquestionably a great
Convention—perhaps the most extraordinary, in many particulars, ever held
in the United States . . . The talent, zeal, and eloquence displayed took our
citizens by surprize [sic]; and we confess, ourselves, even with our expectations,
more than gratified . . . For the first time in the history of this country, the Free
Colored people have banded themselves together nationally, for the defence of
their liberty, and the improvement of their condition." Listing James McCune
Smith, Pennington, Beman, and over a dozen others, the paper boasted that
such an assembly of "men of mark . . . could not be brought together in any
place, in any circumstances, without producing a sensation—and a sensation
they did produce amongst us."[36]

Ethiop, the same paper's "Brooklyn Correspondent," produced a series of
reports on the Conference, including his mixed feeling of fear and delight at
his first experience of railroad travel on his way to Rochester. In addition to
the Convention sessions, there was an afternoon tea which, to Ethiop's astonishment, was held in the "splendid drawing rooms" of a wealthy white citizen
where the arriving delegates found a number of "white ladies and gentlemen"
and "nothing daunted . . . passed into the gay throng as though it was an
everyday affair," which, he thought, might have surprised some of the whites
"who might not have made up their minds to the possibility of meeting so
agreeable companionship in sable skin." Ethiop's columns, providing a personal
perspective on the event, give us also a rare word picture of James W. C. Pennington as he seemed to his contemporaries:

> You never saw the Doctor? Many others have been alike unfortu-
> nate. Let me, in a word or two, speak of him. There is something
> about the Dr., in his quiet deportment—something in both his
> manner and speech so very English—refined English I mean—
> that you would hardly have supposed him to have been bred in
> America. Lively—I may even say jolly—in manners, agreeable,
> with no attempt at austerity, you feel at ease in his presence at
> once. So he appears in the private circle. As presiding officer of the

Convention, he must have made the impression upon every man
capable of an impression, that neither hardships nor undue severity
was necessary to guide through the varied forms of business of a
body of gentlemen! The Doctor is, withal, a clergyman in the fullest
sense of the word—pious, learned, able, skilled in research, and
deep in *lore*—in all things earnest—in nothing insincere.

The editor of *The Christian Witness,* a British journal, painted a similar picture
of James Pennington a few years earlier:

His cast of thought is remarkably English. Were he to be heard
without being seen, he would pass for a thorough English speaker of
a very high order. His leading characteristic, however, is weight,—
solidity of thought, clothed in appropriate language. There is no
burst, no blaze, none of the vehemence which characterizes the
highest order of eloquence; but it is that which constitutes the basis
of all real oratory,—judgment, sobriety, force of thought, conclu-
siveness of argument, aptness of illustration, which an English
audience never fails to appreciate, and which, in truth, constitutes
their favorite mode of address. In the speech of Pennington there
is, moreover, a moving mixture of pathos, with an occasional stroke
of pleasing humor.[37]

This cultivated and urbane leader was a very different James W. C. Pen-
nington from the ragged, illiterate fugitive who had appeared at William
Wright's door more than thirty years earlier, and even from the half-educated
Brooklyn house servant who had journeyed to the first such convention in
Philadelphia in 1830.

The Black Convention movement had also come a long way from the
Philadelphia Conventions of 1831 and 1832 at which it had taken five days on
the first occasion and ten days on the second to denounce colonization, commend the Canada settlement, and approve a plan to raise funds for a manual
school. The Rochester Convention had moved on also from the frustrated
militancy of the Buffalo Convention with Henry Garnet's call for a slave
rebellion, and the 1848 Cleveland Convention's call for the "Colored Freemen
of North America" to learn military tactics so that they could "measure arms
with assailants without and invaders within."[38] Rather, the emphasis was on
creating the kind of structure and organization within the larger society that
would enable change and support progress.

In Rochester, where a massive amount of preparation had been done, the
Convention was able to move through a much more ambitious agenda in only

three days. In the closing session, delegates to the newly created National Council were named[†]—two each from ten states, with Frederick Douglass and James McCune Smith to represent New York—and resolutions were adopted expressing the Convention's thanks to the officers and committees. Then, a resolution having been adopted to adjourn *sine die*, Frederick Douglass came to the front of the hall and led the delegates in singing the Doxology:

> From all that dwell beneath the skies,
> Let the Creator's praise arise . . .

"In which the whole Convention heartily joined."[39]

Pennington hurried home to conduct the Sunday service at the Shiloh Church and to open the church again on Friday, a week after the Rochester Convention had adjourned, to provide a public report to New Yorkers. James McCune Smith opened the meeting and turned it over to other delegates who read parts of the Convention report published in *Frederick Douglass' Paper* and part of the "Address of the Convention to the People of the United States." Some Ohio delegates were on hand, and the editor of the new paper the *Aliened American* spoke of the importance of the Convention. James Pennington, relaxed and confident, told some amusing anecdotes, and resolutions were then adopted endorsing the work of the convention and creating a committee of nine to move forward on the plan to elect members of the proposed State Council.[40] Similar meetings were held in Chemung County, New York, and Chicago, Illinois, and many other places in the following weeks and months to endorse the plan for a Council and elect delegates.[41]

James McCune Smith and James Pennington both had impressive credentials and were providing African Americans with exceptionally talented leadership in the summer of 1853. Before the summer was over, however, both of them would be made aware again of how far pre-Civil War New York had to go if they were to realize their dream of equal citizenship.

A few weeks after the post-Convention meeting, James Pennington set off on a Thursday morning with his wife, Almira, and another woman to take the Fulton Street ferry which connected Manhattan and Brooklyn Heights. In the days before the building of the Brooklyn Bridge, this ferry was an essential connection between the business district of the city and the wealthy suburban community across the East River. The group of three found seats for

---

† At the afternoon session, it had been agreed that the Council would have its office in Pittsburgh, which was amended to Cincinnati, to Chicago, to Portland, Me.; but there is no evidence that the office was, in fact, created.

themselves in the "ladies' cabin," distinguished from the "gentlemen's cabin" by the fact that the air was not filled with smoke nor the floor wet with spewed tobacco. James Pennington was not the only "gentleman" who preferred the ladies' cabin, but the captain came down and ordered him out. When Pennington protested, the captain seized him by the throat and forced him out. An observer calling himself "Equity" wrote to say that "the worst characters with a white skin, may sit, and elbow a lady in silk or satin, in those cabins; but if a decent man with colored skin only wishes to walk through the cabin, he is clutched by the throat and sent reeling." Dogs also, he noted, are admitted to the ladies' cabin, but not the pastor of men and women "who are in our families and at our firesides daily."[42] It was a routine reminder that whatever plans a convention might make to improve the standing of black people in a white world and whatever recognition might be given to their leaders, there was also the daily reality of life in a city that paid little attention to the letter sent them from Rochester asking for recognition as citizens and human beings.

James McCune Smith was confronted with the same reality in early September. A World's Temperance Convention was being held in New York, and Smith, who claimed to have been "an old-fashioned Temperance man" for the last twenty-four years, "relying on my own unpledged will to keep me temperate in all things," was chosen to serve as a delegate from the Fifth Ward Temperance Alliance. At ten o'clock on the morning of the first day of the Convention, Smith arrived at Metropolitan Hall, informed a policeman on guard that he was a delegate, and was admitted. Shortly, a member of the Credentials Committee arrived to tell him that his credentials were not in order and to rebuke the policeman for letting Smith in. When Smith inquired what he would need to provide to gain admission, he was told, "That will depend on the action of the Committee." Smith crossed the street to a tavern, where he was made welcome without regard to color or opinion of alcohol, and used a convenient table to write to the *New York Tribune* to report this event and to say that he had hoped to call the Convention's attention to the relationship between "the Rum Trade, and its twin brother, the Slave Trade." Until Liberia adopted a temperance law, he argued, it would not be able to wash its hands of the slave trade. Finally, he went back to his office to finish the letter and found "an African gentleman" was sitting in his office and telling him that two slaves were often traded in Africa for a small keg of rum. But the Temperance Convention's Credentials Committee prevented the Convention from hearing anything of that.

A small step forward did take place that summer, when the Episcopal Diocese of New York finally admitted St. Philip's Church, where Smith was a communicant, to membership in the Diocesan Convention. The congregation had been organized since 1826, and John Jay had been leading an effort to admit the congregation to membership in the Convention since 1844. Such action is normally a routine matter, but Jay's resolutions were ruled out of order and referred to committee and otherwise turned aside for ten years. When George Templeton Strong, a sophisticated lawyer and member of the Vestry of Trinity Wall Street, recorded the event in his diary, he revealed the common attitude against which Jay and, of course, Pennington and Smith, were contending:

> Another Revolution. John Jay's annual motion carried at last, and the nigger delegation admitted into the Diocesan Convention. John Jay must be an unhappy, aching void, as when one's stomach, liver, and other innards have been dexterously taken out.[43]

Smith was not one of the three delegates to the 1853 Convention who were thus given seats and votes, but he did take his place the following year without interference from a credentials committee.[44]

While Americans, black and white, were debating the merits of colonization, European governments were proceeding rapidly with a rather different kind of colonization, as James Pennington had pointed out to the Convention and as he wrote in a letter to the *American Missionary* magazine in September. European governments might have abandoned the slave trade, but they had found a new and better way to exploit the continent to the south. They had taken possession of the land at the mouth of every important river and so secured the trade with the interior for themselves. In South Africa, Pennington noted, drawing on an article head he had spotted recently in a newspaper, the intention of the governor of the Cape Province was to establish a line of forts to keep the "Kaffirs" north of a certain boundary. All of this, Pennington pointed out, was counter-productive if Christians were interested in proclaiming the gospel in the interior of the continent: "So little sense of justice has been shown [by] those who have represented Christian governments in Africa, that the confidence of the native tribes has been greatly shaken, even in well-intentioned efforts for their good." Pennington also believed that there was a divide between these European governments and their people. "The British Christian people," he wrote, "are ashamed and sick of the cruel conduct of their government; they have remonstrated in every way, and on every fitting occasion; and yet the oppressions and abuses of government continue." But Pennington's contact with European people had been primarily with evangelicals and temperance leaders in England, and these were not the majority nor were they even represented proportionately in the government. Many English Christians saw the rapid expansion of the empire as beneficial to missionary work, and many of the missionaries were grateful for the support the government gave them, even if it was the indirect benefit that forts on the coast provided of an established base to supply communications with the homeland and easier access to necessary supplies. Pennington saw it differently: "The idea, that missions can only be sustained in connection with some colony, or by the potent name of some foreign ruler, is mischievous in practice and false in theory."[45] Most Americans, however, saw the issue through the very narrow lens of the Liberia colony, and what European powers did with the rest of Africa was of little concern. Pennington's broader view of the situation and concern for the future failed to generate much interest.

In November, the first meeting of the National Council took place in New York City as scheduled, with delegates present from Illinois and Rhode Island. Reports were received in the various areas assigned by the Rochester Convention, and McCune Smith spoke of the "fine time, vigorous spirit, the harmony and the determination at work." But there was no report of the establishment of an office or library or of fund raising for a manual labor school, the specific and measurable challenges the Convention had taken on.[46]

In the midst of all this activity, word came that Pennington had been elected president of the Woodstock Manual Labor Institute in Michigan. Located midway between Detroit and Kalamazoo, the school boasted eight buildings, a library of 2000 volumes, and over fifty students. It had been founded nine years earlier by Prior Foster, a black citizen of Ohio, and incorporated in 1848. Foster wrote in November to Henry M. Wilson, a black Presbyterian colleague of Pennington's who had visited the Institute, to ask him to notify Pennington of the action of the Annual Meeting of the Trustees in October. Those two letters were published in the *National Anti-Slavery Standard* in December, along with a copy of a letter from Pennington saying that "the honour was unsolicited and unexpected" but that he would accept the position. The position included a professorship and, not unreasonably, required a move to Michigan. But Pennington did not move to Michigan, and no more is known of the matter except that the main building of the Institute burned down in 1855 and that the Institute's life ended during the Civil War.[47] Pennington might have made a very good academic leader but, for some reason, it didn't happen.

What did happen in the course of the next year was what does happen to many people in the spotlight: he became the subject of vicious personal attacks, he became involved in a very personal matter that attracted unusual publicity because of his position, and he took a leadership role in an issue of both symbolic and practical importance to the black community.

CHAPTER NINETEEN

New York, 1854–1855

Questions had been raised while James Pennington was still in Britain about the use made of the funds he had raised, and those questions seem to have persisted. Wendell Phillips, Parker Pillsbury, and other white New England abolitionists had begun to attack him as early as 1850 with accusations centered on the misuse of funds. Lewis Tappan had raised similar but more specific questions directly with Pennington. What validity those charges may have had is hard to discern in the midst of the fierce rivalry between the New England and New York anti-slavery groups in the one case, and Tappan's distrust of African American abilities in the other. Rumors were continuing to circulate, however, and James Pennington met them head-on by going to the Presbytery in early April of 1854 and asking them to investigate the matter and make a report. In response, two clergy and an elder "were appointed a committee to confer at his own request with the Rev. J. W. C. Pennington, D.D., in relation to his personal affairs." Three weeks later the committee reported back that they had "conferred with Dr. Pennington and received from him a detailed statement of the transactions connected with the purchase of his freedom, which was perfectly satisfactory to the committee."[1] Since Pennington had been out of the country when the arrangements were made to purchase his freedom and since the Scottish church had raised the money, it is hard to see what impropriety Pennington might have committed and who might have been concerned. So that criticism was dealt with; others would not be quieted so easily. Meanwhile, there were very personal concerns that occupied Pennington's attention.

James Pennington had grown up in a family that was out of the ordinary among slaves in that they continued for many years as an unbroken unit deeply devoted to each other. He had spoken of his parents, brothers, and sisters, as "the sun and moon and eleven stars" of his social sky.[2] It was now almost twenty-seven years since he had seen any of them, but he had never forgotten them. In the summer of 1853, Pennington had learned the name of the man who owned his next younger brother, Stephen, and had written to make what he considered "a fair offer" for his purchase, but there had been no reply.[3] Then, very suddenly, in May of 1854, a letter came from William Still in Philadelphia to say that Stephen had arrived in Philadelphia with his two sons, Robert and Jacob, ages 19 and 17, and with their owner in hot pursuit.

Stephen had become the property of a man named Joseph Grove in Sharpsburg, Maryland, a very small community about thirteen miles south of Hagerstown, but had escaped from his master on Sunday, May 20. His two sons, who lived nearby but belonged to David Smith,[†] managed to escape at the same time and flee with their father. Walking all night, they covered fifty miles without stopping and came into Pennsylvania where, undoubtedly with help along the way from people like William Wright and those who had assisted James Pennington—but a new generation of such people, because so much time had passed—they "took the cars for Philadelphia." New and faster transport was available than when Pennington had escaped. In Philadelphia they found William Still, a man known variously as "the Father of the Underground Railroad" and "the Secretary of the Underground Railroad."[4] Still, who was born free in New Jersey, had moved to Philadelphia as a young man and become a member of the Pennsylvania Anti-Slavery Society and chairman of its committee to assist fugitive slaves. He helped an average of sixty fugitives a month on their way, and kept careful records of his work. Whether Still and Pennington had ever met is not known, but Pennington had helped Still's brother Peter at some point and they knew each other by reputation.[5] Still therefore wrote to Pennington on May 22 to tell him of the fugitives and report that they were on their way to New York with "an intelligent guide." Pennington wrote back to thank Still for his "offices of benevolence to my bone and flesh" and alerted the New York Vigilance Committee to be ready to receive them.[6]

Meanwhile, setting off a remarkably dramatic series of events, Grove and Smith had set out to follow their fugitive property and bring them back. They traced them to Baltimore, where they engaged the services of professional slave hunters. A message brought by a carrier pigeon told them that the fugitives were in Philadelphia and preparing to move on to New York, so the owners went on at once to Philadelphia with two agents of the slave-hunting firm, Augustus Briggs and a man named Graham. Arriving in Philadelphia, they

---

† Several articles about this incident reverse the names of the owners, listing Grove as owner of the nephews and Smith as the owner of Stephen, but Pennington had written to Grove in 1853 and it was Grove who later did negotiate with Pennington for Stephen's purchase. Some published reports of the matter include texts of the affidavits filed by the owners, and these also name Grove as the owner of Stephen and Smith as owner of the nephews. ("The Fugitive Slave Law Enforced Peaceably—Three Slaves Surrendered New York," *New York Times*, May 27, 1854.)

succeeded in getting on the same train that was taking the Pembrokes and their guide to New York. Fortunately for the Pembrokes, the train cars were segregated, so they knew nothing of the other passengers, and the guide was clever enough to get them off the train in Newark to throw the pursuers off the scent of their quarry. The hunters, as a result, rolled on through Newark and arrived in New York ahead of the fugitives and used the time to round up confederates and plan their next moves.[7]

The hunters may well have been watching as the fugitives came into the city, but they were content to wait for a better time to spring their trap. Pennington's home on Sixth Avenue was far too centrally located and well known to make it a safe place for the fugitives, so they were taken off to spend the night with a less-well-known family on Thompson Street,[†] a few blocks away. James Pennington was reunited there with his brother and met his nephews for the first time, but, after two hours, the fugitives retired for the night and Pennington returned to his home, confident that all was well. The New York Vigilance Committee routinely dealt with forty or fifty fugitives a year, and this was simply one more case.[8] But this time, they were not careful enough. Someone had been watching, and when all was quiet, the hunters pounced. At three-thirty the next morning, the hunters broke the lock on the front door, seized the three fugitives, and carried them off to the Eighth Ward police station to await the arrival of the proper authorities. U.S. Marshal Abraham Hillier arrived promptly at 8:30 A.M. and took them to Commissioner G. W. Morton, who had been appointed to deal with fugitive slaves. At about 9 A.M., a hearing was held in which the owners were represented by the law firm of Dunning & Smith. The fugitives, completely ignorant of the law, were unrepresented, since there was no need for them to have counsel under the Fugitive Slave Law. The relevant documents from the State of Maryland were presented to the Commissioner, who listened to the claims of the owners and found that the three men before him were indeed the property of the claimants. He therefore ordered that they be placed in irons and held in jail until transportation could be arranged.

When James Pennington awoke that morning and learned that his relatives had been seized, he went first to the station house and was told that there would be a hearing at 11 A.M. He then went off to find legal counsel while Almira set out to locate the kidnaped men. John Jay was the lawyer most familiar with fugitive slave cases, so Pennington found him, told him what was happening, and sent him to provide legal counsel while he himself continued

---

† Still says Thompson Street but Thomas Pennington, quoting an article in the *Liberator*, says Broome Street. Thompson Street would have been a very short distance from Pennington's home, but Broome Street is more than half a mile further away.

his search for assistance. He went to the Marshal's office between 10 and 11 and was told that the hearing (which had, of course, been held at 9 A.M.) was now scheduled to be held between 12 and 1. When he called again at 12, he was told that he could see the captives between 4 and 5. Almira, meanwhile, had found the fugitives locked in a room in the same building as the Commissioner's office, but when John Jay arrived, shortly after noon, he met Morton on the street and was told that the prisoners wanted no counsel, that their case had been adjudicated, that he had made out the warrant, and that the prisoners had been taken away. Next to arrive was Judge Erastus D. Culver,[†] who was also told that he was too late: the formalities had been completed and the prisoners, who admitted they were slaves and were willing to be taken back, were no longer there. Culver asked the deputies what time they went and in whose charge, and was repeatedly assured that they had been taken away earlier in the day in charge of a U. S. officer. Culver, however, decided to ask further and find some witnesses not in the pay of the government. That led him to "Mrs. Dr. Pennington," who told him the facts and took him to the room where the fugitives were being held. They, not surprisingly, told Culver a very different story: they wanted their freedom and therefore wanted counsel and the support of friends. Culver then went to another judge and obtained a writ of *habeas corpus* and a warrant. By the time he returned, late in the day, to the Commissioner's office he was informed that he was ten minutes too late. Pennington also came back about 3:30 P.M. and was also told he was ten minutes too late. A crowd had gathered, but the prisoners had, in fact, been carried off long before under a heavy guard of police, taken across the Hudson River to Jersey City, and put in a railroad car headed south. Ironically, they had been placed under guard in the private room of the ladies' car which was normally a segregated place for whites only.[9]

On Sunday the 28th, two days later, a large congregation thronged the Shiloh Presbyterian Church to express their feelings and to listen to indignant speeches by Pennington, Culver, and others. Pennington told the gathering the story of his own escape and spoke of the family he had left behind, tracing their descent from a young Mandingo prince, his grandfather, who had been captured and enslaved some hundred years earlier. He had a surprising amount of information about his family, and he was not the only one who had found a way to freedom. His parents, he told the audience, had also escaped from slavery at some point, but his mother had been recaptured, taken back to Maryland, and then sold to new owners in Missouri. His father, meanwhile, had managed to

---

† Erastus D. Culver had served one term in the State legislature and one term in the House of Representatives in Washington. Elected to serve as a judge of the City Court in Brooklyn in 1854, he ruled in favor of a fugitive slave in 1857. (*Wikipedia*.)

reach Canada and safety. One brother, Robert, had also escaped to Canada but had died there. Horace, Richard, and Vernon had also died. His sister Maria had escaped to Canada with her husband and lived there still. Another sister, Margaret, had married a free man who had bought her freedom as well, but she had subsequently died. The remaining sister, Emmeline, had been sold to owners in Missouri. The two remaining brothers, Bazil and Daniel, remained in slavery and were said to belong to one of the wealthiest merchants in Boston. Apart from Stephen, then, and James himself, three remained in slavery, one was living in freedom, and five had died. Two more children, Maurice and Jane, had been born after his escape, but Jane had died young and he had no report on Maurice.[10]

E. D. Culver, the judge who had arrived on the scene too late, was cheered when he told the assembly that although he thought of himself as "a man of peace, and never counseled resistance to the laws," he was nevertheless now quite prepared to call for the pulling down of the house over the head of any minion of the Fugitive Slave Law and the "battering of his head on his shoulders." Resolutions were passed sympathizing with the victims of slavery and expressing sympathy for Pennington and his family in their "crushed affections and hopes under these most trying and painful circumstances." One further resolution, finding a bright side to the affair, was able to "rejoice" that it was no longer possible to carry out the provisions of the Fugitive Slave Act "except through the infamy of lies and subterfuges by United States officers."[11]

Two letters arrived from Baltimore during the next few days, one from Stephen and one from Jacob Grove. Both were short and to the point. Grove had written on Saturday, immediately after reaching Baltimore. He said he would not have written except for Stephen's "earnest solicitation," but that he was willing, as a result, to sell Stephen to his brother. He would wait to hear from Pennington, he said, before selling Stephen "to the drivers." The letter from Stephen, which a friend had written for him and posted three days later, begged, "Do, my brother, make arrangements, and that at once for my relief. Oh; do make them; I will work daily when I get there to pay you back. If you only knew my situation and my feelings, you would not wait one moment. Act promptly, as I will have to be sold to the South . . . My two sons were sold to the drivers . . . I am confined to my room with irons on."[12]

In response to these appeals, James Pennington published an appeal for assistance that copied the two letters and continued: "Those who may wish to aid me in this painful hour with money can remit their sums to the following gentlemen . . ." He then lists ten addresses including those of Senator Francis Gillette of Connecticut, Horace Greeley of the *New York Tribune*, Henry Raymond of the *New York Times*, John Hooker of Hartford, and Simeon Jocelyn, now of New York. There was a generous response to this appeal, but

Grove had stated no price and proved to be a hard bargainer. When funds had been donated, Pennington wrote to Grove with an offer of $600, saying he had heard that was his price, and asking what his expenses would be. Grove write back to say that his price was $1000 plus expenses. He added that he had been offered $800 in Baltimore and that he could get $1500 for him in Richmond.[13] At this point, Pennington made use of the telegraph to say that he would provide the amount asked. Grove telegraphed back that his expenses were $333, making a total demand of $1333. This was far beyond what Pennington had available, but he finally decided that "I must try to redeem my brother even at this extravagant price" and responded to Grove accordingly. Two days went by before Grove replied from Sharpsburg that he was there with Stephen, awaiting orders.

The pressure of these negotiations had made an impact on Pennington. Once before, in the midst of a convention in Hartford that he was responsible for, he had had an attack of illness. Now, again, when the response finally came from Grove, Pennington was "confined to my bed with a critical attack of illness." Nevertheless, against the advice of his doctor, he went out and began arrangements to raise the money. He also deposited the $850 that had been donated to that point with "a respectable house" and authorized them to contact "a good house in Baltimore" and ask them to transact the business. From Baltimore came a response that they had sent at once to slave dealers called Duke & Donauris, who had Stephen in custody. The slave dealers replied that they were authorized to release Stephen for $1333 plus their expenses of $42 and that this charge would increase daily. All this, Pennington laid out in a new appeal to the newspapers. He was no longer in a mood to plead. "I am an American to the backbone," he wrote, "but I am ashamed of my countrymen . . . This expense is going on every day," he concluded. "My brother is there."[14]

Heartsick over his brother's captivity and his inability as yet to find the funds required to buy his freedom, James Pennington found himself under attack for a position taken by his Presbytery and his relationship to the Presbyterian Church. After the Rochester Convention, Pennington's increased prominence seemed to intensify the attacks on his integrity and broadened them to include a range of issues from personal morality to theology. Lewis Tappan had confided a broadside against Pennington to his letter book in February 13, 1854, with an entry saying "Rev. S. E. Cornish spent the evening with me and communicated the sad intelligence that Dr. P has become a confirmed drunkard, has used friends wrongfully, is greatly in debt, is neglecting his parishioners, and contriving, with the aid of P. Foster, to obtain money under wrong pretense. This is sad news, but from facts known to me many months ago it was not wholly unexpected by me."[15] Others, presumably, were

saying such things in Tappan's hearing. But were they true? Christians who are above reproach in most things can still be careless in regard to the Ninth Commandment and repeat rumors without being sure of their truthfulness.†
Lewis Tappan had, in fact, been warned years earlier that he was all too apt to form and share negative opinions of other people. In 1836, Theodore Weld had written to tell him that he was given to forming such views "on too slight grounds, too summarily."†† A twentieth-century biographer speaks of Tappan's "appalling disregard for the feelings of others."[16]

Nonetheless, the letter book report of a conversation with Samuel Cornish has generally been taken as true and therefore requires a very careful analysis. The careless way in which rumors were passed on in the 19th century (and today!) has already been noted. Is it, then, credible that a pastor who required an abstinence pledge from every member of his congregation and preached frequently on the subject, had suddenly become "a confirmed drunkard," and what do those words imply? The "temperance movement" in the nineteenth century was, in fact, not advocating temperance but total abstinence, and any use of alcoholic beverages was likely to be denounced as "drunkenness." It is also true that no one in those days understood alcoholism as a disease. Then, too, although Samuel Cornish had been present at the tribute to Pennington a year earlier, he had angrily attacked the clergy and Christian churches many years earlier for their treatment of black people. In an editorial written when he was editor of the *Colored American*, Cornish had accused "the American Church" of being "the strong hold of an unholy prejudice against color, more oppressive and fatal in its results than any other sin. It is not only a generator of . . . darkness, but it is an extinguisher of *the light*."[17] Now that Pennington was being attacked for his membership in the Presbyterian Church, Cornish may have begun to see him as part of a corrupt system and may have decided to join in the attack himself. So the implications of the language are unclear and the attackers can hardly be seen as impartial witnesses. Pennington's life would continue to make its own witness, but such attacks would drastically cripple his future role in the abolition movement.

---

† In 1844, Harriet Beecher Stowe's husband, Calvin Stowe, a rather dull theologian, passed on to her the claim that "A Philadelphia bishop, long addicted to drink, while half boozled has caught young ladies who were so unfortunate as to meet him alone, and pawed them over in the most disgusting manner." Typically of rumormongers, Stowe has confused the bishop of Pennsylvania, who was accused of alcoholism, with the bishop of New York, who was accused of "pawing young ladies," and he passes on as fact charges that were never proved.

†† Weld, Theodore, to Lewis Tappan, May 21, 1836, cited in Mabee, *Black Freedom*, p. 17.

Unlike the gossipy charges of alcoholism and misuse of funds, the theological questions were raised in the public press and could be dealt with openly. In June 1854, just four days after Pennington had appealed again for help in freeing his brother, *Frederick Douglass' Paper* printed a letter from Washington Stickney, a minister in Canastota, New York, who had been involved in the "Jerry Rescue," one of the famous incidents of the fugitive slave era. When a black tailor named William Henry but known to everyone as Jerry was seized in Syracuse in October 1851, Stickney was one of a large group of local residents who planned his rescue. A crowd broke into the courthouse and spirited Jerry away to Canada. So Stickney was a man with strong convictions, and he used violent language to condemn James Pennington for his association with the Presbyterian Church. "That Dr. Pennington—a man that has felt the iron of slavery in his own soul—who has passed through the torturing fires of this Moloch—a man who could find no foot of American soil, free from the desecration of the kidnapper, who at any moment, was liable to be torn from the horns of the altar, even by the kidnappers of his own ecclesiastical communion—a man who owes his freedom to foreign gold—that this man, who should be a Moses, to lead Israel out of bondage—worse than Egyptian—should continue to hug slavery to his bosom, ecclesiastically, is truly for a lamentation."[18]

What brought on this tirade? Pennington was a member of the Third Presbytery of New York, a constituent member of the New Light Presbyterian Church, or, as Stickney put it, "a body in full communion with men thieves [who] have labored to make it easy for the dragon of slavery to slime his way through these Northern States." That Presbytery had adopted a resolution which declared: "We believe in the present aspect of Divine Providence, the agitation in our General Assemblies, by any portion of our churches, of our relations to slavery, in this country, is *undesirable* and *inexpedient*." And what, asked Stickney, was Pennington's position on that "anti-christian and dastardly resolution, in reference to the crime of trafficking in human flesh, in the merchandise of souls? Does his soul burn with a lofty indignation? . . . Does he, indignantly, rebuke the guilty proposition? Far from it. Doctor Pennington gets down, even as low as the white Doctors of Divinity, and endorses 'concurs in the resolution' . . . Does not Dr. Pennington thus betray the cause of the slave, and shake hands with the allies of the slaveholder and the slave driver?" After a good deal more such language, Stickney summed it up with the charge that Pennington, by concurring in the resolution, "throws his church shield over the diabolical crime of slavery . . . If God shall enter into judgment with men, for their political offences against the slaves, of how much sorer judgment shall they be thought worthy who baptize it in the name of God, and do it reverence in the temple of Jesus."[19]

William Lloyd Garrison and his followers, having abjured all relationship with slave holders and, indeed, the government of the United States, were apt to criticize abolitionists not associated with them for being connected in some way to slavery. As a recognized leader among African Americans, Pennington became an obvious and visible target for such attacks. Pennington, however, had more important concerns that summer than defending himself against the Canastota clergyman. His brother had been carried off in chains and his first priority was to do whatever was necessary to redeem him. His last, desperate appeal for help was ultimately successful and by the end of June,[20] Stephen Pembroke was back in New York and appearing before rapt audiences to tell the story of his escape, his recapture, and finally of his freedom. He had been taken back to the South and kept in chains constantly for fifteen days, eating and sleeping in chains until his arms swelled and his appetite was gone. "Some suppose slavery not to be what it is said to be," Pembroke told his audiences, "but I am right down upon it. I was fifty years in it and it has many degrees. I have been in three of them." He had been sold three times and for twenty years served a "rigid and wicked" man. He saw men "tied up, whipped, shot, and starved." But it was the "moderate degree" of slavery that he left after twenty years of service to a man who wanted a thousand dollars for him "after starving me and depriving me of all the comforts of life and the worship of God." "I used to say to my master, 'I am getting old, and ought to have some rest'; but he would answer, 'No, sir; if you speak about freedom, I will sell you further South.'" Such were the stories Stephen Pembroke told from his experience. Somehow he had also gained a perspective on American economics: "I think it is the North that keeps up slavery," he said. James Pennington spoke also at several such gatherings and told the audiences that his brother was finding it difficult to shake off the fear of recapture and find the courage to go out and walk freely in the street.[21] Stephen stayed on in New York, settling for a while in Brooklyn, and then moved to Monticello, Florida, when the war was over. His two sons were auctioned off to a lumber merchant from North Carolina, "well reported of as a master," to work in a cypress shingle factory.[22] They were reported as living in Alabama in the spring of 1893.[23]

Simultaneously with these events, another drama was playing out in the courtrooms and streets of Boston around the arrest and final extradition of Anthony Burns. On the same day that Stephen Pembroke was seized in New York, Anthony Burns, who had managed to escape from Virginia to Boston on a ship three months earlier, was arrested and brought before a commissioner to be identified and taken back into slavery. This drama played out over a longer time than the Pembroke case and therefore drew larger crowds and even wider attention. At one point, a small group stormed the Court House and a deputy was killed, but the crowd was beaten back. White abolitionists rallied to the cause as well, and for days the crowds in the streets of Boston attempted to block the carrying out of the law. National attention was drawn to the situation, and President Pierce, determined to see the Fugitive Slave Act enforced, ordered marines and artillery to reinforce the Boston guards and sent a ship to carry Burns back to Virginia. On June 2, 50,000 people lined the streets of Boston to see Burns, heavily guarded, walk in shackles to the waiting ship. Once again, however, a purchase was arranged and Burns was back in Boston in less than a year. In March of 1855, Burns came to the Shiloh Church in New York to be introduced by James Pennington as "the last Victim of the Fugitive Slave law in Boston." The phrase was indicative of the rising anger of the black population, implying as it did that the next time an attempt was made to enforce the law, the victim would be the judge.[24] Indeed, one paper summed up the anger in Boston at the judge who ruled in the Burns case in an article titled "Off With His Head."[25]

Even before Burns and the Pembrokes had been returned to slavery, playing out before the public of two major cities the implications of the Fugitive Slave Law, President Pierce signed into law a bill that would raise tensions even further. The "Missouri Compromise" of 1820 had prohibited slavery in territories north of a line running west from the southern border of Missouri, but the Kansas-Nebraska Act, signed on May 30, re-opened the question of slavery in the territories, putting it in the hands of the voters and virtually ensuring that battles would be fought to assure one side or the other a majority in Kansas and the ability to make it a slave state or free. The *New York Herald* called it "one of those great events which, in a nation's history inaugurate a political revolution, and a new cycle in political affairs."[26] The *Albany Register* said, "The great battle between slavery and freedom must one day be fought, and it may as well begin now as at any time."[27]

James Pennington, however much he shared the inevitable anger of those who were frustrated by the Fugitive Slave Law and its consequences, held on to a perspective that gave him confidence in the future in spite of the seeming lack of progress toward the goal of equal rights, and even regression from that goal. In July of 1854, less than two weeks after his brother's return, he was called on to speak at the Seventh Annual Meeting of the New York Central College Association in McGrawville, New York, a tiny community 75 miles southeast of Rochester. The New York Central College had been established five years earlier by anti-slavery Baptists and included three African Americans on the faculty. The college admitted both women and African Americans and was strongly supported by Gerrit Smith. As he had done in his sermon on Christian zeal, Pennington took advantage of the opportunity to step back from the immediate controversies and to outline the theological and Biblical worldview that persuaded him to trust God's providence when current events seemed anything but hopeful. It was a viewpoint based solidly on the teaching of Nathaniel Taylor at Yale concerning the "moral government of God," and Pennington had frequently referred to it ever since his days in New Haven. In McGrawville, he provided the first systematic analysis of African American progress in term of Taylor's theology. The sermon, appropriately in an academic setting, is scholarly, even pedantic, and certainly the least exciting of Pennington's sermons that have survived, but it shows more clearly than the more interesting sermons the perspective that guided Pennington in his daily life and ministry. Unlike some of his angrier contemporaries such as Henry Garnet, who shifted focus from calls for rebellion to calls for emigration, James Pennington saw no need for violence or despair. He could trust God's moral government to bring justice.

Beginning with a text from Psalm 22, verse 28, that says "God is the governor among the nations," Pennington pointed to the existence of a government "resting its power upon infallible laws" and "competent to exercise jurisdiction over all men, all angels, all devils, as well as over all irrational creatures . . . The existence of such a government alone meets the wants of our nature, by giving the rational mind assurance that there is one high, central and supreme POWER ruling and subduing all others." He proceeded to analyze that claim by showing first that "God is governor among the nations" as his text asserted. He found proof of this doctrine in the history of separate nations and the rise and fall of empires such as those of Babylon and Rome. He then demonstrated the appropriateness of God's law to the government of nations and pointed to the parable of the last judgement (Matthew 25:31-48) as proof that such government exists and will determine the ultimate destiny of individuals and nations. "His eye," Pennington asserted, "is in all places beholding the evil and the good. His ear hears and understands every language and speech beneath the sun. His superintending hand is in all national matters. He has to do with the Throne, and with the Chair of State, the Bench, the Bar, and the Jury Box.—The hearts of all men are in His hands and he turns them as the rivers of water are turned. The minds of all men are in His hands. He can control the thinking powers. He can communicate His own mind unto men. He can fasten conviction upon the souls of men. In all his operations as our moral governor He has in view the best welfare of nations."

That being the case, Pennington went on to show how "THIS TRUTH AFFECTS OUR INDIVIDUAL RELATIONS." Every individual conscience "responds to the judgments of God" in matters of human duty, and "the government of God extends to all the duties between man and man . . . There is a voice from the inner man directing, ordering and commanding, and enforcing justice to man. This voice condemns all injustice, fraud and wrong, no matter whether sanctioned by legislation or not." This perspective brings with it the rights of human beings under God's government, and here Pennington finds the Declaration of Independence directly in line with his teaching. "Every human being has a right to be, and to act as such. To possess life, liberty, and to pursue happiness. This right is given by the author of man's being—God; and it cannot be taken away by any power in the world." God-bestowed rights are common to all men. They may be invaded, but man never surrenders them. They may be impaired by oppressive legislation, but they are never abandoned. If misfortune ever snatches them from his embrace, the prompting of his conscience moves him to recover them."

All of this, Pennington was convinced, spoke directly to the present situation of the American slave, and it was in applying it that the sermon came most fully to life: "What rouses the most enlightened and spirited of the slaves from the Southern house of bondage, and sends them at all hazards in search of a place where they can enjoy liberty? The loud voice of natural conscience . . . tells the suffering slave what are his rights, and what are his wrongs. It prompts him to escape from his oppressors. Chains cannot bind him. Bolts and bars cannot confine him. The horse whip cannot deter him. Every fugitive who comes to our free district is a living monument of the power and daring of silent prompting by the sacred whisperings of the voice of God, and of nature." Moreover, "God is bringing the national conscience into sympathy with the oppressed. The whole world is now astir upon the great question of the liberty of conscience." From Pennington's perspective, the wars in Europe were part of the same drama as the conflict in America. Kossuth might not have seen it that way, but it was clear to James Pennington that events in Hungary and Poland were very much connected with America's struggle. England, France, Prussia, and Austria were also involved, though "for some reasons known to their own conscience, [they] are ill at ease. . . [T]hey have awakened a spirit like to that which moved upon the face of the waters," the Spirit that brought order out of chaos in the beginning of Creation (Genesis 1).

On this basis, Pennington moved toward the inevitable conclusion, a vision of a "final campaign" that will be "fought in our land." Four years later, William Seward, United States Senator from New York, in a similar speech analyzing the same collision of social systems from a more political perspective, called it the "irrepressible conflict." Pennington saw it as a continuing conflict that had been going on since the creation of the United States. "We profess to be the freest nation in the world," he pointed out, and yet "We have the largest number of slaves of any nation in the world, excepting the Brazilians . . . For three quarters of a century the descendants of Ethiopia have been waging a powerful warfare against the tyranny of this Republic. Success has attended that warfare in this, that the race has preserved itself from annihilation; and now stands physically among the first class in the

Races of the world." The United States owed the "Ethiopians," as Pennington called them, an enormous debt for services rendered: "The race has served the Republic in all the domestic relations, giving patriotic leisure for study, and preparation for affairs. It has served the Republic in the Revolutionary field; and produced for the nation the enriching luxury of the plantation." But in spite of this, slavery continues—and for one reason only: "The cotton plant which has done more than any thing else to enrich and refine the Saxon, has also done most to brutify and bind fast the slave." Every aspect of American society is responsible for perpetuating the system but they have failed: "The American horsewhip; the American Senate; the American Pulpit; and the American Press, have all in part lent their efforts to annihilate the race; but without success."[28]

James Pennington returned to New York City with a contribution of $25 "for the aid of the Pembroke family"[29] and in time to keep a speaking engagement with his brother and to conduct the usual Sunday service at the Shiloh Church. On that same day and only a few blocks away, new events were taking place that would help shape his future. On that Sunday, July 16, 1854, Elizabeth Jennings, a twenty-four-year-old school teacher, set out to go with a friend to the First Colored American Congregational Church, where she was the organist. She was the daughter of Thomas Jennings, a tailor and a leader in New York's black community. He had served as assistant secretary of the First Annual Convention of the People of Color in 1831, and ten years before that had invented a dry cleaning process that won him the first patent ever held by an African American. Elizabeth Jennings and her friend, Sarah Adams, walked to the corner where they could take the streetcar, and Jennings held up her hand for it to stop as she had been doing for some six months. The driver stopped the cars and they boarded the platform, but Edward Moss, the conductor, told them to get off and wait for the next car. Jennings replied that she was in a hurry to go to church and could not wait. The conductor continued to insist that she must get off, and she continued to refuse. Meanwhile, the next car came up and Jennings asked whether there was room there and was told that there was not. The conductor then said she might go in but would have to leave if any of the other passengers objected. Jennings responded that she had never before been insulted while going to church and "that he was a good for nothing impudent fellow for insulting decent people on their way to church." That ended the possibility of a peaceful ride to church. It had been a summer of "paralyzing heat" and tempers were undoubtedly short.[30] Jennings described the result in a subsequent statement: "He then said I should come out and he would put me out. I told him not to lay his hands on me; he took hold of me and I took hold of the window sash and held on. He pulled me until he broke my grasp and I took hold of his coat and held on to that, he also broke my grasp from that (but previously he had dragged my companion out) she all the while screaming for him to let go. He then ordered the driver to fasten his horses, which he did, and come and help him put me out. They then both seized hold of me by the arms and pulled and dragged me flat down on the bottom of the platform, so that my feet hung one way and my head the other, nearly on the ground. I screamed murder with all my voice, and my companion screamed out 'you'll kill her; don't kill her.' The driver then let go of me and went to his horses; I went again in the car, and the conductor said you shall sweat for this; then told the driver to drive as fast as he could and not to take another passenger in the car; to drive until he saw an officer or a Station House. They got an officer on the comer of Walker and Bowery and the conductor told that him his orders from the agent were to admit colored persons if the passengers did not object, but if they did, not to let them ride . . . The officer, without listening to anything I had to say, thrust me out and then pushed me, and tauntingly told me to get redress if I could; this the conductor also told me, and gave me some name and number of his car; he wrote his name Moss and the car No. 7, but I looked and saw No. 6 on the back of the car; after dragging me off the car he drove me right away like a dog, saying not to be talking there and raising a mob or fight."[31]

Jennings then went home to nurse her bruises and the church made do without their organist that Sunday. A protest meeting was held at Jennings's church the next day, and her account of the incident was read by the clerk since she was too injured to attend in person. Resolutions were passed, demanding equal rights in the use of the streetcars, and copies of the resolutions were sent to the *New York Tribune* and *Frederick Douglass' Paper.* More important, Thomas Jennings, James Pennington, and others formed a Legal Rights Association to provide a way to fight back against injustice. They would begin by suing the 3rd Avenue Street Car company on behalf of Elizabeth Jennings. Such suits had been brought before, but this was the first time such a suit was taken seriously. To represent her, the Legal Rights Association found a young lawyer, interested in the abolition movement, named Chester A. Arthur. Twenty-seven years later, Arthur would become President of the United States, but in July of 1854 he was only twenty-four years old and recently admitted to the bar. A young lawyer with ideals but not heavily burdened with other work seemed the perfect choice. The case would not go to trial for many months, so Arthur had ample time to prepare.

Beyond these local dramas—and to some degree as a result of them—tensions between North and South continued to rise, first under the stress of enforcing the Fugitive Slave Law, and then when President Pierce signed the Kansas-Nebraska Act on May 30, 1854 and so re-opened the possibility of expanding the slave territories. As tensions rose, the number of African Americans willing to emigrate rose also. In early January of 1854, the American Colonization Society had reported its most successful year in fundraising and the sailing of over a thousand emigrants to Liberia in that same year.[32] And now there was organized support for emigration among African Americans as well. Henry Garnet wrote from Jamaica to say that there were planters eager to hire American workers and provide them with help in building houses,[33] and while Philadelphia and New York had come together in support of the Rochester plan, western Pennsylvania had now gone astray and was organizing to support the emigrationist cause.

Martin Delaney in Pittsburgh signaled his dissent by sending Frederick Douglass a letter that poured scorn on him for consulting with Harriet Beecher Stowe; "she *knows nothing about us*, 'the Free Colored people of the United States,'" he wrote, "neither does any other white person." He was doubtful that a National Council would bring together the "intelligence, maturity and experience" to make it more than a "mere mockery."[34] Delaney, who had studied medicine at Harvard and founded, in 1842, one of the first black newspapers, published a book in 1852 on *The Condition, Elevation, Emigration, and Destiny of the Colored People of the United States, Politically Considered*, calling for a separate black nation outside the United States.

"Charlotte K," another of Frederick Douglass's pseudonymous correspondents, wrote from Pittsburgh to report a conversation among Delaney and other western Pennsylvania leaders, Lewis Woodson, John Vashon, and John Peck. "How they did pitch into the Rochester Convention! [Woodson] rolled up his sleeves, and knife in hand, 'went in' at the constitution, poor thing— reminding one of a great big cook . . . cutting up a poor little reed bird. . . . [They] were getting along pretty slick when the tickets arrived from Philadelphia, containing both their names [Woodson and Vashon] as candidates for the State Council. Then, Presto! Whew! John Zuille[†] never saw J. Smith turn a corner quicker nor sharper than these two old fogies flapped right around, calling upon the people to vote for them."[35]

There was, no doubt, some prestige associated with being named as a candidate for the new State Council, but a "National Emigration Convention" was held, nonetheless, in August, in Cleveland, Ohio. There were over one hundred and forty delegates present from ten states, including the mid-South states of Missouri, Kentucky, and Tennessee as well as Canada, but the majority from the Pittsburgh area.[††] Among the resolutions passed was one "That the

† Zuille was an early leader in the New York African American community, as was John McCune Smith.

†† One of the two delegates from New York was J. Theodore Holly, an Episcopal priest, who was convinced that African Americans could find freedom and self-government in Haiti. He emigrated to Haiti with a small group of followers in 1861, and in 1874 he was consecrated Bishop of Haiti, the first African American so designated by the Episcopal Church.

frequent seizure in the North of colored men, women, and children, who are sent into slavery, have measurably alienated our feelings toward this country; dispelled the lingering patriotism from our bosoms, which compels us to regard as our common enemy every white, who proves not himself to the contrary." The Convention, emphasizing that they were tired of talking and ready to act, sent out "Foreign Commissioners" to scout out possible destinations in "the Western Continent" for emigration and report to the next Convention, which, they hoped, would be the last one necessary.[36]

The conflicting aims of the two convention movements shattered whatever national unity the Rochester Convention had hoped to symbolize and achieve, and for the remainder of the pre-Civil War years neither was able to regain a sense of momentum. State and local meetings would provide most of whatever organized action was possible.[37]

Still, there was considerable prestige associated with presiding at the National Convention in Rochester, and that may have encouraged James Pennington to approach the trustees of the Shiloh Church with a request for financial help. Five hundred dollars a year may have seemed adequate when Pennington first came to New York, but a good mechanic could earn that much[†] and the cost of housing and feeding a family of three in the city was undoubtedly greater than he had expected. There may have been some small income from speaking engagements and his writing, but there would also have been considerable cost involved in traveling to various places. George Templeton Strong, a young lawyer in his late twenties, records constant concern in his diary about making ends meet on an invested income of $3000 and earnings of $2500.[38] But a white lawyer and a black pastor lived in very different worlds. To accommodate their pastor, the trustees and elders of the congregation felt it necessary to send a letter in August to the secretaries of the American Home Missionary Society, requesting further help. The letter did not offer the kind of complete picture of the congregation's membership and financial situation that the secretaries might have found helpful, but the trustees and elders seemed not to have that kind of information; the Presbytery had already complained of their record keeping. In neatly numbered summary, they reported:

1. Our present no of members it is difficult to state. Since the commencement of the church (1822) 648 have been added. For the past year we have at each communion 85 as an average.
2. These persons are entirely laborers.
3. The Trustees pay the Pastor $500.

† *Connecticut Courant*, January 16, 1856.

4. The Pastor feels that $700 is the lowest sum he can subsist upon in N.Y. as rents, provisions, now are.

5. The Shiloh, or Prince St church, therefore hereby as [sic] for $200 from the year commencing September 1, 1854 to be paid to the Treasurer of our church to aid them in paying said Pastor a salary of $700 per annum.

The wording of point 4 may indicate that the trustees were able to subsist on less themselves and were not wholly persuaded of their pastor's need. Pennington's August report to the American Home Missionary Society supported the request by pointing out that "up to this date" the trustees of the Shiloh Church had paid his salary of $500 "punctually and satisfactorily" in addition to the special collections made for various purposes.

Although James Pennington had had no time to respond to Washington Stickney's attack in the midst of his other activities, there was a response in September 1854, from an unexpected quarter. William Nell, a Bostonian and Garrisonian open-minded enough to have attended the Rochester Convention but closed-minded enough to have voted against every resolution there presented, published a letter in the *Liberator*, a journal more inclined to agree with Stickney in condemning any slightest appearance of unity with slaveholders. Nell's letter was, in fact, not a direct reply to Stickney but a report on a meeting he had attended in New York where "a large audience" had gathered in the Southac Street Baptist Church "to hear an anti-slavery lecture from Rev. J.W.C. Pennington." Pennington, Nell wrote, had spoken about his escape from slavery and that of his brother and nephews and provided some "reflections on American slavery." At the end of the lecture, one of those present asked Pennington about the resolutions adopted by the Third Presbytery of New York as they had "created much remark" and Pennington "was reported to have agreed to their passage." The questioner said he knew nothing of the facts but wished "to afford Dr. Pennington the opportunity to set himself right before the people." The resolution was quoted as Stickney had reported it, though without the italics, and had concluded by "committing this whole subject . . . to the government of Eternal Providence" and calling on the churches "to offer unceasing prayer for our country in all its sections, and for our church in all its interests."

Pennington told the audience that the Presbytery was composed entirely of white men except for himself, and he should not be blamed for their faults. He told his hearers that he had opposed the resolution and had told the Presbytery that whatever resolution was passed would not be binding on his conscience. Another member of the audience then said that he had thought the question "an impropriety" when it was put but was now glad it had been asked and answered; he hoped "those who were attempting to destroy the usefulness of those men of God, who were making great sacrifices for humanity, would feel rebuked." The meeting then went on to other subjects.[39]

Nell's letter should have set the record straight, but charges continued to be made nonetheless. In October, *The National Anti Slavery Standard* published a letter Parker Pillsbury had written to the *Glasgow Sentinel* in October 1854, which denounced Pennington for directing English and Scottish audiences to the support of vigilance committees and Canadian refugees "instead of aiding the anti slavery cause." Pillsbury's opinion, endorsed by a Glaswegian writing as "Nicholas," was that even if abolitionists were infidels, it was still a duty to overthrow slavery, and that "no amount of churches or ministers for the colored race, whether bond or free; nor of coloured schools or colleges; nor of vigilance committees . . . nor of missions to assist those who have effected their escape to Canada, can do much for the anti-slavery cause." The immediate concerns of African Americans were irrelevant to Pillsbury and Nicholas; only changing public opinion was important. "The true Abolitionist," as Nicholas summed it up, "is uncompromising. He knows and feels that his object is right, and that no pretence of religion or policy which opposes him is worthy of respect. If the interests of sects or parties be incompatible with his object they must be wrong" and that is why the true Abolitionists are the "champions and only true friends" of "the colored race."[40] It was a viewpoint that welcomed no allies and tolerated no divergence from the party line; it seemed sometimes to be angrier at moderate Northerners than at Southern slave owners. Pennington, Nicholas and Pillsbury complained, "comes to Great Britain as an Abolitionist . . . representing vigilance committees as anti-slavery instrumentalities on the one hand, and, in the other, misrepresenting the only genuine active Abolitionists in America as infidels. . . . And then Dr. Pennington goes home to New York, to sit in the bosom of one of the most corrupt pro-slavery bodies this world of wickedness has produced." Not to be overlooked in this lengthy tirade is a sentence noting that a result of Pennington's work had been that "he perverts the sympathies of many of the humane and good who really wish well to the cause of the slave and would gladly aid it."[41] Pillsbury, in other words, had gone to England to raise money and was annoyed to discover that people had already given to the causes Pennington espoused rather than those supported by Pillsbury. The resolution passed by the Third Presbytery that had so outraged Washington Stickney outraged Pillsbury as well, but Pillsbury told his readers that Pennington had not only said "he concurred in the resolution" but that he also voted for it, which was simply mot true.[42] Even Stickney did not charge that.

The *Liberator* returned to the attack in January of 1855, publishing a letter from "S. W. W." who had attended a lecture in Newport, R.I., that Pennington had given just before Christmas, 1854. S. W. W. had not been at the lecture but had a written report from a friend who was there. W wanted the *Liberator* to know that Pennington's "sectarian religion is of more consequence to him than the emancipation of the slaves. I believe this is the man," he continued, "who went to England, and kept away from a large congregation in New York City—in consequence of the passage of the Fugitive Slave Law, fearing he might be caught by some of Millard Fillmore's officials, and sent back to slavery, from which he had run away." The friend's rather lengthy report quotes Pennington as saying that "*He first wished it expressly understood, by all, that he was not connected with that class of abolitionists, or reformers, called infidels*" and he hoped that fact "would secure to him a candid hearing!"†

According to W's friend, Pennington had spoken also of the Northern Church and said he thought they did not design to avoid the subject of slavery but had not "given it proper thought" or "considered its effect on the colored people." Likewise he was reported to have thought that the political parties were not so much evil as "misled." He spoke also of the commercial interests and how he had come to understand in England that "it was for their interest" to act in a way that benefitted the slaveowners. He hoped the Northern merchants "would not foster, encourage and abet" the "despotic designs" of the slave owners. He had advocated a boycott of Southern merchandise and hoped petitions would be sent to Congress to prevent the domestic slave trade. He had spoken of "the great evils of slavery," but W's friend saw it as a very "mild and temperate speech" that "would do for a Newport audience" and perhaps "open the way . . . for a more thorough, fearless anti-slavery lecturer than the present one."[43] Such a second-hand report before an unknown audience is, of course, difficult to assess. Perhaps, indeed, it was exactly the right speech for an audience that had not been persuaded of the abolitionist cause and might have been alienated by Garrisonian jeremiads. But it was another example of the continuing criticism that Pennington had to deal with as a recognized leader in the New York school of abolitionism. He might denounce the evils of slavery, call for a boycott of Southern goods, and refuse slave owners communion in his church, but it would not satisfy the Boston abolitionists or those still affiliated with them.

The *National Anti Slavery Standard*, the New York paper of the Garrisonian abolitioniists, summarized the *Liberator*'s article briefly and added its own comments. "He [Pennington] has so little moral principle and self-respect," the

---

† Presumably the italics and exclamation mark were provided by W's friend.

paper editorialized, "as to be willing to remain a minister of the man-stealing Presbyterian Church, half of whose clergy and membership would unhesitatingly consent to his reënslavement, were it not for the fact that British gold[†] had made him the owner of his own body. It is equally natural that a clerical associate and toady of the Rev. Dr. Cox should go about the country, uttering lying insinuations that real Abolitionists are 'infidels.' Is it our duty to spare such men on account of their complexion?"[44]

Perhaps as a deliberate balance to such attacks, supporters in New York arranged a special program in early February. The announcement of "an intellectual entertainment" at the Broadway Tabernacle of which "the Rev. Dr. Pennington of the African Church" would be the beneficiary appeared in the *New York Daily Tribune* but, since none of the surviving newspapers reported the event itself, we can only guess what it may have been like.[45] An "intellectual entertainment" might well have included James McCune Smith reading one of his carefully researched papers on immigration trends or comparative death rates among African Americans in the North and in the South. Writers and speakers like Charles Ray might have been called on to speak on a subject of interest to them. Pennington himself might have contributed to the evening by talking about his research into African civilization. Probably there was singing and undoubtedly there was food contributed by the ladies of the church. Presumably those present were given an opportunity to contribute to a fund to help Pennington with his finances. Pennington, in any event, would not afterwards have felt that he needed to face his attackers alone.

---

† "British" was still often used as an epithet less than a century after the American Revolution. It was, however, partly the contest to acquire British gold for their own organization that intensified the conflict between Garrisonian and non-Garrisonian abolitionists.

CHAPTER TWENTY

New York, 1855

While James Pennington was being attacked and defended, Chester Arthur was preparing his case against the 3rd Avenue Railroad Company and, in February 1855, the jury found in Jennings's favor. Judge William Rockwell, agreeing with the jury, declared that "Colored persons if sober, well behaved and free from disease, had the same rights as others and could neither be excluded by any rules of the Company, nor by force or violence." Jennings had sued for $500 in damages and the majority of the jury was prepared to give her the full amount, but a persuasive minority argued them into settling on an award of $225—still a substantial amount in those days—and another $22.50 in costs. The 3rd Avenue Company ordered its cars integrated the next day.[1]

The *Tribune* editorialized that "Railroads, steamboats, omnibuses and ferry-boats will be admonished from this as to the rights of respectable colored people. It is time the rights of this class of citizens were ascertained, and that it should be known whether they are to be thrust from our public conveyances, while German or Irish women, with a quarter of mutton or a load of codfish, can be admitted."[2]

But the rights of all to ride the omnibuses was not that easily "ascertained." On Saturday of the same week in which the Jennings case was decided, a woman was ordered off an Eighth Avenue car. She refused to leave and told the conductor that her rights had been established by a judicial decision in Brooklyn. The conductor told her that he was under orders and, when she still refused to leave, he called the driver to assist him. After "a desperate struggle of some minutes, [he] forced her out into the middle of the street, where she was left in the bitter cold, her clothes badly torn and herself somewhat injured." The next Monday another woman was refused entrance to an Eighth Avenue car in spite of the cold, and James Pennington called on the mayor to restrain the company and its conductors and compel them to obey the law.[3] These very personal struggles, victories and defeats at the local level, often did more to shape public opinion than the carefully worded "addresses to the American people" issued by conventions. One small victory in a Brooklyn courtroom would give some reason to hope, while the capture and return to slavery of an Anthony Burns or James Pennington's nephews would give others cause for despair. It was to ensure that small victories would not be lost and defeats be less likely, that Thomas Jennings, James Pennington, and a few others had formed the Legal Rights Association.

With the Jennings case decided, James Pennington felt free at last to respond to the various attacks that had been made on him in the public press. He was familiar with the press and had used it often to set out his opinions and goals, frequently writing a series of articles over a period of many months. Now he wrote to Frederick Douglass, taking note of the fact that "statements have been going the rounds . . . tending—I will not say designed—to convict me of pro-slavery sentiment and action" and saying that "My aversion to controversy is one of the reasons why I have not, ere this, taken notice of these statements in this public manner. Those who know me, personally, will appreciate this reason." But Pennington wrote that "there is a point . . . beyond which even forbearance ceases to be a virtue." It was, he wrote, "beyond endurance" that "men belonging to a race which has done so much to oppress, wrong, and outrage my race, should take so special pains to convict me of treachery to my own race." Therefore he was asking Douglass for "space in your columns, from time to time, to defend myself against these cruel and unreasonable aggressions. My motto is *the race is not to the swift, nor the battle to the strong.*' Give good old Truth time, and she will beat the world."

This opening letter was comparatively brief but cited, first of all, "deeply engraven on my soul's memory twenty-one years' awful experience of Slavery, in all its forms; and twenty-nine years of self-denying, hazardous, odious, expensive abolition in which I will yield to no man the palm—no, sir, not even to yourself. I think, therefore, I may afford to speak a few words, when accused of treachery to my race." There had been, he pointed out, no vigilance committee in existence when he came out of slavery, nor any of the anti-slavery societies now in existence, and "no one of the present anti-slavery leaders had appeared upon the platform." Pennington was clearly angry and wanted the world to know that he felt the attacks against him to be not only unfair but deeply unprincipled. He would not only defend himself but challenge anyone to bring their criticism forward openly. No one, he wrote, could tell him what opinions to hold in the pulpit or public platform; his views on slavery and "kindred subjects . . . are neither bought nor borrowed from any class of men—I inherit them from the bosom of my dear enslaved mother, and as I love her memory, I will stand by them till I die. If the time has come, when colored men are to be persecuted for freedom of opinion in regard to their own cause, let us know it, and let us prepare for an open and manly fight."[4]

Theology, for Pennington, was also very often a local matter. In March of 1855, he wrote to the *New York Tribune* to tell the story of how an African American New Yorker, going about his business, had been suddenly seized as a criminal. The man was a deck hand on the *George Steer*, a pilot boat, and was about to step on board when two plainclothes officers, looking for a burglar, demanded he go with them. The man asked them to show a warrant for his arrest or evidence of their authority, but the officers continued to insist that he go with them. Two passers-by stepped up to support the man and say that a warrant was needed. Two officers in uniform then appeared to identify the first men as officers and say "he had better go with them to the Court's office." The man, with his two friends, then went to the court where, "after some examination," he was discharged. So the matter might have been said to have ended happily, but James Pennington was not content to let it rest. "This matter calls for explanation," he wrote. "Officers, starred or unstarred, have no right to arrest a man on charge of a serious crime without a warrant, or without knowing his name." Nor was it only a matter of insisting on proper forms and procedures. Black citizens could not be certain of the protection of the law even inside a courthouse. "It is certainly not safe in these times," Pennington told the *Tribune* and its readers, "for a colored man to be led into a place surrounded by so many gates and bars, without the protection of a legal warrant."[5]

Such incidents were constantly occurring, and Pennington was constantly working to make a larger public aware of them. In July of 1855, when a Southern slave owner, newly named as ambassador to Nicaragua. came through Philadelphia en route to his new assignment with his slaves, Passmore Williamson and a group of local abolitionists forcibly abducted Jane Johnson, one of the slaves, and her two small children. Charged with "riot, forcible abduction, and assault," Williamson was convicted and spent three months in prison, drawing attention to the case and visits from Frederick Douglass and Harriet Tubman, among others. Pennington sent Williamson and his colleagues an open letter on behalf of the Shiloh Church, assuring them of the sympathy of the congregation. "The shadow of the law, without a shade of justice," might condemn them, but "many other true lovers of liberty" were "awake to the value of men who aim to extend freedom."[6]

Meanwhile, in April, Part Two of James Pennington's self-defense appeared in *Frederick Douglass' Paper*. His letter, when it came, was dated simply "March," so it may have been written fairly soon after his February 23rd letter and been delayed by the newspaper's priorities. "I am accused of pro-slavery sentiment and action," he begins, and charges his accusers instead with "the guilt of false accusation." But where, he asks, is the proof: "Come, let me have it." And now, for the first time, he pushes back against his attackers as unqualified to understand him. "I am a black man," he writes, "and of 3rd generation from pure Mandingo stock." The attacks, Pennington asserts, have not come from "any descendant of my race or nation . . . then, why should white men seek this quarrel with me? . . . Can they emancipate my enslaved brethren by abusing, and misrepresenting me? I think not." As in the February letter, Pennington stresses the fact that he has achieved what he has largely without assistance. "I have emancipated myself," he writes, "and have worked my way up to a standing amongst the *Men* of this land, and of the world; and I ask, why should these men pounce upon me as if I were an Alabama slaveholder?" In this perspective, he quotes at length from the letter he wrote to the *Long Island Star* after the first Negro National Convention in 1830, putting heavy emphasis on the claim he made to the rights and privileges of American citizenship and saluting his attackers as "Brethren." "We are not strangers," he had written, "neither do we come under the alien law; our Constitution does not call upon us to become naturalized; we are already American citizens. Our forefathers were among the first that peopled this country . . . and shall we forsake their tombs, and flee to an unknown land?" He goes on to tell the story of how Adrian Van Sinderen had questioned him about his letter to the paper and his opposition to the Colonization Society, and how Van Sinderen, who might have chosen to "take umbrage at my daring," had instead resigned from the society of which he was president. "Such," he concludes, "were some of the difficulties that beset my way," and why had he persisted? It was, he writes, because he was "moved by my own patriotic spirit." The contrast is clear between his conduct and that of the Garrisonians, who took their stand in opposition to the government and refused to pay taxes or accept the responsibilities of citizenship. His concern is to reform the government and make it recognize its own stated ideals, not to destroy it, and certainly not to abandon the three million still living in slavery by dividing the nation into two entities, one slave and one free. But he emphasizes also, again, that he has come to his present position without help, and certainly without the help of the Garrisonians. "I stole my freedom, and I took my licence, and have gone on studying the system of slavery from my own standpoint—that of one who knows it from the inside as his attackers do not—[and] opposing it in all its forms." The final line repeats the opening challenge: "[I]f any man knows to the contrary, let him bring the proof."[7]

The third installment in James Pennington's self-defense came just one month later and focused on an editorial that had been published some two years earlier in the *Pennsylvania Freeman*. Like the other attacks, it found Pennington's membership in the Presbyterian Church reprehensible and his election as moderator of the Third Presbytery of New York grounds for a violent attack on his character. It considered also that the situation was worse because Samuel Cox was another member of the same Presbytery. "That Dr. Pennington, who has felt in his own person, the miseries and horrors of slavery, should be a member of that Presbytery, or any other forming a constituent part of the Presbyterian Church, is a fact which we cannot explain without supposing him to be either ignorant of that church in respect to slavery, or lacking in self-respect and sympathy for them [sic] in bonds." Pennington responds to that with scorn: "[T]o dispose of a question of such grave importance . . . by three sweeping suppositions, without a single argument, is a specimen of logic I have not met with in any book on that science I ever read . . ." Like any good preacher, Pennington here is "reminded of a story" that was told by "Uncle Taff," a blacksmithing master workman under whom he had worked as a young man. Uncle Taff in turn liked to tell stories of a man named "Wise Peter," who could give a reason for any fact with the result that the slaves would resort to him to settle questions in dispute. One day some slave children had brought him a dead bat that had flown into a building with such force that it was more than a little deformed. Wise Peter surveyed the thing from several angles and turned it over with a stick and finally, "with a very sage-like nearer glance," announced that it was "either a ground mole or a flying squirrel." The story (like many preachers' stories) is not terribly relevant but does put the *Pennsylvania Freeman*'s editor down as likewise dealing with things beyond his level of competence.

"[T]o be serious," Pennington goes on, the paper seems not to understand "that colored men have as strong a jealousy of their rights of private judgment and conscience as white men have." So the editor "mends his pen" and attempts to explain a fact "by three suppositions and no argument." If the editor chose to attack the Presbyterian Church, that would be his right, Pennington writes, but it has no right to tell him what church he can belong to or where his "fugitive heel" can find a resting place. That is a matter of private judgment and individual conscience. "Has the *Freeman* read the history of the Pilgrims," Pennington asks, "and others who have suffered for their right of private judgment? . . . I recognize no Lord of my conscience but God only." Pennington provides a flurry of Biblical references to Pharaoh and the Amalekites, but the gist of his argument is that as a free man he has a right to make choices and he rejects completely the notion "that a mere profession of abolitionism gives any white man a right to take me by the coat button and lead me where he will." It is at last a matter of white men unwilling to recognize black men as equals. "We become obnoxious to some of our professed friends, because we do not gee and haw, and come into and out of the traces at their bidding."[8]

In April, the Third Presbytery of New York held its annual meeting, and James Pennington "officiated as secretary."[9] The Presbytery might not agree with him on the issue of slavery, but surely the fact that he was chosen to serve as an officer at their meetings was not without significance. Should he have withdrawn from their meetings as a protest against the Presbytery's stand on slavery, or presided as a witness to the Presbytery's willingness to recognize his abilities? James Pennington and his attackers obviously saw the question very differently.

One more letter in the series of Pennington's answers to his attackers appeared in Douglass's paper a week later. It came in response to a letter from "M. H. Tuttle" of Albion, Michigan, who had written to Pennington almost a year earlier at the request, he said, of the Albion Anti Slavery Society. Tuttle had written to say that the Society had received an appeal for help in setting Stephen Pembroke and his sons free from slavery. They had decided not to respond with assistance since they believed Pennington to have concurred in the vote of the New York Presbytery that it was "undesirable and inexpedient" to take a stand on slavery and "If you thus joined hands with the pro slavery hypocrites, to thus treat the system of *stealing your fellow man* and your brother, then *we desire to say to you* that *we* think it undesirable and inexpedient to offer you any aid in your pretended deep affliction." Pennington called the letter "a gross and cruel insult" and surely not less cruel for being, apparently, a private communication made public only in his response. That reply is brief: he had made no appeal to Tuttle for aid to his brother; what Tuttle states in regard to Pennington's action in Presbytery is "not true," and a thousand dollars had come in response to his appeal from members of Congress, governors, and many others, even inmates of orphan schools, who rejoiced when his brother was redeemed. "No word or sentence of congratulation," however, had come from Albion. "Let the world judge between us."[10]

Publication of the last two of these letters would have framed, before and after, the days of the second week of May that had become the traditional time for organizations to hold their annual meetings in New York City. They called it "Anniversary Week," and at least twenty-seven various societies participated in 1855.[†] Many of them used the Broadway Tabernacle for at least one major session, and sometimes two organizations met there on the same day, though at different times. Some organizations found New York so crowded with charitable societies that they held their meetings in Brooklyn. The National Council of the Colored People began its session on the 8th of the month at the Shiloh Church, and the next day the American Anti-Slavery Society took up its twenty-second anniversary meeting at the Metropolitan Theatre on Broadway, but there was no conflict of dates because there was no overlap of membership. The Anti-Slavery Society was

† Organizations meeting in New York included the American Anti Slavery Society, the American and Foreign Anti Slavery Society, the American Colonization Society, the American Bible Society, the New York Institute for the Blind, the American Swedenborgian Printing and Publishing Society, the American Temperance Union, the American Female Guardian Society, the New York Asylum for Idiots, etc. (*New York Herald*, May 14, 1855.)

almost as vehemently anti-church as it was anti-slavery. Men like Pennington and Smith would have not been comfortable with a resolution that was "warmly approved" by William Lloyd Garrison's followers in their opening session:

> Resolved, that for the continuance and extension of slavery on our soil the American Church and clergy, with honourable but rare exceptions, are preeminently guilty, and that they have thrown over it the mantle of Christianity, declared it to be in accordance with the will of God, branded the Anti-Slavery movement as infidel in its spirit and object, and admitted to the communion table such as make merchandise of human bodies and immortal souls.[11]

Pennington as a Presbyterian and Smith as an Episcopalian were clearly members of churches that had incurred Garrisonian wrath by doing their best to avoid taking sides on the slavery question. That each had in one way or another moved his church toward a greater openness toward black Americans, Pennington by serving as moderator or secretary of his presbytery and Smith by serving on the vestry of a church which was finally accepted into union with the diocese, made no difference to the Garrisonians. Their policy was separation and denunciation, thus cutting themselves off from those with whom they differed. Smith and Pennington might, of course, have considered themselves to be among the "honourable but rare exceptions," but they would have been uncomfortable among idealists who seemed sometimes more anxious to condemn than to reform. One resolution alone condemned more than a dozen Christian organizations, from the American Bible Society and American Home Missionary Society to Presbyterian, Methodist, and Moravian missionary societies. All these, they agreed, "ought to be instantly abandoned by every one claiming to be a friend of liberty and a disciple of Christ the Redeemer."[12]

James McCune Smith was in New York that week, as was Frederick Douglass, to press ahead with the National Council of the Colored People, to which Smith especially was deeply committed. The third semi-annual meeting of the Council met at "Dr. Pennington's Church"[†] in response to a notice from Smith that called on delegates to "take such . . . steps as shall prove, that although among the oppressed and down-trodden, you are prepared to resist and overcome oppression in your own behalf, and in behalf of your bleeding brethren of the South . . . Wo [sic] be to you if you do not faithfully struggle to carry out at whatever cost the Gospel of Abolition, Elevation and Affranchisement!"[13] Six states were finally represented, though Connecticut and Vermont missed the opening session. Seven states were said to have organized state councils. In his

† The terminology is that of the *Anti-Slavery Bugle*, May 19, 1855.

opening address, Smith sounded the same notes as in the notice of meeting and urged that they had no need to rely on others; they had the power themselves to change their circumstances. "From the mere act of riding in public conveyances up to the immediate and entire abolition of Slavery in the slave states, the law and the Constitution of the country are clearly on our side." He noted the integration of public schools in Massachusetts, actions of the Connecticut legislature to grant equal suffrage, action in New York State to abolish the property requirement for black voters, signs of progress toward enfranchisement in Pennsylvania. All this he attributed to "the almost isolated labors of less than a hundred colored men; I had almost said of five." What, then, he asked, could be accomplished by ten thousand? "It is emphatically our battle," he urged; "no one else can fight it for us." Instead of depending on the anti-slavery movement, Smith told the delegates they must take the lead themselves.

All this, however, led to only one specific recommendation: to create an "Industrial School; and a plan by which our rising youths may forsake menial employments for mechanical and mercantile occupations." Such a school had been recommended first in Philadelphia more than twenty years earlier, but it was still a dream; John Bonner of Illinois, who chaired the committee, reported that nothing had been done. "Owing to a combination of circumstances wholly unavoidable and unexpected by us we have been prevented from making any successful efforts toward establishing the contemplated school, but we are not without hope . . ." The remainder of the day was spent debating the proposal, and it was clear that there was no consensus at all as to either the feasibility or usefulness of such a school. Smith had said in his opening address that the free colored people of New York and Pennsylvania alone had the means to establish and richly endow such a school, but Bonner thought economic conditions in the country were such that fund raising had been impossible. James Pennington, one of four New York delegates, suggested that education of every sort was a good thing for black and white alike, but if blacks must do it separately, so be it. One delegate wanted to know what the cost would be, and Smith said $30,000 would be needed. Douglass, however, thought $5,000 would be enough to make a start. One delegate thought they would never find white men to teach black children a trade, but another thought they had all the skills needed themselves. Still another delegate thought that even if they learned a trade, no white man would employ them. Pennington, whose interventions seemed more theoretical than practical, said that he thought schools for white as well as black might be founded. George

---

† George Downing (1819–1903) was the son of Thomas Downing and became a wealthy man in his own right. He traveled between Newport, RI, New York, and Washington and worked to desegregate Rhode Island schools, the Baltimore and Ohio Railroad, and the Senate galleries in Washington. (Alexander, op. cit.)

Downing† of Rhode Island thought the plan was impractical. Stephen Meyers, another New York delegate, noted that even the strongest white abolitionists (he may have had Lewis Tappan in mind) "might employ a colored boy as a porter or packer, but would as soon put a hod-carrier to the clerk's desk as a colored boy, ever so well educated though he be." In the evening session, Smith turned over the chair to Bonner and urged that "There is no use further holding these Councils and passing first-rate resolutions, unless we do something tangible and show our people what may be accomplished . . . We must start this school and make it work." But Phillip Bell of New York still thought "the whole plan was impracticable," and Charles Remond of Massachusetts thought whatever gains the black man had made were due to the abolitionists and he "was not prepared to turn his back on them." At the end of the evening the question was put, and the plan for a school was affirmed by a vote of seven to five. Pennington was either absent or abstaining. The second day moved on to the question of calling another national convention and agreed to set one in place for Philadelphia in October. Efforts were made to appoint a finance committee and agents for the industrial school, but one after another of those appointed asked to be excused and finally the matter was left in the hands of the Manual School Committee. On the third day it was agreed to constitute the Council as a "Committee in Trades and Employment" to try to match young people interested in learning trades with white employers willing to train them. And so, with "the customary compliments to their officers the Council adjourned *sine die*."[14]

That evening a public meeting was held at the Shiloh Church, attended by a large and "decidedly mixed" audience. Pennington opened the meeting with prayer and spoke briefly in opposition to colonization and in favor of the proposed industrial schools for blacks. Frederick Douglass then spoke for nearly two hours, covering a wide range of subjects, before Charles L. Remond closed with some dissenting remarks defending Garrisonian abolitionism.[15]

Frederick Douglass came away from the meeting believing that it "evinced the dawning of organic life of a people long scattered by ignorance and crushed by slavery and oppression."[16] William C. Nell, on the other hand, writing for Garrison's *Liberator*, had attended the meeting but was "predisposed against any participation . . . [and] negatived all the questions submitted during his stay."† He reported for his paper that "It is an undeniable fact that the colored people of the several States are not in harmony with the National Council and their proceedings." Nell quoted resolutions adopted by another meeting held

† Nell was not listed as a delegate, so it is unclear that he could have voted or that he did. He is mentioned in the minutes as having declined to serve on the Finance Committee "from conscientious scruples." "W. C. Bell" was listed as voting in the negative on the only recorded vote and, since there was no W. C. Bell listed as a delegate, that may have been Nell.

in New York that took issue with the Council's goals. Taking note of the call for a convention in Philadelphia next October, he suggested that "much good might be anticipated" if that convention were made an anti-slavery convention and invited "those friendly, irrespective of complexion."[17] But the majority of the black leadership had experience of the way white people tended to take over such meetings and had long ago decided that they needed to have their own agenda even if there were few measurable results. The interracial anti-slavery societies had little to show for their work in any event.

"A man's reach should exceed his grasp," said the poet, "or what's a heaven for?" But the hopes and dreams of the series of African American conventions were for real-world accomplishments and exceeded their grasp precisely because the leaders were dreamers, clergy and teachers, speakers and writers, men of ideas without experience of administration. They could create a structure on paper but not make it function. They were a very few black men who had run a business, but they were mostly the Pennsylvanians who had come to the first conventions and then focused their efforts on moral reform. James Forten had run a sailmaking business with white employees and made a fortune. William Whipper and Stephen Smith had run a successful lumber business. Richard Allen, the African Methodist bishop, had also been a successful businessman. New Yorkers, on the other hand, like James McCune Smith and Frederick Douglass, did their best to make the Councils useful and create the school that the Tappan brothers and Simeon Jocelyn had first proposed so long ago, but they had neither the skills nor the resources to make it happen. So their plans failed, but the ideals they voiced so eloquently made a difference, forcing white Americans to consider the basic immorality of their society and inspiring black Americans to believe in a better future.

The *New York Herald* compared the National Council meeting with the meeting of the American Anti Slavery Society and found that Garrison and his followers attracted more attention, although the audience at the Council meeting was described as "quite large and decidedly mixed." The *Herald* also found that the two gatherings reflected "the cause of religion and Christianity" on the one hand and "treason and infidelity" on the other. The *Herald* preferred the Council's "moderation, common sense and reasoning ability"[18] but may not have remembered a speech of Frederick Douglass's four days earlier in which he remarked that "The idea prevails everywhere in this country that as a people, however much we may talk of our love of liberty, and the regard for our rights and the knowledge of our rights . . . that we care too little about them to defend them when assailed by force. I would have every colored man defend them when the law does not protect them and surrender his liberty only with his life. I would have you fight for your liberty when assailed by the slave hunter. This will gain you some respect. . . . Fear inculcates respect. I would rather see insurrection for the next six months in the South than that slavery should exist there for six more years."[19]

There was another very practical issue that James Pennington was deeply involved in that spring that mattered deeply to him and his parishioners. He took the occasion after his first Sunday sermon in May to advise his congregation to remind any of their friends who would be coming to the city for these meetings "that colored people could no longer be excluded from the City public conveyances as was formerly the usage." He told them that a judicial decision had already placed the matter of public conveyances in the hands of the colored people themselves, and they would be to blame if they long continued subject to the great disadvantages involved by the proscriptions of conductors and drivers of cars and omnibuses. Individual leaders like Frederick Douglass had long resisted segregation in public transportation, but now Pennington was calling on the rank and file to resist also. He said that "nothing short of the utmost tameness and cowardice, would induce colored men and women who valued their rights, to surrender the privilege of common transit along the regular thoroughfares of the busy City."[20]

That message was then reinforced with a notice that Pennington had published in *Frederick Douglass' Paper*: "To the numerous colored ladies and gentlemen who may visit this city during the coming anniversary week, let me say:

1. That all our public carrier conveyances are now open to them upon equal terms.
2. No policeman will now, as formerly, assist in assaulting you.
3. If any driver or conductor molests you, by laying the weight of his finger upon your person, have him arrested, or call upon Dr. Smith, 55 West Broadway, Mr. T. L. Jenning, [sic] 167 Church-st., or myself, 29 Sixth-av., and we will enter your complaint at the Mayor's office.
4. You can take the conveyances at any of the Ferries or stopping places. Ask no questions, but get in and have your five cents ready to pay. Don't let them frighten you with words; the law is right and so is the public sentiment.
5. J. W. C. Pennington, New York, May 1855.[21]

Anniversary Week was barely started when one delegate tested the reliability of Pennington's advice. Sidney McFarland, who had made a similar attempt ten years earlier, refused to leave a Sixth Avenue Railroad car when the conductor told him to, with the result that the driver was summoned and together they pitched McFarland over the back railing of the car. As he had done in the first case, McFarland went to court accusing the conductor and driver of assault and battery, and this time the judge responded to his complaint by having the two trainmen arrested. There was no immediate decision, but the newspaper reported that the case had "created a great sensation among the conductors on the various city railroads."[22] The Jennings case had not apparently persuaded a good many railroad men that anything much had changed, but if judges were no longer dismissing such cases out of hand, they might have to pay attention.

Two weeks later, James Pennington himself was ordered to leave a Sixth Avenue streetcar. Having told his congregation what to do unless they were afflicted with "the utmost tameness and unjustifiable, indeed impious cowardice," he found himself without much choice except to provide an example. He therefore refused to leave, and the conductor and driver proceeded to remove him by force. Once outside, Pennington held on to the car and, since the horses drawing the car were proceeding at a walk, managed to run behind it, although the conductor stamped on his hands to try to force him to let go. When the car reached the depot, Pennington found an officer and asked him to arrest his assailants. The officer had never before been asked by a black person to arrest a white person and told Pennington he had no intention of doing so. The train left on its return trip and Pennington, insisting on his rights, found himself arrested and taken to court where the case was dismissed by a Justice Connelly—with a warning of severe consequences if he were brought there again.[23] [24]

Now, however, there was a Legal Rights Association and the New York justice system could not simply dismiss a case and have it go away. Pennington went the next day to a lawyer prepared to deal with such issues and filed a complaint. Had he not done so, the case would still have drawn attention. Fernando Wood, the mayor of New York, was informed of the case and wrote to the streetcar company for an explanation. The secretary of the company, T. Bailey Myers, responded indignantly that his company had generously provided one car every half hour for colored persons (as compared with one every three or four minutes for others) and that they were also free to ride on the platform of the other cars. He knew of no other company in the country, he said, that did as much. The railroad's business, Myers told the mayor, was to carry passengers and "we have nothing to do with the color of their skin, only with the color of their money, and the comfort and convenience of all." But Pennington had been causing trouble, Myers complained, by urging his parishioners to assert their right to ride in all public conveyances. One member of Pennington's congregation, he said, had done so the next day, had been removed, had obtained a warrant for the arrest of the conductor and driver, had had his charges dismissed, and was suing the company. Since then a number of others had attempted to do the same, he wrote, and finally Pennington himself. Myers was willing to give him credit for attempting "to practise as he had preached," but he must know that many people were unwilling to sit beside a black passenger, and he would do better to waive his rights than "force himself in where a large majority do not wish him" and he would lose more by success than failure. "Even the metaphysical air of Heidelberg, where he took his degree is not free of prejudices, if not those of color," Myers told the mayor, "and many, in this more practical country, who are willing to recognize a black in the abstract, as a man and a brother, are not quite prepared to carry it into practice into our cars."[25] That, of course, was all too true.

Frederick Douglass, on the other hand, cheered Pennington on: "We hope that the matter will not be allowed to rest here," he wrote. "We do not believe that the people . . . would prefer sitting by the side of a white man, a dirty white man, with a cod-fish, or a bunch of onions in his hand, to sitting by the side of a respectable colored man. And in this case, the conductor has ejected *the right man*, a respectable Doctor of Divinity! What will his brother Doctors say? Suppose Dr. Bethune had been ejected from the same car, for his *physical rotundity*, what a time there would have been in New York! And yet the conductor had no more right to eject Dr. Pennington than Dr. Bethune. We anxiously await the issue of the present struggle of the colored people in New York to ride in the public conveyances. They will ultimately triumph; let them persevere, let them develop their manhood, and it will, at length, be recognized."[26]

The Legal Rights Association called a public meeting to encourage broad support for Pennington and to reiterate their contention that public conveyances should be open to all. Pennington told the meeting that if he was beaten in one court, he would take his case to another, and if he were defeated there he would carry the campaign to the ballot box. A "sense of the meeting" resolution expressed outrage at the continuing denial of this basic right and urged everyone present to enroll in the Association.[27]

The case did not come up for trial until December 1856, which meant that the Sixth Avenue line saw no immediate need to change its policies. With that trial hanging over him, Pennington found himself forced to pay attention to some complex financial matters, the aspect of his life that he was least able to control successfully. At the end of June, Lewis Tappan, reviving a matter that had first emerged four years earlier, wrote to Pennington to tell him that he owed money to Lord Elgin, whom he had come to know while in Jamaica nine years earlier. Now, apparently, Lord Elgin had sent word to Lewis Tappan concerning twenty pounds owed by James Pennington to Elgin because, as Tappan put it, Pennington had "improperly secured money for an object that did not exist" and "milked" the name of Lord Elgin for that purpose. Pennington apparently responded that he had offered to refund the money to Elgin's messenger four years earlier and he had declined to take it. Tappan wrote again on July 18 to say that, if that was the case, then Pennington owed no interest on it but was still under obligation to pay it if requested. "I advise you to pay the money without delay," Tappan wrote; "You would not like to have publicity given to the fact that you solicited the money under wrong pretenses." Eight days later Tappan wrote again to say that a man named Thomas Oughton had come to settle the accounts and that the amount owed was £131.6.3, money that had been given to Pennington by various individuals and refunded to them by Oughton's father, a clergyman in Jamaica. This was in addition to the £20 owed to Lord Elgin. "I will show you the papers," Tappan wrote, "and adjust the whole matter, if you will call at my home for this purpose. Your early attention is requested."[28]

Lacking any information on the subject except Lewis Tappan's letters, the matter remains somewhat mysterious. While in Jamaica, Pennington had written letters concerning several schemes to benefit the Jamaican churches and, since his return to the United States, had also suggested various projects to benefit those churches. Nothing specific is known about any of these projects or whether they came to fruition. It is certainly possible that money was contributed for some of these purposes and then used for other purposes when the initial project died. Pennington was never nearly as interested in money as Lewis Tappan, and the evidence would indicate that he did not keep careful financial records.[†] Presumably Tappan did "adjust the matter," since there is no further reference to it, but Tappan added a P.S. to his last letter to Pennington on the subject, suggesting that Pennington should have shown "heartfelt contrition." Whatever financial adjustment was made failed to satisfy Lewis Tappan's narrow conscience.[††]

Undeterred by Lewis Tappan's criticism of his financial stewardship, Pennington served that summer as coordinator of an attempt to come to the help

---

† It has already been noticed that William Lloyd Garrison saw no need to connect stated purposes, actual purposes, and accurate reporting. Harriet Beecher Stowe likewise has been suspected of announcing a purpose such as educating former slaves, but then using money for herself. (cf. Fladeland, op. cit., p. 357.) Charities were not held to account in the 19th century, and fund raisers felt free to use the money where it seemed to them it would do the most good.

†† Tappan was very busy advising black people about their financial affairs that summer. Just days after "adjusting" Pennington's affairs, he met with Charles B. Ray "at my request to confer about money in his hands." Tappan spent three hours trying to persuade Ray that he had misused some funds, but "he did not appear to think he had done wrong." Ray went away saying that "he would ask his atty and do what is right." (Tappan, L., *Lewis Tappan Papers*, Journals and Notebooks, Microfilm in the Library of Congress, Container 10, Reel 5.)

of a congregation in Brooklyn. He and the pastors of other African American congregations in the city organized a "mass meeting" at the end of July centered on three services, morning, afternoon, and evening, that raised over $200 for "our beloved sister church in Bridge-street, Brooklyn."[29] It was a minor event in the larger pattern of Pennington's life but evidence of the variety of events that crowded his schedule without, ordinarily, drawing sufficient attention to be recorded.

Matters of more concern to most African Americans were being faced in the streets and the courts. Lacking a definitive statement from the courts, attempts to integrate the New York City rail system continued. In September, Thomas Downing, one of the wealthiest and most prominent African Americans[†] in the city, wrote to the *Evening Post* to describe an attempt that had been made to put him off a car of the Sixth Avenue Railroad. Like Jennings, McFarland, and Pennington, he had refused to leave the car, but the conductor, rather than take matters into his own hands, threatened to call an officer. Downing told him that was the very thing he wanted him to do, because officers were there to keep the peace and the conductor was disturbing him. Unwilling to admit defeat, the ill-fated conductor asked other riders to assist him in removing Downing, and some were prepared to do so. Downing told them if he were breaking some law, he would give them his card and they would know where to find him. Handing out his card, however, made it clear who he was and at that point passengers began to rally to his side. One man came and sat beside him, saying he had known him for thirty years, others called "Stay in, Downing," and still others set up a shout of "Three cheers for Downing." As the car went on its way, Downing noticed that the conductor was looking closely to see who had pulled the cord for the car to stop and surmised that the conductor might be unwilling to stop for him. Nothing daunted, Downing simply asked the man beside him to pull the cord when the car came to his stop, and Downing then "got quietly out, and no one was hurt."[30] But Thomas Downing was a popular public figure. Not everyone would fare as well and, of course, Downing's successful flaunting of the system changed nothing for anyone else, since it led to no legal action.

Undaunted by the lack of concrete achievements in the National Council meeting, Pennington and Smith were among forty signers of a call for a State Convention to be held in September in Troy. This, however, had a narrow and

† Downing (1791–1866) had been born free in Virginia and had come to New York as a young man. Gradually he built up an oyster business, and by this time his oyster house, at the corner of Broadway and Wall Street, was the fashionable place for New Yorkers to indulge themselves in this local specialty. (Hewitt, John, "Mr. Downing and his oyster house: the life and good works of an African-American entrepreneur—19th century New York, New York restaurateur, Thomas Downing." *American Visions*, June-July 1994.)

specific agenda: "to give the ear of our Legislature no rest till every legal and political disability, with all its depressing and degrading tendencies, shall be swept from the Empire State."[31]

If conventions could have changed the world, the world would have been changed in the fall of 1855. The State Convention in Troy was followed by a National Convention in Philadelphia that opened on October 16th and a "General Convention of Radical Political Abolitionists" in Boston the following week. James McCune Smith was actively involved in all three but, when the time came to attend the meetings he had helped arrange, Pennington could find time for none of them. He was, after all, pastor of a large congregation and had a court case hanging over his head.

Parish affairs did need attention. There had been previous indications that record keeping at the Prince Street Church was not always up to standard. In January of 1852, shortly after Pennington's return from Scotland, the Presbytery had given its approval of the required records from the Prince St. Church "except in two cases of delinquency in which a summary was provided instead of the steps prescribed in the Book of Discipline." Again in July 1855, the Presbytery records noted, "Exceptions to Records of the Prince St. Church"; there were "irregularities in reference to discipline" and "no record of reading and approval of minutes." Technically, these records were the responsibility of the trustees, but the trustees were men of little education for the most part and less likely to be attentive to their duties if the pastor were frequently absent.[†] Tensions between pastor and congregation seem to have been constant. Pennington's report to the American Home Missionary Society in June of 1855 reports that he had been "prevailed upon to withdraw my resignation of the pastorate which I tendered some time ago" and expresses the hope that the relationship will continue "as now we are using efforts to improve our financial condition."[32]

It does seem evident that Pennington, in the fall of 1855, was concentrating more on his local responsibilities and directing his energy toward an issue that was less controversial in polite society. When the Colored National Convention met in Philadelphia in mid-October, he was listed as a delegate but wrote a letter instead asking to be excused because of "circumstances unseen and entirely beyond my control." Ethiop's column reported that he had looked around and missed many of the faces familiar from Rochester, especially "one of the great lights of the East, Dr. Pennington."[33] Pennington's

† The 1855 Colored National Convention received a report of "trades and professions" followed by African Americans. New York reported on 744 individuals, among whom were 35 teachers, 21 clergymen, 7 physicians, 4 merchants, and one lawyer. Since St. Philip's Episcopal Church drew off the elite of the black community, it is unlikely the Shiloh trustees could have included many members with experience in keeping records.

letter, sounding in part like a valedictory address, recalled fondly the "glorious gatherings" held in Philadelphia in the early 1830s and urged the delegates "to return to the good old path;—better late than never." But Pennington, not lacking yet in ambition, suggested that the time had come to begin "a new series of national conventions of our people" and that such a convention should include "gentlemen of talent" from the British, French, Spanish, and Danish dominions, as well as Mexico and Central America, and that it be held "at some point where civilized law and order prevail" such as Jamaica or Haiti.[34]

What it was that prevented James Pennington from being in Philadelphia that month is unknown. He had scheduled a major event at his church for the following week but presumably the date of the National Convention was set long before Pennington scheduled his local meeting. It seems likeliest that he was responding to pressure from his congregation to give them more of his time. In his absence, the Convention, with Amos Beman presiding, quickly agreed to drop further consideration of an industrial school but did agree, after a "spirited discussion," to admit a woman, Mary A. Shadd of Philadelphia, as a delegate. William C. Nell, a not unbiased observer who believed that the National Council had "proved itself (to say the least) too cumbersome and complicated to promote the desired good," reported that this Convention "was far transcended by the Convention of 1853."[35] The most extended debate centered on the question of whether the Constitution of the United States, which Garrisonians denounced as a "covenant with hell," could be best described as a pro- or anti-slavery document. The "address to the people of the United States" issued by the Convention centered its attention on this issue and maintained that slavery existed "in violation of the Constitution, which is the supreme law of the land." Not only does slavery violate the Constitution, they said, but so also has the Constitution been violated by laws which violate the freedom of every citizen. "There can be no higher praise of the Constitution," the address proclaimed, "than that its workings are absolute—if rightly interpreted, for Freedom—if wrongly, for Slavery—to all."

But James Pennington was not there. For reasons which he considered more important, he remained in New York and addressed a different issue entirely. In a rapidly changing society, questions about women's role in marriage and society were increasingly raised. The American Anti Slavery Society, of course, had divided on that issue in 1840, but that had to do with the right of a woman to speak in society and take a role in organizational leadership. In 1855 a small group of New Yorkers was raising more basic issues still and questioning the commonly accepted understanding of marriage. A "free-love society," claiming some five or six hundred members, was meeting every other week and attacking what they called "compulsory morality." An October entry in George Templeton Strong's diary undoubtedly spoke for many in suggesting that "'passional attraction' was its watchword; fornication and adultery its apparent object."[36]

James Pennington had frequently commented on political issues where they impacted the status of African Americans in society, but now he weighed in on a rather different subject on which orthodox Christians, black or white, would have been in general agreement. Notices were placed in the papers announcing a talk on "free love" on a Friday afternoon in October. In response, an "attentive audience, about equally composed of white and colored" and with "the fair sex" well represented, came together to hear what Pennington might say. If they hoped for scandal, they were disappointed. However much a revolutionary and disturber of the peace James W. C. Pennington might be on racial matters, when it came to doctrine and morality he was there to uphold the traditional faith. He would not apologize for introducing any subject from his pulpit, he told the audience, and he would not do so now. "If from indifference or false delicacy the pulpit shrinks from this discussion," he said, "the result will be that vast numbers of our youth will be drawn in the path of shame and sorrow." The doctrine Pennington set out was the system he had learned at Yale from Nathaniel Taylor almost thirty years earlier: God's moral governance provides laws by which to live, and to violate those laws is to substitute chaos for order. The "Free Love system" as Pennington understood it "means indiscriminate love between the sexes," and that violates the "law of affinities which has been enacted by God and nature for the regulation of the attachment of the sexes," and it violates the law of marriage which "leaves man without a home." "Show me a man who is either too lazy, too selfish, or too stingy, or corrupt, or anything else," he proclaimed, "to provide a home for a fair partner, and I will show you a thing in the shape of a man that should be marked and shunned. But just such a one is one of these free lovers."

It was the sort of address that enables an audience to shiver comfortably at the thought of the wickedness being perpetrated somewhere else by others and only to be condemned by all right-thinking people such as they. But Pennington then added another specter at which his hearers might similarly shudder: "the poluted [sic] elements of socialism from Germany, France, and England, at work in the veins of society." It behooved "the pulpit and parents to be on the lookout, and guard against the invading evil." Karl Marx and Friedrich Engels had published *The Communist Manifesto* in 1848, and a wave of revolution had swept through Europe in the same year, but neither the document nor the revolutionary mood had much appeal in America. Indeed, Karl Marx had been employed by the *New York Tribune* as a "foreign correspondent" for a short time in 1851. But preachers and politicians have been warning against various foreign evils almost from the beginning of American settlement, and "socialism" was simply the latest convenient label for anything disturbing to the established order. This rather unique event in James Pennington's life is typical of his fundamentally conservative approach to social change. Garrison, Pillsbury, and many of the New England abolitionists were radicals, attacking the establishment in church and state, but men like James W. C. Pennington and James McCune Smith were fundamentally conservative in their approach, proud to be Americans and confident that society needed only to uphold its own ideals and all would be well. The *New York Tribune* reported that "The discourse, which was lengthy, appeared to give great satisfaction to all present."[37] It was a role in which James Pennington was very much at home.†

But perhaps it was already too late to satisfy the discontented. The swelling chorus of criticism finally became too personal and immediate. In December, the Presbytery received a communication from the Session of the Prince Street Church, stating that they were "aggrieved at certain conduct on the part of their pastor, and asking advice or a speedy relief." The communication was referred to a three-member committee consisting of two clergy and one layman. Christmas was not celebrated in the mid-nineteenth century with the same ferocity as it would be a century later, but late December even then was not a convenient time for meetings, and the committee did not report back for a month. When it did report, on January 9, there seem to have been differences of opinion, because the Presbytery postponed consideration of the report and five days later, the clergy member of the committee resigned and was replaced. Finally, at the end of January, James Pennington himself came before the Presbytery "in relation to certain rumors which had been referred to a committee of conference." It seems odd that the committee that had been formed to deal with specific complaints from the congregation is no longer mentioned and the Presbytery itself was now dealing with "certain rumors." Nevertheless, the Presbytery, after discussion, adopted a resolution "that the confessions made by Dr. Pennington, his expressions of penitence, and his professed purpose carefully to guard against a repetition of the acknowledged offense, are satisfactory to the Presbytery, and that, with their hearty forgiveness of the past, they commend him for the future to the grace of the Great Shepherd and Bishop of souls."[38]

All this is very mysterious, since the conduct complained of and the rumors are never named. Neither the Session nor the Presbytery had shown

---

† Pennington seems to have said nothing about it, but the term "free love" was applied to a broad range of subjects in that era. A few months later, the *New York Tribune* wrote of missionaries in India who were worrying about whether or not to accept polygamy among new Christians. The *Tribune* was concerned that accepting polygamy among the "Mohammedans" and "Hindoos" in India might lead to the acceptance of polygamy among Mormons in Utah and set out its views on the subject in an article headed "FREE-LOVE IN THE CHURCH."

any reluctance to identify misconduct on other occasions. Adultery, drunkenness, slander, and profanity on the part of specific church members are clearly named in the Session records. Over the next ten years the only issue not specifically labeled has to do with "several matters of grievance" between Henry Garnet, who succeeded Pennington as pastor, and some members of the congregation.† Issues between pastor and congregation continued to rise, and Henry Garnet clearly also found it difficult to work with church members. On two or three occasions the congregation turned to the Presbytery with complaints, and at least three times Garnet resigned and had to be persuaded to continue. In view of all this and apart from Lewis Tappan's conversation with Samuel Cornish, the obvious reading of the minutes would suggest that the congregation was upset by Pennington's frequent absences and that Pennington admitted this "offense" and promised to pay more attention to the congregation. The evidence is clear, in fact, that he was well aware of such complaints and was already changing his behavior in this respect. Had there been more serious violations, the Presbytery might have been expected to call for something more than a simple admission of mistakes and to respond with something more than "hearty forgiveness" and good wishes. Nonetheless, it was obviously an unpleasant business, and James Pennington after the roller-coaster ride of the last two years was not prepared to deal with it. One month after receiving forgiveness from the Presbytery, James Pennington returned to ask them to dissolve his relationship with the Shiloh congregation so that he could accept a call from the Fifth Congregational Church (Talcott Street) in Hartford.[39] The court case with the Sixth Avenue Railroad Company remained unresolved, but Pennington was unwilling or unable to deal with that and a troublesome congregation at the same time. Hartford was familiar ground, the congregation had been unable to obtain a "settled pastor" since Pennington's departure, so there, perhaps, he could find release from the constant pressure of recent years.

James Pennington's adopted son, Thomas, provided his own commentary over forty years later. "Critics may pass judgment," he wrote, "upon some of the acts of his life in later years, which might not be favorable; but did they know, and could fully appreciate and realize, the extreme tension of mind to which he was subjected at that time, followed by an experience of ingratitude, they would descend from their rostrum, and cast the broad mantle of charity, over any and all overt acts from that time onward."[40]

---

† Henry Garnet had recently returned from several years in England and Jamaica to his old parish in Troy, New York.

CHAPTER TWENTY-ONE

Hartford and New York, 1856–1864

J ames Pennington had been gone from Hartford for nearly eight years by February 1856, but only a few months earlier had he cut his last material tie with the city by selling his remaining interest in the yellow frame double house on Village Street. The house had been a continuing source of supplemental income since Pennington had been able to rent his half of the house when he moved to New York. In October 1854, he mortgaged a quarter share in the property, to Stephen Rogers of New York City for three hundred dollars, and then, in October 1855, he had sold the quarter-interest to Noble Jones, his original partner in ownership of the property. Of course, in October 1855, Pennington had probably not been thinking of moving back to Hartford, so when he did make that move a few months later, he had to find new housing. He located a place to rent at 3 Baker Street, over a mile from the Talcott Street church, in what was then a very new blue-collar area of Hartford and is now a predominantly black section of the city known as "Frog Hollow."† Two other black families are listed as living in the eight houses on the street, and twelve white families.[1]

Hartford had continued to grow while James Pennington was in New York and, with a population nearing 30,000, was almost three times the size of the city he had first come to sixteen years earlier, in 1840, but there were no streetcars in Hartford, and whereas the New York congregation clung to its fond memories of their only former pastor, Theodore Wright, the Hartford congregation's fond memories were of their only former pastor, James W.

---

† Baker Street, so new an address that it was unlisted in the city directory three years earlier, ran from Washington Street west to Zion Street. It was renamed Ward Street in 1871. Number 3 Baker Street would have been on the corner of Baker Street and Washington Street. Although the other houses on the street were multi-family units, only Pennington is listed at number 3 in the 1856 directory.

C. Pennington. Pennington might not have been able to satisfy yearnings for Wright, but he could satisfy yearnings for himself. When the African American community in Hartford made plans for a major celebration of the abolition of slavery in the West Indies at "Gillette's Grove"[†] on August 1, they naturally asked Pennington to be the orator, and he responded with one of his most eloquent speeches, a stirring reiteration of confidence in "God's moral governance" and the ultimate triumph of the cause of freedom. Subsequently published as a pamphlet, the address was given the unexciting title "The Reasonableness of the Abolition of Slavery in the South, a Legitimate Inference from the Success of British Emancipation."

Ever the scholar, Pennington began the speech with a detailed, even pedantic, review of the introduction of slavery to the American colonies[††] and then recited the list of states and nations in the New World that abolished slavery beginning with Chile in 1683 through Massachusetts in 1780. His point was to show "that a constant series of acts of emancipation have been going on upon this continent for seventy-five years." He could not, of course, resist the urge to provide a number of historical details: that Queen Elizabeth had serious doubts of the lawfulness of slavery, for example. He spoke of the controversy in England as to whether slaves brought to England and "baptized with English water, and by English clergyman" were set free by virtue of that act. He told his audience how that issue was tested "by an appeal to Talbott and York, the attorney, and solicitor-generals." That decision, in 1729, was that baptism did not invalidate the master's right, but the effect of that decision was "to awaken the abolitionists to greater efforts." He talked about the Somerset case in 1769 testing whether a slave became free by coming into England, and the positive outcome of that case after a struggle of forty-three years. He talked about the long struggle led by Clarkson and Wilberforce to outlaw the slave trade and finally to abolish slavery on August 1, 1838. He pointed out that the abolitionists in England insisted that this was a moral question, and he insisted that when a question is placed squarely on moral grounds "even in the most corrupt ages of the world . . . it will seldom fail to be decided according to its true character." And this long development he compared to Jesus' parable of the mustard seed, the smallest of all seeds, which, even if "sown . . . in tears" will in time become a tree where "the birds of the air may have a jubilee in its branches, while the care-worn prisoner may shade himself beneath it." Jesus, of

† Senator Francis Gillette had established himself in Hartford a few years earlier and had contributed to the fund to rescue James Pennington's brother. "Gillette's Grove," also known as Gillette's Woods, was south of Farmington Avenue and east of Laurel Street, within the present city limits but well beyond them in 1856.
†† Oddly, he dates the beginning of slavery in America to New England in 1638 rather than Jamestown in 1619.

course, said only that the birds would *rest* in its branches and he said nothing about care-worn prisoners resting beneath a tree, but Pennington needed to balance his historical detail with an occasional rhetorical flourish.

Having brought his history nearly up to date, Pennington moved from being a historian to an orator in describing the work of the British abolitionists. "They condemned slavery in all its length and its breadth—in its total character. They pushed their arguments to the throne, and they spoke in thunder tones to the Parliament, declaring, that the enslavement of man was a monstrous crime, which endangers the very existence of a nation, by exposing it to the wrath of heaven; that freedom is the slave's birth right; that the only way to do them justice is to set them free immediately and unconditionally; but the slave's ignorance which has been entailed upon him by slavery, is no argument for delaying his emancipation; but whatever preparation he may need for freedom, can not be made while in a state of slavery. And moreover, that as the best way to fit a man for slavery is to place them in a state of slavery, so the best way to fit in a man for freedom is to lay upon him the responsibility of acting the part of the freeman." All of which, of course, was directly relevant to the debate then going on in the United States. Pennington was careful to point out also that the apprentice system introduced in the West Indies as a necessary transition from slavery to freedom had proved to be unnecessary.

Having given his audience a lesson in history, Pennington moved on to give them a lesson in geography. He described what he called "that grand string of islands lying partly in the Atlantic Ocean, and partly in the Caribbean Sea, constituting the great islanded pathway between the northern and southern hemispheres of the Western continent, belting the shore from Florida, the great toe of the United States, down to the neck and shoulders of South America," and told his audience that God had chosen those islands well to provide an example for the United States.

If stubborn advocates of slavery would like to know "what we mean by immediate emancipation," Pennington said, "we ask him to read this chapter" in history. "If he talks bloodshed and murder, we would ask him to read this chapter, and tell how much blood he finds in it. Nay did not this event blot out the blood which had stained the land before? Murder or homicide may have been the result of slavery, but never of emancipation. Does he talk about the slaves not being capable of taking care of themselves? We only ask him to review and study this chapter, and see how much pauperism it has inflicted upon Great Britain. We can but rejoice in the happy results of this benevolent achievement . . . and that it therefore presents the best argument why it should take place in this our land."

With all this as background, Pennington came at last to his rhetorical climax; he had never been more eloquent. "What slave in ours or any other country need despair of liberty since the British slave has gone free! His case was a desperate one; literally imprisoned in the sea, dark waters were the boundary of his habitation of sorrow. No free states or Canadas bounded him on either side, to which he could fly. But God, who ordained that the isles should wait for his law, enforced that law in due season . . . the law came in to restore the bondman his body; his body that was marked, bruised and lacerated; but it was his body, dear to him still, as was the body of his oppressor to him, whose skin had never been broken by the scratch of a pin. The law came, and the bondman received back his soul; his soul long benighted and vexed, but it was still his soul, possessed of its own immortality, an immortality of which the cart-whip and other instruments of torture, plied with deadly effect to the body that enshrined it, could not divest it.

"And here is an eternal truth that is destined to beat away every refuge of lies that can be brought by the ingenuity of critics, tyrants and cavilers, to support slavery. When you have made of man a slave by a seven-fold process of selling, bartering and chaining, and garnishing him with that rough and bloody brush, the cart-whip, and set him to the full by blowing into the eyes of his mind cloud after cloud of moral darkness, his own immortality still remains. Subtract from it what you *can*, immortality still remains; and this is a weapon in the bosom of the slave which is more terrible and terrifying to the slaveholder than the thunder of triumphal artillery in the ears of a retreating army. . . . Oh, what moral sublimity is here, when the law spoke with such stirring eloquence to the tyrant, in regard to the personal liberty and rights of the slave, and the mandate was, *'give them, give them back!'* and when the man of chains and stripes came forth and reached out his hand to receive the precious trust!

"Echo, songs of praise; echo, ye sacred chapels; echo, schoolhouses, echo, ye railroads of beautiful cottages; ye villages, VICTORIA and WILBER-FORCE; echo, ye colored magistrates, lawyers, merchants, members of assembly, governors and secretaries, and still the echo comes, how are they acting? Look over and see. Then let us make a bold push, for our day is nearby."

So far as James Pennington was concerned, history established the truth that he had learned from Nathaniel Taylor at Yale: God rules in human affairs and God's will must be done. "They tell us that slavery is here, and that it must remain; and that it is useless to discuss it. They say that however desirable it may be that slavery should be abolished, it cannot be done. It is impossible. So said the British slaveholder. We lay down as a general truth, that what is desirable is possible with God; is possible unto us, with his aid. *Upon this basis, what have we to do in order to success?* Why, to concentrate our energies upon this desirable object. Let our means harmonize with the moral government of God. Let our plans harmonize with His wisdom. Let our plans harmonize with the perceptible economy of Providence. And what becomes of the impossibility? It is annihilated." The speech summed up the paradox of Pennington's life and ministry: he appealed to reason, to combat an institution founded not on reason but economics and emotion, but he advanced his reasons in rhetoric that appealed as much to the heart as to the mind.

Such a speech would have demonstrated to the Garrisonians that such leaders as James Pennington obviously had no plan and would accomplish nothing. But to James W. C. Pennington it was equally obvious that God had a plan and was working it out. Faithful people needed to be aware of God's purposes and work patiently with God toward that end.

The great oration on August 1, however, was not typical of James Pennington's second tour of duty in Hartford. Through most of the year, the emphasis needed to be on the rebuilding of pastoral relationships and the ordinary work of parish ministry. The congregation had withered away in Pennington's absence to fewer than fifty members, and the viability of the church had become a serious question. Even this work, however, did sometimes have a social dimension; apart from the one published sermon, the only published evidence of James Pennington's work in Hartford that year is a brief letter in the *Hartford Courant* of August 21 inquiring about the progress of a needed sewer installation. "Dear Sir," James Pennington wrote to the paper, "The dry season has passed, and the wet season has commenced; the property-holders and the tenants on Talcott street, are suffering for the want of the public sewer through that street. We have petitioned for it, and are patiently waiting the action of our City Fathers. Will they give us a sewer?"[2]

Petitions and letters to the paper are a relatively mild form of protest, but James Pennington still had a court case pending in New York, and the ill health that seemed to attack him in times of stress now made it impossible for him to continue his pastoral duties or take part in the meetings that had always been an important part of his life. There is no evidence that he even attended meetings of the Hartford clergy associations.[†] In late October a "Convention of Ministers of the Congregational and Presbyterian Churches of the United States of America" was held at the Shiloh Church in Manhattan and, although James W. C. Pennington had been expected to be present, he was not there.[3] It seems very likely that Pennington knew the Hartford congregation could no longer support a full-time pastor and that he never intended to stay in

---

† The Hartford Central Association had divided in 1851 because of the conflict between Horace Bushnell and Joel Hawes, with Hawes and a few colleagues forming a "Hartford Fourth" association. Pennington would probably have preferred to associate with Hawes both because of his more conservative theology and because of his greater sympathy for the abolition movement, but there are no records of that association's meetings.

Hartford for any length of time since he retained his home on Sixth Avenue in Manhattan. Perhaps the move to Hartford was simply a convenient excuse for leaving the conflicts and tensions of the Shiloh Church behind. In any event, on November 12, he resigned his ministry in Hartford because of his health and returned to New York after less than a year away and only a month before the streetcar case finally came to trial.[4]

In spite of the fact that a Legal Rights Association had been formed and James Pennington was represented by its lawyers, he evidently felt insecure with the advice being given him and deeply concerned as to the outcome of the trial. The presentation of the case had finally been scheduled for December 15 but then postponed again for two more days. On December 15, very much at the last minute, Pennington wrote to Gerrit Smith seeking further advice. Smith was not trained as a lawyer, but he had served in Congress and his immense wealth and business experience made his opinion valuable. Pennington had several questions for him. If the decision went against him "through the prejudices of the jury," what would be Smith's advice, he wondered, as to an appeal? And if an appeal were made, should it be to the same court or to the Supreme Court or to some other district court? He asked Smith also whether a plaintiff can challenge the jurors in a civil case and what the law of the State was as to a man's right to plead his own case in a civil suit. "An immediate reply," Pennington wrote, would "greatly oblige" him because "for the last four or five years [I have] been the object of untold outrages, by several powerful corporations in and about this wicked city." They could only hope to succeed, he told Smith, "because the object of their abuse has not the pecuniary means to cope with them at the Bar."[5]

All the evidence indicates, however, that James W. C. Pennington was well represented. The lawyer presenting his case was Frederick A. Tallmadge, who was a graduate of Yale in the class of 1811 and who had studied at the Litchfield law school. Tallmadge had been practicing law in New York City since 1813. He had served in the state legislature and had served one term in the United States Congress. Later he would serve for five years as superintendent of the Metropolitan Police and then as clerk of the New York Court of Appeals. These would certainly seem to be more than adequate credentials.

Tallmadge began his presentation of the case by making it clear that the question at issue was not any injury that Pennington might have received but "whether in this country, the colored man can or cannot ride in these public conveyances." He also wanted the jury to understand that he was not a fanatic. "I come not here," he said, "to make any abolition harangue, or to talk of Sharp's rifles, but simply to test this simple question of right." He told the jury what "Mr. Pennington," as he called him, had said to him when first they met: "I know the prejudice which the people of this country have against our color.

We do not claim, however, to be their equals. We do not expect to be invited to sit at their tables, or share their beds. But I have yet to learn that I cannot pass from one part of the country to another in your rail cars and steamboats. In that I claim no equality, except the right of passage."

The defense, Tallmadge told the jury, would claim that they could restrict ridership to white people. But if they have that power, he argued, "could they not say that you, who are only five feet and ten inches high, should not ride?" The streetcar company, Talmadge pointed out, was granted a monopoly and, in return for that, expected to convey the citizens of the city. Why, then, should they not also convey James Pennington? "Does he not eat, drink, sleep and think like a passenger? He is a citizen. He goes to the polls and votes for you, or for his honor there, to sit—and the laws uphold them. What more constitutes a citizen?"

Tallmadge then called a 13-year-old boy, Joseph Mitchell, who was apparently the only witness to the event. He described what he had seen and was cross-examined. So ended the first day of the trial.

Waldo Hutchins, a younger man but also an experienced New York lawyer and a future member of Congress, opened the case for the defense. He pointed out that this case was by no means the only one of its kind, but never had the Company "been mulcted" for their conduct. Briefly he reviewed the evolution of the Company's behavior. At one time it had been accustomed to refuse to carry "persons of color" in any of its cars. Then a deputation of colored persons had asked the company to provide a car in which they could ride, and that was done. Later a request was made for additional cars, and they were provided "to the exclusion of the whites." Then a Legal Rights Association had been formed, of which "Mr. Pennington was at the head," that was "determined to possess the right to ride in any and all of the City cars." We have nothing to say, Hutchins continued, "of the color, the character, or the position of the reverend gentleman." They had no doubt that he was "one of the most respectable colored men in the city," and that was why he had been chosen to test the law. But "corporations have no souls," the lawyer told the jury. "They are willing to carry all the law compels them to—white or black—so long as they pay their five cents." They believed that they had furnished "quite ample accommodation for all passengers, of whatever kind, as required by law." Unfortunately, Hutchins told the jury, "there is a great prejudice, as has been said, among many people, about riding with colored persons, and to provide for that we've done all we could, and put on different cars, so that they can go separate if they might desire." It seemed to him quite unreasonable to ask the company to do any more than was already being done.

The defense then called the superintendent of the 6th Ave. Railroad, who discussed at some length the rules of the company and the way in which they were enforced. He pointed out that colored persons were allowed to ride on the front platform of the car where they were somewhat sheltered by a roof but otherwise exposed to the weather, and that he had seen as many as thirteen or fourteen people on the platform at one time, though the testimony was that only four or five could be so accommodated. Depending on the time of day, "white" cars were scheduled at two-, three-, or four-minute intervals, and "colored" cars every half hour.

John P. Early, a merchant, was then called on to describe what he had seen that day as a passenger. Early had been sitting on the left side of the car when Pennington came in and sat down on the right side of the car. He said the passengers near him then "rose up and left a vacant space on either side of him of three or four seats." He said that some of the passengers had then gone to the conductor, who requested Pennington to move to the front platform in accordance with company rules. When Pennington refused to do so, the conductor insisted, and Pennington said "he was prepared to maintain his rights." Since the car had now arrived at the Carmine Station, the conductor asked the driver to stop the car and remove Mr. Pennington. The conductor, Early testified, "approached Mr. P., took him in his arms, and embraced him and moved him backwards through the car, the doctor making all the resistance apparently in his power." Early believed that "no more force was used than was necessary" and that the conductor did not assist the driver, although "there was such a crowd that he might have done so." He also testified that the car had not been crowded, that there were "some fifteen or twenty" passengers at the time, and that some of them said they would leave unless the conductor removed Pennington. The witness did not remember whether any passengers had left the car, nor did he see any stamping on the plaintiff's feet, though they "might have been trodden upon leaving the car." Early also testified that he had no interest in the company. Under cross-examination, Early described Pennington as very well-dressed—"better dressed than now"—and said that he had on gold spectacles and carried a cane. The driver on the car was also called and gave very much the same testimony as the previous witnesses.

The plaintiff's lawyer then called Henry Highland Garnet, who testified that he was "a City Missionary of the Shiloh Presbyterian Church." Garnet testified that he had frequently been inconvenienced by the lack of available cars, sometimes having to wait half an hour in a storm and sometimes having to pay twenty times the streetcar fare for a private carrier. Sometimes, he testified, he found it impossible to get to the front platform on account of the crowd. He also told the jury that he had sometimes seen a "colored car" go by full of white people, and that on occasion he had found it necessary to take a car to the terminal in the opposite direction in order to get a car going in the right direction and therefore had to pay a double fare. It was his testimony that the three cars provided were far from adequate for the colored population of the city. Thomas Jennings also testified that the provision of cars was inadequate for the colored population along the Sixth Avenue line.

The third day of the trial began with a presentation of the defense case. Lawyer Hutchins attempted to prove that if colored persons were allowed to ride in public cars, it would also be necessary to let them sit at public tables in hotels. He argued that nature had made the races distinct "and that they must necessarily remain so." He stated that the company provided more cars for the colored population in proportion to their number than they provided for white people.

Frederick Tallmadge was involved in another trial, and so another member of the firm, Edward Phelps, summed up the case for the plaintiff in a speech lasting well over an hour. He maintained that the defendants, as common carriers, "were not justified in refusing to convey any passenger who might present himself" and that the rule prohibiting colored persons from riding in some of the cars was not a reasonable regulation. He spent some time discussing the differences between the races and claimed that the "free negroes" in the city were "equal, morally and intellectually, with those of the same station in life among the white population." As to the assertion that white people were unwilling to ride with negroes, he claimed that prejudice existed nowhere except in New York and that in New England "respectable negroes were admitted into the cars." In Europe, he said, "a negro who was properly attired could ride in the same car with any of the nobility, without anyone imagining themselves to be demeaned by reason of his presence."

The *New York Times* report of the case said that both lawyers had paid tribute to the "very high-minded and particularly intelligent jury, who had listened to all this evidence with such patience, &c. &c."

James Pennington's lawyer, Edward Phelps, then asked Justice John Slosson[†] to instruct the jury on two matters: 1) that the defendants, as common carriers, were bound to admit into their cars any passengers who presented themselves in accordance with the company's reasonable regulations, and 2) that a regulation excluding a passenger because of his color was not a reasonable regulation. Justice Slosson agreed to charge the jury on the first point but not the second. The second point, he said, was for the jury to decide. The defendants' counsel asked the justice to instruct the jury 1) that the company had a right to make regulations distinguishing between white and colored persons, 2) that the

---

† Justice John Slosson was coming toward the end of a distinguished career as a New York lawyer and judge and retired in 1860. It may be of interest that the defendant's lawyer, Hutchins, had begun his career in the law firm of which John Slosson was a senior member.

defendants had made reasonable rules and regulations for the transportation of colored persons, they had done their duty and were not liable in this action, 3) that the plaintiff was bound to follow the regulations if he was given notice of them, 4) that the defendants' obligations do not extend beyond the furnishing of three cars for the special use of colored persons and privilege of riding on the platforms of the other cars. Justice Slosson responded that the first point was a question for the jury, that the second point would be charged, that the third point would be charged if the jury agreed with the first point, and that he would not charge the jury as to point four.

Having clarified all that, His Honor gave the jury their instructions. The case before them he said is "one of great nicety and difficulty." It would require of them "the special exercise of great wisdom, candor and fairness" and "any admixture of prejudice or passion in determining the question, may seriously compare [sic], on one side or the other, the rights of these parties." No one denied that the company had an obligation to provide for the general public and no one denied that they could exclude individuals who would "give offense and discomfort to the other passengers." But that, he told them, "is not the present case." The question, he told them, could be narrowed down to this: "had [Pennington] the general right to sit in any car he might select, promiscuously with the whites, notwithstanding the regulation of the company to the contrary?" This, the justice said, is "a very serious question," because the principle could be applied equally to "hotel keepers, omnibus proprietors and all others of that description." If the jury felt that the company's regulations were reasonable, then the plaintiff had no claim to damages; but if they were not reasonable regulations, then he had such a claim to such damages as they might deem reasonable.

The jury spent several hours in their deliberations, but returned with a verdict for the defendants, apparently on the grounds that the admission of colored persons "would tend to diminish the profits of the company"—an issue that no one had raised. Justice Slosson indicated to the jury that he expected the case to be appealed to a higher court.[6] There had been every indication, in the judge's statement and in Pennington's letter to Gerrit Smith, that the case would be appealed, but there is no record of such an appeal. Possibly James Pennington and the Legal Rights Association had used up their resources in his case and had no ability to carry it further, but it is also possible that the black leadership had decided to throw its resources behind another pending case, that of Peter Porter, in which they seemed likelier to prevail. Pennington had successfully put the issue before the public, and now it would not go away. Over the next several years there were more incidents and more cases.

In January 1857, there was a public meeting at which James McCune Smith complained of his inability as a doctor to reach sick children. But the next time a black man was assaulted for asserting his right to ride, he was arrested and put in jail. The case of Peter Porter and his wife, however, was still making its way through the courts. Porter was an officer of the Legal Rights Association who had been riding the Eighth Avenue line with his wife when a conductor attempted to force them from the car. In the ensuing struggle, Porter was beaten "most ferociously" and she was taken by the neck and strangled. The Porters survived the attack, but Mrs. Porter had been pregnant and her child died as a result of her injuries. Clearly this was a more dramatically appealing case, and in February 1858, that priority was vindicated when Judge Rockwell, speaking for the highest court in the state, ruled that "colored people have the same rights in public conveyances" as any other members of the public. A great celebration took place, at which Porter told the crowd that at last "the five cents of a colored man were as good as those of a white man." But James Pennington had thought that was proven after the Jennings case and had learned that judicial decisions do not always alter conduct. Now he told the victorious crowd that they should be prepared for "the bitterest opposition" from conductors.[7] Before the year was out, he was shown to be right when another black man was attacked on the Sixth Avenue line. This time, however, the passengers divided over the issue, with a large number chanting "let the man ride." The possibility of violence was narrowly averted when company officials let the man reboard the car and continue his ride.[8] The tide was turning, and Pennington's leadership had played an important part in the transformation.

Even while James Pennington's case was being argued out, two other important cases were being tried, one in New York and one in Washington—though various contemporaries tended to be concerned about only one. For ordinary black people living in New York, the decision in James Pennington's case was of immediate importance for their lives, as it involved their ability to travel freely around their community, to get to work or church, or to visit friends. Of no concern to them was the trial of Charles B. Huntington, a financier charged with forgeries involving some $300,000 that had enabled a life-style with a mansion, a dozen servants, half a dozen carriages, and "a colossal tailor's bill." Frederick Tallmadge was involved in that case as well as Pennington's. Charles Templeton Strong's *Diary*, on the other hand, discusses the Huntington trial but makes no mention at all of the streetcar case. Six and a half million people rode the 6th Avenue Railroad in a typical year,[9] but Strong seldom rode in a streetcar.† The *New York Times* gave equal attention to the two cases but placed the streetcar story first. The abolitionist papers, on the other hand, provided no report at all on the streetcar case; they were

---

† On February 13, 1865, he notes, "At two o'clock resigned myself to one of those foul, over-crowded mephitic Third Avenue railroad cars which took me to Forty-ninth Street for a meeting . . ."

interested in abolition and stories of slave rebellions in the South, not the immediate, practical problems of black people and any protests they might be making against their treatment in the North. The hearing of the Dred Scott case drew little attention from the New York papers or Strong's *Diary*—even the decision drew no attention from Strong—but three months later, the New York papers and abolition papers reported that decision at great length.

The Dred Scott decision was a blunt rejection of everything James W. C. Pennington and his colleagues had worked for and an affirmation of the claims of William Lloyd Garrison and his associates, that the Constitution was a slavery document offering no hope of change. Those who framed the Constitution, Chief Justice Roger Taney ruled, believed that negroes are "beings of an inferior order, and altogether unfit to associate with the white race, either in social or political relations, and so far inferior that they had no rights which the white man was bound to respect." If James Pennington was not completely crushed by the outcome of the railroad case, this might have been the final blow. For twenty-five years he had been a rising star and leading light of the emerging African American community, speaking and writing to set forward that community's claim to an equal place at the American family table. Now that claim had been rejected by the final authority in the American system, and James Pennington, in addition, no longer had a pulpit from which to continue the struggle. With the precedent of the Jennings case, he might reasonably have hoped for an award of damages to cushion a transition to a new career, but that hope also had been turned aside. The consolidated impact of these events was catastrophic, leaving him without position or resources. Many people under such circumstances have disappeared from the public stage, struggling simply to survive. It is hardly surprising that James Pennington, over the next year, seemed to be moving in that direction. During the calendar year 1857, there is no evidence of his existence: no speeches, no writing, no presence at the meetings in which others continued to press their claims. But the story was not over. James Pennington could not reconstruct his shattered career, but he would regain his feet and once again make his voice heard.

It would be easy to understand if James Pennington had felt the need for some time away from all the pressures with which he had been dealing for most of his adult life, but sabbaticals and vacations were not possibilities for African Americans in the days before the Civil War and were rare for white clergy also.[†]

---

† Horace Bushnell had found time for a year-long trip to Europe because of ill health in 1845 and an extended visit to California in 1856 for the same reason, but there is no record that Joel Hawes ever traveled except to church conferences in the Northeast.

Lacking a congregation, Pennington had to turn more than ever to the lecture hall to support himself. Thomas H. S. Pennington, his adopted son, says that his father "traveled considerably in the middle and Eastern states" after his return from Hartford.[10] It seems likely that he set out to recapture those relatively carefree years in Scotland when he could travel from place to place speaking to audiences of supporters and raising enough money not only for his own needs but to contribute to the New York vigilance committee and pay off the church mortgage as well. In Scotland, however, there was a network of abolition societies eager to hear a black American who had escaped from slavery; but New York and New England in the 1850s had heard many such stories—and besides that, there was still a civil war between the abolition societies, and Pennington would not have been welcome in the communities where Garrisonian abolitionists were established.

New England nevertheless reminded James Pennington of those earlier days in "old England," and he spoke of the parallels in a speech given in a Manhattan church after returning from a tour of the Eastern states, where he had been speaking in schools and churches. It seemed to him, he reported, that public opinion in New England on the subject of "the colored man, as a man, is as sound as it is in England." African Americans could vote in every state except Connecticut, public conveyances and hotels were open to them, and he had felt as free as he did when traveling abroad. The former governor of New Hampshire had come to the railroad station to see him off when he left that state and had spoken with him cordially. It seemed to him that only a lack of education prevented black people from taking a full and equal place in New England society. He was also struck by the way in which the families with whom he stayed joined in family devotions with Bible reading, singing, and prayer. This, he felt, was "one of the great secrets of the progressive refinement of the whites," and he commended such practices to black families.[11]

The primary thrust of Pennington's speeches on this tour was on the need for education, but he was willing now to speak anywhere on any subject. He even went to a Masonic meeting in Tarrytown, New York, and spoke about John the Baptist. He needed the money, but making ends meet proved far harder than it had been in Great Britain.

In March 1858, James Pennington wrote a letter to Gerrit Smith that reveals just how difficult it was. "Dear brother," Pennington wrote, "you have been so kind to me, that I am ashamed to trouble you more; but in the service of the free colored people now for the second time [I] have exhausted the last dollar of my fortune and myself and family are without the necessities of life. For the past year I have had no income except from the sale of my printed addresses and my lectures. For some months past I have not been able for want of money to travel to such points in the lecturing field as would make my labors pay.

My wife is ill; my son is in Albany at a trade, yet an expense to me. Many of my friends here to whom I looked in days past for material aid in these times are among the embarrassed. Can you help me, and oblige Yours truly, J. W. C. Pennington."[12]

It is a letter of desperation. The address given is not the 6th Ave. address at which Pennington had lived while at the Shiloh Church and at first after returning from Hartford. Now he is on West 26th Street and living in a multi-family building. Ironically, Pennington's letter to Gerrit Smith was sent only three weeks before both Smith and Pennington received a plea for help from John Brown. Brown had come from Kansas to make a last plea for funds and to search for recruits for the small army he was forming. Thomas Pennington never forgot coming to breakfast one day when he was a teenager and finding John Brown seated at the table in earnest conversation with his father. Brown and Pennington had met at the Albany Convention several years earlier, and now Brown was reaching out to everyone he could talk to because he had a definite plan for action but was finding neither the money nor the volunteers on which his plan depended. He had traveled through New England and come back to New York to make one last effort there. Leaving New York on March 23, he traveled back to his home in North Elba in the Adirondacks and met again with Gerrit Smith. Smith was one of the "secret six" who had committed themselves to Brown and raised hundreds of dollars in the cause. But James Pennington had no money to give, and as a pacifist was not yet ready to endorse Brown's violence.

The two years during which James Pennington was attempting to support himself as a traveling speaker and preacher were also, unfortunately, the two years of his life in which financial assistance would have been hardest to find. A recession had begun late in 1856 and by the next year it had developed into what was called "the Panic of 1857." Railroads and other businesses failed, and Europe, South America, and Asia soon joined in the economic catastrophe. In October 1857, George Templeton Strong wrote in his diary, "we are a very sick people just now. The outward and visible signs of disease, the cutaneous symptoms, are many. In Wall Street every man carries pressure, anxiety, loss, written on his forehead." Building construction came to a standstill while shops cut their prices below cost and stayed open well into the evening on the chance that someone might come in. It was, Strong wrote, "far the worst period of public calamity and distress I've ever seen."[13] Lewis Tappan hoped that God would "sanctify losses and trials to individuals and to nations" and took grim satisfaction in noting in his journal that "The extravagance, specula-tions, financial gambling, and other sins of the people have brought about the commercial distress" and consoled himself with the thought that "it will be good for the people to be thus afflicted." Even though "many poor working persons will be [in] great distress the coming winter," he was confident that "God can temper the wind to the shorn lamb & will do so."[14]

At Thanksgiving, 1858, someone with a cruel sense of humor amused himself by advertising free bread and meat in Union Square at noontime. Several thousand came, "worn sewing-women, hungry children, . . . all the poor of every type, and there they sat and waited hour after hour in vain, and went away, reluctantly at last, with empty baskets, weary and cold and sad and disappointed." Strong speculated on the appropriate way to torture whoever had done it.[15] One wonders whether James Pennington might have been there.

Even in these circumstances, however, Pennington continued to make a difference. One of his friends was Evan Johnson, an Episcopal clergyman who served St. John's Church in Brooklyn. Johnson had fought hard, and successfully, for the admission of St. Phillip's Church to the Diocese of New York. One "snowy, sleety morning" in February, Johnson met Pennington on the Brooklyn ferry and, taking him by the arm, ushered him into the ladies' cabin, a refuge many men took in preference to the cigar smoke and tobacco spitting of the men's cabin. A deck hand followed them and ordered Pennington out. "Then I must go, too," said Johnson and followed the deck hand out. Johnson was irate at this treatment and told Pennington, "I will do some good for the wrong just perpetrated. They are about to establish street railroads all over Brooklyn, my son is one of the Board of Directors. I will give him no peace until he establishes the rule that there shall be no exclusion from the cars on account of color." He was as good as his word, and the Brooklyn railroad system was saved from the troubles that had caused so much trouble in Manhattan.[16]

That was a bright moment in an otherwise difficult time in Pennington's life. In spite of the rumors spread by Lewis Tappan and others, however, Pennington remained a pastor in good standing in the Presbyterian Church. When the Third Presbytery of New York held its semiannual meetings in April and October 1858, James Pennington was present.† And when an opening came in his former congregation in Newtown late in 1858, he was glad to return to parish ministry and teaching.††

Income from the Newtown congregation would help, but it had never been generous and Pennington continued to travel as often as possible to lecture. A letter to Gerrit Smith in early September of 1859 asked for help in arranging

---

† Henry Garnet, on the other hand, was not present to represent the Shiloh Congregation.

†† The Newtown congregation had been a Congregational church when Pennington organized it, but it had been received into the Third Presbytery as a Presbyterian church in March of 1857. The first pastor to serve it in its new relationship was Benjamin Lynch, who had succeeded Henry Garnet in Troy. (Weise, Arthur James, *The City of Troy and its Vicinity*. Troy, New York, Edward Green, 1886.)

"two or three lectures in your neighborhood." He was planning two lectures, Pennington told Smith: one on the progress of anti-slavery in New England based on a two-month lecture trip through the area from which he had just returned, and the other on a recent convention of slaveholders in Baltimore. "Like other preachers," he told Smith, "I am obliged to lecture in part for usefulness and for the support of my family."

As he had done in writing Smith the previous year, he let his discouragement show. It was said of Smith that he was that rare white man who had a black heart.[†] Clearly Pennington felt that he could be honest with Smith in a way that he never was with others. He could tell him about his family "whose circumstances are suffering on account of my limited income. I do not know in my own case," he wrote, "whether most to blame the South for enslaving me, or the North for oppressing me. For since I have been North few men have been required to make more bricks without straw than myself." But even in these years of hardship, Pennington's central faith and confidence in God's governing providence remained firmly in place. He concluded the letter in lines placed on the page like poetry:

> But it is no time
> for despair is a
> sin under God's
> moral government.
> Work and Hope,
> Hope and Work
> must be our motto.[17]

Whether it paid or not, however, he was continuing to write. There had been fewer vehicles for his writing in recent years, but in 1859 a new magazine had been established. Thomas Hamilton, who had worked in the New York newspaper district since he was a boy, had finally realized "the dream of his youth . . . and the aim of his manhood" by establishing the *Anglo-African Magazine*. Like the recently established *Harper's Magazine* and the *Atlantic Monthly*,[††] the *Anglo-African Magazine* would include poetry, fiction, editorials,

† James McCune Smith, a close friend of Gerrit Smith's, had suggested that whites needed to shed their white skins and acquire black hearts. Gerrit Smith and John Brown were perhaps the only white Americans of their day who were accepted on those terms by black colleagues. *The Ram's Horn*, a back abolitionist newspaper, said, "Gerrit Smith is a colored man." (Stauffer, John, *Black Hearts of Men*, p. 1.)

†† *Harper's New Monthly Magazine* began in June 1850, and the *Atlantic Monthly* in 1857. Unlike those magazines, which are still published, the *Anglo-African* survived only until 1865.

and essays on a wide variety of subjects, but exclusively by black writers. For a brief time, there was a *Weekly Anglo-African* as well. James McCune Smith wrote for it, and so did Martin Delaney and the poet Francis Allen Watkins Harper.[18] James Pennington wrote frequently for the magazine, beginning with a letter responding to a recent article in a New York newspaper that pointed with pride to America's hold on the cotton market and suggesting that slave labor made that preeminence possible.[19] In a more leisurely and lengthy mode, he indulged his interest in history by reviewing the early meetings of the Conventions of Colored People and providing a history of the slave trade.

James Pennington's "Review of Slavery and the Slave Trade" was a lengthy, scholarly, and somewhat repetitive examination of the subject published in three consecutive numbers of the *Anglo-African Magazine*. His sources range from Homer, Terence, Plutarch, and Quintilian in the ancient world, to such classical English writers as Alexander Pope, Adam Smith, and Edward Gibbon. He quotes as well the late 18th-century African American poet Phyllis Wheatley. There is a lengthy discussion of slavery, voluntary and involuntary, in the ancient world, a chronicle of its development in the Western world from the time of the Spanish settlement to the present, and a description of the horrors of slavery in the American South. Perhaps most biting is his analysis of the way in which "when men once consent to be unjust, they lose at the same instant with their virtue, a considerable portion of that sense of shame, which, till then, had been found a successful protector against the allies of vice. (Slavery) hardens their hearts and makes them insensible to the misery of their fellow creatures, it begets a turn for wanton cruelty . . . The slaveholder does not murder his horse, on which he only rides; he does not mutilate his cow, which only affords him her milk; he does not torture the dog, which is but a partial servant of his pleasures, but these unfortunate men, his slaves, from whom he derives his very pleasures and his fortune, he tortures, mutilates, murders at discretion."[20] All of these arguments, of course, had been made by Pennington before and by many others as well, yet it remained necessary to restate the case against slavery again and again so long as slavery existed and so long as, even in the North, there were still some who did not understand.

That Pennington wrote so much for the *Anglo-African* would not have been surprising if the magazine had paid its writers, but none of its authors was paid. Pennington may have gained some publicity by such writing and he was often reworking themes he had spoken about or written about on other occasions, but sometimes he was writing, as people today write for the Internet, simply for the joy of writing. It was in that vein that he wrote two essays about Newtown with the heading "From the Old 'Long Island scribe.'" "At home again, at the old school desk, Newtown avenue," he wrote, "I have had charge of the church and school here . . . for the past year, preaching and teaching from house to house, and from pulpit to pulpit, among both white and colored people. The field opens and widens as I labor." The essay deals not so much with his ministry, however, as with the changing population of Newtown and the changing position of "the colored people of this town." Not least important, Pennington notes that the two railroads serving Newtown "make no distinction of color among the passengers; but regard one man's money as just as good with them as another's." Indeed, one of the depots was in charge of an African American. Most of the population, however, were farmers still. In the various markets of New York City, Pennington believed that "the old Long Island Garden will be found to be well represented in all the luxuries of the domestic board, which are now being consumed by your returning hungry travelers, and laid up by your cautious housekeepers for the winter, which already begins to breathe significantly through your doors and windows evenings and mornings. Let them lay in well; winter is no respecter of persons."[21] This is clearly writing for its own sake; perhaps for the first time, Pennington could write as an essayist without a social agenda but with a delight in words. In spite of his various troubles, the tone is consistently positive. In the second issue, "The Old Long Island Scribe" devoted himself to a discussion of the railroad lines running near the church, then tells how he had gone out one afternoon when school classes were over to walk along the railroad line and see exactly where it went. He thought the existence of two lines in the neighborhood, one within a stone's throw of the church, would enhance the value of the church property as well as that of the nearby black farmers.[22]

Pennington's longest piece of writing that fall was titled "The Self-Redeeming Power of the Colored Races of the World" and is a strange amalgam of a rather philosophical essay about the struggle for black freedom combined with a very detailed analysis of recent legislation in the state of Maryland. White slave owners in Maryland had been concerned for some time about the growing number of free black people in the state and had attempted to win the passage of legislation for their general removal from the state. A committee appointed for that purpose had concluded that a general removal of the free black population was "inexpedient" but that that population "should be well and thoroughly controlled by efficient laws, to the end that it may be orderly, industrious, and productive," while emancipation of others should be forbidden or else those subsequently set free should be removed from the state. The various reports and resolutions are all reproduced in the essay, so that what began as a philosophical discussion ends as a legislative report. It is, of course, the philosophical framework that matters, and inevitably it has to do with "the moral government of God" in which "no provision is made for waste human materials."[23] Nathaniel Taylor had taken no particular interest in slavery, but his principles continued to serve James Pennington well. Finally, his message always was one of confidence both in God and in the innate strength of black people: "If there is a human being on the face of the earth who can hope alone, and even hope against hope, it is the colored man. And this is the secret of the amazing power of endurance. . . . Every attempt of our oppressors to swallow us up, has ended in their defeat. Whether we look at court-decisions or malicious legislations, or the preaching of false theology, all have ended in their confusion. . . ."[24]

Even as people were reading these words, however, John Brown, who had shared a meal with James Pennington a week earlier, was taking violent action to enforce his own version of the "moral government of God." On the night of Sunday, October 16th, John Brown and his little band seized the United States Armory and Arsenal at Harpers Ferry, in a narrow river valley on the border between Maryland and Virginia. They cut the telegraph wires, so it was not until noon of the next day that word reached Baltimore. On Tuesday morning, however, Colonel Robert E. Lee stormed the building and five days later John Brown was brought to trial in Jefferson County Courthouse. On October 31 he was found guilty of treason and sentenced to death, a sentence carried out on December 2. George Templeton Strong, like many other New Yorkers of his class, had no sympathy with the South but saw no alternative to the jury's verdict. Even so, the affair made him uncomfortable and fearful of the consequences. "He will undoubtedly be hanged," he wrote in his diary. "Were I his jury, I could not acquit him, and twelve terrified Virginians will have little difficulty about a verdict. This insane transaction may possibly lead to grave results. If Gerrit Smith and other fanatics of the extreme left are compromised by the papers found upon Brown, they may be indicted, and a requisition for them from the governor of Virginia would embarrass the governor of New York a little."[25]

Indeed, Gerrit Smith and several others across the North who had had close contact with John Brown spent the next few days burning potentially incriminating papers. The governor of Virginia was anxious to have any co-conspirators extradited for trial, but Frederick Douglass and a few others fled to Canada. Gerrit Smith, worn down already by a severe attack of typhoid in 1857 and a grueling campaign for governor of New York in 1858, collapsed under the strain and, when he began having hallucinations, was committed to an asylum, where he remained for a month before returning home, still too weak for any normal activities. James Pennington also may have destroyed relevant records. His stepson remembered clearly the breakfast meeting between Brown and his father, but beyond that his recollections were vague. "I know that there were several meetings at various places," he wrote years later, "but I think all information either written or printed was destroyed during the excitement, following the Harpers Ferry, so called insurrection."[26] When Thomas asked his stepfather to talk about Harpers Ferry, it "seemed always to be a subject which was gracefully retired to a more convenient season."[27] Whether Pennington himself had records that were destroyed is unclear, but James W. C. Pennington was one Northerner, perhaps the only one of those close to John Brown, who took a public stand in support even while the trial was going on. "History is always faithful to the memory of the martyr," he wrote, only a week after the news of Harpers Ferry reached New York. "He may be ahead of his age. He may be regarded as imprudent, unfortunate, or conscientiously wrong . . . but truthful history will be sure to vindicate his memory." Meanwhile, he urged that Brown should be the subject of prayer. "Shall any of our ministers be lacking in moral courage to bring this case squarely and openly before the people? I hope not. It is certainly no murder nor treason to pray for men in distress." He himself, he said, had offered prayer for Brown the Sunday after the event and would continue to do so. "Pray for old John Brown of Osawatamie! that he may be delivered or die like a man, and that his blood may be sanctified to the cause of freedom."[28]

Another year would go by before the election of Abraham Lincoln, but the violence at Harpers Ferry seemed to mark a turning point in the chain of events leading directly to the Civil War. The *Weekly Anglo-African* editorialized that "Henceforth forever there is no peace in the South until the morning of universal emancipation."[29] James Pennington was equally clear that "God must soon work, . . . and let us not doubt it." How then should believers respond? By faith, always the great watchword of the Protestant churches: "The Great Conflict Requires Great Faith" was the title of an essay Pennington wrote just afterwards in an attempt to spell out exactly what was required in this time of crisis. Slavery had fortified itself "in the church, and in all the high places of power," but "God has not forgotten how to use His right hand for the deliverance of the poor and oppressed. If tyrants have forgotten the history of the doings of that right hand in olden times, He is able to write a new one for their especial benefit." All this must have seemed frustratingly vague to those who, like John Brown, were ready to take events in their own hands and force the issue, but James Pennington had learned long ago to trust in God's moral government. "The strongest weapons we can use against oppression," he urged, "are moral courage and trust in God; trust in Him as the unchanging foe of tyrants . . . [for] their day is almost drawn to a close, and the year of jubilee is at hand!"[30]

The Year of Jubilee was, perhaps, at hand for African Americans as a group, but James Pennington was struggling more than ever simply to survive. In December he felt compelled to turn again to begging from wealthy whites. He called on John Jay to ask for help and, not finding him at home, wrote a letter telling Jay that his salary was only $200 and "For the winter I am much in want of [a] small amount of pecuniary help." "Can you give me $5.00," he asks. There was no response, so Pennington wrote again five days later, telling Jay that his people in Newtown "are poor" and therefore he has "called on several gentlemen—such as Francis Hall, Stracy B. Collins etc. who have aided me in sums of $2, $3, $5, etc." "Can you, sir, do anything for me. My family wants induce me to ask."[31]

Whatever his financial needs might have been, Pennington could still find reasons to write. There were still, always, sermons to write, but there were other ways as well to transmute daily life into prose for publication. In February 1860, the *Weekly Anglo-African* published an essay on "How to Keep Coal Stoves Free from Clinkers." Pennington had noticed an item in a local paper reporting that oyster shells were said to prevent clinkers from adhering to the insides of a stove when anthracite coal was burned in it and asking for someone to let the paper know the facts and the cause of the effect. Since no one else had responded, Pennington wrote the paper to tell them that oyster shells were indeed effective and to tell them why. Step by step, he described the way a fire should be built in a stove, how the oyster shells should be placed, and why the lime in the shells improved the burning of the coal. Lay a good base, he wrote, and start your fire, place a layer of oyster shells on it, then "I put on such a quantity of coal as I may need for the morning's use, and in a few moments I hear pop, pop, crack, crack, clink, clink, often so sharp that a nervous person might fear some injury would happen to the stove . . . The effect is that my coal kindles more thoroughly, burns more regularly to ashes, and prevents the lining from being matted with those hard masses of clinker substance which often carry away portions of it, to the great injury of the stove." "I can only speak as a practical blacksmith," he added, "long accustomed to the kindling and use of different kinds of coal fire."[32] Writing such essays was also, no doubt, a way to put aside for the moment the constant, pressing need to find money.

Neither financial worries nor essays on oyster shells, however, could long distract James Pennington from pursuit of the goals that had shaped his life for thirty years. God's moral government was moving affairs toward those goals and Pennington would continue to work for them and to oppose those who lacked his confidence in ultimate victory. An increasingly vocal minority was beginning to question their future in America and African Americans found themselves seriously divided for the first time on the subject of African colonization. Always impetuous and volatile, Henry Garnet and others created a new organization in 1859 called the African Civilization Society. Their goal was not the sort of indiscriminate exporting of African Americans promoted by the African Colonization Society, but rather a more selective emigration of educated leaders whose goal would be nothing less than the transformation of Africa as a result of the infusion of American skills. In an 1860 speech, Garnet defined the goal of the new organization by saying, "We believe that Africa is to be redeemed by Christian civilization and that the great work is to be chiefly achieved by the free and voluntary emigration of enterprising colored people."

But how would this siphoning off of talent benefit those who remained? Opposition was quick to organize, and Pennington took a leading role in condemning his colleague's efforts. When a great meeting in support of Garnet's project was scheduled for the Cooper Institute in early March of 1860, Pennington wrote to Thomas Hamilton at the *Anglo African* to denounce the plan and to point to the lack of black leadership among the speakers announced. "The colored people," he wrote, "desire to know whether this one-horse team is running in opposition to or in connection with the odious colonization scheme."[33] It did, of course, sound very much like the colonization plans that African Americans had been resisting for thirty years. A lecture Pennington gave at St. Paul's Church, Brooklyn, was poorly attended,[34] but when he and more than a dozen others called for a meeting at Zion Church, Manhattan, over a thousand responded and the meeting became tumultuous when Garnet and his supporters showed up also and insisted on having their views heard. The reporter for the *Anglo African* said the meeting at one point looked like "a lot of toads caught in a July shower." At last, "something like order being restored," it was suggested that prayer for God's blessing and presence might help, and Pennington was called on for the purpose. After that, things went better. A letter was read from Gerrit Smith, still too shaken by the aftermath of Harpers Ferry to leave his home but honored to be the one white man invited. His opinion was that there was a considerable danger in schemes to emigrate to Haiti or Africa if they were to "create or rather to increase the feeling that this land is not the home of these Americans . . . and that they have as much reason as the whites have to look upon it as their home." That was also the sense of the meeting, and Garnet with his followers had to accept the fact that most blacks were not yet ready to consider leaving the land of their birth, whatever the hardships might be. Hamilton's *Weekly Anglo-African* ran a series of letters by prominent African Americans denouncing the scheme as "disadvantageous" at best. "It is here," wrote John C. Bowers, a Philadelphian, "where their presence is wanted; it is here where the great battle for our rights is to be fought." "Shall we, in this day of conflict and struggle, desert our country and the sorrow-stricken bondman?" asked John Waugh of Rhode Island. "Shall we, sirs, in this day of light and hope, unsettle our relations with this country when white men are laying down their lives for black man's liberty . . . I say again, we will not leave our country, and the silent graves of our sleeping fathers."[35] James

McCune Smith wrote to Garnet in biting sarcasm at the end of the year to say, "The diamond owes its brilliancy to the numerous facets which it presents, and doubtless, in like manner, is your reverence indebted for the manifold luster with which you illuminate your times. There is scarcely a subject, or any side of a subject, connected with the recent history of us blacks for which you have not a corresponding face. . . . And now, my dear Sir, if Jamaica, with a fine church and ample salary, was not a fit place for you to shine in, why do you urge upon us, your brethren, to go to Abbeokuta, or Hayti, or any other climate equally hot, or hotter. Are we not constituted like you? Have we any qualities . . . so superior to yours that we will be able, under circumstances where you failed, to shine generally and abolish slavery in particular? . . . For my own part, I ask to be excused from emigrating either to Abbeokuta or Hayti . . ."[36] By the end of the year, however, Garnet himself was having second thoughts and, showing another face, inclined to favor Haiti over Africa.

But events were overtaking that particular debate. The moral government of God was moving Americans toward a final resolution of the slavery question by force of arms. Abraham Lincoln was inaugurated as president in March of 1861, and in April Confederate forces fired on Fort Sumter. In January, black clergy and lay people came together at Shiloh Church and spent two days listening to speeches and agreeing to call on Christians throughout the free states for "a day of humiliation, fasting and prayer. . . that God would avert the judgments about to fall upon the nation—that he may bring to naught the counsels of the wicked and cause righteousness and truth to prevail."[37]

In spite of the looming conflict, Garnet was not ready to abandon the emigration cause entirely; without the benefit of hindsight, no one could be sure that slavery was doomed. As late as May of 1860, fugitive slaves were still being arrested in New York and returned to slavery.[38] In February 1861, Garnet wrote to the *Anglo-African* attacking James McCune Smith, Martin Delaney, and an unnamed "D. D." who was almost certainly James Pennington, for their opposition to his program, and in March he accepted the post of resident agent for the Haitian Immigration Bureau in New York. Before the year was over, however, he was removed from his position at Shiloh Church and was off to England to look for support for the African civilization agenda.† Angry as usual and readier to attack than to conciliate, he wrote back to New York criticizing Theodore Bourne, another agent of his own society, and referring scornfully to James Pennington as "an unfortunate old negro, a Presbyterian minister of New York."[39]

† The trustees reversed their decision before Garnet's return from England, but the relationship continued stormy, and in 1864 he accepted a call to the Fifteenth Street Presbyterian Church in Washington, D.C. (Pasternak, Martin B., *Rise Now and Fly to Arms: the Life of Henry Highland Garnet*, pp. 102, 104.)

Far more single-minded, Pennington spoke again that summer at an August 1 celebration, this time in Yonkers, New York, near enough to the city that a number of celebrants could get there by traveling up the Hudson by ship. As principal speaker, Pennington saw it as his role to spell out the position African Americans should take in relationship to a contest whose goals were not yet clear. Lincoln and the North were fighting to preserve the Union, but whether slavery would be abolished as a result was not yet evident. What was not in doubt was the South's determination to maintain and extend slavery. Therefore, Pennington told his audience, "colored patriots" had a duty to support "Union without Slavery" and emancipation of the slaves. And, since the issue was now to be fought out on the battlefield, Pennington was ready to abandon pacifism and call for the creation of an army of 25,000 black troops to "recapture king cotton." "Our race in America has by its blood, tears, and sweat crowned it a king," he told the gathering, "and are therefore entitled to the benefits of his reign." Cotton had, in fact, made slavery profitable to the South, so it was critical to take that weapon away. The war to do that would be costly; Pennington saw that new taxes would be needed and that there would be opposition from those "who have fled the old world . . . to escape direct taxation." Nevertheless, he saw it as essential that black politicians support direct taxation. To "sit back in the shade and take no part, is unpolitical, unphilosophical, unmanly, and I had almost said traitorous to our own race."[40]

James Pennington might have lost his central pulpit and be desperate for support, but he could still take a leadership role in the black community. The speech in Yonkers was followed up by an effort to enlist support for a petition to Congress from colored citizens stating their view that "African Slavery . . . is the prime cause of the present Crisis and that permanent peace cannot be restored until said cause be removed."[41]

Pennington might have been concentrating his energy on the war effort, but the idea of colonization would not go away. A long letter came to him from Daniel Fraser, a writer unknown to him in upstate New York, outlining in great detail the essentials, as he saw it, for planting a colony. Salt pork, meat, and fish had resulted in diseases "which ought not to exist anywhere," Fraser wrote; "the nearer you can bring your people to living on penaceous substances, with suitable additions of fruit, the better it will be for them as regards health, clearness of intellect, and morality." American soil, he believed, had been "sugared, tobaccoed and cottoned to destruction to gratify the depraved appetites, tastes and whims" of the public. Yams were a better crop and "the African character" also "requires a goodly degree of personal religious freedom . . . Staid, sleepy sermons shut up the avenue of spiritual revelation . . . and shuts out the light of the oil of life. A little religious noise now and then will not hurt anybody." Somewhat puzzled by all this, Pennington wrote back that he was really not much involved in colonization projects, though he knew of efforts being made in England; he would have the letter published in view of its many valuable suggestions.[42]

Perhaps Fraser had Pennington and Garnet confused. Garnet was about to embark for England in support of his colonization project, but Pennington was planning to travel there with the purpose of enlisting English support for the Northern cause. Although the two clergy headed for England with different goals, both attempted to score the same point in their departure by applying for a passport. Pennington had been given a passport on his first trip to England, but the Dred Scott decision had raised the question whether African Americans could be citizens with all the rights and privileges of white people. A passport, certifying that the holder was, indeed, an American citizen, would attest to that. Pennington wrote to Secretary of State Seward:

> Being about to visit a foreign land, I wish as a loyal American citizen to obtain a passport. Maryland is my native state. My profession is that of a Presbyterian minister. I refer to ex governors Clark and Hunt, and to Hon. Gideon Welles secretary of the Navy and Gerrit Smith. Please send me a blank to be filled out as I wish to leave on the 14th instant. Mr. Buchanan gave me a passport in 1846 which I exchanged in London afterward for one in French when I was going to Paris.[43]

Both Garnet and Pennington received their passports, and the English *Anti-Slavery Reporter* hailed Garnet's document as making him "The First Black Citizen of the Dis-United States."[44]

Pennington's last speech before leaving was given at the Zion Baptist Church in Manhattan. He called for loyalty to the Union cause: "anything short of that was defying the wrath of heaven, and trampling under foot the eternal love of God."[†] A final farewell gathering took place at the Shiloh Church just two days before his departure on October 12 on the steamer *Edinburgh*.[45]

Pennington's first report from England made no report of speeches delivered, but spoke instead of a recent and dramatic incident in which a Confederate ship had captured an American merchant ship in the English Channel, taken its crew, and burned the ship. "A column of smoke from the burning of an American ship in British waters has been added to the dingy atmosphere of

---

† There is an odd foreshadowing in this phrase of Julia Ward Howe's "Battle Hymn of the Republic" with its phrase about "trampling out the vintage where the grapes of wrath are stored." Both draw on Biblical imagery (cf. especially Jeremiah 25:30), but the parallels between Howe and Pennington are much closer.

this land of November fogs and mists," wrote Pennington, "and created in this country a strange development of feeling and opinion." Some thought that the intrusion of the "American War in British Waters" was a deliberate attempt to involve England in the war, but the British Foreign Office managed to keep the incident from escalating out of control. There was also, Pennington reported, intense interest in England in the passport he had been issued and an inability to understand how the American government could issue him a document asserting his rights as a citizen although that same document gave him no security on a New York City streetcar. More important than the steam-ship and passport, but given only passing attention in Pennington's report, was the pressure on England from the cotton merchants. "A solid conviction rests upon the minds of the people," he told his American readers, "that they (the British) will not in future be dependent upon a cotton aristocracy." There was, in fact, considerable support for the Northern cause among English people generally, but the government's policy remained in doubt for several years. Pennington's journey was intended to help rally the public to the Northern cause and counter pressure from the merchants concerned for their profits from the cotton trade. Garnet dealt with that issue by asking support for his African civilization society: the remedy for dependence on the South, he told his audiences, was the creation of cotton farms in Africa.[46]

Pennington meanwhile had used his first weeks in England on behalf of a fugitive slave, J. H. Banks, who had reached England and turned to Pennington for help in telling his story. Published in November, the *Narrative of Events of the Life of J. H. Banks, an Escaped Slave from the Cotton State, Alabama, in America*, was written by Pennington and included a lengthy preface reviewing the course of the conflict between North and South in America and calling on "the friends of freedom to renew their fidelity to the principles of Sharpe, Clarkson, and Wilberforce," which would have preferred a peaceful solution to the crisis. It was the South, however, Pennington told his readers, that had brought on the crisis, "and to them must the account be placed . . . They have shed the first blood; and on them rests the blame for all the confusion which now fills the land, and which threatens the peace of the world."[47] As he had done on his first visit to England, Pennington used a fugitive slave narrative to reach a wider audience than he could do by lectures alone, but he traveled also telling his story, appealing for support for the Northern cause, and also asking for money to help instruct African Americans for missionary purposes.[48] William Crafts, J. Sella Martin, and other former slaves were also in England and, like Garnet and Pennington, trying to bring what pressure they could on the government to throw its weight behind the Union armies or, at the least, to maintain neutrality. The difficulty was that the policy of the Northern government on slavery remained unclear, and it was difficult to rally British enthusiasm for preserving the American union. The travelers found themselves reciting again the stories of their escape from slavery and unable to attract a large audience for a familiar story.

Pennington's English journey came to a disastrous end in June 1862, when he was arrested in Liverpool and sentenced to a month's hard labor for allegedly stealing a copy of Pope's translation of the *Odyssey* from a secondhand bookstore. Pennington claimed that he had absentmindedly slipped the book into his pocket, that he had every intention of paying for it, and that he had offered to do so when accosted by the clerk. The clerk, however, insisted on pressing charges, and the magistrate felt he had no alternative except to pronounce sentence.[†] Pennington was back in New York before the end of the summer. Garnet had returned earlier, also in straitened circumstances and delighted when the members of the Shiloh Church brought him and his wife a supply of groceries.[49] Colonization schemes remained at the center of his attention. President Lincoln had spoken of his belief that it would be useful to find a place to resettle emancipated slaves in Central America, and Garnet provided public support for the notion, saying that "neither the North nor the West nor the East will receive them. Nay, even our colored people of the North do not want them here [because it will] reduce the price of labor and take the bread out of our mouths."[50]

Pennington was quickly back on the lecture circuit and spoke in early September at a series of meetings in Montreal. One of his speeches was given at a temperance meeting where, if Tappan's charge of alcoholism was true, it seems odd that Pennington made no reference to personal experience in his address but drew a parallel between "the involuntary slavery of the slave and the voluntary slavery of the inebriate."[51] In his other speeches, Pennington gave his view of the war and the future of African Americans. Without referring specifically to Lincoln's ideas or Garnet's support for them, he acknowledged that some still wanted to send black people away, but he contended, as he had always done, that America had become now "as much the property of the black man as of the white man." As in England, he appealed for funds to educate African Americans for "missionary purposes among the population."[52]

Preoccupied as he was with traveling a widening lecture circuit, earning a living, and urging support for the Northern cause, James Pennington was not present in January of 1863 when the president's Emancipation Proclamation was celebrated with songs and oratory by a great gathering at the Cooper

---

† "Hard labour" was a standard sentence in mid-eighteenth century England, commonly used as punishment for petty theft and other minor offenses, and graded according to the severity of the offense. First offenders would usually be put in the "Star class" and might be set to work at shoemaking or bookbinding.

Institute. Henry Garnet presided, read the president's proclamation, and called on Lewis Tappan, William Wells Brown, and other veterans of the abolition movement to deliver addresses as well. The music and speeches went on until after midnight and were followed by a "Soirée" at Mozart Hall and dancing that lasted well into the "small hours" of the morning. Similar celebrations took place in Rochester, Buffalo, Brooklyn, and elsewhere.[53]

Pennington was back in New York that spring to deal with several pending issues. Colonization remained a contentious matter, and the return of a group of would-be emigrants to Haiti offered an opportunity to excoriate the ancient foe or, as the meeting termed the Colonization Society, "the old Hag" and "its pet daughter," Garnet's African Civilization Society. Pennington chaired a meeting at Zion Church at which the colonists told their story of "troubles and sufferings" from which they had escaped with "shattered constitutions and barely their lives, leaving husbands, wives, parents and children in premature graves, victims of cupidity and deception." Resolutions were passed denouncing schemes for "expatriation of our people from their homes" and creating an "Anti-Emigration League" to assist victims of such plots and "counsel and deter" those tempted to colonize distant lands.[54]

Just as the emancipation proclamation united African Americans in celebration, so the war in its various aspects was beginning to unite black leadership around other issues as well. Pennington and Martin Delaney had differed sharply on the subject of colonization, and Pennington, as a pacifist, had disagreed also with Delaney and Garnet on policy toward the slaves. But it was hard for Pennington to remain a pacifist now. In March, he wrote to Delaney to tell him "that our views so nearly harmonize in reference to arming the slaves . . . [that] our duty is to . . . organize, plan, and go forward." Pennington was anticipating action by the Confederates to arm the slaves, and he told Delaney that he had been speaking to this issue. "It would be an awful state of things to see the 200,000 union colored soldiers confronted by 200,000 of our own race, under the rebel banner! . . . No, this must not be. It shall not be. It cannot be if we do our duty. That is, to go to our brethren, and tell them what to do."[55] A more immediate issue was responding to the president's call for black troops and here, too, Pennington's former pacifism was not allowed to stand in the way.

Important as the campaign to enlist black troops was, James Pennington was well enough acquainted with the reality of life in New York City to be aware of an impending disaster. Two years had gone by since war had broken out between North and South, and the contest seemed to have become stalemated. The South could not, and the North would not, force the issue to a conclusion, yet the price in blood and money continued to grow, and the Northern dissenters, or "Copperheads," a sizeable force to begin with, were emboldened by the apparent inability of the administration to move decisively toward its goals. What Pennington understood was that the longer this situation persisted, the more dangerous it was for black people. The strength of Northern opposition to the war was to be found in the ranks of merchants and manufacturers who were cut off from their Southern suppliers, but wealthy men were not likely to rage in the streets, nor were the ordinary laborers likely to turn against the administration because business had become less profitable. Far more immediate to the working people who had so often rioted in the past was the threat of the draft that could sweep up young men for cannon fodder. What the merchants and bankers could do, therefore, was instill in the working poor a fear of the draft and a fear that abolition would bring a wave of black laborers surging up from the South to compete for the unskilled labor positions that went predominantly to the poorest and most uneducated immigrants, who were largely the Irish. A riot inspired by such fears would inevitably threaten not the Irish or the authorities, as previous riots had done, but black people.

What could black people do? A meeting was held at the Shiloh Church in May 1863, to encourage black enlistment in the Union Army. Massachusetts was raising a back regiment and Frederick Douglass, the principal speaker, told his audience that there were already 800 black soldiers in training. Here was an opportunity, he pointed out, to upset the Copperheads and to bring retribution to slaveholders. Henry Garnet and James Pennington both addressed the meeting and the *Liberator*, no fan of either man, termed Garnet's speech "eloquent" and Pennington's both "eloquent" and "most impressive."[56] Pennington did more than appeal to others; he offered his own services to the Union League Club of New York to assist in securing volunteers, and volunteered to go himself with such a regiment when it was ready.[57]

Less than a month after the rally at Shiloh, Pennington published an essay calling on black people to support the war and the enlistment of black troops or risk the establishment of an uncontrollable dictatorship or, worse still, a Southern triumph that would open the whole continent to slavery. The country, he understood, was, of necessity, "passing through the narrow and rockbound straits leading from the sea of republicanism to a military government." Military necessity had led Lincoln to abrogate some of the normal freedoms of peacetime, and there would be still further movement in that direction unless black people did their utmost to support the Union. Pennington saw white people attempting to encourage black resistance to military service. Worse still, he heard of black women discouraging their husbands and sons from enlisting. "The government may not give you all you wish," he wrote, "but you have more than you could expect in a state of anarchy, or under a dictator, or in a military despotism." Black troops in the North were not paid as well as white troops, but "see what the despotism of the South is compelling our black brethren to do without pay." Black troops in the North were being offered "a just cause to defend, good pay, good rations, good clothing, and in short every honorable motive calculated to move the patriot to action." All this on the one side, and on the other, a conspiracy—"a deep, desperate, wicked and treacherous scheme to break the government down." How wicked or dangerous to African Americans the scheme might be, Pennington may not fully have understood, but he was shortly, along with other New Yorkers, to learn for himself at first hand. Meanwhile, he saw the rising animosity expressed by the "stones, potatoes, and pieces of coal . . . hurled by idle young loafers [while] the language addressed to colored men, not seemly to record on paper, became the common language of the street, and even of some of the fashionable avenues. The streets were made to ring with words, and sayings, the most filthy, and yet no effort was made by magistrates, the press, or authorities, to suppress these ebullitions of barbarism . . . Every loafer . . . who could throw a stone of half a pound's weight, across the street at a colored man's head, might anywhere about the city, on any day, and at any hour, salute colored persons with . . . words surcharged with filth, malice, and brutal insult." Storm warnings were flying, but nothing was being done.[58]

Barely a month after Pennington's warning, the great draft riot of 1863 broke upon New York City like a firestorm, burning buildings and driving helpless black citizens out of their homes. The first Federal draft had begun on July 11, a Saturday, and proceeded peacefully, but opponents of the draft spent the weekend agitating, and mobs were in the street before the sun was properly up on Monday morning and streaming toward the draft office at Third Avenue and 46th Street, leaving destruction in their wake. Telephone poles were hacked down, rail lines rooted up, and the Superintendent of Police was beaten, tossed down an embankment, and nearly killed. For five days, from July 13 to 17, the mob raged through the city streets, burning and killing as the authorities pondered what to do. The state militia had been dispatched to Gettysburg to help block General Lee's invasion of the North, and the police were completely unprepared to deal with insurrection on this scale. George Templeton Strong watched the mob attack one house until he turned away in disgust. "I could endure the disgraceful, sickening sight no longer," he wrote in his diary, "and what could I *do*?" He and others pleaded with Mayor Opdyke and General John Wool, commander of the Army's District of the East with headquarters in New York, to declare martial law, but the mayor thought it was up to the general and the general thought it was up to the mayor; neither was willing to take decisive action. "Jefferson Davis rules New York today" wrote Strong and, indeed, this greatest riot in American history was more like a civil war within the Civil War, potentially a greater disaster to the Union cause than defeat on the battlefield.[59]

The Irish made up the largest number in the ranks of the mob, but James Pennington saw clearly that they were tools in the hands of others: it was "an Irish Catholic mob prompted by American Protestant demagogues and negro haters . . . an attempt by the southern rebels to plant the black flag of the slavery propagandist on the banks of the Hudson."[60] The mob, nevertheless, was intent on punishing the black population, seeing them as responsible for the war and the draft, and New York City's black citizens were in the greatest danger. Homes, boarding houses, and businesses, not only of black people but of whites who were known to be their friends, were attacked, vandalized, and burned. An orphan asylum for black children was burned down and the children barely escaped. William Powell wrote to Garrison to tell how he had guided his family to the roof of their five-story house when the mob began to break the ground-floor windows, and how a Jewish neighbor had brought them a rope to slide down to a lower roof and so to the ground.[61] Others were less fortunate. Some who fell into the hands of the mob were strung up on lampposts; others were beaten, mutilated, and tortured. A black woman whose son was serving in the Union Army was clubbed to death with her daughter and grandson, by members of the mob using a cart rung.[62] "Surely never was wickedness to parallel this, committed before in a Christian land," wrote an English observer. "It drove five thousand men, women, and children home-less and helpless, to seek refuge in the outskirts of the city, in the swamps and Woods, in barns and out-houses, anywhere so they could escape, even temporarily, the awful fury of that infuriate mob."[63]

James Pennington had found employment that spring as a school teacher in Poughkeepsie, New York, and in June had gone north, leaving his wife and son living still in a four-story brick house at 312 West 26th Street in New York.[64] They needed to stay in the city since they had bought the building they lived in three years earlier and were running it as a boarding house for seven other families.[65] From July 16 to 17, while the mob raged in New York, James Pennington was in Poughkeepsie presiding over a state convention of African Americans who had come together to urge support for the war as "a combat for the sacred rights of man," to call for the raising of 200,000 black troops, and to appoint a central committee to help coordinate enlistment efforts.[66]

Reports of the violence inevitably came north to Poughkeepsie, and as soon as the convention ended, Pennington took the evening ship south to Manhattan to look for his family. Arriving on Saturday morning, he went on foot "cautiously and peaceably" toward 26th Street but, just four doors away from his home, he was attacked with stones and brickbats and cries of "*kill the d——d nigger.*" He had only to put his hand on the door knob to learn that the

mob had been there first and his family was gone. Retreating to the river, he
was greeted for the first time by a friendly white face, a German acquaintance,
who said, "Why, Doctor, is it not too soon for you to be back in the city? Do be
careful which way you go!" This man walked with Pennington as he headed
back into the city to look for his family among other black residents, "and at
every step death and desolation stared me in the face." Far from finding his
wife and son or learning whether they were dead or alive, he found himself,
more than once, running for his life when an element of the mob caught sight
of him and, at other times, outfacing the mob by refusing to show any fear.
Thousands had fled the city, and those who remained were keeping themselves
well hidden. Whether Almira and Thomas had escaped from the city or found
a place to hide, Pennington could not find them. At last there was nothing to
be done except go back to Poughkeepsie and wait for order to be restored.[67] At
last it required the arrival of federal troops from the battlefield at Gettysburg
to occupy the city and put an end to the violence.[68]

From Poughkeepsie, Pennington drew up the first indictment of the authorities for their failure to prevent a crisis that he had long foreseen, and a demand
for reparations that would enable those uprooted by the riots to replace their lost
possessions. "I have facts in my possession," he wrote, "to prove that the recent
onslaught upon the colored people of New York, and other cities, is the result
of a deliberate arrangement."† There should be a commission created at once,
he said, to lay bare the whole scheme, and the city and state should pay for the
property destroyed and take responsibility for the "lives lost, the limbs broken,
the families broken up." Winter would soon be coming, and how would the
"poor scattered families" survive without such aid?

One answer to that question came from a committee of merchants who
came together as soon as the riots were over to see what could be done for
the relief of the African American community. In less than a week, they had

---

† Whether there was a deliberate plot concocted by Southern leaders and Northern
sympathizers was never demonstrated, but the possibility that a Confederate victory at
Gettysburg would have emboldened Southern sympathizers and made Northern victory
difficult or impossible was very real. Looking back only two years later, George Templeton
Strong wrote in his diary, "Gettysburg seems to have been the turning point of the four-
year struggle. I believe, moreover, that Lee's failure on that field saved us from an organized
Copperhead rising in New York. . . . Meade's victory and the fall of Vicksburg disheartened
the conspirators, but the draft riots of July were a partial deflagration and explosion of the
combustible ruffianism that have been stored away for yet worse mischief on a larger scale.
Had Meade been routed at Gettysburg, Seymour would have screwed his courage up to a
coup d'état backed by the mayor and aldermen of this city and all the rest of its rascaldom
in office and out. With Lee riding in triumph over Pennsylvania and New York arrayed
against government, the national cause would have been nearly hopeless. . ." (Strong, op.
cit., v. IV, pp. 14–15.)

raised money, created an office, and begun distributing assistance. Henry Garnet served on a small committee to assist the merchants in determining need and facilitating the distribution of aid. By the end of August, they had given assistance to over 6000 individuals, and they eventually distributed over $40,000. The final "Report of the Committee of Merchants for the Relief of Colored People Suffering from the Late Riots in the City of New York" not only details the money raised and distributed, but also the concern of merchants to restore "the confidence of colored people in the community, from which they have been driven," and their intention to assist them in pursuing their claims for assistance from the city. "The colored people of this city," said the report, "are a peaceable, industrious people. . . . As a class, they seldom depend upon charity; they not only labor to support themselves, but to aid those who need aid. This is their general character, and it is our duty to see that they are protected in their lawful labors . . ." The report also included story after story of men, women, and children beaten, mutilated, and killed, and a few stories of white people who stood up to the mob or assisted black people to hide or escape.[69] Garnet helped draft a remarkably generous statement of gratitude that said in part:

> When in the pursuit of our peaceful and humble occupations we had fallen among thieves, who stripped us of our raiment and had wounded us, leaving many of us half dead,[†] you had compassion on us. We were hungry and you fed us. We were thirsty and you gave us drink . . . We have now learned by your treatment of us in these days of our mental and physical affliction, that you cherished for us a kindly and humane feeling of which we had no knowledge . . . [B]y your generous moral courage you rolled back the tide of violence that had well-nigh swept us away.[70]

The generous response of the merchants' committee was offset to some degree by the employers who refused to take black employees back to the jobs they had held, from fear of the consequences and by new restrictions on travel. The Eighth Avenue Railroad Company, for example, issued an order on August 1 that "Colored persons are not allowed to ride on the cars of this company." Pennington was quick to call attention to the order and to point out that the railroad company's conduct was not only contrary to the injunction of the Supreme Court of the State but also "has attracted the attention of the parties in aristocratic England, infidel France, and despotic Russia, so-called. . . . It is in vain that we tell them we are fighting to put down slavery, at the South,

† Garnet might have added "and many dead in fact."

while we are mobbing, murdering, and turning respectable colored people out of our cars, in New York." It was right, Pennington said, that money be spent "for the relief of colored people, but let some be spent for justice."[71]

Six months later, Pennington, ignoring the merchants' belated response, weighed in with a much longer analysis of the riot and the specific lessons to be learned. Most strikingly, the first lesson he drew from the event was that "We must study of the use of arms, for *self-defense* . . . Self-defense is the first law of nature." The second recommendation was almost as aggressive: "We must enter into a solemn free colored *protestant industrial or labor league*. Let the greedy foreigner know," he wrote, "that a part of this country belongs to us; and that we assert the right to live and labor here. . . . No part of our influence has been used to prevent foreigners from coming to this country and enjoying its benefits. We have done them no wrong. What we ask in return is non-intervention. Let us alone." The third and fourth lessons were that young African-Americans should take whatever positions they could find, however humble. They should respond to the many applications they would see for "colored help" and be useful to applicants. Able-bodied men should go into the Army and Navy "for the sake of the strength that will give them, the education they will obtain, the pay they will get; and the good service they will do for God, the country, and the race. . . . we are bound to support the government, and the government is bound to protect us. . . . the plain and safe course for colored men, is *to do service and claim their rights*."[72]

Part two of this lengthy essay dealt first of all with the old question of colonization. Pennington spoke of the way in which colonization had divided the ranks of African-Americans: "many angry discussions had taken place. Old friendships were broken up, and a bitter spirit had been engendered among us." The worst effect of this as he saw it was that no training was being offered for teachers or ministers in the Southern field that was opening. Garnet was not mentioned by name, but it was clear that Pennington had him in mind when he wrote of "a colored Presbyterian clergyman" who had counseled a young man hoping to obtain an education for the ministry to "join a body where it would require less education to be a minister." It seemed to Pennington that Garnet and others like him were neglecting the opportunity opening in the South to support instead the president's interest in colonizing the freed slaves elsewhere. Patriotism was the next theme of the essay. Pennington saw the hand of God in the events taking place, and a need to be earnest to do God's will when it was so clearly shown.

The next to last section of the essay dealt with the danger that Confederate leaders would arm the slaves and send them into battle with promises that might induce them to fight for the Southern cause. "Every week's delay in crushing out this rebellion increases the danger that the slaves may be brought into the field against us. . . . If the slaves are brought into the field by the Confederates," Pennington wrote, "it will be a sad and awful day for us."

Finally, Pennington looked again at the riots that took place and insisted that the history of those days must not pass unrecorded, nor could the belated offering of the merchants atone for what had happened. "Shall a few thousand dollars of relief money, and a few words of good counsel, and consolation be a sufficient inducement to neglect our own history?" It was not simply the loss of life and property Pennington wanted recorded, not "the breaking up of families and business relations . . . the loss of precious harvest time which will never again return; the feeling of insecurity engendered; the confidence destroyed; the reaction; and lastly, the gross insult offered to our character as a people." All this, he concluded, was "a weight of injury which can only be realized by the most enlightened and sensitive minds among us. . . . Relief, and damage money, is well enough. But it cannot atone, fully, for evils done by riots. It cannot bring back our murdered dead. It cannot remove the insults we feel; and finally it gives no proof that the people have really changed their minds for the better, towards us."[73]

The summer of 1863 was the turning point of the war. When Lee drew back from Gettysburg and the New York rioters were subdued, the South had lost its last best chance of a victory, or at least a negotiated settlement leaving the South to go its way with its peculiar institution in place. Instead, the Union armies began their inexorable advance and in April 1864, the Senate passed the Thirteenth Amendment to the Constitution, which, after the House passed it in January 1865 and the ratification process ended in December 1865, abolished slavery. Garnet, who had left the Shiloh Church early in 1864 for a congregation in Washington, was asked to address a special Sunday morning session of the Congress and complied with an address centered primarily on a denunciation of the evils of slavery. "We plead for justice," he said, in a brief paragraph toward the end of his address. "We demand the right to live and labor, and enjoy the fruits of our toil." He looked toward the future and envisioned a time when "caste and prejudice in the Christian churches shall be utterly destroyed . . . When the blessings of the Christian religion and of sound religious education shall be freely offered to all, then, and not till then, shall the effectual labors of God's people and God's instruments cease."[74] †

---

† Garnet's stay in Washington was brief. He spent some months after the war touring the South and writing reports on the early days of Reconstruction. In April 1868, he resigned to take the presidency of a newly organized college for black students in Pittsburgh, but in 1870 he returned to New York to be pastor of a reorganized Shiloh Church, so small now that it could offer no salary. He continued in that position, though largely in retirement, until 1881, when President Garfield appointed him ambassador to Liberia. He sailed for Liberia in November and died there in February of the following year. (Pasternak, Martin B., *Rise Now and Fly to Arms, the Life of Henry Highland Garnet*. New York, Garland Publishing Inc., 1995, pp. 136, 143, 152, 155.)

But the war was not yet over and slavery had not yet been defeated. Indeed, Abraham Lincoln's first term of office was coming to an end; and if he were not reelected, the long and costly struggle on the battlefield might well end in a political compromise that would leave the South free to keep its "peculiar institution." It was all very well for Garnet to speak to the Congress about the evils of slavery, but there were immediate and practical concerns to be dealt with, and there was no consensus among Northern abolitionists as to the best way forward. Lincoln had signed an emancipation proclamation, but he had also suggested the wisdom of colonizing American blacks in Central America rather than help them find their place in a reconstructed American society. Some black Americans found Lincoln vacillating and unprincipled; African American soldiers resented the unequal treatment they were given and thought John C. Fremont would be a better choice.[75] Pennington had fought consistently against colonization schemes, but he could also be a pragmatist. Lincoln might not be the perfect candidate for African Americans, but neither was this a perfect world. In June, Pennington wrote the editor of the *Weekly Anglo-African*, Robert Hamilton, to suggest that the immediate need was to rally behind the president: the confidence he had acquired long ago in the "moral providence of God" was still shaping his understanding of events. "There was," he wrote, "a kind and wise Providence in bringing Mr. Lincoln into the Presidential chair, and I believe the same all-wise Providence has directed him in everything he has done as our President. I say OUR President because he is the only American President who has ever given any attention to colored men as citizens." In a short list of reasons to reelect Lincoln, courage and vision were not mentioned, but the more practical values of honesty, faithfulness, the respect of the world, and the fact that he was "more cordially hated by the Copperheads of the North and the rebels of the South than any other man." Blacks, he urged, should do all in their power to secure Lincoln's reelection.[76]

Those sentiments were endorsed by a National Convention of Colored Men held that Fall in Syracuse, New York. Henry Garnet called the meeting to order and was a principal speaker but spoke defensively of his connection with the African Civilization Society and was unable to prevent a convention vote condemning that society for its relationship with the Colonization Society. The Congress of the United States had listened to him more patiently than the Colored Convention. James Pennington, who had been present at almost every such gathering for over thirty years and had been president of the convention ten years earlier, was there in the New York delegation but made no speeches and served on no committees.[77] His days of national leadership were over; he was already preparing to move away from New York and serve again as a pastor and teacher in an area he had always wanted to serve and which was now, at last, becoming accessible.

CHAPTER TWENTY-TWO

Mississippi, Maine, and Florida, 1864–1870

While Henry Garnet was leaving the Shiloh congregation for a new charge in Washington and lecturing the Congress on the evils of slavery, James Pennington was looking ahead to the new world coming into being with the end of slavery and imagining a role for himself in that world.

It had come as an astonishing revelation to James Pennington, shortly after his escape from slavery, to learn how many others were still enslaved. The question he then began to ask himself was, "What can I do for that vast body of suffering brotherhood I have left behind?" As the Civil War drew slowly and painfully to an end, that question came to the fore once again and with new force, since now that "vast body of suffering brotherhood" was accessible and Pennington had an education and experience as a teacher. To bring his skills to bear on that need was, however, not much easier than it had been before. The Union armies had opened the South to all the skills and humanitarian concerns of the Union government and Northern churches, but none of them had given much thought to the task they now faced or put structures in place to prepare the freed slaves to make use of their freedom.

Complicating the situation even further for James Pennington was the fact that the church he belonged to had lost any connection with its Southern congregations. At the outbreak of Civil War, the General Assembly of the Presbyterian Church had passed resolutions denouncing secession as treason. Southern congregations of the Presbyterian Church had therefore created a separate denomination for themselves, and the end of the war brought with it no desire to forget past differences. The Southern church had no interest in the freed slaves, and the Northern church had no structure in the South. If Pennington were to serve the freed slaves, his own church could not provide any structure to support or enable him. There was, however, another church, undivided by the war and eager to reach out to the freedmen. The African Methodist Episcopal Church, the church of Richard Allen, had been created by free African Americans in the North and had already reached out to those few free African Americans in the South. By the time of the Civil War, AME congregations had been established in Maryland, Kentucky, Missouri, Louisiana, and South Carolina. The end of the war opened a vast mission field for this church, and its clergy moved aggressively to capitalize on the opportunity. Two AME clergy, Alexander Wayman and Theophilus G. Steward, took the Biblical text "I seek my brethren" as their watchword and preached on that text over and over in the first post-war years as the church expanded rapidly through the South.[1]

James Pennington felt that same impulse to seek his brethren but needed to find a road into the new South that would be open for him. He had friendships inevitably with AME members and clergy, and as early as 1852 had even attended an AME General Conference in New York City as a "distinguished guest."[2] To join the AME Church, which was actively recruiting Northern clergy in order to maintain a high standard of clerical leadership in its new mission field,[3] would give him access to the South, but he had endured so much for his membership in the Presbyterian Church that a change of allegiance was not easy. Finally, in October 1864, however, he took the necessary step, requesting "letters of dismission" from the New York Presbytery and a recommendation to the St. Louis Conference of the African Methodist Episcopal Church.[4] The request was granted, but the war was not over, so Pennington would have to wait for events to play themselves out on the battlefield to begin the next chapter of his life.

When Robert E. Lee surrendered on April 9, 1865, the Civil War was essentially over, although Confederate forces in the deep South and West held out for another month or more. Pennington continued on in New York through the summer, writing and speaking on various occasions. In late July, he attended the graduation ceremonies of Colored Grammar School No. 2 and gave an address on the "Use of Language,"[5] on August first he was the featured speaker at a Brooklyn celebration of the anniversary of West Indian Emancipation,[6] and in September he contributed an essay to the *Anglo-African* denouncing the notion that black people must still endure. Patience and endurance would continue to be recommended for America's black population for another century, but James Pennington was becoming impatient with that philosophy, and said so in an editorial in the *Anglo-African* titled "The New Evangel":

> We have fulfilled the gospel of endurance; thoroughly, completely, exhaustively, in such a way as gospel never was fulfilled before,

never can be fulfilled again. . . . We have fulfilled it as individuals; each and every one of us, we have fulfilled it as a race through six generations; we have fulfilled it in all the relations of life, family, social, political, through all the recesses of the soul, mind, and body, drenched, drained, filled to the overflowing, saturated, crushed, from birth to death with this doom of endurance under slavery and caste.

Endurance indeed! That game is "played out." There is nothing left of it . . . There must be a new deal . . . We must exchange the gospel of endurance for the gospel of resistance. . . . Let this new gospel of resistance, or self-assertion, be clearly understood.[7]

Not until October 1865 did Pennington finally leave New York and travel to New Orleans to attend the first annual conference of the newly organized Louisiana Conference of the African Methodist Episcopal Church. Clearly, Pennington's reputation had preceded him, since he was appointed a "Travelling Elder" and placed on a three-member committee on education for ministry several days before the service at which he officially took the ordination vows of the African Methodist Episcopal Church.[8] After several weeks in New Orleans, he decided he could best serve his new church in Natchez, Mississippi, perhaps because it was a commercial center for the region. Appointed to serve in Natchez, he journeyed up the river with Bishop Jabez P. Campbell and arrived there on November 9.[9] Local leaders had called a meeting the next day to plan for the building of a school and acquisition of a church building, and took the occasion to complain of Northern missionaries who insisted on controlling funds and buildings and leaving black women in subordinate roles: "We very much dislike the idea of those Missionary Associations sending men down here who, while in the North made loud pretensions to Abolition, and when they get in the south partake so largely of that contemptible prejudice that they are ashamed to be seen in company with colored men. We say it is decidedly wrong."[10] There were evidently leaders in the congregation with strong views and an ability to express them. Among the members were a plasterer, a carpenter, a gunsmith with a shop to sell his wares, a silversmith with a jewelry store, two blacksmiths, an undertaker, and a brick mason.[11] Several members of the congregation had letters published in the denomination's national newspaper. "Some of them are quite wealthy," Bishop Campbell wrote in his journal, "and the majority are in comfortable circumstances."[12] Pennington's objective may have been to serve the freedmen, but the congregation he would serve was not a collection of illiterate and helpless former slaves.

On the following Sunday, Pennington preached in Natchez for the first time and took his text from the Old Testament: "Arise, therefore, and be doing, and the Lord be with thee." Bishop Campbell reported that it was "a good practical discourse, just such as we like to hear a minister deliver on taking charge of a congregation. The Doctor's manner of speaking is very pleasant, and we think his sermon was quite satisfactory."[13] A member of the congregation calling himself "Occasional" wrote that, in his opinion, "I think he [Pennington] is the right man in the right place. The A.M.E. Church should certainly feel proud of such a man, and duly appreciate him."[14] Pennington's salary in the new post would be only $300, but provision was made in the budget for rent, board, and travel for a total stipend of over $1700.

The city of Natchez, less than two hundred miles north of New Orleans on the Mississippi River, had actually been a part of the Confederacy for barely a year before it surrendered peacefully to a naval force commanded by future Admiral David Farragut in April 1862. Three and a half years under Union control had not, however, enabled the Union forces to establish a re-ordered society. Slaves had been set free, but there was no established policy for dealing with them. The Union army, inevitably, saw things from a miliary point of view and declared the slaves to be contraband, that is, goods seized from the adversary. Slaves, in other words, were still seen as property and the army's instinctive response to the possession of this property was to use it for its own ends. Freedmen were therefore organized into either military units or labor brigades to serve the military.† Some freedmen, nevertheless, managed to set themselves up in business or take possession of small plots of land, while others remained contentedly with their former owners.

By the time Pennington arrived in Natchez, the former slaveowners were beginning to work out strategies for dealing with the new situation and were hiring back the more able of their former slaves to work under contract. Emerging one day from the store where he had bought a copy of the *New York Tribune*, Pennington was hailed by a man on the other side of the street: "Uncle, what is the news?"

"Well," said Pennington, "what sort of news do you wish to hear?"

"I come a good ways from here," was the answer; "away from the swamp, and I would give half a dollar to know the news about dis here hiring business. Now de way day tell us out dere, it seems, when my year is out, next Christmas, I can't hire for another year without being bound for five years."

"You are willing then to hire for another year—are you?" asked Pennington.

"O, yes; but then I don't want to bind myself for five years."

---

† The freedmen's "wages" were not paid to them, however, but used to buy food, clothing, and other necessities for the black population, a system that differed little from slavery since the black laborers had no control over their compensation. (Davis, Ronald L. F., "The U. S. Army and the Origins of Sharecropping in the Natchez District—A Case Study." *The Journal of Negro History*, v. 62, n. 1 (January 1977), pp. 60–80.)

As the conversation went on, Pennington learned that the man was part of a group of four or five who had come some forty miles to find out what the new laws required. No law required five-year contracts, but word was being circulated that it did, and those refusing to sign on those terms were then charged with being lazy. Part of the difficulty was the lack of clear guidance as to the government's intentions. Land and property of slaveowners "in open rebellion" had been declared confiscated, but just what land that was or how it could be purchased remained uncertain as a succession of administrators came out from Washington and issued various orders on the subject.[15] Pennington set himself the task of gaining clarity on everything related to land, labor, and wages and announced a course of lectures so that "right and truth shall go from this point throughout the state." In a lengthy report to the *Anglo-African*, he said that the freedmen needed "nothing more than a fair chance in the market to buy or lease lands upon just terms and good titles."[16]

Perhaps even more urgently, he felt, Southern whites needed steady guidance from Washington and an end to trouble-making advice from New York. One day, when Pennington bought a copy of the *New York Herald*, he found an editorial in it suggesting that "The idea . . . of giving the negro possession of and control over the fairest portion of the American continent . . . is the most insane and impossible one that ever entered into the mind of man." Eventually, the *Herald* believed, the freedmen would settle in "the rice and cotton lands of the Atlantic coast and south Georgia . . . [in] regions adapted to his constitution . . . [where he can] luxuriate under a tropical sun in canebrakes and rice swamps, where the white man cannot."[17] Equally disturbing to Pennington was an article copied into a local paper from the *New York Day-Book* under the title "Can we amalgamate with the negroes?" Pennington's rejoinder was caustic: "Why, this is fifty years behind the age." "The waves of the Black Sea, the Red Sea, the Yellow Sea, and the White Sea had already been mingled," he wrote, by the "canals" of slavery, and the aftermath of the war had continued the process through the agency of "some of the proudest and bravest of your Northern soldiers and officers." The Southern population was not only "of every possible mixture," but so depleted by the war that it would now be "her wisdom to measure her population by manhood and vitality, and not by the mere color of the skin."[18]

Southern whites, it seemed to Pennington, were fortunate to have come through the war and its aftermath so easily. "They know that educated freedmen and freed-women could speak burning words, and write with biting pens." Instead of "troubling the blacks of the South about ignorance, laziness, vice and immorality, they have every reason to congratulate themselves that they have escaped with so little exposure." They did, however, stand in need of "improvement in their spirit and manners." But the freedmen, of course, "who have been so long sunk down and brutified by custom and legislation" needed the "full standard of Christian civilization . . . set before their minds, and every effort made to impel them up to it." The time had come, Pennington believed, when, if Southern whites would "let bygones be bygones, accept the state of facts which their own gotten up war has created, [and] stop their croaking about amalgamation and the inferiority of the negroes, things will go well."[19] A recent act of the legislature allowing blacks to testify in all cases except between whites seemed to him evidence that events were moving in the right direction;[20] nonetheless, he thought that "for the welfare of all parties, it is to be hoped that the military forces will not be withdrawn and especially the colored forces."[21]

Military men may have seen the situation more clearly, hearing from the white population more fully than Pennington could. Colonel Samuel Thomas, assistant commissioner of the Freedmen's Bureau for the state of Mississippi, toured the State and reported, "The negroes have almost everywhere gone to work and their good conduct is the subject of universal praise." But he saw clearly that the South was not ready to adjust to new relationships. "No one known to represent the Government," he reported, "is treated with respect or decency unless backed by military force."[22]

> The reasons why I think the negro has so little chance for justice at the hands of Mississippians is, that into whatever place I go the street, the shop, the house, the hotel, or the steamboat I . . . hear the people talk in a way that indicates that public sentiment has not come to the attitude in which it can conceive of the negro having any rights at all. Men . . . cheat a negro without feeling a single twinge of their honor; to kill a negro they do not deem murder; to debauch a negro woman they do not think fornication; to take property away from a negro they do not consider robbery. The reason for this is simple and manifest: they esteem the negro the property of the white man by natural right. . . .[23]

Even as Pennington was writing his optimistic report in November, however, the Mississippi state legislature was enacting a set of laws, known collectively as the Black Code, designed to restore the pre-war relationship between the races. Blacks might no longer be slaves, but they could not be idle or disorderly or use "insulting" gestures. They could not own a gun or even preach the Gospel without first obtaining a special license. Their children were required to work as "apprentices" for white planters, often their former owners, until they turned eighteen. The state penal codes simply replaced the word "slave" with "freedman," and left all the penalties for slaves in full force for the newly emancipated. The newly elected governor, Benjamin G. Humphreys, a former Confederate general, laid out the thinking of many for the legislature in his inaugural address: "The Negro is free, whether we like it or not; we must realize that fact now and forever. To be free, however, does not make him a citizen, or entitle him to political or social equality with the white race."

The local consequences of this perspective were realized when Pennington's congregation, lacking as yet a building of their own, asked permission to use the City Hall for a church fair and were turned down. A subsequent request to use two basement rooms in the Natchez Institute was "respectfully declined." "What a terrible thing is prejudice!" wrote Pennington. "And more so now than ever before as their prejudice has settled down into positive hatred." Prejudice, it seemed to him, could only be removed by granting all citizens equal rights, and that would require a Constitutional amendment.† "Time, aided and abetted by equal rights, will, I am confident, remove all prejudice, envy, and hatred."[24]

Meanwhile, Pennington's primary concern was to create a stable and growing congregation, and his largest harvest field would be among the black members of the Southern Methodist Church. The Methodist Church had become divided in 1844 over the issue of slavery, and by the beginning of the Civil War the southern Methodist Church had built up a membership of nearly 750,000, of whom nearly 200,000 were black. As the war came to an end, however, the black membership began a massive exodus in favor of black-led churches like the A.M.E. By 1866 only 78,742 black members remained in the Methodist Church, and by 1870 the number had dwindled to less than 20,000; meanwhile, the A.M.E. Church had grown from an 1860 membership of 70,000 to nearly 400,000 ten years later.[25] The Northern Methodist Church hoped to capitalize on this exodus itself, but Southern Methodists, angry over the Northern church's aggressive invasion of the South in the wake of Union armies,†† encouraged their black members, if they must leave, to join a black-led church rather than the Northern church. For the same reasons, the Southern church acted to cede use and even possession of its buildings to

---

† The Fourteenth Amendment, proposed in June 1866 and adopted two years later, provided that "No State shall make or enforce any law which shall abridge the privileges or immunities of citizens of the United States; nor shall any State deprive any person of life, liberty, or property, without due process of law; nor deny to any person within its jurisdiction the equal protection of the laws." Lacking Federal enforcement, however, the Amendment did little to alter the situation.

†† The War Department in Washington had gone so far as to give Northern Methodist Bishop Ames authority over Methodist property in major Southern cities, apparently on the theory that the Northern branch would take over the Southern church as the war ended.

black congregations where they had sole possession,[26] especially those aligned with the AME Church.[27]

In Natchez, as a result, the black congregation hoped to buy a building belonging to the Southern Methodist Church, but negotiating the terms was not easy. Since Washington had given the Freedmen's Bureau supervision of schools and clergy,[28] Pennington wrote in January to Major G. D. Reynolds, the Freedmen's Bureau's representative in Natchez, that the negotiations had been going on for three months and had become tedious. Since he needed to return to New York to visit his family and attend to business, he asked the Major to certify that the AME Congregation would not, in his absence, be required to vacate the building they had been using to move to the other site.[29] By the middle of May 1866, they had managed to raise $3000 as a partial payment and agreed to pay an additional $6000 in two annual installments.[30] Opposition came not from the Southern branch of the Methodist Church but from the Northern. John Turner, a colleague of Pennington's serving in New Orleans, wrote to the national AME newspaper to report the difficulty and included a memo from Pennington. A Methodist elder from the Northern church had appeared at the church one Sunday in March and asked permission to address the congregation. After a "long, tedious, and somewhat offensive statement," he asked for a show of hands of those who were willing to join his party. Pennington decided "he had gone far enough" and objected to any further such discussion, but the Northern elder found a room elsewhere in the city and received ten or twelve members of Pennington's congregation as well as some others. His approach, as Turner reported it, was to tell church members that they need not give their money since the Northern church had created a special fund for their benefit, and they need only come back to "the old Mother Church." Turner described this as simply one of a number of such incidents.[31]

Awkwardly for Pennington, this had come to a head at the end of May and on the last Sunday before he was to leave again "to visit my family in New York." He speaks fondly of leaving "my people" and clearly expected to return,[32] yet the need to make two visits several weeks long to New York in six months indicates that Pennington was not really free to commit himself to the Natchez post. There is no evidence that he returned a second time to Mississippi. When the New Orleans Conference met in the fall, someone else was appointed to Natchez and Pennington's name is not listed. On April 1 of the following year, the Third Presbytery of New York received a letter from Pennington, now stationed at the other end of the country with the Abyssinian Congregational Church in Portland, Maine, to the effect that "owing to the dissolution of the ecclesiastical body, to which he had been dismissed by this Presbytery, he had not presented his testimonials, and now asked leave to return his certificate, with a request that his name be restored to the Roll." The request, strange though the language seems, was granted. Hardly had Pennington's request been granted, however, when he was called back from Maine since, once again, his wife had died in his absence. Falling ill on April 3, she died three days later. The cause of death was peritonitis, and the death certificate states that she had been sick for three days.[33]

It is hard to know what to make of this sequence of events. One possible reading would be that Pennington went to Mississippi to fulfill a lifelong dream of ministry to freed slaves, even though Almira was not well. She might have stayed in New York for health reasons, or simply to manage the boarding house and provide additional income. Pennington then would have returned to New York after three months to see her condition, and felt the situation was such that he could return to Mississippi. When he came back to New York in June, however, he may have found that she was in such poor health that he felt he could not return to Mississippi. That meant, of course, that someone else would be appointed in his place, and he would not be re-appointed in the African Methodist system. The language in the Presbytery minutes about the "dissolution of the ecclesiastical body, to which he had been dismissed by this Presbytery" may represent an awkward attempt by the clerk to say that the relationship between Pennington and the African Methodist Episcopal Church had been dissolved since both the denomination itself and the Natchez congregation were evidently still in existence. So Pennington could not return to the AME Church, and if Almira then seemed better, Pennington would have been able to take a Congregational position; and the one opening available was in Maine. Pennington would be serving a Congregational church there, but could do so and remain in good standing with the Presbyterians. Portland, Maine, of course, is some distance from New York, but not as far away as Mississippi. The pay was not generous, however, so Almira would have stayed in New York to manage the boarding house. Peritonitis is typically a disease of sudden onset but can also be the result of underlying causes, and Pennington had spoken of his wife ten years earlier as being in only "tolerable health."[†] Almira's death left James Pennington with no reason to stay in New York, and he could continue to serve the congregation in Portland for the short term. He still wanted to go south, but there was no immediate way to arrange it.

The Abyssinian Religious Society in Portland had been established to serve the four hundred or so African Americans in the area, many of them fugitives from the South, and a church had been built in 1828. Many of the men "followed the sea" for a living.[34] Pennington had known of the Portland congregation for thirty years because Amos Beman had written him a series of

---

† See above, November 6, 1852.

long letters when he was there in 1840 and 1841. He had written of the "gloomy fact" that the average daily attendance in the school was not more than 30 or 35 out of sixty black children of school age. "Such," he wrote, "ought not to be the case," and he begged Pennington to "dip your pen in fire" and let parents know the importance of education.[35] Beman returned to Portland after his marriage in 1858, leaving the congregation he had been serving in Hartford since 1841, but the congregation in Maine refused to provide the usual furnishings for the pastor's home when they learned that his wife was white and he stayed less than a year. Pennington's service there would also be brief.

There are few records of the nearly three years Pennington spent in Portland. The church record book, full of details for the early years of the congregation, has no entries at all for that period and the local newspaper seldom reported church news, and this lack of news indicates that Pennington was apparently accepted as a colleague by the other Congregational and evangelical clergy in the city. When an Evangelical Conference convened in January of 1868 "to devise measures to advance the cause of Christ in our community," Pennington was one of several clergy to address the gathering. In April 1869, a Fast Day was marked by a Union service "particularly with reference to national affairs, such as was formerly held 'before the fire'"[†] and Pennington was one of five clergy to lead the prayers.[36]

The few records that exist also show that Pennington continued to make his voice and presence felt beyond this small city in Maine. He continued to work for the education of African Americans for the ministry, serving as the only black trustee of a fund created for that purpose.[††] In December 1868, he wrote to Lewis Hayden, a black leader in Boston, about plans for a society to increase the fund. He suggested calling together a group of supporters and electing officers. "Give me the Secretaryship," he wrote, "and I can set the thing at work without expense." There were two young men in need of financial assistance in their studies and Pennington felt it was urgent that they move quickly. "I desire to have this body formed on or near the 1st of January," he wrote; "I want this matter attended to at once . . ."[37]

Pennington continued to make his views known on larger issues as well and, as always, believed that conventions were an essential tool for progress. In a letter to the *National Anti-Slavery Standard* early in 1869, he noted with approval the fact that a recent Colored Convention had recommended annual

---

† The Great Fire of Portland, in July 1866, destroyed a large part of the city and left 10,000 people homeless. The Abyssinian Church was one of the few structures that survived.

†† This may be the fund Pennington referred to in the *Christian Freeman*, November 6, 1845. cf. p. 310.

conventions until full suffrage was obtained. "It was a blunder," Pennington wrote, "to give up our regular conventions years ago." He took the occasion to report that prejudice was far from dead in Maine. When Wendell Phillips had come to Portland to speak, condemning distinctions of race and color, Pennington heard a woman seated directly in front of him say, "I wish someone had gone up and knocked him down! How dare he come here and talk that way!" He spoke of the incident less in anger than with amusement at this survival of a dying way of thinking: "While we have such mothers in Maine, we cannot be at all surprised that her sons are not up to the times."[38]

Far to the north though Portland is, it was no more enlightened on racial matters than the rest of the country. The local paper reprinted an item from the *New York World* about a lecture by "Prof. Agassiz," who "pointed out a hundred specific differences between the bonal and nervous systems of the white man and negro. . . . The whole physical organism of the negro differs as much from the white man as it does from the chimpanzee—that is, in his bones, muscles, nerves and fibres, the chimpanzee has not much further to progress to become a negro, than the negro has to become a white. This fact science inexorably demonstrates. . . . The negro is no more the white man's brother than the owl is the sister of the eagle, or than the ass is the brother of the horse. How simple is the doctrine that the Almighty Maker of the universe has created inherent species of the lower animals, to fill different places and offices in the grand scenery of nature."[39] Six weeks later, the same paper reported its view on "the ultimate result of the Negro experiment the Radicals are making in the South. . . . The black will not succeed in raising himself to the dignity of the freeman, but he will succeed in depressing the character and obstructing the progress of the white."[40] Such were the insights into the state of American civilization that could be read in the morning paper. When Portland celebrated the Fourth of July in 1867 a dozen teams competed to "hit off" effigies of "colored folks, State Constables, Horace Greeley, Jeff Davis" and other objects of derision.[41]

But Pennington could console himself with the thought that Portland was not "up to the times" nor on the front line of progress like other cities, and he yearned to be once again where the action was. He continued to go to New York for meetings, attending the Stated Meeting of the Third Presbytery on April 6, the first anniversary of Almira's death.[42] The evidence seems to indicate that he was away from Portland with increasing frequency. *The Eastern Argus*, Portland's newspaper of record, found room for the announcement of church services less than half the time but, when it did, the Newbury Street Church services were usually listed with "Preaching by Rev. Dr. Pennington" morning, afternoon, and evening every Sunday until the summer of 1868. From August of 1868, however, until March of the following year, the

Newbury Street Church was seldom listed and, when it was, "the Rev. Mr. Brown of Chelsea" was announced as the preacher. Pennington was present in March and April of 1869, but the next notice in June lists no preacher and Pennington's name does not appear thereafter.[43] By September, he was on the move again.

In 1863, James W. C. Pennington's former colleague William Wells Brown had described him as being "of the common size, slightly inclined to corpulency, with an athletic frame, and a good constitution,"[44] but for at least thirty years he had been living with little regard for his health. More than once, he had succumbed briefly to the pressure of events. Never had he been able to settle in one place for more than a few years, and he had often lived for years at a time, in England and Scotland, with no fixed residence at all. Even when he did have a fixed residence, he was often traveling and away from that home for months at a time. By 1869, the effects of that life were becoming visible. He was about 60 years old, but in place of the "erect bearing" of his early years, he was described as being "in broken health, and bending under the infirmities of years."[45] Portland had provided a home and community and ministry, but the climate was not the most healthful and the pull of the South and a ministry to the former slaves remained strong. Impatient with the Presbyterians, Pennington had joined the African Methodist Church, but only a year or two later the Presbyterian Church had finally taken action to create a Committee of Missions for Freedmen to provide its own ministry to the former slaves. Thus the way was open for Pennington to go back to the South under Presbyterian auspices.

In September 1869, Pennington left Portland and wrote, "I have taken a mission to Florida for the coming winter, which will embrace the cause of education in the State, and also a mission under the direction of the presbytery."[46] A mission in Florida with an opportunity to do something about "the cause of education" must have seemed very nearly ideal. He could do the things he cared most about doing while moving to a climate that might also improve his health.

Like the editor of the *Weekly Anglo-African,* Pennington also had become impatient with the philosophy of endurance. He had abandoned his pacifist principles to help raise troops for the Northern armies, but once the war was over, education became the priority. Only an educated citizenry would be in position to claim the benefits of freedom. The Presbyterian Church was ready at last to move in that direction and, lacking many qualified candidates, was prepared to take Pennington back and send him again to the South. They had a specific situation for him in Jacksonville, Florida, where the leading Presbyterian congregation had become divided. One faction thought the time had come to reunite the church, while another faction was not ready to make peace with the Northern church. The result of this division was that there were now two Presbyterian churches in Jacksonville. The reunionists, whose church building had been coopted for use as a school for black children, were prepared also to work with the Northern church in creating a mission to the Freedmen. Funding, of course, would be a problem; the Presbyterian Committee offered a salary of $200, exactly what Pennington had been paid when he began as a school teacher in Newtown almost 40 years earlier, but there the schoolroom was also provided.† American churches have often encouraged their mission-minded members to raise their own funds for missionary work, and Pennington had been doing that for years. Among others, he turned quite naturally in this new situation to Gerrit Smith, telling him, "Duty calls me to go to the State of Florida and assist my brethren and others in that interesting field in the great cause of education and christian Reconstruction. There is a fine prospect in that state and a pressing call for education. I wish to enter this field. I need a little means; will you aid me?"[47] Help came also from a Philadelphia Committee that provided a set of communion vessels.[48]

For those enjoying the rush of prosperity that came to the North at the end of the Civil War, the lure of a subtropical climate in Florida was a great discovery, and "Florida fever" broke out all over the Northern states. Some were quickly disillusioned; a correspondent for the New Haven *Palladium* thought it the most "miserable and forlorn" country he had ever seen, but also noted that those "with nothing to do, can do it easier and better" in Florida than anywhere else. People who thought Florida was "a land of oranges and mockingbirds . . . where flowers bloom in luxuriance . . . where well people never get sick and sick people never die" would, he thought, "receive some new impressions on going there."[49] Harriet Beecher Stowe liked it well enough to create a winter home for herself on the banks of the St. John River just south of Jacksonville. She improved her time there by working with the Episcopal bishop and the Freedmen's Bureau to build a combined school and church to serve both the black and white communities. She earned some additional income by writing a book about her experience in Florida that offered a remarkably balanced appreciation of the area:

> To be able to spend your winter out of doors, even though some days be cold; to be able to sit with windows open; to hear birds daily; to eat fruit from trees, and pick flowers from hedges, all winter long,—is about the whole of the story. This you can do; and this is why Florida is life and health to the invalid. . . . [But there are] three formidable summer months, July, August, and

---

† The cost of living, however, was generally stable through the 19th century. The Civil War caused an inflationary spike, but prices declined again afterwards.

September, when the heat is excessive, and the liabilities of new settlers to sickness so great, that we should never wish to take the responsibility of bringing anybody here. It is true that a very comfortable number of people do live through them.[50]

It was also true, she added, that "some invalids do come here, expose themselves imprudently, and die. People do die in Florida . . . it is true we have sometimes severe frosts in Florida; it is true we have malaria; it is true that there are swamps in Florida . . . All these are undeniable truths."[51]

Perhaps, then, Florida was not the ideal place for someone whose health was as uncertain as Pennington's. But he took passage on a coastal steamer to Savannah and then journeyed on by train to Jacksonville. There he introduced himself to the pastor of the First Presbyterian Church, who told him that a small group had already begin to think about creating a new congregation. On February 12, 1870, Pennington met with that committee in the pastor's office and, on February 27, he preached the first sermon for the new congregation.[52] The *Palladium*'s correspondent filed reports on February 17 and 24 and mentioned the number of "Connecticut people" in the area, lawyers, judges, and even the clerk in the hotel, but his path did not cross that of James W. C. Pennington.[53] Pennington did, however, find one of his long-lost brothers and several other families, one from a friend's church in Brooklyn, who formed a nucleus for the new congregation.[54] Also in the congregation was another African American Presbyterian pastor, J. C. Gibbs, a graduate of Dartmouth College and the Princeton Theological Seminary, who had been made secretary of state for Florida and who later served as superintendent of public instruction for the state.[55] But these were not the people Pennington had come to serve. His great concern, inevitably, was for the freedmen and to help create "social and domestic organization" out of a population that had for generations been controlled by a government and "dominant race [so] averse to all the social and domestic virtues" that the result was "a fearful moral chaos." Slavery, Pennington wrote, was "a malignant cancer [that] leaves its roots after being apparently cured." The cure, Pennington was still convinced, was to be found in the "Remedial power of the Gospel." Relying, as always, on that power, Pennington remained optimistic and wrote that "under God, I have confidence in our cause and a cheerful hope of our ultimate success. I have always believed even in the darkest days that God had some great use for the race. And I believe now that the gospel and education can do for the race what they did for the Britons. Let us, my venerable brother, continue to use these standard remedies and look for a glorious moral resurrection."[56]

In May, the Committee of Mission for Freedmen, meeting as usual in Pittsburgh, officially commissioned "J. W. Pennington, D.D. . . . to labor as a

Missionary at Jacksonville, Florida, at a salary of ($900) nine hundred dollars."
This is surprising, since Pennington had arrived in Florida as their representative six months earlier believing that his salary was to be $200 annually, and
because the Committee had resolved the previous June that "the salaries of
colored Ministers [be set] at $50 per month maximum." On June 15, Pen-
nington, Gibbs, a pastor from St. Augustine, and two elders, representing a
total of three congregations with 149 members, met to organize the Presbytery
of East Florida as authorized by the General Assembly that had met in May.[57]
Ten days later, the Committee of Missions for Freedmen, which seemed to be
operating in some confusion, resolved that Pennington's salary should be paid
at the $900 rate until the first of July and after that reduced to the amount
previously set for "colored Ministers" the year before, so, presumably, bringing
his salary into line with other "colored Ministers."[58] †

No report of the next two months has been found, but in September Pennington wrote with his usual optimism that his mission was "successful and
prospering." One month later, on October 22, he died suddenly after a short
illness.[59] ††

---

† It is also possible that the Committee had not been aware of Pennington's color since
they had in January agreed to pay $800 to a certain M. Riley who is not listed as "colored"
and therefore was presumably white.

†† Pennington was 61. It might be noted that his predecessor at the Shiloh Church,
Theodore White, died at the age of 50, James McCune Smith at the age of 52, and Henry
Highland Garnet at the age of 66. Frederick Douglass, like Lewis Tappan and William
Lloyd Garrison, lived well into his 70s.

EPILOGUE

When James Pembroke decided that he could no longer be a slave, he had no alternative vision of who or what he could be. He knew only what he could *not* be. William Wright taught him what he could be when he greeted him on his doorstep as a human being. Pembroke told Wright he was looking for work. He had always been treated as a worker, and he could only visualize a future in which he continued simply to be a worker, though in a condition of freedom. William Wright changed all that in one short sentence: "Well, come in then and we will talk about it." To "talk about it" implies a human relationship: no longer master and machine, but human beings exploring together how to live.

A second transforming moment came when William Wright told James Pennington about some of the African Americans whose genius had been recognized by some, at least, of those around them. Phyllis Wheatley and Francis Williams had been poets, and Benjamin Banneker had been a scientist. Black people had demonstrated an ability to be as creative as the white people around them. To be black did not mean to be limited.

A third transforming moment came in a Brooklyn schoolroom when James Pennington was astonished to learn that there were 700,000 children in slavery and his instinctive reaction was to wonder "what can I do for that vast body of suffering brotherhood I have left behind?" The proper human response to a gift is to share its joy. The smallest child runs off to show someone else what she has been given. Freedom also is a gift to be shared, and the sharing of that gift can become a life's work. A teacher and pastor can provide others with the tools, the understanding, with which life can be lived more fully.

A fourth transforming moment came when Samuel Cox brought James Pennington into the Christian church. With conversion came membership in a community with a larger vision of human life and destiny and the faith that God is at work in the world to bring about that vision. Confidence that God's purpose will prevail is a powerful remedy for discouragement. Pennington's presence within the Presbyterian Church also, inevitably, helped to transform that church by bringing its clergy and members into a working relationship with an educated and articulate African American.

Still a fifth transformation came about as a result of the Negro Convention movement. There were those in America who thought the solution to America's racial dilemma was to send black people "back" to Africa. But James Pennington had not come from Africa. His grandfather had been brought to the Western Hemisphere unwillingly, but Bazil and James had been born and brought up in America. This, for better or worse, was their country. Rather than "return" to a continent they had never known, they would prefer to reshape America to include them in its self-definition. In the struggle to do so, James Pennington came to realize that he was "American to the backbone." It was no solution to his situation to go elsewhere. He would spend a large part of his life exhorting black Americans to work to transform their country by getting the education and skills that would enable them to play their part in the nation's life. In doing so, he would help white Americans to see the wholeness of their country and broaden their vision of what it means to be American.

The Negro Convention movement was a response to the American Colonization Society's effort to define America as a country for white people. James Pennington played a critical role in that response, consistently and eloquently making the case that America must be an interracial nation and must make a place for all those who considered it their home. In Scotland, he told an audience:

> The colored population of the United States have no destiny separate from that of the nation in which they form an integral part. Our destiny is bound up with that of America. Her ship is ours; her pilot is ours; her storms are ours; her calms are ours, if she breaks upon any rock, we break with her. If we, born in America, cannot live upon the same soil upon terms of equality with the descendants of Scotchmen, Englishmen, Irishmen, Frenchmen, Germans, Hungarians, Greeks, and Poles, then the fundamental theory of America fails and falls to the ground.[1]

Today the alternative notion of a monoracial society is no longer imaginable, and that is primarily due to the insistence of James W. C. Pennington and his colleagues on a broader vision. They, too, were Americans and they dedicated their lives to making that vision a reality.

It was, after all, America's charter document, the Declaration of Independence, that had told James Pennington, Frederick Douglass, Theodore Wright, Henry Garnet, James McCune Smith, and others of their generation what needed to be set right. If, indeed, "all men are created equal" and "endowed by their Creator with certain unalienable rights," including life and liberty and the pursuit of happiness, then there was work to be done. The American Revolution had begun the job but not finished it. The nation could not exist indefinitely, "half slave and half free" as Lincoln put it. Until all were free, no one was truly free. The slave holder who walks uneasily with a lash in his hand and sleeps with a gun beside his bed is as much a captive as the black man he fears.

James Pennington and his colleagues were a tiny and all-but-powerless minority. There were fewer than half a million free blacks in a nation of twenty-three million, less than two per cent of the population, and the largest part of them in the South. Free Northern African Americans, most of them disenfranchised, were not a significant pressure group. There were also, of course, white people who abhorred slavery and made it their life's work to abolish the institution, but they too were a tiny minority and bitterly divided as to goals and methods. William Lloyd Garrison would take no active step to change the nation. He would rather divide it and separate himself from the evil. John Brown, on the other hand, would confront the evil with armed force and pay the price in blood to change the nation. Lewis Tappan was deeply committed to the fight against slavery but never understood that it was at least as important to create opportunities so that black Americans could be not only not-slaves, but positive contributors to American life. Furthermore, while Garrison and Tappan might agree that slaves should be free, they could not agree on the role women might play in their organizations, nor could they agree as to whether the church was the rock on which the movement was founded or an impediment to be swept aside. James Pennington and his colleagues had a larger vision than Garrison, Tappan, or Brown, and it was their vision—not yet fulfilled—that has finally won broad acceptance.

It is, of course, astounding, that a man could begin his life at the age of about twenty without education or family or supportive social structures and become not only an educated man but a leader. Those who argued that black people could never equal white people in accomplishment were silenced simply by James Pennington's witness. If Pennington had been only a teacher, writer, and scholar, he would have left a significant mark on American society. Like Wheatley and Banneker, he would have given evidence of black potential. But Pennington was not content with that. He had learned at Yale to trust in a God who, as Martin Luther King Jr. would say, "bends the arc toward justice." That theology might enable a Christian to let God do the bending, and most of those taught by Timothy Dwight were content to do so, but Pennington believed, as King did, that God could use human agents to help bend the arc.

Here, also, a range of options was available. Henry Garnet called on the slaves to rebel. John Brown collected guns and used them. James Pennington simply insisted on taking his place in the world. He would play his part in churches that had never imagined a church other than white. He would come back from England and chide his colleagues for their unwillingness to open their pulpits to him. They had never thought of it before, but when he pointed it out, they realized that he was right and began to act on this new understanding. When a judge ruled that color barriers in the New York City streetcars were wrong, Pennington exhorted his parishioners to live into this new freedom and face the consequences. When it turned out that the streetcars were not yet open, Pennington challenged the law in person, perhaps at the cost of his career, but others followed his lead and before long another barrier to America's future had been swept aside.

Looking back, all this may seem natural and even inevitable. It did not seem so at the time. In the last years before the Civil War the country seemed to be moving in the opposite direction, as the Fugitive Slave Act put even free black people in jeopardy and the Supreme Court, in the Dred Scott decision, ruled that black people had no rights. Those who had hoped to move the country in the opposite direction had every right to be discouraged. When Gerrit Smith wrote to James McCune Smith in 1847 asking him to write an address to the black people of New York State, McCune Smith responded in words that must have expressed the feelings of many others:

> I have not heart to write it. Each succeeding day, that terrible majority falls sadder, heavier, more crushingly on my soul. At times I am so weaned from hope, that I could lay me down and die, with the prayer, that the very memory of this existence should be blotted from my soul. There is in that majority a hate deeper than I had imagined. . . . Labouring under these views, I cannot write a cheering word & will not.[2]

In that same mood, almost ten years later, Smith deplored the lack of leaders in the African American community. "I deny, absolutely," he wrote, "that the colored people in the United States now have, or ever had, leaders." There were, indeed, he admitted, "men of public spirit, earnest for the general good and zealous for the advancement of the down-trodden, men willing to spend and be spent," but what he saw happening to such men was condemnation and rejection even by their own people. "Ten colored men to one white, have I heard blame Dr Pennington and Frederick Douglass for their manly resistance against caste in cars and steamboats." And this was why such potential leaders as Garnet, Ward, and Alexander Crummell were not in New York. "It would not do for such a man as I am," Crummell had written, to live in New York, the Rector of a colored congregation, amid all the moral confusion in church and State which pertains to the question of the rights of our poor and oppressed race. The galling pressure of the whites would be sad enough: but to have to endure the malignant spite of our own people ever ready to lick the dust before our common oppressors, and to turn with venom upon their black vindicators and to crush their hearts as they did mine, is something which I cannot learn over again.[3]

There must have been many days when James Pennington felt equally discouraged. Certainly he had often looked in vain for followers and support in his own community,[†] but somehow he remained faithful to his original commitment: through the ministry of the church, he would do what he could for his fellow African Americans. He would teach and exhort and inspire and help build up structures to serve his community. When the opportunity came, he would answer his own question, "What can I do for that vast body of suffering brotherhood I have left behind?" and go first to Mississippi and then to Florida to serve those who had not escaped from slavery as he had done or had the opportunities that had opened up for him.

When Pennington wrote from Florida that "I believe now that the gospel and education can do for the race what they did for the Britons," we are reminded that Pennington was first and always a teacher and pastor. It is easy to lose sight of that, since that work is not documented in the way that the abolitionist movement is. There are records of Pennington's speeches and committee work, but hardly any records of his "day job." We see him two or three times making parish calls and going about his parish work, but there is not a single record of an ordinary Sunday sermon, though he delivered many more sermons than speeches. Yet it might be argued that his example and leadership in the local community and congregation, where individuals were encountered and educated and inspired, was at least as important as the headline appearances. It was the lack of an educated base that constantly vitiated the initiatives of the community leaders.

In 1853, when James W. C. Pennington was at the height of his influence, he wrote to a white Presbyterian colleague on behalf of an African American pastor named Wilson.[††] Wilson was attempting to negotiate to buy a church

---

† Smith tells a story of an unnamed "leader," who may have been Pennington, who had gone to great lengths to organize a city-wide celebration of August 1 in 1855 and had brought together a gathering of some five thousand, but "after all this toil, and trouble, and invention . . . he was scarcely permitted to say a word."

†† This is presumably Henry M. Wilson, an 1848 graduate of Princeton Seminary and the man who had mediated the offer from the Woodstock Institute.

on Thompson Street, Manhattan. Pennington had called on several colleagues to ask them for assistance with the project, but J. M. Kebbs was never at home when he called, with the result that a letter had to be written. In the letter, Pennington said of Wilson that he is "not a popular preacher" but, he continued, "my testimony is that he is an excellent pastor, a cautious, judicious and good advisor and leader of a flock, just such an one as is needed among the better class of our people." He had more to say about the need for another church to serve the black population and about the particulars of the proposed negotiation, but in commending specific virtues in Wilson, Pennington tells us much about himself. Pennington himself undoubtedly *was* a "popular preacher," but "pastor . . . advisor . . . and leader" were the roles he valued because they were essential to the building of community, and without an educated community the "popular preacher" would make no lasting difference. It is, of course, as a speaker and abolitionist that Pennington is remembered, if he is remembered at all, but in his own mind it may have been his work as a pastor and teacher that contributed the most.

Even today, for all the interest in "Black History," such men as James McCune Smith and James W. C. Pennington are generally unknown. They were, we might say, ahead of their time; they were visionaries who saw and longed for a day when a man like Martin Luther King could speak of their dream and his before tens of thousands, black and white, and help bring about significant change. It would take another century for that to happen, but the great moments never come without first the "day of small things" and the pioneers, like James W. C. Pennington, who blaze a trail for others to follow.

"Small things," however, seems hardly a fair assessment of men who, without for the most part either votes or influence, dared to challenge the recognized people of power in their world. The First Negro National Convention was called specifically to challenge the American Colonization Society, which had the support of the president himself and such other leading Americans as Henry Clay, Daniel Webster, Francis Scott Key, and the presidents of Princeton, Harvard, Yale, and Columbia. Richard Allen, who presided at the first convention, had been born in slavery, as had many of those in attendance. James Pennington was still a fugitive slave with a price on his head. It is hard to imagine two more contrary visions of America than those offered by the Colonization Society and the Negro Convention, but it was the fugitive slave and his colleagues, rather than the President of the United States and his colleagues, who changed the terms of the debate and who ultimately prevailed.

APPENDIX

Concerning James Pennington's Initials

In the text of *The Fugitive Blacksmith*, James W. C. Pennington transcribes a letter of reference given to him less than a year after his escape from slavery as James Pembroke. In that letter, his name is given as James W. C. Pennington, but Pennington himself says nothing about his name change or the reason for it. In signing his name, he always used the first and last names with two initials or the last name with three initials. There seems to be no document of his in which he gives the names that go with the middle initials, and only a few other documents spell them out. One of those documents is the honorary degree from the University of Heidelberg, and it gives the middle names as William Charles; but one of his closest associates, Amos Beman, gives the middle names (see below) as "William Cox."

Some of those who have written about Pennington have suggested that the name "William" was chosen to honor William Wright, but no one has offered an explanation of "Charles." Of course, if Amos Beman is correct, the "W" would honor the man who welcomed him into Northern freedom and the "C" would honor the man who welcomed him into the Christian Church. It is easy to understand that Pennington might have chosen those names for that reason and then changed the reference to Cox when he and Cox walked apart on the church's stand on abolition. The difficulty with that explanation is that Beman's undated poem speaks of "new honors" in "distant lands." That reference would most logically be related to one of Pennington's European journeys, the first of which was in 1843, while the most honors came on the journey from 1849 to 1851. The division between Pennington and Cox would have come at the latest in 1846 and well before the honorary doctorate, so, logically, the name change should have occurred before the honorary degree and, most probably, before Beman wrote his poem. But since Pennington seldom, if ever, used his middle names, it is quite possible that Beman simply did not know that Pennington had changed the second of them.

All this, however, is only an informed guess. The mystery remains.

Acrostic

by Amos Beman

REV. J. W. C. PENNINGTON

J ustified by wisdom's high behest
A slave no more—a man confessed—
M any have read from thy eloquent pen,
E nnobling thoughts for the freedom of men.
S till upward and onward is thy way.

W hich thousands admire, blessing God for the day
I n which you have toiled, so nobly and true—
L ike Garnet and Douglass, and Delaney, too—
L ifting the bondman from darkness and death—
I nvesting him with rights—inspiring him with breath,
A nd sending him forward in virtue's career,
M ajestic and noble, divested of fear.

C ontinue then faithful and true to the end;
O n God you rely—He is strong to defend.
X ylographican skill let others unfold.

P resent thou thy record to ages untold,
E mblazoned with the deeds of light and love;
N one will deny thee a mansion above.
N ow awaiting to crown thee in thy new field,
I n heart and in hope as your power you wield,
N ew honors shall deck thee as in distant lands,
G iving thee joy amid the work of thy hands.
T o heaven we commend thee in all the way
O n which thou goest from home far away—
N one can more warmly adieu to thee say.

NOTES

Chapter One (pages 1–16)

1. Pennington, James W. C., *The Fugitive Blacksmith; or Events in the History of James W. C. Pennington, Pastor of a Presbyterian Church, New York, Formerly a Slave in the State of Maryland, United States*. Second Edition London: Charles Gilpin, 1849, p. 15.
2. Ibid., p. 10.
3. Ibid., p. 13.
4. Ibid., p. 15.
5. Ibid., p. 14.
6. Ibid., p. 15.
7. Ibid., p. 15.
8. Ibid., p. 16.
9. Ibid., p. 16.
10. Ibid., p. 17.
11. Ibid., pp. 17–18.
12. Ibid., p. 18.
13. Douglass, Frederick, *Life and Times of Frederick Douglass Written by Himself, His Early Life as a Slave, His Escape from Bondage, and His Complete History to the Present Time*. Elbiron Classics, Adamant Media Corporation, Cleveland, 2001. pp. 238–240.
14. Pennington, op. cit., p. 19.
15. Ibid., pp. 19–20.
16. Ibid., pp. 20–21.
17. Ibid., p. 21.
18. Ibid., p. 22.
19. Ibid., p. 23.
20. Ibid., p. 23.
21. Ibid., p. 24.
22. Ibid., p. 25.
23. Ibid., p. 26.
24. Ibid., pp. 26–27.
25. *Torch Light and Public Advertiser*, November 1, 1827.
26. Ibid., November 22, 1827.
27. Pennington, op. cit., p. 27.
28. Ibid., p. 28.
29. Ibid., pp. 28–30.
30. Ibid., p. 33.
31. Ibid., p. 34.
32. Idem.
33. Ibid., p. 36.
34. Idem.
35. Ibid., p. 37.
36. Ibid., p. 38.
37. Idem.
38. Ibid., pp. 39–40.
39. Ibid., p. 41.

Chapter Two (pages 17–31)

1. Ibid., p. 7.
2. Ibid., p. 8.
3. Ibid., p. 9.
4. Ibid., p. 12.
5. Kemble, Frances Anne, *Journal of a Residence on a Georgian Plantation in 1838–1839.* Athens, Georgia, University of Georgia Press, 1984, p. 86.
6. Ibid., p. 342.
7. Pennington, op. cit., p. viii.
8. Ibid., p. v.
9. Douglass, op. cit., p. 53.
10. Pennington, op. cit., p. 9.
11. Ibid., p. 10.
12. Ibid., pp. vii–viii.
13. Ibid., p. viii.
14. Douglass, Frederick, *My Bondage and My Freedom.* New York, Miller, Orton & Mulligan, 1855.
15. Kemble, op. cit., p. 314.
16. Pennington, op. cit., p. 10.
17. Douglass, op. cit., pp. 122–123.
18. Pennington, op. cit., pp. 10–11.
19. Ibid., p. 11.
20. Douglass, Frederick, *Autobiographies: Narrative of the Life of Frederick Douglass, an American Slave; My Bondage and My Freedom; Life and times of Frederick Douglass.* New York: The Library of America, 1944, p. 37.
21. Ibid., p. 80ff.
22. Ibid., pp. 498–500.
23. Brown, William Wells, *Narrative of William W. Brown, a Fugitive Slave. Written by Himself.* Boston: Published at the Anti-slavery Office, No. 25 Cornhill. 1847, p. 16.
24. Weld, Theodore D., *American Slavery As It Is: Testimony of a Thousand Witnesses. New York: American Anti-slavery Society, Office, 1839*, p. 53.
25. Ibid., p. 54.
26. Ibid., p. 23.
27. Ibid., p. 24.
28. Ibid., p. 23.
29. Ibid., p. 55.
30. Ibid., p. 23.
31. Pennington, op. cit., p. 10.
32. Ibid., p. 72.
33. Ibid., p. 69.
34. Ibid., pp. 69–70.
35. Ibid., p. 70.
36. Ibid., p. 72.
37. Ibid., p. 73.
38. Pennington, Thomas H. Sands, *Events in the Life of J. W. C. Pennington, D.D.,* an unpublished letter to Marianna Gibbons, Lancaster Historical Society.
39. Pennington, J. W. C., op. cit., p. 3.
40. Ibid., p. 4.
41. Idem.
42. Ibid., pp. 10–11.
43. Ibid., pp. 66–67.

44. Douglass, op. cit., p. 132.

45. Pennington, op. cit., p. 67.

46. Douglass, op. cit., p. 102.

47. Pennington, op. cit., p. 67.

48. Ibid., p. 5.

49. Ibid., p. 5.

50. J. W. C. Pennington to H. B. Stowe. Stowe, Harriet Beecher, *A Key to Uncle Tom's Cabin; presenting the original facts and documents upon which the story is founded. Together with corroborative statements verifying the truth of the work.* Boston: J.P. Jewett & Co., 1853, p. 51.

51. Pennington, *Fugitive Blacksmith*, p. 6.

Chapter Three (pages 32–43)

1. Ibid., pp. 41–42.

2. Ibid., p. 42.

3. Idem.

4. McCauslin, Debra Sandoe, *Reconstructing the Past: Puzzle of a Lost Community.* For the Cause Productions: Gettysburg, PA, 2005.

5. Ibid., pp. 51–53.

6. Smedley, R. C. *History of the Underground Railroad in Chester and the Neighboring Counties of Pennsylvania*, pp. 41–42.

7. Pennington, op. cit., pp. xiv–xv.

8. Ibid., p. 43.

9. Idem.

10. Ibid., p. 44.

11. Ibid., p. 45.

12. Ibid., pp. xiv–xv.

13. Ibid., pp. 46–47.

14. Ibid., p. 45.

15. Ibid., pp. 47–48.

16. Ibid., p. 50.

17. In his autobiography, Pennington, still concerned not to reveal identities, refers to his host as "J. K." Since there was no prominent J. K. in the Nantmeal Quaker community, it seems likeliest that "I. K." was misread as "J. K." Isaiah and Elizabeth Kirk fit perfectly with Pennington's description except for that first initial. It is also noteworthy that the Nantmeal Friends community was merged with the larger Uwchlan Meeting after Elizabeth Kirk's death.

18. Obituary notice, *The Friend*, Fourth Month, 9, 1831.

19. *Minutes of the Uwchlan Monthly Meeting*, microfilm in the collections of the Friends Historical Library of Swarthmore College.

20. Obituary notice in *The Friend*, Seventh Day, Fourth Month, 16, 1831.

21. Idem.

22. Pennington, op. cit., pp. 50–51.

23. Ibid., p. 51.

24. Idem.

Chapter Four (pages 44–62)

1. Idem.

2. *A Statistical Inquiry into the Condition of the People of Colour of the City and Districts of Philadelphia*, Philadelphia: Kite and Walton, 1849.

3. Pennington, James W. C., *A Lecture Delivered before the Glasgow Young Men's Christian Association; and also before the St. George's Biblical, Literary, and Scientific Institute, London,* 1850, *BAP,* 06:0264. cf. also, Lepore, Jill, "The Tightening Vise: Slavery and Freedom in British New York" in Berlin, Ira and Harris, Leslie M., (eds.) *Slavery in New York.* New York: New Press, 2005, pp. 78–87.

4. Douglass, Frederick, *Narrative of the Life of Frederick Douglass, an American Slave, written by himself.* Edited by Benjamin Quarles. Cambridge, Mass., Belknap Press, 1960, pp. 143–144.

5. Ibid., p. 52.

6. Douglass, op. cit., p. 145.

7. Riker, James, *The annals of Newtown, in Queens County, New York, containing its history from its first settlement, together with many interesting facts concerning the adjacent towns: also, a particular account of numerous Long Island families now spread over this and various other states of the Union.* New York: D. Fanshaw, 1852, p. 224.

8. Douglass, Frederick, *Life and Times of Frederick Douglass,* Hartford, Park, 1882, pp. 325–326.

9. Pennington, *Fugitive Blacksmith,* p. 52.

10. Alexander, Leslie M., *African or American?: Black Identity and Political Activism in New York City,* 1784–1861. Urbana: University of Illinois Press, 2008, p. 13.

11. Ibid., p. 44.

12. Ibid., pp. 52–53.

13. Pennington, *Fugitive Blacksmith,* p. 52.

14. Ibid., p. 53.

15. Ibid., p. 54.

16. Idem.

17. Cox, Samuel Hanson, *Interviews Memorable and Useful.* New York, Harper and Brothers, Publishers, 1853, pp. 222–228.

18. Cox, Stephen H., *Salvation Achieved,* New York, Jonathan Leavitt, 1831, pp. v–vi.

19. Pennington, op. cit., p. 55.

20. Alexander, op. cit., pp. 31ff.

21. Ibid., p. 77.

22. Walker, David, *Walker's Appeal, in Four Articles; Together with a Preamble, to the Coloured Citizens of the World, but in Particular, and Very Expressly, to Those of the United States of America,* Boston, 1829, p. 30.

23. Mayer, Henry, *All On Fire: William Lloyd Garrison and the Abolition of Slavery,* New York, St. Martin's Press, 1998, pp. 82–84.

24. Walker, op. cit., pp. 80–81.

25. Pennington, J. W. C., "The First Colored Convention," *The Anglo-African Magazine,* October 15, 1859.

26. Idem.

27. Massachusetts Colonization Society, "The American Colonization Society and the Colony at Liberia," Boston, Perkins and Mervin, 1832, p. 3. Bound with Garrison, William Lloyd, *Thoughts on African Colonization.* New York, Arno Press, 1968.

28. Pennington, J. W. C., "The First Colored Convention." *The Anglo-African Magazine,* October 18, 1859.

29. Idem.

30. Idem.

31. Idem.

32. Idem.

33. Gross, Bella, *The Journal of Negro History,* v. 31, n. 4, 1946, p. 435.

34. Swift, David, *Black Prophets of Justice,* p. 41.

35. Alexander, op. cit., p. 74. According to Alexander, there was a riot in response to Russworm's decision, and crowds hung his effigy and pelted it with rocks.

36. *The Rights of All*, October 16, 1829.

37. Gross, Bella, *Clarion Call; The History and Development of the Negro People's Convention Movement in the United States from 1817 to 1840*. New York, 1947, p. 4.

38. *Freedom's Journal*, November 2, 1827.

39. *Constitution of the American Society of Free Persons of Colour for improving their condition in the United States; for purchasing lands; and for the establishment of a settlement in Upper Canada*, also *Proceedings of the Convention with their Address to the Free Persons of Colour in the United States.* J. W. Allen, Philadelphia, 1831, p. 9.

40. *The Frederick Douglass Paper*, April 6, 1855.

41. Bell, Howard Holman, *A Survey of the Negro Convention Movement, 1830–1861*. New York, Arno Press and the *New York Times*, 1969, p. 1.

42. Ibid.

43. Pennington, *Fugitive Blacksmith*, p. 38.

Chapter Five: Brooklyn (pages 63–76)

1. Garrison, William Lloyd, *Thoughts on African Colonization*.

2. Ibid., p. 24.

3. *Liberator*, July 2, 1831.

4. *Liberator*, January 1, 1831.

5. Warner, Robert, *New Haven Negroes, a social history*. New York: Arno Press, 1969, p. 54.

6. *Liberator*, July 9, 1831.

7. *Liberator*, July 9, 1831.

8. Howard Bell, in *Minutes of the Proceedings of the National Negro Convention, 1830–1864*, says, ". . . the national conventions of the 1830s were sometimes almost overrun by whites pleading a particular cause or offering gratuitous advice on a multiplicity of subjects . . ."

9. *Thoughts on African Colonization*, p. 12.

10. Ibid., p. 11.

11. Staudenraus, P. J., *The African Colonization Movement, 1816–1865*. New York: Columbia University Press, 1961, pp. 207–210.

12. *Liberator*, September 14, 1831.

13. *Liberator*, September 17, 1831.

14. *Liberator*, October 22, 1831.

15. *Connecticut Herald*, October 4, 1831, quoted in Warner, op. cit., p. 57.

16. *Connecticut Journal*, September 13, 1831.

17. Letter from Peter Williams, Thomas Downing, Peter Vogelsang, Boston Cromwell, and Philip Bell to Simeon Jocelyn, New York, October 12, 1831. Ripley, Peter, and Jeffrey S. Rossbach, *BAP*, p. 487.

18. Letter from Simeon Jocelyn to Peter Williams, Thomas Downing, Peter Vogelsang, Boston Cromwell, and Philip A. Bell, New Haven, October 15, 1831. Ripley, op. cit., p. 490.

19. *Minutes and Proceedings of the First Annual Convention of the People of Colour held by adjourments in the City of Philadelphia, from the sixth to the eleventh of June, inclusive, 1831.* p. 5.

20. *Beecher Family*, p. 258.

21. *Liberator*, August 6, 1831.

22. *Liberator*, August 13, 1831.

23. *Liberator*, May 19, 1832.

24. *Liberator*, March 3, 1832.

25. *Liberator*, February 18, 1832.

26. *Liberator*, April 21, 1832. (The masthead of this issue carries the date 1831, but all the material is dated 1832.)

27. Gurley, Ralph Randolph, *Life of Jehudi Ashmun, late colonial agent in Liberia*. Freeport, N.Y.: Books for Libraries Press, 1971.

28. *Minutes and Proceedings of the Third Annual Convention for the Improvement of the Free People of Colour in these United States held by adjournments in the City of Philadelphia from the 3rd to the 13th of June inclusive, 1833*, pp. 32–33.

29. Ibid., p. 34.

30. Ibid., p. 36.

31. Ibid., p. 32.

Chapter Six: School Teacher in Newton (pages 77–94)

1. *Fugitive Blacksmith*, p. 54.

2. Jortner, Jortner, "Cholera, Christ, and Jackson: The Epidemic of 1832 and the Origins of Christian Politics in Antebellum America," *Journal of the Early Republic*, v. 27, n. 2.

3. *FDP*, August 18, 1832.

4. Beardslee, G. William, "The 1832 Cholera Epidemic in New York State, 19th Century Responses to Cholerae Vibrio," *The Early America Review, Fall 2000*.

5. Ibid.

6. *New York Times*, September 8, 1892.

7. *Fugitive Blacksmith*, p. 56.

8. "Convention at Syracuse," *National Anti-Slavery Standard*, December 16, 1843.

9. Swift, David E., *Black Prophets of Justice Activist Clergy before the Civil War*. Louisiana State University Press, Baton Rouge, 1989, p. 49.

10. *Fugitive Blacksmith*, p. 56.

11. Pennington, as previously noted, dates his escape as October 28, 1828, but the Hagerstown newspaper advertised for his return in 1827. Taking the latter date as correct, the date of Pennington's new position would be February 10, 1833. This must be the date on which he agreed with the trustees, since Pennington later says that he actually began his new position on March 5. There is also an essay of Pennington's in an 1840 issue of the *Colored American* (July 25) in which he says he began to teach school in 1830, but that would have been less than three years after his escape from slavery and seems highly unlikely.

12. Hourahan, Richard, "Turning Point: The Newtown Years of James C. Pennington, Fugitive Slave and Black Abolitionist," in Warren, Wini, *Friends of Freedom: the Underground Railroad in Queens and on Long Island*, The Queens Historical Society, Flushing, New York, 2006, p. 99.

13. *CA*, August 12, 1840.

14. Hourahan, Richard, op. cit., p. 101.

15. Pennington, J. W. C., "Common School Review" n. 2 and 3, in the *CA*, July 25 and August 22, 1840.

16. Pennington, J. W. C., "Common School Review n. 7," in the *CA*, v. 1, n. 39; November 28, 1840.

17. I prefer not to use the annoying "sic." There is no way of knowing whether the error here is Pennington's or the typesetter's.

18. "Common School Review—n. VII," *CA*, v. 6, n. 39, November 28, 1840. (Two consecutive essays are labeled "n. VII.")

19. Pennington, J. W. C., "Common School Review" n. 6, in the *CA*, v. 1, n. 37; November 14, 1840.

20. Nathan Daboll published *Daboll's Schoolmaster's Assistant* in New London, Connecticut, in 1812 and it was widely used to teach mathematics in the early 19th century.

21. "Common School Review—n. IV," *CA*, October 24, 1840.

22. "Common School Review—n. V," *CA*, November 7, 1840.

23. "Common School Review—n. V," *CA*, August 22, 1840.

24. *CA*, January 30, 1841.

25. *CA*, January 24, 1837.

26. "Common School Review—X," *CA*, May 5, 1841.

27. *CA*, December 19, 1840; April 10, May 8, August 7, 1841.

28. *Minutes of the Third Annual Convention, for the Improvement of the Free People of Colour in These United States*, Philadelphia, 1833.

29. Tappan, Lewis, *The life of Arthur Tappan*. New York: Hurd and Houghton; Cambridge: Riverside Press, 1871.

30. Ibid., pp. 201–202.

31. Swift, David E., *Black Prophets of Justice: Activist Clergy before the Civil War*, p. 49.

32. *A Pastoral Letter Addressed to the Colored Presbyterian Church, in the city of New York, June 20th, 1832* (New York, 1832).

33. Pennington to American Home Mission Society, August 1833, and November 1, 1833. *BAP* 01:0325.

34. *Minutes: Fourth Annual Convention for the Improvement of the Free People of Colour.*

Chapter Seven: Yale (pages 95–104)

1. Davis, Hugh, *Joshua Leavitt, Evangelical Abolitionist*. Baton Rouge: Louisiana State University Press, 1990, pp. 117–118.

2. Cole, Donald B., *Martin Van Buren and the American Political System*. Princeton, New Jersey, Princeton University Press, 1984, p. 285.

3. Sorin, Gerald, *The New York Abolitionists; a case study of political radicalism*. Westport, Conn., Greenwood Pub. Corp., 1971, p. 74.

4. The deeds are available in the Connecticut State Library.

5. Warner, Robert A., *New Haven Negroes: A Social History*. New Haven: Yale University Press, 1940, p. 2.

6. Wayland, John Terrill, *The Theological Department in Yale College, 1822–1858*. New York: Garland Pub., 1987, p. 349.

7. Sweeney, Douglas A., *Nathaniel Taylor, New Haven theology, and the legacy of Jonathan Edwards*. Oxford; New York: Oxford University Press, 2003, p. 56.

8. Sweeney, op. cit., p. 56.

9. *FDP*, August 14, 1851. This article gives Pennington's own account of his status at Yale and is cited in Warner, Robert A, *New Haven Negroes: A Social History*. New Haven: Yale University Press, 1940. Other reports of Pennington's status at Yale usually cite Warner, often inaccurately.

10. Idem.

11. Wayland, op. cit., pp. 229–240.

12. Cross, Barbara, *Horace Bushnell: minister to a changing America*. Chicago, University of Chicago Press, [1958].

13. Wright, Henry B., *Christian Activity at Yale*. New Haven, 1901.

14. Wayland, op. cit., p. 92.

15. Ibid., p. 108.

16. Sweeney, op. cit., p. 57.

17. Ibid., pp. 57–58.

18. Ibid., p. 57.

19. Wayland, op., cit., pp. 352–354.

20. Messenger, J. P., *An Interpretive History of Education*, p. 302, cited in Wayland, op. cit., pp. 356–357.

21. Wright, Henry B., op. cit., pp. 55–74.

22. Bainton, Roland Herbert, *Yale and the ministry: a history of education for the Christian ministry at Yale from the founding in 1701.* New York: Harper & Bros., 1957, p. 80.

23. Wright, Henry B., op. cit., pp. 55–74.

24. *FDP*, August 14, 1851.

25. Wayland, op. cit., pp. 302–311.

26. Wayland, op. cit., pp. 360, 375–376.

27. *New Haven West Association Records, 1734–1909*, v. 5–6 (1832–1903).

28. Schmoke, Kurt, "The Dixwell Avenue Congregational Church, 1829 to 1896," *New Haven Colony Historical Society Journal*, v. 20, n. 1, May–June 1971, p. 6.

Chapter Eight: Return to Newton (pages 105–119)

1. Ward, Samuel Ringgold, *Autobiography of a Fugitive Negro: His Anti-Slavery Labours in the United States, Canada, & England.* London: John Snow, 1855, pp. 30–31.

2. *CA*, August 5, 1837.

3. Ibid., October 28, 1837.

4. Pennington, J. W. C. to American Home Missionary Society, March 29, August, November 1, 1839, and January 21, 1840. *BAP*, 02:0247, 03:0023, 3:0040, 03:0159, 03:332.

5. Swift, op. cit., p. 84.

6. *CA*, August 12, 1837.

7. *CA*, November 7, 1837.

8. *CA*, November 7, 1837.

9. Ibid., June 17, 1837.

10. *CA*, August 18, 1837.

11. Idem.

12. *The New York Evangelist*, November 4, 1837.

13. *CA*, October 20, 1838.

14. Register of the Third Presbytery of New York.

15. *CA*, March 22, 1838.

16. *CA*, June 16, 1838.

17. *CA*, June 2, 1838.

18. *CA*, July 21, 1838.

19. *CA*, August 4, 1838.

20. Bacon, Margaret Hope, *But One Race: the Life of Robert Purvis.* Albany: State University of New York Press, 2007, p. 9.

21. Winch, Julie, *Philadelphia's Black Elite: activism, accommodation, and the struggle for autonomy, 1787–1848.* Philadelphia: Temple University Press, 1988.

22. Bacon, op. cit., p. 9.

23. Foner, Philip Sheldon (editor), *Frederick Douglass on Women's Rights.* Westport, Conn.: Greenwood Press, 1976, p. 9.

24. Douglass, Frederick, *Life and times of Frederick Douglass: His Early Life as a Slave, His Escape from Bondage, and His Complete History. Written by himself.* London, Collier Books, 1962, p. 205.

25. *CA*, August 14, 1839.

26. Bainton, Roland Herbert, *Yale and the Ministry: a History of Education for the Christian Ministry at Yale from the Founding in 1701.* New York: Harper & Bros., 1957.

27. Pennington, J. W. C., *An Address Delivered at Newark, N. J. at the First Anniversary of West Indian Emancipation, August 1, 1839.* Newark, N.J., Aaron Guest, 1839.

28. The editor failed to notice until too late that as a result of a typographical error, the first column in the series was headed "Refector."

29. *CA*, September 23, 1839.
30. *CA*, November 2, 1839.
31. *CA*, November 16, 1839.
32. *CA*, November 16, 1839.
33. *CA*, March 28, 1840.
34. *CA*, March 28, 1838.
35. Tappan, Lewis to [Bartholomew] Welch, May 26, 1840. Library of Congress, *Lewis Tappan Papers*, Journals and Notebooks, Container 2, Reel 1.
36. "Intelligent Action of Our Colored Friends," *The Colored American*, May 30, 1840, from the *Emancipator*; Charles B. Ray to James G. Birney and Henry B. Stanton, May 20, 1840, Ripley, op. cit., v. III, p. 331.
37. *Connecticut Observer and New York Congregationalist*, June 20, 1840.
38. Ibid., May 23, 1840.
39. Ibid., May 23, 1840.

Chapter Nine: Hartford (pages 120–147)

1. Pennington, Thomas H. Sands, *Events in the Life of Rev. James W. C. Pennington*. p. 4.
2. Idem.
3. *CA*, September 28, 1839.
4. Strother, Horatio T., *The Underground Railroad in Connecticut*. Middletown, CT, Wesleyan University Press, 1962, p. 70.
5. *CA*, June 7, 1840.
6. Strother, op. cit., p. 70.
7. Linder, Douglas, *Famous American Trials, Amistad Trials, 1839–1840*, on-line resource, 1998.
8. *CA*, November 16, 1839.
9. *Hartford Courant*, January 27, 1840. It is estimated that as many as 250,000 Africans were imported to the United States as slaves between the date when the slave trade was outlawed and the beginning of the Civil War. The fact that the trade was illegal raised the value of the slaves and made it more worthwhile.
10. "The Amistad Africans. Farewell Meetings and Embarkation," *CA*, December 25, 1841.
11. *Hartford Courant*, January 15, 1840.
12. *Hartford Courant*, May 7, 1840.
13. *Boston Recorder*, reprinted in the *Hartford Courant*, August 28, 1840, and *Connecticut Observer*, October 17, 1840.
14. *Hartford Courant*, December 28, 1840.
15. *Geer's Hartford City Directory*, Hartford, Hartford Steam Printing Co., 1840 et al.
16. Mullin, Robert Bruce, *The Puritan as Yankee: a life of Horace Bushnell*. Grand Rapids, Michigan. W. B. Eerdmans Pub. Co., 2002, p. 52.
17. *Martinson's New Directory and Guide Book for the City of Hartford*. Hartford, Isaac N. Boles, 1841, pp. 9–10.
18. Cross, Barbara M., *Horace Bushnell: minister to a changing America*. Chicago, University of Chicago Press, 1958, p. 39.
19. Pawlowski, Robert E., and the Northwest Catholic High School urban studies class. *How the other half lived; an ethnic history of the old East Side and South End of Hartford*. [West Hartford, Conn., 1973], p. 20.
20. *Liberator*, v. 1, n. 9, February 26, 1831.
21. *Liberator*, v. 1, n. 30, July 23, 1831.
22. "A Brief Historical Sketch of the Talcott Street Congregational Church" privately published by the Faith Congregational Church.

23. *Contributions to the Ecclesiastical History of Connecticut prepared under the Direction of the General Association to Commemorate the Completion of One Hundred and Fifty Years since its First Annual Assembly.* New Haven, William L. Kingsley, 1861, p. 406.

24. Bushnell Park web site, www.bushnellpark.org

25. Cross, Barbara M., *Horace Bushnell: minister to a changing America.* Chicago: University of Chicago Press, 1958, p. 12.

26. Lawrence, op. cit., p. 202.

27. Mitchell, op. cit., pp. 53–55.

28. Lawrence, op. cit., p. 210.

29. *The Charter Oak*, v. 1, n. 1, March 1838.

30. *CA*, February 10, 1838.

31. Cross, *Horace Bushnell*, p. 41.

32. Ibid., p. 27.

33. Ibid., p. 37 [citing "Sermons on Living Subjects," pp. 248, 263]

34. *The Beecher Family*, p. 568.

35. Cross, op. cit., p. 39.

36. Bushnell, Horace, *The Crisis of the Church.*

37. Bushnell, Horace, *The census and slavery: a Thanksgiving discourse, delivered in the Chapel at Clifton Springs, N.Y., November 29, 1860.* Hartford: Lucius E. Hunt, 1860, pp. 12–13.

38. Hawes, J., *Two Discourses Delivered in the First Church in Hartford, March 5, 1848.* Hartford, Press of Case, Tiffany & Co., 1848.

39. Cheny, op. cit., p. 74; Munger, Theodore T., *Horace Bushnell: Preacher and Theologian.* Boston: Houghton, Mifflin and Company, 1899, p. 51.

40. *CA*, June 13, 1840

41. *CA*, July 25, 1840.

42. *CA*, August 15, 1840.

43. *CA*, August 8, 1840.

44. *CA*, September 1, 1840.

45. *CA*, August 8, 1840.

46. Idem.

47. *CA*, March 11, 1837.

48. J. W. C. P. at the Anti-Slavery Convention in 1843—Benjamin Quarles, *Black Abolitionists*, p. 71.

49. *CA*, September 19, 1840.

50. Idem.

51. *Connecticut Observer*, July 4, 1840.

52. *Connecticut Observer*, February 6, 1841.

53. *Connecticut Observer*, January 16, 1841.

54. "Common School Review—n. X," *CA*, May 5, 1841.

55. *CA*, June 26, 1841.

56. Idem.

57. *CA*, July 17, 1841.

58. *CA*, August 14, 1841.

59. "Common School Review—n. XIV," *CA*.

60. "Common School Review—n. XIII," *CA*, August 14, 1841.

61. White, David, "Hartford's African Schools." *Connecticut Historical Society Bulletin*, v. XXXIX, 1974, pp. 51–53.

62. White, op. cit., pp. 48, 53.

Chapter Ten (pages 148–172)

1.   *Connecticut Observer*, "The Freshet," January 16, 1841.

2. Pennington, J. W. C., "Freshet and Great Distress," *CA*, January 23, 1841.
3. *Connecticut Observer*, January 16, 1841.
4. Pennington, op. cit.
5. *Connecticut Observer*, January 16, 1841.
6. Reported in *CA*, January 16, 1841.
7. *CA*, January 9, 1841.
8. Pennington, James W. C., *A Text Book of the Origin and History, &C. &C. of the Colored People*. Hartford, L. Skinner, 1841.
9. Staudenraus, P. J., *The African colonization movement, 1816–1865*. New York, Columbia University Press, 1961, p. 28.
10. Ibid., p. 6.
11. Ibid., p. 31.
12. Pennington, James W. C., *A Text Book of the Origin and History, &c. &c. of the Colored People*. Hartford, L. Skinner, 1841, p. 4.
13. Ibid., pp. 6–7.
14. Ibid., pp. 37–38.
15. Ibid., p. 41.
16. Ibid., pp. 47-52.
17. Ibid., p. 68.
18. Ibid., pp. 72–73.
19. Ibid., p. 74.
20. Ibid., February 27, 1841.
21. Pennington, op. cit., pp. 74–76.
22. Ibid., pp. 77–85.
23. Ibid., pp. 79, 81.
24. Ibid., pp. 86–87.
25. Ibid., pp. 87–89.
26. Ibid., pp. 95–96.
27. Sinha, Manisha, "Coming of Age: the Historiography of Black Abolitionism," in Stauffer, John and McCarthy, Timothy Patrick McCarthy (ed.), *Prophets of Protest: Reconsidering the History of American Abolitionism*. New York: New Press, 2006, p. 28.
28. Priest, Josiah, *Slavery as it relates to the Negro, or African Race, examined in the light of circumstances, history and the Holy Scriptures; with an account of the Origin of the Black Man's Color, causes of his state of servitude and traces of his character as well in ancient as in modern times: with Strictures on Abolitionism*. Albany: C. Van Benthuysen and Co., 1843, pp. 33, 337.
29. Martin, op. cit., p. 186.
30. Ibid., p. 196.
31. *Hartford Courant*, March 10, 1841.
32. Strother, Horatio T., *The Underground Railroad in Connecticut*. Middletown, CT, Wesleyan University Press, 1962.
33. Ibid., pp. 203–204.
34. Martin, Christopher, *The Amistad Affair*. New York, Tower, 1970, p. 206.
35. *CA*, April 17, 1841.
36. Ibid., April 24, 1841.
37. Ibid., May 15, 1841.
38. Ibid., July 3, 1841.
39. Ibid., July 10, 1841.
40. *CA* (letter dated May 1840).
41. White, David, "The Fugitive Blacksmith of Hartford." *Connecticut Historical Society Bulletin*, v. XXXXIX, n. 1, (Winter, 1984), p. 13.

42. Plato, Ann, *Essays Including Biographies and Miscellaneous Pieces, in Prose and Poetry.* Hartford: Printed for the author, 1841. James W. C. Pennington, "To the Reader," pp. xviii–xx.

43. *CA,* June 26, 1841.

44. *Christian Freeman,* July 24, 1845.

45. *Union Missionary Herald,* February 1842.

46. Ibid., pp. 76–77.

47. *CA,* September 4, 1841.

48. *CA,* November 20, 1841.

49. Pennington, J. W. C. to Executive Committee, October 9, 1841.

50. *CA,* October 30, 1841.

51. *CA,* November 20, 1841.

52. "Impromptu: on hearing a Missionary Sermon from Rev. Dr. P." *Union Missionary Herald,* May 1842.

53. Blasingame, John W., *Slave Testimony: Two Centuries of Letters, Speeches, Interviews,* p. 201.

54. From the Lynn *Record, Liberator,* November 19, 1841.

55. "The Amistad Africans. Farewell Meetings and Embarkation," *CA,* December 25, 1841.

56. "Departure of the Mendians," *CA,* December 4, 1841.

57. *New York Journal of Commerce,* November 27, 1841.

58. "Departure of the Mendians," *CA,* December 4, 1841.

59. Ibid., p. 210.

60. Pennington, J. W. C. to Thomas Lafon, June 17, 1845. (BAP 5/0053).

61. J. W. C. Pennington to Lewis Tappan, October 9, 1843. (BAP 2567/7130).

62. Tappan, Lewis to J. W. C. Pennington, October 10, 1844. (BAP 7614/954).

63. Letter from Lewis Tappan to J. W .C. Pennington, November 6, 1844. (BAP 7646/955).

64. *Contributions to the Ecclesiastical History of Connecticut prepared under the Direction of the General Association to Commemorate the Completion of One Hundred and Fifty Years since its First Annual Assembly,* v. II, June 8, 1839.

Chapter Eleven: The Mendi Mission (pages 173–185)

1. Jonathan Edwards to the Reverend Thomas Prince in Boston, December 12, 1743.

2. Cox, Stephen H., *Salvation Achieved,* New York, Jonathan Leavitt, 1831, pp. v–vi.

3. Wayland, op. cit., p. 366.

4. Other phrases include "a precious season of revival," "effusions of renewing grace," "a quickened state of feeling," "dews of divine grace," etc. cf. *Contributions to the Ecclesiastical History of Connecticut prepared under the Direction of the General Association to Commemorate the Completion of One Hundred and Fifty Years since its First Annual Assembly,* v. II, 1861, pp. 13–14.

5. *Contributions to the Ecclesiastical History of Connecticut prepared under the Direction of the General Association to Commemorate the Completion of One Hundred and Fifty Years since its First Annual Assembly of Connecticut,* v. II, 1842, p. 14.

6. Mitchell, Mary Hewitt, *The Great Awakening and Other Revivals in the Religious Life of Connecticut.* New Haven, Published for the Tercentenary commission by the Yale University Press, 1934, p. 42.

7. Ibid., p. 43.

8. *Contributions to the Ecclesiastical History of Connecticut prepared under the Direction of the General Association to Commemorate the Completion of One Hundred and Fifty Years since its First Annual Assembly,* v. II, June 1, 1847, p. 26.

9. Ibid., pp. 49–50.

10. Pennington, J. W. C. to Joshua Leavitt, April 4, 1843. *BAP* 04:0560.

11. *CA*, November 20, 1841.
12. Garrison, William Lloyd, *Thoughts on African Colonization*. Boston: Garrison and Knapp, 1832, Part II, pp. 28–29.
13. *Christian Freeman*, February 24, 1843.
14. Records of Faith Congregational Church, Hartford.
15. *Pennington, J. W. C. to Secretary, American Home Missionary Society*. American Home Missionary Society Papers, Amistad Research Center, Dillard University, New Orleans, LA.
16. *Contributions to the Ecclesiastical History of Connecticut prepared under the Direction of the General Association to Commemorate the Completion of One Hundred and Fifty Years since its First Annual Assembly of Connecticut*. New Haven, J. H. Benham, p. 16. This annual publication shows same payment to the church each year and various amounts received.
17. *The Connecticut Observer*, March 26, 1842.
18. Idem.
19. Idem.
20. *Hartford Courant*, September 16, 1850.
21. *Hartford Courant*, May 15, 1841, January 8, 1848, and November 20, 1865.
22. Microfilm records of the deeds involved are at the Connecticut State Library in Hartford.
23. *Hartford Courant*, April 4 and May 13, 1842.
24. Tappan, Lewis, *History of the American Missionary Association: Its Constitution and Principles, etc.* New York: J.A. Gray, 1860.
25. Mars, James, *Life of James Mars, a Slave Born and Sold in Connecticut*. Hartford, Press of Case, Lockwood & Company, 1868, pp. 34–35.
26. *Nantucket Inquirer*, reprinted in the *Liberator*, August 5, 1842.
27. Pennington, J. W. C., "Origin and Furthering Cause of the Philadelphia Riots," Connecticut Observer in *Charter Oak*, September 1842.
28. Schneider, Janet M. and Bayla Singer, *Blueprint for Change: The Life and Times of Lewis H. Latimer*, http://edison.rutgers.edu/latimer/blueprnt.htm.
29. Pennington, J. W. C., *Covenants Involving Moral Wrong Not Obligatory Upon Man: A Sermon Delivered in the Fifth Congregational Church, Hartford, on Thanksgiving Day, November 17, 1842 by J. W. C. Pennington, Pastor of the Church*. Hartford, John C. Wells, 1842.

Chapter Twelve: England (pages 186–201)

1.   Farewell Letter of Rev. Mr. Pennington. *BAP* 04:0486.
2.   Leeds *Mercury*, August 5, 1843 *BAP* 04:0624.
3.   Davis, Hugh, *Joshua Leavitt, Evangelical Abolitionist*. Baton Rouge: Louisiana State University Press, 1990, p. 201.
4.   *Christian Freeman*, May 19, June 22, 1843.
5.   *Christian Freeman*, June 22, 1843.
6.   *Wikipedia*, John Morison.
7.   *The Clarksonian*, November 1842.
8.   *Christian Freeman*, September 14, 1843.
9.   Rice, C. Duncan, "Controversies over Slavery in Eighteenth- and Nineteenth-Century Scotland," in Perry, Lewis and Michael Fellman, *Antislavery Reconsidered: New Perspectives on the Abolitionists*. Baton Rouge, Louisiana State University Press, 1979, pp. 43–44.
10. Philips to Thompson, July 29, 1839, Garrison Papers—quoted in Temperley, H., *British antislavery, 1833–1870*, p. 193.
11. Fladeland, op. cit., pp. 260–261.
12. Temperley, Howard, *British antislavery, 1833–1870*. Longman, London, 1972, p. 195.

13. Hochschild, Adam, *Bury the Chains: Prophets and Rebels in the Fight to Free an Empire's Slaves*. Boston, Houghton Mifflin, 2006, pp. 6–7.

14. British and Foreign Anti-Slavery Society, Minute Book I, 206, May 15, 1840, quoted in Fladeland, op. cit., p. 266.

15. Howard, Percy, "Disappearing London: The Passing of Exeter Hall," *The Civil Service Observer*, May 1907.

16. British and Foreign Missionary Society, Minute Book II, pp. 66–67, June 3, 1843, in Fladeland, op. cit., p. 285.

17. *Anti-Slavery Reporter*, June 14, 1843.

18. Idem.

19. *Proceedings of the General Anti-Slavery Convention in London, 1843*. London, 1843, pp. 28, 62, 121, 322.

20. Swift, David Everett, *Black Prophets of Justice: activist clergy before the Civil War*. Baton Rouge: Louisiana State University Press, 1989, pp. 253, 155.

21. *Patriot*, July 3, 1843. *BAP* 04:0406.

22. *Anti-Slavery Reporter*, June 28, 1843. (*BAP*, Doc. n. 06951).

23. "American Slavery," *Liberator*, October 26, 1849, *BAP* 6:0206.

24. *Emancipator*, October 26, 1843. *BAP* 04:0686.

25. *Nonconformist*, June 28, 1843. *BAP* 04:0591.

26. Clarkson, Thomas, *The History of the Rise, Progress and Accomplishment of the Abolition of the African Slave-trade by the British Parliament*, New York, John Taylor, 1836, v. 1.

27. Ibid., p. 168.

28. Quarles, Benjamin, *Black Abolitionists*. New York, Oxford University Press, 1969, p. 136.

29. *Emancipator and Free American*, September 7, 1843.

30. *Christian Freeman*, September 7, 1843.

Chapter Thirteen: New Beginning in Hartford (pages 202–219)

1. Hartford *Courant*, August 28, 1843.

2. *Palladium of Liberty*, March 27, 1844. *BAP*, 4:0770.

3. Gross, Bella. *Clarion call; the history and development of the Negro People's Convention Movement in the United States from 1817 to 1840*. New York, 1947, p. 42.

4. Swift, David Everett, *Black Prophets of Justice: activist clergy before the Civil War*. Baton Rouge: Louisiana State University Press, 1989, p. 126.

5. *Minutes of the National Convention of Colored Citizens held at Buffalo, on the 15th, 16th, 17th, and 18th of August 1843*. New York, Piercy & Reed, 1843.

6. *Garnet's Address to the Slaves of the United States of America*. New York, J. H. Tobitt.

7. Pennington, J. W. [C]. et al to the Ministers, Elders, and Members of the Church Worshipping at Surrey Chapel, London. *BAP* 04:0667.

8. Pennington, James W. C., *Speech Given at the Middletown Anti-slavery Convention*, October 28th and 29th, 1843. University of Detroit Mercy, Black Abolitionist Archives.

9. *Contributions to the Ecclesiastical History of Connecticut prepared under the Direction of the General Association of Connecticut*, Volume II. New Haven, William L. Kingsley, Printer. 1861.

10. *Contributions to the Ecclesiastical History of Connecticut prepared under the Direction of the General Association to Commemorate the Completion of One Hundred and Fifty Years since its First Annual Assembly*, v. II, December 5, 1843.

11. *Minutes of the Hartford Central Clergy Association*. Connecticut State Library microfilm.

12. *Contributions to the Ecclesiastical History of Connecticut prepared under the Direction of the General Association of Connecticut*, v. II. New Haven, William L. Kingsley, Printer. 1861.

13. *Christian Freeman*, January 11, 1844. (Report of action taken November 20, 1843.)

14. Hooker, John, *Some Reminiscences of a Long Life; with a few articles on moral and social subjects of present interest.* Hartford, Conn., Belknap & Warfield, 1899, p. 342.
15. *The Clarksonian*, November 1843.
16. J. W. C.Pennington to Thomas Clarkson, September 4 and December 14, 1844. *BAP* 04:0966.
17. Clarkson, Thomas to Pennington, J. W. C., February 20, 1844. (*BAP* 7209/7934).
18. From the *Liberty Bell*, "Thomas Clarkson," *Liberator*, January 2, 1846.
19. Pennington, J. W. C. to Thomas Clarkson, December 14, 1844.
20. "Prevention Better Than Cure," *Public Ledger*, May 13, 1844.
21. J. W. C. Pennington to Joseph Sturge, September 4, 1844. *BAP* 04:0912.
22. Pennington, J. W. C., *The Fugitive Blacksmith*, p. 74.
23. Stowe, Harriet B., *A Key to Uncle Tom's Cabin*, p. 51.
24. Hooker, John, Letter to the *Hartford Courant*, June 23, 1851.
25. Pennington, op. cit., p. 81.
26. Ibid., p. 82.
27. Idem.
28. Ibid., pp. 83–84.
29. Ibid., p. 76.

Chapter Fourteen: Hartford (pages 220–245)

1. Wyatt-Brown, Bertram. *Lewis Tappan and the Evangelical War Against Slavery.* Cleveland: Case Western Reserve University Press, 1969, pp. 254–255.
2. Smith, James McCune, *The Destiny of the People of Color: A Lecture Delivered before the Philomathean Society and Hamilton Lyceum.* New York, 1843.
3. Pennington, J. W. C. *The Star*, co-edited with James McCune Smith, and quoted in *The Liberator*, June 28, 1844.
4. Idem.
5. Pennington, J. W. C. to Thomas Clarkson, September 25, 1844. *BAP 04:0922.*
6. Pennington, J. W. C. to Thomas Clarkson, December 14, 1844. *BAP 04:0966.*
7. *Eighth Annual Meeting of the Connecticut Anti-Slavery Society*, Christian Freeman, June 5, 1845.
8. Idem.
9. Idem.
10. DeGrasse, Isaiah, "The American Churches the Bulwark of Slavery," *Christian Observer*, November 1845.
11. "Soul or Skin?" *Pennsylvania Freeman*, October 7, 1845.
12. Idem.
13. Pennington, J. W. C., to "Esteemed Friend" (probably Joseph Sturge). No date given, but Pennington says his wife died fifteen months earlier, so the date would be in September 1847.
14. Pennington, J. W. C. to Thomas Lafon, June 17, 1845. *BAP* 05:0054.
15. Pennington, J. W. C., to Editor, *Christian Freeeman*, October 30, 1845.
16. Pennington, J. W. C., "Why Put a Difference Between Them?" *Christian Freeman*, November 6, 1845.
17. Pennington, James W. C., *A Two Years Absence or a Farewell Sermon preached in the Fifth Congregational Church, by J. W. C. Pennington, November 2, 1845.* Hartford: B. T. Wells, 1845, p. 9.
18. Ibid., p. 22.
19. Ibid., p. 29.
20. Ibid., pp. 30–31.
21. Ibid., pp. 4–5.

22. Ibid., p. 6.
23. Pennington, J. W. C., "Who Will Go and Do Likewise," *Christian Freeman*, November 6, 1845.
24. Pennington, J. W. C. to H., *Christian Freeman*, December 18, 1845.
25. Ibid.
26. Stowe, Harriet Beecher, *A Key to Uncle Tom's Cabin*, p. 51.
27. "History of Jamaica," *The Baptist Magazine* 33:361.
28. Pennington, J. W. C. to A. A. Phelps, February 26, 1846. *BAP* 5:0170.
29. Pennington, J. W. C. "Letter from Rev. J. W. C. Pennington," Kingston, Jamaica, February 10, *Union Missionary Herald*, May 1846.
30. Tappan, L. to James Pennington, October 10th, 1844. *BAP* 4:0931.
31. Pennington to "Esteemed Friend," op. cit.
32. Wyatt-Brown, p. 292.
33. *Proceedings of the National Convention of Colored People and Their Friends held in Troy, N.Y., on the 6th, 7th, 8th, and 9th October 1847.* J. G. Kneeland and Co., Troy, New York, 1847.

Chapter Fifteen: New York, 1848–1849 (pages 246–257)

1. "Obituary," *American Missionary*, May 1847.
2. *Register of the Third Presbytery of New York*, p. 10.
3. "The Wedding of the Rev. Dr. Pennington," *Hartford Courant*.
4. "Colored Ministers," *North Star*, April 7, 1848, (from the *Ram's Horn*) *BAP*.
5. "Churches In This City," *CA*, March 28, 1840.
6. Minutes of the Third Presbytery of New York, April 5, 1848.
7. *Charter Oak*, August 13, 1848; Records of the Third Presbytery of New York, April 5, 1848.
8. Pennington, J. W. C. to Lewis Tappan, July 5, 1848. *BAP* 5:0696.
9. Pennington to "Esteemed Friend," op. cit.
10. Tappan, A., et al., "To The Friends of Liberty," the *National Era*, July 6, 1848.
11. Cole, Donald B., *Martin Van Buren and the American Political System*. Princeton, New Jersey, Princeton University Press, 1984.
12. Ward, Samuel Ringgold, "Address to the Four Thousand Colored Voters of the State of New York," *North Star*, September 1, 1848.
13. Smith, Page, *The Nation Comes of Age: a People's History of the Ante-bellum Years*, p. 240.
14. Pennington, J. W. C. to Gerrit Smith, November 23, 1848. *BAP* 05:0830.
15. Pennington, J. W. [sic] to Frederick Douglass, *North Star*, January 12, 1849. *BAP* 5:0950.
16. "Slave Case in New York and the Colored Meeting," *Pennsylvania Freeman*, January 4, 1849.
17. Williams, Geo. R., to J. W. C. Pennington, *North Star*, January 19, 1849. *BAP*, 5:0955.
18. "Colonization and Emigration; H. H. Garnet's reply to S. R. Ward." *North Star*, March 2, 1849.
19. Douglass, Frederick, *North Star*, "Calling Him Out" and "He Comes" September 7, 1849.
20. "Great Anti-Colonization Mass Meeting," *National Anti-Slavery Standard*, May 3, 1849. *BAP* 5:1071.
21. Idem.
22. Tappan, L. to J. W. C. Pennington, March 25, 1848. *LTP*, v. 7, Letterbook November 4, 1847 to June 30, 1852.

Chapter Sixteen: Great Britain, 1849–1851 (pages 258–288)

1. Pennington, J. W. C. to Editor, *New York Herald Tribune*, June 24, 1849. *BAP* 6:0193.

2.   Pennington, J. W. C. to William Harned, *Boston Semi-Weekly Republican*, May 25, 1850.
3.   Pennington, *Fugitive Blacksmith*, p. 54.
4.   Ibid., pp. 41, 42.
5.   Ibid., p. 56.
6.   "The Peace Congress," *North Star*, September 28, 1849.
7.   Brown, William Wells, *Three Years in Europe; or, Places I Have Seen and People I Have Met*, with a memoir of the author by William Farmer. London, C. Gilpin, 1852.
8.   http://www.gavroche.org/vhugo/peacecongress.shtml.
9.   Ripley, op. cit., "Speech by J. W. C. Pennington," pp. 157–158. *The Non Conformist*, August 29, 1849.
10. "Americans and Englishmen Feted in Paris," *Hartford Daily Courant*, October 4, 1849.
11. Brown, William Wells, *The Black Man: His Antecedents, His Genius, and His Achievements*. New York: Thomas Hamilton, 1863, p. 277.
12. *Hartford Daily Courant*.
13. Garrison, William Lloyd, *The Letters of William Lloyd Garrison*. (Editor) Walter M. Merrill. Cambridge, Belknap Press of Harvard University Press, 1971–1981. v. III, p. 624.
14. *Encyclopaedia Judaica*.
15. *BAP* 6:0166.
16. Thomas, op. cit., p. 185.
17. Pennington, James W. C., *The Fugitive Blacksmith; or, Events in the History of James W. C. Pennington . . . Formerly a Slave in the State of Maryland*, United States. London, C. Gilpin, 1850. 3rd edition, p. iii.
18. Ibid. (2nd edition), p. iv.
19. Swift, *Black Prophets of Justice*, p. 247.
20. Brown, William Wells, *A Description of William Wells Brown Original Panoramic Views of the Scenes in the Life of an American Slave*, pp. 8, 9, 18.
21. *Gateshead Observer*, September 28, 1850; Blackett, op. cit., p. 47.
22. Pennington, J. W. C. to P. Bolton, November 13, 1849. *BAP* 6:0214.
23. Thomas, Herman E., *James W. C. Pennington, African American Churchman and Abolitionist*. p. 184.
24. Ibid., p. 185.
25. Ibid., p. 184.
26. Ibid., p. 54.
27. Pennington, J. W. C. to the editor of the *British Banner*, January 4, 1850.
28. "American Slavery," *Christian News*, January 3, 1850.
29. "Anti-Slavery Meeting," *NonConformist*, January 2, 1850.
30. Smith, Page, *The Nation Comes of Age*, p. 1072.
31. Ibid., p. 1073.
32. "A Fugitive Doctor of Divinity Set Free," *Hartford Daily Courant*, June 23, 1851.
33. Pennington, J. W. C. to George Whipple, February 20, 1850. *BAP* 6:0406.
34. Pennington, James, W. C., *A Lecture Delivered Before the Glasgow Young Men's Christian Association*. H. Armour, Edinburgh, 1850.
35. Idem.
36. Idem.
37. Pennington, J. W. C. to George Whipple, April 21, 1850. *BAP* 6:0449.
38. Blackett, op. cit., p. 50.
39. Pease, Jane H. and William H. Pease, *They Who Would Be Free: Blacks' Search for Freedom, 1830–1861*. New York: Atheneum, 1974.
40. Ripley, op. cit., v. 2, p. 419.

41. Blackett, op. cit., p. 52.
42. Ibid., p. 51.
43. *Christian News* (Glasgow), June 27, 1850.
44. Ripley, op. cit., pp. 228–229.
45. *Christian News* (Glasgow), September 26, 1850.
46. Ibid., September 26, 1850.
47. "Anti-Slavery Meeting at Frankfort on the Maine," *BAP*.
48. Garnet, H(enry) H(ighland), to Editor, *Non-Slaveholder*, November 1850.
49. Blackett, op. cit., p. 48.
50. "Slavery in the United States," *Gloucester Journal*, November 2, 1850. *BAP* 6:0662.
51. Garnet, H(enry) H(ighland), to Editor, *Non-Slaveholder*, November 1850.
52. "Slavery in the United States," *Gloucester Journal*, November 2, 1850. *BAP* 6:0662.
53. Pennington, J. W. C. to Editor, *Christian News*, December 12, 1850. *BAP* 6:0684.
54. "The New York Slave Case," *Voice of the Fugitive*, January 15, 1851.
55. Anti-Slavery Meeting, *Kelso Chronicle*, January 3, 1851, *BAP* 6:0723.
56. "A Fugitive Doctor of Divinity Set Free," Hartford *Daily Courant*, January 23, 1851.
57. Hooker, John, *Some Reminiscences of a Long Life*. p. 41.
58. "Rev. Dr. Pennington," *FDP*, August 14, 1851.

Chapter Seventeen: New York, 1851–1852 (pages 289–320)

1. "Rev. Dr. Pennington an Exile from his Native Land," *North Star*, April 4, 1851.
2. "Rev. J. W. C. Pennington, D.D.," *American Missionary*, July 1851.
3. Blackett, R. J. M, *Beating Against the Barriers*, pp. 48–49.
4. Tappan, Lewis, *Lewis Tappan Papers, Journals and Notebooks*, September 9, 1851.
5. "From Our Brooklyn Correspondent," *FDP*, January 17, 1852.
6. Smith, Page, *The Nation Comes of Age*, p. 760.
7. *Philadelphia Freeman*, October 3, 1850.
8. *Hartford Courant*, October 24, 1850.
9. "Kidnapping Children," *North Star*, April 10, 1851.
10. Smith, Page, op. cit., p. 632.
11. Quarles, Benjamin, *Black Abolitionists*. pp. 205–207.
12. "Great Excitement in Boston," *Voice of the Fugitive*, April 9, 1851.
13. "Cradle of Liberty," *Voice of the Fugitive*, April 23, 1851.
14. Berlin, Ira and Leslie M. Harris (editors), *Slavery in New York*. New York: New Press, 2005.
15. White, David, "Augustus Washington: Black Daguerreotypist of Hartford," *Connecticut Historical Society Bulletin*, v. XXXXIX, n. 1, pp. 6–8.
16. Blackett, op. cit., p. 54
17. "Hunting of Men Recommended by the Governor of New York," *FDP*, January 22, 1852.
18. "Colored People's Meeting," *Liberator*, April 4, 1851.
19. "Report on the Social Condition of the People of Color around New York City, and on the best means of ameliorating the same," *National Anti-Slavery Standard*, March 27, 1851. *BAP*.
20. Pennington, J. W. C. to Editors, *New York Independent*, reprinted in *FDP*, April 22, 1852.
21. http://en.wikipedia.org/wiki/Millard_Fillmore.
22. McKivigan, John R., *The War Against Proslavery Religion: abolitionism and the northern churches, 1830–1865*, pp. 132–135.
23. Slaughter, Thomas P., *Bloody Dawn, the Christiana Riot and Racial Violence in the Antebellum North*, p. 47.

24. "Fugitive Slave Law—Trial for Treason," *Christian News*, December 12, 1851.
25. Slaughter, op. cit., p. 134.
26. Pennington, J. W. C., to John Jay, March 2, 1853. *BAP* 8:0150.
27. Slaughter, op. cit., p. xi.
28. "Another Freeman sent into Slavery," *Voice of the Fugitive*, August 27, 1851.
29. "Fugitive Slave Law Ripening," *Voice of the Fugitive*, September 24, 1851.
30. "Another Fugitive Remanded Back To Slavery," *Voice of the Fugitive*, October 22, 1851.
31. "Another Slave Dragged of [sic] into Bondage," *Voice of the Fugitive*, December 17, 1851.
32. "Another Fugitive Returned," op. cit., December 17, 1851.
33. November 18, 1851. *BAP*.
34. "Interesting Incident," *Hartford Daily Courant*, November 25, 1851.
35. Wikipedia: Lajos Kossuth.
36. "Kossuth and American Slavery," *Voice of the Fugitive*, January 1, 1852.
37. Pennington, J. W. C. to Gerrit Smith, December 2, 1851. *BAP* 7:202.
38. "Kossuth at the Irving House," *NAS*, December 18, 1851.
39. "Kossuth and Slavery," *NAS*, December 18, 1851.
40. "Address of the Coloured People to Kossuth," *NAS*, December 18, 1851.
41. "American and Foreign Anti-Slavery Society. Presentation of an Address to M. Kossuth," *NAS*, January 1, 1852.
42. "Kossuth," *NAS*, December 11, 1851.
43. "The Kossuth Excitement: A Letter from the Hon. William Jay, President of the American Peace Society," *NAS*, January 29, 1852.
44. "Kossuth and His Cause," *Liberator*, March 19; "Mr. Garrison and His Cause," *Liberator*, March 25, 1852.
45. "American and Foreign Anti-Slavery Society and Kossuth," *NAS*, January 1, 1852.
46. Idem.
47. Idem.
48. "Meeting of the Colored People of New York," *National Anti-Slavery Standard*, January 22, 1852.
49. "Address to the People of the State of New York," *National Anti-Slavery Standard*, February 5, 1852.
50. "Letter from Observer," *FDP*, January 22, 1852.
51. Pennington, J. W. C. to Lewis Tappan, November 26, 1852. *BAP* 7:0837.
52. Pennington, J. W. C. to Rev. Dr. Badger. *BAP* 7:0266; Pennington, J. W. C. to Secretaries American Home Missionary Society, August 2, 1852, *BAP* 7:0686; Pennington, J. W. C. to Secretaries American Home Missionary Society, November 1, 1852, *BAP* 7:0813.
53. Smith, P., op. cit., p. 845.
54. "Presbyterian Church in Prince Street," *New York Evangelist*, December 28, 1852.
55. Pennington, J. W. C. to Rev. Dr. Badger. *BAP* 7:0266; Pennington, J. W. C. to Secretaries American Home Missionary Society, *BAP* 7:0686.
56. Pennington, J. W. C., to the *New York Evangelist*, December 28, 1852. *BAP* 8:0108.
57. Pennington, J. W. C. to Dr. Badger, November 1, 1852, and to *New York Evangelist*, December 28, 1852. *BAP* 08:0108.
58. "Pro-Slavery: Dr. Cox," *New York Evangelist*, September 17, 1846.
59. "Reply of Frederick Douglass to Dr. Cox, Salisbury Road, Edinburgh, October 30, 1846." *The National Anti Slavery Standard*, December 3, 1846.
60. "From the New York Evangelist; Samuel H. Cox to the Rev. John G. Fee of Kentucky." *The National Anti Slavery Standard*, September 16, 1846.
61. "Dr. Cox Twenty-Five Years Ago," *National Anti Slavery Standard*, September 15, 1860.
62. "Dr. Cox Twenty-Five Years Ago," *National Anti Slavery Standard*, March 20, 1851.
63. "Selections: Dr. Cox's Letter," *National Anti Slavery Standard*, June 11, 1846.

64. "Rev. Dr. Cox," *Cleveland True Democrat*, reprinted in *FDP*, April 8, 1852.
65. "General Assembly of the Presbyterian Church—New School," *American Missionary*, July 1847.
66. "The New School General Assembly and Slavery," *American Missionary*, July 1853.
67. "The Slavery Question in the Presbyterian Church," *FDP*, June 10, 1853.
68. "From Our Brooklyn Correspondent," *FDP*, December 11, 1851.
69. *Hartford Courant*, February 19, 1841.
70. "From Our Brooklyn Correspondent," *FDP*, July 30, 1852.
71. "Mass Convention of the Colored Citizens of the State," *Voice of the Fugitive*, October 7, 1852. *BAP*, 7:0768.
72. Dann, Martin E., *The Black Press, 1827–1890: the Quest for National Identity*. New York: G. P. Putnam's Sons, 1971, pp. 50–52.
73. nyhistory.com/gerritsmith/voters.htm
74. "Gerrit Smith Elected," *Voice of the Fugitive*, November 18, 1852.
75. Pennington, J. W. C. to Gerrit Smith, November 7, 1852. *BAP* 7:0821.
76. Pennington, J. W. C. to Editor, *Christian News*, December 16, 1852.
77. Pennington, J. W. C. to Horace Greeley and William Harned, November 27, 1852. *BAP* 7:0839.
78. Smith, Page, op. cit., p. 1089.
79. Stowe, Harriet Beecher, *A Key to Uncle Tom's Cabin*, pp. 51–52.

Chapter Eighteen: New York, 1853 (pages 321–342)

1. Pennington, James W. C., January 1853. *BAP* 8:0151.
2. "Obituary," *American Missionary*, May 1847.
3. *The Tappan Papers*, p. 323.
4. Pennington, James W. C., to Secretaries, American Home Missionary Society, August 6, 1853. *BAP* 8:0996.
5. Pennington, James W. C. to the Secretaries of the American Home Missionary Society, February 14, May 2, August 1, and November 1, 1853. *BAP* 8:0138, 8:0237, 8:0389, 8:0466.
6. Badger, Milton to James W. C. Pennington, February 4 and 20. *BAP* 8:0136.
7. Ethiop, "Presentation of a Gown to Dr. Pennington," *New York Evangelist*, March 17, 1853.
8. Ottley, Roy and William J. Weatherby, editors, *The Negro in New York; an informal social history*, p. 105.
9. *Slavery in New York*, Ira Berlin and Leslie M. Harris, editors, p. 251.
10. Douglass, Frederick, *My Bondage and My Freedom*, pp. 399–400.
11. "A Hard Case," *New York Evangelist*, September 1852.
12. Stowe, Harriet Beecher, *A Key to Uncle Tom's Cabin*, p. 32.
13. "A Hard Case," *Maryland Colonization Journal*, October 1852. *BAP*, 8:0148.
14. *CA*, January 19, 1839.
15. "The Sixth-avenue Railroad vs. Colored Passengers," *National Anti-Slavery Standard*, May 12, 1845.
16. "From Our Brooklyn Correspondent," *FDP*, January 27, 1852.
17. "A Correspondent of the Times," *National Anti-Slavery Standard*, November 25, 1852.
18. Pennington, James W. C. to Elizabeth Greenfield, March 30, 1853. *BAP* 8:0197.
19. Greenfield, Elizabeth to James W. C. Pennington, March 31, 1853. *BAP* 8:0198.
20. "From our Brooklyn Correspondent," *FDP*, April 1, 1853.
21. "Concert," *New York Tribune*, April 2, 1853.
22. "The Black Swan," *The Liberator*, April 8, 1853.
23. "A Week in New York," *FDP*, March 16, 1855.

24. "Freedom and Re-Union of the Trainer Family," *New York Tribune*, January 10, 1854; and May, Samuel, *The Fugitive Slave Law and Its Victims*, p. 26.
25. Pennington, J. W. C., "Christian Zeal: A Sermon Preached before the Third Presbytery of New York, in Thirteenth-St. Presbyterian Church, July 3, 1853, by J. W. C. Pennington, D.D., Moderator." New York: Zuille & Leonard, 1854. *BAP* 8:0320.
26. *Proceedings of the Colored National Convention held in Rochester, July 6th, 7th, and 8th, 1853.* Rochester: Printed at the Office of *Frederick Douglass' Paper*, 1853.
27. Ibid., pp. 18–19.
28. Idem.
29. Bell, Howard Holman, *A Survey of the Negro Convention Movement, 1830–1861*, p. 29.
30. "From our Brooklyn Correspondent," *FDP*, December 3, 1853.
31. Ibid., pp. 16–17.
32. Ibid., p. 22.
33. "National Convention of Colored Men," *New York Times*, July 8, 1853.
34. Ibid., pp. 9–11.
35. Ibid., pp. 47–57.
36. *FDP*, July 15, 1853.
37. *Christian Witness*, 6:461-462 (1849) in Blasingame, James W., *The Frederick Douglass Papers*, p. xxxvi.
38. *Report of the Proceedings of the Colored National Convention held at Cleveland, Ohio*, pp. 14–15.
39. *Proceedings of the Colored National Convention held in Rochester, July 6, 7, and 8, 1853*, p. 46.
40. *FDP*, July 22, 1853.
41. Ibid., March 17, 1854.
42. To the Editor, *NAS*, August 20, 1853.
43. Strong, op. cit., p. 131.
44. Townsend, Craig D., *Faith in their Own Color: Black Episcopalians in Antebellum New York*. New York, Columbia University Press, 2005.
45. To the Editor, *American Missionary*, September 1853.
46. "From our New York Correspondent," *FDP*, December 2, 1853.
47. *NAS*, December 10, 1853.

Chapter Nineteen: New York, 1854–1855 (pages 343–362)

1. *Presbyterian Church in the U.S.A. Third Presbytery of New York. Minutes, 1831–1870.*
2. Pennington, J. W. C., *The Fugitive Blacksmith*, p. 76.
3. "The Pembroke Family," *New York Tribune*, June 15, 1854.
4. Pennington, Thomas H. S., *Capture, trial, and return of the fugitives Stephen Pembroke and his two sons, to Slavery*, p. 1.
5. Idem.
6. *Capture, trial, and return of the fugitives Stephen Pembroke, and his two sons, to Slavery. Brother and nephews of the Rev. J. W. C. Pennington, D.D.*, Document Collection Archives, Lancaster County Historical Society, Box 17, Folder 16.
7. "Man-Hunting in New York," *NAS*, June 3, 1854.
8. Still, William, *The Underground Railroad*, pp. 175 ff.
9. Idem.
10. "Another Fugitive Slave Law Case: Three more Victims Hurried into Slavery," *The New York Tribune*, May 27, 1854.
11. Idem.
12. "Letter from Rev. Dr. Pennington—Appeal for Help," *Pennsylvania Freeman*, June 8, 1854.

13. Ibid.
14. "The Pembroke Family," *New York Tribune*, June 15, 1854.
15. *Lewis Tappan Papers, Journals and Notebooks*, p. 88, February 13, 1854.
16. Wyatt–Brown, op. cit., p. xiii.
17. *CA*, March 11, 1837.
18. "Dr. Pennington, Ecclesiastically," *FDP*, June 9, 1854.
19. *FDP*, June 9, 1854.
20. "Pembroke Returned a Freeman," *New York Times*, June 29, 1854.
21. *New York Tribune*, July 18, 1854.
22. *New York Times*, June 29, 1854.
23. Pennington, Thomas H. S., *Capture, trial, and return of the fugitives Stephen Pembroke and his two sons to Slavery*, p. 5.
24. "Anthony Burns a Freeman," *NAS*, March 10, 1855.
25. *BAP*, 8:088.
26. "Passage of the Nebraska Bill—The Constitution Triumphant—The Great Revolution at Hand," *New York Herald* in *NAS*, June 3, 1854.
27. "The Treason Consummate," *The Albany Register* in *NAS*, June 3, 1854.
28. Pennington, J. W. C., "Sermon: The Government of God over Nations; its Evidences; and the Manner in which it Affects Individuals." *BAP*, 8:0914.
29. Ibid., "Minutes." *BAP*, 8:0914.
30. Strong, George Templeton, *Diary of George Templeton Strong*, p. 229.
31. "Outrage Upon Colored Persons," *FDP*, July 28, 1854.
32. *NYT*, January 16, 1854.
33. Ibid., September 2, 1853.
34. "Letter from M.R. Delaney," *FDP*, April 1, 1853.
35. *FDP*, December 2, 1853.
36. *Proceedings of the National Emigration Convention of Colored People; held at Cleveland, Ohio, on Thursday, Friday and Saturday, the 24th, 25th, and 26th of August 1854.* Pittsburgh: A.A. Anderson, 1854.
37. Pease, Jane H. and William H. Pease. *They Who Would Be Free: Blacks' Search for Freedom, 1830–1861.* New York: Atheneum, 1974, p. 123.
38. Strong, op. cit., v. I, p. 324.
39. "Meeting at Southac St. Church," *Liberator*, September 22, 1854.
40. Nicholas, "The Orthodox Faith" and Pillsbury, Parker, "Rev. Dr. Pennington and His Compeers," *Glasgow Sentinel* in *NAS*, October 28, 1854.
41. Pillsbury, Parker, "Rev. Dr. Pennington and His Compeers," *Glasgow Sentinel* in *NAS*, October 28, 1854.
42. Ibid.
43. "Dr. J. W. C. Pennington," *Liberator*, January 5, 1855.
44. "Rev. Dr. Pennington," *NAS*, January 13, 1855.
45. *New York Daily Tribune*, February 9, 1855.

Chapter Twenty: New York, 1855 (pages 363–382)

1. "Wholesome Verdict," *New York Times*, February 23, 1855.
2. *New York Herald Tribune*, February 23, 1855.
3. *Provincial Freeman*, March 10, 1855.
4. "Letter from Rev. Dr. Pennington," *FDP*, February 23, 1855.
5. Pennington, J. W. C., to the Editor of the *New York Tribune*, "Look Out for the Slave-Catchers," in *FDP*, March 16, 1855.
6. "Letter of Sympathy," *FDP*, August 24, 1855.
7. "Letter from Rev. Dr. Pennington," *FDP*, April 6, 1855.

8. "Letter from Rev. Dr. Pennington," *FDP*, May 4, 1855.
9. "Third Presbytery Meeting," *New York Times*, April 22, 1855.
10. *FDP*, April 6, 1855.
11. "Anniversary of the American Anti-Slavery Society," *National Anti-Slavery Standard*, May 19, 1855.
12. "Garrisonians in Council," *New York Times*, May 11, 1855.
13. "To the Members of the National Council of the Colored People of the United States," *FDP*, March 30, 1855.
14. "National Council of the Colored People," from the *New York Tribune*, *FDP*, May 18, 1855.
15. New York *Morning Express*, May 10, 1855; New York *Daily Times*, May 12, 1855.
16. Blasingame, James A., *The Frederick Douglass Papers*, v. I, p. 52.
17. W. C. N. (William C. Nell), "Colored National Council," *Liberator*, July 27, 1855.
18. *New York Herald*, May 14, 1855.
19. *New York Herald*, May 10, 1855.
20. "Rights of Colored People," *New York Tribune*, BAP, 9:0648.
21. Pennington, J. W. C. to *FDP*, BAP, 9:0635.
22. "Police Intelligence: Ejecting a Negro from a City Railroad Car—Arrest of the Conductor and Driver for Assault and Battery," *New York Herald*, May 10, 1855.
23. "Outrage upon a Doctor of Divinity," *New York Daily Times*, May 25, 1855.
24. "The Case of Rev. Dr. Pennington," *FDP*, June 8, 1855.
25. "Colored People in City Cars," *New York Times*, May 29, 1855.
26. "The Case of Rev. Dr. Pennington," op. cit.
27. "The Legal Rights Association," *FDP*, September 7, 1855.
28. L. Tappan to J. W. C.Pennington, July 26, 1855. *BAP*, 9:0750.
29. "Colored Churches," *New York Daily Times*, July 31, 1855.
30. "Colorphobia on a City Railroad," *FDP*, October 5, 1855.
31. "Call for a State Convention of the Colored People of the State of New York." *FDP*, July 20, 1855.
32. Pennington, J. W. C. to American Home Missionary Society, June 1, 1855. *BAP*, 9:0678.
33. "From Our Brooklyn Correspondent," *FDP*, October 26, 1855.
34. *Proceedings of the Colored National Convention Held in Philadelphia, October 16, 17, and 18, 1855.* Salem, New Jersey: National Standard Office, 1855.
35. Nell, William C., "National Convention of Colored Americans," November 1855. *BAP* 09:0974.
36. Strong, op. cit., p. 235.
37. "Dr. Pennington on Free Love," *New York Tribune*, October 26, 1855.
38. Minutes of the Third Presbytery, January 28, 1856.
39. Idem.
40. Pennington, Thomas H. S. to Marianna Gibbons. Handwritten letter, 1897. Document Collection Archives, Lancaster Historical Society.

Chapter Twenty-One: Hartford and New York, 1856–1864 (pages 383–418)

1. Geer's Hartford City Directory, 1856–1857.
2. Pennington, J. W. C., "Sewer Wanted in Talcott Street," *Hartford Courant*, August 21, 1856.
3. Rogers, E. P. and Wilson, Henry M., et al. *Minutes of the Convention of Ministers of the Congregational and Presbyterian Churches of the United States of America held October 22, 1856, at the Shiloh Presbyterian Church, cor. of Prince and Marion Sts., New York City.*
4. Pennington, Thomas H. S., *Prominent Events in life of Rev. J. W. C. Pennington*, p. 7.

5. Pennington, J. W. C. to Gerrit Smith, December 15, 1856. *BAP,* 10:0426.
6. "Important and Interesting Trial—Can Colored People Ride in the City Cars?", New York *Daily Times,* December 18, 19, 20, 1856.
7. Alexander, Leslie, *African or American? Black Identity and Political Activism in New York City, 1784–1861.* University of Illinois Press, Chicago, 2008, p. 129.
8. Ibid., pp. 129–130.
9. New York *Daily Times,* January 19, 1854.
10. Pennington, Thomas H. S., *Prominent Events,* p. 8.
11. "Lecture by Dr. Pennington," *Weekly Anglo-African,* October 15, 1859.
12. Pennington, J. W. C., to Gerrit Smith, March 1, 1858. *BAP,* 11:0165.
13. Strong, op. cit., v. II, p. 367.
14. *Lewis Tappan Papers, Journals and Notebooks,* September 1857, p. 246.
15. Ibid. v. II, p. 422.
16. "Rev. Evan M. Johnson," *Elevator,* May 26, 1865. [told in an 1865 obituary as having happened "six or seven years ago."]
17. Pennington, J. W. C. to Gerrit Smith, September 5, 1859. *BAP, 12:0018.*
18. Katz, William Loren, editor, *The Anglo-African Magazine.* New York: Arno Press and the *New York Times,* 1968.
19. "Cotton Growing in Africa," "J. W. C. P." *Weekly Anglo-African,* September 3, 1859.
20. Pennington, J. W. C., "A Review of Slavery and the Slave Trade," *Anglo-African Magazine,* March, April, May 1859.
21. Pennington, J. W. C., "From the Old 'Long Island Scribe'," *Anglo-African Magazine,* September 24, 1859.
22. Ibid., October 1, 1859.
23. Pennington, J. W. C., "The Self-Redeeming Power of the Colored Races of the World," *Anglo-African Magazine.* October 1859, p. 314.
24. Ibid., pp. 315–316.
25. Strong, op. cit., v. II, pp. 464–465.
26. Pennington, Thomas H. S., to Marianna Gibson, Handwritten letter of August 1, 1897.
27. Idem.
28. "Pray For Old John Brown," *Weekly Anglo-African,* November 5, 1859.
29. "The Emeute at Harper's Ferry," *Weekly Anglo-African,* October 22, 1859.
30. "The Great Conflict Requires Great Faith," *Anglo-African Magazine,* November 1859.
31. Pennington, J. W. C., to John Jay, December 5 and 12, 1859. *BAP,* 12:0288 and 12:0295.
32. Pennington, J. W. C., "How to Keep Coal Stoves Free from Clunkers." *Weekly Anglo-African,* February 18, 1860.
33. Pennington, J. W. C., to Thomas Hamilton, *Weekly Anglo-African,* March 17, 1860.
34. Ibid., April 7, 1860.
35. John F. Waugh, John C. Bowers, et al, *Weekly Anglo-African,* May 12, 1860.
36. James McCune Smith to Henry H. Garnet, December 30, 1860. *Black Abolitionist Papers,* v. 2, p. 38.
37. "The Christian Union Convention," *Weekly Anglo-African,* February 2, 1861.
38. "More Slave-Hunting in New York," *Weekly Anglo-African,* May 5, 1860.
39. Garnet, Henry Highland to Henry M. Wilson, September 27, 1861.
40. "A Word to Colored Politicians," *Weekly Anglo-African,* August 10, 1861.
41. "A Petition," *Weekly Anglo-African,* August 17, 1861.
42. "Letter of Daniel Fraser to Rev. Dr. Pennington, and Reply Thereto." *Weekly Anglo-African,* October 12, 1861.
43. Pennington, J. W. C. to William Seward, September 6, 1861, *BAP,* 13:0740.

44. "The First Black Citizen of the Dis-United States," *Anti-Slavery Reporter*, October 1, 1861.

45. "Departure of Dr. Pennington," *Weekly Anglo-African*, October 19, 1861.

46. "Rev. H. H. Garnet's Speech at Birmingham," *Weekly Anglo-African*, November 16, 1861.

47. Pennington, James W. C., *A Narrative of Events of the Life of J. H. Banks*. Liverpool, M. Rourke, 1861, p. 7.

48. "Pennington on Slavery," *Manchester Examiner*, February 20, 1862, copied in *Weekly Anglo-African*, March 15, 1862.

49. "A Great Surprise by the Members and Congregation of Shiloh Presbyterian Church Manhattan," *Weekly Anglo-African*, February 22, 1862.

50. "Rev. H. H. Garnet on President Lincoln's Central American Colonization Plan," *Pacific Appeal*, October 11, 1862.

51. "Sabbath Afternoon Meeting," *Montreal Witness*, September 6, 1862. "The Colored Race—Its Relations to the Present Struggle," *Montreal Witness*, September 6, 1862.

52. "Dr. Pennington on Slavery," *Weekly Anglo-African*, March 15, 1862.

53. "The Proclamation Among the People," *National Anti-Slavery Standard*, January 10, 1863.

54. "Anti-Colonization Meeting," May 1863, UDM.

55. Pennington, J. W. C. to Martin R. Delany, in Rollin, Frank A., *Life and Public Service of Martin R. Delany*, BAP, 14:0778.

56. "Great Meeting at Shiloh Church," *Liberator*, May 22, 1863.

57. Pennington, Thomas H. S., *Prominent Events*, p. 7.

58. Pennington, J. W. C., "Colored Men, Beware," *National Principia*, June 11, 1863.

59. Strong, op. cit., v. 3, p. 336.

60. Pennington, J. W. C., "The Position and Duties of the Colored People," *National Principia*, January 7, 1864.

61. "The New York City Draft Riots: William P. Powell to William Lloyd Garrison," Ripley, op. cit., v. 5, Document 47, pp. 229–233.

62. Hodges, op. cit., p. 264.

63. "The Late Riots in New York," *Anti-Slavery Reporter*, November 1863.

64. United States Census, 1860.

65. Ripley, op. cit., v. 5, p. 237.

66. Pennington, J. W. C., "Rebel Rule in New York: Six Hours Walk Over the Blood-stained Pavements of New York," *National Principia*, July 30, 1863.

67. Ibid.

68. Hodges, op. cit., p. 265.

69. "Report of the Committee of Merchants for the Relief of Colored People Suffering from the Late Riots in the City of New York," New York, George A. Whitehorne, 1863.

70. Schor, Joel, *Henry Highand Garnet*. New York, Greenwood Press, 1977.

71. Pennington, J. W. C., "Railroad Lawlessness," *National Principia*, August 4, 1863.

72. Pennington, J. W. C., "The Position and Duties of the Colored People," *National Principia*, January 7, 1864.

73. Pennington, J. W. C., "The Position and Duties of the Colored People (concluded)," *National Principia*, January 14, 1864.

74. Ofari, Earl, *Let Your Motto Be Resistance*. Boston, Beacon Press, 1972, p. 200.

75. "Africano" to Robert Hamilton, *Weekly Anglo-African*, August 6, 1864.

76. Pennington, J. W. C. to Robert Hamilton, *Weekly Anglo-African*, June 25, 1864.

77. *Proceedings of the National Convention of Colored Men held in the City of Syracuse, New York, October 4, 5, 6, 7, 1864; with the Bill of Rights and Wrongs and the Address to the American People*. Boston, 1864.

**Chapter Twenty-Two: Mississippi, Maine,
and Florida, 1864–1870 (pages 419–433)**

1. Steward, Theophilus Gould, *Fifty Years in the Gospel Ministry from 1864 to 1914.* A.M.E. Book Concern, Philadelphia, Pennsylvania, 1920.

2. Payne, Daniel Alexander, *History of the African Methodist Episcopal Church*, Charles Spencer Smith (editor). Nashville, Tenn.: Publishing House of the A.M.E. Sunday-School Union, 1891.

3. Watkins, Ralph C., *The Institutionalization of the African Methodist Episcopal Church*, Doctoral Thesis, University of Pittsburgh, 1997.

4. *Minutes of the Third Presbytery*, v. I, October 20, 1864.

5. "Colored Grammar School No 2," *Anglo African*, August 12, 1865.

6. "The First of August," *Elevator*, September 15, 1865.

7. "The New Evangel," *Anglo African*, October 7, 1865.

8. Payne, op. cit.

9. Occasional, "Letter from Mississippi," *Christian Recorder*, December 2, 1865.

10. "Editorial Correspondence: Notes by the Wayside," *Christian Recorder*, December 2, 1865.

11. "Letter from Natchez," *Christian Recorder*, November 3, 1866.

12. Editorial Correspondence: Notes by the Wayside," *Christian Recorder*, December 2, 1865.

13. Idem.

14. Occasional, "Letter from Mississippi," *Christian Recorder*, December 2, 1865.

15. Davis, Ronald L. F., "The U. S. Army and the Origins of Sharecropping in the Natchez District—A Case Study." *The Journal of Negro History*, v. 62, n. 1 (January 1977), pp. 60–80.

16. Pennington, J. W. C., *Weekly Anglo-African*, December 23, 1865.

17. Ibid., p. 397.

18. Ibid., p. 398.

19. Ibid., pp. 399–400.

20. Ibid., pp. 400–401.

21. Ibid., p. 395.

22. "Mississippi: The Freedmen—Report of Col. Samuel Thomas," *New York Times*, February 25, 1866.

23. Phillips, Jason, "Reconstruction in Mississippi, 1865–1876," *Mississippi History Now*, Mississippi Historical Society, May 2006.

24. "Letter from Natchez, Miss.," *The Christian Recorder*, December 2, 1865. (This letter is unsigned, but sounds like Pennington's work.)

25. Bucke, Emory Stevens (editor), *The History of American Methodism*. New York: Abingdon Press, 1964, p. 280.

26. Ibid., p. 284.

27. Dvorak, Katharine L., *An African-American Exodus: the Segregation of the Southern Churches*. Brooklyn, New York: Carlson Publishing Inc., 1991, pp. 158–159.

28. *Records of the Mississippi Freedmen's Department ("Pre-bureau Records"), Office of the Assistant, Commissioner, Bureau of Refugees, Freedmen, and Abandoned Lands, 1863–1865*, United States Congress and National Archives and Records Administration, Washington, D.C., 2004, p. 7.

29. Pennington, J. W. C. to Major Reynolds, February 2, 1868. *UDM Black Abolitionist Archives.*

30. "Good News from Natchez, Miss.," *The Christian Recorder*, June 2, 1866.

31. "Letter from Rev. John Turner," *The Christian Recorder*, June 30, 1866.

32. Idem.

33. Municipal Records, New York Public Library.

34. Beman, Amos to James W. C. Pennington, *CA*, November 7, 1840.

35. Ibid., November 14, 1840.

36. *Eastern Argus*, February 21, 1868, April 17, 1869.

37. Pennington, J. W. C. to Lewis Hayden, December 16, 1868.

38. Pennington, J. W. C. to the Editor, *National Anti-Slavery Standard*, February 8, 1869.

39. *Eastern Argus*, November 2, 1867.

40. Ibid., December 24, 1867.

41. Ibid., July 6,1867.

42. *Minutes of the 3rd Presbytery*, April 6, 1868.

43. *Eastern Argus*, dates cited.

44. Brown, William Wells, *The Black Man: His Antecedents, His Genius, and His Achieve-ments*. New York: Thomas Hamilton, 1863, p. 277.

45. *The Palladium*, February 17, 1870.

46. Pennington, Thomas H. S., *Prominent Events*, p. 7.

47. Pennington, J. W. C. to Gerrit Smith, September 17, 1869.

48. Pennington, J. W. C. to "Esteemed Friend," May 25, 1870. *BAA UDM*.

49. "From Florida: a Few General Impressions About the Land of Flowers," *The Palladium*, February 17, 1870.

50. Stowe, Harriet Beecher, *Palmetto-Leaves*. Boston: James R. Good and Company, 1873, p. 37.

51. Ibid., p. 120.

52. "Our Church History," woodlawnpresbyterian.org, Woodlawn Presbyterian Church, Jacksonville, Florida.

53. *The Palladium*, February 17, 1870.

54. Pennington, J. W. C. to George Whipple, May 25, 1870. AMA Archives.

55. Wight, J. K., *Historical Notes of the Presbytery of East Florida*, p. 6.

56. Idem.

57. Lyons, J. L., *Report of Historian of Presbytery of East Florida*, December 1887. Archives of the Presbyterian Historical Society. The *Minutes of the East Florida Presbytery* give the same date. Wight (op. cit.) gives June 5 as the date but notes that he was writing without benefit of the Minutes.

58. *Minutes of the Presbyterian Committee of Missions for Freedmen*, June 11, 1869, May 2, 1870, June 27, 1870.

59. Pennington, Thomas H. S., op. cit.

Epilogue (pages 435–440)

1. Brawley, Benjamin Griffith, *A Social History of the American Negro*. New York: The Macmillan Company, 1921, p. 239.

2. Smith, James McCune to Gerrit Smith, December 28, 1846. Stauffer, John, *The Works of James McCune Smith*. New York: Oxford University Press, 2006, p. 303.

3. Ibid., pp. 125–126.

BIBLIOGRAPHY

NEWSPAPERS AND MAGAZINES
American Missionary
American Visions
Anglo-African Magazine
Brooklyn Evening Star
Charter Oak
Christian Freeman
Christian Recorder
Clarksonian
Colored American
Connecticut Observer
Connecticut Observer and *New York Congregationalist*
Elevator
Emancipator
Frederick Douglass' Paper
Friend (Philadelphia)
Hartford Courant
Independent
Liberator
Long Island Star
National Anti-Slavery Standard
National Principia
National Reformer
New York Herald
New York Morning Express
New York Times
New York Tribune
North Star
Provincial Freeman
Publications of the Mississippi Historical Society. Centenary series. Vol. 1-2.
The Rights of All
Torch Light and Public Advertiser (Hagerstown, MD)
Weekly Anglo-African

PRIMARY SOURCES
The annals of Newtown, in Queens County, New York, containing its history from its first settlement, together with many interesting facts concerning the adjacent towns: also, a particular account of numerous Long Island families now spread over this and various other states of the Union. Riker, James (ed.), New York: D. Fanshaw, 1852, p. 224.
Beman, Amos Gerry, *Amos Beman Scrapbooks I-IV,* original document in the Beinecke Library at Yale.
Bell, Howard H., *Minutes and Proceedings of the National Negro Convention, 1830-1864.* New York: Arno Press, 1969.

Bushnell, Horace, *The census and slavery: a Thanksgiving discourse, delivered in the Chapel at Clifton Springs, N.Y., November 29, 1860.* Hartford: Lucius E. Hunt, 1860.

Bushnell, Horace, *Discourse on the slavery question. Delivered in the North Church, Hartford, Thursday evening, January 10, 1839.* [CT Hist Soc]

Bushnell, Horace, *Sermons for the New Life.* New York: Charles Scribner, 1861.

Bushnell, Horace, *Sermons on Living Subjects.* New York: Scribner, Armstrong & Co., 1872.

Contributions to the Ecclesiastical History of Connecticut prepared under the Direction of the General Association to Commemorate the Completion of One Hundred and Fifty Years since its First Annual Assembly. New Haven: William L. Kingsley, 1861.

Constitution of the American Society of Free Persons of Colour, for improving their condition in the United States; for purchasing lands; and for the establishment of a settlement in Upper Canada, also The Proceedings of the Convention with their Address to the Free Persons of Colour in the United States. Philadelphia: J. W. Allen, 1831.

Dominic, Randolph P., *Down from the Balcony: The Abyssinian Congregational Church of Portland, Maine,* unpublished thesis, 1982.

Extracts from the records of Newtown, L.I., and other newspaper clippings relating to Newtown, L.I. Brooklyn, N.Y.: Paul Grosser, stationer & printer, 18–.

Garnet, Henry Highland, *Garnet's Address to the Slaves of the United States of America.* New York: J. H. Tobitt, 1848.

Garnet, Henry Highland, *Walker's Appeal, with a brief sketch of his life and also Garnet's address to the slaves of the United States of America.* New York: J. H. Tobitt, 1848.

Geer's Hartford City Directory, Hartford: Hartford Steam Printing Co., 1840-1846, 1856-1857.

Hartford Central Association, Records 1843-1901, Microfilm, Connecticut State Library.

Hartford North Consocation, Records 1802-1842, Microfilm, Connecticut State Library.

Hawes, Joel, *Memoir of Norm and Smith, or The Christian serving God in his business.* New York: The American Tract Society, 1839[?].

Hawes, Joel, *Two Discourses delivered in the First Church of Hartford, March 5, 1848,* Hartford: Case, Tiffany and Co., 1848.

Lewis Tappan Papers, Journals and Notebooks, Library of Congress, Manuscript Division, microfilm.

Lyons, J. L. *Report of Historian of Presbytery of East Florida,* December 1887. Archives, Presbyterian Historical Society.

Martinson's New Directory and Guide Book for the City of Hartford, compiled and published by Isaac N. Bolles, 1841.

Minutes of the fourth annual Convention for the Improvement of the Free People of Colour in the United States held by adjournments in the Asbury Church the 2d to the 12th of June inclusive 1834. New-York: Published by order of the Convention, 1834.

Minutes of the National Convention of Colored Citizens held at Buffalo, on the 15th, 16th, 17th, and 18th of August 1843. New York: Piercy & Reed, 1843.

Minutes and Proceedings of the First Annual Convention of the People of Colour held by adjournments in the City of Philadelphia, from the sixth to the eleventh of June, inclusive, 1831. Published by Order of the Committee of Arrangements, Philadelphia, 1831.

Minutes of the East Florida Presbytery. Archives, Presbyterian Historical Society.

Minutes of the Uwchlan Monthly Meeting, microfilm in the collections of the Friends Historical Library of Swarthmore College.

New Haven West Association Records, 1734-1909, Vols.5-6 (1832-1903). Archives, United Church of Christ, Hartford, CT.

Pendleton, Lawson Alan, *James Buchanan's Attitude Toward Slavery*. Unpublished thesis, University of North Carolina, 1964.

Pennington, James W. C., *An Address Delivered at Newark, N.J. at the First Anniversary of West Indian Emancipation, August 1, 1839*. Newark, N.J., Aaron Guest, 1839.

Pennington, James W. C., Common School Review, *Colored American*, 1840.

Pennington, J. W. C., "The First Colored Convention," *The Anglo-African Magazine*, October 15, 1859.

Pennington, James W. C., *A Lecture Delivered before the Glasgow Young Men's Christian Association; and also before the St. George's Biblical, Literary, and Scientific Institute, London, 1850, BAP* 06:0264.

Pennington, James W. C., *A Narrative of Events of the Life of J. H. Banks, an escaped slave from the cotton state, Alabama, in America, written, with introduction, by J. W. C. Pennington, D.D.* Liverpool: M. Rourke, 1861.

Pennington, J. W. C., *The Reasonableness of the Abolition of Slavery at the South, a legitimate inference from the success of British Emancipation, An Address delivered at Hartford, Conn., First of August 1856*. Hartford: Press of Case, Tiffany and Company, 1856.

Pennington, James W. C., "A Review of Slavery and the Slave Trade," *Anglo-African Magazine*, Volume I, 1859. New York: Arno Press and *The New York Times*, 1968.

Pennington, James W. C., *A Two Years Absence or a Farewell Sermon preached in the Fifth Congregational Church, by J. W. C. Pennington, Nov. 2, 1845*. Hartford: B. T. Wells, 1845.

Pennington, Thomas H. S., *Capture, Trial, and Return of the Fugitives Stephen Pembroke and his two sons to slavery, brother and nephew of the Rev. James W. C. Pennington D.D.*, (handwritten) Document Collection Archives, Lancaster Historical Society, 1893.

Pennington, Thomas H. S., *Prominent Events in life of Rev. J. W. C. Pennington, D.D. by his adopted son, Thomas H. Sands Pennington of Saratoga Springs, N.Y.* 1897. (handwritten) Document Collection Archives, Lancaster Historical Society.

Pennington, Thomas H. S., to Marianna Gibbons. Handwritten letter, 1897. Document Collection Archives, Lancaster Historical Society.

Portland Directory and Reference Book for 1869, Vol. IX. S.R. Beckett: Portland: B. Thurston and Company, 1869.

Presbyterian Church in the U.S.A. Third Presbytery of New York. Minutes, 1831-1870. Presbyterian Historical Society.

Priest, Josiah, *Slavery as it relates to the Negro, or African Race, examined in the light of circumstances, history and the Holy Scriptures; with an account of the Origin of the Black Man's Color, causes of his state of servitude and traces of his character as well in ancient as in modern times: with Strictures on Abolitionism*. Albany: C. van Benthuysen and Co., 1843.

Proceedings of the Colored National Convention Held in Philadelphia, October 16th, 17th, and 18th, 1855. Salem, New Jersey: National Standard Office, 1855.

Proceedings of the Colored National Convention held in Rochester, July 6th, 7th, and 8th, 1853. Rochester: Printed at the Office of *Frederick Douglass' Paper*, 1853.

Proceedings of the General Anti-Slavery Convention in London, 1843. London, 1843.

Proceedings of the National Emigration Convention of Colored People; Held at Cleveland, Ohio, on Thursday, Friday and Saturday, the 24th, 25th and 26th of August 1854. Pittsburgh: A. A. Anderson, 1854.

Proceedings of the National Convention of Colored Men held in the City of Syracuse, N.Y., October 4, 5, 6, 7, 1864; with the Bill of Rights and Wrongs and the Address to the American People. Boston, 1864.

Proceedings of the National Convention of Colored People and Their Friends held in Troy, N.Y., on the 6th, 7th, 8th, and 9th October 1847. Troy, N.Y.: J. G. Kneeland and Co., 1847.

Publications of the Mississippi Historical Society. Centenary series. Vol. 1-2.

Records of the Mississippi Freedmen's Department ("Pre-bureau Records"), Office of the Assistant, Commissioner, Bureau of Refugees, Freedmen, and Abandoned Lands, 1863–1865, United States Congress and National Archives and Records Administration, Washington, D.C., 2004.

Register of the Third Presbytery of New York, Archives of the Presbyterian Historical Society, Philadelphia, Pennsylvania.

Report of the Committee of Merchants for the Relief of Colored People Suffering from the Late Riots in the City of New York, New York: George A. Whitehorne, 1863

Report of the Proceedings of the Colored National Convention held at Cleveland, Ohio, on Wednesday, September 6, 1848. Rochester: North Star Office, 1848.

Rogers, E. P. and Wilson, Henry M., et al. *Minutes of the Convention of Ministers of the Congregational and Presbyterian Churches of the United States of America held October 22, 1856, at the Shiloh Presbyterian Church, cor. of Prince and Marion Sts., New York City.*

Roper, Moses *Narrative of the Adventures and Escape of Moses Roper, from American Slavery.* London: Harvey and Darton, 1842.

A Statistical Inquiry into the Condition of the People of Colour of the City and Districts of Philadelphia, Philadelphia: Kite and Walton, 1849.

Strong, George Templeton, *Diary of George Templeton Strong,* Vols. I and II, edited by Allan Nevins and Milton Halsey Thomas. New York: Macmillan, 1952.

Walker, David, *Walker's Appeal, in Four Articles; Together with a Preamble, to the Coloured Citizens of the World, but in Particular, and Very Expressly, to Those of the United States of America,* Boston, 1829.

Walker, George Leon, "The Historical Address," in *Commemorative Exercises of the First Church of Christ in Hartford at the Two Hundred and Fiftieth Anniversary, October 11 and 12, 1883.* Hartford, Conn.: Case, Lockwood & Brainard Company, 1883.

Wight, J. K., *Historical Notes of the Presbytery of East Florida.* (Printed paper without date or publisher)

SECONDARY SOURCES

ARTICLES

Burkett, Randall K., "The Reverend Harry Croswell and Black Episcopalians in New Haven, 1820-1860." *The North Star: A Journal of African American Religious History,* Volume 7, Number 1 (Fall 2003).

Davis, Ronald L. F., "The U. S. Army and the Origins of Sharecropping in the Natchez District—A Case Study." *The Journal of Negro History,* Vol. 62, No. 1 (Jan., 1977), pp. 60-80.

Gravely, William B., "The Dialectic of Double-Consciousness in Black American Freedom Celebrations, 1808-1863," *The Journal of Negro History,* Vol. 67, No. 4 (Winter, 1982), pp. 302-317.

Hourahan, Richard, "Turning Point: The Newtown Years of James C. Pennington, Fugitive Slave and Black Abolitionist," in Warren, Wini, *Friends of Freedom: the Underground Railroad in Queens and on Long Island,* The Queens Historical Society, Flushing, New York, 2006.

Jortner, Adam, "Cholera, Christ, and Jackson: The Epidemic of 1832 and the Origins of Christian Politics in Antebellum America," *Journal of the Early Republic*, 27 (Summer 2007).

Phillips, Jason, "Reconstruction in Mississippi, 1865-1876," *Mississippi History Now*, Mississippi Historical Society, May 2006. http://mshistory.k12.ms.us/articles/204/reconstruction-in-mississippi-1865-1876

Schmoke, Kurt, "The Dixwell Avenue Congregational Church, 1829 to 1896," *New Haven Colony Historical Society Journal*, Vol. 20, Number 1, May-June 1971.

White, David, "The Fugitive Blacksmith of Hartford," *Connecticut Historical Society Bulletin*, Vol. XXXXIX, No. 1 (Winter, 1984).

White, David, "Hartford's African Schools," *Connecticut Historical Society Bulletin*, Vol. XXXIX (1974).

UNPUBLISHED THESES

Watkins, Ralph C., *The Institutionalization of the African Methodist Episcopal Church*, Doctoral Thesis, University of Pittsburgh, 1997.

BOOKS

Alexander, Leslie M., *African or American? Black Identity and Political Activism in New York City, 1784-1861*. Urbana: University of Illinois Press, 2008.

Bacon, Margaret Hope, *But One Race: the Life of Robert Purvis*. Albany: State University of New York Press, 2007.

Bainton, Roland Herbert, *Yale and the Ministry: a history of education for the Christian ministry at Yale from the founding in 1701*. New York: Harper & Bros., 1957.

Barnes, Gilbert Hobbs, *The Antislavery Impulse, 1830-1844*. New York: D. Appleton-Century Company, 1933.

Berlin, Ira and Harris, Leslie M. (eds.), *Slavery in New York*. New York: New Press, 2005.

Blackett, R. J. M., *Beating Against the Barriers: biographical essays in nineteenth-century Afro-American history*. Baton Rouge: Louisiana State University Press, 1986.

Blasingame, John and Henderson, Mae (editors), *Antislavery Newspapers and Periodicals*, Boston: G. K. Hall, c1980-c1984.

Blasingame, John W., *The Frederick Douglass Papers*. New Haven: Yale University Press, 1979.

Blasingame, John W., *Slave Testimony: Two Centuries of Letters, Speeches, Interviews, and Autobiographies*. Baton Rouge: Louisiana State University Press, 1977.

Borneman, Walter R., *Polk: The Man Who Transformed the Presidency and America*. New York: Random House, 2008.

Brown, William Wells, *The Black Man: His Antecedents, His Genius, and His Achievements*. New York: Thomas Hamilton, 1863.

Brown, William Wells, *Narrative of William W. Brown, a Fugitive Slave. Written by Himself.* Boston: Published at the Anti-slavery Office, No. 25 Cornhill, 1847.

Brown, William Wells, *The Rising Son; or, The Antecedents and Advancement of the Colored Race*. Boston: A. G. Brown & Co., 1874.

Bucke, Emory Stevens (editor), *The History of American Methodism*. New York: Abingdon Press, 1964.

Budney, Stephen P., *William Jay: Abolitionist and Anticolonialist*. Westport, Conn.: Praeger Publishers, 2005.

Burton, N. J., "The North Congregational Church," *in* Trumbull, James Hammond, *The Memorial History of Hartford County, Connecticut, 1633–1844*. Boston: Edward L. Osgood, 1886.

Calhoun, Daniel, *Professional Lives in America: Structure and Aspiration, 1750-1850*. Cambridge, Massachusetts: Harvard University Press, 1965.

Cheney, Mary Bushnell, *Life and Letters of Horace Bushnell*. New York: Harper and Brothers, 1880.

Christian, Charles Melvin, and Sari J. Bennett, *Black Saga: the African American Experience*. Boston: Houghton Mifflin, c1995.

Cox, Samuel Hanson, *Interviews Memorable and Useful*. New York: Harper and Brothers, Publishers, 1853.

Cox, Stephen H., *Salvation Achieved*. New York: Jonathan Leavitt, 1831.

Cross, Barbara M., *Horace Bushnell: Minister to a Changing America*. Chicago: University of Chicago Press, 1958.

Dann, Martin E. (editor), *The Black Press, 1827-1890: the Quest for National Identity*. New York: G.P. Putnam's Sons.

Davis, Hugh, *Joshua Leavitt, Evangelical Abolitionist*. Baton Rouge: Louisiana State University Press, 1990.

Davis, Thomas, *A Rumor of Revolt*. New York: The Free Press, 1985.

Dershowitz, Alan, *America Declares Independence*. Hoboken, New Jersey: John Wiley & Sons, 2003.

Dick, Robert C., *Black Protest; Issues and Tactics*. Westport, Conn.: Greenwood Press, 1974.

Douglass, Frederick, *Life and Times of Frederick Douglass: his early life as a slave, his escape from bondage, and his complete history. Written by himself*. London: Collier Books, 1962.

Douglass, Frederick, *My Bondage and My Freedom*. New York: Miller, Orton & Mulligan, 1855.

Du Bois, W. E. B., *Suppression of the African Slave-trade to the United States of America, 1638-1870*. New York: The Social Science Press, 1954.

Edwards, Robert L., *Of Singular Genius, of Singular Grace: a biography of Horace Bushnell*. Cleveland, Ohio: Pilgrim Press, 1992.

Fellman, Michael and Lewis Perry, *Antislavery Reconsidered: New Perspectives on the Abolitionists*. Baton Rouge: Louisiana State University Press, 1979.

Fladeland, Betty, *Men and Brothers; Anglo-American Antislavery Cooperation*. Urbana: University of Illinois Press, 1972.

Foner, Philip Sheldon (editor), *Frederick Douglass on Women's Rights*. Westport, Conn.: Greenwood Press, 1976.

Fox, Early Lee, *The American Colonization Society, 1817-1840*. Baltimore: Johns Hopkins Press, 1919.

Garrison, William Lloyd, *Thoughts on African Colonization, or, An impartial exhibition of the doctrines, principles and purposes of the American Colonization Society: together with the resolutions, addresses and remonstrances of the free people of color*. Boston: Garrison and Knapp, 1832.

Goodrich, Samuel G. *Recollections of a Lifetime, or, Men and Things I Have Seen: in a series of familiar letters to a friend, historical, biographical, anecdotical, and descriptive*. New York: Miller, Orton, and Mulligan, 1856.

Grant, Ellsworth Strong and Grant, Marion Hepburn, *The City of Hartford 1784-1984, An Illustrated History*. Hartford: the Connecticut Historical Society, 1986.

Gross, Bella. *Clarion Call; the History and Development of the Negro People's Convention Movement in the United States from 1817 to 1840*. New York, 1947.

Gurley, Ralph Randolph, *Life of Jehudi Ashmun, late colonial agent in Liberia*. Freeport, N.Y.: Books for Libraries Press, 1971.

Headley, Joel Tyler, *The Great Riots of New York, 1712-1873*. Indianapolis: Bobbs-Merrill, 1970.

Hinks, Peter P. *To Awaken My Afflicted Brethren: David Walker and the Problem of Antebellum Slave Resistance*. University Park, PA.: Pennsylvania State University Press, 1997.

Hochschild, Adam, *Bury the Chains: Prophets and Rebels in the Fight to Free an Empire's Slaves*. Boston: Houghton Mifflin, 2005.

Hodges, Graham Russell, *David Ruggles: a Radical Black Abolitionist and the Underground Railroad in New York City*. Chapel Hill: University of North Carolina Press, 2010.

Hodges, Graham Russell, *Root & Branch: African Americans in New York and East Jersey, 1613-1863*. Chapel Hill: University of North Carolina Press, 1999.

Howard, George Elliott, *History of Matrimonial Institutions chiefly in England and the United States; with an introductory analysis of the literature and the theories of primitive marriage and the family*. Chicago: University of Chicago Press, Callaghan, 1904.

Jacobs, Donald M., editor, assisted by Heath Paley, Susan Parker, and Dana Silve, *Antebellum Black Newspapers: Indices to New York Freedom's journal (1827-1829), The Rights of all (1829), The Weekly advocate (1837), and The Colored American (1837-1841)*.

Katz, William Loren, editor, *The Anglo-African Magazine*. New York: Arno Press and the *New York Times*, 1968.

Katz, William Loren, *Eyewitness: The Negro in American History*. New York: Pitman Publishing Corporation, 1967.

Kemble, Frances Anne, *Journal of a Residence on a Georgian Plantation in 1838-1839*. Athens, Georgia: University of Georgia Press, 1984.

Lawrence, Edward Alexander, *The Life of Rev. Joel Hawes, D.D., tenth pastor of the First Church, Hartford, Conn*. Hartford: Hamersley & Co., 1871.

Mabee, Carleton, *Black Freedom; the Nonviolent Abolitionists from 1830 through the Civil War*. New York: Macmillan, 1970.

Mabee, Carleton, *Black Education in New York State from Colonial to Modern Times*. Syracuse: Syracuse University Press, 1979

Mars, James, *Life of James Mars, a Slave, Born and Sold in Connecticut / Written by himself*. Hartford: Case, Lockwood & Co., 1867.

May, Samuel, *The Fugitive Slave Law and Its Victims*. New York: American Anti-slavery Society, 1861.

Mayer, Henry, *All On Fire: William Lloyd Garrison and the Abolition of Slavery*. New York: St. Martin's Press, 1998

McCarthy, Timothy Patrick and John Stauffer (editors), *Prophets of Protest: Reconsidering the History of American Abolitionism*. New York: New Press, 2006.

McCauslin, Debra Sandoe, *Yellow Hill: Reconstructing the Past, Puzzle of a Lost Community*. Gettysburg, PA: For the Cause Productions, 2005.

Mitchell, Mary Hewitt, *The Great Awakening and Other Revivals in the Religious Life of Connecticut*. New Haven: Published for the Tercentenary commission by the Yale University Press, 1934.

Mjagkij, Nina, *Organizing Black America: an encyclopedia of African American associations*. New York: Garland Pub., 2001.

Mullin, Robert Bruce, *The Puritan as Yankee: A Life of Horace Bushnell*. Grand Rapids, MI: Wm. B. Eerdmans Publishing Cp., 2002.

Munger, Theodore T., *Horace Bushnell: Preacher and Theologian*. Boston: Houghton, Mifflin and Company, 1899.

Murray, Andrew E., *Presbyterians and the Negro; a History*. Philadelphia: Presbyterian Historical Society, 1966.

Nell, William C., *Colored Patriots of the American Revolution, with sketches of several distinguished colored persons: to which is added a brief survey of the condition and prospects of colored Americans*. Boston: R. F. Wallcut, 1855.

Ofari, Earl, *Let Your Motto Be Resistance*. Boston: Beacon Press, 1972

Pasternak, Martin B., *Rise Now and Fly to Arms: the Life of Henry Highland Garnet*. New York: Garland Pub., 1995.

Pawlowski, Robert E., and the Northwest Catholic High School urban studies class. *How the Other Half Lived; an ethnic history of the old East Side and South End of Hartford*, [West Hartford, Conn., 1973].

Payne, Daniel A., edited by Charles S. Smith, *A History of the African Methodist Episcopal Church*. Nashville, Tenn.: Publishing house of the A.M.E. Sunday-school union.

Pease, Jane H. and William H. Pease. *They Who Would Be Free: Blacks' Search for Freedom, 1830-1861*. New York: Atheneum, 1974.

Pillsbury, Parker, *Acts of the Anti-slavery Apostles*. Concord, N. H.: Clague, Wegman, Schlicht & Co., 1883.

Rugoff, Milton Allan, *The Beechers: An American Family in the Nineteenth Century*. New York: Harpercollins, 1981.

Sernett, Milton C., *Black Religion and American Evangelicalism*. Metuchen, N.J.: The Scarecrow Press, 1975.

Simmons, William J., *Men of Mark Eminent, Progressive and Rising*. Cleveland, Ohio: G. M. Rewell & Co., 1887.

Sinha, Manisha, "Coming of Age: the Historiography of Black Abolitionism," in Stauffer, John and McCarthy, Timothy Patrick McCarthy (ed.), *Prophets of Protest: Reconsidering the History of American Abolitionism*. New York: New Press, 2006.

Smedley, R. C., *History of the Underground Railroad in Chester and the Neighboring Counties of Pennsylvania*. Lancaster, Pa.: Office of the Journal, 1883.

Smith, James Eugene, *One Hundred Years of Hartford's Courant: from colonial times through the Civil War*. New Haven, Conn.: Yale University Press, 1949.

Smith, Page, *The Nation Comes of Age: a people's history of the ante-bellum years*. New York: McGraw-Hill, 1981.

Stauffer, John, *The Black Hearts of Men: Radical Abolitionists and the Transformation of Race*. Cambridge: Harvard University Press, 2002.

Stauffer, John, *The Works of James McCune Smith, Black Intellectual and Abolitionist*. New York: Oxford University Press, 2006.

Steward, Theophilus Gould, *Fifty Years in the Gospel Ministry from 1864 to 1914*. Philadelphia, Pennsylvania: A.M. E. Book Concern, 1920.

Stowe, Harriet Beecher, *The Key to Uncle Tom's Cabin*. New York: Arno Press, 1968.

Stowe, Harriet Beecher, *Palmetto-Leaves*. Boston: James R. Good and Company, 1873.

Strangis, Joel, *Lewis Hayden and the War Against Slavery*. North Haven, CT: Linnet Press, 1999.

Strother, Horatio T., *The Underground Railroad in Connecticut*. Middletown, CT: Wesleyan University Press, 1962.

Sweeney, Douglas A., *Nathaniel Taylor, New Haven theology, and the legacy of Jonathan Edwards*. New York: Oxford University Press, 2003.

Swift, David Everett, *Black Prophets of Justice: activist clergy before the Civil War*. Baton Rouge: Louisiana State University Press, 1989.

Tappan, Lewis, *The Life of Arthur Tappan*. New York: Hurd and Houghton; Cambridge: Riverside Press, 1871.

Temperley, Howard, *British Antislavery, 1833-1870*. Columbia: University of South Carolina Press, 1972.

Thomas, Herman E., *James W.C. Pennington, African American Churchman and Abolitionist*. New York: Garland Publishing, 1995.

Townsend, Craig D., *Faith in Their Own Color*. New York: Columbia University Press, 2005.

Trumbull, J. Hammond, *The Memorial History of Hartford County, Connecticut, 1633-1884*. Boston: E. L. Osgood, 1886.

Walker, Peter Franklin, *Vicksburg; a People at War, 1860-1865*. Chapel Hill: University of North Carolina Press, 1960.

Ward, Samuel Ringgold, *Autobiography of a Fugitive Negro: His Anti-Slavery Labours in the United States, Canada, & England*. London: John Snow, 1855.

Warner, Robert A., *New Haven Negroes: A Social History*. New Haven: Yale University Press, 1940.

Wayland, John Terrill. *The Theological Department in Yale College, 1822-1858*. New York: Garland Pub., 1987.

Weld, Ralph Foster, *Slavery in Connecticut*. New Haven: Yale University Press, 1935.

Weld, Theodore D., *American Slavery As It Is: Testimony of a Thousand Witnesses*. New York: American Anti-slavery Society Office, 1839.

Williams, Robert C., *Horace Greeley: Champion of American Freedom*. New York: New York University Press, 2006.

Winch, Julie, *A Gentleman of Color: the Life of James Forten*. New York: Oxford University Press, 2002.

Winch, Julie, *Philadelphia's Black Elite: activism, accommodation, and the struggle for autonomy, 1787-1848*. Philadelphia: Temple University Press, 1988.

Woodson, Carter G. *The Education of the Negro Prior to 1861*. New York: Arno Press, 1968.

Wright, Henry B., *Christian Activity at Yale*. New Haven, 1901.

Wyatt-Brown, Bertram. *Lewis Tappan and the Evangelical War Against Slavery*. Cleveland: Case Western Reserve University Press, 1969.

ONLINE SOURCES:

Fisher, Mel, *The Last Slave Ships*, www.melfisher.org

Linder, Douglas, *Stamped With Glory: Lewis Tappan and the Africans of the Amistad*, 1998. http://ssrn.com/abstract=1109114

Schneider, Janet M. and Bayla Singer, *Blueprint for Change: The Life and Times of Lewis H. Latimer*, http://edison.rutgers.edu/latimer/blueprnt.htm.

ACKNOWLEDGMENTS

A book like this depends on help from many others who contributed in big ways and small, but all of it valuable and valued. I am grateful especially to the following:

Barbara Bair, Manuscript Division, The Library of Congress
Marjorie R. Bardeen, Librarian, Lancaster County Historical Society
Elizabeth Call, Reference Librarian, the Brooklyn Historical Society
Christopher Densmore, Curator, Friends Historical Library, Swarthmore, PA
Dennis C. Dickerson, Historiographer of the African Methodist Episcopal Church
Paul Stuehrenberg, Joan Duffy, and the staff of the Yale Divinity School Library
Joellen ElBashir, Moorland Spingarn Research Center (MSRC) at Howard University
Leonard Cummings at the Abyssinian Church in Portland, Maine
David R. Gaewski, Conference Minister, Maine Conference, United Church of Christ
Leah Gass and the staff at the Presbyterian Historical Society
Patricia Higo, of the Acquisitions and Archive Collections University of Detroit Mercy
    Libraries
Phil Lapsansky, Curator of African American History, and the staff at the Library
    Company of Philadelphia
Richard C. Malley and Nancy Finlay of the Connecticut Historical Society
Margot McCain of the Portland Room, Portland Public Library
Dan Rolph and the staff at the Historical Society of Pennsylvania
Evans Sealand, archivist of the Connecticut Conference of the United Church of Christ
Paul Stuehrenberg, Joan Duffy, and the staff of the Yale Divinity School Library
Mariam Touba, Reference Librarian, The New-York Historical Society
Frank Turner and the staff of the Beinecke Library at Yale
John Witte, Jr., and Frances Smith Foster at Emory University

Stan and Libby Browne, Tony Grant, Michael J. Webber and Muzz Laverty, and Peter
    and Katie Basquin for generous hospitality and technical support
Harlon Dalton, Mark Gruner, Caroline Grant, Eugene Leithiser, Al Tisdale, and
    Joseph L. Yannielli for help in many ways
Debra K. McCauslin for orientation to William Wright's neighborhood

and Peter Riva, who first told me to write this book

Staff at the following institutions:
    Robert Frost Library of Amherst College
    Brooklyn Historical Society
    Brooklyn Public Library
    Connecticut State Library, esp. Mel Smith
    Chester County Historical Society
    New York Public Library
    Olin Library of Wesleyan University
    Presbyterian Historical Society
    Watkinson Library of Trinity College
    Yale University Libraries

INDEX